WAP—The Wireless Application Protocol

Writing Applications for the Mobile Internet

Sandeep Singhal

Thomas Bridgman

Lalitha Suryanarayana

Daniel Mauney

Jari Alvinen

David Bevis

Jim Chan

Stefan Hild

ADDISON–WESLEY

Boston • San Francisco • New York • Toronto • Montreal
London • Munich • Paris • Madrid • Capetown
Sydney • Tokyo • Singapore • Mexico City

Many of the designations used by manufacturers and sellers to distinguish their products are claimed as trademarks. Where those designations appear in this book, and we were aware of a trademark claim, the designations have been printed in initial capital letters or in all capitals. All trademarks are the property of their respective companies.

The authors and publisher have taken care in the preparation of this book, but make no expressed or implied warranty of any kind and assume no responsibility for errors or omissions. No liability is assumed for incidental or consequential damages in connection with or arising out of the use of the information or programs contained herein.

This book is published as part of ACM Press Books—a collaboration between the Association for Computing Machinery (ACM) and Addison-Wesley. ACM is the oldest and largest educational and scientific society in the information technology field. Through its high-quality publications and services, ACM is a major force in advancing the skills and knowledge of IT professionals throughout the world. For further information about ACM, contact:

ACM Member Services
1515 Broadway, 17th Floor
New York, NY 10036-5701
Phone: (212) 626-0500
Fax: (212) 944-1318
E-mail: ACMHELP@ACM.org

ACM European Service Center
108 Cowley Road
Oxford OX4IJF, United Kingdom
Phone: +44-1865-382338
Fax: +44-1865-381338
E-mail: acm.europe@acm.org
URL: *http://www.acm.org*

The publisher offers discounts on this book when ordered in quantity for special sales. For more information, please contact:
Pearson Education Corporate Sales Division
One Lake Street
Upper Saddle River, NJ 07458
(800) 382-3419
corpsales@pearsontechgroup.com
Visit AW on the Web: *www.awl.com/cseng/*

Library of Congress Cataloging-in-Publication Data
WAP—the Wireless Application Protocol : writing applications for the mobile Internet /
Sandeep Singhal . . . [et al.].
        p.   cm. -- (ACM Press series)
    Includes bibliographical references and index.
    ISBN 0-201-70311-4
    1. Computer network protocols.   2. Internet.   3. Wireless communication systems.
    4. Mobile communication systems.   I. Singhal, Sandeep.
    TK5105.55.W37 2001
    004.6'--dc21   00-060555

ISBN 0-201-70311-4

1 2 3 4 5 6 7 8 9 10 – CRW – 04 03 02 01 00
First printing, October 2000

Contents

Foreword   *ix*

Preface   *xi*

Acknowledgments   *xv*

About the Authors   *xvii*

PART I   **INTRODUCING THE MOBILE INTERNET**   **1**

Chapter 1   **The Mobile Internet Is Here!**   **3**
Mary Beeker   4
Bob Fisherman   6
Conclusion   7

Chapter 2   **The Rise of Mobile Data**   **9**
Market Convergence   9
Enabling Convergence   11
What Is in It for the User?   17
Conclusion   18

Chapter 3   **Key Services for the Mobile Internet**   **19**
Productivity Applications   19
Information and Transactional Services   27
Life-Enhancing Applications   35
Telephony Account and Subscription Management   42
Vertical Services for the Enterprise   46
Conclusion   48

Chapter 4   **Business Opportunities**   **51**
End User   54
Terminal Manufacturer and Browser Vendor   55

Mobile Internet Access Provider   56
Infrastructure Vendor   58
Content Aggregator (Portal)   59
Application Service Provider   60
Content Provider   62
Content Developer   62
Conclusion   63

PART II   WAP: THE MOBILE INTERNET STANDARD   65

Chapter 5   Making the Internet "Mobile": Challenges and Pitfalls   67
What Is So Different about Wireless?   67
Using Current Web Technologies for Wireless Applications   79
Conclusion   86

Chapter 6   Overview of the Wireless Application Protocol   89
The Origins of WAP   90
Overview of the WAP Architecture   102
Components of the WAP Standard   107
Network Infrastructure Services Supporting WAP Clients   124
WAP Architecture Design Principles   132
Relationship to Other Standards   139
Conclusion   141

PART III   IMPLEMENTING WAP SERVICES   143

Chapter 7   The Wireless Markup Language   145
Overview   145
The WML Document Model   149
WML Authoring   159
URLs Identify Content   160
Markup Basics   161
WML Basics   166
Basic Content   176
Events, Tasks, and Bindings   188
Variables   217
Other Content You Can Include   221
Controls   235
Miscellaneous Markup   257
Sending Information   261
Application Security   264
Other Data: The meta Element   272

Document Type Declarations   273
Errors and Browser Limitations   274
Content Generation   275
WML Version Negotiation   276
Conclusion   277

Chapter 8   Wireless Binary Extensible Markup Language   279
Overview   279
Content Structure   280
Document Structure   281
Content   285
The Encoding Process   292
Binary WML   300
Conclusion   306

Chapter 9   Enhanced WML: WMLScript and WTAI   307
WMLScript Overview   308
Language Basics   311
WMLScript Standard Libraries   340
Other WMLScript Libraries   369
WMLScript Development   374
Binary WMLScript   382
Conclusion   384

**Chapter 10   User Interface Design: Making Wireless Applications
Easy to Use   385**
Web Site Design: Computer Terminals versus
    Mobile Terminals   386
Designing a Usable WAP Site   389
Structured Usability Methods   390
User Interface Design Guidelines   412
Design Guidelines for Selected WML Elements   420
Conclusion   454

PART IV   ADVANCED WAP   457
Chapter 11   Tailoring Content to the Client   459
Techniques Using HTTP 1.1   461
A Standard Capability Negotiation Mechanism   464
Putting It All Together   473
Conclusion   488

Chapter 12   Push Messaging   489
Overview of WAP Push   490
Push Access Protocol   493
WAP Push Addressing   497
Push Message   499
MIME Media Types for Push Messages   501
Push Proxy Gateway   505
Push Over-the-Air Protocol   507
Push Initiator Authentication and Trusted Content   508
Conclusion   509

Chapter 13   Wireless Telephony Applications   511
Overview of the WTA Architecture   512
The WTA Client Framework   514
The WTA Server and Security   525
Design Considerations   527
Application Creation Toolbox   531
Future WTA Enhancements   535
Conclusion   538

Chapter 14   Building and Deploying End-to-End WAP Services   541
Mapping the Deployment Chain to the Business Value Chain   543
Security Domains   545
Linking WAP and the Internet   548
WAP Service Design   554
Conclusion   564

PART V   WHERE NEXT?   567

Chapter 15   The Mobile Internet Future   569
Better Content, Easier Access   570
Beyond Browsing   574
Beyond Cellular   577
Mobile Data Unleashed   579

APPENDICES

Appendix A   WAP Development Tools, Browsers, and Resources   583
Development Environments   583
Other WAP Browsers   584
Other Useful Resources   585

Appendix B   WML Reference   587

Appendix C   WMLScript Standard Libraries Reference   601
Crypto Library (Optional)   601
Dialogs Library   602
Float Library   603
Lang Library   604
String Library   607
URL Library   611
WMLBrowser Library   614
WTAPublic Library   616

Appendix D   User Agent Profiles Vocabulary   617

Appendix E   Mobile Internet and WAP Acronyms   623

Bibliography   627
Index   643

Foreword

According to industry analysts, there will be "over 1 billion wireless subscribers" by 2003, and with the introduction of micro-browsers on wireless devices many believe there will be more people accessing the wireless Internet using WAP-enabled devices than PCs around that same time as well. In just three short years the Wireless Application Protocol (WAP) has become the de facto worldwide standard that can provide wireless Internet services on digital mobile phones, pagers, personal digital assistants, and other wireless devices. Wireless devices represent the ultimate constrained computing devices with limited CPU, memory, and battery life, and a need for a simple user interface. Wireless networks are constrained by low bandwidth, high latency, and unpredictable availability and stability.

The WAP specification addresses both market and technical needs by using the best of existing standards and developing new extensions where needed. The WAP specification leverages existing technologies, like digital data networking standards, and Internet technologies, such as IP, HTTP, XML, SSL, URLs, scripting, and other content formats. It enables industry participants to develop solutions that are air-interface independent, device independent, and that are fully interoperable. The WAP solution leverages the tremendous investment in Web servers, Web development tools, Web programmers, and Web applications, while solving the unique problems associated with the wireless domain. The specification ensures that this solution is fast, reliable, and secure. It enables developers to use existing tools to produce sophisticated applications that have an intuitive user interface. Ultimately, wireless subscribers benefit by gaining the power of information access in the palm of their hand.

This book is an example of a unique partnership of motivated technical teammates and would-be competitors coming together to develop a real "how-to" book on the Wireless Application Protocol. This team is distributed across several countries and companies. It was not written by academics, but by talented individuals actively working in the wireless and Internet industry, on the "front line" helping to develop and deliver services to customers using a new wireless Internet standard that is destined to change the world.

I believe this book will end up on every bookshelf of the tens of thousands of Internet developers around the globe looking for a way for their application to become the next household name synonymous with the *Wireless World Wide Web*. Because of the skills and talents of the authors, you have a WAP reference that will become "required reading" for anyone planning to create applications, author content, deliver or deploy services to wireless devices.

WAP makes mobile devices first-class citizens of the Internet!

Gregory G. Williams
Chairman of the WAP Forum

Preface

The past few years have witnessed a radical shift in the way we work, play, and communicate. Today, the Internet and the World Wide Web allow people to exchange messages at the speed of light and access information from any source around the globe. These services are always on, always available, and easy to use. They are also relatively affordable, requiring only a simple browser, desktop personal computer, and modem. The power of these services and their global reach is enriching people's personal lives and reducing costs for businesses.

At the same time, people around the world have jumped to wireless communications at a frenzied pace. Today, cellular telephones are critical companions for active consumers and mobile professionals. In fact, many people have abandoned their wireline telephones altogether, drawn in by the lower costs and greater convenience afforded by wireless handsets. In many parts of the world that do not have sufficient terrestrial telephone service, cellular infrastructure represents an inexpensive, easy-to-deploy alternative to the traditional telephony infrastructure. In some countries, as much as 70 percent of the population now uses cellular phones.

These two trends—the expansion of the Internet's reach and the burgeoning of mobile communications—are now converging. Enter the *mobile Internet*. The mobile Internet extends the traditional Internet to wireless devices such as cellular phones, personal digital assistants (PDAs), and even automobiles. It brings information and services to users' fingertips when and where they need it, anytime, anywhere.

The mobile Internet involves more than simply accessing existing Web pages, however. Mobile users want personalized services that match their individual preferences and needs. They are demanding greater ease of use and immediate results. In this market, services should be tailored to suit the user's current physical location. In addition, services geared toward the mobile environment can push critical information such as news and stock price alerts asynchronously to the user. These new types of Web clients offer the opportunity to integrate Internet access with traditional telephony operations. In summary, the mobile Internet combines data and voice, information and communication, and global reach and personalization.

The realization of the mobile Internet relies on a new set of standards, known as the Wireless Application Protocol (WAP). WAP extends the Internet by addressing the unique requirements of the wireless network environment and the unique characteristics of small handheld devices. This exciting technology enables efficient access to information, applications, and services from a wide range of mobile devices. It also facilitates the interaction between browsing and telephony services, and it defines how to deliver pushed content. The WAP standard provides the necessary network protocols, content types, and run-time application environments to deliver a broad set of new and existing services to consumers and professionals alike.

WAP is an enabling technology that is heralding a revolution in the way we think about building and deploying Internet services. Some analysts predict that Internet traffic from mobile devices will outpace traffic from traditional desktop systems within a few years. Consequently, developers need to keep the mobile environment in mind when they are building and deploying Web site content. A failure to do so could eventually translate into the loss of a significant percentage of available traffic. Conversely, exploitation of the mobile Internet as enabled by WAP creates opportunities to reach new customers, provide more personalized service, and sell new applications.

Organization of This Book

WAP—The Wireless Application Protocol: Writing Applications for the Mobile Internet focuses on the mobile Internet, the technology that powers it, and strategies for writing content and applications for this new environment. It is divided into five parts, plus appendices:

• Part I introduces the mobile Internet. It discusses how the mobile Internet is emerging at the nexus of the traditional World Wide Web and wireless communications. The mobile Internet is driving new business models, partnerships, and competition. In this environment, providers are seeking to expand their existing Internet content and applications, as well as to deploy new services that take advantage of handheld devices' unique capabilities.

• Part II introduces WAP, the mobile Internet standard. The wireless environment brings with it several unique challenges that make traditional Internet Web browsing impractical from mobile devices. The WAP standard was defined to address these user interface and network challenges. This suite of protocols defines a complete mobile Internet platform, along with the mechanisms needed to bridge the gap between the mobile environment and the wired Internet.

- Part III discusses how the WAP standards can be applied to implement mobile Internet content and services. The Wireless Markup Language (WML) is a content format that is attuned to devices having small screens and limited user input capabilities. The Wireless Binary eXtensible Markup Language (WBXML) enables the delivery of arbitrary data over low-capacity networks. The WMLScript language provides a rich execution environment for client-side application logic. The mobile Internet introduces its own set of usability requirements, many of them arising from its non-Internet-savvy user population. Hence, the creation of mobile applications requires that the developer follow a rigorous usability design process.

- Part IV describes how to build and deploy sophisticated WAP services. WAP User Agent Profiles (UAProf) allow application developers to customize their content to match the unique capabilities of the individual devices targeted. WAP provides sophisticated capabilities for push messaging. The Wireless Telephony Application (WTA) environment offers capabilities that bridge the gap between the data and voice environments. In the end, the holy grail is the deployment of integrated, reliable, and secure Web applications that can serve existing desktop, emerging mobile, and future clients; accomplishing this goal requires the cooperation of many business entities.

- Part V peers into the future of the mobile Internet, commenting on WAP's role in its evolution.

- The appendices include information describing how to obtain the freely available WAP development environments, as well as reference guides to WML, WMLScript, and WAP User Agent Profiles.

The companion Web site (**http://www.aw.com/cseng/titles/0-201-70311-4**) includes a full WAP simulation environment, including a browser, along with all of the code examples from the book and some additional example applications.

Who Should Read This Book?

WAP—The Wireless Application Protocol: Writing Applications for the Mobile Internet examines both the business and the technology of the mobile Internet. It can serve both as a tutorial and as a reference for several audiences:

Business strategists and service planners: The book describes the market forces that are driving the creation of the mobile Internet, as well as the ways in which the mobile Internet is shaping business models, partnerships, and competition. Parts I, II, and V should be of particular interest to these readers.

Content and application developers: The book discusses application development in detail. Parts II and III form the heart of this material. Part I provides background information, and Part IV describes strategies for taking advantage of WAP's more advanced features. The appendices are useful references, and the companion Web site contains the software needed to get started writing mobile Internet content.

University students and researchers: The book highlights the unique qualities of the mobile environment, including networking, information design, and usability issues. It not only teaches readers about the mobile Internet, but also explains how the traditional Internet infrastructure can be adapted and extended in unforeseen ways. Parts II, III, and IV provide the most important lessons.

The reader is expected to have a basic familiarity with the World Wide Web, including the notion of Web browsers, servers, and proxies. A basic knowledge of TCP/IP, the Internet protocol stack, HTML, and XML will contribute to understanding the motivations behind various aspects of the WAP standards.

Acknowledgments

This book would not have been possible without the willing help from our friends and colleagues throughout the industry and around the world. We are deeply indebted to the following wonderful people who contributed technical and historical information, suggestions on the text, and advice and guidance: Alastair Angwin, Dick Augustsson, Virinder Batra, Jacques Beneat, Carl Binding, Alex Bobotek, Jim Colson, Abha Divine, Philip Enslow, Jr., Dan Garza, Ajei Gopal, Mike Grannan, Chuck Green, Johan Hjelm, Yen-Min Huang, Bashar Jano, Peter King, R. Adam King, Jerry Lahti, Bo Larsson, Henry Liao, Michael Luna, Bruce Martin, Jennifer Mauney, Michael Moser, Mikael Nilsson, Hidetaka Ohto, Garland Phillips, Richard Tam, Greg Williams, Fergus Wills, and Sachiko Yoshihama.

We would particularly like to thank the people listed above who reviewed the manuscript and contributed generously to its improvement. As reviewers, Virinder Batra and Andrew Capella even went beyond the call of duty and drafted a section to complete Chapter 6. We thank Amy Porento for providing administrative and research support, particularly as the manuscript neared completion.

Finally, we thank our employers—IBM, Mobileum, Nokia, ReefEdge, and SBC Technology Resources and SBC Communications—for supporting us in this project.

We are indebted to Helen Goldstein, Peter Gordon, and the staff at Addison-Wesley who offered continuous encouragement, advice, and support.

Finally, we dedicate this book to our families, whose patience, understanding, and encouragement made this book possible.

Credits

The authors and publisher would like to thank the following companies for permission to use some of the artwork, screenshots, and photographs contained in this book.

Figures 6.11, 6.12, 7.3, 7.7, 7.11, 7.14, 7.15, 7.17b, 10.7, 10.13, 10.16, 10.19a, 10.19b, 10.22a, 10.22b
   Nokia WAP browser simulator screenshots used with permission from Nokia Wireless Software Solutions, Burlington, MA.

Figures 7.3, 7.8, 7.12, 7.17a, 7.18, 10.12, 10.15, 10.18, 10.21
   From the WAP SDK (The WapIDE). WAP browser simulator screenshots used with permission from LM Ericsson, Inc.

Figures 7.4a, 7.7, 7.9, 7.17d, 7.19
   Used with permission from International Business Machines, Research Triangle Park, NC.

Figures 7.4b, 7.10, 7.16, 7.17c, 10.11, 10.14, 10.17, 10.20
   UP.Simulator, UP.SDK, and Phone.com™ examples and images © copyright 1995–1999 by Phone.com, Inc. (freely available at *http://www.phone.com*). All rights reserved. Reprinted with permission.

Figures 10.5, 10.9, 10.10
   Used with permission from Ericsson Mobile Communications.

Figure 10.6
   Used with permission from NeoPoint.

Figure 10.8
   Reproduced with permission from Motorola, Inc., Libertyville, IL. MOTOROLA and the Stylized M Logo are trademarks of Motorola, Inc. Registered U.S. Patent and Trademark Office, © 2000 Motorola, Inc.

Figure 14.7
   Reprinted with permission of Travelocity.com, LP, a Delaware limited partnership. Travelocity® and Travelocity.com are trademarks of Travelocity.com LP.

About the Authors

Sandeep Singhal is CTO of ReefEdge, Inc.—a wireless applications and infrastructure company based in Fort Lee, New Jersey. He was formerly Chief Architect and a Senior Technical Staff Member for IBM's Pervasive Computing Division, where he was responsible for product design to support network connectivity from a broad range of sub-PC devices to Web servers and application infrastructure. He previously worked as a Research Staff Member in IBM's T. J. Watson Research Center and as a Software Engineer for the National Aeronautics and Space Administration (NASA). He is also an adjunct assistant professor on the graduate faculty at North Carolina State University in Raleigh.

Sandeep's interests include network protocol design for large-scale collaborative and real-time systems, object-oriented software engineering, and network computing for pervasive computing devices. His credits include dozens of publications, including *Networked Virtual Environments* (Addison-Wesley, 1999), and ten issued patents. He served for the Defense Advanced Research Projects Agency (DARPA) on an advisory board that defined a long-term networked virtual environment research agenda, and participated in a National Research Council effort to link military and entertainment applications of simulation technology. Sandeep also played a key role in defining and implementing the Defense Department's High Level Architecture (HLA) for distributed simulation.

Sandeep has participated in the WAP Forum since February 1998. He currently chairs the User Agent Profile drafting committee and the Architectural Consistency Group at the WAP Forum. He is a member of the W3C Mobile Access Interest Group and is actively working toward converging WAP technologies with the larger Web.

Sandeep holds M.S. and Ph.D. degrees in computer science from Stanford University, as well as B.S. degrees in computer science and in mathematical sciences and a B.A. in mathematics from Johns Hopkins University.

Tom Bridgman is a software engineer in IBM's Research Division located in Yorktown Heights, New York. He joined IBM in 1989, working on network-based managed client environments for OS/2 and Windows. Since 1997, he has concentrated on development for pervasive computing devices, and he was one of the principal designers for the first release of Lotus Wireless Domino Access (now Mobile Services for Domino)—IBM's first product supporting HDML smart phones. Tom has been an IBM representative to the WAP Forum since February 1999, concentrating on the Wireless Application Environment Subgroup of the Wireless Applications Group. He has recently assumed editorship of the WML 1.x specification.

Lalitha Suryanarayana is a senior member of technical staff at Austin, Texas, based SBC Technology Resources (TRI), the applied research arm of the SBC Communications family of companies. She is responsible for developing a new services architecture strategy for wireless and other emerging data technologies. She has been with SBC TRI since 1997 and was formerly a member of technical staff in NYNEX (now Bell Atlantic) Science and Technology in White Plains, New York.

With nine years in telecommunications research and development, Lalitha has had extensive experience in developing services in the voice and data worlds. She led the implementation of NYNEX's CallAbility Feature Access℠. She has participated in the design of Southwestern Bell's first AIN mass-market service— Outgoing Call Control℠—and, more recently, in the architecture design of Online Office℠. Lalitha's research interests include defining network and device agnostic architectures for interactive and collaborative data applications.

Lalitha has participated in the WAP Forum since October 1998. She is currently serving on the WAP–W3C Coordination Committee, representing the WAP Forum in the coordination of activities associated with the convergence of the mobile Internet with the larger Web. In addition, she is on the drafting committee for WAP User Agent Profile where she has been responsible for authoring the schema and vocabulary specifications for UAProf. She also participates in CC/PP standardization efforts within the World Wide Web Consortium.

Lalitha holds an M.S. degree in electrical engineering from Polytechnic University in New York and is currently working toward an MBA at the University of Texas in Austin.

Daniel Mauney has designed wireless software and hardware user interfaces for more than six years. Currently, he is the director of the Human Factors Engineering Group at Mobileum, Inc., a leading provider of solutions designed to power the global wireless e-commerce market. Dan is responsible for defining and designing the user interface for wireless Internet sites, and he participates in the WAP Forum.

Formerly, Dan was a senior member of technical staff in the Human Factors Engineering Group at SBC Technology Resources, the applied research and development arm of SBC. He was responsible for defining, designing, and evaluating the user interface of WAP applications offered by the SBC Communications family of companies (including Southwestern Bell Wireless, Pacific Bell Wireless, Ameritech, and Cellular One). Prior to joining SBC, Dan was with Jabra Corporation—a small company that makes hands-free communications devices.

Dan holds a Ph.D. in industrial and systems engineering, with an emphasis in human factors, from Virginia Tech. He has published numerous papers and has been granted five patents, with two additional patents pending.

Jari Alvinen is a senior specialist for Nokia Mobile Phones based in Tampere, Finland. He is responsible for standardization activities in the Wireless Application Protocol Forum and other WAP-related technologies. Jari has been with Nokia since 1999 and was formerly manager of technology research and architecture at TeamWARE, Wireless Solutions.

He has been working with mobile applications since 1994 and has participated in the WAP Forum since February 1998. He currently chairs the WAP Push drafting committee of the Forum and is a member of the WAP Specification Committee.

Jari holds a B.Sc. degree in computer science from Espoo-Vantaa Institute of Technology, as well as a B.Sc. degree in telecommunications from Riihmäki Institute of Technology in Finland.

David Bevis is an architect for IBM's Pervasive Computing division based in Hursley, England. He is responsible for mobile data communications system design.

He has worked in the mobile communications arena for more than 10 years, in development of both hardware and software, and more recently as a consultant. Dave qualified in telecommunications and radio and line transmission while working for the Marconi Company in England, and, subsequently, has worked for IBM in both Germany and the United States.

Dave has been a telecommunications representative for IBM on several mobile computing forums, such as the European Community ACTS projects on mobility and the European Telecommunications Standards Institute (ETSI) that is working on applications for Trans European Trunked Radio Association (TETRA). He currently serves as secretary for the WAP Forum's Wireless Application Group (WAG) and as editor of the WBXML specification. Previously, he represented IBM on the WAP Forum's Board of Directors.

Jim Chan is the director of Wireless Network Technologies at Mobileum, Inc. He contributes to the WAP Forum's WTA and WAP NG working groups, and the Location-Based Services Drafting Committee. Prior to this position, Jim was a senior member of technical staff of the Wireless Systems Division at SBC Technology Resources, Inc. His projects included Wireless Telephony Applications (WTA), emergency and location-based services (LBS), wireless number portability, wireless communications for law enforcement, and speech recognition for wireless applications. From 1990 to 1997, Jim was with BellSouth's Science and Technology group where he worked on specification and development of Advanced Intelligent Network (AIN) services. His background includes working on several telecommunications and data communications start-up projects.

He received his MSEE from Georgia Tech and is a registered Professional Engineer (PE) and Certified Computing Professional. He has been granted three patents and has one patent pending.

Stefan Hild has been involved with mobile communications research and development since 1992, working in IBM laboratories at Heidelberg (Germany), Hursley (UK), and Zurich (Switzerland). He holds doctorate and undergraduate degrees in computer science from the University of Cambridge, England, and the University of London, respectively. Stefan has presented at a number of conferences and has published articles in several journals and trade magazines. He is a member of the IEEE and a Fellow of the Cambridge Philosophical Society.

Most recently, Stefan and his colleagues at IBM Zurich Research have been involved with the on-going standardization of the Wireless Application Protocol and have made contributions in the area of WAP security and WAP prototyping.

Part I
Introducing the Mobile Internet

Chapter 1
The Mobile Internet Is Here!

In a matter of just a few years, the ubiquity of the Internet and the World Wide Web has changed the way we work and live. Both individual users and businesses can now reach people—whether they are family, friends, merchants, customers, or suppliers—around the globe instantly. Individuals are using the Internet to find information, buy and sell goods, communicate with friends or relatives, and be entertained. Businesses are enhancing their customer relationships and streamlining relationships with suppliers and distribution channels.

The numbers are staggering. Today almost 60 percent of U.S. households have Internet access from their homes. Each household spends an average of 12.2 hours per week online. In Europe, 50 million users will have Web access by the end of 2000. Even more people are expected to go online in the future, with the user population reaching a total of 171 million people in 2004. Furthermore, nearly 8.3 million businesses are projected to be Internet-enabled by 2004.

The growth of the Internet has resulted, in part, from its simplicity. To get onto the Information Superhighway, the user requires only a simple browser on a desktop terminal with a modem connection. This ease of accessibility, along with the wealth of Internet services available for both consumers and businesses, has made the Internet into one of the most valuable technology tools.

Now imagine that, instead of using a desktop PC, you are running an Internet browser on a device that is portable, mobile, and, most importantly, wireless. With the click of a button or two from this untethered browser, you can not only connect to the World Wide Web, but also access the same information that you can reach from your desktop. Moreover, this device would be nothing more than the handy cellular mobile phone or personal digital assistant (PDA) that you might already be carrying around. It is always turned on, meaning that the browser does not require a lengthy "boot up" procedure every time you want to reach the Internet or access information such as your list of contacts. If the terminal is a cellular phone, you could even make phone calls from it!

Although this scenario might sound like a dream, the truth is that the technology is here today and rapidly gaining acceptance. The "mobile Internet" stands ready to revolutionize the way that we think about the Internet, the way that we access information in our day-to-day lives, and the way that we think about communications. You might wonder, What can the mobile Internet do for you? How can it enhance your personal lifestyle? How can it make you more productive at work?

The concept of mobile browsing is fraught with technical challenges. How could a browser fit into a tiny phone? How will you browse the Web from a small screen? How does this process work over the wireless network? Who delivers the technology? Does it require writing special content? How does one author such content?

In this book, you will find answers to these questions and more. Before we dive into these topics, however, we will visit with two users benefiting from the mobile Internet.

Mary Beeker

Mary Beeker is a typical working woman living in Houston. She works from home as a freelance graphic designer, which gives her the flexibility to adjust her work schedule around the schedules of her 9- and 11-year-old children. Like other kids their age, Mary's children have a hectic schedule on weekdays, thanks to their after-school classes and extracurricular activities.

For example, on Monday and Thursday afternoons, Mary must first pick up her son from school, then bring him home, and later drive him to his karate class. Her daughter needs to be picked up from her after-school piano lessons. Tuesdays, Wednesdays, and Fridays are Little League practice days: The children must be picked up from school, taken home for a change of clothes and snacks, and then rushed back to the playground in time for baseball practice.

Like other moms, Mary has worked out a schedule that meets her children's deadlines. Unfortunately, she often runs late, particularly when she has to drive across town to meet with her clients. Sometimes she becomes stuck in rush-hour traffic between dropping her son off to his karate class and picking up her daughter, who does not like to be kept waiting.

Now suppose that Mary purchases a cellular phone that is equipped with a Web browser. From this phone, she can access her e-mail and calendar, and she can view Internet content such as traffic, weather, and directory information. The online calendar application could remind Mary of her appointments and her children's schedules for each day. She could check up-to-the-minute traffic conditions with the push of a button and receive suggestions for alternative routes during the rush-hour congestion. When her meetings across town are running long, she could send a brief text message to John, her husband, asking him to pick up their daughter. On rainy days, Mary could also get weather updates on her mobile phone: This information will help her determine whether the baseball game has been canceled. Alternatively, the coach might send an e-mail to all of the parents about the game being canceled; Mary would be notified about this e-mail via her mobile phone. On other days, she could use her data-enabled phone to catch up on the latest news and events of the day or to pay her bills electronically while she is waiting for the game to finish. Taking advantage of the location-based capabilities on her phone, she could inquire about the closest Pizza Hut, call the restaurant and order takeout, and even get directions to the place so that she can pick up dinner on her way home.

Equipped with this data-enabled phone, Mary can get her work done without missing the highlights of her children's lives. Her life becomes more organized, and she has more time to spend with her children. A browser-equipped phone acts as a radio for weather forecasts or the latest news and entertainment, a personal co-pilot that provides her traffic updates and directions, a set of Yellow Pages for restaurant information, a map for directions, a device to check e-mail, and a phone to return calls. This gadget is light and compact, fitting into her bag. Mary can take it with her anywhere, so she can always depend on it when she needs information.

Bob Fisherman

Now let us take a peek at Bob Fisherman's typical day at work. Bob is the regional sales manager for a computer company in Chicago, where he oversees the large corporate accounts in the Midwestern states. His job requires him to make frequent day visits to client sites.

Like several other traveling professionals, Bob takes his "office" with him on his trips. His gear includes the following items:

- A five-pound laptop (and associated power and telephone cables, floppy disk drive, and extra batteries) for checking e-mail, giving presentations, storing customer data, and so on.
- A pager and cell phone to keep in touch with the office and clients.
- His day planner, which lists contact numbers and appointments.

A typical day for Bob begins with a trip to the airport. If he arrives early, he looks around the terminal for a data port to dial into the office and download his e-mail. Of course, he uses the time on the flight to catch up on his work. As soon as Bob arrives at his destination, he checks his voice mail and returns his pages. He then rents a car and heads to the client site. At the meeting, if his client requests information on the order status and schedule for shipment, Bob excuses himself from the meeting to call the office, where his administrative assistant checks one of the databases and gives him the latest information. After the meeting, he heads back to the airport and realizes that he can take an earlier flight. He scrambles to rearrange his ticket at the last moment and barely manages to touch base with his boss for the day before boarding the plane.

Now imagine that Bob has a personal digital assistant, integrated with wireless data and voice capabilities. He can store his contact list and address book in the personal information manager on the device. The device is always turned on, and Bob receives notification of new e-mail and important appointments. It connects him with the office, regardless of the time and place. His device provides him with a map and directions to the client site. The handy terminal acts as a telephone, organizer, pager, and perhaps even a laptop, all rolled into one. Bob can therefore travel lighter and get a chance to relax at the airport instead of searching for a data port.

It is easy to imagine other ways that this browser-equipped PDA would improve Bob's work. At the client meeting, his always-on device would come in handy when he needs to connect with the office to check on the order status and availability in the corporate database. Bob can use the same tool to search for local restaurants and make reservations for lunch with the clients. He can accomplish all of these tasks without even leaving the room or making a phone call! If the meeting concludes earlier than planned, Bob simply connects to his airline's Web site and re-arranges his flight schedule so that he can head home early. He even can quickly fire a short e-mail message to his boss, informing him about the results of the meeting.

In short, the integrated device improves the quality of Bob's life: He can keep up with his work, office, travel, and family while away from the home or office. He no longer needs to learn how to use three or four different devices or tools. Instead, he can rely on a single, versatile wireless handset or terminal that is Internet-enabled and telephone-enabled. This smart device can perform complex tasks with minimal instruction. The convenience is compelling, and Bob's work and productivity depend on it.

Conclusion

As we see from the examples of Mary and Bob, the mobile Internet can be valuable to both consumers and professionals. It can give users access to personalized information when and where they need it, empower them to make decisions more quickly, and bring them closer to friends, family, and work colleagues.

This book focuses on the mobile Internet, the technology that powers it, and ways to write content and applications for this new environment. The mobile Internet relies on a new set of standards, known as the Wireless Application Protocol (WAP). This exciting technology will provide efficient access to information and services from a wide range of mobile devices. In particular, WAP extends the Internet by addressing the unique requirements of the wireless network environment and the unique characteristics of small handheld devices. The standard defines the network protocols, content types, and run-time application environments needed to deliver a broad set of new and existing services to consumers and professionals alike.

We begin our discussion in the next chapter by exploring the forces that are shaping the mobile Internet: the convergence between the Internet-based World Wide Web and wireless communications.

Chapter 2
The Rise of Mobile Data

Just as the online industry has boomed over the last few years—and continues to grow at a rapid pace—the wireless (cellular) telecommunications industry has experienced a tremendous growth spurt in the past decade. In parts of Europe, nearly 70 percent of the population already uses cellular phones. According to a 1999 Yankee Group Mobile User Survey, almost 75 percent of wireless phone users also access the Internet. Cap Gemini America predicts that by 2001, 78 percent of Internet subscribers will tap into the mobile Internet as well! This overlap, along with an ever-growing need for mobility in business environments, has spurred a natural demand for *convergence* between the wireless and online information industries.

Market Convergence

This convergence between the wireless and wired worlds leads to the notion of *mobile Internet services*, which would empower the user to access the same suite of rich value-added applications at work, at home, and on the road. Such a blended market offers more opportunities than the sum of the two individual worlds: access to services at any moment in time, from any device, at any place, instantly, and over any network. By 2004, the device of choice for accessing information will be the hand-held mobile phone, as shown in Figure 2-1.

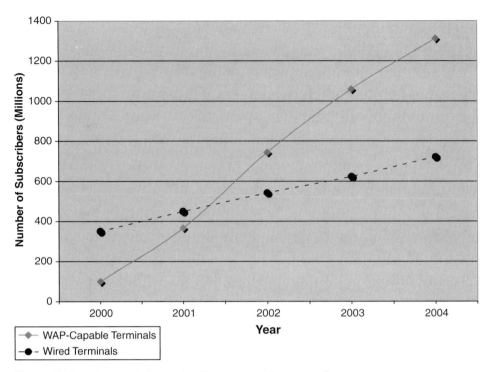

Figure 2-1   Connectivity to the Internet: A five-year forecast

Source: Based on information in Iain Gillott, "Wireless Access to the Internet: Everybody's Doin' It," IDC Report #W21187, December 1999.

The word "convergence" is derived from the verb "converge"; the latter word, in its truest sense, means to "meet" or to "come together and unite in a common interest or focus." In the context of mobile devices and the classic web, convergence encompasses the seamless integration of heterogeneous networks, terminals, applications, and content. The World Wide Web is evolving into a truly ubiquitous, worldwide wireless web with inherent support for mobility. One can envision the day in the not-too-distant future when browser-based devices of every shape, form, and processing capability will coexist, with each accessing the Internet over a variety of networks.

In such a world, user experience would naturally vary according to the terminal and the access network. For instance, the users of the mobile Internet would typically be on the move and use the Web for key value-added services: accessing the Internet for short periods at a time. This usage contrasts with a desktop user who may have a high-speed connection and prefer to simply surf the Web for extended periods of time.

The browsers and applications running on mobile devices need to be easier to use than those on the desktop. After all, mobile users typically operate in a highly dynamic environment and may not be as tightly focused on the task at hand. Moreover, their devices have limited display sizes, keypads, and battery power. Achieving an enhanced user experience on this mobile Internet therefore necessitates that highly personalized value-added services be made accessible with just a few key clicks. In contrast to the classic Web, the mobile Internet delivers value by providing services dynamically based on the user's preferences or context, including the current location, and by integrating voice telephony with asynchronous notification features.

Enabling Convergence

Historically, the market for wireless data has been driven primarily by the evolution of technology. In contrast, the World Wide Web, while a "disruptive innovation," is being driven primarily by a demand for electronic business. If the experience of the classic Internet serves as any indication, the mobile Internet will likely create its own snowball effect, driving the development of new markets, opportunities, and technological innovations. It will continue to improve business's bottom line and enhance people's lifestyles.

The Technology Adoption Life Cycle framework[1] provides insights into how the mobile Internet market might evolve. In the early days of wireless data, the first people to accept the new gadgets were high-end business users known as *Early Adopters*. These users were willing to pay more and explore untested technology to realize significant improvements in their productivity or achieve a sizable competitive advantage. Now, however, the mobile Internet capability is poised to "cross the

---

[1]In his landmark book *Crossing the Chasm*, Geoffrey Moore uses the Technology Adoption Life Cycle to describe the market penetration of a new technology product as a progression in the types of consumers whom it attracts throughout its useful life. A product's market is initially dominated by Innovators and Early Adopters ("visionaries"). The bulk of the market is attributable to acceptance by the Early Majority ("pragmatists") and Late Majority; the Laggards adopt the product only late in the life cycle. A so-called *chasm* separates the visionaries and the pragmatists because this customer transition demands a fundamental shift in the way that a technology company must market its products. Once a technology has crossed the chasm, it enters a market "tornado" characterized by rapid volume growth and high profitability.

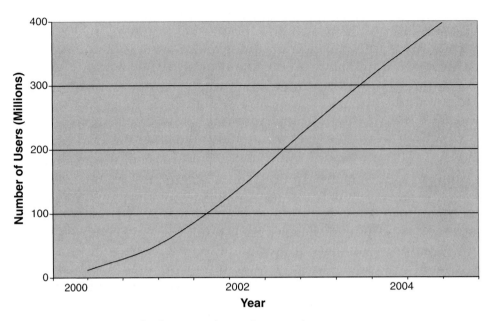

Figure 2-2 Forecast for location-dependent services

Note: Services include location-based information, traffic and navigation, location-based billing, and roadside assistance.

Source: Based on information in Strategis Group report, as quoted in "Wireless Location Services Will Generate More Than US$81.9 Billion for European Cellular Operators by 2005," *Cambridge Telecom Report,* April 10, 2000.

chasm." The emergence of Short Message Service (SMS) capability combined with the advent of location technology and browser-enabled mobile devices offer prospects for accelerated growth within the mainstream consumer market. Projections from the Strategis Group indicate that in Europe alone, such services will generate almost $82 billion in revenues over the next five years (see Figure 2-2).

Table 2-1 summarizes some of the key drivers that will allow this market to thrive.

Technology Drivers

One key technology driver focuses on the emergence and standardization of the wireless data network infrastructure, application development, and rendering technologies. At the forefront of this movement lies the Wireless Application Protocol (WAP). This suite of specifications enables the delivery and rendering of Web-based content to mobile devices. WAP provides a set of data protocols that are simultaneously optimized

Table 2-1 Summary of the Drivers Enabling Convergence

Technology drivers	Emergence of standards Network ubiquity and interconnection Emergence of affordable and powerful terminal devices
Usage drivers	Mobility needs among business professionals, such as access to intranet information while at a customer site Need for people to be in touch with friends and family all the time; need for people to access information as part of an "on-the-go" lifestyle
Business drivers	Explosive growth of the Internet Opportunity for new revenue models Need to differentiate services and improve customer retention Need to expand reach to new customers

for the restrictive wireless network environment and independent of the underlying type of wireless network. The WAP protocols can work with standard Internet protocols as well. In addition, WAP includes an application environment that supports development of applications suitable for use with a wide variety of thin-client mobile devices.

A second key enabler for mobile data is a set of technological advances that will provide network ubiquity and offer efficient network architectures for connecting devices to applications. At the forefront of these advances are the emerging "2.5-generation" and "third-generation" wireless networks.[2] These networks span countries and continents, and they connect to the classic Internet, thereby interconnecting a plethora of devices, switches, gateways, proxies, and servers. These networks are engineered for efficient use of bandwidth and network resources that are critical for always-on, always-available, ubiquitous accessibility from millions of devices across the globe.

Yet another technology driver focuses on the ever-increasing capabilities and computational power of mobile user terminals. The new-generation handsets are light, versatile, and user-friendly. Some support

---

[2]First-generation cellular networks used analog radio technologies. Second-generation (2G) networks use digital technologies and can support both voice and data calls. Third-generation (3G) networks are packet-based networks that support simultaneous voice and data traffic, including multimedia. So-called 2.5G networks represent an intermediate step, adding higher capacity to existing 2G networks.

intelligent data entry, as enabled by emerging technologies such as predictive text entry capability. Browsers on these phones even support graphics, and the devices generally can perform increasingly complex tasks at the mere touch of a button.

Another key technological motivation is the evolution and applications of smart-card technology for e-commerce and security purposes. Over-the-air (OTA) programming of end-user terminals enhances the mobile Internet by providing automatic updates to the software and settings without any user intervention.

These technologies, together with the advent of simpler tools for content development, demonstrate the feasibility of bringing the Internet to the mobile user's fingertips.

Usage Drivers

Unlike today's online user who browses the classic Web, the mobile Internet user is expected to use the mobile device for small, specific tasks that need to be accomplished fairly quickly. Whereas e-mail turned out to be the killer application on the classic Internet, users will be motivated to adopt the mobile Internet by the promise of a combination of services that will be customized to the individual user as well as his or her current location. Besides messaging, the combination of compelling horizontal applications will likely include real-time information retrieval, electronic commerce, and communications management services, to name a few. There is also the opportunity to participate in online virtual communities and plug into the community discussions even when mobile.

Consider the results of a survey of 1000 people carried out by Yankelovich. More than two-thirds valued the use of data-enabled mobile phones for receiving e-mail, directions, and important information and content. More than half expected to use wireless phones equipped with digital cameras to take and send pictures to family and friends or to conduct videoconferences. For a mother who is rushing from work to pick up her infant before the day-care center closes, it is not difficult to imagine how valuable it would be to receive real-time traffic information updates suggesting the least crowded route. In Chapter 1, we saw in detail how these services would add intrinsic value to Mary Beeker's life.

On the other hand, vertical applications such as fleet dispatch service or personal information management (PIM) applications will likely be specifically targeted toward a niche business market characterized by a large number of mobile professionals and field personnel. In the enterprise environment, for example, timely access to corporate information, whether from a database or from an e-mail repository, is vital to business success. Mobile access would augment the existing desktop access to that data.

Our friend Bob Fisherman (from Chapter 1) would fit the profile of a typical mobile business user. It is not difficult to understand the need and urgency of these workers to stay in touch with the office and clients, whether it is to communicate via e-mail, check appointments, or access the corporate intranet for specific information. Research carried out by Gartner Group reveals that more than 40 percent of the workforce will be location-independent by 2001. A report from Cahners In-Stat Group estimates that by 2002, medium and large businesses will spend more than $117 billion on wireless equipment and services as a means of achieving competitive advantage. In the area of small and large business markets, Booz Allen Hamilton predicts that the number of mobile users in the United States will rise from 33 million in 1999 to 50 million in 2000.

The forecasts being made for the mass-market acceptance of mobile data reveal the momentum and market readiness for this technology. International Data Corporation predicts that by 2004, almost 1.3 billion users worldwide will be connected to the Internet via Web-capable mobile phones; only 700 million users are expected to maintain connectivity via traditional means. That is indeed a large number of eyeballs from mobile devices, which naturally attracts businesses striving to capture a share of the market!

Business Drivers

Innovation often brings with it new markets and revenue opportunities, new channels of distribution, new partners and management teams, and—most importantly—new business models. The life cycle for high-technology markets is typically characterized by three phases. The first phase is the "tools" phase, where products—primarily tools and utilities—are targeted toward the Early Adopters. It is followed by the "platforms" phase, during which infrastructure providers bring products to market and seek increasing returns by focusing on the Early Majority users who are looking for pragmatic solutions to business problems. These two phases together account for 50 percent of the market. The most profitable phase, however, is the "applications" phase, where the focus is on value-added applications. In this phase, the technology gains mass acceptance among members of the Late Majority market. The cascading model of market economics assures increasing returns when businesses position themselves to take advantage of this life cycle.

The mobile data industry appears to be following this life cycle model. An entirely new value chain, enabled by the device-independent and network-independent capabilities of WAP, is emerging (see Figure 2-3). This value chain brings together the experience of the wireless and the Internet industries and offers a global reach to customers and users.

Near one end of the value chain lie the traditional wireless operators, who are competing on the basis of differentiated services to improve subscriber loyalty and boost airtime usage. For them, WAP offers a means of providing value-added services that can be used to target, capture, and

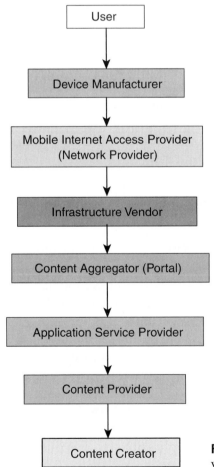

Figure 2-3   The mobile Internet value chain

retain key subscribers. At the other end of the value chain lie content creators and providers, who seek to bring more users to the content already offered over the classic Internet and to gain wider brand-name recognition. With these different motivations, wireless operators and content creators/providers will drive the emergence of new and untested pricing and bundling models for subscription-based services, electronic commerce, and targeted advertising.

In the middle of the value chain lie the infrastructure vendors, who see opportunities in extending the traditional wireless telephony infrastructure to provide data services, thereby capturing greater value and differentiation, or in extending the traditional data infrastructure into the telephony environment, which offers the promise of higher transaction rates and market growth. In addition, handset manufacturers see the mobile Internet as an opportunity to enhance the value of their devices and provide additional personalized services. Along this value chain, an entirely new set of players, such as portal providers and online intermediaries, are also emerging. These new entrants seek to resegment the market through unique value propositions aimed at taking advantage of the potential richness or reach of the mobile Internet.

According to a recent study by Strategy Analytics, by 2003 more than 95 percent of the mobile handsets shipped by handset manufacturers and operators will include a browser. This trend promises to bring a dramatic increase in the number of WAP-enabled handsets available in the market over the next five years. Early indications suggest that the size of the market opportunity will be on the order of $10.8 billion by 2003 for manufacturers, service providers, "infomediaries," and carriers. According to analysts at Warburg Dillon Read, this market will grow explosively to reach $31 billion by 2008! No one can predict exactly how this revenue pie will be shared among the value chain players or who the winners and losers will be. However, the participation of companies from each of these industry segments in the WAP Forum standardization effort serves as a clear indication of the pronounced importance of the converged mobile Internet industry. We will analyze the evolving dynamics of the WAP value chain in greater detail in Chapter 4.

What Is in It for the User?

This question is a very good one. End users do not perceive value in the technology itself; instead, they value the various concrete applications and services that the technology provides. For consumers, the core value proposition is the possibility of higher productivity levels at work and home, as well as the availability of a portfolio of options with which to keep in touch with people and receive personalized information anytime, anywhere, instantly, with an overall promise for improved quality of life. Users perceive immense value in receiving highly contextual, personalized, and spontaneous services that they associate with convenience rather than a simply "nice to have" luxury. As we will see in Chapter 3, the WAP protocol suite opens the door for an untethered culture dominated by contextualized and instant access to applications like e-commerce, messaging, and directory services from small, yet powerful devices. In other words, WAP allows its users to transcend the barriers currently imposed by the wired world.

Conclusion

The Internet and wireless communications are converging to meet the needs of anywhere, anytime access to information and services. As we have seen, wireless data services promise to unleash a broad range of new opportunities to both consumers and businesses. The Wireless Application Protocol will provide a common software foundation that will enable the rapid development of these mobile data applications. Greater demands for WAP expertise will surely arise as the business world tries to find ways to make money from mobile Internet access.

Chapter 3
Key Services for the Mobile Internet

The mobile Internet—enabled by the Wireless Application Protocol (WAP)—allows users to access services over high-latency, low-bandwidth cellular networks from thin-client terminals such as mobile phones and personal digital assistants (PDAs). The applications may deliver data that is currently available on enterprise intranets, the World Wide Web, and any other repository on an Internet Protocol (IP) network. Applications may also deliver data that is specifically valuable in the mobile context; this data may be time-sensitive, location-sensitive, or secure in nature. Whatever the circumstances, the user experience depends on the usability of the applications themselves, as well as the devices' ability to render that information. The challenge lies in developing and rendering suitable real-time interactive services that provide spontaneous value to the end user in mobile environments.

This chapter analyzes the most common applications that we believe will be deployed in the mobile Internet context. Table 3-1 summarizes these applications. We expect several more types of value-added services to emerge as WAP becomes more ubiquitous.

Productivity Applications

Productivity applications enable users to manage information and enhance their day-to-day communications with friends and colleagues.

Table 3-1   Summary of the Key Applications for the Mobile Internet

Category	Application	Explanation
Productivity applications	E-mail/text messaging	Native access to electronic mail, with features such as reading a message, replying to it, and so on.
	Personal information management (PIM)	Access to calendar for schedule and appointments, reminders and notifications, address book and contacts, and to-do lists.
	Unified messaging and universal inbox	Integration of voice mail, e-mail, and fax into the same inbox that can be accessed by the user by various means.
	Instant messaging	Awareness of online users and instant messaging with them.
Information and transactional services	Kiosk to content	News, stock quotes, weather, traffic updates, sports scores, directions to restaurants and ATMs, bus and train schedules, and other information. Also includes searching for directory information such as that found in the White or Yellow Pages.
	E-commerce	Online transactions such as banking, purchase of goods and services, day trading, bill payment, and so on.
Life-enhancing applications	Telematics	In-vehicle information systems that enable navigation, infotainment services, and roadside assistance.
	Entertainment services	Games, puzzles, ring tones, image downloads, betting services, and recipes.
	Multimedia services	Video mail, graphical directions, traffic reports, and speech synthesis.
	Enhanced telephony applications	Visual voice mail, multiway conference setup, and incoming call treatment.
Telephony, account, and subscription	E-care	Electronic customer care for billing information, service-related information, service plan options, minutes of use, and other applications.
Vertical services	Fleet management and dispatch	Ability for the fleet to receive and view information about schedules, location of pickups and drop-offs, and so on.
	Sales force automation	Access to corporate intranet information such as a database of information regarding customer orders, product pricing, and so on.

E-Mail/Text Messaging

Electronic mail has traditionally been the "killer application" on the wired Internet. It has allowed employees to be more productive, improved the speed and quality of business decision making by facilitating communication with external clients and vendors, and enabled collaboration. It can also improve a business's bottom line by permitting online customer care and support. For instance, Amazon.com uses electronic mail to confirm orders and answer queries regarding e-commerce transactions. The power of e-mail in overcoming the barriers of time zones, languages, land-line phones, and postal mail has made it a de facto medium of business communication.

In the consumer market, electronic mail has changed the paradigm of keeping in touch with family and friends. Like the telephone, e-mail has eliminated the barrier posed by long distances. For many of this book's authors, e-mail links family across several continents, including Australia, Europe, America, and the Far East.[1]

Wireless e-mail makes traditional e-mail even more powerful. It allows users to read and reply to e-mail messages from anywhere, without being chained to the office or home.

Mobile e-mail has been available for quite some time in a variety of forms. For example, users can send and receive e-mail messages using two-way paging systems and the Short Message Service (SMS) that is available in many mobile phone networks. Other existing implementations of e-mail access to or from a PDA, pager, or wireless device include e-mail forwarding through the desktop PC and e-mail downloading and synchronization through the desktop or over the air. In addition, e-mail has been implemented as a Java-enabled SIM-card application.

All of the existing systems have a number of limitations. For instance, they can be clumsy and inefficient for busy professionals to use. They lack the ability to send or receive large messages and, more importantly, to access the e-mail repository in real time. Instead, all of these e-mail systems require the creation and handling of multiple copies of the same message: on the server, on the client desktop, on a store-and-forward e-mail gateway, or on the device itself. As a result, the user must review,

---

[1]This book could not have been written without the use of e-mail to link eight highly mobile authors from around the world with one another and with the editorial staff of Addison-Wesley Professional!

manage, and store messages in multiple locations. Synchronization mechanisms are necessary to keep the various e-mail repositories consistent with one another; unfortunately, these synchronization mechanisms tend to be inefficient over low-bandwidth wireless networks and difficult to configure for devices having limited storage.

Mobile e-mail, as enabled by WAP, allows for native ("live") access to the original copy of the information residing on an enterprise or Web-based e-mail server. Only one copy of the information exists, so updates made from the WAP device are automatically and immediately updated at the user's e-mail box on the server. Thus the user processes each message only once. Such WAP-based e-mail can support features such as reading messages, replying to them, acknowledging receipt of a message, and even rerouting file attachments for printing at a nearby fax machine.

Such a messaging application will enhance the productivity of mobile business professionals like Bob Fisherman (Chapter 1), who constantly need to be in touch with clients or co-workers. There is no need to find a data-capable phone at the airport, mess with the hotel's phone system, or search for a kiosk. E-mail messaging is considered to be a core offering for a WAP service, and capabilities such as personalization, friendlier user interfaces, and alert notification will make the service extremely compelling in the coming years. When packaged with unified messaging and personal information management, wireless electronic mail is surely an indispensable tool for staying in touch.

Personal Information Management

Personal information management (PIM) is one of the key applications that a business professional depends on to be productive in his or her work. This application suite includes tools such as a calendar, scheduling, contact lists or address books, and to-do lists. Along with e-mail, PIM is considered to be one of the powerful groupware applications, allowing the user to schedule meetings and maintain a directory of contacts while on the road.

WAP-enabled PIM solutions allow the user to download and synchronize databases over the air, giving the user access to a global phone book, the organizational diary database, and other information at all times. Imagine a Web site or Web user interface through which the user enters information about a new contact. That information could be uploaded to a central PIM repository and made instantly available to the desktop calendar application and, at the same time, downloadable to one or more wireless devices. A friendly visual interface for contact lists on the user's terminal would permit the user to employ a one-touch dial for a voice call and would save keystrokes on addressing a text message. When a PIM application is used in combination with speech recognition, the user in effect can voice-dial the contact in the address book. What makes the PIM capability particularly compelling, however, is that users may be reminded of appointments using alert notifications delivered through the wireless network.

Consider our friend Bob Fisherman (Chapter 1), who is planning to visit a client site in Peoria today. He uses an online directory application to look up the contact information, then saves it to his personal contacts list, which is also stored centrally on an Internet server. If Bob needs to refer to the address while he is driving, he presses a few keys on his WAP phone to access the information. The native PIM application on the device could interact with the telephone itself, allowing Bob to call the phone number listed in the contact record.

As another example, consider the difference a PIM application would make in Mary Beeker's hectic life (Chapter 1). Using push notification technology, her online calendar application would remind her of her appointments and her children's schedules for the day. Up-to-the-minute access to her calendar and to-do lists would help Mary organize or plan her day or week for visiting clients.

Unified Messaging and Universal Mailbox

The Unified Messaging Consortium (UMC) defines unified messaging as the ability of users to respond to multimedia messages without concern for the sender's message format. Unified messaging enables the integration of voice, e-mail, and fax into a single inbox that can be accessed by the user. Ovum has forecast that 14 million active mailboxes will exist worldwide by 2002, growing to 170 million by 2006. As shown in Figure 3-1, the Pelorus Group has predicted that revenues from unified messaging will reach $2.3 billion by 2002.

The advent of wireless phones, telephony capabilities such as voice mail and call forwarding, and the penetration of e-mail subscription on the Internet has forced the user to deal with several mailboxes: a voice mailbox for the wireline telephony line, another voice mailbox for the wireless account, a multimedia mailbox for Internet e-mail, a text mailbox

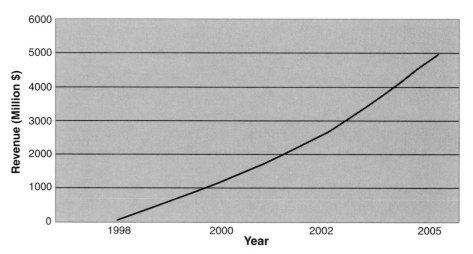

Figure 3-1 Unified messaging forecast

Source: Based on information in Pelorus Group report, as quoted in O'Keefe, S., S. Masud, and D. Allen, "The 10 Hottest Technologies," *Telecommunications Online,* May 1998; available from http://www.telecoms-mag.com/issues/199905/tcs/hottech.html.

for the pager, and so on. Indeed, many people carry multiple portable devices and, therefore, multiple mailboxes tied around their waists!

Unified messaging allows the user to use a variety of devices to not only access a single message store containing multiple message types, but also respond to those messages in a format that is acceptable to the original sender. It is a key application that streamlines and simplifies messaging in both the voice and data worlds. For an enterprise, the net result is an increase in the productivity of employees, who would now spend less time each day checking fewer messaging platforms,[2] as well as a tangible cost saving in consolidating directories associated with multiple messaging systems.

Going back to our earlier example, Bob and other mobile professionals would greatly benefit from the concept of a single, universal mailbox. Messages in the inbox could be retrieved from any device and using any interface at any time. Bob is free to use a touch-tone telephone, a voice-controlled phone interface with speech recognition capabilities, a multimedia-enabled PC, a Web-based interface, or even a mobile phone integrated with a WAP micro-browser. With the help of push alerts from the

---

[2]The Radicati Group estimates that unified messaging can provide a net saving of 25 to 38 minutes each day, with annual productivity gains of $3600 to $7800 per employee.

wireless network, Bob can be notified of waiting messages through his pager, cell phone, or handheld device. He can identify urgent messages by viewing the sender's identity, the message time and date, the message length, and the subject of the mail. He can compose or create, route, comment on, and save messages such as e-mail and voice mail.

The messaging service provider also benefits from the ability to integrate and package offerings across product lines. Consider a telecommunications provider such as AT&T or SBC that offers wireline and wireless telephony, as well as Internet e-mail and fax services to its customers. With unified messaging, such operators can offer subscribers a single solution, combining the inbox for all of their messaging accounts.

Instant Messaging

Instant messaging (IM) permits two or more people to carry on a private conversation online. Unlike with e-mail, the interaction is instantaneous; unlike with anonymous chat, the user can create a personalized directory of people with whom to converse and determine whether those people are online at a given moment.

The first implementation of this application occurred in the mainframe world, where users connected to a common server could send instant messages to other users who were logged in at that time. The technology has since evolved, and the ubiquity of the World Wide Web has now made it possible for online users to interact through their PCs with people around the world. Popular features include the ability to know when buddies are online or receive alerts when they come online; the ability to exchange instant messages, pictures, and documents with conversants; and the ability to participate in group chat rooms. When network problems disrupt the delivery of real-time messaging, the IM application can function as a "store-and-forward" system, mimicking e-mail until real-time connections can be restored. Some instant messaging applications include complementary features such as voice capabilities. Users can communicate using either a custom client or a browser-based application.

Today's desktop instant messaging market is fragmented. Proprietary offerings are available from America Online (Instant Messenger [AIM] and ICQ applications), Yahoo!, Microsoft Network, and other companies. Other products include Yabumi Instant Messaging (CyPost), which is targeted toward Japanese Apple Macintosh users, and PowWow (TribalVoice), which allows interaction with AIM buddies.

According to Jupiter Communications, instant messaging is one of the top ten online activities today.[3] In fact, many consider IM to be the next "killer application," and it is in the process of surpassing e-mail in popularity and usage. America Online's AIM service has more than 90 million users, who exchange more than 1 billion instant messages a day, compared with the service's 110 million e-mails daily. This service has gained a steady following consisting of both teenagers and adults.

With WAP, IM is likely to be extended to several billion additional devices around the globe. Users will be able to communicate and collaborate with their buddies who are using PCs, set-top boxes, or handheld phones. With advances in text input software (such as that available from Tegic), mobile IM applications will be optimized for use from handsets with keyboard limitations. AOL, for instance, has teamed with Nokia, Motorola, and other wireless device makers to develop the new AOL Mobile Messenger service to be delivered over mobile devices.

Imagine a scenario in which a mobile user strolls into a mall and receives a notification, sponsored by the local McDonald's, about the presence of her friends in the mall. At the touch of a button, she could send them an instant message suggesting that they meet at the food court in five minutes. The sponsor can also push coupons to the user and her friends, encouraging them to purchase from McDonald's.

No longer only a consumer application, instant messaging is beginning to make inroads into the enterprise world as well. Enterprise IM offerings, such as Sametime from Lotus and BizBuddy from FaceTime, can be a source of competitive advantage for their users. Already, instant messaging is being used within the companies to improve the speed of communications and information dissemination. Corporate call centers, customer-support operations, and supply chains are also benefiting by using real-time IM to improve customer relations and boost business. Ferris Research predicts that in the next five years, two-thirds of corporate e-mail users will begin to use IM regularly.

Like wireless push notification and alerts, IM enables real-time transactions in business-to-business online marketplaces and digital exchanges. On the business-to-consumer side, Wingspan Investment Services, the online brokerage unit of BankOne, is exploiting IM to communicate with its customers. The company notifies customers about the execution of trades or fulfillment of orders using IM. The benefit to the business derives

---

[3]Mobile Insights projects that the number of IM users will reach 175 million by 2002.

from its ability to provide greater access to customers and users, greater efficiency by having customer support staff carry on multiple conversations at any time, and differentiation by offering superior customer service. The user benefits because he or she does not have to wait on hold (as is required with a telephone call) and because he or she can use a familiar application.[4]

Information and Transactional Services

As mentioned earlier, the mobile Internet gives users immediate access to relevant information and allows them to subsequently take actions on that information. In this section, we consider some common applications that are particularly interesting in the mobile context.

Kiosk to Content

The World Wide Web is the largest distributed database system in the world. Indeed, it is a gold mine of information when you need it. People regularly visit the Internet in their spare time to catch up on areas of interest, whether the latest news event, technology updates, or even the coolest recipes. Occasionally, all of this information can seem overwhelming when accessed from a wireline PC. With the WAP-enabled device, this information overload does not have to happen! The relatively limited device capabilities dictate not only that the information presentation be simple and friendly but also that it provide clear and immediate value. More importantly, the user can retrieve just the desired information, at the desired time, and in the preferred dosage (amount). This information can be personalized to meet the user's preferences (such as the language of choice) and made relevant depending on the location of the user at any given time. For example, if someone based in Austin travels to New York, he might be interested in the weather in New York or the local events there. Furthermore, if this user is looking for a restaurant listing in the phone directory, he might want directions to the establishment from his current physical location in New York.

---

[4]For example, Yellow Freight Systems has found IM-based customer service to be a natural complement to its toll-free telephone number. The company's customer service representatives can respond to inquiries for rate quotes and delivery times from America Online users.

The World Wide Web will no longer be a destination in the mobile world. Rather, it will be a means to an end: information retrieval. Users are unlikely to surf the Web in the same way that they do from a wired connection on the desktop; instead, they will frequently access sites to obtain up-to-the-minute, time-critical, location-sensitive, value-added information. Users may access business-critical information, key financial transactions, or simply entertainment and games. For generic Web content of interest, the user can simply select the appropriate listing on the menu and retrieve the information. Alternatively, the user might enter the destination URL of a Web site.

Just as frequently accessed sites can be bookmarked and saved on the desktop browser, so too can mobile bookmarks be stored in the local WAP-capable device or at a network server, in which case the bookmarks will be accessible from all terminals accessed by the user. This capability is particularly useful in devices with limited keyboard capabilities. At the touch of a button, the menu of bookmarks is retrieved and displayed on the terminal. The user simply scrolls to the desired one and is connected to the selected site.

Finally, the user can also have personalized content pushed to the mobile devices, based on a priori settings or a Web-based profile. Such content might include the following items:

• *News.* News such as major social, political, or rare events; sports scores; and regional and local content can be delivered in the preferred language and format. Several content providers, including CNN and Reuters, already provide such information to mobile users. WAP also provides a channel for direct and targeted advertisements ("phonecasting"), based on user preferences and location, that can be pushed to the device.

• *Traffic reports and updates.* When text is combined with graphics, traffic information is a highly desirable application for commuters in metropolitan areas. As part of its emedi@ service, for example, Cegetel SFR offers a graphical application that provides traffic updates of the Paris Peripherique. Subscribers can determine the traffic conditions on Paris highways during any time of the day and plan to take alternative routes under heavy traffic conditions. Similarly, technology from Webraska provides GSM users in France and other parts of Europe with maps and directions.

• *Weather forecasts combined with location data.* This information can provide the user with up-to-the-minute information such as forecasts,

Doppler radar maps, or satellite pictures implicitly based on the user's location. When combined with alerts, these forecasts can be a powerful vehicle for notifying the public about severe thunderstorms or tornadoes, hurricanes, or snow. The information can be personalized to users' active lifestyles so as to provide boat and beach reports, ski forecasts, or golf weather. The ability to receive weather forecasts anytime, anywhere helps consumers make better everyday decisions.

- *Directory information.* The user may search for specific information, such as the phone number and directions to the nearest Italian restaurant, the nearest ATM location, bus or train schedules, and so on. Users will want to access moving maps from their WAP phones to navigate around unfamiliar areas. The localized maps could include real-time traffic updates and potentially be linked to local and regional advertising. According to a recent Jupiter Communications report, this type of advertising is expected to account for 24 percent of all Internet advertising by 2003.

Given the broad range of applications possible, it should be apparent that enabling instant access to this world of information at any time will make WAP into a life-enhancing technology.

Electronic Commerce

Electronic commerce is the concept of carrying out trade over the Internet by establishing a marketplace or digital exchange. It involves an outlet with an electronic storefront on a Web server, online catalogs identifying the merchandise, an application that can perform dynamic pricing and deliver selected promotions, and a back end connecting to transaction, payment, and fulfillment systems. E-commerce is the most popular and fastest-growing segment of transactional services on the Internet. According to a study conducted by Boston Consulting Group in the area of business-to-consumer (B2C) commerce, online retailers in the United States and Canada will collect roughly $268 billion in revenue by 2002.[5] The opportunities on the business–to-business (B2B) side of e-commerce are even more promising, with Forrester Research projecting a market of almost $1.3 trillion for 2003.

---

[5]B2C e-commerce is led by hardware and software merchants (total revenues of $7.4 billion in 1999), travel retailers ($7.3 billion), financial brokerages ($5.8 billion), and collectibles ($5.4 billion).

Motivations for Mobile E-Commerce

Mobile e-commerce extends e-commerce's transactional capabilities to any customer with a mobile terminal, essentially putting the electronic store in the customer's hand—anywhere. McKinsey consultants estimate that by 2002 the worldwide market for e-commerce from mobile devices will total between $10 billion and $15 billion. Advancements in digital certificate technology will ensure that secure transactions can be conducted between Web merchants/e-businesses and their mobile customers and suppliers. The merchants are motivated by the following attractions:

- Mobile e-commerce can expand the customer base and therefore generate more revenue through a wider sales and distribution channel. Mobile devices allow Web-based merchants to sell products and services that they already offer through a traditional means.

- Customer acquisition and retention are enhanced through repeated visits by loyal customers.

- Mobile e-commerce offers opportunities for brand recognition unlike any seen before.

- Further reductions in the infrastructure and transactional costs associated with online retailing are possible by, for example, delivering instantaneous online price change notifications and advertisements.

- Customer access improves because the customer can carry out e-commerce transactions from anywhere, spontaneously.

As the Chairman of the Global Mobile Commerce Forum (GMCF) said recently, "Anything you can sell over the Internet can be sold with the brand intimacy of a device that is held close to the user's heart." Returning to our earlier examples from Chapter 1, Mary Beeker could check her bank balances, transfer money between accounts, or pay her bills electronically, all without missing the highlights of her children's lives. This capability has already become ubiquitous in Hong Kong, where electronic trading has become extremely popular because it addresses Hong Kong's distinctive need for mobility while ensuring a greater level of privacy than that available with other trading methods.

Mobile Commerce Applications

The GMCF has identified four key mobile e-commerce groups that will be among the first to reach the market: mobile banking and financial services, information services, tickets, and contracts. Key applications in these areas include the following:

- *Electronic banking.* The user can check account balances, transfer funds between accounts or banks, or obtain temporary lines of credit. Customers are attracted by the new freedom of banking from anywhere, not just from a PC, ATM, or bank teller. Most importantly, mobile banking allows the customer to avoid using the unfriendly voice response systems typically encountered in traditional phone banking. For the bank, mobile phones are simply another way of doing business. Because customers already possess the necessary equipment, very little cost is involved. The bank benefits by providing differentiated banking services, increasing the number of transactions, and promoting e-cash. Mobile online banking has 250,000 users in the United Kingdom today, and all of Japan's leading banks are now offering e-banking services compatible with NTT DoCoMo's i-mode wireless Internet service. According to Meridien Research, almost 40 million users are expected to use wireless electronic financial services by 2003, with more than 70 percent of European banks offering such services.

- *Bill payment.* Online bill presentment and payment represents an opportunity for the provider to save costs on paper billing and distribution and to improve customer service by providing more details regarding the bill online. The Gartner Group predicts that the percentage of U.S. households paying bills electronically will increase from 4 percent in 1999 to 70 percent by 2009. Another forecast from International Data Corporation suggests that a $1 billion market opportunity will emerge for electronic bill presentment and payment businesses by 2004.

We can envision several methods of bill payment for the mobile user. For example, a user might first access the provider's Web site from a desktop PC and personalize it by entering information such as credit card or bank account details. Using a mobile phone, the user can later check for—or be alerted to—the due date and amount of the bill. At the touch of a button, the user can authorize payments from a correctly configured credit card or bank account. Alternatively, the user might establish electronic funds transfer from a bank account. On a specified date

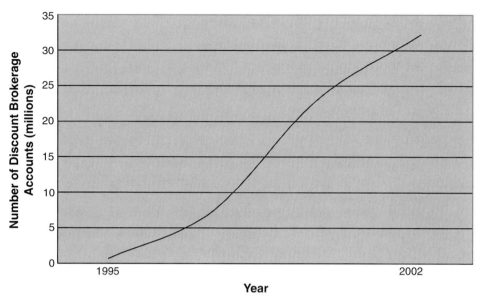

Figure 3-2   Growth in online trading

Source: Based on information in Tabb, L., "New Frontiers for Internet Trading Technology," Tower Group, 1997. Also see Levinsohn, A., "Online Brokerage, the New Core Account?" *ABA Banking Journal Online*; available from http://www.banking.com/aba/trustinvestments_0999.asp.

every month, the user could receive a reminder on the mobile phone about the pending financial transfer. The user could then authorize or cancel the bill payment from the mobile device.

• *Online trading.* Online day trading has become very popular with a large number of individual investors. With the boom in the stock market over the past few years, it has become as lucrative to the end user as it is to the discount brokerage firm. According to U.S. Bancorp's Piper Jaffrey, the total number of online retail trading accounts is expected grow to more than 30 million by 2002 (Figure 3-2). Approximately 340,000 online trades are currently made every day, with the Internet accounting for 30 percent to 35 percent of all stock trading by individuals. These figures will only increase as WAP devices proliferate in the mainstream consumer market.

The combination of Internet-based portfolio management with mobile e-commerce enablement and push notification puts control into the investor's hands as never before. The mobile user does not have to wait for the broker to deliver the information, but can instead receive alert messages automatically when a trade is executed. These transactional capabilities come in addition to real-time quotes, news reports and events, personalized buy or sell recommendations, and up-to-date account balances and summaries that the user will soon take for granted.

- *Electronic purchases of goods and services.* Mobile e-commerce allows users to purchase and trade goods and services using wireless devices. Examples include airline reservations, movie and theater tickets, flower deliveries, and even purchases from vending machines. The user experience can be enhanced immensely with personalization. For example, using a profile-based personalization capability, the server can make intelligent recommendations based on the individual's tastes and preferences, resulting in an overall faster and more satisfying experience. The payment could be made by debiting a prepaid account, by direct charging a bank account or credit card, or by charging the transaction to the phone bill. The last option is particularly popular in Japan and Europe, where the user receives one consolidated phone statement at the end of the month. This statement lists not only the phone calls and data charges for the month but also the charges from goods and services consumed while on the mobile Internet.

In addition to supporting online purchasing, the advent of short-range Bluetooth radio technology will further extend the reach of mobile devices to perform tasks beyond the initial purchase. Whereas a WAP device can support the ability to make a reservation or purchase tickets online, the Bluetooth technology would allow the passenger to check in prior to boarding as well. Swissair currently is testing an early form of this service in some airports in Switzerland.

- *Contracts.* Electronic contracts via mobile devices constitute yet another emerging application of electronic commerce. Key elements of such a service include nonrepudiation of the transaction and authentication of the parties involved. Typical applications include agreeing to insurance policies, agreeing to corporate papers, and gambling (although these contracts are legally enforceable in only some countries). Another popular contract application is online auctions, which could represent a market as large as $27 billion by 2003[6] (Figure 3-3). With the emergence of push notification to mobile devices, auctioneers and bidders can participate in real-time bidding, effectively spurring a real market for commerce from the wireless device.

---

[6]This market includes B2C, B2B, and reverse auctions.

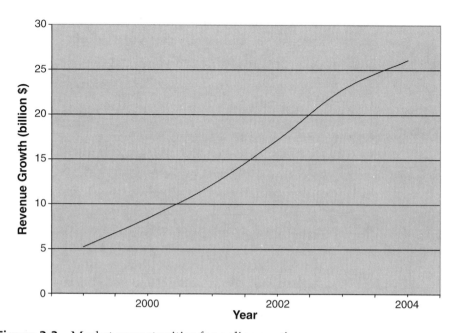

Figure 3-3   Market opportunities for online auctions

Source: Based on information in May, M., "Auctions and Classifieds Online Forecast," Jupiter Research, Vol. 1, April 18, 2000.

Another emerging application for mobile e-commerce relates to e-coupons. Merchants can provide digital promotional coupons to shoppers using smart-card technology. The coupon industry is already huge, with 4.8 billion coupons redeemed in the United States in 1998, and has bright prospects for the future—online retail sales are forecast to be on the order of $184 billion by 2004, with the Web influencing buying decisions for another $500 billion of goods.[7] Online coupons allow companies to strengthen their relationships with loyal customers or provide incentives for new customers to buy their wares. Based on customer buying behavior (as defined in terms of most recent purchasing, monetary value, frequency, or even the customer's location), e-coupons may be pushed to the phone at the right time to influence the consumer's purchasing decision.

Clearly, mobile commerce will bring about the convergence of several industries—e-commerce and finance, smart-card technologies, and wireless communications, to name a few. For example, in some parts of the

---

[7]Information from Forrester Research, 2000.

world, downloading e-cash into a second smart card (such as a Visa cash card) via the phone is gaining popularity as a means of payment for financial transactions. Motorola's StarTAC-D phone comes with an extra slot for a second smart card or debit card. Such cards hold prepaid cash values and are useful for applications that are charged on a pay-per-use basis. In addition, they offer a means to verify the identity of the consumer paying for the goods and can be used to track loyalty points or deliver discounts such as from frequent airtime usage or frequent transactions.[8] WAP allows such a card to be provisioned over the air, enabling downloading of cyber-cash.

Life-Enhancing Applications

A third broad class of mobile applications enables a user to be more informed, safe, productive, or entertained in performing everyday tasks.

Telematics

The term *telematics* was originally used to identify capabilities associated with the convergence of telecommunications data and information processing. More recently, it has been associated with wireless communications systems in automobiles. Also known as In-Vehicle Information Systems (IVIS) and automotive PCs, telematics devices support the development of a new breed of applications, such as in-car systems management and monitoring, emergency signaling to the police and medical authorities, access to Internet information and applications including PIM and e-mail, and "infotainment" solutions that include multimedia, navigation, and wireless data retrieval.

Including telematics in vehicles is not a novel idea. According to the Strategis Group, approximately 430,000 commercial vehicles are currently equipped with automatic vehicle location devices. In Japan, demand is high for autonomous navigation systems because of the overcrowded and highly complex road structures there. In contrast, North American consumers tend to prefer safety and security services, including emergency response functions from Internet-enabled wireless devices in the vehicle. For example, in its luxury vehicles, General Motors offers a communications system called OnStar that provides a number of

---

[8]According to Dataquest, 3.4 billion smart cards will be in use by 2001.

services geared toward safety, security, and convenience. The company's high-end cars include an onboard Global Positioning System (GPS) and wireless communications to link the driver to the OnStar Center, where advisors provide real-time, person-to-person help around the clock. In collaboration with Motorola, BMW has introduced a telematics system called Mayday, which triggers emergency services once the car's airbags have been activated and communicates with the BMW response center when the customer needs roadside assistance, stolen vehicle notification help, and remote door unlocking. Other features include the ability to synchronize the car's phone book automatically with the phone and muting of the radio when a call is sent or received.

These systems now available in Japan, Europe, and the United States represent only the first-generation wireless IVIS. The telematics market is rapidly evolving, driven by technology development, an inevitable increase in the number of wireless and Internet-enabled devices, and a decrease in service and equipment costs. Over time, the trend will be toward equipping all automobiles with telematics capabilities as a standard option. Strategis Group predicts that more than 1.2 million vehicles in North America will be equipped with telematics devices by 2003. Allied Business Intelligence and Frost and Sullivan have projected that the global telematics market for in-vehicle systems will exceed $7 billion per year by 2005[9] (Figure 3-4).

The next-generation telematics systems will greatly benefit automotive drivers, especially mobile professionals. These "Internet on wheels" systems will allow drivers to take their world with them as never before. The market is clearly ready for the new technology: According to a recent Gartner survey of U.S. households that bought a new car in late 1999, 70 percent had a mobile phone and 65 percent had Internet access.

Clearly, future telematics systems will implement WAP not only to communicate with an emergency center but also to access the World Wide Web. Users will access services such as the following:

- Up-to-the-minute travel news (traffic updates, directions, maps, alternative routes, parking, and airline status)

---

[9]Beyond the initial device sales, Ovum projects $4 billion in service revenues from 17 million cars equipped with telematics devices in the European continent alone by 2005. These 17 million cars represent nearly 10 percent of the 185 million cars that will be on the road.

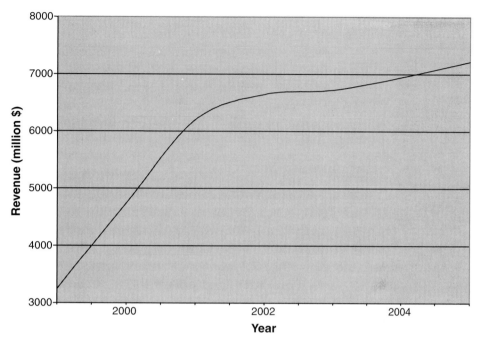

Figure 3-4 World Telematics Forecast

Source: Based on information in Frost and Sullivan, "Telematics Markets (World)," Report #5812-18, March 1999; as quoted in "Your Car: The Ultimate Portable Wireless Data Device," *Wireless Data News,* June 23, 1999.

- Location-based services (locating the nearest gas station, hotel, or ATM)
- Information (sports, weather, stock market updates, and other general Internet access)
- Toll payments via smart cards
- Entertainment (audio games, books, magazines, and newspapers)
- Automotive amenities (roadside assistance, concierge services, stolen vehicle tracking, and diagnostic checks)

All of these services will be enhanced through advanced voice activation and speech recognition capabilities, essentially a voice browser.

Industry players are now scrambling to provide this next wave of IVIS systems. For instance, Toyota, Toshiba, and Fujitsu recently announced a venture named Nihon Mobile Broadcasting Corporation aimed at transmitting multimedia services such as in-vehicle audio and video entertainment. The Intelligent Transport Systems Data Bus Forum has been established to develop a standard interface that will allow installation of the most current telematics offerings regardless of the car's age. The Automotive Multimedia Interface Consortium (AMIC) is seeking to standardize the services and interfaces provided by IVIS systems to achieve greater economies of scale within the marketplace.

Entertainment Services

Taken at face value, online games and betting do not seem to be alluring as a market opportunity for revenue. This intuitive assessment was confirmed by early needs analyses and customer surveys carried out by mobile operators for WAP services. Despite these research findings, however, the experiences in Japan and Europe have proved just the opposite, taking service providers and operators by surprise. Entertainment has emerged as one of the most addictive and highly used applications in the mass market.

One might well wonder about the relevance of mobility to entertainment, especially over a narrow-band network and with a limited device. Although almost one-third of all wireline Internet users now play games online, game companies are still trying to figure out the recipe for riches in the domain of mobile game playing.

The most likely scenario is that these applications will prove appealing to children and teenagers who find that it is fashionable to walk around with a cell phone that lets you do all of these cool things. The handheld game market among children today serves as a useful analogy. Justin, a friend of one of the authors, recently purchased a handheld Nintendo Game Boy game device at his son's insistence. Before buying this device, Justin—convinced that it was a temporary craze—tried to talk his son out of the purchase. Justin could not understand why his son wanted a small device, when he already had all the latest and greatest multimedia game players and gadgets in his collection. He thought that the Game Boy fad would disappear in no time at all, given the small black-and-white screen and limited processor horsepower. When later asked about it, Justin just shook his head, accepting defeat! But the device has become his son's constant companion for over a month now: He takes it everywhere he goes. It appears to be the coolest thing among kids his age, and he absolutely loves it!

Consider Pokémon, one of the most popular games for kids today. Nintendo is planning to unveil an Internet-based Pokémon game for its

Game Boy handheld player soon. The market will really take off when the company begins to sell an adapter that will allow pre-teens to connect the Game Boy to a cellular phone and play the game online with other players in remote locations. Soon to follow will be the ability to access Nintendo's server for swapping Pokémon characters and downloading new creatures.

Interactive games that do not require guaranteed quality of service or high bandwidth are suitable applications for WAP and the mobile Internet. Examples include chess and blackjack, to name a few. Early wireless data subscribers in Japan seem to have become addicted to network games such as Bandai and Tamagochi. Additionally, users are willing to pay for fee-based entertainment services such as Dai-chi Kosho, horoscopes, betting, and fortune telling. One of the most popular i-mode (from NTT DoCoMo) entertainment applications is the Photonet service, where users can take a digital photograph, upload it to a server, and then download it to a phone. As new high-bandwidth wireless networks emerge, these and other multimedia applications will attract the younger generation toward the mobile environment.

Other potential entertainment services include lotteries and small-time betting for fun. For example, some WAP Web sites offer the ability for users to guess which team will win the next NBA championship or World Cup cricket series or who will be elected as the next president or prime minister. Correct guesses win a small prize. In Hong Kong, mobile phones could potentially be used for horse-race wagering—a favorite local pastime. The Hong Kong Jockey Club is considered to be the ultimate place for horse racing—and wagering. Others can indulge in gambling on dog races or fantasy (virtual) sports games played on the Web. Several gambling portal sites offer non-casino-style games like Hearts and Tetris, with incentives offered to winners. These ventures will naturally be extended to the wireless data world.

Christiansen/Cummings Associates, a market research firm, expects the gambling market to amount to $3 billion worldwide by 2002. WAP technology offers entertainment to users of all ages, tastes, and interests all around the world.

Multimedia Services

Multimedia content is often considered to be the ultimate test of a networked application. In the context of the Internet, *multimedia* refers to content that incorporates voice or audio, images and graphics, text data, and video. Here, the whole (the final multimedia delivered) is greater than the sum of the parts (the individual technologies). Our experiences with television, radio, and the Internet have proved that multimedia-enabled applications deliver higher impact than applications having only plain text or audio. Significant strides have now been made in defining Internet standards for streaming video and audio at the network and application levels.

Multimedia applications for mobile terminals are not wishful thinking destined for the distant future. They represent the natural next step—consumers will soon insist on multimedia capabilities as a basic service, rather than as a desirable add-on. Some key applications in the area of multimedia are as follows:

- *Video mail and electronic postcards.* With next-generation network and mobile terminal capabilities, users will be able to receive and send mail with video, sound, music, and image attachments. In their messages, users could simply point to URLs on a Web server where the actual multimedia content is stored. A good example of applications involving this capability is the storage and retrieval of family pictures. One could imagine compact video cameras attachments that would be integrated with the mobile handset or PDA and communicate with the application running on the device. Still images, audio, or video could be captured from the camera, attached to a message, and uploaded to the mail server wirelessly.

- *Surveillance and videoconferences.* Video-enabled devices such as phones and PDAs would allow anxious parents to get a glimpse of their infants in day care or remotely monitor their babysitters without requiring access to a high-end desktop machine. If both parties on a phone call have multimedia phones, they would be able to carry out a video conversation from their mobile devices. Compelling applications include allowing far-off grandparents and family members to see the newborn in the hospital instantly or allowing children to preview the local attractions or amusement park rides when on a family trip. In a valuable application in the business world, store managers or security guards could approach shoplifters while watching live security camera images transmitted to their phones. Business professionals might also be able to participate in conference calls (audio and video) while traveling or vacationing.

- *Multimedia entertainment, streaming, and broadcast.* WAP technology integrated with multimedia would support "news on the move," whereby users would be able to watch live coverage of important events such as the President's speech or a football game. From online music sites set up to promote and distribute music, mobile users would be able to download clips of their favorite music or songs on a subscription basis.

- *Online games.* Several types of games, all of which require access to multimedia content from mobile terminals, are possible. Specifically, a user might download a game to his or her mobile device and play against a server or against another user. Other network games might allow groups of users to play together across the Internet. Depending on the type of the game, the handset will evolve to become a combination of television screen and joystick controller. The i-mode interactive game Duwango offers an early hint of how multimedia capability might be employed in mobile data terminals. Duwango users can, for instance, play fishing strategy games. The content (fish) is updated regularly depending on the season and the availability of the fish.

- *Multimedia catalogs for online shopping.* Online catalogs that are multi-media-enabled with color, graphics, sound, and text serve as a rich source of advertising for the products being sold online. Although several e-commerce sites on the Internet already provide this capability, it is really the end-user device that must be able to display and present the multimedia content to facilitate the enhanced user experience. Imagine a mobile user who wants to purchase movie tickets online from her wireless device. Being able to see previews or snippets of the latest James Bond movie will be valuable to the user when trying to select which movie to watch. In another application, a real estate agent could operate more effectively by showing her client a video preview of a prospective house, thereby avoiding a wasted trip to the other end of town to show the home to an uninterested client.

As yet, the WAP specifications do not support multimedia content. However, the WAP Forum is actively working to identify key multimedia applications and define technologies for enabling mobile multimedia as quickly as possible. Obviously, the interest level is quite high!

Other Services

Network operators and service providers are implementing several other creative applications around the globe. The potential of WAP appears limitless, based on the type of wireless data applications already being offered. For example, NTT DoCoMo has implemented a "child finder" capability in its wireless network. Children carry a toylike phone, shaped like a clown. If the child becomes lost, the parent can find him or her by going to a fax machine and entering a phone number and access code. The machine prints out a map indicating the location of the child within a radius of about 100 meters. The child can also locate the parent by pushing a button on the phone. Without a doubt, this service would garner interest from parents worldwide!

In Finland, users can pay for soft drinks or a car wash with a mobile phone. Sonera has undertaken a pilot project with its partners in which users do their daily grocery shopping using a wireless data-enabled service. As with the Peapod.com home grocery ordering service for PCs on the Internet, the goods ordered via the wireless system are delivered to the home from the supermarket. If the service is successful, it will not be long before it becomes WAP-enabled.

Another compelling application relates to health care. Destination sites facilitating e-business with medical professionals—including doctors, pharmacists, and managed care organizations—are emerging. One such secure site is LogonHealth, which allows physicians to write prescriptions, check health plan coverage information, and access vital patient information via a wireless PDA. The prescription is forwarded to the pharmacy. In the WAP-enabled world, the user would receive an alert notification when the prescription is ready for pickup.

Telephony Account and Subscription Management

The mobile Internet enables network operators to provide improved telephony services and enhance the customer service relationship. Besides providing service differentiation, these capabilities can enhance customer retention.

E-Care

Electronic customer care, or *e-care,* is the ability to provide customer care and support to subscribers and users over the World Wide Web. As shown in Figure 3-5, 40 percent of all calls to a telephony customer call center are related to billing (for example, to inquire about the bill due date or mailing address), 30 percent involve the subscriber's service

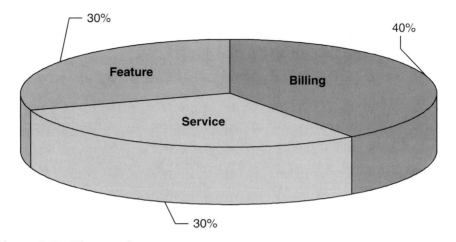

Figure 3-5 The case for e-care

Source: Based on information in Luna, M., "e-Care." Presentation at Unwired Universe Conference, 1999.

plan, and 30 percent deal with the features included in that plan. Clearly, most of this information can be delivered in an automated fashion.

Current methods of automated customer care include interactive voice response (IVR) systems with audio menus that provide help with commonly asked questions. Users can become frustrated, however, by the need to listen to and navigate through several menus before they reach the desired information or are connected to a live customer care representative who can provide the necessary support. Navigating such a system often takes a considerable amount of time. Although it results in cost savings for the service provider, it is less than a satisfying experience for even a savvy user.

Enter e-care on the mobile Internet. With micro-browser visual interfaces on a mobile phone, the information provided previously through IVR menus is now made much more palatable. With a properly designed e-care application, users can find information to frequently asked questions about the coverage area, subscription fees, and so on. They can access up-to-the-minute billing information, bill due dates, amounts due, mailing addresses, and other data about their accounts. In addition, users can find information such as the calling area and minutes of use at any time, in the language of their choice. Advanced capabilities might include secure online credit card transactions for electronic bill payment or subscription to new features, as well as fax capabilities to obtain an instant copy of a current or past bill.

The service provider benefits by providing a superior level of customer service without any drain on resources such as time and money. Delivering customer care and billing services in this manner reduces call center costs, cuts costs associated with payment processing and bill printing, and helps the carrier create a positive relationship with subscribers. This improved customer relationship can be used to differentiate the provider from its competitors and represents a potential sales channel for new services.

As subscribers become accustomed to the convenience of online customer service and begin to trust the accuracy and efficiency of online mobile customer care, carriers can introduce new service offerings designed to boost revenues and increase the perceived value of their services. For example, a WAP-based electronic customer care application might be combined with features such as notification and alerts for bill payment reminders or targeted advertisements for new service offerings.

The enhanced service might be supplemented with the ability to call the customer service number at the touch of a button. Such seamless voice and data integration is necessary for subscribers who still prefer to talk to a human being about the subscription or for those with unique requests that are not addressed by self-help options.

A new level of customer care is enabled by means of over-the-air provisioning methods. Such an approach allows operators to automatically update the subscriber's phone with the most recent versions of network information, such as roaming lists and area code information. Over-the-air provisioning also facilitates instant activation of new services.

From an implementation standpoint, the challenge lies in integrating the e-care application with back-end legacy systems (such as the billing system). This integration takes time and effort, and attention must be paid to security concerns. Fortunately, providers with existing Web-based e-care facilities have already tackled many of these integration and security issues, and the wireless e-care service can typically reuse most of the mechanisms they developed.

Enhanced Telephony Applications

Ironically, many consider voice to be the most compelling application for mobile data. Indeed, WAP is a unique technology in that it enables this convergence of voice with data—that is, the blending of the wired Internet with the wireless handset. Imagine the ability to be notified of an incoming call while you are looking for some information on the Internet. Depending on the importance of the data session and the caller's identification (learned through caller ID), you might want to answer the phone call and resume the data session later where you left it. Alternatively, you might want to direct the call to voice mail.

Enhanced telephony applications in the wireless context include capabilities such as mobile visual mailboxes, visual call handling and treatment, and enhanced services such as a call waiting indicator or conference calling. Some of these applications are described below:

- *Mobile visual mailbox.* Such a service would provide the ability to visually access a network-based unified mailbox for retrieving multimedia messages such as voice, e-mail, and fax messages. The visual interface offers several advantages over voice. For instance, voice mail is sequential and therefore not very convenient. Messages cannot be retrieved out of sequence, and the navigation is not intuitive. In contrast, a visual interface, such as that enabled by WAP, provides enhanced and personalized navigation, including prioritization of messages.

- *Incoming call treatment.* WAP, when integrated with wireless network systems such as intelligent networks (IN), provides the subscriber with the ability to determine how to handle an incoming call. Based on who is calling, the time of the call, or other preset options, the user can decide whether to answer the call immediately, forward it to another phone, or direct it to voice mail. For example, imagine that Bob Fisherman, the traveling professional introduced in Chapter 1, receives an incoming call while he is dining with his clients. Based on the caller identification (caller ID) associated with the call, he can decide whether to answer the call. If the call comes from his boss, Bob might react differently than when his mother is calling!

- *Saving caller ID information to the contact list.* If caller ID information is included in an incoming telephony call, a WAP subscriber can save the phone number and name of the caller to the phone book or contact list in the mobile device or on the server. In this way, WAP uniquely combines telephony and data capabilities.

- *Multiway conference setup.* A WAP-enabled phone is clearly the device of choice while handling the setup of a multiperson conference call. With a visual interface, the user can follow a simple set of instructions to establish such a call. No longer must he or she deal with hook flashes or access codes.

- *Other features including telephone service management and preprogrammed call macros.* WAP supports several other telephony control and management applications. For example, WAP enables a user to manage a telephone call that is already in progress. The user can forward the call to another person or to voice mail. These transfers may be appropriate when the user needs to obtain assistance from a co-worker or from a secretary or when the caller needs to record information that the user can write down at a more convenient time. Another potential service management application allows the user to create, store, and modify a personalized call screening list. Parents might want to restrict their child's phone so that it can only connect with designated numbers, or they might want to block calls to or from certain numbers. Yet another telephony service might provide personalized WAP application macros for navigating through IVR systems. For example, these macros might incorporate long numeric sequences such as credit card or ATM card numbers required to access an account balance. These sequences can be downloaded directly from the service provider and installed into the phone when the user first registers for the service.

- *Voice recognition.* Speech recognition technology has come a long way. Today, users can speak into the phone to dial a number or navigate through a interactive menu. Voice recognition is particularly convenient in a mobile environment, where the user may be busy driving and would prefer hands-free interaction with the terminal or phone. This simple capability will soon evolve to support not only verbal commands but also voice language translation. Voice browsing involving speech synthesis and recognition, integrated with WAP, might bring real value to services such as directory lookup or information searching on the World Wide Web. Voice-controlled e-mail, where e-mail messages can actually be automatically dictated and sent, are in early trials.

Vertical Services for the Enterprise

Specialized wireless data applications are critical to the successful operations of various types of organizations with large mobile workforces. In particular, utilities, chauffeur services, public safety agencies, firefighters, courier services, and manufacturing firms are always looking to improve the productivity of their employees on the move. WAP applications might assist police officers in checking car registrations or license plates, driver's licenses, or felony records on the roadside. In time-critical situations, such applications might help fire trucks or emergency ambulance services determine the best route to the crisis site. Field technicians of utility companies could query legacy databases to obtain accurate customer information, delivery status, or equipment and parts inventory.

Other companies may choose to develop their own specialized applications for workflow management, with these applications soon becoming accessible via WAP devices. For example, a construction company in San Francisco has provided Palm Pilots to all of its geographically dispersed construction team members to help them communicate about and collaborate on their paperwork. A Web-based application was then developed to organize and manage the construction process. Architects, engineers, and city officials could view blueprints, note changes in plans, and even get information about the weather. The team members could work offline on the data and later synchronize their devices with the application to receive the latest updates. Before long, one might imagine this application expanding to allow users of WAP-enabled devices to receive real-time updates and alerts at construction sites.

One emerging application for WAP will be in the area of e-business and business-to-business electronic commerce. In this area, getting real-time information and executing transactions to buy, sell, or trade products and services from a wireless device will be mission-critical for businesses.

According to the Yankee Group, at least one-third of all large U.S. corporations are expected to use wireless intranet access by 2000. Next, we describe two vertical services to illustrate how enterprises might grow to depend on mobile data capabilities as part of their streamlined and efficient operations.

Fleet Management and Dispatch Service

Although fleet management and operations control have been used by dispatch companies for some years, the ability to receive and review the frequent schedule changes made from a mobile terminal is proving to be extremely beneficial for fleet drivers. The result is a dramatic saving in mileage costs, system maintenance, and customer response time. In Europe, studies have shown that data dispatching increased fleet efficiency by as much as 30 percent. Business Class Transportation, a New York City–based car service company, claims that the use of data-enabled mobile handsets eliminates the need to install expensive radio hardware in the cars, as well as the expense associated with maintaining a radio frequency for operations. The cellular solution also offers ubiquitous service coverage in areas not reached by the private radio spectrum.

As one example of this application, consider a Dutch distribution company that has begun tracking and tracing consignments using WAP-enabled handsets. Customers that ship their goods with this company, as well as those that receive parcels or pallets from the firm, can readily learn about a deviating consignment. This service provides the user with the same experience whether the user accesses the classic Internet or the mobile Internet.

Using WAP, fleet dispatch services could be augmented with GPS, which helps the dispatchers track the fleet and select the closest available vehicle for a service call or pickup. Notification alerts can be used to transmit new assignments or inform the fleet of specific changes to schedules. The fleet can confirm the notification and update the status with a single keystroke.

Sales Force Automation

Having immediate and easy access to comprehensive product, inventory, and pricing information can be extremely useful to a sales representative while he or she is negotiating a sales deal with a prospective customer. WAP provides the mobile sales force with a convenient and effortless way to obtain cost, availability, configuration, promotional sales, discount rules, new product release dates, and other types of data, regardless of the salesperson's location. After collecting information from the product database, the sales force automation application on a micro-browser handset allows the mobile professional to process orders electronically at the touch of a button, track pricing and order status, or even generate a report or invoice to be faxed or e-mailed to the client. The mobile worker can then be reminded of upcoming sales calls in order of priority.

Conclusion

The mobile Internet has opened up opportunities for a broad range of services geared toward both consumers and professionals. Some of these services are natural extensions of applications already available on the Internet; others are innovative applications that take advantage of features, such as location awareness and push, that are unique to the mobile environment.

In this chapter, we merely scratched the surface of potential applications for the mobile Internet. Many other applications have been envisioned, and, of course, others will emerge over time.

To bring mobile Internet applications to the user, much work must be carried out behind the scenes. Delivering mobile services requires the cooperation of several different business entities, each offering a different expertise, product, or service. In the next chapter, we explore the members of this application delivery chain and see how the mobile Internet is reshaping companies and even whole industries.

Chapter 4
Business Opportunities

Now that we understand and appreciate the potential of WAP in delivering value-added services to the user in a mobile environment, it is time to take a more in-depth look at the various stakeholders and the roles that they play in making these services possible. We have already introduced some of these stakeholders in passing. After all, it is not difficult to envision who the critical players are, given that WAP services represent the convergence of the existing wireless communications and Internet services businesses.

Let us first look at the various components that must fall into place for a user to receive information from a Web site:

- The user must have a WAP-enabled mobile device or terminal.
- The user must subscribe to a wireless Internet service from a wireless Internet service provider.
- The user may need to subscribe to content, services, or premium information.
- The mobile Web application must be developed.
- The application must be hosted at a well-known site and made accessible for downloading.

Thus the key components for engaging the wireless Internet are the device, the network access and infrastructure, the service subscription, the application and its development, and the server that hosts the application. Table 4-1 summarizes this service fulfillment chain.

To get a good idea of the end-to-end picture, we need to take a closer look at the businesses that will play a part in providing one or more of these components. Collectively, these businesses define a *value chain* for delivering services to end users. Each member of the value chain offers a specific revenue-generating value proposition either to end users or to other businesses within the value chain.

Like the pattern seen with other emerging high-tech industries, the implementation of WAP will give rise to new business paradigms and open up new opportunities in the Internet, wireless communications,

Table 4-1   Summary of the WAP Service Fulfillment (Value) Chain

Stakeholder	Function	Examples
End user	Is the primary consumer of the service	Mary, Bob
Handset manufacturer	Manufactures the terminal device and the micro-browser or other user agents running on it	Ericsson, Nokia, Motorola, Panasonic, Sharp
Wireless network operator and Internet service provider (ISP)	Operates the wireless network; may implement the WAP capability and provide connectivity between the device and the Internet	AT&T, NTT DoCoMo, SBC, Vodaphone Airtouch
Infrastructure vendor	Manufactures gateways, switches, servers, and tools that implement WAP technology and allow WAP applications to be built and hosted	Ericsson, IBM, Nokia, Phone.com
Content aggregator or content portal	Aggregates and packages a variety of content offered by various content providers; may implement the WAP capability and provide connectivity between the device and the Internet	Excite, Infospace, Phone.com, Yahoo!
Application service provider/service bureau	Provides and aggregates services such as e-mail, PIM, and enterprise application access	Aether, AOL, Concentric, IBM
Content provider	Owns the specialized content and makes it available to end users by hosting it on the Internet or intranet	CNN, Mapquest, Reuters
Application and content developer/ author	Develops the application, service, or content	Various ISVs

and computer industries. Indeed, industry research indicates that by 2003, one-third of all Internet users will also access the Internet via mobile devices, most likely enabled by WAP. Not surprisingly, businesses are now seeking to uncover, develop, and experiment with new business models that will provide them with a competitive edge with their core competencies in the mobile Internet.

Generally speaking, each player in the service fulfillment chain seeks to maximize profit and gain market share by means of one of the following models:

- Acquire and retain an ever-expanding customer base (reach)
- Gain brand name recognition and Web identity through differentiated products that are of value to the customer (richness)
- "Own" the end customer's total experience

Before diving into a discussion of how the wireless Internet marketplace will evolve, we will first look at the historical trends affecting the classic Web marketplace. First, the costs of network connectivity and transport are decreasing, causing access and bandwidth to become commodities. At the same time, typical end-user expectations are continually increasing. For businesses competing in such an environment, new products and services will be the key source of sustainable revenues in the long run. Second, businesses are increasingly vying to become the primary "customer facing point" in the service fulfillment chain. In doing so, they seek to create a sense of "stickiness," thereby spurring the fragmented customer base to become "loyal" to their individual brands. The current trend is toward storing customer personalization, profile, or subscription information, making it more difficult for the end user to move between brands. The economics of information and the Internet are causing resegmentation and disintermediation like never before, giving rise to new business models such as "infomediaries," service bureaus, horizontal and vertical portals, and digital marketplaces. Traditional "brick and mortar" companies are competing with these emerging entities to become the focal point for the user's Internet experience. They do so by executing innovative strategies not only for investments, partnerships, product development, marketing, and customer care, but also for relationships, communities, transactions, and interactions in the Net economy.

One can expect the mainstream mobile Internet marketplace to closely follow along the lines of the classic Web. Thus, in an effort to be customer-centric, businesses entering the mobile Internet space are likely to focus on building and enhancing their existing relationships with the end users. Alternatively, as in the case of the classic Internet, they could attempt to provide a new set of compelling services that will reel in a whole new set of customers and establish new long-term customer relationships. Like the Internet, success in the mobile data marketplace is achieved by harnessing the Web to let enterprises integrate, collaborate, outsource, and bid out noncore activities to gain competitive advantage. In doing so, firms would constantly reinvent or refine current value propositions and operating models to meet the evolving demands of the mobile e-consumer.

Of course, the mobile Internet market is in its infancy, and it would be premature to predict how its value chain will mature. Indeed, it is anybody's game. As both the market and the technology mature over the coming years, however, a continuous realignment of the value chain will be inevitable.

Let us now analyze the roles of the key stakeholders identified in Figure 2-3 on page 16.

End User

The end user plays the most important role in the success of WAP and the mobile Internet. Clearly, without this consumer, there would be no market for any applications, which means that no one would want to develop, host, or enable such applications in the first place. Market forecasts presented in earlier chapters support the existence of a potentially large user base for WAP-enabled mobile applications. They indicate that users would accept and demand these services as long as they remain affordable, usable, personalized, and valuable.

The end-user market can be broadly segmented into enterprise customers and mass-market consumers, all with varying degrees of sophistication, expectations, and enthusiasm for new, sometimes unproved, capabilities. For example, an enterprise user might be willing to pay a higher price for a solution, feature, or capability that may not be truly easy to use, reliable, or mature. These users are seeking competitive advantage, and for them the potential benefits of a successful solution far outweigh its costs. In our example from Chapter 1, Bob Fisherman would demonstrate these characteristics: He is always looking for niche applications that will improve his work productivity, even if he has to endure a suboptimal product in the short run.

On the other hand, the demographic of a typical mass-market consumer (such as Mary Beeker, our other example from Chapter 1) is generally characterized by a different set of expectations. Such a user is less experienced in configuring and navigating through online applications and might potentially be turned off by a feature that is, for instance, not intuitive. This user is typically willing to pay less for a service and is seeking more immediate and tangible value for her money.

Despite their differing demographics, both types of users benefit by gaining access to personalized services that can be customized according to their individual preferences and can be available at their fingertips at any time, wherever they are. Furthermore, users claim to value being able to subscribe to a bundled package containing multiple services from a single provider—that is, from one-stop shopping. Studies carried out by the Strategis Group indicate that 66 percent of businesses and 63 percent of consumers are interested in purchasing bundled telecommunication services. A recent Cahners Instat study validated that view, finding that consumers perceive simplified billing and discount pricing as the most important benefits to purchasing multiple services from one provider.

It is not clear who the preferred WAP service provider will be in the long run. Will it be the operator or a third-party content aggregator (mobile portal)? Will the user prefer a default menu of services offered through the home page, or will he or she prefer to bookmark favorite sites on the Internet? These interesting questions open up spectacular opportunities for the remaining players in the value chain.

Terminal Manufacturer and Browser Vendor

Terminals are a key element in enabling the delivery and interactive use of mobile data services. A terminal can be anything from a data-enabled smart phone with a built-in micro-browser (a "WAP phone"), to an enhanced personal digital assistant (PDA), or even to a handheld companion PC running several applications at once. Over time, we can expect to see advances in processor, memory, battery, keyboard, and display technologies, leading to an overall reduction in the cost of computing power. Consequently, these devices are likely to evolve into terminals that would not only be lighter to carry and have longer battery life but also perform extremely complex tasks that were inconceivable not too long ago.

Some evidence suggests that users demonstrate a personal attachment to their terminal devices, to the extent that these devices are even claimed to represent the user's personality through their color, shape, and ring tones. In a highly competitive market, terminal vendors will seek to differentiate themselves by identifying and implementing new ways to allow users to personalize their devices. Among mobile handsets, Nokia phones have become popular because of their flashy covers and attractive back cases that help uniquely identify your phone from others. A ring tone composer (harmonium) for the phone allows subscribers to generate and download their own ring tones over the air for a small fee. There have been stories of a Finnish user having a heart symbol displayed on the phone to notify him that the call is from his wife; Japanese teenagers can pay for images of Pokémon characters as screensavers for their phones. Also in Japan, one can buy little fuzzy animals whose eyes flicker to indicate that the phone is ringing. On the other hand, a typical user of a Palm Pilot device fitting the demographic of a "corporate user" often carries this device in sleek, designer leather cases or accompanied by voice recorders. Thus, these devices are evolving from simple communications tools into personal information appliances that take on the user's personality.

The Strategis Group predicts a ninefold increase in sales of mobile Internet handsets—rising from $867 million today to $7.8 billion by 2005. This revenue level is equivalent to the sale of 60.3 million units. In an attempt to grab market share and enhance their long-term relationships with end customers, first-tier phone manufacturers, such as Nokia, have already built their own WAP micro-browsers. Other phone manufacturers have licensed and customized micro-browsers from suppliers such as Phone.com and AU Systems. Some handset manufacturers have announced partnerships with content aggregators and portals to provide a WAP offering that could be directly marketed to mobile ISPs or even enterprises. Besides generating incremental revenue for their infrastructure, the companies intend to provide a richer affinity between the content and their phones.

Mobile Internet Access Provider

WAP has been designed to run over multiple wireless networks. Consequently, it offers a "write once, run over any network" ubiquity that allows the user to have a common view of services and applications across multiple, disparate networks. The wireless operator, or carrier, plays a critical role in enabling seamless coverage and connectivity to both voice and data applications, regardless of the location from which the services are accessed.

To support WAP, the carrier implements, maintains, and upgrades the necessary wireless network and data (ISP) infrastructure; it also ensures high availability of the network at all times. For large carriers that operate and support not only the wireless network but also a traditional wireline ISP infrastructure, the mobile Internet provides an opportunity for seamless integration of services, complementing and extending the carriers' existing infrastructure and offerings. On the other hand, a wireless operator whose core competency has so far been traditional value-added voice services faces a more difficult decision. It might choose to function as a simple transport or access provider, or it might implement a revenue-sharing business model with content providers. It might even extend its role into niche areas such as services hosting, service aggregation, or customization and rendering.

Early wireless data offerings have demonstrated all flavors of these business models. Some operators have chosen to act as primary service providers to their WAP customers. They support private-labeled or co-branded WAP sites consisting of a carefully selected suite of content and applications developed in strategic collaboration with content providers. Such a "walled garden" approach has the advantage of providing a common look and feel across the various applications and is typically optimized for one-click access from the main menu. Users may have the option to go to the World Wide Web directly by entering the destination URL. Depending on the relationship, the operator could charge the content providers for the placement (on the main menu) or for the incremental traffic to their sites, while subsidizing the service and cost of the handset for the subscriber.

On the other hand, some carriers do not foresee how they could directly profit from providing data services. They may therefore forego branding and instead opt to earn a small commission from the millions of transactions carried out over their wireless networks; this model can generate a significant profit stream. Still other carriers might serve as core connectivity enablers, seeing their revenues grow through their wider reach and increased airtime use by data customers.

In the long run, what will likely emerge are new partnership ventures between operators and service/content providers that allow for co-branding of services and co-ownership of customer data. Clearly, the operator has access to a large subscriber base from the voice world. The operator also has the infrastructure needed for billing and payment collection.

These capabilities make it extremely attractive for other stakeholders, such as portals and content providers, to partner with carriers to obtain access to their customers and infrastructure. The operator would likely function as a service bureau, continuing to act as the primary interface to the subscriber.

Thanks to its partners, the carrier has the opportunity to bundle, package, and market differentiated services such as online subscription management to better lure the end customer. For example, the AT&T Personal Network product bundles wired telephony (local and long distance), wireless telephony, Internet access, and wireless data services into one attractively priced offering, with one consolidated bill for all services. This model could be a potential win-win situation for both the individual consumer and the wireless ISP. The end user has to maintain a relationship with only one provider and can receive a single bill. In return, the wireless operator is assured stickiness and the opportunity to cross-sell and up-sell services. In some cases, particularly in Europe, the bundling might potentially extend to e-commerce transactions from the phone that would be charged to the monthly phone bill.

Infrastructure Vendor

In the context of WAP, the infrastructure includes the wireless network and Internet components for enabling service delivery to the end user, as well as tools for developing WAP content and applications.

Wireless network components include both the switches and the base stations that enable the wireless environment. On the Internet side, the system must include Web servers, caching, and proxies that permit hosting of the content and rendering to the mobile terminal in an optimal way. Most of this wireline infrastructure is already in place on the existing Web. Finally, the wired and wireless network and the wired Internet come together at the *WAP gateway*, which implements the suite of WAP protocols. The WAP gateway may also be coupled to an enhanced proxy that provides vendor-specific capabilities such as methods for content conversion or optimization of specific WAP features.

Content and application development tools already exist for building Web applications (servlets, JSPs, ASPs, CGIs) and content (HTML, JavaScript, applets). Several companies have delivered tools specifically intended to simulate the WAP client application environment (see Appendix A). However, the ultimate challenge lies in extending existing Web tools to support both the classic Web and WAP technologies. Such tools would allow both mobile and desktop clients to communicate with common server-side applications. Tools that promote a separation of application logic from the generated markup language, such as IBM WebSphere Studio, are best positioned to provide this flexibility.

Today, WAP infrastructure vendors are developing WAP gateways, proxies, and solutions for deployment in the network. Phone.com, for example, is one of the pioneer developers of WAP technology and a market leader in providing WAP gateways to operators. IBM offers WAP infrastructure as part of a network solution to enterprises and service providers that desire wireless access to intranet and Internet applications. Its approach supports connectivity to legacy systems from WAP devices and integrates WAP with existing Internet and Web infrastructure.

As part of their attempt to provide end-to-end (packaged) offerings to carrier and enterprise customers, some infrastructure vendors are also extending their traditional business models. They are developing services or content in-house and partnering with content providers and aggregators, not only to jump-start the market but also to develop revenue streams from usage and transactions. As gateway and browser products proliferate in the marketplace, versatile and interoperable end-to-end solutions will most likely be the winners.

Content Aggregator (Portal)

The powerful concept of the consumer portal grew out of the classic Internet, where it was originally targeted toward the novice user who browsed the Web in search of useful content. For a fairly unsophisticated user population, the portal initially served as a launching pad or doorway to the wild Web by providing easy links to the desired content. As users became more comfortable with online surfing and navigation, the function of the portal evolved into its current form: a personalized destination—a one-click, one-stop shop showcasing a broad range of services including search engines, directory services, e-mail and chat, e-commerce, and local and regional content. On the e-business side, portals now serve as online intermediaries and market aggregators. They support business-to-business (B2B) e-commerce within vertical industries, provide economies of scale to fragmented supplier or customer bases, and reintermediate the traditional supply chains in niche markets.

With these changes, the portals' business model also has evolved. Portal vendors no longer earn revenue only from selling advertising banner space. Some charge commissions for directing users to commerce sites. Others seek to more directly complement other parts of the value chain: operators, e-commerce vendors, and content providers. These cobranded efforts are aimed at engaging and retaining users, as well as establishing brand differentiation through personalization and breadth of services. Because the sophistication of the common user is continually increasing, portal vendors must work at evolving their role and value proposition to meet the dynamics of the virtual marketplace.

According to a study carried out by the Strategis Group, almost 25 million users in the United States are expected to use wireless portals by 2006. The size of this prospective customer base, combined with the promise of the mobile Internet, gives portal vendors an incentive to reestablish themselves as destination sites for WAP applications in an attempt to become the primary "owners" of the customer's total (wired and wireless) experience. Recently, some existing portals have announced joint ventures with mobile operators and wireless ISPs to cater to the existing wireless voice market. Using the portal Web sites, end users have the ability to customize and configure exactly what information they want, when and how frequently they receive it, and on which device the data is displayed. One can expect these mobile portals to offer personalized information and local/regional content that takes advantage of user preferences and tastes. Transaction-based and advertiser-supported applications are also a potential source of revenue.

What will make the wireless content aggregator and broker successful in the long run remains to be determined. The Chevy Chase consulting firm claims that consumer portals are currently positioned to cater to horizontal markets, whereas the most successful wireless data applications so far have targeted vertical markets. It is also not clear whether sophisticated business users and mobile professionals, who have access to wireless e-mail and PIM capabilities provided through their employers, will find generic portal-based services worthwhile. However, these users might find significant value in using vertical portals that support niche markets in key business-to-business areas.

Application Service Provider

Application service providers (ASPs) and *service bureaus* are emerging as a new channel for applications on the Web. Traditional ISPs also seem to be gradually moving into the application services hosting space. These providers host and rent niche applications to ISPs, enterprises, and consumers alike. Service bureaus generally offer "horizontal" applications such as e-mail and content hosting, whereas most ASPs also support specialized business software such as enterprise resource planning (ERP) or sales force automation within specific "vertical" market segments (for example, finance, manufacturing, transportation).

The opportunity for ASPs lies in the largely untapped and lucrative market resulting from the universal adoption of IP technology by businesses for their day-to-day operations. Their value proposition lies in offering economies of scale while hosting applications and servers within virtual domains for multiple small or medium-size businesses. The typical revenue model is based on the number of seats per customer per application per month. The enterprise benefits from the significant cost savings that result from outsourcing the implementation and ongoing maintenance of the infrastructure associated with in-house IT functions, as well as from the more predictable costs. According to Forrester Research, the ASP industry is expected to garner $21.1 billion in revenues by the end of 2000, with e-mail outsourcing alone generating $1 billion!

WAP provides these traditional ASPs with the ability to extend their reach to the heretofore untapped wireless market. In addition, these vendors could find opportunities for new horizontal and vertical applications specifically tailored for the mobile data space. The new applications would likely require ASPs to incur only an incremental infrastructure cost because they already operate data and network operations centers. Ultimately, wireless data promises to strengthen ASPs' prospects for customer retention and brand recognition. The business model, however, must account for the costs associated with conversion or repackaging of data for low-end terminals.

Groupware (e-mail and PIM) is an application that many enterprises might choose to outsource to a service bureau or ASP for integrated wired and wireless access. In this case, the service bureau would provide the enterprise with secure solutions that enable access to the corporate groupware application from any device over any network at any time. Other integrated access scenarios could include Web hosting, supply chain management, sales force automation, and field service dispatch services. In the area of e-business, ASPs would host managed security offerings, audio and video streaming, and e-commerce transaction and fulfillment capabilities.

Content Provider

Content providers play many different roles on the Internet. For example, one type of content provider syndicates and brands the content developed by the content authors and hosts that content at a Web site that attracts users from near and far. Examples in the media business include *Rolling Stone* (**www.rollingstone.com**). In another scenario, the content provider and the content author might be the same; thus, the site hosts content from only that author. This case is typically seen when the content already has some brand recognition and does not need promotional services or resources from an aggregator. A site dedicated to Dilbert cartoons would fall under this definition. Under a third scenario, the content provider is synonymous with the service provider. The content provider can therefore act as an aggregator of multiple services, each of which is provided by an ASP.

Different revenue models are possible, of course. One source of revenue might involve licensing the rights to the content and splitting the income with the content author. Premier content, such as the *Wall Street Journal,* could also be made available on a subscription basis. In addition, revenue might be generated by syndicating the content to portal providers and aggregators. A third model could involve paying a commission fee to sites based on the amount of traffic directed to the content provider's site. Paid advertisements on the site could also boost the revenue stream.

WAP offers content providers the opportunity to extend their brands through wider distribution channels for the content and products and through increased Web site circulation as a result of return visits. With this technology, content could reach customers any time of day, wherever they are. Competitive advantage is realized through support of asynchronous notification features based on personal preferences and location-aware services. Site navigation from WAP terminals can be greatly improved by means of implicit or explicit personalization. In addition, studies have shown that it is less expensive to retain existing customers than to attract new ones. The challenge, therefore, lies in erecting sufficient barriers to prevent customers from switching to alternative content providers and in maintaining barriers to entry for competitors. Content providers must refresh the content frequently to continually provide value to their loyal customers.

Content Developer

Content developers are the people who actually author or create the content. They include application architects, HTML and WML developers, human factors professionals, programmers, artists and musicians, story-writers, news reporters and editors, and so on. According to a forecast developed by International Data Corporation (IDC), worldwide Web authoring and design revenues could exceed $290 million by 2002. Already a lucrative opportunity, the Web content publishing and media business continues to explode and is becoming increasingly complex as competition grows unabated.

Internet access from mobile devices and smart phones, however, introduces new challenges for content developers: The mobile Internet requires development of content scaled toward low-end, sometimes black-and-white, sometimes text-only devices. It is no longer enough to simply develop a Web site and expect users to use it. Instead, content must be attractive and constantly provide enough unique value to attract customers to the site. Differentiation strategies include supporting an intuitive, simple-to-use interface, as well as frequent updating of content that lures the user back for more. It also means keeping a close eye on usage patterns to verify that the user continually perceives the services offered by the site as having real value.

Content developers will play a key role in the proliferation of WAP to the mass market. With sufficient content from which to choose, the user will perceive the mobile Internet offering as being attractive and valuable. Likewise, with sufficient users, content developers will be motivated to create content tailored for specific mobile terminals. As the success of i-mode in Japan has demonstrated, this process could feed on itself and become the driving force for "crossing the WAP chasm." The good news is that the outlook for the mobile Internet is extremely optimistic. With the growing availability of tools that make the task of content creation easier, developers can pursue this opportunity now. This book will show you how!

Conclusion

The next few years will likely witness dropping prices for phones and PDAs, as well as wireless network access. The resulting market will be even more competitive. In a fluid market environment, business models and relationships will evolve rapidly, as members of the value chain seek to maximize their profits either in conjunction with or at the expense of other players. Strategists must understand where their businesses currently lie within the WAP value chain so as to identify potential partners, customers, and competitors. Finally, a key to success in this fast-paced, dynamic business is to "start early," thus gaining a foothold in the market. In essence, the first-mover advantage can help create a market share leader.

The next part of this book delves into WAP technology. We begin our journey into WAP in Chapter 5 by exploring the challenges to delivering data within the wireless environment. WAP was designed to overcome many of these limitations, and it is important to understand why extending the existing Internet to the wireless world is not a straightforward task.

Part II

The Wireless Application Protocol: The Mobile Internet Standard

Chapter 5

Making the Internet "Mobile": Challenges and Pitfalls

Having whet your appetite about the glorious new future that awaits us in a world enabled by the emerging mobile Internet, we must now deliver the bad news. It is tempting to consider wireless connectivity to be simply "copper in the air" and expect that the computing assumptions traditionally made about connection methods and application usage will hold true. It is also easy to assume that existing applications will migrate to the mobile Internet world without significant change. Unfortunately, both of these assumptions are rarely valid.

This chapter will address the major technology challenges, making specific reference to those that pose the largest obstacles for deploying applications in the wireless environment. The chapter concludes with an evaluation of existing Internet technologies and their suitability for the wireless application world.

What Is So Different about Wireless?

This section considers the major differences between the wireless world and the wireline world as they relate to an application writer or user. Suppose that we simply want to connect a laptop PC to a remote server

Table 5-1   Characteristics of the Mobile Internet

Wireless network characteristics	Latency
	Bandwidth and run-time costs
	Error rates and unreliability
Wireless device constraints	Memory
	CPU power
	Battery life
	Variable device capabilities, possibly even changing dynamically
	Graphical user interfaces (GUIs) and nongraphical user interfaces
	Location independence or dependence
	Security
Service requirements	Huge user base
	Management and control
	Roaming

over a cellular phone: The engineer would say "No problem!" In truth, knowledge is required to configure dial-up connections and TCP/IP, set up server authentication, be aware of network coverage and connection characteristics, and worry about error correction protocols. In many respects, therefore, almost everything is different when we consider today's average cellular phone user wishing to jump into the mobile Internet.

Table 5-1 lists the major issues that are quickly encountered by a wireless application user. Of course, the non-wireless user may also be affected by these characteristics, but they take on a new significance in the wireless world. Because a huge range of wireless communication types and variants are possible, it is difficult to make statements that will apply to all of these networks. For example, packet-based networks have connection characteristics that differ from those of circuit-switched networks. Nevertheless, each of the attributes listed in Table 5-1 is still important to consider in all cases.

Latency

Network latency, or "delay," is the amount of time required for a message to travel between two points in the network. To send a byte of information over a telephone line to a server and back again usually takes about 250 milliseconds. This latency, once established, will remain reasonably constant for each byte sent via the connection.

Wireless networks typically have considerably longer latencies than their wired counterparts. GSM (Global System for Mobile Communication) wireless networks for circuit-switched data connections have round-trip latencies on the order of 800 milliseconds, whereas packet-based networks such as Mobitex have latencies between 2 and 4 seconds on average, although variations up to 30 seconds are not unknown. A message delivered via Short Message Service (SMS) over the GSM system has been known to take several minutes to arrive! Some packet-based networks even demonstrate variable latency between one packet and the next, due to packet routing changes that may occur during transmission.

Response time matters in many places within a wireless system architecture. For example, an application may make assumptions about the expected performance of the server, or the transport protocol may make assumptions about lost packets and the need to retransmit. In a wired world, these times are usually short and within reasonably tight tolerances, but these assumptions are invalid in a wireless world.

The Effect of Latency on Applications

Consider a typical logical application flow of request–response, where the application expects the response to arrive within a predefined time. A wireless system will need to take account of the network latency to operate effectively, otherwise false errors will be detected. Miscalculation of the expected response time has dire consequences for an application's behavior. For example, many applications time the response between an SQL query and its expected result, using this information for error routine triggering or statistical monitoring purposes.

Variable wireless network latencies can introduce other side effects as well. For example, if each packet incurs a different latency, then packets may be received out of order. For example, suppose that packets 1, 2, and 3 are sent sequentially, but packet 2 is routed via a longer path due to network congestion. The result is that packets arrive in the order 1, 3, and then 2.

Reassembling the packets in the correct order requires each packet to have some form of sequence identifier. These identifiers, which can "tag" packets of data, are often added in the packet address fields. Reassembly software in the protocol stack is responsible for buffering packets that arrive out of order and delivering them to the application when the preceding data has arrived. High-performance reassemblers can be quite complex, as they must decide when to deliver partial data "chunks" of reassembled packets and when to discard packets from the buffer to conserve space.

Although reassembly software is commonplace on wireline networks, it is invoked only rarely because most packets arrive in order. Out-of-order delivery is more likely in cellular systems, however, so the reassembly software requires additional buffer space and consumes more CPU cycles. Moreover, packet resequencing can affect application performance when the number and frequency of out-of-sequence packets are high, because the application typically sees larger gaps between the delivered data bursts. Applications tend to need twice as much buffer size to accommodate this bursty behavior.

The Effect of Latency on Transport Protocols

Wireless network latency also affects the underlying transport protocols. Protocols such as TCP/IP can get into all sorts of trouble if network latency exceeds what the transport considers a reasonable time to receive a response.

It should be noted that, strictly speaking, TCP has the difficulties, not IP. This fact reflects the reality that the major error recovery protocols are implemented in TCP, rather than as part of IP. TCP includes a very complex set of rules to ensure that it can handle slow-responding networks, and it tries to adjust itself to work with the response times discovered. Because these discovery mechanisms were not designed for high-latency networks, the protocol frequently retransmits data. These retransmissions will themselves be seen as a failed transmission, and therefore retried again. Before long, the protocol link either stops working entirely or slows so dramatically that it becomes unusable.

TCP Behavior with High-Latency Environments   The transport problems arise because of the way that TCP attempts to adjust its transmission speed to account for network congestion and avoid flooding the network. TCP sends two basic acknowledgments from the receiver:

1. ACK, the normal positive acknowledgment that the data was received correctly and in sequence order
2. DUPACK, indicating that the data was received correctly but "out of sequence"

TCP has two types of triggers for error recovery:

1. Timeout
2. DUPACK

Although both triggers are linked to the TCP congestion control mechanisms, each employs a slightly different algorithm.

If a timeout is detected, the sender reduces its transmission speed to one segment per Round-Trip Time (RTT), in the belief that either serious congestion or link failure has occurred. Neither of these situations would be helped by faster retry attempts. If this drastic rate reduction is successful, the sender then ramps up the transmission speed exponentially in the "slow start" phase, reaching half the original transmission rate. Finally, in the "congestion avoidance" phase, the transmission rate is increased linearly.

The DUPACK recovery mechanism begins with the sender halving its data rate (that is, segments sent per RTT). The rate is then increased in the same way as in the congestion avoidance phase.

Neither of these mechanisms was specifically designed for the random effects often produced in wireless systems. In these environments, the network may "disappear" for a second or more, although the data is preserved within the network. The network may experience a rapid latency variation that causes enough reordering to trigger a DUPACK threshold and consequently reduce the transmission rate sharply. If multiple latency bursts occur, the sender backs off repeatedly, halving the throughput each time.

This approach presents a problem for many applications that might seek to use TCP/IP as the underlying connection layer. The issue is just as relevant to middleware such as messaging, databases, or encryption software intended to provide SSL or TLS security. Such middleware makes assumptions about the reliability of the connection transport mechanism and requires the TCP transport protocol to ensure correct operation. Unfortunately, the lighter-weight UDP protocol does not offer the reliability characteristics required by these applications.

Improving TCP Behavior   Much research has been done, and some practical implementations for overcoming these TCP "problems" have emerged. The most recent publications by Mark Allman of the NASA Glenn Research Center, for example, provide useful insight into how the TCP slow-start algorithms for congestion avoidance and control seriously affect protocol performance over high-latency, low-bandwidth networks. Allman also draws attention to the problems associated with packet loss when switching between slow-start termination and "normal" processing. Typically, papers published in this area have dealt with attempts to extend or enhance the use of TCP to cope with the environments that a wireless network brings. Most authors have suggested using various byte-counting techniques to more effectively use the slow-start and congestion window thresholds.

Until these techniques, or other similar ones, become commonly accepted within the major implementations of TCP stacks in the marketplace, it will be impractical to expect widespread usage of TCP in wireless environments. Specific protocol solutions for the mobile Internet environment will be required.

Bandwidth and Run-Time Costs

Bandwidth is the speed, or capacity, of the data network, measured in bits per second (bps). The higher the network bandwidth, the greater the potential for transfer of more data in a defined period. Network bandwidth is often the most obvious difference between the wired and wireless worlds, with wireless networks being several orders of magnitude slower than their wireline counterparts. Network operators manage the finite network capacity—the radio-frequency spectrum. Consequently, the user is charged according to the amount of that spectrum requested. Typically, network operators charge for accessing the wireless network based on either the amount of time or the amount of data being passed.

As mentioned earlier, a variety of wireless networks are used for cellular communications. Most analog cellular networks are gradually being superseded by the newer digital networks. In Europe and Asia, most users already use the digital networks. In Australia, the analog networks were turned off at the start of the new millennium. Although analog networks could be used for transferring data, this approach has proved unreliable and slow. Typically, data transfer rates could not top 4800 bps. Digital networks, however, have proved to be much more reliable, and much faster data rates have been achieved already.

The most commonly encountered digital networks in the Western world are GSM and CDMA (Code Division Multiple Access). GSM is almost universally accepted across Europe and much of Asia, with CDMA being the most popular option in North America and South Korea.

GSM typically provides a 9600 bps data service, with the network providing the error correction capability. Slightly higher data rates are possible by using uncorrected network service and handling the error correction within the end user's device; however, devices rarely support this approach because of the complexity of function and the corresponding computing power required in the device. CDMA has a data service rate of 14,400 bps.

Both the GSM and CDMA networks also provide SMS, which is a much more bandwidth-constrained service. SMS is typically implemented by using part of the digital control channel. In GSM networks, SMS has a bandwidth of about 600 bps; because it is basically a packet service, however, SMS is more often characterized in terms of 160 characters per message with a variable latency in the range of seconds.

Some methods to enhance the data speeds available in these networks and improve the effective bandwidth are available today, whereas others are scheduled for deployment within the next few years. Note, however, that although the technology and the standards exist, it is the network operators that will choose when and if they are deployed. GSM enhanced with data rates as high as 14,400 bps will probably be deployed across Europe in 2000, with services based on EDGE (Enhanced Data for Global Evolution) offering rates of 384 Kbps and UMTS (Universal Mobile Telecommunication System) providing data transmission at 2 Mbps in subsequent years.

Early rollouts of GPRS (General Packet Radio Service) probably will appear in late 2000. As a packet data system, it will not only have a potentially greater speed capability (up to 115 Kbps) but also give an "always available" characteristic to the service. The word "potentially" was used deliberately, as the bandwidth offered to users remains at the discretion of the service provider and may vary. That is, a user may request a 14,400 bps link, but be granted only a lower-speed link. This variation in the quality of service will pose a serious challenge for application developers, who must contend with dynamic notification of service capabilities and negotiation of service availability. Imagine, for instance, a wide-band video data stream being transferred, only to have the network dynamically decide that due to increased voice traffic demand, the data link will have only a 9600 bps data rate!

The traditional Western cellular phone networks are not the only contenders for mobile data traffic, of course. The Japanese systems evolved in a very different geographical and social environment. Consequently, these networks, which include PHS and PDC, have high-speed, small-cell architectures that can support high-bandwidth applications. In Europe, other standards also exist for the new digital PMR (Private Mobile Radio) and PAMR (Public Access Mobile Radio) services, as typified by TETRA

(Trans-European Trunked Radio). These networks offer the ability to mix voice and data traffic on the same call, and the bandwidth for each service can be varied dynamically based on total user demand or a specific request. These new capabilities provide both exciting opportunities for applications and challenges for implementations.

In summary, the bandwidth of existing wireless networks is usually at least two orders of magnitude slower than that offered by traditional local area networks. Higher-speed networks will undoubtedly become available as operators decide to implement them, but even these will come nowhere close to matching the wireline bandwidth capacity. These networks may not guarantee a certain level of data service, or they may be required to dynamically select or manage the services offered. Applications will therefore need to be cognizant of the network bandwidth either at source or through intelligent middleware.

Error Rates and Reliability

The *bit error rate* (BER)—the ratio of corrupted bits to total bits transmitted—is the unit of measure usually quoted for telephony purposes. As it turns out, because the mobile Internet usually involves both wired and wireline communication links, the application and user must contend with the error rates from both media.

Communications Errors

The actual data error rate figures quoted for modems and telephone lines are getting better over time in most countries, and the BER is often better than 1 in 10^5. Wireless usage figures are often worse by at least an order of magnitude, resulting in a BER of 1 in 10^4 or worse.

Data performance over the wireless network is also affected by the connectivity from the network operator to the Internet. This connection may take place over analog lines. Analog lines, such as those used in the average home telephone service, may suffer from errors due to the low modulation level of the signals and due to the low received signal strength caused by lossy transmission lines. These errors make it very difficult for devices such as modems to establish a stable communication channel and work properly. Although the acceptable levels for BER and modulation are specified across most of the world, the levels in reality may be somewhat different, even in developed countries. Because of these limitations, it is preferable to maintain a digital link from one end of the connection to the other end. Most operators offer services such as

ISDN at primary (2 Mbps) or basic (64 Kbps) rates—enough to support as many as 30 simultaneous wireless calls.

The error distribution over wireless links has also been shown to have somewhat different characteristics from that seen with traditional wireline links. Wireless error spectrum analysis shows a much broader distribution of errors in both the frequency and time domains. The latter (time) error distribution implies that error recovery protocols must not only detect and configure themselves based on initial connection characteristics, but also monitor the link over time and alter the recovery protocols dynamically. For instance, a wireless user may initially establish a connection while stationary, in a high-signal area, with few buildings or large obstructions. The negotiated error protocols, speeds, and compression techniques will not be appropriate moments later, when the user is mobile in a car moving at 100 kilometers per hour. In that case, the data may be disrupted by the Doppler shift effects of information arriving at slightly different time intervals, reflection signals from a nearby large vehicle that swamp the direct signal, or complete signal loss as the user passes through a ravine or tunnel.

Cellular networks use a process called "handing off" to move a user from one transmitter to another so as to better manage capacity or maintain user proximity to transmitters. In an analog system, these handoffs typically cause a 10-millisecond loss of the wireless signal. In digital networks, they occur more quickly but are still noticeable. Why do cellular network users not notice such high error rates? Wireless networks were designed to service a vast user base of voice traffic (usually representing more than 95 percent of all wireless traffic), and many characteristics of digital networks assume the dominance of voice traffic. The human brain is remarkably adept at correcting slightly fuzzy information and masking, or removing, extraneous signals. However, while we may not notice the occasional pops or quiet sections during a voice conversation, we would not be too pleased if similar errors occurred during the transfer of bank account details.

Just as the human brain corrects errors to present what seems to be an error-free conversation stream, the network transport protocol typically corrects these errors on behalf of the application. Consequently, although they are significant in both their magnitude and their nature, these errors are usually hidden from the application.

User Errors

More relevant sources of errors include those that result from a user action. Wireless application writers must be aware that their users are not necessarily literate with personal computers. Users cannot be expected to "be kind" to the applications, and they may perform actions that are non-intuitive to the application designer. For example, closing down applications cleanly is unnatural to a phone user, who simply hangs up or turns off the phone, so applications should take this into account.

The new user will be mobile, which brings all sorts of new challenges. Mobile (cell) phones, for instance, typically are used while propped next to one ear. Combining voice instructions with data entry therefore is very difficult—a fact known by anyone who has tried to navigate through a voice mailbox from a cell phone, unless the user employs an ear bud. User mobility may mean that connections are lost in an abrupt manner, as the user enters elevators or subway stations. Being able to cope with the unexpected lack of response is a common requirement for an application. The ability to save and restore state and data at significant process points within the application will be required—or at least the ability to close and restart without generating a user error notification.

Note that this last requirement often requires the establishment or resumption of the call, and applications may be called upon to both detect and initiate this connection management activity. This demand has proved very cumbersome in many applications that were not designed for the wireless environment, as applications generally do not bother to ask for the current connection state before attempting to transmit data. In reengineering these applications, convoluted timer response algorithms and polling loops need to be employed.

Wireless Device Constraints

The end-user device's capabilities also need to be considered. For example, portable wireless devices typically have only a limited amount of processing power available. Modern digital phone technology is very computing-intensive, and the dedicated DSPs (*digital signal processors*) and single-chip microprocessors employed will be only as powerful as the average desktop personal computer. The power left over for application data processing is therefore limited. Processing performance improvements are happening regularly, following Moore's law, but with those improvements come requirements for more data storage; with both of these demands come new demands on battery technology.

Even when the computing power does increase, the user interface remains limited. Whereas the personal computer world boasts keyboards with more than 100 keys, multifunction pointing devices, and very-high-definition displays, the wireless devices are often limited to a handful of keys, low-definition displays, and small form factors.

An added complication is the diversity of facilities on wireless devices. In Chapter 4, we saw the vast market opportunities for members of the mobile Internet value chain. This potential has forced handset manufacturers to differentiate their products to gain market share. This differentiation often occurs in the user interface, which makes maintaining a consistent look and feel for an application very difficult to accomplish.

Finally, when considering constraints, the wireless application developer must note that the client device may change its capabilities at any time. Sound can be turned on and off, keys can be switched between alphabetic and numeric functions, and visible alerts can become useless as a device is moved away from view. In short, the device may be a chameleon, and detecting these changes in a standard manner that all applications can use has proved an elusive goal.

These factors combine to affect the application writer in several ways. If the processing power is limited, then designs that expect the client device to have large caches of data or carry out complex calculations such as those required by traditional encryption methods will always perform poorly. The constrained user interface implies the need for new usability and design paradigms. The wide variations in which device features are available—and when and where those features can be used—mean that the application must be tailored toward specific devices and even may need to change its behavior dynamically based on how the device is currently being used.

The wireless device, however, should not be envisioned only in terms of limited function. First, the mobility of the device provides several new possibilities due to its location. Initially, wireless devices were considered ideal for providing *location independence,* allowing the user to receive information anywhere. Although this remains true, recently these devices have also been recognized for their ability to deliver *location-dependent* applications. For instance, by notifying the application about its current location, the device can access a broad range of services, such as locating the nearest bank, ATM, or pizza restaurant.

Second, the wireless device must identify itself to the wireless network to confirm that it has access to network service. Thus every device must have a unique identifier. Applications can use this identifier to drive an authentication and security system, as long as the identifier can be guaranteed to be delivered to the application. Unfortunately, network operators often withhold this information for security reasons.

Service Requirements

In building wireless applications, developers must consider the challenges of scale and wide geographic acceptance.

Scalability

Application writers for traditional PC environments may expect client-server ratios of perhaps tens or hundreds of clients to one server. If the wireless device is a mobile phone, then this ratio needs to scale up to hundreds of thousands or millions of clients for each server. This scale implies the need for larger, faster content servers, network routers, and wireline network capacity.

Scalability is particularly significant for the application writer when considering managing and controlling the client environment. It will be unreasonable to expect real-time control of individual clients on this scale without considering the number of requests that could be reasonably generated by a few million users, which is not uncommon for most cellular network subscriber bases. Such management and control could also consume considerable over-the-air bandwidth. In comparison to wired device environments, device control and application management are more server-centric for wireless devices, where applications typically are not locally installed but may be remotely loaded. Limited-function devices will be unlikely to provide the client-side infrastructure required to support this management, as typical MIBs *(management information blocks)* would add reasonably large code overheads for a small-footprint client.

Roaming and Network Services

In the traditional personal computing realm, the network environment connecting the client device to the application or service is well known—or at least under the control of the client or end user. The user plugs into the enterprise's local area networks or connects through a predetermined service provider. Wireline networks tend to be quite uniform, providing a standard suite of TCP/IP and UDP/IP protocol connectivity and standard services such as DHCP and DNS.

In contrast, wireless network environments tend to far less uniform. In this world, the wireless network service providers control the available facilities and services, and different service providers may provide different services. For instance, the services provided by wireless connections in Rome may differ dramatically from those available in Chicago. In addition, the user may transparently swap service providers as he or she moves from place to place. For example, while in downtown Chicago, the user might enjoy call forwarding and caller ID facilities, but these facilities may not be provided by the network in Rome—or even by the network in suburban Chicago.

As the user moves, neither the application nor the source of the information changes; however, the network route does change and alter the capabilities available so that the application may be rendered useless. This "roaming" problem, which is well known to cellular providers in the United States, has largely been overcome for GSM voice users in Europe. Unfortunately, the situation has not always been overcome for data services, and the issue must be considered by application developers.

Applications need to be aware of the environment in which they are executing, and they need to adjust to compensate for changes to the available network capabilities. This adaptability becomes more complex as applications are more closely tied to the mobile network environment itself. For example, mobile applications may use location information provided by a network operator. An e-commerce application may access usage data and billing services provided by the home service provider. In these environments, if a user "roams" to a new service provider, then the new service provider needs to provide these data and services, and the application must dynamically adapt to the new services (or lack of services) offered by that provider.

Work has been under way for some time now within the World Wide Web Consortium (W3C) to define standards for passing information about service capabilities from all parties, including intermediaries in the data path. This issue will gain more significance as the wireless application market matures. Chapter 11 discusses these emerging standards in more detail.

Using Current Web Technologies for Wireless Applications

In the opening paragraphs of this chapter, we posed the question, What is so different about wireless? So far, we have discussed the wireless environment and the ways in which it affects the assumptions about the network protocol and application design. Despite these differences, one might expect that wireless applications could still be built using standard Internet and Web technologies; indeed, the concept of seeing the wireless device as a type of network client in which the user simply has an Internet browser has many advantages and solves many of the problems that we have discussed. Nevertheless, the Internet was not designed to be used over wireless networks. Just as we saw when considering TCP/IP earlier, difficulties arise when we try to use Web technologies without due care and attention to detail.

HTTP

The Hypertext Transfer Protocol (HTTP) has been a major contributor to the success of the World Wide Web. This text-based protocol implements a basic request-and-response interaction. HTTP is simple to implement and has been universally accepted. The session capability provided by this protocol is well suited for Web browser applications.

HTTP is not very efficient in terms of either communications or computational overhead. These inefficiencies were especially evident in HTTP version 1.0, where each request-and-response pair required a separate network communications session and network-level acknowledgments. Typically, the protocol introduced a communications overhead ranging from 50 percent to 70 percent.

The situation is made worse by the design of modern Web pages. Typical Web pages today combine text with links to multiple in-line graphics; a single page may consist of more than 20 such elements. Because retrieving each element requires an individual HTTP session (and the associated network overhead), a single-page retrieval can generate significant data traffic. In the wireless link, the most problematic performance inhibitors are often the network delay times. Thus HTTP design has tremendous implications for browser performance over wireless networks. The browser must request each element of content and wait for a response. With complex pages containing multiple embedded elements, the overall delay can be significant. HTTP version 1.1 has done much to improve this deficiency, with its ability to stream data with implicit acknowledgments. Nevertheless, session establishment and teardown remain the primary cause of slow data retrieval in network environments, such as wireless connections, characterized by a relatively high network delay.

HTTP overhead is not limited to aggravated round-trip delays. The establishment of connections usually consumes both processor cycles and operating system thread capacity. Applications could minimize these problems by streaming data over single HTTP sessions and by encoding the data into a binary form to convey more information with each byte. However, these optimizations rapidly begin to change the Web as we know it today.

HTML and XML

Most documents published to the World Wide Web are written in HTML (Hypertext Markup Language). HTML itself is based on another standard (ISO 8879) called SGML (Standard Generalized Markup Language), which defines a generic document syntax. HTML and SGML differ from formats such as PostScript in that they define the document structure and content rather than simply describing how it must be rendered.

HTML is a simplified form of SGML in which a specific set of formatting and structure commands, or *tags*, has been chosen and standardized. As the requirements and demands of the Internet community have matured, the HTML specification has itself evolved to cope with the new requirements. The current version of HTML supports more than 80 tags covering the following items:

- Document structure
- Forms
- Frames
- Graphics and multimedia
- Lists
- Links
- Paragraphs and lines
- Titles and headings
- Text styles
- Tables

This rich set of tags represents a powerful tool, but HTML rendering has also become complex and computationally expensive within today's Internet browsers. The most popular browsers require tens of megabytes of storage to implement this level of functionality and demand significant processing power. For the mobile client, many of these HTML tags may be irrelevant because of the device's inability to render the content. For example, wireless devices usually support only limited graphics or have constrained displays in which a table would be impossible to usefully render. The functional capabilities of HTML are very much directed toward the needs of a PC-based browser, with all of its implied capabilities, and it is expected that browsers will implement the full set of capabilities. For this reason, new versions of HTML need to be defined to add or supersede functions as appropriate.

SGML is more flexible than HTML in that it is extensible, supports the definition of many document types, allows complex structures to be described, and allows receivers of SGML documents to validate the correctness of the content. These attractive attributes come at a cost, however. HTML can lead to large implementations, but SGML, being more comprehensive, is even more computing-intensive!

XML (eXtensible Markup Language) was created by the W3C to bring the benefits of SGML in a limited form to the Internet world. Because SGML was originally targeted to the more general document management arena, many of its features were not applicable to Internet documents and could safely be omitted. Unlike HTML, XML is a "meta" markup language; that is, it defines a syntax, so that other markup languages (MLs) can be defined. A chemist may define chemistML, a mathematician create mathML, and a wireless application writer use wirelessFriendlyML. These new MLs can be defined to include tags having meaningful names within their particular application domains. Note that XML describes the structure for all of these MLs but does not define how documents authored in these languages will be displayed or output. This flexibility is a major advantage of XML, as it allows for a separation of the ML from the rendering environment within which it will be used.

The challenge lies in mapping the ML to the rendering. The W3C has defined XSL (eXtensible Stylesheet Language) as a way of describing the formatting. Over the Internet, XSL documents are used to convert the domain-specific ML to HTML. Cascading Style Sheets (CSS) are then used to instruct the browser about the details of the HTML formatting.

The removal of extraneous SGML functions and the separation of document structure from document rendering mean that XML holds significant promise for building efficient, flexible wireless applications. However, it is important to remember that enabling a mobile Internet was not the primary goal in designing XML. For example, XML documents are linked to DTDs (document type definitions), which can be used to verify that the document structure and syntax are correct. If these DTDs are large and must be transmitted across wireless links, then they have limited value in wireless environments. Similarly, although XML allows the document structure to be separated from its rendering, it has also introduced the high data-transmission, storage, and processing overhead involved with style sheets. These difficulties have typically hindered the unaltered use of XML technology in the wireless application space.

The W3C's work with XHTML, where "modules" of XML may be selected, is a promising technology direction. Its success will depend on whether a suitable minimal optimized set for mobile use can be defined.

Web Scripting Languages

Web scripting languages add computation and content manipulation capabilities to the browser environment. Scripting transforms what would otherwise be dull content presentations into lively and often interactive experiences. Just as many programming languages exist, several Web scripting languages have become popular. JavaScript, Jscript, ECMAScript, and Visual Basic are the most well-known scripting languages in use today.

For the sake of simplicity in the following discussion, we will ignore the differences between these scripting languages. Despite their differences, they share many similarities, and implementing them requires similar processing capabilities.

ECMAScript is a formal standard (ECMA-262); its second edition was approved as international standard ISO/IEC 16262 in April 1998. (Version 2 enhances some of the base language functions and introduces additional error-handling mechanisms.) ECMAScript is based on the original technologies of JavaScript (from Netscape Communications Corporation) and Jscript (from Microsoft Corporation). The language is object-based, but not in the same way that Java is an object-oriented language. Instead, objects in ECMAScript employ a prototype-based object model and prototype-based inheritance.[1] The prototype object model

---

[1]This model is similar to that used in the Self programming language.

does not have classes in the traditional sense; instead, *constructors* are used to create an object or even a primitive value or string from an existing instance. The code to perform this task must allocate storage and manage any required data initialization. The prototype-based inheritance means that ECMAScript objects inherit not only structure and behavior, but also state from their ancestors. This feature is well suited to Web-based functions.

ECMAScript includes a set of built-in objects such as Array, String, Math, and Date. It is capable of providing 32-bit computation, and it uses "host objects" for integrating capabilities offered by other providers.

Such object models have great value where large programs can reuse common or similar functions or objects, but this characteristic imposes a significant overhead to handle the ensuing complexity and cope with dynamic memory management issues resulting from the allocation of objects and properties. Arrays, for instance, can be passed to functions, so memory needs to be dynamically allocated when the function is invoked and released when the array is no longer required.

Given the nature of the wireless environment and the limited processing power found on most wireless devices, care must be exercised when deploying Web scripting languages on these devices. The application developer must limit the set of functions offered by the languages' supporting libraries to reduce the required memory footprint. One of the larger components required by script engines is the parser, whose job is to process the script and select the appropriate computational elements. In memory- and processor-constrained devices, this operation can soon eat up precious resources, and it should be minimized or perhaps removed altogether. In Java environments, for example, compiled executables have proved effective at boosting performance. To apply this technique within a Web scripting language, the execution environment must lose the dynamic binding capabilities provided by the ECMAScript interpreter. Any additional functions required by the wireless application writer, such as telephony services, would be added as external objects or functions.

Java

Java technology has become synonymous with the Web and Internet, which seems strange when one considers its roots. In 1990, Sun Microsystems' Patrick Naughton was assigned to overcome the problems associated with the proliferation of application programming interfaces

(APIs). This effort soon grew into a project, called OAK, aimed at building a programming environment allowing appliances to talk to one another. On May 23, 1995, Sun announced the development of the Java programming language. Because the Internet permitted users to access data using any type of client platform, the platform independence offered by Java applications was an obvious match for the Web.

Today, Java is used in everything from mainframe computers for vast computation in machines like the IBM 390 series to tiny embedded processor solutions such as the iButton. The latter is a 16-millimeter computer chip armored in a stainless steel can. Some iButton models incorporate cryptographic technology with a Java virtual machine (VM); for example, the Java-powered Cryptographic iButton uses a microprocessor for additional arithmetic functions to enhance the cryptographic speed. The Java VM is compliant with the Java Card 2.0 specification, so the Java programming community can easily program it for inclusion for instance in jewelry (a Java-powered ring) in the same way developers program Java on a mainframe! See **http://www.ibutton.com** for more details.

Java is a simple, object-oriented, distributed, interpreted, robust, secure, architecture-neutral, portable, high-performance, multithreaded, and dynamic language. Its execution environment achieves many of these properties by using an interpreter and a virtual machine. The *Java Virtual Machine* (JVM) itself is an abstract computing machine: It has an instruction set and uses memory areas much as a real computer does.

Java source code is compiled into byte codes that are independent of the operating system on which they ultimately will be executed. At run time, an interpreter translates these byte codes into the machine's native instructions. These instructions are executed within the JVM, which provides security, dynamic class loading, and scheduling services. Dynamic class loading is a particularly important feature, because it allows the execution environment to bind the application to its requested services—and particular implementations of those services—at run time. Java application portability is enhanced by the use of a standard set of class libraries that include basic data types, networking, and GUI classes.

Over the Web, users typically access applets. An *applet* is a Java class, which is normally downloaded over a network into a viewer (typically a browser). The browser needs to execute a JVM to run the applet.

All of these attributes of Java can prove difficult to implement in the constrained memory, processor, and bandwidth environments found on most wireless devices. JVMs have traditionally been both large and processor-hungry. Moreover, modern desktop environments enhance Java performance by using techniques such as just-in-time (JIT) compilers, which themselves are computationally expensive and demand considerable memory. With the applet model, downloaded Java classes are costly in terms of bandwidth, delay, memory, and performance.

Java execution on mobile devices is complicated further by the limited user interfaces available on these devices. Recall that Java application and applet portability relies on the presence of a standard set of Java class libraries. These class libraries were not designed with limited screen sizes and input capabilities in mind. They do not naturally integrate speech into the user interface or support mixed display and speech interfaces. Over time, this variation of platform requirements on limited-function devices has prompted the development of various "flavors" of so-called embedded Java or "micro-Java" standards. Unfortunately, these versions are largely incompatible with one another, which limits their ability to easily extend existing Web applets to the mobile device space.

With all of these limitations, early Java solutions for wireless devices were soon labeled as being processor- and memory-hungry, slow to start, and often slow to execute. Many of these deficiencies have been minimized or rectified over recent years, but they persist as issues that native code implementations can more easily overcome. Java technology is advancing rapidly, however, and reduced-function Java environments such as IBM VisualAge Micro-Edition are beginning to become viable on mobile devices.

Even with Java on the client, application writers still need to be aware of the fallacies inherent in expecting browsers with Java applets to be an appropriate model for wireless users. Developers need to consider the size of the applet, in terms of both transmission costs and device processing and storage requirements. Typically, Java applets are downloaded each time they are used, which further increases network bandwidth requirements and perceived delays. In the end, a locally stored and reusable Java application model would be much more efficient—possibly with client-side servlets that allow data to be posted to the client application for processing and display.

Conclusion

The chapter began by considering the wireless environment, with all of the challenges that it introduces for data applications. The experience has been compared with trying to suck a very expensive, thick milkshake through a narrow straw, when you are short of breath! It is a reasonable metaphor.

In light of these constraints, we have considered the viability of using the existing Internet technologies of HTTP, HTML, XML, scripting languages, and Java in this environment. Each of these technologies appears to bring valuable assets to the mobile environment, but each comes with a set of design assumptions that makes it difficult to apply outside the traditional wired computing world. Naturally, each technology holds the potential and promise of being adapted or modified to extend the reach of the application writer and bring wireless applications into commonplace reality. Unfortunately, the very large scope of these standards, and the range of industries affected, make a single "upgrade" initiative problematic; it would be virtually impossible to solve the wireless application problem by using such a piecemeal approach. In Chapter 6, we will see that a unified approach—the Wireless Application Protocol—is succeeding in establishing both the critical mass of users and the full range of technologies required to bring wireless data to reality.

Finally, it is important to observe that we have evaluated Internet technologies based solely on their technical merits, with little regard to their ease of use or appropriateness for wireless application users. As the technology problems and pitfalls are overcome, we must also focus on a whole range of new requirements and challenges for wireless application writing. If we enable these new devices, we enable a new range of users, too. These users probably have no previous Internet experience or background from which to approach these applications. When navigating through information, they may not expect "back" buttons. Instead, the users may expect to interact with location-based services as a matter of course; hence the term *wireless information appliance* becomes much more appropriate than *personal computer*. These changes in the user audience will affect the application writer perhaps even more dramatically than any of the issues discussed so far; we will consider these issues more fully later in the book.

Chapter 6

Overview of the Wireless Application Protocol

Over the years, the industry has made numerous attempts to extend wireless access to enterprise data, consumer information, and the Web. However, none of these efforts has achieved significant traction. After experiencing several failures in this area, industry leaders realized that the only way to bring data to users over wireless networks—and to achieve the requisite critical mass of developers, applications and services, devices, and network availability—was to establish a single world-wide standard for the delivery of these services.

The Wireless Application Protocol (WAP) suite has emerged as the standard underlying this vision of a mobile Internet. During its short existence, it has succeeded in unifying most of the fragmented wireless data connectivity efforts around the world. As a result, WAP is establishing the critical mass required for widespread deployment of wireless data services to both business and consumer users. Moreover, this standard continues to evolve as it incorporates new technologies, provides more seamless connectivity with the existing Internet, and enables the development of new functional capabilities.

The WAP standard consists of a variety of components, including network transport protocols, security capabilities, and an application environment integrating a browser markup language, scripting, and telephony. A modular architecture underlies its design and supports a wide variety of physical implementations, deployment configurations, and integration points with the existing Web and information services. The WAP architecture itself adheres to a set of guiding principles intended to ensure that future enhancements to the standard will remain consistent with the overall goals and design of the suite.

This chapter discusses the architecture of the WAP standard. It begins by discussing how the WAP standard was developed and how the WAP Forum continues to extend the standard. Next, it discusses the components of the WAP standard, including network infrastructure and protocols, security, and the application environment. In considering the design principles that form the foundation for the WAP architecture, the chapter explores how this architecture enables these components to be deployed in various network infrastructure configurations. The chapter concludes with a discussion of the relationship between WAP and other existing and emerging industry standards.

The Origins of WAP

The WAP standard represents the first successful attempt to establish a broadly accepted environment for delivering information, data, and services to both enterprise and consumer users over wireless networks. This section highlights the origins of the standard and its growth into an industrywide consortium, including network operators, device manufacturers, infrastructure suppliers, and application developers. It then discusses the processes used within the WAP Forum to continue enhancing and evolving the standard.

Many Successes with No Success

The technology to deliver wireless data to mobile devices is not new, and many have long proclaimed its impending adoption. Over the years, several companies have attempted to establish standards that would drive widespread commercial adoption of wireless data.

Analog Modem Technologies
Analog data communications typically supports between 4800 and 9600 bits per second, although variations in signal strength and quality may

lower the effective throughput considerably. Several attempts have been made to enhance the data capabilities of these networks.

Probably the most notable effort was Enhanced Throughput Cellular (ETC), a technology developed by AT&T Paradyne and rolled out in 1994. ETC-equipped cellular modems operate on the physical and link layer protocols, optimizing V.42 and V.32bis for improved data compression, error detection, and error correction. For example, ETC reduces the signal transmission by 6 dB so as to improve the reliability of data transmission over a wireless connection that is optimized for voice traffic. This technology monitors the network link to recognize distortions, and it can dynamically adjust the transmission speed as often as once every five seconds to account for these changes. ETC transmits small, 32-byte chunks to reduce retransmission time and improve throughput, and it increases the number of permitted retransmission retries.

Similar technologies for optimized analog modems include Enhanced Control Cellular (EC²), which was developed by Motorola, and Enhanced Cellular, which was created by Microcom.

Wireless Middleware Solutions

Several companies have deployed wireless middleware solutions that extend the transport protocols in an effort to improve throughput, reliability, or user experience. Middleware solutions include the following offerings:

- *Secureway Wireless Gateway (formerly Artour) from IBM.* In this approach, software on the client and the server transparently manages the use of the air link beneath any standard TCP/IP applications. Optimizations include compressing the data, encrypting the packets, shutting down the cellular link during periods of inactivity, fast reconnection, and delayed acknowledgments. Application-layer middleware optimizes Web and mainframe applications by providing additional caching and data reduction capabilities.

- *ExpressQ from NetTech Systems (now BroadBeam).* The ExpressQ middleware provides asynchronous messaging, push, encryption, and roaming capabilities on a variety of networks and devices. This technology includes a developer's kit for building applications.

- *Handheld Device Markup Language (HDML) and Handheld Device Transport Protocol (HDTP) from Unwired Planet (now Phone.com).* This technology includes a micro-browser and optimized protocol stack for supporting Web access from mobile phones. Authors write content in HDML, with the content then being sent to a gateway for encoding and transmission over the air.

- *AirMobile from Motorola.* This middleware solution provides optimized access to Lotus Notes and cc:Mail over wireless networks.

- *Narrowband Sockets (NBS) from Nokia and Intel.* NBS provides optimized data transport services for using UDP over circuit-switched data and GSM Short Message Service (SMS). The server implementation resides beneath the Microsoft WinSock API, thereby supporting seamless application development. NBS supports both delivery of notifications and pushed content. This technology is now part of the Nokia Smart Messaging Platform.

Each of these technologies has achieved some measure of success within particular markets and industries. None, however, has inspired mass-deployment of a mobile Internet.

Data-Optimized Networks

Several wireless networks have been deployed to specifically support wireless data:

- *Cellular Digital Packet Data (CDPD).* CDPD transmits digital data in idle space within an analog voice network. It offers raw 19.2 Kbps throughput, with effective data throughputs in the 9.6 to 14.4 Kbps range. Network latencies are approximately one second. Coverage is available throughout most of the United States and Canada.

- *ARDIS.* Developed by Motorola and IBM, the ARDIS packet network offers effective throughputs of approximately 2.4 Kbps. Latencies range from four to ten seconds. Coverage is available in major U.S. metropolitan markets.

- *RAM Mobile Data.* Developed by RAM and BellSouth, this packet network offers an effective throughput of approximately 4 Kbps with latencies ranging from four to eight seconds. The RAM Mobile Data network is being used to support the Palm.net service offered by Palm Computing.

- *Ricochet.* Metricom's packet network uses low-power base stations placed atop light poles. The network offers up to 128 Kbps throughput with one-second latencies. It has limited coverage areas but is often deployed in campus or corporate environments.

All of these data-optimized networks have several things in common. First, many of them have limited coverage. Second, they require the purchase of special radios. Third, they have rather high per-packet costs. As a result, these networks' market penetration has been limited to specialized vertical applications supporting mobile workers—particularly in the public utility and public safety industries. With this set of users, little economic impetus exists to drive costs even lower or to provide greater coverage for the mass consumer market.

The Need for a Mobile Internet Standard

Previous efforts to establish mobile Internet standards shared the same fate: They all failed. None succeeded in attracting the requisite number of content and application developers, handsets, and network operators to sustain a growth business. In large part, these efforts failed for similar reasons:

- Content and application developers were reluctant to support systems that did not have a sufficiently large customer market.
- Handset manufacturers were reluctant to build devices unless a sufficient number of network operators and service providers were willing to market and distribute those handsets.
- Software and hardware providers and tools vendors were unwilling—and often unable—to support proprietary systems in such a fragmented market where no one could generate sufficient sales volume to recover the development costs, let alone make a profit.
- Network and service providers were reluctant to deploy expensive, proprietary services that locked them into a single infrastructure vendor and unwilling to invest in infrastructure unless a sufficiently rich set of services and quality handsets were available.

As shown in Figure 6-1, the wireless industry was deadlocked in its effort to create a mobile Internet standard in mid-1997, preventing the establishment of a successful, growth-oriented business. For handset

Figure 6-1   The wireless data market, 1997

manufacturers, infrastructure providers, and content developers to invest, sufficiently large-scale service deployments were needed. For network operators to deploy services, sufficiently high-quality handsets, infrastructure, and content were required. Each attempt at defining a standard had been initiated by one of these industry segments, but each eventually failed to gain the necessary acceptance from other segments.

A single standard for the mobile Internet was clearly needed to help galvanize and unify the market. A standard would benefit all players:

- Content and application developers would be able to create content and services in a single format that could be delivered over all networks and to all phones.

- Software and hardware providers and tools vendors would be able to develop technologies to support that standard and be assured that their products would be useful to the broadest audience of network operators, content developers, and handset manufacturers.

- Handset manufacturers would be able to rationalize their product lines and sell data-ready phones through network operators to customers around the world.

- Network operators would be assured of an open, competitive market for handsets, infrastructure, and applications and services.

In this way, an industry standard would establish a global marketplace for wireless data solutions and, given sufficient end-user demand, foster industry growth.

Initiation of the WAP Standard

It was against this industry backdrop that AT&T Wireless Services (AWS) sought to roll out wireless data services in time for Christmas 1997. The network operator faced the quandary of selecting a wireless data infrastructure that was supported by multiple handset manufacturers. Unfortunately, no existing infrastructure satisfied these requirements.

In June 1997, AWS hosted a meeting in Seattle, Washington, that brought together representatives of Ericsson, Motorola, Nokia, and Unwired Planet (now Phone.com). Each of these companies had previously made an independent attempt to develop and deploy a wireless data solution, and, to a large extent, each had failed to gain significant market traction. In hosting this meeting, AWS sought to reach agreement on a single wireless data infrastructure standard.

The resulting effort to develop a standard, known as the Wireless Application Protocol (WAP), was announced on June 26, 1997. Representatives from each of the four companies that participated in the meeting were allocated seats on the Board of Directors for the WAP Forum. In establishing WAP as the standard, these four companies sought to jump-start the wireless data market:

> The initiative is aimed at aligning the companies' efforts to bring advanced applications and Internet content to digital mobile phones. This alignment will result in numerous benefits, among them providing operators differentiation and new business opportunities. In addition, developers of applications and content will be aided, since a single protocol and markup language will work with any vendor's compatible handsets.[1]

The four companies promised to publish a public standard by September 1997. Two weeks after the initial announcement, Alcatel, Mitsubishi

---

[1]"Ericsson, Motorola, Nokia, and Unwired Planet Unite to Create an Open Common Protocol for Interactive Wireless Applications," June 26, 1997. Available from **http://www.wapforum.org/new/jun26971.htm**.

Electric, Nortel, Philips, and Siemens endorsed the establishment of a common standard for the mobile Internet.

As envisaged at the June 1997 meeting, the WAP standard would incorporate three existing technologies:

- HDML, developed by Unwired Planet, would become the common markup language.
- NBS, developed by Nokia as part of its Smart Messaging Technology, would become the optimized transport protocol, and HDTP, created by Unwired Planet, would become the optimized session protocol.
- Intelligent-Terminal Transfer Protocol (ITTP), developed by Ericsson, would provide the foundation for the telephony application services.

Throughout the summer and fall of 1997, representatives from the four companies met frequently. Indeed, they worked almost full-time to integrate the core proprietary technologies, adopt existing and emerging Internet technologies, and establish a viable public standard.

The technical work to integrate these technologies into a single standard proved far more complex than originally thought. The core technologies had been designed with different basic assumptions, and considerable duplication of function (including reliability, session management, and other aspects) existed among them. Moreover, the four founding companies did not want to establish a standard that would tangibly benefit any one of them at the others' expense. The resulting need to "shoot everyone in the foot" further complicated the design. In fact, the difficulties were so great that by September 1997 the standard was still far from complete. The four companies were able to publish only a WAP architecture document at that time.

Several key issues had to be faced during the specification design process:

1. *Should the standard be layered?* A tightly integrated stack would enable greater levels of network optimization and a more efficient implementation, but would require more significant work to integrate the core technologies. On the other hand, a layered approach would allow for partial implementations of the standard, the possibility of providing APIs at each layer, and a better segmentation of design responsibilities.

Resolution: In September 1997, this issue was brought to the WAP Forum's Board of Directors, who declared that the standard would be layered, although implementers would remain free to merge the layers so as to provide a smaller implementation. This compromise essentially allowed for purity and manageability of design, while supporting efficient implementations—something that most traditional layered protocol stacks such as OSI had not permitted. As a side effect of this decision, however, the designers could not define standard interlayer APIs because implementers were not required to internally maintain the layer boundaries.

2. *Should IR-OBEX or HDTP be used as the session layer?* The Infrared Data Association (IrDA) had already developed and standardized a session-layer protocol, the Object Exchange protocol (IrOBEX). This binary protocol supports both push and pull semantics for accessing various types of data. It was designed to provide "HTTP-like" semantics for wireless devices that cannot support a full HTTP stack. In this respect, the IrOBEX protocol appeared to meet many of the needs of WAP. Nevertheless, it was not deemed capable of running over the full range of wireless networks being targeted by the WAP standard.

Resolution: The WAP standard included a new protocol stack that could easily be targeted to run on many bearer networks. It borrowed ideas from both HDTP and NBS, but ultimately differed quite significantly from both of these technologies.

3. *How should connection-oriented and connectionless sessions be supported?* In the original WAP design, HDTP rested on top of an optional security layer; this layer, in turn, rested on top of NBS. However, these core protocols conflicted in several ways. The resulting stack contained redundancy because both protocols provided data reliability. Moreover, NBS offered both a connection-oriented abstraction (stream) and a connectionless (datagram) abstraction. The security layer therefore had to support both datagrams and connections. Adding to the complexity, because the security layer was optional, HDTP essentially had to support four configurations (secure connection, insecure connection, secure datagram, and insecure datagram). Even worse, the connection-oriented NBS mode was overkill for the transaction-oriented operation provided by HDTP. Finally, because the security layer ran on top of a datagram layer, its state machine was susceptible to attack from an intruder that introduced illegal datagrams to the mobile terminal requiring processing by the security layer.

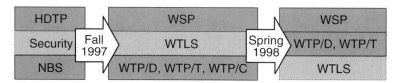

Figure 6-2   Evolution of the WAP protocol stack—from core technologies to version 1.0

Resolution: These layering issues were resolved in two stages, as shown in Figure 6-2: (1) During the fall of 1997, HDTP (now the Wireless Session Protocol [WSP]), the security layer (now Wireless Transport Layer Security [WTLS]), and NBS (now the Wireless Transport Protocol [WTP]) were redesigned. WSP emerged as a strict session protocol, similar in spirit to HTTP. The reliability layer was moved out of WSP, and WTP became responsible for providing reliable datagrams (WTP/D) and request–response transactions (WTP/T). The connection-oriented features of WTP were relegated into a third mode (WTP/C), which was subsequently dropped from the standard. (2) During the first quarter of 1998, the WTLS protocol was moved beneath WTP, allowing it to enable only secure datagrams. Besides simplifying WTLS, this shift addressed concerns about potential denial-of-service attacks on the protocol.

By early 1998, the first version of the WAP standard was nearing completion, and the WAP Forum was ready to go public with its work. A draft of version 1.0 of the WAP standard was formally released to the public via the WAP Forum's Web site in February 1998. The standard covered the full suite of wireless data functionality, including a complete protocol stack, security layer, and browser-based execution environment, as well as a cohesive architecture and high-level statement of direction.

The WAP Forum Goes Public

Although the development of a WAP standard had been announced in June 1997, the initiative received relatively little attention because virtually no information had been made publicly available about the capability and design of WAP.

In January 1998, however, the WAP Forum announced that the standards were nearly ready and that it was ready to recruit new members.

Informational meetings were scheduled in both London and Miami to discuss the standard and encourage other companies to join.

Of course, no network operators had yet committed to developing or deploying WAP-based services, and the founding members could make only vague promises to deliver WAP-based handsets and infrastructure "soon." However, despite the lack of any product or deployment commitment, the WAP Forum began to be perceived by the industry as a viable entity, offering a complete wireless data solution. Although its success was not assured, it was recognized as having the potential to lead the convergence of the wireless data industry.

Throughout the spring of 1998, the founding members continued to refine the initial specification to resolve additional security concerns and fix numerous specification bugs. Finally, in May 1998, version 1.0 of the WAP standard was published. With this event, the founding members officially declared the WAP Forum to be active and invited its newly joined members to participate in further enhancing the emerging standard.

Evolution of the WAP Standard

By late 1998, broad experimentation with version 1.0 of the WAP standard had revealed several errors and ambiguities in it. Moreover, WAP members expressed interest in introducing several minor enhancements to the suite to enable the standard to be used in more versatile ways. Finally, liaison activities with the World Wide Web Consortium (W3C) and European Telecommunications Standard Institute (ETSI) had begun to reveal ways in which the WAP specifications could be changed to enable greater interoperability with other existing and emerging standards. Unfortunately, instituting these changes would eliminate backward compatibility with version 1.0 of the WAP standard.

Given that no WAP equipment was available yet and, consequently, no WAP 1.0 deployments had reached the market, the WAP Forum decided in early 1999 to declare version 1.0 of the specification to be obsolete; instead, a one-time "baseline" version 1.1 would be adopted for use in all initial commercial deployments. Throughout early 1999, changes were made in the specification, and version 1.1 of the standard was formally adopted in May 1999. Version 1.2 of the standard was formally adopted in December 1999, and a maintenance release (version 1.2.1, known as "WAP June 2000") was adopted in June 2000 to improve interoperability.

In the future, the WAP Forum intends to update the standard on a regular basis, perhaps once every six to nine months.

The WAP Forum Today

The WAP Forum currently includes nearly 600 members,[2] which range from network operators and service providers, to handset manufacturers, to hardware and software infrastructure providers, to content and application developers. The Forum has defined two classes of membership:

- *Full members* include operators and industry suppliers. They have full voting rights, including the ability to run for a seat on the Board of Directors.
- *Associate members* include affiliates of full members, as well as non-infrastructure suppliers such as content suppliers, application developers, and tools vendors. They have limited rights and may neither run nor vote for the Forum's Board of Directors.

An up-to-date list of WAP Forum members can be found on the WAP Forum Web site, **www.wapforum.org**.

The WAP Forum meets five times each year, with meeting attendance now rapidly approaching 1,000 delegates. Each week-long meeting includes meetings of the Board of Directors, specification committee, architecture group, various technical working groups and specification drafting committees, expert groups, and marketing and requirements groups. Time is also reserved for workshops discussing future WAP standards, relationships with other standards bodies, and other issues.

The WAP Forum includes several subgroups:

- The Board of Directors is elected by the membership and manages the direction and policies of the Forum. It may sanction various nontechnical groups, including the Marketing and Communications Expert Group.
- The Specification Committee is nominated by the Board of Directors (each member of the Board has the right to nominate one member of the Specification Committee). It manages the day-to-day technical operations of the Forum and its technical

---

[2]This number reflects the membership as of September 2000.

roadmap. This committee also serves as the WAP Interim Naming Authority (WINA). Much like IANA (the Internet Assigned Numbers Authority) on the Internet, WINA manages the assignment of global numbers and identifiers required by the WAP specifications.

- The Architecture Group includes members of the Forum at large. It maintains the technical architecture of the Forum's standards, ensures that draft standards and proposed standards activities conform to that architecture, and defines the Forum's relationships with other standards bodies.

- The Specification Working Groups manage various areas of the WAP specifications. Currently, six working groups exist: Architecture, Application, Telephony, Protocol, Security, and Interoperability. Each working group includes several Drafting Committees, which are responsible for drafting or maintaining particular specifications.

- Expert Groups meet to discuss various topics that span multiple areas of the specifications. They play an advisory or monitoring role. The WAP Forum has many active expert groups, including the Carrier Expert Group, Multimedia Expert Group, Smart Card Expert Group, Telematics Expert Group, and WAP Developer Group.

Forum representatives who are interested in proposing a new WAP standard typically organize a workshop to discuss the proposed topic and assess the need for the standard. If the idea draws sufficient interest, members develop an *activity proposal* that defines the scope and role of the proposed standard. This activity proposal is submitted to the Specification Committee for its approval. After approval of such a proposal, the drafting committee holds an organizational meeting and elects a chair.

The drafting process typically encompasses several stages:

1. A *requirements document* is created that defines the measure of a successful standard.

2. Active discussions take place, which eventually lead to an architecture for the standard.

3. Several *working drafts* are developed. The final working draft is delivered to the applicable working group, which votes to promote it to a *proposed specification*.

4. The proposed specification is made available for public review and comment. Editorial changes are applied to it, but material changes cause the specification to be demoted to the drafting committee for further consideration.

5. After the open comment and review period, the general Forum membership votes on whether to promote the proposed specification to an *approved specification*.

New WAP standards must conform to the WAP architecture, which defines not only how the WAP specifications fit together but also which design points the WAP standard seeks to meet. This architecture is discussed in the next section.

Overview of the WAP Architecture

The WAP standard is actually a suite of standards that together define how wireless data handsets communicate over the wireless network and how content and services are delivered and executed to those same handsets. Using these standards, the handset can establish a connection to a WAP-compliant wireless data infrastructure, request content and services from that infrastructure, and present the retrieved content and services to the user. As shown in Figure 6-3, the standards affect not only the imple-

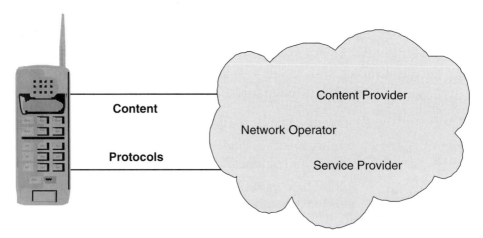

Figure 6-3   The WAP standard—defining both handset behavior and network infrastructure behavior

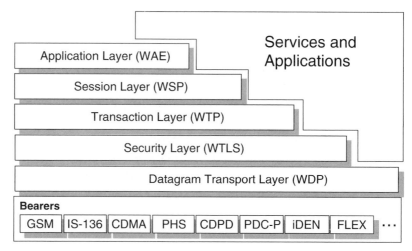

Figure 6-4 The WAP architecture

mentation of the handsets but also the server-side infrastructure that may be present in the network operator, service provider, or content provider.

Figure 6-4 depicts the WAP architecture, which consists of a set of standard services encompassing network protocols, security, and the application environment. As shown in the figure, the WAP standard is *layered*, meaning that the standards rest on top of one another and, therefore, depend on one another to provide services.[3] Protocol layering is commonly employed to simplify networking designs by dividing them into functional layers and assigning protocols to perform each layer's task. Protocol layering essentially decomposes the problem so that simpler protocols can perform well-defined tasks. These protocols collectively provide a complete service infrastructure.

In addition to exposing an interface to the layer above it, each layer may expose an interface directly to applications and services. For example, if a particular application or service requires only the services provided

---

[3]You should not confuse the WAP logical architecture with the physical architecture in a WAP implementation. The WAP standard says nothing about how stacks are implemented, and implementers are not required to actually employ a layered structure, expose interfaces between different layers of the stack, or even expose interfaces from those layers to the application. Indeed, the WAP specification makes no attempt to define these interfaces, so any interfaces, should they be provided, would be entirely proprietary.

by the datagram transport layer, it may request those services directly without incurring the overhead introduced by higher-level, but unnecessary, layers.

Most of these layers are *symmetric*, meaning that they run both on the client device and within the network infrastructure, as shown in Figure 6-5. For example, the transaction layer on the handset communicates with an instance of the transaction layer running somewhere in the network infrastructure. Server-side and client-side applications communicate by residing atop the same layer in the WAP standard.

The layering provided by the WAP architecture offers many advantages:

1. *Layering allows the design of each protocol to evolve independently of the other protocols.* In particular, each layer assumes that the layer below it has a particular set of capabilities and provides a particular set of capabilities to the layer (or applications) above it. As long as these *service interfaces* are maintained, the standard that defines each layer may change independently from the others.

2. *Layering allows subsets of the standard to be implemented.* On a resource-constrained device, an implementation of the standard may choose to provide only a subset (for example, only the lowest layers) of the available WAP functionality.

3. *Layering permits effective bridging to the Internet.* As shown in Figure 6-6, the protocols that are used over both the Internet and World Wide Web are layered. Note that the layers in the figure are not pairwise-compatible with one another, which complicates protocol conversions. The layering, however, allows protocol converters, gateways, and proxies residing within the network infrastructure to effectively bridge the two standards by operating pairwise, according to corresponding layers within each protocol stack.[4]

4. *Layering supports the* Principle of Separability. This principle ensures that functionality is distributed among different elements of the network infrastructure. (This principle will be explored later in this chapter.)

---

[4]Unfortunately, this bridging turns out to be far more complex than one might think. The WAP protocol layers *have different semantics* than the Internet layers. Consequently, bridging can occur only at certain "equivalence" layers—in particular, the datagram transport layer, session layer, and application layer. These bridging configurations are discussed briefly later in this chapter, and Chapter 14 considers them in more detail within the context of end-to-end security and manageability.

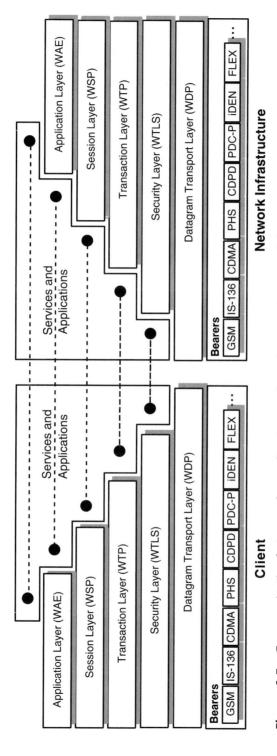

Figure 6-5 Communication between the applications and services running at each layer on the client handset and those running at corresponding layers within the network infrastructure

105

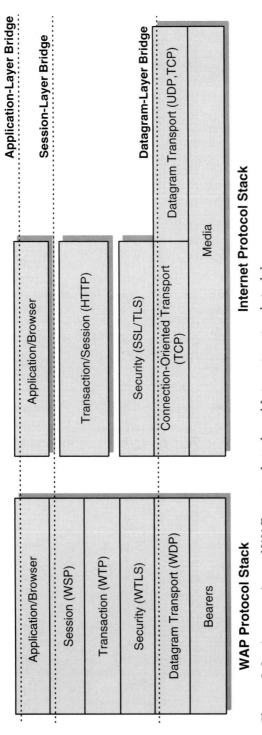

Figure 6-6 A comparison of WAP protocol stack and Internet protocol stack layers

5. *Layering potentially allows the implementation of each layer to change independently of the other implementations.* If the implementation follows the logical architecture and preserves the service interfaces, a developer may refine the implementation of any one layer without directly affecting the implementation of the other layers.

Layering also has several disadvantages:

1. *Layered protocol implementations are more difficult to optimize and, once optimized, more difficult to maintain.* If the protocol specification is layered, the natural implementation preserves this layering structure. However, optimization (for performance or code size) typically requires the designer to break the protocol layering boundaries, merging code and protocol operations where possible. Once the layering is broken, the implementer must work more diligently to incorporate changes to the layered protocol specifications into his or her code.

2. *Layered protocols tend to be less efficient.* Layered protocols typically reside above abstract protocol services (the layer below) and, in turn, provide abstract protocol services upon which the layer above is implemented. Because these layers are often designed independently, duplication and inconsistencies may easily crop up in the design.

In light of these potential drawbacks, layered protocol design requires careful oversight to ensure that inconsistencies and inefficiencies do not find their way into the specifications.

Components of the WAP Standard

The layers of the WAP suite cooperate to enable a sophisticated environment for content, applications, and services delivered to and executing on mobile clients. These layers may be divided into three groups, corresponding to the three interoperability layers shown in Figure 6-6:

1. *Bearer Adaptation:* Hides the differences between the myriad signaling and channel protocols used over wireless networks around the world.

2. *Service Protocols:* Includes protocols providing various higher-level services for moving application data through the wireless network. These services include security, reliability, and caching.

3. *Application Environment:* Includes a powerful, browser-based environment that supports content and application portability across a broad range of device types and form factors, independent of the manufacturer.

In this section, we consider each of these components in turn, defining the basic capabilities of the constituent layers and their role within the overall WAP architecture. In the rest of this book, we concentrate our attention on the components of the application environment.

Bearer Adaptation

Wireless networks employ a variety of protocols for exchanging messages, packets, or *frames* to and from the client device. Dozens of these network protocols, also known as *bearer protocols*, exist. Each bearer protocol is associated with a particular type of network infrastructure, and each type of network infrastructure is typically associated with a particular set of suppliers or with particular regions of the world.

The most common wireless network infrastructures in use today include the following:

• The *Advanced Mobile Phone System* (AMPS) is an analog communications infrastructure that is still used throughout much of the world, including North America. Geographic *cells* are used to separate conversations taking place over the same frequency.

• *Cellular Digital Packet Data* (CDPD) is a 19.2 Kbps digital packet service that uses free space in a voice network to transmit data. It uses *Frequency Division Multiplexing* (FDM), in which the transmitter sends each packet on a different frequency. CDPD is deployed in various parts of the United States and Canada.

• IS-54/IS-136/ANSI-136 (commonly referred to as North American TDMA, or *Time Division Multiple Access*) is used primarily in the United States and Canada. It takes advantage of *Time Division Multiplexing* (TDM), which works by dividing a radio frequency into time slots and then allocating those time slots among multiple calls.

• IS-95, or *Code Division Multiple Access* (CDMA), was developed during World War II by Qualcomm for the U.S. military and is now widely used within the United States, Canada, and parts of Asia. CDMA is a spread-spectrum technology that tags each conversation with its own digital sequence.

- The *Global System for Mobile Communications* (GSM) standard runs in the 800 MHz band and has emerged as the standard in Europe, Australia, and most of Asia. It relies on a combination of TDM and FDM to achieve benefits similar to those provided by CDMA. In the United States, GSM operates at different frequencies and is commonly known as DCS 1800 (at the 1800 MHz band) and PCS 1900 (at the 1900 MHz band).

- The *Personal Digital Cellular* (PDC) system provides both telephony and data services and is widely used in Japan. Like GSM, it combines TDM and FDM capabilities.

- The *Personal Handy Phone System* (PHS) represents an evolution of digital cordless phone technology for wide-area telephony. It is popular in Japan.

- The Flex protocol, developed by Motorola, supports one-way paging. The ReFlex protocol adds two-way paging capabilities.

- New network standards, including EDGE, GPRS, and UMTS, provide greater capacity either by enhancing existing networks such as GSM or by replacing them.

Unfortunately, this multitude of bearer network protocols complicates the task of providing a network-independent system for delivering content to devices. In particular, each network provides a different level of reliability, latency, throughput, and error rate. Some of these bearer networks transmit *packets*, where each transmission is routed independently to its intended destination. Other networks rely on fixed *circuits*; like telephone calls, these circuits involve point-to-point connections between the client and its destination. A network may also provide *Short Message Service* (SMS), which is similar to a paging service for transmitting text-based messages to an intended recipient within the wireless network.

The lowest level of the WAP standard—the *Wireless Datagram Protocol* (WDP)—is used to hide these differences between the underlying bearer networks. WDP is not a protocol in the traditional sense but rather a *service abstraction*—that is, an assumed set of capabilities upon which the higher layers of the protocol stack may build their function. The WDP layer is responsible for ensuring that this common service abstraction is provided over the full range of supported bearer networks.

The WDP service abstraction is a datagram service, which simply enables one endpoint to send a message point-to-point to another endpoint in the network. The service abstraction neither guarantees the reliability and security of the transmission nor guarantees the ordering and timeliness of the data's arrival at the destination. Instead, WDP defers these services to higher levels of the protocol stack.

Of course, each bearer network provides a different level of service. Therefore, WDP is actually a *collection* of protocols, with a WDP protocol being associated with each supported bearer network protocol. Consequently, when the application transmits a message through the WAP stack, a different WDP protocol is invoked depending on the bearer network in use. Indeed, a device that is capable of communicating over multiple bearer networks may use different WDP protocols at different times.

Naturally, some networks provide bearer protocols that deliver precisely the service abstraction represented by WDP. In those cases, the WDP specification simply mandates use of that bearer protocol to achieve the service abstraction. In particular, if the underlying network supports the User Datagram Protocol (UDP), as do most IP-based networks, then WDP simply uses UDP/IP to achieve the service abstraction.[5]

On the other hand, some bearer networks provide richer functionality than the service abstraction defined by WDP. In these cases, the WDP specification makes direct use of the bearer network protocol and simply ignores the extra functionality provided by that bearer protocol. This situation arises with circuit-switched connections, for example. These connections guarantee packet ordering (although not necessarily reliability). Consequently, the higher-level WAP protocols may provide duplicate functionality, which wastes some network bandwidth (and code memory on the device) in providing capabilities already available from the bearer protocol. These situations are relatively rare, however, and tend to arise in networks over which bandwidth is a lesser concern. The interoperability benefits of the WDP abstraction far outweigh these costs.

---

[5]A useful side effect is that the WAP service protocols may be used over the Internet by simply encapsulating them within UDP/IP packets. As a result, a specialized Web server (commonly referred to as a *WAP application server*) can be deployed on the Internet to deliver content to WAP clients without any intermediate protocol conversions. This feature of WDP has important implications for end-to-end security, as will be discussed in Chapter 14.

Service Protocols

The datagram abstraction guaranteed by WDP is rather limiting. Applications are difficult to implement in a network environment that does not guarantee reliability, ordering, timeliness, or security. The *service protocols* provide these additional capabilities in a layered fashion for use by the application environment.

Unlike WDP, the service layers are protocols in the traditional sense. That is, each defines a set of packet formats and a protocol *state machine* that determines when each type of packet should be transmitted. Because these protocols are deployed over WDP, they are designed and implemented independently of the underlying bearer network. A gateway may bridge the service protocols between two bearer networks by simply changing the type of WDP adaptation associated with the transmission.

The service protocols include three protocol layers: Wireless Transport Layer Security, Wireless Transaction Protocol, and Wireless Session Protocol.

Wireless Transport Layer Security

The *Wireless Transport Layer Security* (WTLS) protocol is modeled after the Transport Layer Security (TLS) protocol (formerly, Secure Sockets Layer [SSL]) that is typically used over the Internet. WTLS provides authentication using specially optimized client and server certificates that demand less bandwidth than traditional X.509 certificates sent over the Internet. This protocol includes data encryption, which prevents third parties from seeing or modifying the data. Finally, the protocol defends against various security attacks, including *replay attacks* in which a third party attempts to access services by replaying the requests and/or responses generated by a client during a previous session.

From its position near the lowest level of the protocol stack, WTLS helps to defend against *denial-of-service attacks*. In this type of attack, a third party bombards a client or server with a sequence of invalid packets. Because the target host must receive, parse, and discard the illegal packets, the third party can effectively consume the available computational resources on the target host, leaving that host unable to process any valid packets that it might receive. The security protocol layer is best suited to detecting and discarding invalid packets, so by placing it near the bottom of the protocol stack, the WAP suite ensures that invalid packets are identified and eliminated as quickly as possible. Consequently, precious computational resources are not devoted to performing higher-layer processing on these packets that would otherwise be discarded.

The WTLS protocol is an optional layer in the WAP stack. A device is not required to support WTLS; even when it is present, its use is optional. The authentication and encryption functions of WTLS consume computation and bandwidth. Because WTLS is optional, the WAP suite can still be deployed on devices having minimal resources and over networks offering minimal bandwidth.

Wireless Transaction Protocol

The *Wireless Transaction Protocol* (WTP) resides on top of a (secure or insecure) datagram service; it is loosely modeled after Transactional TCP (T/TCP), an experimental Internet protocol designed to support efficient request–response operations. In addition to supporting unreliable and reliable one-way messages, WTP introduces the notion of a *transaction*, an explicit pairing between client requests and server responses. It does not embrace the notion of a stream or connection, such as that introduced by TCP over the Internet. The transactional model enabled by WTP is well suited for Web content requests and responses, but it handles stream-based communications such as Telnet poorly.

WTP supports reliable message exchange between the device and the server by transmitting acknowledgment messages to confirm the receipt of data and by retransmitting data that has not been acknowledged within a suitable timeout period. In addition, it includes options that query the user to acknowledge the data receipt, thus establishing true *end-to-end reliability* between the sender and receiver.

WTP takes great pains to minimize the additional bandwidth consumption introduced by this reliability layer. The protocol reduces its bandwidth requirements by permitting the piggybacking of fresh data with each acknowledgment that is sent. Moreover, WTP delays the transmission of outbound data and acknowledgments in the hope of concatenating multiple data messages and acknowledgments into a single transmission. Piggybacking and concatenation reduces network overhead, as fewer WDP packet headers need to be sent.

Wireless Session Protocol

The *Wireless Session Protocol* (WSP) layer of the WAP stack supports efficient, long-term "conversations" between two application peers. In particular, WSP supports the efficient operation of a WAP micro-browser running on the client device and communicating over the low-bandwidth, high-latency wireless network. The WSP layer is modeled on the existing HTTP 1.1 standard that is the lingua franca of the World Wide Web; indeed, the two protocols are semantically equivalent. Typically, a WAP gateway transforms WSP requests received over the air into HTTP requests sent over the Internet; similarly, the gateway transforms HTTP responses received over the Internet into WSP responses sent over the air. A WAP-enabled Web server (a WAP application server) may also speak WSP directly.

WSP introduces features that address many of the limitations that are inherent to HTTP: sessions, modularity, and binary encoding.

Sessions   WSP establishes a long-lived *session* between the client and the WAP gateway. This session provides a context within which several requests and responses are exchanged. Some WAP gateways even include a session ID with each forwarded HTTP request, allowing a WAP-aware origin server to avoid the use of cookies or encoded URLs to recognize several requests from the same client.

WSP sessions should not be described in the same terms as HTTP "sessions," as the latter tend to define the lifetime of a user's interaction with a particular content server. Instead, as shown in Figure 6-7, WSP sessions between the device and gateway survive across requests to multiple content servers. The session may even survive across power cycles of the client device! The WSP protocol allows the client to suspend and resume the session at any time. Session resumption requires a simple client–gateway handshake and occurs considerably more rapidly than session establishment. The suspend–resume capability therefore allows the client to quickly connect, access WAP services, and disconnect from the network. Either endpoint may discard the WSP session state at any time (because the cache is depleted or because an administrative timeout occurs, for example), after which a new session must be established for communication to take place.

When the WSP session is being established, the client and gateway exchange a set of HTTP headers that they cache for the duration of the session. Subsequently, the cached headers need not be transmitted along with each request or response. Instead, the WSP gateway automatically inserts the cached headers into the request when forwarding an HTTP message to the content server, and the gateway automatically removes the cached headers from the response before forwarding it over the wireless network.

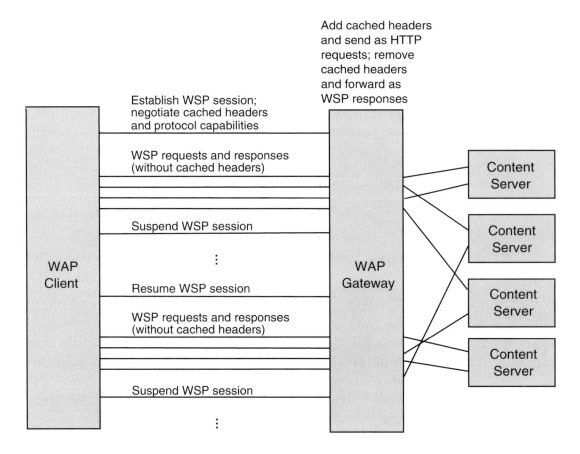

Figure 6-7   Use of Wireless Session Protocol to establish a long-lived session between a WAP client and a WAP gateway

This *header caching* is associated with a significant bandwidth saving, because most HTTP headers do not change across subsequent requests and responses. Instead, most of these headers describe the client and server capabilities, including accepted character set encoding, content formats, and language. In the end, each WSP request and response needs to contain only the information (URL, content) that is unique to that request. WSP also provides features that allow either endpoint to insert additional headers into a request–response pair or trigger renegotiation of the cached headers.

Modularity   The basic WSP protocol supports the same request–response operations as HTTP—namely, "get" and "post." However, while establishing a WSP session, a client and gateway can negotiate additional features or parameters:

1. *Extended methods.* The endpoints can negotiate additional WSP commands beyond the standard "get" and "post." These extended methods are application-specific and have no well-known semantics.

2. *Protocol parameters.* The endpoints can negotiate a variety of protocol configuration and performance parameters, including message size and number of outstanding (unanswered) requests that may exist within the session.

3. *Protocol features.* WSP defines several optional features, which may be used if they are supported by both session endpoints. During session negotiation, for example, the client and gateway agree on whether to support one-way push messages and session suspend–resume. As a result, WSP does not generate additional communications overhead for features that are not required by the applications.

With this session negotiation, the WSP protocol can support a fairly broad range of application styles, from the browser request–response model to more sophisticated push, message-based, and transactional models. The one limitation is that WSP does not easily support a two-way "stream," like that offered by TCP/IP. Various proposals have been made to introduce a WSP/C, a connection-oriented session protocol for use by applications that demand more unstructured communication semantics. Such a proposal is likely to emerge in a future version of the WAP standard.

Efficient Encoding   HTTP uses ASCII text to describe protocol operations, making it both easy for humans to read and debug and expensive to transmit over low-bandwidth networks. In contrast, WSP is designed to operate efficiently over the air. The request and response header names, as well as common values for those headers, are assigned binary values. Consequently, the WSP protocol involves the exchange of small binary sequences, followed by the transmission of the application data.

The number of headers and values is potentially quite large, and assigning a single number space would therefore require that multiple bytes be used for each value. To address this problem, WSP introduces the notion of *code pages*, or groups of token values. Each code page contains a maximum of 255 entries, which is enough to support a one-byte representation. The most common headers and values are placed in code page 0, whereas less common headers and values are placed in code page 1. A single code page is assumed within the WSP protocol header, but a special byte sequence can be used to switch to another code page if necessary. Consequently, most header values can be handled using a single byte (relying on the default of code page 0), but less common headers can be added with a minimal byte expense to switch code pages.

Application Environment

The WAP application environment consists of a set of standards that collectively define a group of recognized formats for downloadable content and applications, as well as instructions on how application servers should deliver that information to the WAP environment. These standards are optimized for use by devices having small display screens, limited input controls (that is, not a full QWERTY keyboard and mouse), and constrained memory capacity. These standards are loosely based on the Internet Web application environment—Hypertext Markup Language (HTML) for content, JavaScript (ECMAScript) for applications, and eXtensible Markup Language (XML) for structured data—but are optimized for use in the constrained device and network environment.

The WAP application environment remains largely independent of the WAP service protocols and adaptation layer standards.[6] Indeed, WAP-based content can be downloaded to a WAP application environment running over a standard Internet protocol suite. This approach would be appropriate for a small-screen telephone connected to a high-bandwidth IP network. Similarly, standard Internet content can be downloaded to a Web application environment running over the WAP protocol suite. This approach would be appropriate for a full-screen, keyboard-equipped device connected over a low-bandwidth wireless network.

Wireless Markup Language

The *Wireless Markup Language* (WML) is a content format designed for use by small-screen devices that do not have a rich input mechanism (such as a keyboard and mouse). In this respect, the markup language seeks to overcome many of the limitations of HTML. WML is designed to

---

[6]Newer capabilities, such as WAP Push and WAP Telephony Applications (WTA), rely on the server-to-client messaging capabilities that are unique to WSP. The closest analogy on the Internet would be an HTTP POST to a Web server embedded into the client browser; however, this structure is rarely seen on the Internet today.

allow the device to perform local processing that reduces the number of network interactions required to retrieve content while the user is navigating through content. Combined with the Wireless Binary XML standard (described later in this chapter), which provides for efficient encoding of WML documents, WML is well suited for use over narrow-band networks. Chapter 7 discusses WML in depth.

WML derives much of its heritage from the Handheld Device Markup Language (HDML), which was originally defined by Unwired Planet (now Phone.com). WML's attributes are described next.

A "Deck of Cards" Document Structure   As shown in Figure 6-8, each WML URL references a document, known as a *deck*. This deck is actually a collection of pages, or *cards*. Although the entire deck is downloaded to the client, only one card at a time is displayed on the client device. Consequently, the card contains a relatively small amount of data. The deck of cards model allows multiple small-screen pages of content to be retrieved in a single network interaction.

An Intradeck and Interdeck Navigation Model   Each card within a deck is assigned a unique name. Navigation commands and anchors

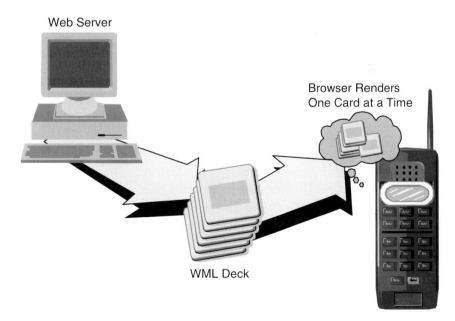

Figure 6-8   A WML document consisting of a deck of cards

within a card may therefore reference any other card in that deck or an arbitrary card within another deck. Moreover, the browser maintains a *history stack*, a last-in/first-out (LIFO) list of the cards that have been navigated by the user. Navigation commands within a card may instruct the browser to "pop" the history stack, thereby displaying the most recently visited card on the history stack.

Document Caching Model   The WAP specification defines how WML documents may be cached in the client browser. When delivering a document to the client, the server can designate how long that document may be safely cached before it must be refreshed from the server. This caching model is essentially the same as that used by HTTP 1.1 over the Internet. Unlike Internet-attached devices that can run a time synchronization protocol such as NTP, however, mobile phones are not assured of always having the current time; therefore, they may misbehave when deciding whether to declare WML documents from their local caches to be expired. The WAP caching specification addresses this issue by providing a mechanism through which the client can retrieve an approximation of the current time from the WAP gateway.

Device-Independent Man–Machine Interface   Mobile Internet devices may have vastly different user input capabilities, ranging from a full keyboard on a PDA, to a numeric keypad on a cellular phone, to two buttons on a pager. To avoid being restricted to a particular class of devices, WML provides an abstract user interface model that allows each device to choose the best way to present the content to the user. Examples of this feature include the following:

- *Browser-supported timers and timer events.* The WML deck can set a timer and bind an action that should be taken when the timer expires.

- *Input forms.* A user can provide input in several ways in WML, including through selection and text entry. When describing a menu, a WML author can request that a menu item be associated with a particular input key. For example, the first menu item might be bound to the "1" key. The browser dynamically makes these key assignments based on requests made by the WML deck and the device's physical capabilities.

- *Soft keys.* A *soft key* is a "virtual" key, programmed by the WML author. The language defines common user event types, such as **Accept**, **Prev**, **Help**, **Reset**, **Options**, and **Delete**, and the WML document defines appropriate actions to take in response to each action. Upon receiving a WML document, the client browser maps these user events to the appropriate physical interactions on the client device. In this way, the user interaction is dynamically tailored to the device's own physical capabilities.

State Management Model   WML browsers maintain dynamic state consisting of a set of attribute–value pairs (that is, a variable name and an associated value). Commands embedded within the WML document can read and write these variables. A new variable is dynamically created when it is first written. Moreover, the markup language includes constructs for making real-time substitutions of these variables into the text that is displayed to the user. This browser state represents a valuable way for communicating information not only between cards in a single deck but also across multiple decks.

Layout and Images   WML inherits many tags from HTML that control text layout and appearance. These tags include line breaking, tables, boldface, italic, underlining, big font, and small font. WML also supports in-line images.

WML is a powerful markup language because it incorporates many capabilities that were traditionally left to scripting languages such as JavaScript. In fact, WML enables rather powerful applications to be deployed on the client without the use of any scripting logic. However, for cases requiring more powerful logic capabilities, WAP includes a scripting language called WMLScript.

Wireless Markup Language Script

The *Wireless Markup Language Script* (WMLScript) language defines the format of the downloadable client logic that can be executed within the client browser. This scripting can be used for many purposes:

- Checking the validity of user input in WML fields.
- Application-controlled selecting and navigating of URLs.
- Generating dialogs dynamically for the user without the need to perform a network round-trip.
- Accessing facilities on the device (such as telephony features, SIM cards, or other smart cards) or, in future releases of the WAP specification, facilities located on other devices attached to the WAP client.

- In the future, allowing the downloading and installation of client software enhancements, the configuration of the device software or hardware, and even dynamic generation of the markup language for the browser.

The WMLScript scripting language is based on the ECMAScript standard, which, in turn, is based on Netscape's JavaScript and Microsoft's Jscript languages. Although WMLScript is considerably smaller and simpler than ECMAScript, it is not a strict subset of the earlier standard because it adds features that support mobile telephony environments.

Unlike ECMAScript or its predecessors, WMLScript is associated with a defined byte code syntax, so the script is typically precompiled at the server before being downloaded to the WAP client. The binary encoding reduces the bandwidth required to download the script. It also means that less memory is required on the client to store the script and fewer processor resources are needed to parse and interpret the downloaded script.

The WMLScript environment includes a set of mandatory libraries, such as a core language library, URI manipulation library, dialog library, and browser interaction library. A floating-point arithmetic library is an optional part of the WMLScript environment and is present on only devices that support native floating-point operations. Device manufacturers, browser vendors, and software developers may define other proprietary WMLScript libraries. For example, a WMLScript library extension might enable access to telephony features that are specific to a particular device. The WAP Forum will standardize those libraries having broad applicability or interest.

Chapter 9 discusses WMLScript in detail.

Wireless Telephony Application Interface

The *Wireless Telephony Application Interface* (WTAI) defines a collection of services that may be used by a WML application to interact with the telephony features of the client device. These services are accessible as WMLScript function calls.

The WTAI services are classified into three categories:

- *Public services* may be accessed from any downloaded WMLScript or WML. Currently, these services include the ability to initiate a phone call and the ability to send DTMF (touch) tones. In addition to being invokable through WMLScript calls, the public functions are associated with specially formatted "`wtai://`" URLs that, when retrieved, invoke the appropriate operation on the client device. Consequently, these WTAI services may be invoked either by using WMLScript logic or by navigating through WML to a WTAI URL.

- *Network-common services* are available on any network, but they can be invoked only from privileged software that is resident in the device. These services include accepting and setting up incoming calls, manipulating the phone book or directory on the device, accessing the device's call log, and sending and receiving network text messages such as those transmitted via SMS.

- *Network-specific services* are available only on certain networks or only within certain network operators. Like network-common services, they may be invoked only by privileged software that is resident in the device. Network-specific services include placing a call on hold, transferring a call, initiating a multiparty call, and transmitting location information.

The public WTAI interfaces are discussed in Chapter 9, and the privileged WTAI interfaces are discussed in Chapter 13.

Wireless Telephony Applications

The *Wireless Telephony Application* (WTA) specification supports the downloading of *catalogs*, or bundles of new telephony libraries and event-handling capabilities. This feature helps users gain easy access to value-added telephony services such as voice mail and call waiting. WTA applications can use the privileged WTAI interfaces.

WTA is discussed in Chapter 13.

Wireless Binary XML

The *Wireless Binary XML* (WBXML) standard supports the efficient binary encoding of XML documents, thereby enabling these text documents to be downloaded over low-bandwidth wireless networks. Binary encoding also reduces the memory requirements on the client device and streamlines the processing needed to parse the document. By encoding arbitrary XML documents, WBXML allows the WAP application environment to support the retrieval of virtually any structured data from a server. Moreover, because WML is itself a valid XML syntax, WBXML can be used to encode WML documents as well.

A WBXML document consists of three parts: a preamble, a string table, and the document body. The preamble includes the version of the WBXML encoding, the XML document type, and the character set used to encode the document. The string table contains a selected list of strings within the source document and assigns a numeric value to each of those entries. Finally, the document body includes the text of the source document, with strings being replaced with numeric tokens. Three types of numeric tokens may be used:

- *Global tokens* that have a common meaning across all types of XML documents. Global tokens are defined in the WBXML specification.

- *Application tokens* that have a common meaning across all documents having the same XML document type. Application tokens must be defined in alternative specifications (for example, specifications that define the particular document type and syntax).

- *Document tokens* defined in the in-document string table.

Many parties have indicated their interest in defining a binary encoding standard for XML. Consequently, the WAP WBXML specification has been submitted to the W3C for consideration in defining an Internet-wide encoding standard.

WBXML is discussed in Chapter 8.

Common Application Content Formats

In addition to supporting WML, WMLScript, and WBXML documents, the WAP application environment explicitly supports three other data types:

- *vCard:* The Internet Mail Consortium (IMC) has defined the vCard standard format for business cards.

- *vCalendar:* The IMC has defined the vCalendar standard for calendar and schedule entries.

- *Wireless BitMaP (WBMP):* The WBMP specification provides an efficient binary encoding of bitmaps and other image data for transmission over low-bandwidth networks.

When combined with WML, WMLScript, and WBXML, these content formats ensure that mobile clients can access, download, and process a full range of graphical data and structured information. Although most uses of the WAP application environment today involve synchronous display and processing of WML and WMLScript content, the supported content types form the foundation for offline information access, data synchronization, and messaging. These future application areas are discussed in Chapter 15.

User-Agent Profiles

Often, content developers need to know about the client that is requesting WAP content so that the server application can tailor the returned content to the capabilities and resources of the user's device. The WAP application environment is flexible enough to be used on a broad range of devices. WAP-capable devices, in turn, may have different screen sizes, input capabilities, and processor and memory resources. Moreover, a device may provide a variety of vendor-specific WMLScript libraries. Finally, WAP devices do not need to implement all of the WAP specifications to be certified as WAP-compliant; in fact, the WAP *Class Conformance Requirements* (CCR) define several WAP specifications as mandatory but leave others as optional.

WAP User-Agent Profiles (UAProf) represent an efficient method for conveying a rich set of information about the client to the various proxies and application servers that provide content and services to the user. UAProf information can be conveyed over both wireless (using WSP) and wireline (using HTTP) networks, can be cached, and can be overridden by intermediate network elements according to network operator or service provider policies. The UAProf standard is based on the Composite Capability/Preference Profiles (CC/PP) specification, which is currently being developed by the W3C to address the same need for the larger Internet.

Chapter 11 discusses UAProf in more detail.

Push Messaging

Like a traditional paging system, the WAP application environment enables a content server to send content to a mobile client, without the need for an outstanding request. Push messaging is useful for delivering time-sensitive notifications to the user. Its potential applications include person-to-person instant messaging, alerts about stock prices and news events, and mobile advertising.

WAP defines how a content server should format, address, and publish content to be pushed to a mobile client. If it conforms to these standards, a content server can provide push-based services compatible with any type of network and browser used by the mobile device. Moreover, the content server can receive information about a particular device's capabilities to support content customization.

WAP Push is discussed in Chapter 12.

Network Infrastructure Services Supporting WAP Clients

The WAP standard enables mobile clients to access data and services residing on servers located at a service provider, in an intranet or extranet, or on the Internet. To support delivery of information to the WAP client, the network infrastructure must perform a variety of services:

- Generate content in standard forms.
- Convert that content into formats (WML, WMLScript, and so on) that are recognized by the WAP application environment, if the content is not originally generated in such a format.
- Compile and encode the content into binary form, using WBXML, WBMP, or WMLScript byte codes.
- Bridge protocols between the WAP suite (WDP, WTLS, WTP, and WSP) and the Internet suite (IP, UDP, TCP, SSL/TLS, and HTTP), if the servers that provide these services cannot handle the WAP protocols directly.
- Bridge the physical wireless network with the wireline network.

In addition to these basic services, the network infrastructure may provide many of the same services that are required by standard Web clients. These services include content caching, content filtering and access control, and content tailoring, among others. Finally, the WAP environment supports other services, such as telephony and server-initiated content push, that are not available through the traditional Web network infrastructure.

The WAP Deployment Chain

Figure 6-9 depicts one configuration of these network infrastructure requirements. Collectively, these elements form a *deployment chain* between

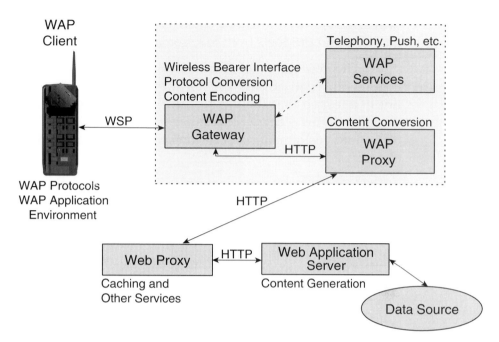

Figure 6-9   A logical view of an end-to-end system supporting WAP client devices

the user and the application or service being accessed by that user. The network infrastructure services required within the deployment chain consist of several logical functions, or logical servers.

- The *WAP client* represents one endpoint for the WAP protocols and executes the WAP application environment. The WML browser, WMLScript engine, push client, and telephony application environment are located on this client. The WAP client may be a mobile phone, PDA, or any other device that supports WAP protocols and content.

- The *WAP gateway* bridges the wireless network protocols with the wireline network protocols. In performing this task, the gateway serves as the other endpoint for the WAP protocols and as a client to the Internet protocols. Here, WSP requests are translated into HTTP requests transmitted over the Internet. In addition, the gateway performs binary encoding of the WML and XML into WBXML, and it compiles WMLScript into its byte code representation. WAP gateways include the IBM Secureway

Wireless Gateway, the Phone.com UP.Link server, the Materna Anny Way gateway, and products from Ericsson and Nokia.

- The *WAP proxy* performs the necessary manipulations to WAP content on behalf of WAP clients. For example, if the retrieved content is not in a format that the WAP execution environment understands, the proxy performs content conversion; it may also perform content filtering or content customization according to the capabilities of the requesting client.

- Various *WAP services* provide capabilities that are not otherwise provided through the existing Web infrastructure. They include a push proxy gateway to support WAP Push and a telephony server to support WAP Telephony Applications.

- The *Web proxy* is a standard proxy capable of providing services to all types of Web clients. These services include content caching, content insertion, and site-based content filtering. IBM's Web Traffic Express (part of IBM WebSphere Performance Pack) is one such Web proxy.

- The *Web server* or *Web application server*, commonly referred to as an *origin server*, generates content in a form that can be delivered to the client, either directly or by relying on downstream proxies to perform conversion. Depending on the capabilities of any proxies in the particular system, an origin server may generate WML, HTML, XML, WMLScript, JavaScript, vCard, vCalendar, and a variety of other content formats. Applications running on the Web server may generate content dynamically based on the requesting client or information contained within its requests. Web application servers include IBM's WebSphere Application Server and BEA's WebLogic Application Server.

- The *data source* is the repository for data being sent to the user or the system that processes transaction requests from the user. For example, the data source may be a relational database system, such as IBM's DB2 or Oracle's 8i databases.

The configuration shown in Figure 6-9 is simply provided as a convenience for the purpose of discussing the responsibilities of the network infrastructure within the deployment chain; it does not correspond to a physical configuration of these services. In fact, one key attribute of the WAP standard is that it does not mandate a particular physical configuration of the network infrastructure services.

In reality, the logical functions are associated with one or more physical network elements. Many physical servers combine two or more of the logical functions shown in Figure 6-9. For example, a "WAP gateway" may actually offer both the WAP gateway and WAP proxy capabilities, or it may be integrated with various other WAP services. Alternatively, the WAP proxy may be integrated with sophisticated Web proxies. Finally, the WAP gateway, WAP proxy, and Web proxy services may all be integrated directly with a Web application server (a *WAP application server*), thereby providing a tightly integrated system for delivering services targeted specifically at WAP clients.

An End-to-End WAP Request[7]

The example included in this section illustrates how a WAP request (to access a checking account balance) travels end-to-end from a mobile device to the data source. In this example, the components—the mobile client device, the WAP gateway, the Web application server, and the data source—are a Nokia 6150 Phone Simulator, IBM Secureway Wireless Gateway, IBM WebSphere Application Server, and IBM DB2 database, respectively.

As shown in Figure 6-10, the mobile client makes a "Checking Balance" query through the WAP gateway to the Web application server.

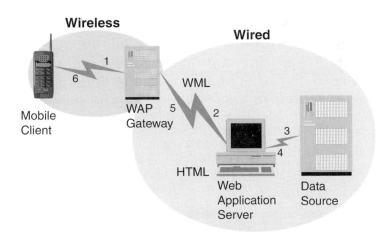

Figure 6-10 An end-to-end WAP checking account balance request

---

[7]We are deeply indebted to Virinder Batra and Andrew Capella for providing the material for this section.

The Web application server obtains the account balance from the data source (database), then converts this information into a generic XML format. Next, an XSL style sheet at the Web application server is used to convert the XML data into WML. The WML content is returned through the WAP gateway to the mobile client.

Request Flow

The WAP request begins at the WAP client and passes to the WAP gateway, Web application server, and data source.

WAP Client Device   The WAP client performs the following functions as part of initiating the WAP request:

1. Obtain the URL, either directly through user input or via the WML card from which the user has selected a link. The sample WML and phone simulator representation for querying the "Checking Balance" can be seen in Figure 6-11.

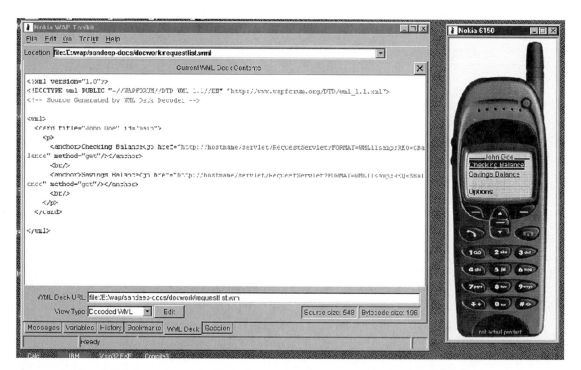

Figure 6-11   A WML and Nokia 6150 phone simulator request for a checking account balance

2. Build a WSP request containing the URL.
3. Encode the WSP request into binary form.
4. Deliver the WSP request to the WAP protocol stack (WDP, WTLS, WTP, and WSP).
5. Establish WAP protocol communication with the WAP gateway and pass the request through the wireless network. The WDP protocol provides the necessary mapping between the protocol stack and the various bearer networks (GSM, CDMA, and so on).

WAP Gateway   The WAP gateway receives the binary-encoded WSP request from the WAP client over the wireless network. It performs the following functions as part of the request processing:

1. Receive the binary-encoded WSP request over the wireless network and deliver it to the WAP protocol stack within the WAP gateway.
2. Process the inbound request through the WAP protocol stack, decode the binary WSP request, and pass it to the WSP/HTTP bridge component.
3. In the WSP/HTTP bridge component, interpret the WSP request and construct a corresponding HTTP request.
4. Establish a TCP/IP connection to the destination Web application server (or to the WAP proxy or Web proxy, if appropriate); over this link, transmit the HTTP request toward its destination.

A sample request to the Web application server might look like the following (the line break is included only for ease of reading):

```
http://hostname/servlet/RequestServlet
                        ?FORMAT=WML11&amp;REQ=CBalance method="get"
```

Web Application Server   The Web application server receives the HTTP request and initiates a request to the data source to obtain the desired data. To process the request, the Web application server performs the following functions:

1. The servlet **RequestServlet** (indicated in the requested URL) extracts the parameter–value pairs "FORMAT=WML11" and "REQ=Cbalance." The application designer defines these

parameters and their values to indicate to **RequestServlet** that a WML output stream is required and that a function called **CBalance** should be used at the server side to construct the WML response.

2. Within the servlet, the request for a **CBalance** function is translated into a request for balance information from the data source. This request leads to a JDBC call, which in turn generates a SQL query to the relational database that contains the desired information.

Data Source   The data source in this example could be any relational database (it is IBM DB2 here). The database could either reside on the same machine as the Web application server or be found on another database server that shares network connectivity with the Web application server.

The database receives an SQL request initiated by a JDBC API call from the servlet running on the Web application server. It returns information about the requested account balance. This data would typically be returned in a JDBC **ResultSet** to the requesting servlet.

Response Flow

The response begins at the Web application server, then passes through the WAP gateway on its way to the WAP client.

Web Application Server   The servlet receives the requested information from the data source and performs the following actions to process the data:

1. The servlet receives the data for the account balance and converts this information into an intermediate XML format, as shown in Listing 6-1. This conversion allows the application to deliver the data in multiple formats, including WML.

2. The Web application server inspects the FORMAT parameter sent with the request, determines that it must generate output in WML 1.1, and selects an appropriate XSL style sheet to transform the balance information from XML into the requested format. Typically, for each function such as "Cbalance," the application server maintains a separate style sheet for each format variant that it is expected to serve (for example, one style sheet for CbalanceWML, another for CbalanceHTML, and yet another for CbalanceVoiceXML). Listing 6-2 gives an example of an XSL style sheet.

3. The servlet invokes the XSL processor, passing the XML describing the account balance and the selected XSL for the requested format. The resulting WML is returned to the calling program (the WAP gateway) over HTTP.

Listing 6-1   XML representation of the checking account balance.

```
<?xml version="1.0"?>
<accountrecord>
   <balancerecord>
      <owner>John Doe</owner>
      <acctnum>0000-1234</acctnum>
      <balance>812.90</balance>
   </balancerecord>
</accountrecord>
```

Listing 6-2   XSL for converting the checking account balance XML into WML.

```
<xsl:stylesheet
     xmlns:xsl="http://www.w3.org/1999/XSL/Transform"
                                            version="1.0">
<xsl:output method="xml" omit-xml-declaration="no"/>
<xsl:output
   doctype-system="http://www.wapforum.org/DTD/wml_1.1.xml"
   doctype-public="-//WAPFORUM// DTD WML 1.1//EN"/>

<xsl:template match="/">
   <wml>
      <xsl:apply-templates/>
   </wml>
</xsl:template>

<xsl:template match="accountrecord/balancerecord">
   <card>
      <p>
         <xsl:apply-templates/>
      </p>
   </card>
</xsl:template>

<xsl:template match="balancerecord/owner">
   <em>Name: <xsl:value-of select="."/></em><br/>
</xsl:template>

<xsl:template match="balancerecord/acctnum">
   <em>Acct# <xsl:value-of select="."/></em><br/>
</xsl:template>
```

```
<xsl:template match="balancerecord/balance">
   <em>Bal: $$<xsl:value-of select="."/></em><br/>
</xsl:template>

</xsl:stylesheet>
```

WAP Gateway   The WAP gateway receives the HTTP response from the Web application server. It then performs the following functions:

1. The gateway processes the response through the TCP/IP protocol stack, then passes the HTTP response to the WSP/HTTP bridge component.
2. The WSP/HTTP bridge component converts the HTTP response into a corresponding WSP response, binary-encodes the WSP response and WML content, and delivers the binary-encoded WSP response and content to the WAP protocol stack.
3. The WAP gateway processes the WSP response through the WAP protocol stack, and forwards the response through the wireless network.

WAP Client Device   The WAP client receives the binary-encoded WSP response and WML content over the wireless network from the WAP gateway. It performs the following functions to complete the end-to-end processing:

1. The client receives the binary-encoded WSP response and WML content over the wireless network.
2. It processes the response through the WAP protocol stack and delivers the WML content to the WAP application environment.
3. The WAP application environment decodes the binary WML content and renders it on the client device display. Figure 6-12 illustrates the WML and visual display of the checking account balance.

WAP Architecture Design Principles

The WAP standard has been designed to satisfy a core set of architectural principles. These principles ensure that the standard not only remains internally consistent, but also achieves its overall goals of enabling interoperability among mobile devices. This section summarizes these archi-

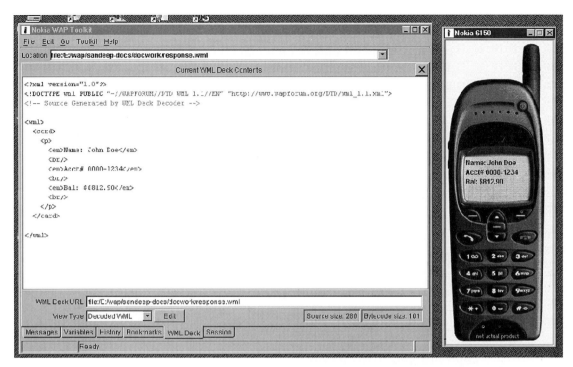

Figure 6-12   A WML and Nokia 6150 phone simulator response to the request for a checking account balance

tectural principles and describes how they affect the design of the WAP standard.

Unfortunately, although the architectural principles are generally reflected throughout the WAP standard, they have never been formally written down and adopted by the WAP Forum architecture group. The principles listed here are therefore intended to give insight into the existing standards, As the WAP standard evolves, however, the architectural guidance will surely evolve as well.

It is no accident that these principles are strikingly similar to the goals of other Internet standards bodies—namely, the Internet Engineering Task Force (IETF) and World Wide Web Consortium (W3C). The WAP standards are largely based on IETF and W3C standards, so design elements within those standards were readily incorporated into the WAP suite. Given the increasing levels of cooperation seen among the WAP Forum, IETF, and W3C, this trend toward common architectural purpose is likely to continue.

Principle of Flexible Deployability
The WAP standard shall not mandate how it is implemented within the network infrastructure.

Flexible Deployability

The Principle of Flexible Deployability ensures that the WAP standard does not mandate the physical structure of the network infrastructure that supports WAP clients. It essentially guarantees that the WAP standard may be deployed across a variety of network infrastructure configurations, as discussed in the previous section. Consequently, the WAP standard does not mandate any particular business model for the entities that deliver content and services to WAP clients. The Principle of Flexible Deployability also maximizes the number of ways in which the WAP standard may be integrated with the rest of the Internet.

Two design elements support this principle: layering and separability.

Layering and Abstraction

The WAP standard is divided into several independent layers, as shown in Figure 6-4 and discussed earlier in this chapter. Because of the existence of these layers, the standard can be separated into several parts as it is mapped against the network infrastructure. Each layer defines a well-defined service abstraction to upper layers and demands a particular service abstraction from lower layers. Consequently, a non-WAP service can use (that is, sit above) a WAP standard that provides a desired service abstraction. Similarly, a WAP standard can use (sit above) a non-WAP service that provides an appropriate service abstraction.

Intrinsic to this idea of layering and abstraction is the elimination of redundancy within the standard suite. A particular function (for example, reliability, authentication, or session management) is associated with a single layer of the WAP standard but is not duplicated across multiple layers. In addition to simplifying the service abstractions used within the layered architecture, this elimination of redundancy removes any unnecessary overhead from the packet flows over the wireless network.

Principle of Separability

Different parts of the WAP standard may be logically and physically separated. These parts should have minimal dependencies, and their interfaces should be well defined.

Principle of Separability

The Principle of Separability asserts that the layers of the WAP standard theoretically may be split, so that different layers are deployed on different servers within the network infrastructure. Moreover, when multiple servers are involved in enabling WAP services, those servers communicate through well-specified protocols and content formats. As a side effect of this principle, clear, nonproprietary interfaces must separate the various layers of the WAP standard.

The Principle of Separability has an important corollary: A WAP network infrastructure may theoretically include server elements from multiple manufacturers (though this is almost never done in practice). As long as each server communicates according to the defined interfaces associated with the standard layers, data may reliably move through the network infrastructure that supports the mobile clients. For example, one vendor may implement the WDP layer, whereas a second vendor implements the WTLS, WTP, and WSP layers. These two servers would communicate by exchanging UDP packets that encapsulate WTLS/WTP/WSP packets.

Although the original WAP 1.0 specifications closely followed the Principle of Separability, newer specifications have begun to deviate from it. For instance, the Push and Wireless Telephony Application (WTA) specifications introduce new network elements (a push proxy gateway and WTA gateway, respectively) whose interfaces with the existing WAP gateway infrastructure are as yet poorly defined. This deviation remains a target of ongoing work within the WAP Forum.

Principle of Flexible Implementability

The WAP standard shall grant maximum flexibility of implementation and support interoperability of those implementations.

Flexible Implementability

In addition to allowing flexible infrastructure deployments from multiple vendors, the WAP architecture seeks to maximize the flexibility offered to implementers of the standard on both the client and the server. This flexibility takes several forms:

- *Language independence.* The WAP standard does not define language-specific bindings for the interfaces between the various protocol layers. Instead, the interfaces are defined in terms of abstract service primitives and in terms of the informational parameters exchanged through those primitives. Implementers are free to define concrete APIs to represent those service abstractions, and those bindings may exist in any programming language.

- *Optimizability.* Although the standard defines service primitives between the layers, it does not actually require that implementations implement or expose those abstractions. A tightly integrated WAP client or server, for example, may integrate multiple layers into a single module, thereby eliminating interlayer overhead to gain additional performance benefits or reductions in the code size.

- *Interoperability.* To the greatest extent possible, the standard is designed to support interoperability testing. Static conformance requirements (SCRs) are published with each standard to allow implementers to verify that all required elements of the specification are implemented. In addition, the WAP Forum has contracted with The Open Group to build a test suite for doing live interoperability testing.

Principle of Global Use

To the greatest extent possible, WAP content, applications, and infrastructure should support all WAP-enabled clients worldwide.

Global Use

The WAP Forum membership includes companies from around the globe that operate virtually every type of wireless network in existence. The Principle of Global Use reflects the WAP design goal of unifying the wireless device and content markets. Within the WAP architecture, this principle is reflected in the ideas of bearer independence and user language independence.

Bearer Independence

The WAP standard is designed for use over every type of wireless network (and can even run over wireline networks). The WDP layer provides a common abstraction to the myriad physical networks available today. For each wireless network supported by the WAP standard, a binding is defined to provide the WDP service abstraction to the upper layers of the standard.

Beyond the WDP bindings, none of the other WAP standards is affected by the choice of bearer network.[8] As a result, application content can be written to the WAP standards and subsequently deployed worldwide without paying attention to the particular bearer network in use. In this way, the WAP standard unifies all mobile clients.

Support for Worldwide Languages

Given that the WAP standard is designed to run on most wireless networks in use today, users of WAP-enabled mobile devices will undoubtedly come from all regions of the world. The WAP standard is designed to support content delivery to users regardless of their native languages. This is not to say that WAP application content can be written once and immediately become accessible to users in any language. Such a goal is laudable, but virtually impossible to achieve.

Instead, the WAP standard allows content to be authored in all major languages, including the double-byte character sets common throughout most of Asia, right-to-left Arabic languages, and European character sets. A WML document may designate which characters it uses, and the standard supports 16-bit Unicode character encoding. In many respects, WML is bet-

---

[8]One small exception to this bearer independence exists. The WTAI library specification includes an addendum providing interfaces to telephony services that are available over only certain types of wireless networks (such as GSM). Applications that restrict themselves to the core WTAI interfaces are guaranteed to work over all telephony networks. The network-specific service interfaces should be used by applications that are aware of the network environments in which they run.

ter attuned to internationalization than alternatives such as HTML, because WML client browsers have greater freedom to determine appropriate character layout within the display and input event processing.

Consistency with the Web and Internet Architectures

Most of the WAP standards are derived from or heavily influenced by their existing counterparts on the Internet and World Wide Web. (The two notable exceptions are the WTA and Push standards, for which no counterpart exists on the Internet today.) Consequently, most of the core aspects of the World Wide Web architecture are retained in WAP:

1. Use of request–response interactions between clients and content servers.
2. Use of proxies to provide protocol and content conversion functions.
3. Separate transport and session protocols.
4. Use of XML-based content markup for rendering within the client browser.
5. Use of URLs as a global resource naming system.

Although the WAP standard departs from many of the details of the Web and Internet protocols and content formats, the reuse of the core architecture means that the different standards have not yet parted ways irreconcilably.

To the contrary, the WAP Forum has stated its desire to work toward integrating the WAP standard with the larger Web and Internet environments. This integration may occur either by adoption of the WAP standards for use over the Web through W3C or IETF standardization or by mutual evolution of Internet and WAP standards to provide an environment suited for both mobile and desktop clients. This goal can be summarized as the Principle of WAP, Web, and Internet Consistency.

Principle of WAP, Web, and Internet Consistency
The WAP standards will adhere to the Web and Internet architectures and be designed to support evolution toward a unified content and application model for all Web clients.

In the short term, the WAP architecture and standards seek to coexist with the existing Internet and Web standards. Moreover, they are designed either to be adopted by other standardization bodies or to support unification with existing standards.

The Principle of WAP, Web, and Internet Consistency raises the issue of how the WAP standards relate to those adopted by or under development by other standards bodies. These relationships are the topic of the next section.

Relationship to Other Standards

Throughout this chapter, we have noted several standards that form the foundation for the WAP specification:

- XML (eXtensible Markup Language), which forms the basis for WBXML and WML.
- HTML (Hypertext Markup Language), from which several WML constructs are adopted.
- HTTP (Hypertext Transfer Protocol), the model for WSP.
- T/TCP (Transactional TCP), from which WTP borrows several concepts.
- SSL (Secure Sockets Layer) and TLS (Transport Level Security), which define WTLS.
- X.509 certificate format, a subset of which became the WAP certificate format.
- UDP, which represents the quality-of-service semantics offered by WDP and the WDP adaptation protocol over IP networks.
- ICMP (Internet Control Message Protocol), the model for WCMP.

The WAP Forum is working with other bodies to ensure that emerging standards can coexist and do not duplicate one another. The most important relationships include those between the WAP Forum and the World Wide Web Consortium (W3C), Internet Engineering Task Force (IETF), and Mobile Station Application Execution Environment (MExE)/ Third-Generation Protocol Project (3GPP).

World Wide Web Consortium

The WAP–W3C relationship dates back to 1998. It emerged for two reasons: (1) most WAP Forum members are already W3C members, and (2) a number of individuals participate in both groups. A formal liaison and coordination committee supports this relationship.

The areas of cooperation between the WAP Forum and the W3C include the following:

• *XHTML and HTML-NG.* Both groups seek to "converge" HTML and WML into a common markup language or framework that can support the broadest range of Internet-connected clients. WML is already an XML-based language, and the XHTML specification defines an XML-compliant syntax for HTML. Over time, the two groups aim to define a single "core" markup language, with various modular extensions supporting particular types of browser environments.

• *CC/PP.* The W3C and WAP Forum have been working in parallel to define standards for conveying device, user, and network capabilities and preferences to content servers. The W3C's CC/PP specification defines a framework for this information, and the WAP Forum's UAProf specification extends the W3C framework with a particular vocabulary and binary encoding. Over time, the W3C expects to define a core vocabulary for all Internet-connected devices, leaving extended characteristics to be developed by other bodies, including the WAP Forum.

Internet Engineering Task Force

The WAP–IETF relationship did not develop nearly as quickly as that between the WAP Forum and the W3C. Traditionally, this relationship has been more informal in nature. However, the two groups do share several areas of common interest:

• *HTTP-NG.* The IETF has long sought to revise HTTP to address its known limitations, including the lack of session support and its "chattiness." The WAP Forum's WSP specification has precisely the same goals.

• *Wireless TCP (W-TCP).* TCP is the most commonly used protocol on the Internet today, but typical implementations of the protocol are not well suited for the low-bandwidth, high-latency wireless environment. As the WAP Forum extends its specification with a streaming protocol to support multimedia and messaging, it seeks to interoperate seamlessly with existing servers that use TCP.

Mobile Station Application Execution Environment and Third-Generation Protocol Project

The European Telecommunication Standards Institute (ETSI) sanctions the MExE group, whereas 3GPP is an independent body operating on a worldwide basis. These two groups are working together to define standards for "third generation" wireless networks offering always-available, packet-based communications with considerably higher bandwidth than is found in today's cellular environments. Such networks can support sophisticated applications running on handheld devices. The standards bodies therefore seek to extend the WAP environment to include the necessary application enablement functions.

In most cases, MExE and 3GPP have not sought to define new standards on their own; instead, they intend to adopt standards created by other bodies. For this reason, these bodies typically convey their requirements to the WAP Forum. In the past, such requirements have included device capability information, data synchronization, and multimedia messaging.

Other Groups

Several other bodies are related to the WAP Forum:

- *Bluetooth Special Interest Group (SIG).* The Bluetooth standard supports low-power, short-range wireless communications. It defines how the WAP protocols may be run over the Bluetooth radio environment.

- *Automotive Multimedia Interface Consortium (AMIC).* AMIC seeks to define common standards for In-Vehicle Information Systems (IVIS). These systems need to support not only communication within a vehicle but also communication with services provided by an external service provider. To provide the latter capability, AMIC relies on the WAP standards.

Conclusion

The WAP standard emerged from an industry need to bring together several proprietary approaches so as to drive device development, content availability, and service deployments. By defining this suite of standards, handset manufacturers, wireless carriers, and content providers hoped to reduce costs and create widespread user acceptance of the mobile Internet.

The WAP standard itself provides a comprehensive environment for efficient, device-independent delivery of applications and services. The specification suite includes adaptations for a broad set of wireless networks; transport, security, and session protocols; and a rich application environment. These standards can be bridged to the Internet in various ways, and they are serving as the basis for standards geared toward next-generation wireless and wireline networks.

The application environment defined by WAP arguably represents the most interesting—and lasting—advance offered by the standard. It offers device independence (while allowing for device extensibility), a link between data and telephony, application-level scripting, and push capabilities. These tools will support the development of sophisticated client-side and client-server applications that are tailored for the mobile environment and run on existing Internet infrastructure. In the next part of the book, we will look at WAP application development in more detail.

Part III
Implementing WAP Services

Chapter 7
The Wireless Markup Language

This chapter introduces the Wireless Markup Language (WML), the WAP markup language for content intended for lightweight, wireless devices. If you will be writing WML applications, you should find this and the following chapters to be useful references.[1] The companion Web site for this book includes a completely self-contained WML and WMLScript application, Code Breaker, that illustrates the use of the language in much more detail than is possible in the simple examples in this chapter. See the file **readme.txt** in the **CB** directory for more information.

Overview

Chapter 6 described the rationale underlying the design of WML in detail. In brief, WML applications are expected to supplement, rather than

---

[1]Although we provide brief background information when necessary, you will find it helpful to have a basic understanding of HTML, Internet protocols (such as HTTP), XML, and Web application design. This chapter is not intended to serve as a primer on general programming or Web application development techniques.

replace, Web sites accessed from traditional personal computers. Consider these three scenarios:

1. A financial services Web site offers current and historical stock prices, charts and graphs, market analysis, financial statements, news, and the ability to buy and sell securities. Using WML, the site could be adapted to offer its clients a crucial subset of information: current quotes, news headlines, market indicators, and the ability to contact a broker by phone or e-mail to make a sale or trade. A more sophisticated WML site could add access to the client's personal portfolio or the ability to buy and sell securities.

2. A map services Web site offers online maps of every city and state, including locations of points of interest, information about travel services, and personalized driving directions. A WML application running on a text-only device would be incapable of offering much of this functionality but could provide point-to-point driving directions—a great time saver for a lost traveler. A PDA with a larger, graphical screen could display small overview maps pinpointing the location of a requested landmark, such as a gas station or drugstore.

3. A travel Web site offers the ability to search flight schedules and fares, book tickets, locate hotels, and reserve a rental car. A WML application could give real-time information about flight times and gate locations, alert you to delayed or canceled flights, and even allow you to check in for a flight.

In each case, the WML application may not offer access to all features of the Web version of the site, but it gives clients access to critical information without requiring immediate access to the traditional Internet connection and PC. The additional value provided by the WML support makes the site as a whole that much more attractive to customers.

Markup for a Tough Environment

When it comes to the types of devices for which WML is intended, the operative word is "constrained." Personal, portable, pervasive—these small devices provide busy people with untethered access to information. Unfortunately, in their current incarnations, they are characterized as much by their limitations as by their strengths:

- *Screens are small.* Devices such as portable phones are tiny, and getting tinier. With only so much room to house a display, the screen may be as small as 4 lines by 12 characters—and perhaps even smaller. It may not be capable of displaying color, graphics, or multiple fonts.

- *Input is challenging.* Keys and controls can shrink only so much and remain usable. Many of these devices, such as phones, pagers, and PDAs, lack a full keyboard.

- *Memory is tight, and CPU cycles are limited.* Hardware advances will ensure that the situation improves, but the advent of increased memory and faster processors will tend to drive up cost, size, weight, and power consumption—all of which are undesirable in a portable device. Manufacturers must juggle these factors to produce a device that is both usable and useful.

- *Network connections are troublesome.* Wireless data connections currently are slower than the least expensive wireline modems, and they are subject to interference, obstructions, and dead areas.

WML is one of the technologies that the WAP Forum has defined in an effort to make wireless computing more palatable. Use of this markup language depends on the availability of a *browser,* a software program that can read WML and interpret it for display to a human. Some devices, such as phones or pagers, may contain embedded browsers that are seamlessly integrated into the other functions of the device. On other devices, such as PDAs and handheld computers, the browser might be either embedded or an add-on program.

WML: A Matter of Influence

WML did not develop in a vacuum. It shares common characteristics with the language of the Web, HTML (Hypertext Markup Language); an earlier wireless language, HDML (Handheld Device Markup Language); and an emerging document structure language, XML (eXtensible Markup Language). Although it has been greatly influenced by all of these languages, WML is not a subset of any of them.

In matters of syntax, WML often draws on HTML, particularly HTML version 4.0. Recognizing that similar concepts underlie both wireless and wireline browser application design, the WAP Forum has adopted HTML's syntax where appropriate. However, WML is not just a slimmed-down version of HTML, and you should not expect WML elements to share completely the semantics of any corresponding HTML tags.

From HDML, WML draws its application model. Unlike HTML, which was primarily created as a language for electronic documents, HDML was designed from the outset to support applications: interactive operations performed at the behest of a human. WML adopts this view. Consequently, WML "documents" are not intended to be read as you would read articles in a newspaper. Although they do contain readable content, they also instruct the browser on how the reader can interact with the document and how the browser should react to the user's actions.

The third major influence on WML's character is another emerging standard, XML. Its name is somewhat of a misnomer, because XML is not a markup language. Instead, it is a *meta-language*—a set of rules for defining markup languages. WML is XML-compliant, meaning that it conforms to XML's syntax rules. You do not have to be an XML expert to write WML, however; despite the length of the proposed XML standard and the myriad books available on the subject, the rules as they apply to authors are quite simple.

The WAP standards have been through a number of revisions, and this chapter covers a number of different versions of WML. The numbering can get somewhat confusing. WML 1.1 is part of WAP 1.1 (released in June 1999) and is the language baseline. As this book is written in June 2000, virtually all shipping WAP implementations support only WAP (and WML) version 1.1. WML 1.2, part of WAP 1.2 (released in November 1999), is mostly an information release providing corrections and clarifications to the version 1.1 specification, although it did introduce a few new features. Few implementations are likely to support WAP (and WML) version 1.2. Instead, most will support the subsequent release, tentatively titled WAP 1.2.1. However, the WAP Forum is moving to a date-based identification scheme, so the release name will probably be similar to WAP June 2000. Regardless of how the suite is named, the corresponding version of WML is numbered 1.3.

Where differences or ambiguities are known to exist between versions, we highlight them in a box like this one. Changes in WML 1.3 are described based on the proposed draft standard; you should refer to the WAP Forum Web site (**http://www.wapforum.org**) for the most up-to-date information. For information on determining which version of WML to use, see "WML Version Negotiation" at the end of this chapter.

WBXML

WAP Binary XML (WBXML) is a compact form of XML that can succinctly represent any document written in any XML-compliant markup language. We will look at WBXML and the binary encoding for WML in Chapter 8.

The WML Document Model

A WML document is called a *deck*, and it is similar to an HTML page. Both a WML document and an HTML page require a browser that will format them for the benefit of the user, but the analogy ends there. Whereas each HTML file is a single viewable page (or, when frames are used, a portion of a single page), a WML deck can contain multiple *cards*, each of which is a separate viewable entity.

Figure 7-1 shows a simple WML deck containing three cards. Cards contain both *content*—material intended for the viewer—and *instructions* to the WML browser. The browser is responsible for *rendering* the cards; that is, it interprets them, formats their content, and presents the result to the user. A *WML application* unfolds as the browser presents a series of cards to the user, one at a time, in response to a user action.

You might envision a WML application as one of those interactive storybooks where each paragraph of narrative is followed by several choices of action. You pick which action you want to take, then turn to the indicated page to continue the story. The "narrative" in WML consists of *user interface elements*: text, pictures, lists of choices, and places where the user can enter information. The "actions" that define what happens next are contained in *event bindings*, which link *events* (such as the user pressing a key) to a *task* (such as displaying another card). When the browser detects the occurrence of an event, it executes the corresponding task.

Some content, such as images, are not actually contained in the WML document. Instead, the WML deck contains a *reference* to pictures. (HTML works in much the same way.) When the deck is viewed on a device and browser that are capable of displaying pictures, the referenced graphics are retrieved and merged with the rest of the document. Pictures are just one example of an *external resource*—a portion of the content not stored with the deck. Another very important type of external resource is the *script*, which we will explore in Chapter 9.

```
<!-- sample WML deck -->
<wml>
  <card>
    <p>
      This deck contains 3 cards.
      <br/>
      <a href="#c2">See next.</a>
    </p>
  </card>

  <card id="c2">
    <p>
      This is the second.
      <br/>
      <a href="#c3">See last.</a>
    </p>
  </card>

  <card id="c3">
    <p>
       This is the third and last
       card.
    </p>
  </card>
</wml>
```

```
<!-- sample WML deck -->
```

This deck
contains 3
cards.
[See next.]

This is the
second.
[See last.]

This is the
third and last
card.

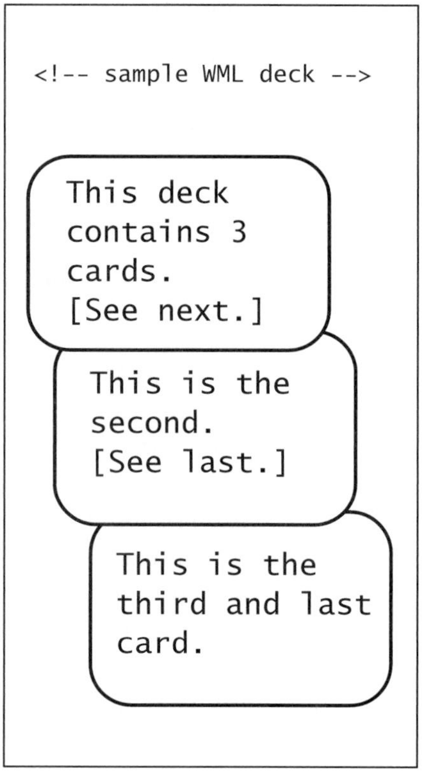

Figure 7-1   A deck of WML cards

Plot a Course, Mr. Chekov

WML cards are relatively uninteresting in isolation. A wireless application consists of many different cards that are joined together: cards contain *links* to other cards, and the user directs the browser from one card to another, in a process called *navigation*. You can establish links to cards in the same deck, in different decks, and even on a different server. In the most basic type of linking, WML adopts the HTML notion of *anchors*, which are "hotspots" in the document content that the user can select. WML also uses links in the definition of *event bindings*, which map other user actions (such as pressing a button) to navigation requests. When the user activates a link, the browser uses the *link pointer* to determine which card to display next.

The Historical Record

As you navigate from card to card, the browser records your path in its *navigation history*. Conceptually, this history comprises a stack of card locations; as you navigate to each new card, the browser pushes its location onto the stack. The browser needs to know where you have been in case you decide to return to a previous card. To do so, it pops the stack to retrieve the previous location.

Each entry on the history stack must include, at a minimum, the following information:

- The address of the card, stored as an absolute Uniform Resource Locator.[2] See "URLs Identify Content" later in this chapter.
- The HTTP[3] method (GET or POST) used to retrieve the card.
- Any postfield data associated with the request for the card (see the section "Passing Data—The `postfield` Element").
- Any request headers that accompanied the request.

The card content itself is not stored in the history but may be stored in a cache.

As we will see when we discuss variables later in this chapter, some WML content can change dynamically, at run time. The browser, however, stores only static information in the history. If any of the information being recorded was specified using a variable, the data is replaced with the variable's current value. Past history entries are therefore unaffected by future changes to variables. In short, the history entry contains the necessary information both to locate the referenced card in the cache and to request it again from the content server when necessary.

This concept of history is one area where familiarity with HTML browsers may lead you to expect different behavior. Web browsers typically allow you to move both "backward" and "forward" via their history

---

[2]Technically, WAP identifies resources by their Uniform Resource Identifier (URI), which can be either a URL (Uniform Resource Locator) or URN (Uniform Resource Name). Current implementations use only URLs, so we will use that term. For more information, see RFC 2396.

[3]Strictly speaking, the browser issues a WSP request that the WAP gateway translates into HTTP. In reality, the two protocols can be mapped one-to-one. Therefore, for clarity throughout this chapter, we will refer to HTTP whenever both WSP and HTTP apply.

mechanism. That is, moving backward does not alter the history; after re-visiting a card, you can return (navigate forward) to the current card without explicitly reactivating the link. In contrast, backward navigation in WML is "destructive": as you move backward, the browser removes from the history the location of the card you were previously viewing. In other words, in a WML browser, the card currently being displayed always appears at the top of the history stack.

Are You Coming or Going?

WML also differs from HTML in that the former language enables you to distinguish between the two directions of navigation. An HTML document has no way of "knowing" whether you have reached it via a link from another page or whether you have returned to it via the history mechanism. With WML, you can not only distinguish between the two directions quite easily, but also program different behavior depending on how the card was reached.

When you access the browser's history to return to a previous card, you are engaging in *reverse* (or *backward*) *navigation*. All other types of navigation involve *forward navigation;* you can usually think of forward navigation as proceeding deeper or further into the application. (We say "usually" because the document can exercise great control over navigation, as you will see in our later discussion, "Logical versus Physical Navigation.") Forward navigation is sometimes referred to by the opaque term *positive acceptance*, presumably because the user accepts whatever has transpired so far and takes the opportunity to continue. Figure 7-2 illustrates navigation between cards and its effect on the history stack.

The WML 1.1 standard included language that seemed to require all browsers to provide a mechanism for returning to the previous card in the history. Unfortunately, the wording was somewhat ambiguous and led to inconsistent interpretations by vendors. The WAP Forum addressed this problem in WML 1.2 by removing the requirement; browsers need now enable backward navigation only when a card explicitly requires it by defining a <prev> task (see "Backward Navigation—The prev Element").

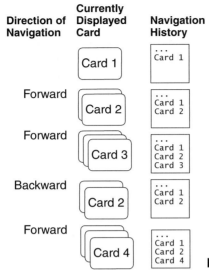

Figure 7-2 Navigation between cards

Note that entries are placed on WML's history stack solely through forward navigation, irrespective of the location of the particular card being visited. In particular, if forward navigation takes you to a card that already exists in the history, its location is added to the stack again. This duplication occurs even if you let the user navigate to the same card that he or she is already viewing. When such "in place" navigation occurs, the user may not think that anything has happened, but the history stack will be changed and backward navigation will therefore be affected. To avoid confusing the user in this case, you should control all navigation explicitly. Alternatively, you might consider whether you could achieve the desired effect by simply instructing the browser to *redraw* the current card, instead of *navigating* to it. We will discuss these techniques later in this chapter when we talk about <prev> and <refresh> tasks.

Some WML 1.1 browsers do not implement this behavior correctly and will not add another entry to the history if it would duplicate the current entry. However, if you always explicitly control backward navigation, your decks should work correctly on all 1.1 and 1.2 browsers. The deck **HistoryStack.wml**, on the companion Web site for this book, lets you test this approach on your browser.

Cache Value

A *cache* is storage set aside for maintaining a copy of previously re-quested content; it can be used to improve response time and reduce net-work use on future requests for the same data. Obviously, the amount of time that information can be kept in the cache before it is out of date will vary, and the browser has no way to know how long is appropriate with-out being told. The HTTP protocol (RFC 2616) includes mechanisms for allowing the content server to control the browser's cache, and WAP's WSP layer adopts the HTTP caching mechanism mostly unchanged.

In the WAP (and HTTP) caching model, the origin server can use *response headers* to indicate whether the data can be cached and for how long. Response headers are additional data, not part of the content, that allow the server to give the browser instructions or other information. When the user navigates to a new page, the browser investigates whether it is available in the cache and, if so, whether it has expired. If a valid copy exists in the cache, the browser uses it instead of requesting a fresh copy over the network.

WAP caching differs from the HTTP model in two ways. First, during reverse navigation the browser will check a cached copy for the `Cache-Control: must-revalidate` response header. The deck will be requested again from the server only if the `must-revalidate` header was specified and the deck is stale. Otherwise, the browser uses the cached copy even if it has expired. Second, navigation within a single WML deck or a function call within a single WMLScript file does not cause revalidation of the deck.

> Some WML 1.1 browsers always use the cached copy of a deck during backward navigation, even if the `must-revalidate` header was set.

The history and the cache are loosely related, but no direct correla-tion exists between them. The presence of a location in the history does not mean that the corresponding card still exists in the cache. Decks will be discarded from the cache when they have expired, and older decks may be removed to make room for new content when cache memory is exhausted. Some browsers may not have a cache at all. In addition, most browsers provide some sort of "reset" option that reinitializes the device to its power-on state, with a clear cache and history. The establishment of a new browser context (see the section "The newcontext Attribute") will clear the navigation history but may not reset the cache, depending on the whim of the browser author.

Your Agent, the Browser

We have already mentioned a few characteristics of the browser without explicitly defining a browser first. In WAP parlance, a *user agent* is a program that acts on behalf of the user and uses the WAP protocol stack in some fashion. A WML *browser* is simply the most common example of a user agent, responsible for rendering WML decks and handling interaction with a user. Over time, a number of cyber-entities will likely evolve that are capable of accessing WAP content for your benefit. For the moment, however, these entities remain purely theoretical creations, so we will stick with the more familiar term "browser."

The Standard That Launched a Thousand Interfaces

In the HTML world, how your Web page looks and behaves depends primarily on which browser is used to view the page. The computer hardware on which the browser happens to be running is practically insignificant. In particular, differences in keyboard layout and screen resolution have minimal effects on the user's experience when viewing your pages. Computers, regardless of their manufacturer or operating system, can be counted on to have a full alphanumeric keyboard, some type of pointing device, and a monitor capable of reasonably accurate color and graphics.

WML browsers, on the other hand, run on a wide variety of devices. The difference between wireless and wireline browsers goes even deeper than that, however. The user's experience depends not only on the device involved and the browser used but also on the integration of the two. As a result, you, intrepid WML author, cannot be quite so cavalier as the HTML author about what happens on the receiving end.

Chaos by Design

This seeming chaos exists, in fact, by design. The WAP Forum recognized that a wide variety of devices would support WML and that considerable differences would exist even within devices of the same class. To keep WML flexible enough to adapt to all the devices on which it might be used, the Forum choose to dictate very little about how WML should be supported by browsers. The standard is clear on *what* can or cannot be ignored, but it is generally mute on *how* this or that must be done. Consequently, browser and hardware providers have much more flexibility in their development options.

This freedom comes at a cost to you, the WML application developer. You will find that WML is as much about hints as it is about commands, and what works remarkably well on one browser (or device) may prove awkward and confusing on another browser (or device). For this reason, it is crucial to test your WML application on as many different platforms as possible. Fortunately, such testing is relatively easy to do by using the software development kits (SDKs) that are available from the various browser providers. It will reveal where you have been seduced by the behaviors of one particular browser and will help you write a better application that works across all platforms.

The Difficult Path to Enlightenment

When producing content, you face a choice between two routes. One approach is to recognize the particular browser and device in use and dynamically deliver the most appropriate version of your content (see Chapter 11). You can generate versions of your content in advance for each type of browser, or you can rely on sophisticated dynamic content generation and conversion capabilities. The danger with this approach is that, to keep up as WAP devices proliferate, you must constantly update your content or increase the complexity of the content generation. The other route is to strive for generic, all-encompassing content, relying on only the explicit promises made by the WML specification. In theory, a little more effort up front would yield dividends down the road, as you could support new devices with no additional effort.

In reality, of course, you will find yourself not on either path but instead struggling through the underbrush that separates the two. The most productive route lies somewhere closer to the second path—striving for generic content where possible, yet bowing to the necessity of living with the quirks of particular browsers.

Promises, Promises

What promises, then, does the WML specification make to developers? First, there will be a way of communicating content to the user. At present, this means a display screen. Although no mention is made of any particular size, the smallest effective display is not likely to be smaller than 4 lines by 12 characters—though someone may yet surprise us with a wireless pen. The most basic screens will be monochrome, use a single, fixed-width font, and be incapable of displaying graphics—in essence, the original IBM PC screen brought to the phone. More capable devices, such as PDAs and higher-end phones or pagers, will add color, rich text, and graphics.

Second, there will be a mechanism for the user to enter information, as most useful applications rely on some form of input. Again, the mechanism will vary widely by device. Some devices will have the luxury of a full QWERTY keyboard, while others will use smaller mechanisms: a "Ouiji board" letter picker, an augmented phone keypad, handwriting recognition, character-based speech recognition, or whatever else you can imagine.

In general, WML is best suited for personal, pervasive devices: PDAs and smaller. Larger devices may make good use of other WAP technologies, but will rarely be an attractive target for WML. The design considerations that make this browser ideal for "constrained" devices means it is relatively underpowered for platforms capable of supporting a more substantial user interface.

Beyond the ability to present and accept data, the device must provide mechanisms for controlling the browser. The physical manifestations of these controls will differ dramatically: push buttons, cursor keys, rocker switches, pointer sticks, touch screens, and jog shuttles, to name a few possibilities. Nevertheless, the browser must adhere to the navigation model and history mechanism that we described earlier.

Rendering versus Display

You may have noticed that we have not said anything about how the browser must display your content. In fact, the specification has very little to say on this subject, other that your content must be displayed in some fashion. For the most part, however, the browser is not required to do so in any particular way.

Perhaps the most difficult concept for new WML authors to grasp is that control over the actual appearance of your application is left mostly to the browser. You can certainly exert some degree of influence, but WML documents will generally look different—often dramatically different—when viewed with different browsers. This apparent anarchy results from WML's fundamental design point: WML is supportable on a wide variety of devices. You will have achieved the "Zen" of WML development when you free yourself from worrying about how your

WML application *looks* and concentrate instead on how it *acts*. Therein lies the road to peace and enlightenment. In general, you can assume only that the user will see all of your text content and all of your defined actions and that no significant reordering of your content will occur.

Of course, it is irrational to presume that you will not be concerned with the appearance of your application. First-time WML developers often have a painful introduction to the reality of the mobile Internet world: After having used only one browser during development, they finally run their application on some other browser, only to discover that it does something ugly and alien. When you first encounter this situation, your immediate reaction may be that the second browser's authors are ignorant cretins. In fact, you have probably been fooled into believing that your original browser's behavior is the Way It Should Be, when in fact it is just one of many possible Ways It Might Be. Your challenge is to avoid relying on such browser-specific behavior and instead write general-purpose WML markup. Of course, when you absolutely cannot obtain the desired effect, you can always resort to identifying the browser making the request and then generating appropriate content on the fly. Before embarking on this approach, which leads to increased maintenance efforts for the resulting application, it is usually worthwhile to make the extra effort to try finding an acceptable generic solution.

WML Browsing Is Not Web Browsing

The Web was originally intended for accessing online documents; only over time did it evolve into a delivery mechanism for online applications. People with mobile devices, however, will not want to browse the Web on a two-inch screen. Reading even a few pages of text five lines at a time quickly becomes tiresome. Mobile users are interested in targeted information, not surfing. Most compelling wireless applications will consist of either request–response interactions or push notifications, giving the user immediate access to a required piece of data, such as a phone number, a stock quote, or driving directions. Interaction between the user and the application should therefore be concise and to the point.

WML provides the tools needed to write such applications: hotspots that designate links for navigation or other tasks, input fields for "fill-in-the-blank" queries, and selection lists for "choose from a list" queries. It provides minimal "document publishing" features because that is not WML's intended purpose.

WML Authoring

WML documents are plain-text files, which you can create with any editor or word processor capable of saving files as text. (Seasoned pros will know that even a concept as seemingly simple as "plain text" is actually a Pandora's box. We discuss some of the issues related to this problem in "Character Sets and Internationalization" later in this chapter.) More elaborate WML editors offer various aids such as syntax assistance and color coding.

Much more important than the editor that you choose is the range of browsers and devices that you use for testing your application. Because of the implementation differences mentioned earlier, a WML application that appears flawless and natural when viewed in one browser may seem confusing or be unusable on another.

Static decks, however created, will take you only so far, because WML is not a programming language. To develop true wireless applications, you must employ dynamic content generation, using some sort of server-side technique. Most mechanisms used for dynamic Web programming, such as CGI programs or servlets, can be used to generate dynamic WML. While server-side application server programming is beyond the scope of this book, we will cover the topic in a little more depth in Chapter 14.

Software Development Kits

Because many browsers come embedded in devices, acquiring a variety of them to test can become an expensive proposition. Indeed, it may be impossible to test some devices if they rely on a data network that is unavailable to you. Fortunately, many of the major browser manufacturers make SDKs for WML testing. At a minimum, these kits allow you to simulate running a particular browser on a variety of hardware devices; usually, they offer a host of other useful features. A listing of SDKs and development tools is included in Appendix A. Bear in mind, however, that simulators do not always function in exactly the same way as the real hardware device they model.

Server Setup

When Web browsers receive content from a Web server, they expect to be told what type of content they are receiving. WML browsers are no

Table 7-1   WAP Media Types

Extension	Media Type	Content Type
wml	text/vnd.wap.wml	WML
wmlc	application/vnd.wap.wmlc	Tokenized ("compiled") WML
wmls	text/vnd.wap.wmlscript	WMLScript
wmlsc	application/vnd.wap.wmlscriptc	Tokenized ("compiled") WMLScript
wbmp	image/vnd.wap.wbmp	Wireless bitmap
dtd	text/plain	XML Document Type Definition

exception. Servers are not omniscient, however, and look to you for this information. For content that is stored in a file on the server, the content type information is carried by the file extension. You will need to configure your Web server to recognize the WAP media types; refer to your Web server documentation for the exact procedure. At a minimum, you will want to define mappings for the file extensions listed in Table 7-1. Although color WAP devices are theoretical at present, they probably will emerge soon. To use color images once such devices become available, you should also add a mapping for the extension "png" to the type "image/png."

URLs Identify Content

WML decks are identified by a name, globally unique on the Internet, called a *Uniform Resource Locator* (URL). URLs also identify external resources, such as images or WMLScript code. All WML browsers must support URLs which specify the Hypertext Transfer Protocol (HTTP), a standard scheme for retrieving files from Web servers; hence, most URLs referring to WML decks will begin with "http."[4] Browsers that support secure transactions over WTLS are also likely to support the secure HTTP scheme "https." Browsers running on telephone devices should also support the Wireless Telephony Application Interface (WTAI) scheme ("wtai"), which is discussed in Chapter 9. Support for other schemes, such as FTP ("ftp"), is optional.

---

[4]Although the URL designates HTTP as the retrieval protocol, the WML browser uses WSP to request and receive the content. The WAP gateway translates the WSP session into a standard HTTP request over the Internet. At the time of this writing, no WAP standard existed for mapping other Internet protocols such as FTP.

Absolute URLs

An *absolute URL* is the complete address of a resource, including the scheme (for example, "http"), the full Internet name or address of the server, an optional network port number at the server, and the location where the content can be found. For static decks, the location is the path and file name of the document; for dynamic decks, it is the path and name of the script to execute, along with any required script arguments. Some examples follow:

```
http://www.xyz.com/entry.wml
http://www.xyz.xom/main.wml#card2
http://acme.com:8080/cgi-bin/main?ns=1
```

Relative URLs

WML also supports *relative URLs*, which specify a document location relative to some base document. Without the base location to provide context, a relative location cannot be resolved, as the missing pieces of the relative URL are replaced by the corresponding parts of the base. In WML, relative URLs are resolved based on the URL of the deck that contains them. Relative URLs are defined in detail in RFC 2396. Some examples follow:

```
http:newdeck.wml
msgs.wml#error8
#searchform
?ns=s&amp;t=x
```

The browser keeps its navigational history in terms of absolute URLs. When a card is loaded via a relative URL, its reference is *fully qualified*—resolved to an absolute URL—before it is stored in the history. The same is true of the cache; cached decks are referenced by absolute URLs.

Markup Basics

If you are familiar with HTML, you will find that WML documents have quite a similar form. Intermixed with the content intended for the user are *markup elements*, which describe the content to the browser. Listing 7-1 shows an exceedingly simple example.

Listing 7-1   A simple WML document.

```
<?xml version="1.0"?>
<!DOCTYPE wml PUBLIC "-//WAPFORUM//DTD WML 1.1//EN"
      "http://www.wapforum.org/DTD/wml_1_1.dtd">

<!-- Extremely simple example -->
<wml>
   <card id="card1">
      <p>
         Hello, wireless world!
      </p>
   </card>
</wml>
```

Elements

Elements are identified by *tags*, which are enclosed in angle brackets. Unlike in HTML, which frequently takes a blasé attitude toward specification of end tags, each WML element must include a start tag, any content contained in the tag, and an end tag:

```
<xyz> some content </xyz>
```

Depending on the type of element, the content may consist of plain text, other elements, or a mixture of both. All elements must be completely contained (that is, started and ended) within their parent element; overlapping start and end tags are not allowed. Empty elements—that is, those not containing any content—either can be represented as you might expect (<xyz></xyz>) or can be abbreviated to a single tag (<xyz/>). The latter form is preferred for human readability and to speed processing but does not affect the meaning of the document in any way.

The deck in Listing 7-1 consists of three elements: a WML deck, marked by the <wml> tag, which contains one card (<card>), which in turn contains a single paragraph (<p>). The paragraph contains no elements but does include a text greeting for whoever might encounter the deck. Note that each start tag has a corresponding end tag.

Attributes

Elements can be embellished with *attributes*, which appear as part of the start tag and alter the semantics of the element in some fashion. In Listing 7-1, the <card> element beginning on line 7 has an id attribute. Attributes consist of an attribute name (id), an equals sign, and a quoted attribute value ("card1"). You can use either single or double quotes; the choice is of no consequence unless the value contains a quote character, in which case the value must be delimited with the other type of quote. XML, and thus WML, does not permit "quote escaping" in any form, but you can use the entities ' and " for single and double quotes, respectively (see the section "Special Characters"). The only time you absolutely must use these entities is when the attribute value contains both types of quote characters.

If an element possesses multiple attributes, they are separated by spaces. It is also legal to use spaces around the equal sign between the attribute name and value; however, it is a common misconception that such spaces are not allowed, so it is safest to omit them:

```
<card id="mycard" class = "c7 c9">
```

A single element cannot possess multiple attributes having the same name.

WML is a case-sensitive language, and all tags and attribute names must occur in lowercase. Furthermore, standard attribute values must be specified in the case required by the standard, which is generally lowercase. Although you can use mixed case in your own attribute values, you must do so consistently.

The Core Attributes—id and class

All WML elements support two attributes, id and class, called the *core attributes* because they apply universally to all elements. The id attribute allows you to assign a name to a particular element; it must be unique within the deck. The class attribute allows you to assign an element to one or more classes (or categories).

For the most part, these attributes are used only for server-side transformations; the browser ignores them. For example, you might use them on the server to facilitate generating WML content from template files. The one exception is the id attribute of the card element, which can be used as a target for links.

The xml:lang Attribute

The xml:lang attribute is not a core attribute, as it applies only to those elements that may contain text. Nevertheless, because it appears quite frequently we will define it here. The xml:lang attribute allows you to specify the natural language used in the element. Consider the following example:

```
<card>
   <p>
      As they say in Latin:
      <b xml:lang="la">Carpe diem!</b>
   </p>
</card>
```

The code used to represent the language can be a two-letter code defined by ISO639, a language identifier registered with the Internet Assigned Numbers Authority (IANA) (beginning with "i-"), or a privately defined identifier beginning with "x-" or "X-". As long as the code does not begin with "x-" or "X-", the first subcode must either be a two-letter ISO country code (as defined by ISO3166) or a subcode for the language in question (as registered with IANA).

For elements that do not explicitly specify a language, the browser uses the xml:lang value for the closest parent element. If none is found, it may employ any language information from the request headers or contained in meta-information. As a last resort, the browser will rely on its default configuration.

Whitespace

The formatting of your source document—where you split lines, how you indent, and so on—generally has no effect on how the application will appear in the browser. Although you can place your entire document on a single line, to enhance readability you should develop a personal style, just as you would for a programming language. For example, you might choose to indent tags to show structure, or you might insert extra blank lines to increase the readability.[5]

Syntax Conventions

As we introduce each WML element in this chapter, we will include a box that summarizes the important details of the element. Each box has the same format, as shown on the next page.

---

[5]You can generally format your document without fear of increasing the amount of time it will take to transmit your deck over the wireless link. As we will discuss later in this chapter, a sequence of whitespace characters is treated as a single space, and most binary WML encoders will remove your excess whitespace before it is sent to the device.

<wml>

Purpose: Defines a WML deck.

Attributes:

`id`	`(novar)`
`class`	`(novar)`
`xml:lang`	`(novar)`

Can contain: `<head>`, `<template>`, `<card>`

This summary includes the name of the element and its purpose, a list of the attributes that the element can possess, and lists of which elements it can contain and within which it can itself be contained. In the preceding case, the `<wml>` element is the top-level element in a WML document, so it cannot be contained in any other.

The attribute summary shows at a glance which attributes are required, what types of values each can assume, and to which version of WML each applies:

- The names of attributes that you must specify are given in **boldface**.

- Default attribute values, which are assumed when you do not explicitly specify the corresponding attribute, are <u>underlined</u>.

- Although we will not discuss them immediately, the values for many attributes can be completely or partially specified using WML variables (see the "Variables" section later in this chapter), which enables you to write decks that can be dynamically adjusted at run time. Those attributes whose values cannot be specified using variables are denoted as "(novar)."

- Elements or attributes that are not present in WML 1.1 are tagged with the version of WML in which they were introduced, such as "[1.2]" or "[1.3]." WML 1.1 browsers will usually consider them to be errors.

- When an attribute accepts one of a set of literal values, the possible values are shown separated by vertical bars (|). Otherwise a brief description may be given, or the discussion of the attribute provides additional details.

For example, the `sendreferer` attribute of the `go` element is optional, and can be either `true` or `false`. If you do not specify a value, the default is `false`. The `href` attribute is required, and it takes a URL as its value. You will find this information presented as follows:

href	*URL*
sendreferer	"<u>false</u>" | "true"

WML Basics

In Listing 7-1, we showed a very simple WML deck. At the time that we introduced this example, we did not demonstrate what happens when the deck is rendered by a browser. Let us now look at how it appears in several different browsers. (All of the sample decks in this chapter are available for downloading on the companion Web site.)

Figure 7-3 shows our deck as displayed in Nokia's SDK (emulating a hypothetical 6110 phone) and Ericsson's SDK (emulating an R320s phone). Figure 7-4 shows the same deck running on IBM's Wapsody browser (emulating an IBM Workpad) and Phone.com's SDK (emulating a Motorola iDEN phone). (Note that the SDKs' ability to emulate different devices does not mean that the emulated devices actually exist or that WML browsers are actually available for them.)

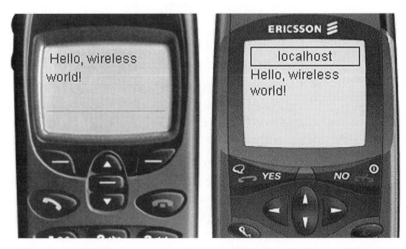

Figure 7-3   A simple document, as displayed by the Nokia and Ericsson browsers

Figure 7-4   A simple document, as displayed by the IBM Wapsody and Phone.com browsers

Aside from the fact that the "devices" in use are quite different, the most noticeable distinction relates to the screens, which differ from each other both in dimension and in the style and size of the characters. Significant differences also exist in the number and types of buttons available to serve as controls. We will find that the differences become more profound as our documents grow more involved.

A WML Skeleton

A complete WML document has the structure shown in Figure 7-5. Each document consists of a *prologue* and a *deck*. The deck, in turn, may contain a *head*, a *template*, and one or more *cards*; the `<head>` and `<template>` elements are optional. The `<head>` element can contain an `<access>` element, which specifies who can link to your deck, and `<meta>` elements, which are used to pass directives to the browser. The `<template>` element allows you to define event bindings that will apply to all of the cards in the deck. As we have seen, cards contain the content intended for the user, as well as the event bindings that define the flow of the application.

```
<?xml version="1.0"?>
<!DOCTYPE wml PUBLIC "-//WAPFORUM//DTD WML 1.1//EN"
      http://www.wapforum.org/DTD/wml_1_1.dtd">

<wml>
   <head>
      ...
   </head>
   <template>
      ...
   </template>
   <card>
      ...
   </card>
</wml>
```

Figure 7-5   Anatomy of a WML document

The Document Prologue

You may be wondering about the first three lines of the document in Figure 7-5, which do not follow the rules that we claimed were required of all elements. This lapse is acceptable because these lines are not elements; in fact, they are not really part of the deck itself. Instead, these lines make up the *XML document prologue*. Recall that WML is an XML-compliant markup language, and XML requires that the prologue be present. All WML documents must begin with a similar prologue, which is case-sensitive. In addition, while not strictly required, some tools become confused if at least one blank line does not separate the prologue from the document body. For the sake of brevity, we will not show the prologue in most of our examples.

Much of the time, you can treat the prologue as boilerplate, exactly as shown here. Nevertheless, let us take a quick tour of what it means. The first line is the *XML declaration:*

```
<?xml version="1.0" ?>
```

It simply indicates that an XML document, conforming to version 1.0 of the XML specification, follows.

The next part, which has been split over two lines for readability, form the *document type declaration*, which specifies the exact type of XML document at hand.

```
<!DOCTYPE wml PUBLIC "-//WAPFORUM//DTD WML 1.1//EN"
      "http://www.wapforum.org/DTD/wml_1_1.dtd">
```

All WML documents will specify wml as the document type. The remainder of the line identifies the *document type definition* (DTD), which actually describes the basic syntax of the language—WML in our case. Again, you can usually take this information as given. We will go into a little more detail about the DTD in the section "Document Type Declarations" later in this chapter.

The wml (Deck) Element

The <wml> element defines a deck and encloses all of its contents. Each deck must contain at least one card; it may also include a <head>, a <template>, or both.

<wml>

Purpose: Defines a WML deck.

Attributes:

id	(novar)
class	(novar)
xml:lang	(novar)

Can contain: <head>, <template>, <card>

The head Element

The <head> element serves as a container for elements that relate to the overall deck: the <access> element, which specifies access control (see the later section "The access Element"), and the <meta> element, which specifies meta-data (discussed in the later section "Other Data: The meta Element"). If neither <access> nor <meta> is specified, the <head> element can be omitted. If <head> is specified, it must be the first element of the deck (after the <wml> start tag).

<head>

Purpose: Defines deck-specific information.

Attributes:

id	(novar)
class	(novar)

Can contain: <access>, <meta>

Valid in: <wml>

The Content Is in the Cards

The <card> element is the basic element of user interaction. It serves as a container for text and user interface elements destined for the user. Although the contents indicate the general layout and the required fields, the browser is free to present the contents in the manner best suited for the hardware on which it is running. For example, on a device with a large screen, the card may be presented as a single page; on a smaller screen, it might appear as a series of pages. In any event, the order of elements within the card is important and must be respected by the browser; the browser cannot reorder the elements at whim.

<card>

Purpose: Contains content and user interface elements.

Attributes:

title	*titletext*
newcontext	"<u>false</u>" | "true" (novar)
ordered	"<u>true</u>" | "false" (novar)
onenterforward	*URL*
onenterbackward	*URL*
ontimer	*URL*
id	*cardname* (novar)
class	(novar)
xml:lang	(novar)

Can contain: <onevent>, <timer>, <do>, <p>, <pre> [1.2]

Valid in: <wml>

The title Attribute   The title attribute has a somewhat ambiguous purpose: It is intended to provide "advisory" information about the card. If you think that statement is a little unclear, you can understand why various browsers interpret this attribute differently. Some treat it as "title bar" text, others use it as a default bookmark name for the card, and still others ignore it entirely. All are equally valid interpretations. Because the title attribute tends to be rendered so differently, you may want to avoid it altogether (unless you are tailoring content for a particular browser). When you do actually want to provide a title as a header for a card and ensure that it is always displayed, it is more reliable to do so directly in the content.

On the other hand, if you want to provide a default bookmark name for the card, you may need to specify a title. Unfortunately, combining both techniques may cause the title text to be displayed twice on some browsers.

The ordered Attribute The Boolean attribute `ordered` specifies the intended organization of the card's fields, which the browser can take into account when it renders the card. When this attribute is `true`, the card is intended to be a linear sequence of fields. This style is best suited for short forms where no fields are optional. A value of `false` indicates that the card is a collection of elements without a linear sequence or in which some elements are optional. The value `false` may also be appropriate when a data record is to be edited, as the user might want to update individual fields in arbitrary order.

The `ordered` attribute is one of many attributes that serve as merely "hints" to the browser about your intentions. The browser is not obligated to respect your hint; in fact, it is not required to do anything differently based on the value that you specify. In theory, an intelligent browser can use this information to advantage, particularly when running on a device with a small screen. For example, it might render an ordered card as a sequence of screens instead of a single screen, and an unordered card as a hierarchy or tree. In practice, specifying `ordered="false"` causes problems on some current browsers or, at best, is ignored.

Exactly how the browser presents the card and allows the user to interact with the content will vary. The browser is expected to render content in a fashion that best suits the user interface and input model of the device on which it is running. In some cases, a soft key or other button may be used to select individual fields for editing or viewing; this approach is common on small-screen devices such as cellular phones. On devices with larger, touch-sensitive screens, graphical buttons that map to the fields may be drawn, or all of the fields may be displayed for direct manipulation.

Because a browser may choose to render an unordered card in ordered fashion, one field at a time, you should avoid packing many fields into a single card. Nevertheless, a browser may not reorder the card's contents, regardless of whether it is ordered or unordered, so you can always rely on the fields being presented to the user in the sequence that they occur in the card.

The browser is supposed to regard a field element (that is, an `<input>` or `<select>`) and any text immediately preceding it as a logical entity and display the two together, with the text serving as a "field prompt."[6] You can also use `<fieldset>` elements (see "Grouping Related Fields—The `fieldset` Element") as a further hint to the browser regarding logical transitions between fields.

You might wonder why, since you do not know how the browser will choose to display your card, you should not do the work yourself. For example, instead of hoping that the browser will treat an ordered card as a sequence, you might decide to write your application as a series of cards, with each card containing one field. The potential problem with this approach is that you have unnecessarily restricted the browser's flexibility. A browser running on a larger device, such as a PDA, is now restricted from taking full advantage of the larger screen. This solution is perfectly valid, however, especially if you are tailoring your content for specific devices.

The onenterforward, onenterbackward, and ontimer Attributes

The `onenterforward`, `onenterbackward`, and `ontimer` attributes are short-hand forms for an `<onevent>` element of the same type that specifies a `<go>` task. We will look at these elements when we discuss `<onevent>` in the section "Trapping Intrinsic Events—The `onevent` Element").

The newcontext Attribute

The `newcontext` attribute allows you to establish a new browser context when a card loads. The *browser context* is the record of the browser's current state, including all defined variables and the navigation history stack. Individual browsers may also keep track of other state information. When the browser loads a card in which you have specified `newcontext="true"`, the browser creates a context with a known, well-defined state. All WML variables become undefined, and the history stack is cleared of all entries except the one for the current card (see Figure 7-6). Any implementation-specific details must also be

---

[6]The break element, `<br>`, was not considered to be part of the text flow in WML 1.0, so a field prompt could not contain a break. Although this specification was changed in WML 1.1, some browsers may still handle this situation incorrectly.

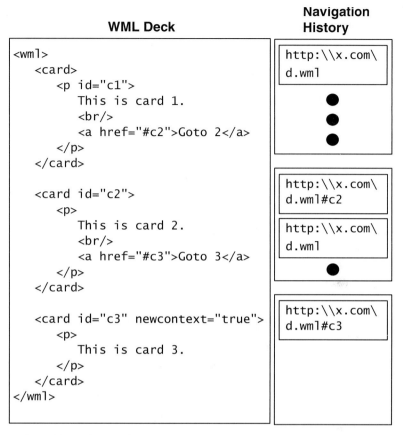

Figure 7-6   Effect of specifying `newcontext`

reset to a well-known state. The WML standard does not define the effect of establishing a new context on the browser's cache, so some browsers may choose to clear it as well.

Resetting the context should not be undertaken lightly, as clearing the history stack may make navigation problematic. In particular, if your application navigation relies on the user being able to move backward through the history stack (using the `<prev>` task), you must ensure that establishing a new context will not interfere with your application flow. In some cases, however, using `newcontext` is desirable, or at least warranted. For example, if you have stored potentially sensitive information in WML variables, clearing the browser context is a simple, if drastic, way to clear the variables. Security issues are discussed in more detail in the section "Application Security" later in this chapter.

Some browsers may provide alternate methods for reaching a WML card, such as via a "Go to URL" prompt or by using a bookmark. When such a mechanism is used to initiate navigation, the browser must always establish a new context, regardless of whether the target card specifies one.

The `id` Attribute   The `id` attribute gives a name to the card. Names must be unique within a deck (in most cases you will not need to name elements other than cards; if you do, all must have unique names). An individual card can be addressed within the deck by using its ID as a fragment anchor.

Identifying Decks and Cards

The WML card is the basic unit that a browser can display, and cards are the smallest "addressable" WML unit. To refer to a particular card, you must have assigned it a name by using the `id` attribute. The card is referenced using the URL *fragment*—the portion of the URL following the hash mark (#). In WML, fragment anchors refer to cards only.

In Listing 7-2, the second card in **nav2.wml** has been given the name "card2." The card in **nav1.wml** refers to the deck (**nav2.wml**) and card (card2) to be displayed next. Neither the card in **nav1.wml** nor the first card in **nav2.wml** has a name. The only time you can refer to an unnamed card is when it appears in the first position in the deck: when a URL does not refer to a specific card, the first card in the deck is displayed by default. The second card in **nav2.wml** refers to the first card in this fashion.

Listing 7-2   Linking example.

```
<!-- This is nav1.wml -->
<wml>
    <card>
       <do type="prev"><prev/></do>
       <p>
       This is deck 1, card 1.
       <br/>
       <a href="nav2.wml#card2">Jump to deck 2, card 2.</a>
       </p>
    </card>
</wml>
```

```
<!-- This is nav2.wml -->
<wml>
    <card>
        <do type="prev"><prev/></do>
        <p>
        This is deck 2, card 1.
        </p>
    </card>

    <card id="card2">
        <do type="prev"><prev/></do>
        <p>
        This is deck 1, card 2.
        <br/>
        <a href="nav2.wml">Jump to deck 2, card 1.</a>
        </p>
    </card>
</wml>
```

The browser will also display the first card in the deck when the URL references a nonexistent card. Although this default usually is undesirable, it may occasionally prove useful. For example, you might define a static deck that contains all of your online help messages. In a perfect world, no one would add a new function without updating the messages, but we often have to cope with the less-than-perfect reality. If you make the first card in the deck contain a message indicating that the specified topic was not found, then the user will see the error message rather than viewing help for an incorrect topic.

Comments

Documents can contain comments that, as in HTML, begin with the sequence "`<!--`" and end with the sequence "`-->`":

```
<!-- A comment -->
```

The body of the comment cannot contain a double hyphen, and comments cannot appear within an element start or end tag. (These restrictions are imposed by XML.) Comments may cross multiple lines but cannot be nested.

Comments are intended for documentation purposes only and will never be displayed by the browser. In fact, you cannot depend on them even reaching the browser, as they may be stripped from the deck before transmission or while en route.

Table 7-2   WML Named Character Entities

Entity	Description
`&amp;`	Ampersand (&)
`&apos;`	Apostrophe (')
`&gt;`	Greater than (>)
`&lt;`	Less than (<)
`&quot;`	Double quotation mark (")

Basic Content

For the near term, most WAP browsers will be primarily text-based, so most of your content will need to be text-oriented. This section describes the text features that WML makes available to you.

Text

Because WML browsers need not support graphics, your content will primarily be text-oriented. In general, any text you can enter from your keyboard is acceptable. (If you are writing in a language that uses characters beyond or other than the basic Roman set, including accented characters or multibyte characters, see "Character Sets and Internationalization.")

Special Characters

If your text contains characters that have special meaning in WML, such as angle brackets or the ampersand, the browser will attempt to interpret these characters in the normal fashion—and fail miserably. To include such "special characters," you must resort to *character entities*, which are nothing more than symbolic names for problematic characters.

Character entities have their own special syntax consisting of an ampersand, the entity identifier, and a terminating semicolon. The identifier can be either a name or a numeric code. WML defines names for its special characters (see Table 7-2); the deck in Listing 7-3 shows how they are used in content.

You can refer to any character by using a *character reference*, which looks similar to a reference to a named entity. The prefix `&#` denotes that the character is being referenced in decimal notation, whereas the prefix

&#x indicates hexadecimal notation. (The WML specification also refers to character references as "numeric character entities.") For example, the exclamation point character, number 33, can be referenced as either ! or its base-16 equivalent !. The sample deck **NumEnt.wml**, on the companion Web site, displays the characters through 1000. Note that not every possible character value is valid; the legal codes are #x09, #x0A, #0x0D, #x0020–#xD7FF, #xE000–#xFFFD, and #x10000–#x10FFFF.

Listing 7-3   Using the standard character entities.

```
<wml>
   <card>
      <p>
      Ampersand: &amp;
      <br/>
      Apostrophe: &apos;
      <br/>
      Greater than: &gt;
      <br/>
      Less than: &lt;
      <br/>
      Double quote: &quot;
      </p>
   </card>
</wml>
```

How are the characters numbered? WML uses the Unicode character set, which is capable of representing any character of any language. (To be strictly accurate, WML uses the ISO/IEC-10646 Universal Character Set, which is essentially identical to Unicode 2.0.) When you specify a character by its code, the reference is always to the same character regardless of which character set your device actually supports.

Not every device is capable of displaying every possible character, however. If you reference a character that the device cannot display, it will substitute its "unknown" character symbol, such as a question mark or dot. You can always safely refer to the characters 9, 10, 13, and 32 through 127, which are the same as the US-ASCII character set and will always be available on any device. We will delve further into the confusing issue of character sets shortly (see "Character Sets and Internationalization").

Literal Dollar Signs

The U.S. dollar sign character, $, is a special case. Because WML uses the dollar sign to identify variables (as described in the "Variables" section later in this chapter), and because entity expansion occurs before variable substitution, the WML specification treats the dollar sign as a variable prefix even if you use the character reference form (&36;). To get around this problem, WML lets you use a doubled dollar sign ($$) to stand for a literal dollar sign in your content, or, if you prefer, you can use the doubled character reference (&36;&36;). To use a literal dollar sign in an attribute value that is a URL, you would use the URL-escaped form (%24).

```
<p>
Your total is $$12.16.
</p>
```

Literal Data—CDATA Sections

Sometimes you will have a block of text that you want to embed in a card but not treat as markup. Although you can go through the block and replace all occurrences of the special characters with their corresponding named entities, it is often easier to use a CDATA section. With this construct, any block of text that begins with the sequence "<![CDATA[" and ends with "]]>" is treated as literal text, including the troublesome dollar sign. The only restriction is that the text cannot contain the sequence "]]>". For example, the two lines in the following paragraph are equivalent:

```
<p>
<![CDATA[The WML special characters include $, &, <, and >.]]>
<br/>
The WML special characters include $$, &amp;, &lt;, and &gt.
</p>
```

Text Emphasis—Adding Weight to Your Words

WML allows you to highlight text by using emphasis elements (Table 7-3). Because devices are not required to support rich text, if you request a form of text emphasis that is not available with the browser, the text will be rendered normally. As a consequence, the *content style* elements <em> and <strong> are preferred over the *physical style* tags <i>, <b>, and <u>. A physical style tag that the browser cannot honor will simply be ignored. The content style elements give the browser more flexibility, permitting more generic markup. Listing 7-4 demonstrates the use of the emphasis elements. Figure 7-7 and Figure 7-8 show some typical renderings.

Style tags can be nested, but nested tags will yield even less predictable results than the rendering of single style elements. The sequence <b><u> can be reasonably interpreted to indicate text that is both bold and underlined, although not all devices will support the combination. Schizophrenic combinations such as <em><strong> or <big><small> are best avoided.

Listing 7-4   Using emphasis elements.

```wml
<wml>
   <card>
      <p>
      Text may be <b>bold</b>,
      <i>italicized</i>, or
      <u>underlined</u>.

      <br/>
      Using <em>emphasis</em> and
      <strong>strong emphasis</strong>
      is preferred.

      <br/>
      Some devices also support <big>larger</big>
      and <small>smaller</small> fonts.
      </p>
   </card>
</wml>
```

Figure 7-7   Full formatting of emphasis elements (Nokia SDK)

Table 7-3   Character Emphasis Elements

Element	Description
`<em>`	Emphasis
`<strong>`	Strong emphasis
`<i>`	Italic font
`<b>`	Bold font
`<u>`	Underline font
`<big>`	Large font
`<small>`	Small font

Figure 7-8   Partial formatting of emphasis elements (Ericsson SDK)

Browsers that comply with the WML 1.2 standard must distinguish emphasized from normal text to the best of their ability, although the actual style requested may not be available. The styles for <em> and <strong> should be different, if possible, but the browser may use the same style for <strong>, <b>, and <big> and for <em>, <i>, <u>, and <small>.

Character Sets and Internationalization

WML uses and supports the Universal Character Set (ISO10646), which is identical to Unicode 2.0. You can write your WML decks using any character set that is a proper subset of Unicode (for example, US-ASCII, ISO-8859-1, UTF-8, or Shift_JIS). If you use anything other than UTF-8 or UTF-16, however, you must identify your choice explicitly. (US-ASCII is a subset of UTF-8, so if your document contains only ASCII characters, an explicit declaration is not required.)

The best mechanism for specifying the character set is the XML encoding declaration in the document prologue:

```
<?xml version="1.0" encoding="ISO-10646-UCS-2"?>
```

The encoding value should be one of the following strings: "UTF-8", "UTF-16", "ISO-10646-UCS-2", or "ISO-10646-UCS-4" (for the various encodings of Unicode and ISO10646); "ISO-8859-1" through "ISO-8859-9" (for the different parts of ISO8859); "ISO-2022-JP", "Shift_JIS", or "EUC-JP" (for the various forms of JIS X-0208-1997); or one of the character sets registered with the IANA. Unlike much of XML, character set encoding names are case-insensitive.

Although UTF-16 is acceptable for encoding WML, a problem will arise if your deck must be converted to binary WML: IANA has not yet assigned UTF-16 an identifier ("MIBenum"). Because WBXML requires a MIBenum for character encoding, and because your deck will almost certainly be converted to binary WML for wireless transmission, it is best to avoid UTF-16 until this discrepancy is resolved.

The WML 1.1 standard dictated that several methods (namely, the HTTP Content-Type header and http-equiv meta-information) had higher precedence than the XML encoding declaration. This priority was changed in WML1.2. Now, http-equiv meta-data is *never* used, and the precedence of Content-Type relative to the XML encoding is specific to the particular higher-level protocol. To be safe, you should always specify the character encoding using the XML declaration. If you are writing for WML 1.1 clients, you may want to set the HTTP Content-Type header to the same value, thereby avoiding any ambiguity.

Probably due to an oversight, the WML 1.2 standard retains the statement that documents should include Content-Type meta-information. Although there is no harm in doing so, statements elsewhere in the standard ensure that such information will never be used to determine character encoding. The Content-Type reference should be removed in WML 1.3.

Text Layout

Although it is not a word processor, WML allows you to influence the layout of your text to some extent. You can group text into paragraphs, control the positioning of line breaks, and specify text alignment and wrapping. Later in this chapter, we will show how tables let you align content into columns.

Paragraphs—The p Element

The paragraph element, <p>, is the generic container for all content and user interface elements; it can also contain event bindings. You can specify where line breaks should occur and how text should be aligned. The browser will provide the user with some means, such as arrow keys or a scroll bar, to view text that is too lengthy to fit on the screen at once.

```
<p>
Now is the winter of our discontent.
</p>
```

Although the term "paragraph" implies a lengthy block of prose, you should keep in mind what Shakespeare would have said had he been a wireless developer: "Brevity is the soul of WML." Your content should be clean, sparse, and to the point. No one wants to read *War and Peace* on a four-line screen.

At a minimum, the use of paragraphs forces the browser to begin a new line. A browser might also provide additional paragraph formatting, such as inserting a blank line or indenting the following text. However, browsers designed for devices with very small screens will usually not "waste" screen real estate in this manner.

The browser is allowed to ignore "insignificant" paragraphs—that is, empty paragraphs or those that contain only whitespace. This is true even if the paragraph specifies a mode attribute that might otherwise affect subsequent paragraphs.

\<p\>

Purpose: Contains a paragraph of formatted content, including text, images, and event bindings.

Attributes:

align	<u>"left"</u> | "center" | "right" (novar)
mode	"wrap" | "nowrap" (novar)
id	(novar)
class	(novar)
xml:lang	(novar)

Can contain: Plain text, emphasized text (\<em\>, \<strong\>, \<b\>, \<i\>, \<u\>, \<big\>, \<small\>), \<br\>, \<img\>, \<anchor\>, \<a\>, \<table\>, \<input\>, \<select\>, \<fieldset\>, \<do\>

Valid in: \<card\>

The align Attribute   You can control the alignment of text and other content within each paragraph by using the align attribute, which can have a value of left, right, or center. If not specified, left alignment is always the default, regardless of the alignment of preceding paragraphs.

```
<card>
   <p align="left">
   Left
   </p>

   <p align="center">
   Center
   </p>

   <p align="right">
   Right
   </p>
```

```
    <p>
    Back to left
    </p>
</card>
```

> The <p> element's preference for left alignment is biased toward languages with left-to-right alignment, such as English. If you are writing content in a right-to-left language, you will need to specify the alignment on every paragraph.

The mode Attribute   You can also control whether long lines of text wrap at the far edge of the screen. WML browsers support two modes, wrap and nowrap, which are specified with the paragraph's mode attribute. In wrap, or *breaking*, mode, lines that are too long to fit on one screen line are broken at word boundaries onto multiple lines.

```
<p mode="wrap">
Behind every great man, there's a great woman.
</p>
```

When nowrap, or *nonbreaking*, mode is specified, long lines are always presented on one line, even when the screen is too small. The browser must then provide some means of allowing the reader to view the remainder of the line. Typically, it will use some form of scrolling. The scrolling may be either (1) initiated manually by the user, via cursor keys or a scroll bar, or (2) performed automatically by the browser, using what is known as *Times Square* or *marquee* scrolling. A browser so equipped will automatically scroll the current line left and right so that it can be seen.

Because you cannot control the browser's scrolling behavior, you should use nonbreaking mode sparingly, if at all. Many people find automatic scrolling uncommonly irritating and awkward. If you must use nonbreaking mode, remember that the eye can easily become lost when the screen is scrolling automatically. Consider giving your users the ability to specify which mode they prefer, and limit the line length to no more than twice the physical width of the screen.

```
<p mode="nowrap">
'Tis better to have loved and lost,
<br/>
than never to have loved at all.
</p>
```

The mode attribute is unusual in that, once set, it stays in effect for the remaining paragraphs in the deck. The default for the first paragraph in the deck, if not explicitly specified, is wrap. If you specify center or right alignment together with nowrap mode, the result will vary depending on the browser. (Typical behavior is to ignore the alignment request.)

When the browser is in wrapping mode, any whitespace between characters becomes a candidate point for splitting a long line. When two words should always appear on the same line, you can use a *nonbreaking space*, represented by the sequence , instead of a space. This character will be displayed as a space, but will not be used as a line break. Use the nonbreaking space sparingly, as its overuse can have a deleterious effect on formatting.

```
<p>
You may order a la carte.
</p>
```

In contrast, the *soft hyphen* (or *discretionary hyphen*), ­, lets you specify where long words can be broken and hyphenated. If it needs to do so for formatting purposes, a browser can replace the soft hyphen with a hyphen and break the line. If they are not needed for a line break, soft hyphens are not displayed. A browser may not support soft hyphens, in which case they will be ignored entirely.

```
<p>
Super&shy;cali&shy;frag&shy;ilistic&shy;expi&shy;ali&shy;docious
</p>
```

Line Breaks—The br Element

The <br> element, the simplest element in WML, forces the browser to place subsequent text on a new line. Breaks have no effect on other formatting characteristics (alignment and wrap mode) that are currently active. Breaks that appear before or after all other content in a paragraph may be rendered as blank lines, but you should not rely on that behavior. Similarly, the rendering of consecutive <br> elements is undefined.

Listing 7-5 demonstrates the <br> element, and Figure 7-9 shows typical formatting using it.

Purpose: Forces subsequent text to begin on a new line.

Attributes:

id	(novar)
class	(novar)

Can contain: Nothing

Valid in: <p>, <anchor>, <a>, <fieldset>, <td>, <em>, <strong>, <b>, <i>, <u>, <big>, <small>, <pre> [1.3]

Listing 7-5   Using line breaks.

```
<wml>
    <card>
        <p>
        Eat
        <br/>
        Drink
        <br/>
        Be merry
        </p>
    </card>
</wml>
```

Preformatted Text—The pre Element

WML 1.2 added a new element, <pre> (see next page), which allows you to mark text that is preformatted and should not be altered by the browser.

Figure 7-9   Typical formatting of line breaks (IBM Wapsody)

<pre> [1.2]

Purpose: Contains preformatted text.

Attributes:

xml:space	"preserve" (novar)
id	(novar)
class	(novar)

Can contain: Plain text, emphasized text (except for <u>, <big>, <small>), <a>, <br>, <input>, <select>. WML 1.3 is expected to allow <u>, <anchor>, and <do>.

Valid in: <card>

The <pre> element is similar to a paragraph, in that it serves as a container for text and various other elements, but it cannot contain everything that a <p> element does. When displaying a block of preformatted text, the browser must do its best to present the text exactly as it appears, including preserving whitespace, using a fixed-pitch font, and disabling automatic word wrap. The actual result will depend on the browser's capabilities; for example, some devices may not have a fixed-pitch font.

> The fact that <pre> cannot contain <u> and <anchor> elements was an oversight. This situation was fixed in WML 1.3.

Remember that WML browsers cannot ignore elements that they do not recognize. A WML 1.1 browser, therefore, will see a deck containing a pre element as erroneous and refuse to display it. A browser can communicate which WML version it expects; see "WML Version Negotiation" at the end of the chapter.

The xml:space Attribute   The xml:space attribute is unusual in that you never need specify it. Because it can take only one value, "preserve," the browser knows about it automatically. XML experts may recognize it, as this attribute is defined by XML to control how whitespace is handled. Consider it a preview of a coming attraction—other elements will likely sport xml:space attributes in a future revision of WML.

Whitespace

In general, you are free to use *whitespace*—spaces (0x020), tabs (0x09), linefeeds (0x0A), and carriage returns (0x0D)—to format your source document in a pleasing fashion. In the examples in this book, we use blank lines and indentation to make our markup more readable. Extraneous whitespace is ignored, in that sequences of consecutive whitespace characters are treated as a single space (as dictated by XML). In addition, WML specifies that whitespace immediately before (preceding a start tag) or after (following an end tag) be ignored. For example, we could have written our sample deck in Listing 7-1 on a single line:

```
<wml><cardid="card1"><p>Hello, wireless world!</p></card></wml>
```

The nonbreaking space entity ( ) is not considered to be whitespace, so sequences of multiple nonbreaking spaces will not be compressed. You might be tempted to use sequences of nonbreaking spaces to achieve certain effects, such as indentation of a paragraph. Because the actual results of such use are not defined, you should avoid this option.

Whitespace can cause problems when used in two particular places. First, any extra spaces within an <a> or <anchor> tag will become part of your link, which may not be desirable. We discuss this issue further in the section "Whitespace in Links".

Second, it is unclear whether the WML rule stating that whitespace before and after an element should be ignored applies to elements that are contained within others. As an example, consider the following card:

```
<card>
    <p>
        <b>Red</b> <i>Alert</i>
    </p>
</card>
```

Depending on how you interpret the rule, it is equivalent to either

```
<card> <p> <b>Red</b> <i>Alert</i> </p> </card>
```

or

```
<card><p><b>Red</b><i>Alert</i></p></card>
```

The latter card is probably not what was intended.

This problem affects only the emphasis elements, and browsers may differ in their renderings. As a result, if you juxtapose two sections of emphasized text, you should place the whitespace within one of the emphasis blocks:

```
<b>Red </b><i>Alert</i>
```

Alternatively, you might use a nonbreaking space character, though it may change the formatting of the text.

Browsers are encouraged to respect the spacing conventions of the language in use, so you may find that some of these guidelines are ignored.

Events, Tasks, and Bindings

Most of the decks presented so far have been static, one-card affairs that illustrate a particular point but are not typical of true WML applications. Real-world applications consist of a number of cards through which the user navigates. Navigation is one type of WML event–task binding.

A WML *event* is some occurrence of interest that can be recognized by the browser. (Dropping your phone does not count.) Two types of events exist: intrinsic events and user-initiated events. *Intrinsic events* are triggered by WML elements; for example, a card can trigger an event when the browser "enters" it. *User-initiated events* are triggered by direct action of the user, such as the selection of an item from a menu. Of all possible events, you tell the browser which are of interest at the moment by defining *event bindings*.

A *task* is an activity that the browser can perform. When the browser detects the occurrence of an event that has an associated task, it executes the corresponding task. Four types of WML tasks exist. The two you will use most often, the go and prev tasks, direct the browser to navigate to another card. The go task initiates "forward" navigation to a new URL, and the prev task instructs the browser to return to the previous location popped from the history stack. The other two WML tasks are refresh and noop. A refresh task causes the browser to redisplay the current card; it can be helpful if the card references variables whose values may have changed. "Noop" is computerese for "no operation"; a noop task tells the browser to do nothing.

If your deck contains multiple cards with similar requirements, you can use the template element (see "The template Element") to define default event bindings that apply to all of them. Events defined in the template act as if they were defined for every card in the deck. To override the template behavior for an individual card, you simply specify an event binding within the card. To hide a template binding for a particular card, you can define a card-level binding for the same event using a noop task.

Tasks

The four types of tasks are each represented by a corresponding WML element.

Forward Navigation—The go Element

The go element declares a go task, indicating forward navigation to a new location. In most cases you will navigate to another card, but sometimes you will specify other WAP content such as a WMLScript program.

<go>

Purpose: Defines a forward navigation task.

Attributes:

`href`	*URL*
`sendreferer`	`"false"` | `"true"` (novar)
`method`	`"get"` | `"post"` (novar)
`accept-charset`	*charsetlist* (novar)
`enctype` [1.2]	`"application/x-www-form-urlencoded"` | `"multipart/form-data"` (novar)
`cache-control` [1.3]	`"no-cache"` (novar)
`id`	(novar)
`class`	(novar)

Can contain: <postfield>, <setvar>

Valid in: <do>, <onevent>, <anchor>

The actual machinations that the browser must go through to execute a go task may surprise you. The required steps are described below:

1. If the <go> task contains any <setvar> elements, the variable name and value are converted to simple strings, and the set of pending

variable assignments is stored in temporary memory. In this way, any variable references within the `<go>` element attributes are expanded using the *current* value of the variables. For example, when the deck in Listing 7-6 is executed, the URL fetched in the second card is foo.wml (not bar.wml).

2. Any variable references in the target URL specified by the `href` attribute are expanded, using the current variable values, and the browser fetches the target URL. The content may come from the cache or be retrieved over the network; if it cannot be obtained for any reason, the browser will report an (ideally, descriptive) error.

3. If the retrieved deck contains access control parameters (see "The `access` Element"), they are checked. If access is not permitted, an error message should be displayed.

4. If the target URL includes a card (fragment) reference and the deck contains a card with the requested name, the named card will be the destination card. Otherwise, the first card in the deck will be the destination card.

5. The pending variable assignments from step 1 are applied.

6. If the destination card has a `newcontext` attribute set to `true`, a new browser context is established (see "The `newcontext` Attribute").

7. The location of the destination card is added to the navigation history.

8. If the destination card contains an `onenterforward` binding, the associated task is executed and processing stops.

9. If the destination card contains a `timer` element, the timer is initialized and started.

10. The destination card is rendered using the current variable state.

Listing 7-6   Reassigning a variable during navigation.

```
<wml>
  <card>
    <p>
    <anchor>Goto card 2<go href="#c2">
      <setvar name="v1" value="foo"/>
    </go></anchor>
    </p>
  </card>
```

```
        <card id="c2">
           <p>
           v1="$(v1)".
           <br/>
           <anchor>Goto next card<go href="$(v1).wml">
              <setvar name="v1" value="bar"/>
           </go></anchor>
           </p>
        </card>
</wml>
```

> Some browsers do not honor this sequence exactly. For example, step 8 implies that, in any card that contains an `onenterforward` binding and a `timer`, the timer will never start. However, you may encounter browsers that start the timer under these circumstances.

The href attribute   The `href` attribute specifies the URL of the destination. If the new location is a card (or a deck, which implicitly names the first card), the current location is pushed onto the history stack and the new card is displayed. If the destination is a WMLScript, however, slightly different behavior results. WMLScript programs do not have quite the same standing as WML cards, and they cannot exist on the history stack. As the script executes, the current card remains unchanged. We show examples of linking to WMLScript in Chapter 9.

You can even specify the URL of a WBMP image or of non-WAP content such as an HTML page. The behavior in these cases is undefined and depends on the capabilities of the browser. Perhaps the image will be displayed, but the user will have no way to continue. A better approach would be to wrap the image in a card that enables the user to navigate elsewhere. Non-WAP content such as HTML will likely generate an error message, so you should avoid it unless you are tailoring your content to a particular browser that supports multiple document types.

The sendreferer Attribute   The `sendreferer` attribute (misspelled for historical reasons) specifies whether the browser should send the URL of the current deck along with the request. The information is sent in the HTTP "referer" request header. You do not need to specify this attribute for static decks but might use it when invoking a CGI program or servlet. The server could, for example, use the information to enforce some measure of access control by examining the source of the request. Alternatively, the server application might customize the returned content based on the location from which the user navigated to the deck.

By default, this feature is disabled to avoid the transmission of extra bytes. When you enable the sendreferer attribute, the browser must provide the URL in the smallest relative form possible; if it cannot be specified as a relative URL, the absolute URL is used. You can find more details on request headers in RFC 2068.

The method Attribute   The method attribute specifies how the data associated with the go task is sent to the server. It applies only if the <go> task contains postfield elements. The value can be either "get" (the default) or "post" (see "Sending Information").

The accept-charset Attribute   The accept-charset attribute tells the browser which character set encodings the server will accept. Its value comprises a list of character encoding names (as specified in RFC 2045 and RFC 2068), separated by either spaces or commas. If the "post" method is used, the browser should select one of the specified character sets to encode the names and values of all postfield elements associated with the go task. The same encoding is used for all of the elements. Note that the browser has no obligation to send the data in one of the specified character sets; however, if it does not do so, then the server probably will not be able to process the data and will return an error.

When developing your own applications, you usually will not worry about specifying an accept-charset value. The default value (when no value is given or when the value is explicitly set to "unknown") is the same character set that was used to encode the deck containing the <go> element. You might need to specify a value if your application links to another application that accepts a different character set.

The enctype Attribute   The enctype attribute, which was introduced in WML 1.2, allows you to specify the content type used to transmit the postfield data to the server. Like accept-charset, it is similar to its counterpart attribute in HTML version 4, and it applies only when the method attribute value is "post." (Specifying an enctype of "multipart/form-data" along with a method of "get" will generate an error.) The default value, "application/x-www-form-urlencoded," is acceptable when the postfield data consists entirely of US-ASCII characters. When the data may include other characters, you should specify multipart/form-data (see RFC 2388 for more details).

Note that the enctype attribute merely informs the browser of your preference as to how the data should be packaged for transmission to the server. The browser can legally ignore the enctype value and always use "application/x-www-form-urlencoded." The enctype attribute will be transparent to your server-side application, as the Web server will handle the retrieval and decoding of the data before passing it to your application.

The cache-control Attribute WML 1.3 added the cache-control attribute, which allows you to bypass the browser cache. When you specify cache-control="no-cache", the browser will always ask the server for a fresh copy of the requested deck. If you omit this attribute, then the browser will look in its cache for a valid copy of the desired information before issuing a request to the server.

Normally the default behavior is desirable, as the cache makes your application appear more responsive. A classic example of when this behavior is not desirable involves an application that includes a list from which the user can delete entries. In most instances, you want the list cached, so the user can navigate it quickly; after a deletion, however, the cached copy will no longer be valid.

To achieve the same effect on a pre-1.3 browser, you must resort to a trick. To force a reload, you must append a unique query parameter to the deck's URL. Listing 7-7 shows a sample deck that demonstrates this technique, using a helper WMLScript (Listing 7-8).

Listing 7-7   Emulating cache-control="nocache".

```
<wml>
    <card onenterforward="EmReload.wmls#Work()">
        <p>
        <a href="?$(Counter)">
        Force reload
        </a>
        <br/>
        $(Counter)
        </p>
    </card>
</wml>
```

Listing 7-8   Nocache helper application.

```
extern function Work() {
    var c = Lang.parseInt(WMLBrowser.getVar("Counter"));
    c = String.toString(typeof c == 0 ? ++c : 0);
    WMLBrowser.setVar("Counter", c);
}
```

Backward Navigation—The prev Element

The prev element declares a prev task, indicating backward navigation. When executed, the browser "pops" the URL of the previous card from the history stack and returns to it. If no previous card appears in the history (for example, if a new context cleared the history), the behavior will depend on the browser. The current card may not change, or the browser may choose to display its "home page."

<prev>

Purpose: Defines a backward navigation task.

Attributes:

id	(novar)
class	(novar)

Can contain: <setvar>

Valid in: <do>, <onevent>, <anchor>

When a prev task executes, the browser will normally use the cached copy of the page if it is available, even if the page has expired. You can override this behavior when the page is cached—rather than when the prev task executes—by including the Must-Revalidate HTTP response header when the server delivers the page.

Do Nothing—The noop Element

The noop element declares a null task. It is used to override a template event binding for a particular card and to ensure that the browser does not add a prev task to your card automatically.

The processing model for a prev task imposes a restriction similar to that for go tasks: if the destination card contains an onenterbackward binding, the associated task executes, and any timer in the destination card is not started. As was the case with go, you may find that some browsers do not enforce this restriction.

Because of the previously mentioned ambiguity in the WML 1.1 specification concerning when backward navigation should be enabled, you should always explicitly define a prev-type <do> element in every card that may be rendered in a WML 1.1 browser. To enable backward navigation, bind it to a <prev> task; to disable it, bind it to a <noop> task.

<noop>

Purpose: Defines a null task ("no operation").

Attributes:

id	(novar)
class	(novar)

Can contain: Nothing

Valid in: <do>, <onevent>

Update the Context—The refresh Element

The refresh task forces the current card to be redisplayed, with any changes to WML variables being reflected in the display. New variable values may be specified as part of the refresh task, or they may be changed by means of a timer. Variable assignments associated with the refresh task are applied before the card is redisplayed.

<refresh>

Purpose: Defines a screen refresh task.

Attributes:

id	(novar)
class	(novar)

Can contain: <setvar>

Valid in: <do>, <onevent>, <anchor>

If you use the refresh task in a card that contains a timer, you should be aware that the interaction between the two is somewhat complicated. See the section "The Clock Is Ticking—The timer Element" for a discussion of this issue.

Linking Events to Tasks

You will recall that two types of events exist, intrinsic and user-initiated. WML lets you define handlers for them using the onevent and do elements, respectively.

Trapping Intrinsic Events—The onevent Element

Intrinsic events are those generated by WML elements. You use the

Table 7-4   Intrinsic Event Types

Name	Description
onenterforward	Occurs when a card is entered as a result of forward navigation
onenterbackward	Occurs when a card is entered as a result of backward navigation
ontimer	Occurs when a timer expires.
onpick	Occurs when a user selects or deselects an option in a list.

onevent element to tell the browser which intrinsic events you are interested in capturing and what should happen when they occur.

There are four types of intrinsic events (see Table 7-4). Two are card entry events, which are triggered whenever the browser begins to process a card. These events are distinguished by the direction of navigation that was used to reach the card, forward or backward. The third type of intrinsic event is triggered when a timer goes off, allowing you to set actions that will occur without user activity. The final type of event is generated when the user makes choices from a selection list.

Event bindings apply only to the element in which they are defined. That is, bindings for events that do not apply to the enclosing element are ignored, and multiple bindings for the same event within a single element are considered an error.

<onevent>

Purpose: Binds an intrinsic event to a task.

Attributes:

type	"onenterforward" | "onenterbackward" | "ontimer" | "onpick" (novar)
id	(novar)
class	(novar)

Can contain: <go>, <prev>, <noop>, <refresh>

Valid in: All except "onpick": <template> or <card>
          "onpick" only: <option>

The type Attribute   You use the type attribute to specify which kind of event binding you are defining. By using the onenterforward and onenterbackward bindings, you can define side effects to be associated with navigation. These events are triggered when the browser enters a new card, as a result of either user-directed navigation or some other mechanism (such as a timer going off). The onenterforward event occurs when the browser enters a card via a go task or any other equivalent method, including navigation caused by a WMLScript go() function. It also applies when the user navigates to a particular card directly, such as from a bookmark list or via input of a URL. Similarly, the onenterbackward event occurs when the browser enters a card via a prev task, a WMLScript prev() function call, or any other method that uses the URL retrieved from the history stack. One particularly common use for these events is for the initialization of WML variables, which we discuss later in this chapter.

You can also specify the onenterforward and onenterbackward bindings in a template element, in which case they will apply to all cards in the deck; see "The template Element" section. This technique is often used to ensure that the user can (or cannot) navigate backward from any point in your application (see Listing 7-9 for an example).

Listing 7-9   A default prev binding using a template.

```
<wml>
   <template>
      <do type="prev">
         <prev/>
      </do>
   </template>

   <card id="c1">
      <p>
      Card 1
      <br/>
      <a href="#c2">To 2</a>
      </p>
   </card>

   <card id="c2">
      <p>
      Card 2
      <br/>
      <a href="#c3">To 3</a>
      </p>
   </card>
```

```
   <card id="c3">
      <p>
      Card 3 - end of the line.
      </p>
   </card>
</wml>
```

The `ontimer` event type lets you specify a task to execute when a timer (see "The Clock Is Ticking—The `timer` Element") expires, allowing completion of the task without user interaction. It also can be specified in the deck's `template` element. The `onpick` binding lets you define a task to be executed when the user selects an option in a select list (see "`onpick` Handlers") and can be specified only within an `option` element.

Abbreviating onevent Elements

WML provides a shortcut that you can use to associate a simple `go` task with an `onenterforward`, `onenterbackward`, or `ontimer` event. Instead of using an `onevent` element, you should use the corresponding attribute on the `card` or `template` element. The resulting deck will be smaller when converted to binary form, and smaller decks are transmitted more rapidly over the wireless link. The two decks in Listing 7-10 are equivalent, for example, but the second is smaller once encoded.

Listing 7-10   Event equivalence.

```
<!-- OnEventA.wml -->
<wml>
   <card>
      <onevent type="onenterforward">
         <go href="#c2"/>
      </onevent>
      <p>
      You don't see this text.
      </p>
   </card>

   <card id="c2">
      <p>
      This is the first card you see.
      </p>
   </card>
</wml>
```

```
<!-- OnEventB.wml -->
<wml>
   <card onenterforward="#c2">
      <p>
      You don't see this text.
      </p>
   </card>

   <card id="c2">
      <p>
      This is the first card you see.
      </p>
   </card>
</wml>
```

Use an onevent element only when you need to specify a task other than go, or when you need to specify attributes, set variables, or associate postfield elements with the go task. Event bindings expressed with this shorthand are identical to those created with the long form, and a binding specified in one form can override one specified in the other form in the template element.

Trapping User-Initiated Events—The do Element

When you write an application for a graphical windowed environment, that environment defines a number of standard controls, either explicitly or by popular convention. These user interface elements—such as menus, push buttons, and toolbars—will be available when any user executes your program.

In contrast, WAP does not define a standard user interface for WML browsers. Indeed, it does not even define a standard reference platform. WML-capable devices will come in many forms, with many different user interfaces. How, then, can you define how users should interact with your application when you have no idea what the user interface will look like? WML's answer to this conundrum is the do element.

The do element lets you specify the actions that the user should be able to perform. The browser will map your defined actions to some user interface widget that the user can activate. This element might appear on screen as a graphical button, it might be added to a menu, it might be linked to a physical hardware control, or it might appear in some other fashion entirely. Regardless of how the control is rendered, the associated task executes when the user activates the control.

It is important not to be influenced by the behavior of one particular browser—if you gear your application toward a specific browser, the resulting WML markup will be less likely to work well on other browsers. In theory, any WML should work on all compliant devices. In practice, it can be very difficult to design a compelling application using generic, "browser-agnostic" WML. In some cases, it may be desirable to tailor the WML at run time to the particular browser being used.

\<do>

Purpose: Binds a user-initiated event to a task.

Attributes:

type	"accept" | "prev" | "help" | "reset" | "options" | "delete" | "unknown" | experimental type | vendor type | other type (novar)
label	*Controllabel*
name	*Bindingname* (novar)
optional	"false" | "true" (novar)
id	(novar)
class	(novar)
xml:lang	(novar)

Can contain: \<go>, \<prev>, \<noop>, \<refresh>

Valid in: \<template>, \<card>, \<p>, \<fieldset>, \<pre> [1.3]

The type Attribute   The type attribute offers a hint to the browser as to the meaning of the do element. Although some browsers will use this information to decide how the element should be mapped to a user interface construct, it is nevertheless perfectly acceptable for the browser to disregard the type information and render all do elements identically. However, as the type attribute is required and is your only option for influencing the browser's handling of the do element, you should make the effort to use an appropriate type. Table 7-5 lists the predefined do types.

The WML standard is nearly mute on the meanings of the various types, providing little information beyond that presented in our table. The following descriptions are designed to give you a feeling for how these types should be used. Bear in mind, however, that the interpretation presented here is not the only one possible. Additional guidelines are given in the section "Using do Elements." Remember that do elements

Table 7-5 Predefined do Types

Type	Description
accept	Positive acceptance (forward navigation)
prev	Cancel, back out (backward navigation)
help	Request for help (may be context-sensitive)
options	Request for options or additional operations (context-sensitive)
reset	Clearing or resetting state
delete	Delete an item or choice
unknown	A generic element

are card-level constructs, so the associated actions should apply to the card as a whole. It is not possible to associate do elements with a particular field in a card.

The accept and prev types can be thought of as opposites (Listing 7-11). The accept type should be used for actions that take you further into the application, whereas prev cancels or returns the user from the current operation. You can often think of these two types as being associated with forward and backward navigation, respectively. It might help to picture how applications behave under Microsoft Windows: Tasks that are associated with the Enter key are analogous to accept tasks, and those associated with the Esc key are similar to prev tasks.

Listing 7-11 Example of accept and prev do types.

```
<wml>
   <card>
      <p>
         Cart:
         <br/>
         "Adventures of Echo", 19.93
         <br/>
         <a href="#conf">Check out</a>
      </p>
   </card>

   <card id="conf">
      <do type="accept" label="Buy It">
         <go href="#sale"/>
      </do>
      <do type="prev" label="Cancel">
         <prev/>
      </do>
```

```
      <p>
      Confirm sale
      <br/>
      Your credit card will be charged
      $$19.93.
      </p>
   </card>

   <card id="sale">
      <p>
      Thank you for your order!
      </p>
   </card>
</wml>
```

The `help` type (Listing 7-12) is associated with a request for help; in a graphical desktop environment, it could be considered the F1 key. You can provide limited context-sensitive help by providing different help actions for the various cards in your application, but you cannot get more specific than that. It is not possible, for example, to provide help that is specific to the active field. Similarly, the `options` type (Listing 7-13) refers to a context-sensitive request for additional operations. (The closest analog in the desktop world is probably the F10 key, which activates the menu bar.)

Listing 7-12   Example of `help` do type.

```
<wml>
   <card id="menu">
      <do type="help" label="Help">
         <go href="#help"/>
      </do>
      <p>
         Account Menu
         <br/>
         <a href="#chk">Checking</a>
         <br/>
         <a href="#sav">Savings</a>
      </p>
   </card>

   <card id="help">
      <p>
      Choose which account you want to work with
      from the list.
      <br/>
      <a href="#menu">Return</a>
      </p>
   </card>
```

```wml
    <card id="chk">
        <p>
        Checking menu goes here...
        <br/>
        <a href="#menu">Return</a>
        </p>
    </card>

    <card id="sav">
        <p>
        Savings menu goes here...
        <br/>
        <a href="#menu">Return</a>
        </p>
    </card>
</wml>
```

Listing 7-13   Example of options do type.

```wml
<wml>
    <card id="menu">
        <do type="options" label="Act">
           <go href="#act"/>
        </do>
        <p>
            Messages
            <br/>
            <a href="#m1">Bullwinkle-10:50</a>
            <br/>
            <a href="#m2">Boris-9:17</a>
        </p>
    </card>

    <card id="act">
        <p>
        <a href="?A=RFR">Refresh</a>
        <br/>
        <a href="?A=NEW">Compose</a>
        <br/>
        <a href="#menu">Return</a>
        </p>
    </card>

    <card id="m1">
        <do type="options" label="Act">
           <go href="#msgact"/>
        </do>
        <p>
        Bullwinkle: Hey Rocky, Watch me pull
        a rabbit out of my hat!
        <br/>
        <a href="#menu">Return</a>
        </p>
    </card>
```

```
<card id="m2">
   <p>
   Boris: Have I mentioned I hate Moose and
   Squirrel?
   <br/>
   <a href="#menu">Return</a>
   </p>
</card>

<card id="msgact">
   <p>
   <a href="?A=RPL">Reply</a>
   <br/>
   <a href="?A=DEL">Delete</a>
   <br/>
   <a href="?A=FWD">Forward</a>
   <br/>
   <a href="#menu">Return</a>
   </p>
</card>
</wml>
```

The meanings of the `delete` and `reset` types are even more vague. The `delete` type is associated with the deletion of an option or choice; because WML does not give you context information down to the level of the individual control, however, you cannot, for example, display a list and use a `delete` binding to remove one item. This type is perhaps most appropriate when the card contains one particular item, and the user should be allowed to delete it. An e-mail application, for instance, might use the `delete` type to let the user delete the message being read. A `reset` binding appropriately might be tied to a task that clears sensitive variables.

The last standard type, `unknown`, is used for bindings that do not fall into any of the preceding categories. (Actually, any unrecognized type will be treated as `unknown`, but as all other type names are reserved, you should use only `unknown`.) Bindings with an `unknown` type probably will not receive any preferential treatment.

Two additional types—actually, families of types—exist: vendor and experimental. Vendor types begin with the string "`vnd.`" (in any combination of uppercase and lowercase) and are intended to allow browser authors and device manufacturers to define types that take advantage of nonstandard capabilities. For example, if all Acme phones have a "home" key, Acme's browser might choose to define a "`vnd.acme-home`" type that would be bound to that key. Experimental types begin with "x-" or "X-". Until vendors take advantage of these types, there is no reason to use them.

The WML deck **DoTestLab.wml**, on the companion Web site, allows you to experiment with the different do types on your device and check their appearances.

The label Attribute   You can define a text string that the browser must use, if possible, to label the user interface control that is bound to the event. (One acceptable reason for a browser to ignore your label is if it binds the task to a physical hardware control.) Your text may be truncated to fit the screen, so try to limit your labels to six characters or less. If you do not specify a label, the browser will use its default. As the default is not likely to be particularly informative, you should always label your event bindings explicitly.

The name Attribute   As we have mentioned, event bindings can be defined either at the card level or, via the template element, at the deck level. Deck-level bindings apply to all cards in a deck unless overridden. Overrides are based on binding names, not binding types. They allow you to override a deck-level binding of one type with a card-level binding of another type, which is sometimes desirable. Most of the time, however, you will seek to override bindings of the same type, so WML provides a shortcut: if you do not specify a name, WML uses the value of the type attribute. For example, an accept binding with no explicit name is assigned the name "accept."

Listing 7-14 demonstrates both kinds of overrides. In the first card, the prev binding in the card overrides the one in the template. Because this override is tied to a noop task, the card should not contain any active event bindings; the only valid action is to follow the link. In the second card, the accept binding also overrides the template binding. It should be the only active binding in the card.

Listing 7-14   Overriding bindings.

```
<wml>
   <template>
      <do type="prev">
         <prev/>
      </do>
   </template>

   <card id="c1">
      <do type="prev">
         <noop/>
      </do>
```

```
      <p>
      Can't back up from here.
      <br/>
      <a href="#c2">To 2</a>
      </p>
   </card>

   <card id="c2">
      <do type="accept" name="prev">
         <go href="#c1"/>
      </do>

      <p>
      Accept should take you back.
      </p>
   </card>
</wml>
```

It is an error to assign the same name to more than one binding in the template or within any one card. Because of the default name assignment, this restriction means that to create multiple bindings of the same type within a card, you must assign each a unique name even when you are not overriding bindings.

The optional Attribute   By default, all active bindings (that is, those not bound to a noop task) must be made available to the user in some manner. If you want to give the browser discretion for some reason, you can set the optional attribute to "true." One possible use for this choice would arise when using a vendor-specific binding. By making this binding optional, a browser from another vendor could, theoretically, ignore it.

The template Element

The template element defines *deck-level* bindings—that is, bindings that apply to all cards in the deck. Deck-level bindings can be overridden in individual cards. If specified, the <template> element must follow the <head> element, if any, and precede the first card in the deck.

<template>

Purpose: Specifies event bindings that apply to all cards in a deck.

Attributes:

onenterforward	*URL*
onenterbackward	*URL*
ontimer	*URL*
id	(novar)
class	(novar)

Can contain: <do>, <onevent>

Valid in: <wml>

Binding overrides are based on binding names: A card-level element overrides a deck-level element if both have a name attribute with the same value. When you do not explicitly name a binding, the browser uses the value of the type attribute as a default name. As a result, when overriding a do element of the same type, the name attribute can be omitted; when overriding an element of a different type, you must give both the same name (Listing 7-14).

The set of *active elements* includes all elements specified in the card, plus any elements specified in the deck that are not overridden in the card, minus any elements bound to a noop task. All active elements must be made available to the user in some manner, and no inactive elements may be presented.

For the purposes of shadowing, bindings defined using the card or template shorthand attributes (such as onenterforward) are treated exactly as if they were defined with a <do> or <onevent> element.

Using do Elements

Suppose that in the course of writing your Next Great WAP Program, you want to display a message and wait for the user to acknowledge it before proceeding. One way to accomplish this goal is to create a card with the message and include a do element binding an accept type action to a go task, as shown in Listing 7-15. If we examine how this particular deck appears on various browsers, we will find some differences worth noting.

Listing 7-15   Rendering of do elements.

```wml
<wml>
   <card>
      <do type="accept" label="OK">
         <go href="#c2"/>
      </do>
      <p>
      Score:
      <br/>
      Computer: 2617
      <br/>
      Human: 4
      <br/>
      Press OK to continue.
      </p>
   </card>

   <card id="c2">
      <do type="prev">
         <prev/>
      </do>
      <p>
         Play again?
      </p>
   </card>
</wml>
```

Many devices take advantage of "soft keys"—hardware controls whose function can change depending on the content. The ways in which soft keys are used vary dramatically, however. Some browsers assign bindings directly to the soft keys, as shown in Figure 7-10. In the figure, the key itself has been dynamically labeled as we requested.

Figure 7-10   An accept binding assigned directly to a soft key (Phone.com SDK)

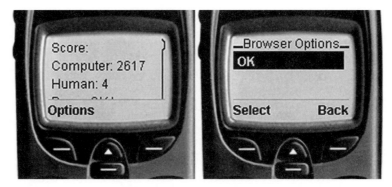

Figure 7-11   An accept binding on a visible menu (Nokia SDK)

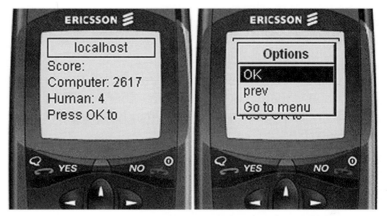

Figure 7-12   An accept binding on a stealth menu (Ericsson SDK)

Other browsers make the binding available indirectly. The browser in Figure 7-11 has a soft key labeled "Options"; the binding is made available on the Options menu (in this case, as the only option). The browser in Figure 7-12 works in similar fashion, except that it does not waste any screen real estate on a label. The user is expected to know that holding down the left key (labeled "Yes") will activate a similar pop-up menu of options.

These variations are probably more confusing to the developer than to the user. A user is unlikely to switch between devices frequently and consequently is likely to be familiar with how his or her particular device works. As a developer, it makes sense to rely on this fact. Jokes about users unable to find the "any" key aside, no one really expects computer programs to give instructions such as "Type in your name using the keyboard and press the key labeled 'Enter' when finished." In our example, it might make sense to dispense with the message "Press OK to continue" entirely and assume that the user will know how to find it.

In fact, you should consider whether users whose browsers tend to use options menus would want to press two keys to continue. This issue might not seem like a big deal in our two-card example, but when required over every step in your application, the two-key strategy could get tiresome. In many cases, the best approach is to include an explicit link (an anchor) that mirrors the "accept" binding, as it offers the best possible experience for most types of browsers without resorting to customized markup.

Although not evident from these examples, a device could conceivably have a dedicated hardware control for use with specific binding types. The device in Figure 7-10, for example, has a key labeled "Back" that is used when the deck contains an event binding for "prev." The point is that you cannot assume that your binding label will be used and therefore must use caution when referring to it in prompts. For example, with binding

```
<do type="prev" label="Cancel"> ...
```

this particular browser would not show the label "Cancel."

Rendering Event Bindings

Some browsers may elect to display do elements intermixed with your content, somewhat like an in-line button. This possibility is easy to overlook, as many current browsers do not exhibit this behavior, but you should nevertheless pay attention to where you define your event bindings. In particular, if you define your bindings at the top of your card, browsers that display them in-line will position them before your content, which may not be intuitive.

For the purposes of rendering, deck-level bindings (that is, bindings defined in a template element) are treated as if they follow all of your card content, including any card-level bindings.

Logical versus Physical Navigation

Because WML gives you control over "accept" and "prev" events, you can, in effect, redefine what these events mean. Just because you have this power, however, it does not mean that you should use it. You should be wary of using do types in an inconsistent manner (although the definitions of the various types are sufficiently vague to make this directive challenging to obey). For example, in the browser shown earlier in Figure 7-10, the binding

```
<do type="prev" label="Continue"> ...
```

would require that the user press the "Back" button to continue, which would hardly be intuitive.

A case when it is arguably acceptable to redefine the "accept" event is on a dead-end card. For example, your online help might consist of a single card of explanation. Having read it and been (hopefully) enlightened, the user will want to return to the application. The prev task will take the user back to this point, of course, but you may also want to define the accept task to do the same (Listing 7-16). Depending on the browser, accept may be easier to invoke than prev.

Listing 7-16   An accept action acting as a prev.

```
<wml>
   <card>
      <p>
      Enter velocity in furlongs per fortnight:
      </p>

      <do type="help" label="Help">
         <go href="#help"/>
      </do>
   </card>

   <card id="help">
      <p>
         A furlong is 40 rods.
      </p>
      <do type="accept">
         <prev/>
      </do>
      <do type="prev">
         <prev/>
      </do>
   </card>
</wml>
```

When does it make sense to change the semantics of the "prev" event? Let us consider the messaging application example mentioned earlier. The application includes a list of messages and allows the user to

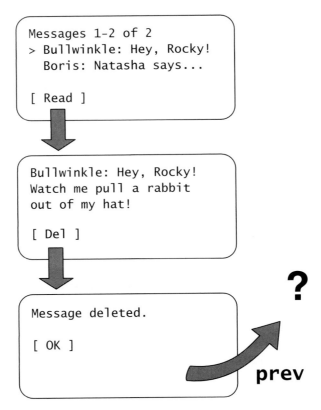

Figure 7-13   The deleted message scenario

delete a message once read. After the message has been deleted, what happens if the user is allowed to invoke a <prev> task (Figure 7-13)?

The answer is "nothing good." If the deck with the message card remains in the cache, the browser would redisplay it. From here, the user could try to delete it again, which is unlikely to be productive. Alternatively, if the deck containing the message card has expired from the cache[7] (or was marked not cacheable to begin with), the browser would request it again from the server, which would most likely generate some form of error. From a usability standpoint, neither option is particularly appealing.

---

[7] Besides having expired, the deck must have been marked "Must-revalidate" when it was delivered, or the browser will not revalidate the deck because it involves a <prev> task. See the "Cache Value" section earlier in this chapter.

One recourse is to dispense with a "prev" action altogether. Although this option may be a reasonable solution, we still have to deal with the issue of returning the user to the message list: That "OK" prompt after "Message deleted" has to lead somewhere. Thus the application needs to request a new copy of the list from the server to ensure that the deleted message does not appear. It would be equally acceptable to bind the "prev" action to share this behavior.

To make effective use of this capability to redefine the direction of navigation, you need to keep straight the difference between "logical" navigation (what the user perceives is happening) and "physical" navigation (what the application is really doing). In the messaging application, when invoking the "prev" task, the user thinks he or she is navigating backward to the message list, skipping over the message body because it had been deleted. In reality, the browser is navigating *forward* to the "same" (albeit updated) view of the message list. This navigational power allows you to define your application flow in a much more natural fashion, but you will need to consider the same question at every card: Will the right thing happen when the user invokes "prev" (or "accept") here?

The Question of Duplicate Bindings

The WML standard says it is acceptable to have multiple active bindings of the same type, but it does not offer any guidance as to what that might mean or how such "twin" bindings should interact. The result, naturally, is that duplicate bindings are treated differently by different browsers.

Consider the "options" type, with which the behavior of some browsers may actually encourage you to use multiple bindings. The standard says only that the "options" type is a "context-sensitive request for options or additional operations," which leaves a lot of room for differences in interpretation. Predictably, at least two behaviors have evolved. One set of browsers expects the "options" type to signal a *request* for actions ("Show me what I can do here"), whereas a second set of browsers expects it to *be* an action ("This is one thing you can do here"). A deck constructed to prefer the first behavior is shown in Listing 7-17, and one that prefers the second behavior appears in Listing 7-18. You can try these decks in various browsers and see how their results differ.

Listing 7-17   Options as a request to display a menu.

```
<wml>
   <card id="menu">
      <p>
         Messages
         <br/>
         <a href="#m1">Bullwinkle-10:50</a>
         <br/>
         <a href="#m2">Boris-9:17</a>
      </p>
      <do type="options" label="Act">
         <go href="#act"/>
      </do>
   </card>

   <card id="act">
      <p>
      <a href="?A=RFR">Refresh</a>
      <br/>
      <a href="?A=NEW">Compose</a>
      <br/>
      <a href="main.wml">Return</a>
      </p>

      <do type="prev" label="Back">
         <prev/>
      </do>
   </card>
</wml>
```

Listing 7-18   Options as an entry in a menu.

```
<wml>
   <card id="menu">
      <p>
         Messages
         <br/>
         <a href="#m1">Bullwinkle-10:50</a>
         <br/>
         <a href="#m2">Boris-9:17</a>
      </p>
      <do type="options" label="Refresh" name="o1">
         <go href="?A=RFR"/>
      </do>
      <do type="options" label="Compose" name="o2">
         <go href="?A=NEW"/>
      </do>
      <do type="options" label="Return" name="o3">
         <go href="main.wml"/>
      </do>
   </card>
</wml>
```

At least you can count on both forms working, regardless of the type of browser employed. As an application designer, however, you need to be concerned with which approach is more usable. Both have their advantages. The second approach, "the options type indicates a menu choice," usually works well on all browsers and requires the least number of keystrokes to activate an entry. However, the first approach, "the options type indicates a menu request," offers a bonus that is not readily apparent from our example: The markup for the menu entries does not need to reside in the same deck.

To understand why the latter option is desirable, think about what happens whenever you use the message application. With the second approach, every deck of messages must also include all of the available options. Consequently, each deck is larger, takes slightly longer to transmit, and—if you are paying for wireless service by the byte or second—costs slightly more. The options also take up space that might better be occupied by additional content within the deck. With the first approach, however, the deck needs to contain only one "options" binding. The card describing the options can be a second deck, which the browser requests only when it is needed. Even better, you can make the options deck "generic," so it can sit in the browser cache and serve across multiple invocations of the messaging application.

In general, the efficiencies possible with the first approach make it attractive regardless of which behavior the browser prefers. Nevertheless, you should consider which approach best serves your particular application.

The prev Mystery

Another problematic area within WML involves the backward navigation mechanism and the issue of "implicit bindings" in general. This concern stems from a WML 1.1 requirement that the browser's user interface must include some mechanism for the user to navigate backward—that is, to access the previous card in the history. What was left unclear was whether the definition of prev event bindings in the content should influence this mechanism. As a result, two approaches evolved (are you detecting a pattern here?). One class of browser allowed "prev" bindings to override the default mechanism. The other presented the user with two "prev" controls; one control always returned the user to the previous card in the history, and the other control was mapped to the prev binding contained in the content.

Realizing that this issue had become a problem, the WAP Forum dropped the requirement in WML 1.2. However, the standard does not forbid a browser from *adding* its own bindings to whatever you specify in your deck. Consequently, even when you do not define an accept or prev binding, you may find that the browser adds one for you! (Usually, the "implicit" bindings are bound to a prev task.)

Fortunately, most browser developers who were in the second camp dropped their default mechanism when WML 1.2 was adopted—even from their WML 1.1 browsers. As a result, an easy technique is available to combat this incompatibility: *Always* define a binding for both accept and prev. When you do not want the binding to be active, link it to a <noop> task. (If your deck includes multiple cards with the same behaviors, define your bindings using the template element.)

Usage Guidelines

We conclude this section by providing a list of guidelines for using do elements. Although they will not apply in every situation, these recommendations serve as a good starting point.

- Always define bindings for accept and prev. If you do not need them, assign them to a <noop> task. Use a template if your deck contains more than one card.

- Use links (<a> or <anchor> elements) at the bottom of your card for the most important (up to three) actions available. Assign the most important action to accept as well.

- Bind the prev event only to return to a previous application state (regardless of whether this state is implemented using a <prev> task).

- Use a single options binding to bring up a contextual menu of additional functions.

- Always strive to give your bindings descriptive labels, but keep them short (six characters at most). Do not rely on the labels, however, and do not refer to bindings in your prompts.

- Define your bindings at the end of your card, after the content, and order the bindings so that those most likely to be used occur first.

- Avoid having multiple active bindings of any of the six standard types (accept, prev, help, options, reset, delete). If you seem to have multiple actions of the same type, consider defining a single binding that calls up a menu.

- Avoid experimental and vendor types unless you have a specific reason to use them. Use vendor types as dictated by the vendor.
- Test your application on more than one browser!

A number of sources have written WML "style guides" that address these and other issues, and it is worth your while to read them. Do not rule out guidelines provided by browser manufacturers, but bear in mind that these recommendations are usually tailored to one particular interpretation of the standard.

Variables

One of WML's most powerful features, variables allow you to alter your content dynamically at run time. You can use variables in most content as well as in certain attribute values; they cannot, however, be used to represent element and attribute names in markup. Variables are also used to capture user input and to control timers.

Variables are considered *set* if they contain any value other than the empty string. A variable that is not set is indistinguishable from one that has been assigned the empty string, and referencing an undefined variable returns an empty string.

The syntax for accessing the value of a variable is the U.S. dollar sign followed by the variable's name in parentheses: $(username). If the variable reference is followed by whitespace, you can omit the parentheses:

```
Your name is $first $(last).
```

Some browsers allow you to omit the parentheses when the reference is adjacent to a character that is invalid in a variable name. However, because not all browsers support this capability, you should always use parentheses unless the variable is followed by whitespace.

Initializing Variables—The `setvar` Element

You use the `<setvar>` element to assign a value to a variable. One inter-esting wrinkle is that explicit variable assignments take place only as a side effect of task execution. The `<setvar>` element must be associated with a task element (`go`, `prev`, or `refresh`). The browser processes variable assignments while executing the task. Variables are also assigned values during the processing of `<input>`, `<select>`, and `<timer>` elements.

`<setvar>`

Purpose: Assigns a value to a variable, or clears a previously assigned value.

Attributes:

name	*varname*
value	*varname*
id	(novar)
class	(novar)

Can contain: Nothing

Valid in: `<go>`, `<prev>`, `<refresh>`

The name *Attribute*

The `name` attribute specifies the name of the variable whose value is to be changed. Variable names are case-sensitive; they must consist of under-scores, ASCII letters, and digits, but cannot begin with a digit. If you specify an invalid name, the `<setvar>` element is ignored.

The value *Attribute*

The `value` attribute specifies the value to be assigned to the variable. You can specify an empty string to clear an existing value.

Using Variables

Variable substitution occurs at run time, within the browser, after the card has been parsed but before it is rendered. Consequently, a variable value can be concatenated with static text or the value of another vari-able. Within a `<setvar>` element, the name of the variable can itself be

Note that the use of variables to store user information may raise security concerns that do not apply to other markup languages. When storing information that could be considered private by a user, you should clear this data from the variable as soon as possible. Try to design your application so that sensitive data are not maintained in variables for multiple transactions; instead, transmit the information to the server and keep track of it there.

named by using a variable. This level of indirection can be used to write cards that are somewhat generic.

Any single dollar sign in your text, even expressed as a character reference, is seen as a variable reference. If you forget to escape a literal dollar sign in your content (see "Literal Dollar Signs"), whatever follows it will be used as the variable name. If the dollar sign precedes an invalid variable name or if the variable reference is found in a location where substitution is not allowed, the deck is considered in error and is not processed. Dollar signs must therefore be escaped even when they occur where a variable would not be valid.

Initial Initialization

As noted earlier, the setvar element must be contained in a task element, and assignment occurs when the task is executed. This approach presents a problem when you want to assign a variable for use in the first card in your application. One option is to use an "invisible" card that precedes the first card and sets up the state. In Listing 7-19, for example, the onenterforward binding is used to set the variables needed by the application. The onenterbackward binding ensures that the browser will pass back through the invisible card if the user backs out of your application.

Listing 7-19   Using onenterforward to initialize variables.

```
<wml>
   <card>
      <onevent type="onenterforward">
         <go href="#c2">
            <setvar name="Name" value="Pandora"/>
         </go>
      </onevent>
      <onevent type="onenterbackward">
         <prev/>
      </onevnet>
   </card>
```

```
<card id="c2">
   <p>
   Name has been set to $(Name).
   </p>
   <do type="prev">
      <prev/>
   </do>
</card>
</wml>
```

An alternative, though less obvious, technique is to use a timer coupled with a refresh task, as shown in Listing 7-20. This method has a slight size advantage—the compiled deck is slightly smaller than the deck with the invisible card—and does not result in an extra entry in the navigation history. The potential drawback is that you cannot return to the card later without reinitializing the variables, which might be a problem depending on your application's design.[8]

Listing 7-20   Using `ontimer` to initialize variables.

```
<wml>
   <card>
      <onevent type="ontimer">
         <refresh>
            <setvar name="Name" value="Candide"/>
         </refresh>
      </onevent>
      <timer name="x" value="1"/>

      <p>
      Name has been set to $(Name).
      </p>
      <do type="prev">
         <prev/>
      </do>
   </card>
</wml>
```

Variable Escaping

Escape encoding is the replacement of some or all characters in a string with an *escape sequence*—a textual representation of the character. De-

---

[8] You can actually work around this problem by assigning a control variable to the time, but doing so will negate the size advantage of this technique and make the working of your deck less obvious (and thus more prone to contain bugs).

scribed in RFC 2396, it is most commonly used in URLs (hence its alternative name of *URL escaping*). Encoding entails replacing characters that might be misinterpreted or incorrectly translated in URLs with a percent sign (%) followed by the relevant character codes. The characters that are considered "safe" and do not need to be encoded are ASCII letters, digits, and a handful of punctuation symbols.

The WML browser must implement automatic escaping behavior and will do what you want most of the time. When you use a variable reference in an attribute that expects a URL (`href`, `src`, `onenterforward`, `onenterbackward`, `ontimer`, or `onpick`), the browser automatically encodes the variable's value when it is substituted at run time. If necessary, you can force or inhibit escaping, or decode an escaped sequence, by specifying a colon and *conversion mode* (Table 7-6) after the variable name—as in `$(foo:escape)`, for example. Specification of a conversion does not affect the value stored in the variable.

Table 7-6　Variable Conversion Modes

Mode	Description
escape	Force URL escaping of the variable's value when used
noesc	Inhibit URL escaping of the variable's value when used
unesc	"Unescape" the variable's value when used

> WML 1.1 allowed you to specify the conversion modes in any case combination (for example, "eScApE"). This requirement was deprecated in WML 1.2. For compatibility reasons, always specify conversions in lowercase.

Other Content You Can Include

Your WML documents may include several other types of content, including images, tables, and links.

Images

As in HTML, WML decks cannot contain images directly; instead, they can include references to images, which exist in separate files. This approach allows you to include images in your documents without affecting the operation of devices that do not support graphics: those browsers simply ignore the image reference when the document is loaded.

A picture may be worth a thousand words, but no matter how they are presented, no one wants to read a thousand words on a four-line screen. Because images are larger than text and take more time to transmit over the wireless network, an excessive number of images can bog down your application. You should seek to minimize your use of images, limit the number appearing in any one deck, and keep each graphic as small as possible.

All WML browsers that support graphics must support WAP's black-and-white wireless bitmap format (WBMP). As of WML 1.2, browsers that support color graphics must also support the Portable Network Graphics (PNG) format. Some browsers may also support additional standards such as GIF or JPEG. Your server program should check the HTTP request headers to determine which, if any, of the non-WBMP image formats the browser supports. However, use of the WBMP format is recommended; all browsers will support it, and it is relatively compact.

Images are rendered in-line with their surrounding content. You can specify the alignment of images relative to this content, as well as the amount of whitespace used to set off an image from its surroundings. Note, however, that some browsers will ignore such requests. Listing 7-21 demonstrates the use of images, and Figure 7-14 shows how they might appear. The deck **ImgTests.wml**, found on the companion Web site, tests many of the possible combinations of the `src`, `alt`, and `localsrc` attributes.

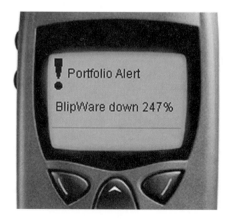

Figure 7-14   Sample rendering of an image (Nokia SDK)

Listing 7-21   Use of the `img` element.

```wml
<wml>
    <card id="c1">
        <p>
        <img src="bang.wbmp" alt="[!] " align="middle"/>
        Portfolio Alert
        <br/>
        BlipWare down 247%
        </p>
    </card>
</wml>
```

`<img>`

Purpose: Includes an image in the card content.

Attributes:

`alt`	*alttext*
`src`	*URL*
`localsrc`	*internalrep*
`vspace`	`"0"` | `pixels` | `percent%` (novar)
`hspace`	`"0"` | `pixels` | `percent%` (novar)
`align`	`"bottom"` | `"top"` | `"middle"` (novar)
`height`	`pixels` | `percent%` (novar)
`width`	`pixels` | `percent%` (novar)
`id`	(novar)
`class`	(novar)

Can contain: Nothing

Valid in: `<p>`, `<fieldset>`, `<td>`

The `alt` Attribute

When the image cannot be displayed for any reason, the text specified by the `alt` attribute is used instead. You are required to provide this alternative text; if no alternative text is appropriate, you can specify an empty string (`""`) instead. Depending on the browser, the `alt` text may run directly into the following text content, so you should usually pad it with a trailing space.

Some browsers may object to a completely empty `alt` attribute, so you may need to specify one space character instead.

The *src* Attribute

The `src` attribute indicates the URL of the image on the Internet. If the browser and device both support images, the graphic will be downloaded and processed. As long as the image is in a form known to the browser and meets any other browser-imposed constraints (such as maximum size), it will be displayed.

The *localsrc* Attribute

The `localsrc` attribute refers to a locally available image on the device, which the browser can display immediately instead of waiting to load the image over the wireless network. The WML standard does not define any `localsrc` identifiers, so currently you can use these identifiers with confidence only if you are tailoring your output to a particular device. If `localsrc` is used and the specified resource exists, it takes precedence over the `src` attribute.

The *vspace* and *hspace* Attributes

You can use `vspace` and `hspace` to request that the browser set the image apart from any surrounding text, although the browser can choose to ignore them. These attributes specify the amount of whitespace to leave to the left and right (`hspace`) and to the top and bottom (`vspace`) of the image. The value may be an absolute number, specifying the number of pixels, or it may be a percentage of the available horizontal and vertical space. If you do not specify any padding, "0" will be assumed, indicating no padding.

The WML 1.1 standard states that the browser's default for these values will generally be a small, nonzero number. This statement is incorrect; the default is "0" even in WML 1.1, as you can see in the WML 1.1 DTD. You must always specify `hspace` and `vspace` if padding is desired.

The *align* Attribute

As noted earlier, images are rendered in-line with their surrounding content. You can use the `align` attribute to control how the image lines up with this content relative to the current line of text, specifying `bottom` (the default), `middle`, or `top` alignment. The browser is encouraged to respect your request but is not required to do so.

The *height* and *width* Attributes

The `height` and `width` attributes give the browser an idea of the image's size in pixels, so that space can be reserved for it. Some browsers may take advantage of this knowledge by rendering the card while waiting for the image data to arrive, thereby shortening the overall time it takes before the user sees the card.

Some browsers and WAP gateways may scale the image to the specified size if necessary, and you can specify the height or width as a percentage of the screen size. This behavior is not required, however, and you should not rely on it. If you specify the `height` and `width` attributes, you should always use the actual dimensions of the image.

Tables

WML supports simple tables for organizing content into columns. These tables are not intended to provide fancy formatting—bear in mind the small size of the screen that most devices will use. Browsers are required only to make their "best effort" to display the table "as appropriate for the device." In practice, attempting to display more than two or three columns of short data is risky, and even that information may not appear as you would expect.

Table data is organized into rows, specified with the `tr` (table row) element; rows, in turn, contain cells indicated by `td` (table data) elements. Within a cell, you can include only text, images, and links; you cannot use controls (such as input or select elements) or other tables. Line breaks (`br` elements) can be used in cells; once again, however, the final effect depends on the "best effort" of the browser (which may choose to ignore the line breaks). Scrolling and line wrapping in tables can also prove problematic, so it is generally wise to avoid table lines that exceed the screen width.

If you include multiple tables in a single card, the browser may choose to create one set of aligned columns for all tables. That is, the browser may set column sizes based on the data in all tables. This decision may lead to adverse formatting if the tables have columns of dissimilar widths. On the other hand, browsers are free to use fixed column widths regardless of the width of the data. In fact, they do not have to display the table in tabular form at all.

Table orientation depends on the layout of the language used for display. For left-to-right languages, the leftmost cell is the first one, and column padding and combination occur on the right. For right-to-left languages, the reverse is true. The WML standard does not currently address other orientations, but presumably they would work in a similar manner. Listing 7-22 demonstrates the use of tables, and Figure 7-15 shows how one might appear.

Listing 7-22   Use of the `table` element.

```wml
<wml>
   <card>
      <p>
      <b>Quote: BlipWare</b>
      <table columns="2" align="LR">
         <tr>
             <td>Last:</td>
             <td>44</td>
         </tr>
         <tr>
             <td>Change:</td>
             <td>-3.19</td>
         </tr>
         <tr>
             <td>Change:</td>
             <td>-3.19</td>
         </tr>
         <tr>
             <td>High:</td>
             <td>51</td>
         </tr>
         <tr>
             <td>Low:</td>
             <td>41</td>
         </tr>
      </table>
      </p>
   </card>
</wml>
```

Figure 7-15 Sample rendering of a table (Nokia SDK)

`<table>`

Purpose: Align output in columns.

Attributes:

`columns`	*number* (novar)
`title`	*titletext*
`align`	*alignspec* (novar)
`id`	(novar)
`class`	(novar)

Can contain: `<tr>`

Valid in: `<p>`, `<fieldset>`

The columns Attribute

You must tell the browser how many columns each row will contain by using the `columns` attribute, which cannot be zero. Rows containing less than the specified number of columns will be padded with blank cells, which appear on the appropriate side for the orientation of the current language; for example, padding occurs on the right for a left-to-right language such as English. If any row contains more cells than the specified number of columns, the excess data will be added to the final cell of the row, separated from the preceding data by a single blank space.

You cannot control column width or layout; instead, the browser sets column widths and dictates the width of the gutter between columns. Browsers also choose how to handle data that is too long to fit in a cell on a single line. Some valid approaches are to apply the mode attribute of the enclosing paragraph, to word-wrap within the cell, or to allow manual or automatic scrolling of the table data.

The *title* Attribute

The title attribute specifies a title for the table. The browser may choose to display the title in some fashion or simply ignore it.

The *align* Attribute

WML allows you to define the alignment for each column of your table in one attribute, align. The browser's default alignment, if you do not provide one or if the browser chooses to disregard your specification, is implementation-dependent. It may be based on the current language, though even this is not required.

Four alignment designators, all of which are specified in uppercase, exist: C (center), L (left), R (right), and D (default, introduced in WML 1.2). The value of the align attribute is a list of nonseparated designators, one per column. These designators are applied to columns in the order that they appear in the document. If you specify fewer designators than there are columns, the unspecified columns will have the default alignment; if you specify too many designators, the browser will ignore the excess ones. Unrecognized designators also are treated as signifying the default alignment.

> The align attribute was poorly documented in WML 1.1, and you may find disparities in its implementation. WML 1.2 clarified how the attribute should be specified and added the alignment designator "D" (default alignment).

Table Structure—The *tr* and *td* Elements

The tr element serves to organize table cells into rows. Each table element must contain at least one tr element, and each tr element must contain at least one td element. Empty rows (rows containing only empty td elements) are legal, and the browser cannot ignore them. Generally, empty rows will be rendered as blank lines.

<tr>

Purpose: Defines a row in a table.

Attributes:

id	(novar)
class	(novar)

Can contain: <td>

Valid in: <table>

A td element holds data for a single cell, which may be empty. Formatting of the data, including handling of long data, images, and line breaks, is left to the best effort of the browser.

<td>

Purpose: Defines a cell in a table.

Attributes:

id	(novar)
class	(novar)
xml:lang	(novar)

Can contain: Text, emphasized text (<em>, <strong>, <b>, <i>, <u>, <big>, <small>), <br>, <img>, <anchor>, <a>

Valid in: <tr>

Links

HTML standardized an unfortunate overloading of the term *anchor*, applying it not only to the point in the document targeted by a link but also to the hotspot in the document that activates the link. WML perpetuates this confusion by using only the second meaning of "anchor," which makes no sense whatsoever. The real "anchor" of a WML link is the URL of another resource such as a card or a deck, which need not be explicitly identified as a possible link target.

WML further occludes the issue by using two tags to define hotspots, <anchor> and <a>, and by broadening the meaning of the term "link." A

WML link is a connection between a document hotspot and a task. This task might be a navigation task (mimicking HTML links) but could also be a prev or refresh task. To avoid confusion, we will use these terms as follows:

- *Anchor* means the <anchor> or <a> elements themselves.
- *Hotspot* refers to the trigger point defined by the anchor.
- *Link task* refers to the action that is bound to the hotspot.
- *Link* refers to the whole ball of wax—a fully specified anchor element.

A WML link, therefore, is similar to an event binding, except that it binds a task to a portion of the document rather than to an abstract event. With an event binding, you pass the task of presentation completely to the browser, trusting that the user will find it obvious and intuitive. In contrast, by using an anchor, you retain some control over the presentation. You do not retain *complete* control, however, because the standard says nothing about how links should be rendered, but you can assume that they will be distinguished in some fashion. If the link hotspot includes text content, for example, the text may be underlined or highlighted. Other browsers may allow the user to cycle among the selectable hotspots using cursor keys. Limitations of the physical device may affect formatting; for instance, some devices may not present more than one link on a physical screen line, even if the screen is wide enough to accommodate multiple links.

Links must contain one and only one task: an <anchor> element must include one go, prev, or refresh element, and an <a> element must include an href attribute. A link may not contain a noop task. Interestingly, WML does not require a link to contain any visible content that serves as the hotspot. Instead, the browser decides how to handle such "invisible" links; usually, it will render them invisibly (and may or may not make them selectable by the user). You can place a link anywhere in your content where text is allowed, except within the text of an option element.

The anchor Element

The <anchor> element is the "long form" for defining a link. When selected by the user, the browser executes the associated task (<go>, <prev>, or <refresh>). Listing 7-23 demonstrates the use of anchor with various types of tasks.

Listing 7-23   Use of the anchor element.

```
<wml>
   <card>
      <p>
         Fruit is now &quot;$(fruit)&quot;
         <br/>
         <anchor>
            Go to card 2.
            <go href="#c2">
               <setvar name="fruit" value="apple"/>
            </go>
         </anchor>
      </p>
   </card>

   <card id="c2">
      <p>
         Fruit is now &quot;$(fruit)&quot;
         <br/>
         <anchor>
            Refresh this card.
            <refresh>
               <setvar name="fruit" value="orange"/>
            </refresh>
         </anchor>
         <br/>
         <anchor>
            Return to card 1.
            <prev>
               <setvar name="fruit" value="banana"/>
            </prev>
         </anchor>
      </p>
   </card>
</wml>
```

<anchor>

Purpose: Defines a link associated with any valid task.

Attributes:

title	*titletext*
accesskey [1.2]	*char*
id	(novar)
class	(novar)
xml:lang	(novar)

Can contain: Text, <br>, <img>, <go>, <prev>, <refresh>

Valid in: <p>, <fieldset>, <td>, <pre> [1.3]

The `title` Attribute   The `title` attribute allows you to specify a brief text string that the browser can choose to display to the user. Typically, you will use the title to give a brief description of the link, which the browser might show as a tool tip or in the dynamic labeling of a button. On devices with small screens, the title will often be ignored.

The `accesskey` Attribute   WML 1.2 introduced the `accesskey` attribute, which allows you to request that the browser assign an *access key* or *accelerator* to the link; the user can then activate the link by pressing a single key. The value of `accesskey` is a single character, such as a digit, a letter, or a symbol. You can also define access keys for the `anchor` and `input` elements.

The browser does not have to support access keys. If it does, it must endeavor to assign a key to every element that has requested one and to respect your requested key assignment. If the browser cannot assign the requested access key to the element (because the requested key is not available on the device or because another element has previously requested the same key), it may choose any unassigned key to be the accelerator.

The browser essentially assigns keys in two phases. First, starting from the beginning of the card and for each element that has requested an accelerator, it checks whether the key exists on the device and is unassigned. If the key is available, it is assigned to the requesting anchor. Second, any element that was not assigned its requested accelerator is assigned an accelerator from the remaining available keys. If not enough keys are available, some elements will not have one assigned.

Because you do not know which key, if any, will be assigned to each element, you should never reference the access key in your content text. Likewise, the activation of the accelerator will depend on the device, so you should not refer to specific activation methods. Some devices may recognize access keys directly, whereas others may require that they be used in conjunction with a "command" key. It is up to the browser to render the access key value in a manner that makes it identifiable, and it is up to the user to recognize the access key cue, realize that the accelerator is available, and know how to activate it.

Note, however, that the recognition of access keys may be inhibited by the context. For example, a device that recognizes access keys directly (without a command key) will probably disable recognition when an input element is active.

To use access keys effectively, you should limit how many you employ. Assign the numbers 0 through 9 to the most important elements in your content, because they will be available on more devices than letters or symbols. This approach will help ensure that your most significant elements have accelerators.

The a Element

The <a> element is a short form for defining a link bound to a <go> task that has no associated variable assignments (that is, one that does not contain any setvar elements). For efficiency reasons, you should use <a> instead of <anchor> when you do not need anchor's added flexibility.

The following link defined with the a element,

```
<a href="somewhere">Go elsewhere</a>
```

is equivalent to this longer form:

```
<anchor>Go elsewhere<go href="somewhere"/></anchor>
```

You have already encountered the a element in many of the examples in this chapter.

<a>

Purpose: Defines a link associated with a simple go task.

Attributes:

href	URL
title	titletext
accesskey [1.2]	char
id	(novar)
class	(novar)
xml:lang	(novar)

Can contain: Text, <br>, <img>

Valid in: <p>, <fieldset>, <td>, <pre> [1.3]

The title and accesskey attributes are identical to those for the anchor element.

The href Attribute The href attribute defines the URL of the card targeted by the link. When the user selects the link, the browser initiates a go task to the indicated card.

Whitespace in Links

Remember that whitespace at the start or end of the link content will be seen as significant in some cases and will not be removed (see "Whitespace"). For example, consider the first link in Listing 7-24. When the whitespace is compressed, this link takes the following form:

```
<a href="http://xyz.com/a.wml"> Click here </a>
```

Listing 7-24   Whitespace in links.

```
<wml>
   <card>
      <p>
        <a href="http://xyz.com/a.wml">
           Click me!
        </a>
        <br/>
        <a href="http://xyz.com/b.wml">No, click me!</a>
      </p>
   </card>
</wml>
```

In most browsers, this extra whitespace will appear when the link is displayed. (Technically, the browser can never legally throw away the space remaining at the beginning or the end of the link; however, depending on how links are rendered, its presence may not be apparent.) To prevent the extra space from making an appearance, as in Figure 7-16,

Figure 7-16   Whitespace in links (Phone.com SDK)

remove the space between the link text and the elements immediately surrounding it, as was done with the second link in Listing 7-24.

Controls

Along with event bindings and links, WML provides two elements that allow the user to provide data to your application: the input element defines entry fields, and the select element defines menus.

Entry Fields—The input Element

The input element defines an entry field—that is, a place where the user enters information that can be referenced directly within your WML decks or can be passed to your application server. The browser stores the entered data in a variable.

As always, the presentation and operation of the input element are primarily left to the browser. Typically, the browser will display the initial value of the input field along with some cue indicating that it is editable. When the user selects an input field, the browser may allow editing in-place or may switch to an edit mode. When the user indicates that editing is complete, the browser must verify that the new value is valid, based on the input element's attributes. If it is acceptable, the value is saved in the associated variable.

In WML 1.1 and 1.2, some aspects of the input element's operation were defined only vaguely, particularly with respect to the interaction between the emptyok and format attributes and the meaning of the format codes. Consequently, you will find some differences between browsers. You should validate all input received from the user, either using a WMLScript program or within your server application. WML 1.3 addresses some of these problems.

<input>

Purpose: Defines an entry field where the user can enter information.

Attributes:

name	*varname* (novar)
value	*defaultvalue*
format	"*M" (novar)
emptyok	"false" | "true" (novar)
size	*number* (novar)
maxlength	*number* (novar)
type	<u>"text"</u> | "password" (novar)
tabindex	*number* (novar)
title	*titletext*
accesskey [1.2]	*char*
id	(novar)
class	(novar)
xml:lang	(novar)

Can contain: Nothing

Valid in: <p>, <fieldset>

The name Attribute

The name attribute identifies which variable is associated with the input element and will receive the user's input. The initial value of the variable also figures in the initial value of the input field, as described below in the section "Input Field Initialization."

The value Attribute

The value attribute provides the default value of the input field. It is used when the value of the variable specified by the name attribute is not valid.

The format Attribute

The format attribute allows you to specify a *mask* to constrain the user's input to particular sequences of characters. It can also be used to accelerate user input by automatically specifying any invariant text in the value. The mask consists of *format codes*, as shown in Table 7-7, plus static text. The browser can never assign a value to the variable unless it conforms

Table 7-7   Input Formatting Codes

Code	Description
A	Any uppercase alphabetic character, symbol, or punctuation mark. Numeric characters are excluded. (Unicode classes Lu, Lm, Pc, Pd, Ps, Pe, Po, Sm, Sc, Sk, So)
a	Any lowercase alphabetic character, symbol, or punctuation mark. Numeric characters are excluded. (Unicode classes Ll, Lm, Pc, Pd, Ps, Pe, Po, Sm, Sc, Sk, So)
N	Any numeric character. (Unicode class Nd) n (Added in WML 1.3.) Any numeric character, symbol, or punctuation mark. (Unicode classes Nd, Pc, Pd, Ps, Pe, Po, Sm, Sc, Sk, So)
X	Any uppercase alphanumeric character, symbol, or punctuation mark. (Unicode classes Lu, Lm, Nd, Pc, Pd, Ps, Pe, Po, Sm, Sc, Sk, So)
x	Any lowercase alphanumeric character, symbol, or punctuation mark. (Unicode classes Ll, Lm, Nd, Pc, Pd, Ps, Pe, Po, Sm, Sc, Sk, So)
M	Any character, uppercase default. (Unicode classes Ll, Lu, Lm, Lo, Pc, Pd, Ps, Pe, Po, Sm, Sc, Sk, So)
m	Any character, lowercase default. (Unicode classes Ll, Ll, Lm, Lo, Pc, Pd, Ps, Pe, Po, Sm, Sc, Sk, So)
*f	(For example, "*A") Zero or more characters matching the format code *f*.
nf	(For example, "3A") Up to *n* characters matching the format code *f*; *n* can be 1 through 9.
\c	(For example, "\-") Adds the literal character *c* to the value.

to the format mask. The default mask (which is used if no mask is specified or if the specified mask is invalid) is "*M", indicating that input is not restricted (but see the discussion of the `emptyok` attribute). If the user enters a value that does not match the mask, the browser must not assign the invalid value to the variable. Instead, it must notify the user that the input was rejected and allow him or her to submit new input.

Each of the eight mask characters—"A", "a", "N", "n", "X", "x", "M", and "m"—matches exactly one character in the input. In the case of "A", "a", "X", and "x", the case of the mask character indicates the required case of the input character. Some browsers will automatically force the character entered by the user to the required case, if necessary. With "M" and "m", the case of the mask character signals the browser as to the requested default case of the input character. Devices can set the "caps shift" mode accordingly as a convenience to the user, though the user remains free to switch between uppercase and lowercase. When a mask is used with a language that does not support the concept of case, there is no difference between any of the uppercase and lowercase codes.

In WML 1.1, the meaning of the numeric code modifier (*nf*) was defined as allowing exactly *n* characters matching *f*; for example, "4A" meant the same thing as "AAAA". The WML 1.2 definition allows for more flexibility by redefining the modifier to enforce an *upper limit* on the length of input. In WML 1.1, such a semantic would have required either an auxiliary WMLScript program or a server-side check after the data had been transmitted. To avoid problems later, it is recommended that you avoid using the "nf" form in decks intended for WML 1.1 browsers.

The asterisk or a single digit from 1 to 9 can modify any of the preceding codes to indicate a sequence of characters. For example, the format string "*x" will accept any number (including zero) of lowercase letters, and "3N" will accept one, two, or three digits. These modifiers can be used only with the final code in the mask, but they can be preceded by other, fixed-length sequences. For example, "N*N" will accept an integer of any length.

The backslash (\) is used to introduce literal characters into the format string; such characters are part of the input value and must be preserved. For example, the format string "N\-N" would match the input "1-2" but not "12" and the value "1-2" would be stored in the control variable. Literal characters must be considered during initialization of the field. An initial value lacking the correct literal characters will be ignored.

Because the literal characters are invariant, a browser can choose to speed user input by automatically inserting these characters into the field during the input process. In the preceding example, for instance, the browser could automatically insert a hyphen after the user enters "1". This behavior is not required, however, nor is the browser required to make the required format known to the user. Therefore, whenever you use an input mask—particularly one that includes literal characters—you should provide a prompt indicating the acceptable format.

The emptyok Attribute

In WML 1.1 and 1.2, the emptyok attribute indicates whether an empty string is a valid value for the input field, even when the format attribute specifies a mask that would require input. By default, its value is false, indicating that an empty string is not acceptable.

The meaning of emptyok when it is used with a format mask that allows empty input (that is, a mask that begins with an asterisk) is not defined. This construction should be avoided.

The WML 1.2 standard is somewhat vague as to the exact meanings of the various formatting characters. The consensus is that a "character" ("M" or "m") refers to any Unicode character, including, on devices that allow it, pictographic characters. Alphabetic characters are those used in words, and numeric characters are digits (0 through 9).

There are some exceptions, however. For "N", some browsers also accept nondigit characters that are associated with numbers, such as plus and minus signs, commas, decimals, exponential indicators, and so on. For "A" and "a", some browsers can handle variations in what are considered punctuation characters. WML 1.3 is expected to clarify the codes to match the classifications shown in Table 7-7. Note that the mask character "n" has been added in WML 1.3 to allow numeric characters plus punctuation.

At present, your best bet is to exercise excessive caution with formatting characters. If you expect the user to enter punctuation, use the "M" codes instead of "A". Similarly, use "M" instead of "N" when formatted numbers are expected. On the server end, do not assume that the input codes have limited the user's input; instead, perform full input validation as if no format code had been specified.

Note also that some languages do not have a concept of uppercase and lowercase. Browsers supporting non-case-sensitive languages should ignore the case of format codes, treating "a" as "A", "x" as "X", and so forth.

Because WML 1.1 and 1.2 were vague regarding the interaction between the emptyok and format attributes, you should expect to encounter differences in browser behavior. In WML 1.3, if emptyok is explicitly specified, it can override the format mask as described above. When emptyok is not explicitly specified, the format attribute completely defines the input requirement. That is, the implied value of emptyok is "true" when the format mask allows empty input and "false" when the mask requires input.

The size Attribute

The size attribute indicates the desired display width, in characters, that the input field should occupy on the screen. The browser can ignore this attribute. If it respects the size attribute and the field contains more characters than can be displayed in the specified width, the browser will have

> If the `format` string is not open-ended (for example, `format="MMMM"`), then the browser *should* ignore `maxlength` because it cannot accept any input that does not match the format string. On the other hand, if your `format` string is open-ended, `maxlength` *should* be respected if it specifies a length that exceeds the fixed size of the format string. For example, the combination of `format="*M"` and `maxlength="10"` should work as planned. However, in the combination `format="MM*M"` and `maxlength="1"`, the length should be ignored; otherwise, the constraints of the `format` string cannot be met.
>
> We emphasize the use of the word "should" here, because some browsers may not see it that way. To ensure maximum compatibility, do not specify a `maxlength` value that is less than or equal to the fixed portion of your `format` mask.

to provide some mechanism (such as scrolling) to give the user access to all of the content.

The `maxlength` Attribute

You can restrict a field to a maximum number of characters using the `maxlength` attribute. By default, the field can accommodate an unlimited number of characters—subject to memory and device constraints, of course.

The `type` Attribute

Most of your input controls will be "text" fields (the default), which allow normal echoing of the characters as the user enters them. If you instead define the `type` to be "password," the browser will obscure the characters as they are entered—for example, by substituting an asterisk. The obscuring affects only the display of the characters as the user enters them, but does not otherwise alter the normal workings of the input control. For example, if the `format` mask contains literal characters, the literal characters will not be obscured. Note that this feature merely guards against someone accidentally observing the characters as they are entered; it does not indicate that the data, once entered, is handled any more securely than other types of fields.

Before using a "password" control in your application, consider that data entry is already difficult on most small devices, particularly those lacking a full keyboard. Obscuring the characters during entry only increases this problem and usually provides few benefits—it is very easy for a user to shield password entry from observers simply by holding the screen appropriately.

The *tabindex* Attribute

Tab support is another optional feature that the browser author may choose to support if it makes sense given the browser's user interface. Essentially, it allows the use of a *tab* control to move the focus from one control to the next, in sequence, much as you can use the Tab key on a desktop PC. Each control element (at present, only input and select) is assigned a position in the tab order. As the user activates the tab mechanism, controls are activated in successive order. The user can interact with the active control or switch to another control if desired.

A browser is not required to support tabbing. If it does, you can control the tab order (at least for input and select elements) with the tabindex attribute. This attribute takes a positive integer value, and the browser initially gives the focus to the element with the lowest index. Each activation of the tab control moves the focus to higher-numbered elements. The browser chooses how to handle multiple elements with the same index.

The browser also chooses whether it will provide default indices for elements where you did not specify one. Likewise, it has the option of assigning tab stops to other types of elements. Such automatic assignments, if any, must come later in the sequence than any that you specify.

The *title* Attribute

The title attribute specifies a title for the input field. The browser may choose to display the title in some fashion or ignore it.

The *accesskey* Attribute

The accesskey attribute functions exactly as it does for the anchor element (see the earlier "The accesskey Attribute" section in "The anchor Element").

Use of *input* Elements

The input element is simply a mechanism for obtaining a value from the user. However, the interplay between the various attributes can be quite complicated, particularly in those areas where the specification is vague or ambiguous.

Input Field Initialization When the browser encounters a card containing one or more input or select elements, it must initialize them in the order in which they appear in the card. After the card is loaded, a change to a variable via one `input` or `select` element will not affect the initial value of any other such elements in the same card.

> Prior to WML 1.3, the order of `input` initialization within a card was not clearly specified. Within a single card, it is therefore risky to use input fields whose control variables are linked in any way.

For each `input` element, the browser first examines the value of the control variable specified by the `name` attribute. If its current value does not conform to the mask specified by the `format` attribute, the browser sets the variable to the empty string.

If the variable is now empty, either because it had no initial value or because the value was unacceptable, the browser looks at the `value` attribute. If its value conforms to the mask, it is assigned to the control variable. If neither the initial value of the variable nor the value of the `value` attribute matches the format mask, the control variable remains set to the empty string. The initial value of the `input` field is the value of the control variable.

Rendering and Operation of Input Fields   The manner in which input fields are displayed and operated is left to the browser's discretion, and you will find a good deal of variety in the implementations. In theory, you should be able to disregard presentation issues and trust the browser to do the right thing. In practice, unfortunately, this is not the case.

One particular area of concern is the interaction between the `title` attribute and the text surrounding the input fields. You might recall—in the context of the card element's `ordered` attribute (see "The `ordered` Attribute" section earlier in this chapter)—that text surrounding the `input` element might be treated as a "field prompt." Basically, the standard gives the browser the option of inserting "screen flips" when a card contains multiple fields. In essence, your single card becomes a number of "virtual cards," in theory making better use of the limited screen real estate. When it takes this approach, the browser is strongly encouraged to treat the text that immediately precedes the field as a "field prompt" and display it with the field (even though the input field has a perfectly good title attribute that could be used for this purpose). The result is that what should be simple is not.

For purposes of illustration, consider the deck in Listing 7-25, which uses input elements to create a small form. We have used a double colon in the `title` attribute text so that you can distinguish it from the static text in the card. As Figure 7-17 shows, different browsers treat this simple form quite differently. (We want to stress that none of these interpretations is wrong, given the latitude granted by the WML specification.)

Listing 7-25 Naive use of the `input` element.

```
<wml>
   <card ordered="false">
      <p>
      Name:
      <input name="Name" title="Name::"/>
      Birthday:
      <input name="BDay" title="Birthday::"/>
      <br/>
      <a href="#c2">Next</a>
      </p>
   </card>

   <card id="c2">
      <p>
      Name: $(Name)
      <br/>
      Birthdate: $(BDay)
      <br/>
      <anchor>Back<prev/></anchor>
      </p>
   </card>
</wml>
```

The first two browsers (Ericsson and Nokia) treat the form in similar fashion. Both display the card text in the form and the `title` label when an input field is activated; Ericsson's browser also displays the label along with the card text. Both display the current value of the field automatically; Nokia's browser displays the empty brackets even when the field has no value. The third browser, from Phone.com, displays only the `title` label. The text has vanished from the card but appears as a prompt when the input field is edited. (The numbers on the left side are access keys, automatically assigned by the browser. The third field, labeled "<no title>," actually hides the anchor.)

Figure 7-17   Various implementations of input fields (Ericsson, Nokia)

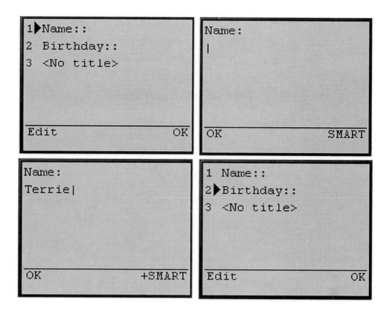

Figure 7-17 *continued*   Various implementations of input fields (Phone.com, IBM Wapsody)

The form is usable in all cases, if not necessarily aesthetically pleasing. You could therefore put it in your application as is. More consistent behavior across all devices could be achieved, however, at the expense of more work. Listing 7-26 shows an alternative approach using a generic data-entry card, "get," to do the work. This deck manages to work in a similar fashion on all browsers but is twice as large and requires the user to press a few more keys.

Listing 7-26   Alternative use of the `input` element.

```wml
<wml>
  <card>
    <p>
    <anchor>Name:<go href="#get">
       <setvar name="Label" value="Name"/>
       <setvar name="OutVar" value="Name"/>
       <setvar name="Default" value="$(Name)"/>
       </go>
    </anchor>
    $(Name)
    <br/>
    <anchor>Birthday:<go href="#get">
       <setvar name="Label" value="Birthday"/>
       <setvar name="OutVar" value="BDay"/>
       <setvar name="Default" value="$(BDay)"/>
       </go>
    </anchor>
    $(BDay)
    <br/>
    <a href="#c2">Next</a>
    </p>
  </card>

  <card id="c2">
    <p>
    Name: $(Name)
    <br/>
    Birthdate: $(BDay)
    <br/>
    <anchor>Back<prev/></anchor>
    </p>
  </card>

  <card id="get">
    <onevent type="onenterforward">
       <refresh>
          <setvar name="Temp" value="$(Default)"/>
       </refresh>
    </onevent>

    <p>
    $(Label):
    <input title="$(Label):" name="Temp"/>
    </p>
    <p>
    -&gt; $(Temp)
```

```
        <br/>
        <anchor>Return<prev>
           <setvar name="$(OutVar)" value="$(Temp)"/>
           </prev>
        </anchor>
        <br/>
        <anchor>Cancel<prev/>
        </anchor>
        </p>
        <do type="accept">
           <prev>
              <setvar name="$(OutVar)" value="$(Temp)"/>
           </prev>
        </do>
        <do type="prev">
           <prev/>
        </do>
     </card>
</wml>
```

Use of Format Codes

Browsers have some freedom in how input is collected. Some will use the format mask "actively," forbidding the entry of characters that do not match; others will not check the mask until input is complete. Whatever the method used, the browser can never allow invalid input to be committed to the variable. Any leading or trailing whitespace characters entered by the user are significant and cannot be stripped by the browser.

You should avoid using format codes when they are not appropriate. Two "obvious" places to use format codes are when collecting phone numbers or dates, but you need to exercise caution. The format of phone numbers, for example, differs widely around the world, and such numbers are usually best handled with a mask of "N*N" (or, if you want to allow phone numbers that include punctuation, "M*M"). Acceptable formats for dates differ by country and individual preference. (Does 03/07 indicate March 7 or July 3? Is the appropriate separator a slash, hyphen, or period?)

Selection Lists—The select Element

The select element allows you to define a selection list—that is, a menu of choices from which the user can pick. WML supports both single-select and multiple-select lists. Individual entries in the list are defined by option elements, and lists may have a hierarchy, defined by optgroup elements.

<select>

Purpose: Defines a list of items from which the user can choose.

Attributes:

multiple	"false" | "true" (novar)
name	(novar)
value	*initialvalue*
iname	(novar)
ivalue	*initialindex*
tabindex	*number* (novar)
title	*titletext*
id	(novar)
class	(novar)
xml:lang	(novar)

Can contain: <option>, <optgroup>

Valid in: <p>, <fieldset>

The multiple Attribute

By default, selection lists are single-select; choosing one option automatically deselects any previously selected option. You can use the multiple attribute to specify that the list should allow multiple selections.

The name Attribute

As with the input element, the name attribute with the select element identifies the WML variable that will receive the list of selected items. For single-select lists, the variable is assigned the string specified by the value attribute of the selected option. For multiple-select lists, the values of the selected choices are concatenated into a semicolon-separated list. If all of the selected options have an empty value, the named variable is set to an empty string. The value of the named variable also determines the initial state of the list.

The value, iname, and ivalue Attributes

The value, iname, and ivalue attributes, together with the name attribute, determine which options are selected when the list is initially displayed to the user. The details are discussed later in the section "Default Value Determination."

In addition, the variable named by the `iname` attribute receives the one-based index of the selected option. For multiple-select lists, it receives a semicolon-separated list of indices.

The tabindex Attribute

The `tabindex` attribute works in the same fashion as it does for the `input` element (see "The `tabindex` Attribute" within the "Entry Fields—The `input` Element" section).

The title Attribute

The `title` attribute specifies additional descriptive text for the `select` control, which the browser may choose to display in some fashion or ignore.

The option Element

You use the `option` element to identify each item that is to be included in a `select` list.

<option>

Purpose: Specifies one option in a selection list.

Attributes:

value	*optionvalue*
onpick	URL
title	*titletext*
id	(novar)
class	(novar)
xml:lang	(novar)

Can contain: Text, <onevent>

Valid in: <select>, <optgroup>

The value Attribute   The `value` attribute specifies a string that is associated with the option. When the user selects an option, its value (that is, the value of the option's `value` attribute) is assigned to the variable specified by the `select` element's `name` attribute.

As semicolons have special significance in index sequences (see "Default Value Determination"), you should usually avoid them within option values.

The onpick Attribute   In our discussion of intrinsic events ("Trapping Intrinsic Events—The onevent Element"), we mentioned that an onpick event is generated when a user selects items from a selection list. You can use an onevent element to associate a task to be executed upon the selection of a particular option; the onpick attribute is a short form that you can use when the task is a simple go with no variable assignments. Thus, the option element

```
<option>
   <onevent type="onpick">
      <go href="someplace"/>
   </onevent>
   Pick me!
</option>
```

can be more succinctly expressed as follows:

```
<option onpick="someplace">Pick me!</option>
```

For the sake of efficiency, when the deck is transmitted over the air, you should use the onpick attribute instead of a go element whenever possible.

In multiple-select lists, an onpick event is also generated when an option is unselected. Note that WML does not provide a simple way to tell whether the event was due to the selection or deselection of an item or which particular item was involved in the action. If this information is important, you will need to keep track of the previous selection state and compare it to the current state.

The title Attribute   The title attribute specifies additional descriptive text for the option, which the browser may choose to display in some fashion or ignore.

The optgroup Element

You can use the optgroup element to place options into a hierarchy, which the browser may then use to compress the selection list or otherwise alter its presentation. Possible presentations include group boxes, cascading menus, collapsed sections, and notebook tabs. A browser can legally ignore optgroup elements, but it must still process any child elements; the effect would be the same as if you had specified all options at the same level. Option groups can be nested, and they can contain a mixture of options and option groups. An empty optgroup element is an error.

As a rule, you should keep your selection lists short, so organizing them into a hierarchy is usually unimportant. If you do use optgroup elements, remember that their presentation may vary widely by browser and that they are often ignored.

<optgroup>

Purpose: Marks a group of related options in a selection list.

Attributes:

title	*titletext*
id	(novar)
class	(novar)
xml:lang	(novar)

Can contain: <option>, <optgroup>

Valid in: <select>, <optgroup>

The `title` Attribute   The `title` attribute specifies additional descriptive text for the group, which the browser may choose to display in some fashion or ignore. Given the intended use of `optgroup`, and given that the title is the only descriptive attribute that browsers possess, browsers that choose to support `optgroup` will likely rely on `title`. Therefore, you should specify a `title` for every `optgroup` you use, and you should try to keep it to one or two short words.

Use of `select` Elements

Selection lists provide the user with a bounded set of choices. Listing 7-27 shows a simple single-selection list, which can be rendered as shown in Figure 7-18. Listing 7-28 and Figure 7-19 illustrate a multiple-select list.

Listing 7-27   A single-choice selection list.

```wml
<wml>
    <card>
        <p>
        Gender:
        <select name="Sex">
            <option value="-">Unspecified</option>
            <option value="F">Female</option>
            <option value="M">Male</option>
            <option value="?">Other</option>
```

Figure 7-18   Sample rendering of a single-choice select (Ericsson SDK)

Figure 7-19   Sample rendering of a multiple-choice select (IBM Wapsody)

```
      </select>
      <br/>
      <a href="#c2">Next</a>
      </p>
   </card>

   <card id="c2">
      <p>
      Selected value: $(Sex)
      <br/>
      <anchor>Back<prev/></anchor>
      </p>
   </card>
</wml>
```

Listing 7-28   A multiple-choice selection list.

```
<wml>
   <card>
      <p>
      Place order:
      <select multiple="true" name="Meal">
         <option value="burger">Krusty Burger</option>
         <option value="fries">Fries</option>
         <option value="cola">Jolt cola</option>
         <option value="snack">Scooby Snack</option>
      </select>
      <br/>
      <a href="#c2">Next</a>
      </p>
   </card>
```

```
<card id="c2">
  <p>
  You ordered: $(Meal)
  <br/>
  Please proceed to window number 2.
  <br/>
  <anchor>Back<prev/></anchor>
  </p>
</card>
</wml>
```

Default Value Determination   The determination of the default values for a `select` element is probably the most complicated area of the WML specification, not only because of the convoluted logic involved, but also because of the terminology used by the standard. Before attempting an explanation, we will define several new terms.

The *default option(s)* are those options, if any, that are initially selected when the list is first presented to the user.

An *option value* is the current value of the option's `value` attribute. Because the `value` attribute can contain variable references, each option's value can change.

An *option value sequence* is a list of one or more option values, separated by semicolons (for example, "xyzzy" or "foo;bar"). Trailing semicolons may or may not be seen as an error; empty entries ("foo;;bar") are illegal in some cases. You should avoid both.

An *option index* is the ordinal position of the <option> element in the selection list, starting from one. Option indices are not affected by the presence of `optgroup` elements; each `option` within one `select` element is assigned a unique index that is independent of any hierarchy.

An *index sequence* is a list of one or more option indices, separated by semicolons (for example, "7" or "1;3"). The standard is not clear on whether trailing semicolons ("1;3;") or null entries ("1;;3") should be allowed, so avoid them.

The *default option index* (DOI) of a list specifies the index or indices of the default options. For a single-choice list, the DOI is a single, non-negative integer equal to the option index of the default option; a DOI of zero indicates no default selection. For multiple-choice lists, the DOI is a semicolon-separated index sequence; as in single-choice lists, zero indicates no initial selection. A zero should not appear in a list containing any other values.

Validating a potential default option index involves removing references to nonexistent elements. The validation process may result in an empty string. Specifically, the process entails the following steps:

1. All non-integer indices are removed from the sequence. For example, "1;apple;-3;1;2" becomes "1;-3;1;2".

2. All out-of-range indices are removed from the sequence, including those with a value of less than one and those with a value greater than the number of options in the list. For example, "1;-3;1;2" becomes "1;1;2".

3. All duplicate indices are removed. For example, "1;1;2" becomes "1;2".

To determine the DOI, the browser looks at the iname attribute first, then ivalue, then name, and finally value. The iname attribute is expected to name a WML variable. If iname has been specified, its value is a valid variable name, and the named variable has been assigned a value, then the DOI is the *validated* value of the variable. (Recall that validation may result in an empty string.) If the DOI is not empty, the process ends.

If the DOI is empty after the check of iname, the browser turns to the ivalue attribute. If it has been specified, then the DOI is the *validated* value of the ivalue attribute. If the DOI is not empty, the process ends.

If the DOI is empty after the check of ivalue, the browser looks to the name attribute. If it has been specified, its value is a valid variable name, and the named variable is assigned a value, then the value is taken to be an option value sequence. The DOI is constructed by taking each entry from this sequence in turn and searching the selection list for the first option whose current value attribute matches that entry. If a match is found, the index of this option is added to the DOI if it is not already present.

Finally, if the DOI is still empty after the check of name, the browser examines the value attribute. If present, it is taken to be an option value sequence, which is evaluated in the same manner as was the variable referenced by the name attribute.

As a last resort, if the DOI is still empty after the check of value, the browser will use a default of "1" (the first option element) for a single-choice list or "0" (no initial selection) for a multiple-choice list.

It is not possible to indicate "no initial selection" for a single-choice list, as the validation process will throw away any zero values you try to set via iname or ivalue. For a multiple-choice select, however, you can rely on the DOI processing to default to "0" if you ensure that any variables referenced by the name or iname attributes do not contain values.

As you can see, initialization of a selection list can be quite complicated. It is likely that some browsers will not behave exactly as described here.

Select List Values During Processing   Once the default option index has been determined, the variables referenced by the name and iname attributes, if any, are updated. If name has been specified, the variable it references is set to the value associated with each option referenced by the DOI. The result will be one value for a single-choice list or an option value sequence for a multiple-choice list. If iname has been specified, the variable it references is assigned the default option index or indices.

The selection list is finally shown to the user, with the option(s) indicated by the DOI selected as defaults. As the user selects or deselects options from the list, the browser continually updates the variables pointed to by name and iname. Note that the displayed card will not reflect any side effects of such changes until an explicit refresh task is executed.

The browser must update the variables referenced by name and iname before executing any new task. For example, if an option element has an associated onpick event handler, the variables must be updated before the handler is called. Thus you can write your handler knowing that the variable state always reflects the user's most recent selection.

For multiple-choice lists, the option value sequence and index sequence will not be ordered in any particular fashion, but you can be assured that they will not contain null ("foo;;bar") entries. The index sequence assigned to the iname variable will never contain duplicate entries; however, the option value sequence assigned to the name variable may contain duplicate values if the list includes multiple options that use the same value.

onpick Handlers   You can use an onpick event handler to manage tasks related to the selection list, such as validating the user's input, updating state variables, or refreshing the current card. Most of the time, you will use a WMLScript program for such activities; sometimes, however, you can accomplish your goals using just WML. Listing 7-29 shows a modified version of our earlier multiple-select list, with an onpick event handler written in WML.

Listing 7-29   Example of an onpick handler.

```
<wml>
   <card>
      <p>
      Place order:
      <select multiple="true" name="Meal">
         <option onpick="#fries" value="burger">Krusty
Burger</option>
         <option value="fries">Fries</option>
         <option value="cola">Jolt cola</option>
         <option value="snack">Scooby Snack</option>
      </select>
      <br/>
      <a href="#c2">Next</a>
      </p>
   </card>

   <card id="c2">
      <p>
      You ordered: $(Meal)
      <br/>
      Please proceed to window number 2.
      <br/>
      <anchor>Back<prev/></anchor>
      </p>
   </card>

   <card id="fries">
      <p>
      Would you like fries with that?
      <anchor>Yes<prev>
         <setvar name="Meal" value="$(Meal);fries"/>
         </prev>
      </anchor>
      <anchor>No<prev/></anchor>
      </p>
   </card>
</wml>
```

You may be tempted to use onpick events to implement an activity menu, but you should resist this urge. Although selection lists and menus are superficially similar, the semantics associated with a menu are not the same as those associated with a selection list. A menu is a construct for launching new tasks, whereas a selection list is a constrained input element within the current task. When you want a menu, you should use a list of anchors, not a selection list. Attempting to use a selection list as a menu works very badly in some browsers.

Miscellaneous Markup

The `timer` element lets you trigger an event after a certain amount of time has elapsed. The `fieldset` element lets you group fields into logical collections.

The Clock Is Ticking—The `timer` Element

The timer lets you trigger events after a certain period of time has passed, allowing actions to take place without the intervention of the user. A timer's life is inextricably linked to the card in which it is defined: it starts to run when the card is loaded, counts down as long as the card is active, and stops when the card is exited. Should the timer reach zero before the card is exited, the action associated with the `ontimer` event is executed. The execution of any task is considered a card exit. No card can contain more than one timer.

The resolution of the timer is specified in tenths of a second, though the actual resolution will depend on the hardware and browser in use. You should not expect the accuracy of a Swiss watch. If the initial value of the timer is not a positive integer, it is disabled, and the `ontimer` event is never triggered.

The interaction of the timer with the device user interface and other device functions is also implementation-dependent. A timer may or may not be able to wrest control away from the user if he or she is actively doing something.

Intrinsic event handlers take precedence over timers. If a card has an active `onenterforward` or `onenterbackward` event binding that is triggered as the result of card navigation, any timer on the card will not be started.

The interaction between timers and WMLScript functions is not well established in the current WML standard. It seems that invoking a script should be considered a card exit, stopping the timer. If the script ends without queuing up any navigation requests, the card containing the timer will still be active; this event should probably be considered a card entry and the timer should restart. However, because this relationship is not well specified, you may encounter differences in behavior.

`<timer>`

Purpose: Specifies an activity to occur after a certain amount of idle time.

Attributes:

name	*varname* (novar)
value	*defaultvalue*
id	(novar)
class	(novar)
xml:lang	(novar)

Can contain: Nothing

Valid in: `<card>`

The name Attribute

The timer optionally can be tied to a WML variable, which is specified with the name attribute. If you specify such a control variable and it has an integer value, its value is used to initialize the timer. In addition, when the timer stops for any reason, its final value is assigned to the variable. If the timer expires, triggering the ontimer event, the value will be zero.

The value Attribute

The value attribute specifies the initial value of the timer, in tenths of a second, to be used when the name attribute is not specified or when the referenced variable does not have a value.

> If the variable given in the name attribute has a nonempty value, the value attribute is always ignored, even if the variable's value is an invalid timer value.

When Is an Exit Not an Exit?—Timers and Refresh

The interaction between a timer and the refresh task is somewhat odd. The execution of a refresh task is considered an exit from the card, so it stops the timer. The value of the timer's control variable, if any, is updated, and the refresh task executes. The completion of the refresh task, however, is considered a card entry, potentially allowing the timer to restart.

In the simplest case, when the timer has no associated control variable, the timer will always be reset to the value specified by the value attribute.

When a control variable has been specified with the name attribute, things become more interesting. If the user initiated the refresh task before the timer expired (by interacting with some other element on the card) and the timer has a control variable specified by the name attribute, the timer will restart. The current, nonzero value of the timer will be saved to the variable before the refresh task executes, and the timer will resume its activity from that value when the refresh task completes.

On the other hand, if the refresh task is triggered when (or after) the timer expires, the value "0" will be stored in the control variable. When the refresh task is complete, the zero value disables the timer. (Of course, this statement assumes that the refresh task does not have an associated setvar element that resets the control variable. Resetting this variable would restart the timer from its new value.)

Timer Demonstration
Listing 7-30 demonstrates basic timer use. The timer in the first card is used to display a "splash screen," a fairly innocuous use. The timer in the second card demonstrates why you should take care when using timers in conjunction with fields. On many browsers, the timer will steal control away from you even when you are interacting with the card.

Listing 7-30   Simple timer demonstration.

```
<wml>
   <template>
      <do type="accept"><noop/></do>
      <do type="prev"><noop/></do>
   </template>

   <card ontimer="#c2">
      <timer value="20"/>

      <p align="center">
      <big>Who wants<br/>to be a<br/>Millionaire?</big>
      </p>
   </card>

   <card id="c2" ontimer="#c3">
      <timer value="150"/>
      <p>
      Brussels sprouts are a type of ...
```

```
    <select name="Answer">
        <option value="no">No idea!</option>
        <option value="no">Animal</option>
        <option value="yes">Vegetable</option>
        <option value="no">Mineral</option>
        <option value="no">Hideous torture</option>
    </select>

    <a href="#c-$(Answer)">Final Answer!</a>
    </p>
</card>

<card id="c-yes">
    <p>
    You just won ONE MILLION DOLLARS!
    <br/>
    <small>(Yeah, right.)</small>
    </p>
</card>

<card id="c-no">
    <p>
    Ooo, sorry.  Should have used a lifeline!
    </p>
</card>

<card id="c3">
    <p>
    Sorry, time's up.  Faster fingers next time!
    </p>
</card>
</wml>
```

Grouping Related Fields—The `fieldset` Element

The `fieldset` element lets you group related fields and text, so that the browser can—possibly—make more intelligent decisions about layout and navigation. You can nest `fieldset` elements, if you think that strategy makes sense, but you cannot have a completely empty `fieldset`. As you might expect, browsers may choose to ignore `fieldset` elements entirely (and, in fact, most do). Any elements contained in a `fieldset` must still be processed.

`<fieldset>`

Purpose: Groups related fields and text.

Attributes:

`title`	*`titletext`*
`id`	`(novar)`
`class`	`(novar)`
`xml:lang`	`(novar)`

Can contain: Text, `<fieldset>`, `<input>`, `<select>`, `<br>`, `<img>`, `<anchor>`, `<a>`, `<table>`, `<do>`

Valid in: `<p>`, `<fieldset>`

The *title* Attribute

The `title` attribute specifies additional descriptive text for the set, which the browser may choose to display in some fashion or ignore. As with `optgroup`, browsers that support `fieldset` elements will likely rely on the `title`, so you should always give each `fieldset` a brief title.

Sending Information

You cannot write very interesting applications without some means of sending the user's input to your application server. WAP supports the two standard methods for transferring data: "get" and "post."

Get versus Post

The "get" and "post" methods differ in the number of connections that they make to the server and in the amount of data that can be transferred. With "get," the browser sends the data as part of the document request by appending the data to the URL that it sends to the server. The data, called a *query string*, is separated from the URL by a question mark as in the following example:

`http://www.whizbang.com/cgi-bin/foo?x=42&y=baz%3f+faz`

Here the query string is the sequence "x=42&y=baz%3f+faz". With a few exceptions, anything other than ASCII letters or numbers in the data must be escape encoded—that is, the character to be encoded is replaced by a percent sign followed by the character's hexadecimal code. Space characters (0x20) can also be encoded as a single plus sign. The query string that is shown in the preceding example, therefore, translates to "x=42&y=baz? faz" (note the space after the question mark).

When "post" is used, the client makes a separate connection to the server to transmit the data. The data does not form part of the URL. Instead, it may be passed in URL escape notation or as a multipart message entity (RFC 2388), which you control with the go element's enctype attribute.

Which method you choose will depend on several factors. If someone else wrote the program on the server, obviously you need to use the method expected by the program. If you control both ends of the process, you should consider the amount of data to be transferred. The "get" method passes the data as part of the URL, and whereas theoretically no limits are placed on the length of a URL, some network components cannot handle more than 255 characters. In contrast, "post" allows you to pass virtually unlimited amounts of data. On the server side, accessing data is equally easy with "get" and "post," although we will not go into the details here. Keep in mind that data passed via "get" is more readily "visible," as it is part of the URL.

Another important consideration is that the "get" method affects caching. As the query string is part of the URL, responses associated with different query strings will be cached separately. Responses to "post" requests cannot be cached, as described in RFC 2616, unless accompanied by either a Cache-Control or Expires response header. In that case, they are cached according to the URL only. (We are oversimplifying greatly here, as the arcane mysteries of HTTP caching are beyond the scope of this book. Refer to the RFC and the WAP Caching Model specification for more information.)

With either method, you are free to format the transferred data as best suits your needs. (Data passed via "get" must be encoded, but the actual data can be in any format.) A common convention is to pass a series of "named arguments"—that is, key/value pairs consisting of an argument key or identifier, an equals sign, and an argument value (for example, "FirstName=Terrie"). This is the mechanism supported by the WML postfield element.

Passing Data—The postfield Element

The postfield element lets you specify one data field to be passed to the server. Its name is misleading, as you can use it with both "post" and "get." The method used is controlled by the method attribute of the go element that contains the postfield; see "The method Attribute" section for more details.

If the go element refers to a card within the same deck, all postfield elements associated with the request are ignored. Because postfield data is intended for use by a server, WML does not provide a way to reference it.

`<postfield>`

Purpose: Specifies data to be passed to the application server.

Attributes:

name	*dataname*
value	*datavalue*
id	(novar)
class	(novar)
xml:lang	(novar)

Can contain: Nothing

Valid in: `<go>`

The name and value Attributes

You use the name and value attributes to specify the key and value to be passed to the server. The browser handles escaping of any special characters in the values as necessary. In addition, it converts the key name and value to an appropriate character set, if required. Acceptable character sets can be explicitly defined by the accept-charset parameter; if more than one is specified, the browser chooses which one to use. If you do not explicitly define acceptable character sets, the browser will use the character set with which the current deck was sent. To code the "get" request in the previous example, you would use two postfield elements:

```
<go href="http://www.whizbang.com/cgi-bin/foo">
   <postfield name="x" value="42"/>
   <postfield name="y" value="baz? faz"/>
</go>
```

Note that when you send data using the "get" method, the browser may not rearrange the postfield elements when it builds the URL.

Application Security

Data security is as critical in the wireless world as it is on the World Wide Web. For true security, WAP defines the WTLS protocol (see Chapter 6) to provide encrypted, authenticated communications. WML and WMLScript provide "application-level" security, allowing you to prevent unauthorized decks from linking to yours. WAP browsers also support the standard Basic Authentication mechanism used on the Web today.

The access Element

The access element allows you to control which other decks can link to your deck. In essence, it makes your deck private. Deck access control is enforced when the browser navigates to a card in a different deck than the current one. In this situation, the browser checks the permissions specified by the new deck to see whether it permits access from the original deck.

The WML specification does not address what should happen when you try to load a deck by some means other than a link, such as from a bookmarks list or by direct entry of the URL. To be safe, your "entry" deck should not specify an access element, thereby ensuring that your application can be reached from all browsers.

What is being secured here is access to the application—not the data contained within the application. Because the access control information is embedded in the content, the browser must be able to read the deck to enforce the access security. Someone could easily write a browser that ignores access information, so you should not rely on the access control information to secure your data.

Legitimate browser manufacturers, of course, will write their browsers to respect the access element. Access control then provides a method to ensure that other content providers do not link into your decks and essentially "steal" your service.

\<access\>

Purpose: Controls access to the deck.

Attributes:

domain	(novar)
path	(novar)
id	(novar)
class	(novar)
xml:lang	(novar)

Can contain: Nothing

Valid in: \<head\>

The *domain* Attribute

The domain attribute lets you limit access to your deck to URLs from a particular domain. The domain specified is "suffix-matched" against the domain of the referring URL. For example, if your deck contains the element

```
<access domain="marx.wapforum.org"/>
```

then access would be permitted from both **groucho.marx.wapforum.org** and **marx.wapforum.org** but not from **harpo.wapforum.org** or from **wapforum.org**. Partial matches of subdomains are not allowed, so access would not be permitted from **rx.wapforum.org**.

If you do not specify a domain, the default is the domain of your deck. That is, only decks from the same domain can access yours.

The *path* Attribute

The path attribute allows you to restrict access to decks residing in a certain path on the application server. The path specified is "prefix-matched" against the path of the referring deck: each element of the specified path must exactly match the corresponding complete element of the referrer for access to be allowed.

Imagine that a document at **http://wapforum.org/abc/example.wml**, for example, contains the following element:

```
<access path="/abc"/>
```

Then the documents at the following URLs would be able to access the deck:

```
http://wapforum.org/abc/d1.wml
http://wapforum.org/abc/
http://www.wapforum.org/abc/d2.wml
http://www.wapforum.org/abc/def/d3.wml
```

The following documents would not be permitted access to the deck:

```
http://wapforum.org/ghi/d4.wml"
http://wapforum.org/ab"
http://scammer.com/abc/d1.wml"
```

For convenience, you can specify the value of the path attribute as a relative URL and the browser will resolve the value using the location of your deck. In the preceding example, the relative path "/abc" was resolved to the absolute URL "http://wapforum.org/abc". If you do not specify a value for path, the default is the root directory ("/"); that is, access is allowed from all decks on the specified domain.

Note that an empty access element is not the same as an omitted access element. A deck that does not contain an access element is public and can be linked from any other deck. A deck containing an empty access element is only accessible to decks residing in the same domain.

Basic HTTP Security

WML browsers must support the HTTP Basic Authentication mechanism (RFC 2617), which allows you to protect a URL with a password. When the user navigates to a protected deck, the server will return an "access denied" status code, and the browser will prompt for a user name and password. The browser then requests the deck again, this time including the user's credentials with the request. If the server accepts the user name and password combination, access is granted and the deck is returned. The browser can cache the user name and password for reuse in the same session; otherwise, the user would be prompted for a password on every access—a very inconvenient approach. If access was not granted, the server will return the same status code and the browser will display a message for the user.

When used over a secure HTTP (HTTPS) connection, the Basic Authentication scheme provides reasonable security, but it offers only rudimentary protection over an unsecured connection. In the latter case, it can prevent casual snooping but should not be relied on as protection against malicious hacking.

Depending on your needs, you can effect Basic Authentication through your Web server or in your application code. Using the Web server makes sense when you want to restrict resource access to a particular group of users. For example, your company may let any salesperson access the order status database. The program that queries the database could be placed in its own directory, which is protected using Basic Authentication at the Web server. The server-side program can then assume that the user has already been authorized by the Web server; if the user's credentials had failed, the program would not have been executed at all.

If a single program needs to grant multiple levels of access to different users, you can implement Basic Authentication from within the server program itself. Essentially, your application code is responsible for checking the user credentials presented by the browser, using whatever means makes sense for your application.

Other Mechanisms

Some browsers may provide additional features relevant for security control. For example, Phone.com's browser sends a unique subscriber identifier with every HTTP request. This ID is tied to the user's particular device (such as a cellular phone) and never changes; it can be preserved if the user upgrades to a new device. Your application could use the subscriber identifier along with basic HTTP security as another check that the user is who he or she claims to be. Note, however, that the use of such nonstandard mechanisms restricts your users to a particular browser, which may not be desirable.

Some browsers support HTTP cookies (RFC 2109), which you might use to enhance your authentication mechanism. Again, you must bear in mind that not all devices or WAP gateways support this feature. You can design your applications to use additional capabilities if they are present, but you should not rely on them unless you are willing to restrict your users to one particular browser.

> A future WAP release should include a state management specification, which will mandate minimum cookie requirements for future browsers.

Securing Variables

The introduction of variables in WML raises security issues that do not exist in other markup languages such as HTML. When you store information that the user would consider sensitive or private, you should take steps to protect this data. In particular, you should ensure that any such data does not remain in variables when the user switches to another application.

Some basic precautions should always be observed. For instance, your application should use a secure connection when it involves sensitive data. The most common mechanism for secure connectivity is the Secure Sockets Layer (SSL), which is signaled when you access a URL whose protocol is "HTTPS." (Over the wireless link, HTTPS requests should be transmitted via the WTLS protocol; however, note that WTLS support is optional, so some browsers may use an insecure connection.) In addition, you should not maintain any sensitive data in variables for longer than necessary; if possible, transmit the information to the server and maintain it there. Once they are no longer required, you should clear the variables used. Simply abiding by these rules will go a long way toward preventing your application from being compromised. Even these steps may not be enough, however.

For purposes of illustration, assume that your application requires the user to enter a credit card number. If a user accessed your program while in a taxi and, on arriving at his destination, left his phone behind with your application active, would the data be safe? Assume that the user put down the phone immediately after entering the card number but before pressing the enter key to signal that he was done.

Your first reaction might be that you could do nothing in that scenario. In reality, you might elect to use the timer element. Normally, having a timer steal focus away from the user would be considered unfriendly. In this case, however, you might decide that giving the user five minutes to enter the number was sufficient. If the user lost the phone, that approach would leave only a five-minute window for someone to find it and copy down the number—a fairly small opportunity.

The deck in Listing 7-31 demonstrates this technique. The process of entering the credit card and completing the order is relatively painless. However, if you stop interacting with the application for a short while, the input card times out and erases the screen. (For purposes of illustration, we have opted here for a timeout of 30 seconds; in practice, you would allow a longer period.) The deck returned by the server, once the transaction is complete, would clear the variables as shown in Listing 7-32. Technically, the variables could be cleared when they are sent to the server, but if a transmission problem occurs, the user will be forced to restart the process from the beginning.

Listing 7-31   Variable security techniques (part 1).

```wml
<wml>
  <template>
    <do type="accept"><noop/></do>
    <do type="prev"><noop/></do>
  </template>

  <card>
    <!-- For purposes of demo, assume we've already
         collected other required information.  -->
    <onevent type="onenterforward">
      <go href="#cc">
        <setvar name="Type" value="VISA"/>
        <setvar name="Name"
          value="Phineas T. Blowfish"/>
        <setvar name="Expires" value="12/2001"/>
      </go>
    </onevent>
    <onevent type="onenterbackward">
      <prev/>
    </onevent>
  </card>

  <card id="cc">
    <onevent type="ontimer">
      <go href="#cctimeout">
        <setvar name="Card" value=""/>
      </go>
    </onevent>
    <timer value="300"/>

    <p>
    Enter your $(Type) number:
    </p>

    <p>
    <input name="Card" title="$(Type) number:"
      format="NNNNNNNNNNNNNNNNN"/>
    </p>

    <p>
    <a href="#cc2">Next</a>

    <do type="accept" label="Next">
      <go href="#cc2"/>
    </do>
    <do type="prev" label="Back">
      <prev>
        <setvar name="Name" value=""/>
        <setvar name="Card" value=""/>
      </prev>
    </do>
    </p>
  </card>
```

```
<card id="cc2">
   <onevent type="ontimer">
      <go href="#cctimeout">
         <setvar name="Card" value=""/>
      </go>
   </onevent>
   <timer value="300"/>

   <p>
   <b>Verify Card</b>
   <br/>
   $(Name)
   <br/>
   $(Card)
   <br/>
   $(Type) $(Expires)
   <br/>
   <a href="#cc3">OK</a>
   <anchor><prev/>Change</anchor>

   <do type="accept" label="OK">
      <go href="#cc3"/>
   </do>
   <do type="prev" label="Change">
      <prev/>
   </do>

   </p>
</card>

<card id="cc3">
   <onevent type="ontimer">
      <go href="https://xxx.com/cgi-bin/transact"
         method="post">
         <postfield name="n" value="$(Name)"/>
         <postfield name="c" value="$(Card)"/>
         <postfield name="t" value="$(Type)"/>
         <postfield name="e" value="$(Expires)"/>
      </go>
   </onevent>
   <timer value="10"/>

   <p>
   Authorizing...
   <br/>
   Please wait.
   </p>

</card>
<card id="cctimeout">
   <p>
   Session timed out.
   <br/>
   <a href="#cc">Restart</a>
```

```
        <do type="accept" label="Restart">
           <go href="#cc"/>
        </do>
        </p>
     </card>
</wml>
```

Listing 7-32   Variable security techniques (part 2).

```
<wml>
   <template>
      <do type="accept"><noop/></do>
      <do type="prev"><noop/></do>
   </template>

   <card>
      <onevent type="onenterforward">
         <go href="#success">
            <setvar name="Card" value=""/>
            <setvar name="Name" value=""/>
            <setvar name="Expires" value="12/2001"/>
         </go>
      </onevent>
      <onevent type="onenterbackward">
         <prev/>
      </onevent>
   </card>

   <card id="success">
      <p>
      Your credit card has been charged.
      </p>
   </card>
</wml>
```

You also need to ensure that sensitive information is not available from within another application. A user can switch from your application to another application in at least four ways:

- Your application can include a link to another application.
- The user can "back out" of your application and resume the previous application.
- The user can use a browser mechanism, such as a bookmark, to jump to a new URL from within your application (not all browsers support such a mechanism).
- On browsers that support a context stack (not a standard requirement), the user can terminate the context in which your application is running and resume the previous context.

Of these possible scenarios, you need worry about only the first two cases, ensuring that variables are cleared at any point where the user can exit your application. In the third case, a browser that supports such a mechanism must start a new context, erasing your variables. The WML standard does not address the final case (and there is little you can do about it, either).

Other Data: The `meta` Element

The `meta` element allows you to specify "meta-data"—data about the deck that is contained within, but is not strictly part of, the content. One common use is to access browser-specific features, such as controlling whether a particular deck can be bookmarked. Refer to the individual browser documentation for details on which special `meta` tags are recognized and how they are used.

`<meta>`

Purpose: Defines meta-information.

Attributes:

name | http-equiv	(novar)
forua	"false" | "true"
content	(novar)
scheme	(novar)
id	(novar)
class	(novar)

Can contain: Nothing

Valid in: `<head>`

The `name` and `http-equiv` Attributes

Each `meta` element must define either the `name` attribute or the `http-equiv` attribute, both of which serve to name the meta-data and specify its purpose. Data named with an `http-equiv` attribute is interpreted as being an HTTP header (RFC 2068). If the content is tokenized before it arrives at the browser, the meta-data should be converted to a WSP or HTTP response header.

On the other hand, the browser will ignore data named with a `name` attribute. In fact, any gateway that processes the deck while it is en route to the user's device should strip such meta-data out of the deck.

You might be tempted to use `http-equiv` meta-data as a mechanism for generating HTTP response headers—for example, when you need to use headers to control browser caching. However, while such data is guaranteed to be delivered to the browser (provided the `forua` attribute is set to "true"), it is not guaranteed to arrive as a response header. Unless the content has been tokenized along the way, it might arrive in the deck in the form of a `meta` element, or it could even be delivered in some other unspecified manner. WML does not require the browser to look for response data anywhere other than in the HTTP (WSP) response headers. Thus, if you want to ensure that the browser sees the response header, you must generate it yourself.

Data specified with the `name` attribute is even odder. The browser must ignore this meta-data, even if it is specified with `forua` being "true." One conceivable use for this feature would be to specify control data for gateways and proxies. Being named with `name` ensures that the browser will ignore the meta-data, but `forua="true"` ensures that it will not be removed from the deck along the way.

The forua Attribute

The `forua` attribute states whether the data is intended for the browser (<u>U</u>ser <u>A</u>gent). If it is set to "true," the data must be delivered to the browser in some format, although the particular format is not defined in the WML specification. If the `forua` attribute is set to "false," any intermediate server between the application server and browser is obligated to remove it.

The content and scheme Attributes

The `content` attribute specifies the value of the meta-data. The `scheme` attribute specifies additional information about how the data should be interpreted; appropriate values would depend on the particular meta-data in use.

Document Type Declarations

When we looked at a skeleton of a WML document (see "A WML Skeleton" earlier in this chapter), we touched briefly on the Document Type

Definition. The DTD describes the basic syntax of an XML-compliant markup language. To be valid, every WML deck must contain a Document Type Declaration that references a WML DTD. Remember the difference between a declaration and a definition—and that the abbreviation "DTD" only applies to the definition.)

Note that we said "a" WML DTD. Our examples have included references to a copy of the DTD that exists on the **www.wapforum.org** Web site, which is certainly valid. However, to process the deck, the WAP gateway may need to retrieve the referenced DTD. If **www.wapforum.org** cannot be reached or the DTD file there is missing, the gateway may not be able to process your deck. The safest action, therefore, is to put a copy of the DTD file on your content server and reference it instead.

Nothing obligates the browser or gateway to look at the DTD. In fact, it may look only at the DTD identifier to verify that the document is a WML deck and then rely on internal knowledge of what constitutes valid WML.

Some browsers may support nonstandard extensions to WML in the form of additional elements or attributes. To use such extensions, you must specify the DTD identifier associated with the extensions and reference a DTD describing them.

Ideally, a browser or gateway encountering a deck with "foreign" markup would just ignore what it did not recognize and process the rest. In practice, this does not happen. An unrecognized document type or markup element is seen as an error regardless of what the DTD may say. Consequently, you would do best to avoid the lure of extensions for now—or at least unless you are tailoring content based on browser type. (As WAP technology matures, interoperability should improve.)

Errors and Browser Limitations

Because WML devices tend to have limited resources, users are much more likely to encounter restrictions imposed by device limitations than they are with a conventional browser. Whenever an error occurs, either due to limitations like those described in this section or when invalid content is found, the browser must report the problem. It cannot attempt to hide errors by guessing the author's intent.

History Stack

If the history stack grows to the point where space becomes exhausted, the browser will drop the oldest entries. Consequently, you should not design your application to rely on deep levels of nesting. Browsers are encouraged to reserve enough memory for at least ten history entries.

Variables and Browser Context

Similarly, the browser will have only a finite amount of space for variable storage, and excessive variable use can consume all available memory. When the browser runs out of memory for variables, it will first attempt to reclaim memory from the cache and the history stack. If sufficient memory is still not available, the browser should notify the user of the error and reset itself to some well-known state.

To help avoid such problems, you should clear variables when they are no longer needed and use short variable names. Besides consuming extra storage, long variable names also take more time to transmit to the device.

Task Failure

If a navigation task cannot be completed, either because the requested deck named by a URL cannot be loaded or because access control restrictions prohibit it, the browser must notify the user of the problem. The browser's current card is left unchanged, any pending variable assignments are not committed, `newcontext` processing is canceled, and no intrinsic event bindings are executed.

Content Generation

When the browser requests some WML content, the deck that arrives may be *static* (that is, a file that resides in the server's file system) or *dynamic* (that is, generated in response to the particular request). Dynamic content also includes content generated from templates, where a basic deck resides in the file system and has areas to be "filled in" in response to a particular request.

A content author creates static pages either directly, with help from a WML authoring tool, or through a program that converts some other data format into WML. Dynamic pages are generated on the fly by a program running on the Web server. Although the choice between static and dynamic pages depends on many factors, it most often reflects the permanency of the underlying data. For example, a company's annual report would probably be stored in static pages, as it changes relatively infrequently. In contrast, a page showing the company's stock price would probably be generated dynamically. A page showing the stock's daily closing price might be a static page that an automated program updates each day.

The examples in this chapter have shown static content, with the goal of demonstrating how WML documents work. As discussed in Chapter 3, such static pages are not particularly useful to mobile users who expect up-to-date, location-based information. The majority of wireless applications, then, will consist of dynamically generated content. The server-side programming needed to create such content is beyond the scope of this book, but many other references exist to guide you in writing CGI scripts, servlets, or other dynamic content generation techniques. Most of techniques they describe for HTML can also be applied to creating WML.

One factor that differentiates WML content development from traditional HTML development is the need to recognize and account for differences among the various devices, browsers, and networks that may receive WML content. Ideally, WML would be a completely generic language, and you could write your WML applications completely independently from concerns regarding which browsers your customers might use to access your content. Unfortunately, that scenario is not yet reality—and it may never be practical, if you want to deliver the best possible experience to each user. Different approaches to this problem are discussed in Chapter 11.

By itself, the WML language is generally insufficient for producing a complete wireless application. Although it has facilities for presenting information and reacting to user input, it does not have the capabilities to produce an entire workable program. Even when coupled with WMLScript (covered in Chapter 9), a complete WML application will usually require additional work on the server end, just as is true for Internet Web applications. A complete WML application, therefore, really encompasses the entire package as seen by the user: WML decks, generated either statically or dynamically; server-side processes such as servlets or CGI programs; WMLScript and image content, and application data residing at the server or downloaded to the client as WBXML.

WML Version Negotiation

The fact that there are numerous versions of the WML standard is not a big issue as this book is published (in the fall of 2000), but it may well become one in the very near future. WML 1.0 was completely replaced by version 1.1, and no WML 1.0 browsers ever shipped. Version 1.2 added one or two new features to the language, but this release was concerned mostly with providing clarifications. As it was not part of a WAP "conformance release," a set of the standards suite backed by certification tests, it is unlikely that any WML 1.2 browsers will be released.

As this is written, however, the next major release of the WAP standards (possibly called WAP June 2000) is being prepared, and a new version of WML, version 1.3, will be included. Furthermore, the WAP Forum has committed to updating the suite on a fixed schedule every six months. The world of the content author is about to get a lot more interesting.

Except for WML 1.0, every new release of WML 1.x will be backward compatible with the previous versions. One approach to development, therefore, is to stick with WML 1.1 constructs. Content written to the 1.1 standard should be usable on any 1.x browser. That may not be very attractive, however. Some useful features have been added in versions 1.2 and 1.3. While it would be nice (especially for the manufacturers) if all users immediately traded in their old WML 1.1 devices as soon as 1.3 versions hit the market, it is virtually a certainty that a mix of browsers will populate the real world. How can you cope with this situation?

A browser is expected to reveal the content types it can handle in the accept headers which it sends along with each request. A WML 1.1 browser is thus likely to send:

```
Accept: text/vnd.wap.wml
```

A WML 1.3 browser, however, needs to indicate that you can send it WML 1.3. It does so using the "level" parameter:

```
Accept: text/vnd.wap.wml;level="1.3"
```

The absence of a level parameter is interpreted as a request for WML 1.1. Thus, if you want to make use of WML 1.3 features, you will need to check the HTTP Accept header to ensure the browser can handle the content. More grisly detail on the use of the HTTP Accept header can be found in RFC 2616.

Conclusion

In this chapter, we explored the construction of applications with the Wireless Markup Language (WML), an XML-based language intended for use on devices having limited processor capability, limited screen size, and limited input capabilities. WML seeks to be a "universal" language, capable of being rendered on a variety of disparate devices. As we saw in this chapter, the wide range of browser implementations complicates content authoring. There is no substitute for testing across as many browsers as possible!

Although WML contains many features, such as timers and variables, that can facilitate the delivery of dynamic, interactive content to the client, WML alone does not provide all of the features required to build complex wireless applications. In Chapter 9, we turn our attention to scripting using WMLScript. The combination of WML and WMLScript transforms the WAP device into a sophisticated, extensible programming platform.

As we have seen, WML is one form of XML. Because of its textual format, the content written with WML is verbose and consumes considerable network bandwidth and computational resources. WAP defines a generic binary encoding format, WBXML, for representing any XML document (including WML). This binary encoding, which we discuss in Chapter 8, accelerates downloads, reduces memory consumption on the client device, and improves the speed of document parsing.

Chapter 8
Wireless Binary Extensible Markup Language

This chapter introduces WAP Binary XML, a compact, binary representation of the eXtensible Markup Language (XML). The chapter also covers the binary encoding defined by the WAP Forum for WML documents. Typically, the WAP gateway automatically transforms WML to WBXML when needed, so as an application developer, you do not need to worry about the encoding of your documents. However, knowledge of the standard may be important when you need to deliver non-WML content to the client or when you want to use WBXML for your own applications.

Overview

The WAP Forum has defined a compact form of XML, called *WAP Binary XML* (WBXML), that can be used to succinctly represent a document written in any XML-compliant markup language. Intended for use in wireless environments, WBXML promotes efficient processing of XML documents by wireless devices. In this case, "efficiency" is measured not only by the time required to transmit the document, but also by the effort required to process it. Because WBXML replaces textual tags with byte codes, it can be easily parsed by a lightweight CPU like those found in today's smaller portable devices. The generic applicability of WBXML's capabilities has prompted broader interest in a binary XML format within the Internet community, and WBXML has been submitted to the World Wide Web Consortium (W3C) for consideration.

The WML standard defines a WBXML encoding for WML, known as "binary WML." Although you can generate such binary-encoded WML documents directly, you will rarely need to do so. Instead, when the binary form is needed, the encoding will be performed automatically by the WAP gateway that sits between the wireless device and your content server. You will, however, need to be concerned with the size of your document once encoded. Although the WML standard imposes no maximum, some networks and gateways will not transmit content that exceeds a certain size. Some client devices may also have a limit on the size of a deck they can process. In general, you will want to keep the encoded size of your content to less than one kilobyte. This size may seem impossibly tiny, but you will find both that it is quite feasible to write applications in such small chunks and that the resulting programs actually perform better on a wireless network than larger counterparts.

WBXML is not intended to be a compression mechanism, however. Although a WBXML document is often smaller than its textual counterparts, it will not be as small as a compressed version of the document. Instead, WBXML was designed to be easily parsed by low-end processors, such as might be found in today's wireless devices. Moreover, the WBXML encoding preserves the parent–child element structure of XML documents, so that (when the content type allows) a client can skip unknown elements or attributes while still processing any child elements.

WBXML encodes parsed "physical" XML documents: the document structure and content. Meta-information, including the Document Type Definition (DTD) and any conditional sections, is removed when the document is converted to WBXML.

Content Structure

An XML document is composed of a sequence of elements, each of which may have zero or more attributes and may contain embedded content. WBXML respects this structure. The following data types are used in the specification: an 8-bit data *byte*, an 8-bit unsigned integer (*u_int8*), and an unsigned 32-bit "multibyte integer" (*mb_u_int32*). The multibyte integer consists of a series of as many as five bytes, with the most significant bit of each byte holding a *continuation flag*. The last byte of the value has a continuation flag of "0," and the remaining bytes have a flag of "1." The other seven bits of each byte—that is, the bits that do not contain continuation flags—hold the data. For example, the integer value 96 (0x60), would be encoded as the one-byte sequence 0x60, while the value 160 (0xA0), would be encoded as the two-byte sequence 0x8120.

Network byte order is "big-endian": The most significant byte precedes the less significant bytes. Bit fields are also big-endian, in that the highest numbered bit is the most significant bit of the byte.

Document Structure

A WBXML document has the format shown in Figure 8-1. Square brackets ("[" and "]") enclose optional elements, a vertical bar ("|") indicates alternatives, parentheses ("(" and ")") group elements, and a bracketed ellipsis ("[...]") indicates that the preceding entity can be repeated.

The WBXML Header

Each WBXML document begins with a header, consisting of a WBXML version number, a document public identifier, a character set identifier, and a string table.

Version Number

The first byte of a document specifies the WBXML version number, with the upper four bits indicating the major version minus one and the lower four bits identifying the minor version. Documents encoded as specified in version 1.1 of the standard will thus begin with the byte 0x01; 0x02 indicates WBXML 1.2; and so on. As the encoded format may change, WBXML decoders need to verify that the document conforms to a known version of the standard.

Public Identifier

Most XML documents are written to conform to a particular DTD, which will be stated in the document type declaration of the XML header. You should remember, for example, that WML documents are required to declare themselves as WML documents and should reference a WML DTD as well.

```
document        :=      header body

header          :=      version publicid charset stringtable
stringtable     :=      length [termstr [...]]
body            :=      [pi [...]] element [pi [...]]
element         :=      [switchpage] stag [attrib [...] END]
                        [content[...] END]

content         :=      element | string | extension | entity | pi |opaque

stag            :=      TAG† | (littag index)
littag          :=      LITERAL | LITERAL_A | LITERAL_C | LITERAL_AC
attribute       :=      attrstart [attrvalue [...]]

attrstart       :=      ( [switchpage] ATTRSTART† ) | ( LITERAL index )
attrvalue       :=      ( [switchpage] ATTRVALUE† ) |
                        string | extension | entity | opaque
extension       :=      [switchpage] (EXT_I termstr) | (EXT_T index) | EXT

string          :=      inline | tableref
switchpage      :=      SWITCH_PAGE pageindex
inline          :=      STR_I termstr
tableref        :=      STR_T index

entity          :=      ENTITY mb_u_int32    // UCS-4 character code

pi              :=      PI attrstart [attrvalue [...]] END
opaque          :=      OPAQUE length [byte [...]]

version         :=      u_int8    // WBXML version number
publicid        :=      mb_u_int32 | ( 0 index )    // public identifier
charset         :=      mb_u_int32
index           :=      mb_u_int32    // integer index into string table
length          :=      mb_u_int32    // integer length
pageindex       :=      u_int8

termstr         :=      // charset-dependent terminated string
```

†The identifiers TAG, ATTRSTART, and ATTRVALUE refer to one token of the specified type from the document-type-specific sets. For example, in WML, TAG refers to a token from Table 8-5, ATTRSTART to one from Table 8-6, and ATTRVALUE to one from Table 8-7.

Figure 8-1   WBXML 1.2 document structure

A WBXML document can encode the DTD in a number of ways. The preferred method is to use the "well-known" identifier (a mb_u_int32 value assigned to the document type), as shown in Table 8-1. When no identifier has been assigned, the document can include the declaration as a literal string (for example, "-//WAPFORUM/DTD WML 1.1//EN") in the string

Table 8-1   WBXML 1.3 Well-Known Public Identifiers

Identifier	Description
0x00	Public identifier is encoded as a literal in the string table (string table index follows)
0x01	Unknown or missing public identifier
0x02	"-//WAPFORUM//DTD WML 1.0//EN" (WML 1.0)
0x03	"-//WAPFORUM//DTD WTA 1.0//EN" (WTA event 1.0, deprecated)
0x04	"-//WAPFORUM//DTD WML 1.1//EN" (WML 1.1)
0x05	"-//WAPFORUM//DTD SI 1.0//EN" (Service Indication 1.0)
0x06	"-//WAPFORUM//DTD SL 1.0//EN" (Service Loading 1.0)
0x07	"-//WAPFORUM//DTD CO 1.0//EN" (Cache Operation 1.0)
0x08	"-//WAPFORUM//DTD CHANNEL 1.1//EN" (Channel 1.1)
0x09	"-//WAPFORUM//DTD WML 1.2//EN" (WML 1.2)
0x0A	"-//WAPFORUM//DTD WML 1.3//EN" (WML 1.3)
0x0B–0x7F	Reserved

table, which we will discuss shortly. Alternatively, you can assign a code of your own; identifiers of 0x80 and higher are available for public use. You probably will not want to rely on an identifier for documents that will be shared outside of a known group, as you cannot guarantee that your choice of identifier will not collide with someone else's number assignment.

If the DTD is embedded in the document, or when no DTD is specified, you will need to use the identifier 0x01, indicating that the document type is unknown. For documents stored in this fashion to be usable, all tags and attributes must be stored as literals; otherwise, there would be no way to decode the file.

Charset
The final piece of information that a reader requires to decode a WBXML file unambiguously is the character set encoding. The encoding is specified using the corresponding IANA "MIBenum" value. The WBXML standard allows a charset value of 0x00 to indicate an unknown character encoding. However, this provision is of little practical use: With an unknown encoding, there is no real way to know which characters are actually contained in the file. Fortunately, most character encodings are registered with IANA and have an assigned value. XML documents that lack an explicit character encoding declaration have a default encoding of either UTF-8 or UTF-16, and the WBXML charset value should be set accordingly.

Note: As mentioned in Chapter 7, UTF-16 does not yet have an assigned MIBenum value and thus cannot be reliably used in WBXML documents as yet.

WBXML can support any string encoding, provided that a specific termination character is used to mark the end of strings unambiguously. When the character encoding specifies a NULL character, that character must be used as the string terminator. For example, the US-ASCII encoding specifies a NULL character of 0x0.

A WBXML document may be accompanied by additional external information that identifies the character encoding, such as WSP, HTTP, or MIME headers. In such a case, the higher-level protocol should specify the priority of the various headers. In most cases, however, the encoding carried in the WBXML file will be authoritative, and any external specification will be redundant. If a source document contains tag or attribute names that cannot be represented in the target character set, then the document cannot be encoded, and the encoder must therefore report an error.

String Table

Following the header, the next entity in the WBXML file is the *string table*, which is simply a concatenated list of each string used in the file (followed by its termination character). Strings will be referenced by a zero-based index, so you generally do not need to worry about the order in which strings are inserted into the table. The only reason why you might care about the string order is related to the fact that the string index is a multibyte value. If the string table contains more than 127 entries, it may be desirable to order the strings by the frequency with which they are used. An index of 127 or less is represented in one byte, whereas an index exceeding 127 will take two bytes (or, if the string table is extremely large, three or four bytes). In practice, this consideration is rarely significant.

All WBXML documents must have a string table, even if it is empty. The string table consists of the length of the table, in multibyte format, immediately followed by the table entries. The length field is not considered part of the table and is not included in the length.

Content

The content and structure of a WBXML document are stored as binary codes (*tokens*) and literal strings. Commonly used strings can be stored in the table and referenced via a pointer, eliminating the need to encode some redundant information.

Tokens

The meaning of WBXML tokens depends on the context in which they appear. Several different types exist. *Global tokens* (Table 8-2), for instance, have the same unambiguous meaning across all document types, regardless of where they appear in the file. They are used to identify in-line data and various control functions. Tokens come in two flavors: Those in the generic set have the same meaning across all types of documents, whereas those in the extension set (with names that are prefixed with "EXT_") are defined according to the particular type of document being encoded.

Besides global tokens, a WBXML document consists of *tag tokens* and *attribute tokens*. Collectively, these are referred to as *application tokens*, and their meaning is defined by the type of document being encoded. Because the values in the tag and attribute sets can overlap, the meaning of a particular application token depends on its context. Tag tokens are single-byte codes representing a specific tag (element) name. Attribute tokens represent attribute prefixes and values.

Because the meaning assigned to tag and attribute tokens is document-type-specific, they can only be used when the type of a binary document can be identified unambiguously. This would be the case when the DTD is well known or when a MIME media type is present (as would be the case when the document is transported by WSP, HTTP, or SMTP). Otherwise, tags and attributes should be represented as string literals, because application tokens would be ambiguous.

Tokens must be defined independently of the version of the DTD being used. That is, the tokens for a given document type must be sufficient to encode any version of the document, and they cannot be reordered.

Code Pages

The tag and attribute code spaces support 256 different *code pages*, which will allow for future expansion of the well-known codes. The global token SWITCH_PAGE is used to switch code pages. The code page for attributes is

Table 8-2   WBXML 1.2 and 1.3 Global Tokens

Token Name	Value	Description
SWITCH_PAGE	0x00	Change the code page for the current state (attributes or tags). Followed by the new code page number (u_int8).
END	0x01	End of current attribute list or end of element.
ENTITY	0x02	A character reference. Followed by the character code (mb_u_int32).
STR_I	0x03	In-line terminated sting.
LITERAL	0x04	An unknown tag or attribute name, possessing no attributes or content. Followed by a zero-based index into the string table (mb_u_int32).
EXT_I_0	0x40	Document-type-specific extension token, as an in-line terminated string.
EXT_I_1	0x41	Document-type-specific extension token, as an in-line terminated string.
EXT_I_2	0x42	Document-type-specific extension token, as an in-line terminated string.
PI	0x43	Processing instruction.
LITERAL_C	0x44	An unknown tag name, possessing content but no attributes.
EXT_T_0	0x80	Document-type-specific extension token, as a mb_u_int32.
EXT_T_1	0x81	Document-type-specific extension token, as a mb_u_int32.
EXT_T_2	0x82	Document-type-specific extension token, as a mb_u_int32.
STR_T	0x83	String table reference. Followed by a zero-based index into the string table (mb_u_int32).
LITERAL_A	0x84	An unknown tag name, possessing attributes but no content.
EXT_0	0xC0	Document-type-specific extension token, as a single byte.
EXT_1	0xC1	Document-type-specific extension token, as a single byte.
EXT_2	0xC2	Document-type-specific extension token, as a single byte.
OPAQUE	0xC3	Document-type-specific opaque data.
LITERAL_AC	0xC4	An unknown tag name, possessing both attributes and content.

distinct from that for tags, and the two pages can be switched independently. The initial page for both spaces is "0." Global tokens have the same meaning across all code pages.

Tag Codes

A tag code is a single unsigned 8-bit byte (u_int8), structured as shown in Table 8-3. Document types with well-known public identifiers will have tag codes assigned. For unknown elements in a document of a well-known

Table 8-3 Tag Code Structure

Bit	Meaning
7	Attribute flag. If 0, the element possesses no attributes. If 1, the tag is followed by a list of one or more attributes, terminated with an END token.
6	Content flag. If 0, the element contains no content. If 1, the tag and attribute list (if any) is followed by a list representing the content, terminated with an END token.
5-0	Tag identifier.

type or for all elements in documents of unknown type, the global literal tokens must be used. The four types are known as LITERAL, LITERAL_A, LITERAL_C, and LITERAL_AC. The last three are equivalent to the LITERAL token with the proper combinations of control bits 6 and 7 set. The literal tokens should not be used when a token encoding exists.

Attribute Codes

An attribute token is also encoded as a single u_int8 value. Values less than 128 represent an attribute name; such codes can optionally specify all or part of the associated attribute value, so a single attribute may have two or more associated attribute codes. For example, the WBXML encoding for WML specifies two distinct encodings for the newcontext attribute, each of which specifies the attribute and complete value:

```
0x22    newcontext="false"
0x23    newcontext="true"
```

The WML src attribute, on the other hand, has three encodings. Two of these encodings specify partial values for the attribute, and the other specifies the attribute alone:

```
0x32    src
0x58    src="http:
0x59    src="https:
```

Unknown attributes must be encoded using LITERAL, and the values of literal attributes must always be encoded separately. That is, the string table entry for a literal attribute cannot contain all or part of the value.

Values of 128 and higher represent well-known strings forming all or part of attribute values. Unknown attribute values are encoded with string, entity, or extension codes. (You can, of course, assign codes to more than 128 attributes or values by using multiple code pages.)

All tokenized attributes begin with either a single attribute start token or LITERAL, followed by zero or more attribute value, string, entity, or extension tokens. Individual attributes are not explicitly terminated; instead, each attribute is ended by the attribute start token (or LITERAL) that begins the next attribute in the list. The final attribute (and thus the entire attribute list) is terminated with an END token.

Depending on the attribute codes assigned, a single attribute might have multiple valid encodings. For example, the WML attribute `src="http://www.wapforum.org/foo"` can be represented in the WML encoding as follows (assuming ASCII encoding for NULL-terminated strings):

```
0x58                             src="http://
0xA1                             www.
0x03                             STR_I (in-line string)
0x7761 7066 6F72 756D 0x00       wapforum\0
0x88                             .org/
0x03                             STR_I (in-line string)
0x666F                           6F00 foo\0 (")
```

Alternatively, it can be represented as follows:

```
0x32                             src (=")
0x8F                             http://www.
0x03                             STR_I
0x7761 7066 6F72 756D 0x00       wapforum\0
0x88                             .org/
0x03                             STR_I
0x666F                           6F00 foo\0 (")
```

In this case, neither method has a size advantage. That may not always be true, however. Although tokenizers are required to use a compact form rather than a literal or string representation when the former is available, they are not required to seek out the most compact form.

Global Tokens

Several tokens always have the same meaning wherever they appear in the document. They include literals, strings and string references, extension tokens, opaque tokens, entity tokens, processing instructions, and control codes.

Literals

We have already discussed literals extensively. When a tag or attribute name has not been assigned a well-known token code, it is represented by the token LITERAL, followed by an index into the string table. To determine whether LITERAL indicates a tag or attribute, you must look at the preceding context.

Strings and String References

Character data can either be represented in-line or be placed in the string table; the succinctness of the approach depends on the length of the string and the frequency with which it appears in the document. In-line string data is represented by the token STR_I, followed by the character data. Remember that strings must be terminated, though the termination character depends on the character set encoding employed and might not be the 0x00 character.

String table references are introduced with the token STR_T, followed by the index into the string table. This zero-based index begins at the start of the table, rather than being a character offset from the start of the document.

Empty strings are usually explicitly encoded as a STR_I token, immediately followed by the string termination character (for example, in ASCII, 0x0300). Well-known attribute codes may include alternative representations.

Character Entities

The character entity token, ENTITY, has the same function as an XML character reference (see Chapter 7) and is used to encode a single character that cannot be represented in the current character encoding. The UCS-4 code for the character (essentially, the Unicode character code left-padded with zeros to become 31 bits) is stored as a multibyte value with any leading zero bits dropped.

For example, the nonbreaking space character (represented in WML as the named character entity) is Unicode character 0x00A0, which cannot be directly represented in a US-ASCII document. Using the ENTITY token, it can be stored as 0x028120, where 0x02 is the ENTITY token and 0x8120 is the mb_u_int32 representation of 0xA0.

All entities appearing in the source XML document must be represented in WBXML as either a string (if the character set can handle it) or an ENTITY.

Extension Tokens

WBXML provides a number of extension tokens for application-specific use. For example, the binary encoding for WML uses extension tokens to encode variable references. Three flavors are available: stand-alone tokens with no associated data, tokens with string data, and tokens with integer data. Three of each kind are available for use.

The stand-alone, or single-byte, tokens (EXT_0, EXT_1, EXT_2) exist on their own. They can be used as flags or switches. For example, you might use them to toggle the meanings of the other extension tokens if you need more such tokens than are available.

The in-line string tokens (EXT_I_0, EXT_I_1, EXT_I_2) are immediately followed by a terminated string; the in-line integer tokens (EXT_T_0, EXT_T_1, EXT_T_2) are followed by an `mb_u_int32` value. The names are somewhat counterintuitive. Although you might expect the EXT_I family to refer to integers and the EXT_T family to refer to terminated strings, in fact their meanings are reversed. The "I" actually stands for "in-line string" and the "T" stands for "table reference" (although any value could follow an EXT_T token).

Extension tokens will have different meanings for different types of documents, but the same meaning will apply to all documents of the same type. For examples of their use, see the WBXML encoding for WML ("Binary WML") later in this chapter.

Processing Instructions

XML processing instructions (PIs) are not part of the document content. Instead, they provide information to applications that process the document. The PIs are bracketed by the sequences <? and ?> and begin with the name of the target for the instruction. (Although the XML declaration might be mistaken for a processing instruction, because both share the same syntax, the XML standard indicates that this declaration is not such a directive. The XML declaration is never encoded in a WBXML document; it is replaced with the WBXML declaration.)

Processing instructions intended for the tokenizer can be removed from the document when it is converted to WBXML (and probably should be removed, unless there is some reason to preserve them), but all other PIs must be preserved. They are encoded much in the same way as attribute lists. That is, the PI target is encoded as the attribute start token, and the PI value or values are encoded as a single attribute value token. Note that well-known codes can be assigned from the attribute token pool to PI targets and values.

Processing instructions are encoded in the same manner as attributes, except that they are introduced with the token PI (`0x43`). Table 8-4 shows

Table 8-4   Examples of Processing Instruction Encoding

0x43	PI
0x04	LITERAL
index	string table index to "foo"
0x01	END
0x43	PI
0x04	LITERAL
index	string table index to "bar"
0x03 STR_I 0x783D 2236 2200	x="6"\0
0x01	END
0x43	PI
0x04	LITERAL
index	string table index to "zed"
0x03	STR_I
0x726F 7461 7465 206C	rotate left 70 pt 8\0
0x6566 7420 3730 2070	
0x7420 3800	
0x01	END

the encoding of the three following hypothetical PIs, in ASCII encoding, with the information being stored as in-line strings:

```
<?foo?>
<?bar x="6"?>
<?zed rotate left 70 pt 8?>
```

As with attributes, the PI identifier cannot appear as an in-line string but must instead either be stored in the string table or be assigned a token from the attribute code space. In addition, the arguments to the PI are always stored as one value, regardless of their format.

Opaque Data

WBXML also allows application-specific data to be embedded in the document; for example, you might define a format that contains embedded images. The exact format and interpretation of the opaque content will depend on the processor, and no explicit provision is made for identifying the data. You will need to define your own scheme, perhaps by using the extension tokens or by defining your own header that precedes the opaque data.

The opaque token is followed by the length of the opaque data (as a multibyte value) and the data itself. The length should not include the OPAQUE token or the length field, and a length of zero is permissible.

Control Codes: End and Switch Page

Finally, a few miscellaneous tokens do not fit into any other category. The END token marks the end of attribute lists and, if they contain content, elements. END is not needed for empty elements, as the lack of content is signaled in the element's start tag.

The SWITCH_PAGE token sets a new code page for the tag or attribute space, depending on which is currently active. It is followed by a single byte identifying the code page to be used. The code page 255 (0xFF) is reserved for implementation-specific or experimental use. You should never use this code page for standard XML documents.

The Encoding Process

A WBXML encoder begins with a text XML document and converts all markup elements (tags, attributes, and so forth) into their corresponding tokenized formats. All comments must be removed, whereas all processing instructions (except those intended for the tokenizer) should be preserved.

All entity and character references must be converted to string form if they can be represented in the target character set; otherwise, they must be encoded using ENTITY tokens. In addition, all XML internal and external parsed entities must be resolved before the document is encoded. Any XML unparsed entities or notations have to be handled on an application-specific basis, perhaps as opaque data.

All element and attribute names must be converted to their corresponding start tokens, if one is available, or to the appropriate LITERAL tokens. Markup—that is, elements and attributes—can never be encoded as a string.

The encoder must handle whitespace characters in the source document as dictated by the type of document. If the encoder does not have knowledge of the DTD and cannot read it at run time, then all whitespace characters must be preserved. Clients therefore cannot assume that encoded documents have been subject to whitespace processing.

The tokenized document must be an accurate representation, structurally and semantically, of the input document. This requirement does not mean that the exact original document can be reconstructed from the encoded version. For example, encoders may omit attributes that match a default value specified by the DTD. Because the encoders may not always be familiar with the latest versions of the token tables, user agents must be capable of handling a mix of tokenized and literal elements, attributes, and values.

An Encoding Example, with No DTD

To demonstrate WBXML encoding, we will use a sample XML document. (This document is intended merely to illustrate the encoding process, not to serve as an example of a well-designed data format.) Listing 8-1 shows our sample file.

Listing 8-1   An XML document to be encoded.

```
<?xml version="1.0" ?>

<!- sample.xml ->
<!DOCTYPE phonelist [
<!ELEMENT phonelist (entry)+ >
<!ELEMENT entry (name, number*, quicklist?) >
<!ELEMENT name (#PCDATA) >
<!ELEMENT number (#PCDATA) >
<!ATTLIST number type (work|home|mobile) #REQUIRED >
<!ELEMENT quicklist EMPTY>
]>

<phonelist>
   <entry>
      <name>Amy Anderson</name>
      <number type="work">212-555-1111</number>
      <number type="home">914-555-2222</number>
      <quicklist/>
   </entry>
   <entry>
      <name>Brian Boitano</name>
      <number type="home">860-555-3333</number>
   </entry>
</phonelist>
```

Because the sample document uses an embedded DTD, all of the attributes and elements must be encoded as strings. In the following section, we will look at the effect of making the DTD external. For this example, we will assume that our document is encoded in US-ASCII (to which the IANA has assigned the MIBenum value of "3." When it is encoded as WBXML, one possible result looks like Figure 8-2. (We have included only attribute values in the string table when they are used more than once, though it would be equally legal for the encoder to include all or none of them in the string table.) You can see that WBXML can be more

Offset	Data	Comment
0x00	0x02	WBXML version=1.2
0x01	0x01	publicid=unknown or missing document identifier
0x02	0x03	charset=US-ASCII
0x03	0x30	length of string table=48 bytes
0x04	0x7068 6F6E 656C 6973 7400 656E 7472 7900 6E61 6D65 006E 756D 6265 7200 7479 7065 0068 6F6D 6500 7175 6963 6B6C 6973 7400	"phonelist" "entry" "name" "number" "type" "home" "quicklist"
0x34	0x44	LITERAL_C (phonelist, with content)
0x35	0x00	index of "phonelist"
0x36	0x44	LITERAL_C (entry, with content)
0x37	0x0A	index of "entry"
0x38	0x44	LITERAL_C (name, with content)
0x39	0x10	index of "name"
0x3A	0x03	in-line string (content)
0x3B	0x416D 7920 416E 6465 7273 6F6E 00	"Amy Anderson"
0x48	0x01	END (of name element)
0x49	0xC4	LITERAL_AC (number, with attributes and content)
0x4A	0x15	index of "number"
0x4B	0x04	LITERAL (type attribute)
0x4C	0x1C	index of "type"

Figure 8-2   A WBXML encoding of the sample document in Listing 8-1

Offset	Data	Comment
0x4D	0x03	in-line string
0x4E	0x776F 726B 00	"work"
0x53	0x01	END (of number attributes)
0x54	0x03	in-line string (content)
0x55	0x3231 322D 3535 352D 3131 3131 00	"212-555-1111"
0x62	0x01	END (of number element)
0x63	0xC4	LITERAL_AC (number, with attributes and content)
0x64	0x15	index of "number"
0x65	0x04	LITERAL (type attribute)
0x66	0x1C	index of "type"
0x67	0x83	string table reference
0x68	0x21	index of "home"
0x69	0x01	END (of number attribute list)
0x6A	0x03	in-line string (content)
0x6B	0x3931 342D 3535 352D 3232 3232 00	"914-555-2222"
0x78	0x01	END (of number element)
0x79	0x04	LITERAL (quicklist, no attributes or content)
0x7A	0x26	index of "quicklist"
0x7B	0x01	END (of entry)
0x7C	0x44	LITERAL_C (entry, with content)

continued

Offset	Data	Comment
0x7D	0x0A	index of "entry"
0x7E	0x44	LITERAL_C (name, with content)
0x7F	0x10	index of "name"
0x80	0x03	in-line string (content)
0x81	0x4272 6961 6E20 426F 6974 616E 6F00	"Brian Boitano"
0x8F	0x01	END (of name element)
0x90	0xC4	LITERAL_AC (number, with attributes and content)
0x91	0x15	index of "number"
0x92	0x04	LITERAL (type attribute)
0x93	0x1C	index of "type"
0x94	0x83	string table reference
0x95	0x21	index of "home"
0x96	0x01	END (of number attribute list)
0x97	0x03	in-line string (content)
0x98	0x3836 302D 3535 352D 3333 3333 00	"860-555-3333"
0xA5	0x01	END (of number element)
0xA6	0x01	END (of entry element)
0xA7	0x01	END (of phonelist element)

Figure 8-2   A WBXML encoding of the sample document in Listing 8-1 (*continued*)

compact than the original; here, the original document's smallest size (with all extraneous whitespace removed) is 243 bytes, whereas the encoded form is 167 bytes.

Using an External DTD

If we make only the DTD external, the encoded version does not change much. The document type identifier is added to the string table, and the public ID byte in the WBXML header changes to `0x00`, followed by the string table index of the document type identifier. If we take the additional step of assigning tokens to the tags, attributes, and values associated with the document type, then the input file can be encoded more succinctly.

> Note that WBXML does not support private (SYSTEM) DTDs: such DTDs have no identifier and are referenced only by their URLs. Because WBXML does not provide a way to encode such URLs, documents using private DTDs must be encoded entirely as literals—the same approach we used in the previous example.

Token Assignment

There are no rules covering the assignment of tokens, other than that the values do not conflict with those assigned to the global tokens. Ideally, any fragment of markup that occurs frequently will have a succinct encoding. For our purposes, we have assigned the tag tokens in the order they appear in the DTD, as shown below:

```
phonelist           0x05
entry               0x06
name                0x07
number              0x08
quicklist           0x09
```

Note that we have started from `0x05` to avoid colliding with any of the global tokens assigned by WBXML. It is also a simple task to assign attribute codes in this case. Because the DTD defines a closed set of possibilities, we need merely assign a token to each one:

```
type="work"         0x05
type="home"         0x06
type="mobile"       0x07
```

Again, our tokens cannot conflict with those in the global space, but they can overlap with the element tokens because the two occupy separate name spaces. With these definitions, the sample document can be encoded as shown in Figure 8-3, requiring 131 bytes.

Offset	Data	Comment
0x00	0x02	WBXML version=1.2
0x01	0x00	publicid=included in string table
0x02	0x00	string table location of public identifier
0x03	0x03	charset=US-ASCII
0x04	0x21	length of string table=33 bytes
0x05	0x2D2F 2F46 6F6F 4261 722F 2F44 5444 2070 686F 6E65 6C69 7374 2031 2E30 2F2F 454E 00	"-//FooBar//DTD phonelist 1.0//EN"
0x26	0x45	phonelist, with content
0x27	0x46	entry, with content
0x28	0x47	name, with content
0x29	0x03	in-line string (content)
0x2A	0x416D 7920 416E 6465 7273 6F6E 00	"Amy Anderson"
0x37	0x01	END (of name element)
0x38	0xC8	number, with attributes and content
0x39	0x05	type="work"
0x3A	0x01	END (of number attribute list)
0x3B	0x03	in-line string (content)
0x3C	0x3231 322D 3535 352D 3131 3131 00	"212-555-1111"

Figure 8-3   The document in Listing 8-1, encoded using a public ID

Offset	Data	Comment
0x49	0x01	END (of number element)
0x4A	0xC8	number, with attributes and content
0x4B	0x06	type="home"
0x4C	0x01	END (of number attribute list)
0x4D	0x03	in-line string (content)
0x4E	0x3931 342D 3535 352D 3232 3232 00	"914-555-2222"
0x5B	0x01	END (of number element)
0x5C	0x09	quicklist, no attributes or content
0x5D	0x01	END (of entry)
0x5E	0x46	entry, with content
0x5F	0x47	name, with content
0x60	0x03	in-line string (content)
0x61	0x4272 6961 6E20 426F 6974 616E 6F00	"Brian Boitano"
0x6F	0x01	END (of name element)
0x70	0xC8	number, with attributes and content
0x71	0x06	type="home"
0x72	0x01	END (of number attribute list)
0x73	0x03	in-line string (content)
0x74	0x3836 302D 3535 352D 3333 3333 00	"860-555-3333"
0x81	0x01	END (of number element)
0x82	0x01	END (of entry element)
0x83	0x01	END (of phonelist element)

Binary WML

The WML specification includes a WBXML encoding for WML documents. The set of element tags and attributes is small enough that multiple code pages are not required. The various sets of tokens are shown in Tables 8-5, 8-6, 8-7, and 8-8.

Table 8-5   Binary WML Tag Tokens

Tag	Token	Tag	Token	Tag	Token
a	0x1C	i	0x2D	refresh	0x36
access	0x23	img	0x2E	select	0x37
anchor	0x22	input	0x2F	setvar	0x3E
b	0x24	meta	0x30	small	0x38
big	0x25	noop	0x31	strong	0x39
br	0x26	onevent	0x33	table	0x1F
card	0x27	optgroup	0x34	td	0x1D
do	0x28	option	0x35	template	0x3B
em	0x29	p	0x20	timer	0x3C
fieldset	0x2A	postfield	0x21	tr	0x1E
go	0x2B	pre	0x1B	u	0x3D
head	0x2C	prev	0x32	wml	0x3F

Table 8-6   Binary WML Attribute Start Tokens

Attribute Name	Value	Token
accept-charset		0x05
accesskey		0x5E
align		0x52
align	bottom	0x06
align	center	0x07
align	left	0x08
align	middle	0x09
align	right	0x0A
align	top	0x0B
alt		0x0C
class		0x54

Attribute Name	Value	Token
columns		0x53
content		0x0D
content	application/vnd.wap.wmlc;charset=	0x5C
domain		0x0F
emptyok	false	0x10
emptyok	true	0x11
enctype		0x5F
enctype	application/x-www-form-encoded	0x60
enctype	multipart/form-data	0x61
format		0x12
forua		0x12
forua	false	0x56
forua	true	0x57
height		0x13
href		0x4A
href	http://	0x4B
href	https://	0x4C
hspace		0x14
http-equiv		0x5A
http-equiv	Content-Type	0x5B
http-equiv	Expires	0x5D
id		0x55
ivalue		0x15
iname		0x15
label		0x18
localsrc		0x19
maxlength		0x1A
method	get	0x1B
method	post	0x1C
mode	nowrap	0x1D
mode	wrap	0x1E
multiple	false	0x1F
multiple	true	0x20
name		0x21
newcontext	false	0x22
newcontext	true	0x23

continued

Table 8-6   Binary WML Attribute Start Tokens *(continued)*

Attribute Name	Value	Token
onenterbackward		0x25
onenterforward		0x26
onpick		0x24
ontimer		0x27
optional	false	0x28
optional	true	0x29
ordered	true	0x33
ordered	false	0x34
path		0x2A
scheme		0x2E
sendreferer	false	0x2F
sendreferer	true	0x30
size		0x31
src		0x32
src	http://	0x58
src	https://	0x59
tabindex		0x35
title		0x36
type		0x37
type	accept	0x38
type	delete	0x39
type	help	0x3A
type	password	0x3B
type	onpick	0x3C
type	onenterbackward	0x3D
type	onenterforward	0x3E
type	ontimer	0x3F
type	options	0x45
type	prev	0x46
type	reset	0x47
type	text	0x48
type	vnd.	0x49
value		0x4D
vspace		0x4E
width		0x4F
xml:lang		0x50
xml:space [1.3]	preserve	0x62
xml:space [1.3]	default	0x63

Table 8-7 Binary WML Attribute Value Tokens

Attribute	Token	Attribute	Token	Attribute	Token
.com/	0x85	http://	0x8E	ontimer	0x98
.edu/	0x86	http://www.	0x8F	options	0x99
.net/	0x87	https://	0x90	password	0x9A
.org/	0x88	https://www.	0x91	reset	0x9B
accept	0x89	middle	0x93	text	0x9D
bottom	0x8A	nowrap	0x94	top	0x9E
clear	0x8B	onenterbackward	0x96	unknown	0x9F
delete	0x8C	onenterforward	0x97	wrap	0xA0
help	0x8D	onpick	0x95	www.	0xA1

Table 8-8 Binary WML Extension Tokens

Name	Token	Description
EXT_I_0	0x40	Escaped variable substitution. The name of the variable follows in-line as a terminated string.
EXT_I_1	0x41	Unescaped variable substitution. The name of the variable follows in-line as a terminated string.
EXT_I_2	0x42	Variable substitution without transformation. The name of the variable follows in-line as a terminated string.
EXT_T_0	0x80	Escaped variable substitution, followed by a reference to the variable name in the string table.
EXT_T_1	0x81	Unescaped variable substitution, followed by a reference to the variable name in the string table.
EXT_T_2	0x82	Variable substitution without transformation, followed by a reference to the variable name in the string table.
EXT_0	0xC0	Reserved.
EXT_1	0xC1	Reserved.
EXT_2	0xC2	Reserved.

The xml:space attribute, introduced in WML 1.2, was not assigned a WBXML token value; however, it applies to only the <pre> element, which has a fixed value of "preserve." Because a WBXML encoder can omit default or implied values, the lack of a token does not prevent the encoding of WML 1.2 documents. The token values listed for xml:space were assigned in WML 1.3.

Binary WML Encoding Example

We will conclude our discussion of WBXML by providing a sample encoding of a WML document. The deck in Listing 8-2 can be encoded as shown in Figure 8-4.

Listing 8-2   A sample WML deck to be encoded.

```
<?xml version="1.0"?>
<!DOCTYPE wml PUBLIC "-//WAPFORUM//DTD WML 1.1//EN"
    "http://localhost/DTD/wml11.dtd">

<wml>
    <card>
        <do type="accept">
            <go href="#c2"/>
        </do>
        <p>
            What's your name?
            <input name="n" format="M*m"/>
        </p>
    </card>

    <card id="c2">
        <p>
            Nice to meet you, $(n).
        </p>
    </card>
</wml>
```

Data	Comment
0x01	WBXML version=1.1
0x04	publicid=WML 1.1
0x04	encoding=ISO-8859-1 (latin1)
0x02	string table length=2
0x6E00	string table: "n"
0x7F	wml, with content
0x67	card, with content

Figure 8-4   Encoding of the WML deck shown in Listing 8-2

Data	Comment
0xE8	do, with attributes and content
0x38	type="accept"
0x01	END of do attributes
0xAB	go, with attributes
0x4A	href= 0x03 in-line string
0x2363 3200	"#c2"
0x01	END of go element
0x01	END of do element
0x60	p, with contents
0x03	in-line string
0x2057 6861 7427 7320 796F 2075 7220 6E61 6D65 3F20 00	" What's your name? "
0xAF	input, with attributes
0x21	name=
0x83	string table reference
0x00	index of "n"
0x12	format=
0x03	in-line string
0x4D2A 6D00	"M*m"
0x01	END of input
0x01	END of p
0x01	END of card

continued

Data	Comment
0xE7	card, with attributes and content
0x55	id=
0x03	in-line string
0x6332 00	"c2"
0x01	END of card attribute list
0x60	p, with content
0x03	in-line string
0x204E 6963 6520 746F 206D 6565 7420 796F 752C 2000	" Nice to meet you, "
0x82	EXT_T_2, variable substitution, no transformation, name in string table
0x00	index of "n"
0x03	in-line string
0x2E20 00	". "
0x01	END of p
0x01	END of card
0x01	END of wml

Figure 8-4   Encoding of the WML deck shown in Listing 8-2 *(continued)*

Conclusion

WBXML is a compact XML encoding, suitable for use in a wireless environment. As XML becomes more widely used, WBXML is expected to evolve into a more capable generic content mechanism.

Chapter 9

Enhanced WML: WMLScript and WTAI

This chapter introduces several areas that allow you to do more with Wireless Markup Language (WML):

- WMLScript, a procedural programming language used to extend the versatility of WML
- The WAP Telephony Application Interface (WTAI), a standard mechanism by which WML decks running on a telephone-based device can access telephone features
- The WMLScript Crypto library, an optional WMLScript library providing cryptographic functions to WAP clients

On the companion Web site you will find a completely self-contained WML and WMLScript application, called Code Breaker, that illustrates the use of these languages in much more detail than is possible in the simple examples in this chapter. See the file **readme.txt** in the **CB** directory for more information.

WMLScript Overview

WMLScript is a lightweight programming language intended to complement WML.[1] Syntactically, this procedural language resembles C. It is inspired by ECMAScript, which you may know as JavaScript 1.1. It differs significantly in some ways from ECMAScript, however, because of the need to support devices with limited capabilities.

WMLScript augments WML by providing additional capabilities that would otherwise be difficult or impossible to achieve with WML alone, and it can sometimes make your application appear more responsive. For example, you can use WMLScript to perform input validation checks on the client side before passing the data to the server. If the user makes a simple mistake in entering data, your WMLScript program can catch the error immediately, without the delay associated with sending the data over the air to the server and waiting for a response. (Prudent developers, of course, will do validation checks at the server as well.)

There is no such thing as a free lunch, of course—loading the WML deck plus the WMLScript function over the network will obviously take longer than loading just the WML deck. However, unlike ECMAScript or JavaScript, WMLScript has a compact, binary format designed for wireless use, so its overhead can be relatively small. Also, browsers can cache WMLScript programs just as they do WML decks, so a script you use frequently need not be loaded over the network every time.

A Simple Example

The WMLScript program in Listing 9-1 is a very simple validation routine that checks whether a given date is in the proper form. The WML deck in Listing 9-2 shows how the script might be used; it calls the script to check a date that has been entered by the user. (Extending the program to handle the correct number of days per month, leap years, and the user's preferred date format is left as an exercise for the reader.)

---

[1]This chapter is an introduction to the WMLScript language, not an introduction to programming. Experience with a procedural programming language such as C, C++, or Java will be helpful.

Listing 9-1   A simple validation routine in WMLScript.

```
/*
 * simple date checking example
 */
extern function CheckDate(TestDate, Sep,
        Continue) {
    TestDate = URL.unescapeString(TestDate);
    Sep = URL.unescapeString(Sep);
    Continue = URL.unescapeString(Continue);

    var Ok = String.elements(TestDate, Sep) == 3 &&
            String.charAt(TestDate, 2) == Sep &&
            String.charAt(TestDate, 5) == Sep;

    if (Ok) {
        var Month = Lang.parseInt(
                String.elementAt(TestDate, 0, Sep));
        var Day = Lang.parseInt(
                String.elementAt(TestDate, 1, Sep));
        var Year = Lang.parseInt(
                String.elementAt(TestDate, 2, Sep));

        Ok = Month >= 1 && Month <= 12 &&
                Day >= 1 && Day <= 31 &&
                Year >= 0;
    }

    if (Ok)
        WMLBrowser.go(Continue);
    else
        Dialogs.alert("Please enter a valid date " +
                "in mm/dd/yy form.");
}
```

Listing 9-2   Using the WMLScript program to check a date.

```
<wml>
    <card>
        <p>
        Enter date (mm/dd/yy):
        <input title="mm/dd/yy:" name="d"
            format="NN\/NN\/NN"/>
        <!-- wrapped for readability only      -->
        <a href="01-CheckDate.wmls#CheckDate(
            '$(d)','/','%23c2')">OK</a>
        <br/>
        </p>
```

```
        <do type="accept" label="OK">
          <!-- wrapped for readability only    -->
          <go href="01-CheckDate.wmls#CheckDate(
             '$(d)', '/', '%23c2')"/>
        </do>
      </card>

      <card id="c2">
        <p>
        You entered $(d).
        <br/>
        <anchor>
           Repeat
           <prev>
             <setvar name="d" value=""/>
           </prev>
        </anchor>
        </p>

        <do type="prev">
           <prev>
             <setvar name="d" value=""/>
           </prev>
        </do>
      </card>
</wml>
```

Typical Uses

Aside from data validation, WMLScript can be put to good use in several areas. It has functions for controlling the browser, including manipulating WML variables and initiating navigation, as well as facilities for rudimentary user interactions. With it, you can imbue your deck with some conditional processing that would otherwise need to be performed on the server. WMLScript includes math and string functions, allowing you to manipulate and transform data. In addition, it provides routines for parsing and manipulating URLs.

Vendors also have the option of providing customized WMLScript libraries that allow access to the special features of their devices. For example, a WMLScript-enabled cell phone might have functions for call control, manipulation of the address book, and so on.

Differences from ECMAScript

If you are familiar with ECMAScript or JavaScript 1.1, you need to understand how WMLScript differs from these languages. WMLScript is not object-oriented and has no object model; instead, it is a procedural language that can be extended via libraries. ECMAScript uses 64-bit floating-point math, whereas WMLScript uses 32-bit integer math with optional floating-point support. WMLScript does not support global variables (although you can use WML variables for this purpose), and it makes use of a simple error-handling mechanism based on a special error value (`invalid`).

Standard Libraries

A *library* is a collection of related functions that extend the basic functionality of the language. WMLScript includes six standard libraries (Table 9-1), although the floating-point library is merely a façade when the implementation does not support floating-point math. An implementation can provide additional libraries encompassing extended or device-specific functions.

Language Basics

The basic syntax of WMLScript should look familiar if you know C++ or Java. It is a case-sensitive language throughout; all language keywords must be specified in lowercase, and variable names, function names, and other identifiers must use consistent capitalization. Whitespace (spaces, tabs, newlines) can appear anywhere between tokens. Each statement must be terminated by a semicolon.

Table 9-1   WMLScript Standard Libraries

Library	Description
Dialog	Rudimentary user interface operations
Float	Floating point math operations (optional)
Lang	Core functions that are closely related to the language
String	String operations
WMLBrowser	Link between WMLScript and the WML browser
URL	Operations on Uniform Resource Locators (URLs)

Comments

Comments follow the C++ convention: *Line comments* begin with a double slash (//) and are terminated by the end of the line, whereas *block comments* are delimited by the sequences /* and */. You cannot nest block comments.

```
// This is a line comment.

/*
   This is a block comment, which can
   span several lines.
*/
```

The `invalid` Value: Error Detection

WMLScript relies on a special value, `invalid`, to represent an invalid value such as one that could result from an arithmetic error:

```
var a = 1 / 0;   // a = invalid
```

The `invalid` value is distinct from all other data types (strings, integers, and so on), and special rules apply when it turns up during execution. We will cover these situations later in this chapter. For now, simply note that the use of the value `invalid` in any expression forces the result to `invalid` in most cases.

Literals

WMLScript supports integer, string, Boolean, and invalid literal values. Floating-point implementations also support floating-point literals.

Integer Literals

You can express integers in decimal, octal, or hexadecimal form (Figure 9-1). Octal values are identified by a leading zero; hexadecimal values are identified by a leading 0x or 0X. Hexadecimal literals are the one place where WMLScript relaxes its case requirements: You can write them using either uppercase or lowercase letters.

Internally, integer literals are represented as 32-bit two's complement numbers, and thus must fall within the range of –2,147,483,648 to 2,147,483,647. You can obtain these constants from the **Lang** standard library by calling `Lang.minInt()` and `Lang.maxInt()`, respectively. The use of an integer literal outside of the valid range will result in an error during compilation; however, during execution, an expression that evaluates

```
1964      // decimal literal
03654     // octal literal
0x7AC     // hexadecimal literal
0X7aC     // hex literals are case-insensitive
```

Figure 9-1 Examples of integer literals

```
6.02e24
32E-1
32.E-1
.167e+5
42.
42e0
3.1415
```

Figure 9-2 Examples of floating-point literals

to a value outside the legal range will result in `invalid`. (The WML deck **Overflow.wml**, which appears on the companion Web site, allows you to test overflow and related scenarios on your browser.)

Floating-Point Literals

Floating-point literals include a decimal point, an exponent, or both. You separate the exponent from the mantissa with a character "E" or "e" (Figure 9-2). Floating-point values are stored in 32-bit, single-precision, floating-point format; the maximum value that can be represented is 3.40282346e+38, and the smallest positive value possible is 1.17549435e-38. These constants can be obtained from `Float.maxFloat()` and `Float.minFloat()`, respectively.

As with integers, using a literal floating-point number that is too large or small will cause an error during compilation, but an out-of-range result during execution, *overflow*, will become `invalid`. However, *underflow*, a literal or run-time result that is too small to be represented (that is, between 0.0 and `Float.minFloat()`), will be treated as a zero (0.0).

On systems that do not support floating-point math, a floating-point constant is converted to `invalid` when the program is executed.

String Literals

A string literal is a sequence of zero or more characters enclosed within either single or double quotes. You must represent any special characters using an escape sequence (Table 9-2). Quote characters represented by escape sequences are always part of the string and never seen as the string terminator. For example, the two strings `'This is a quote: "'` and `"This is a quote: \""` are equivalent.

String literals must be contained on one source line. If your program contains a string that is so long as to become unwieldy, you can concatenate multiple literals (remember to include an intervening space if needed):

```
var s = "This string literal exists " +
        "on multiple lines.";
```

Boolean Literals

The Boolean literals, representing "truth values," are `true` and `false`.

```
var r = (answer == 42);
if (r == true)
   Dialogs.alert("You're not going to believe this...");
```

The Invalid Literal

WMLScript includes a special literal, `invalid`, that can be used to test for the presence of the `invalid` value:

```
var a = 1 / 0;
if (a == invalid)
   Dialogs.alert("Uh oh...");
```

Table 9-2 Special Character Escape Sequences

Escape	Description
\'	Single quote
\"	Double quote
\\	Backslash
\/	Slash
\b	Backspace
\f	Form feed
\n	Newline
\r	Carriage return
\t	Tab
\x*hh*	ASCII character specified by the hexadecimal sequence
ooo	ASCII character specified by the octal sequence
\u*hhhh*	Unicode character specified by the hexadecimal sequence

Variables

A *variable* is a name associated with a value, which you can use to store and manipulate program data. Before you can use a variable, you must *declare* it, thereby instructing the interpreter to reserve space for it. Declaration is accomplished by using the keyword var (see "var Statements" later in this chapter). All variable names within a single function, including function parameters (see "Functions"), must be unique.

You can use the value stored in a variable simply by using the variable's name. In such a case, the interpreter substitutes the current value when the statement executes, as demonstrated by the function in Listing 9-3. As you can see in the listing, variables can be initialized at the same time they are declared. In fact, all variables are initialized on declaration: if you do not supply an initial value, the variable will automatically be set to the empty string ("").

Listing 9-3   Use of variables.

```
function AddTen(InVal) {
   var OutVal = InVal + 10;
   return OutVal;
}
```

WMLScript is a *weakly typed* language, meaning that any variable can hold a value of any type (Figure 9-3). Internally, however, the interpreter stores variable values as one of five types: Boolean, integer, floating-point, string, and invalid. Conversions between types can occur automatically (as we will discuss in the next section) or via explicit library calls.

```
var MyVar = 1;          // A single variable can
                        // hold an integer...

MyVar = true;           // ...a Boolean...

MyVar = 3.14;           // ...a floating point...

MyVar = "Hi, Terrie!"   // ... or a string.

MyVar = 1/0;            // Variables can also hold
                        // the 'invalid' literal
```

Figure 9-3   Variables are not bound to a type

All variables are local to the function in which they are declared. A variable's lifetime begins when it is declared and terminates at the end of the function. Unlike in languages such as C++ or Java, compound statements do not scope variables in WMLScript; that is, a variable defined inside a block is still visible when the block ends. In fact, the variable is accessible even if the block never executes; we will cover this issue in more detail when we discuss the var statement. (To its credit, however, WMLScript does not perpetuate JavaScript's counterintuitive behavior whereby variables become visible to the function before their point of declaration.)

Automatic Type Conversions

Although WMLScript variables can hold values of any type, some operators and library functions expect operands of a specific type. The language defines automatic conversions—that is, conversions that occur without explicit action when the interpreter deems them necessary. When more than one automatic conversion is possible, a set of precedence rules (see "Conversion Precedence Rules") determines which one is used.

Depending on the situation, this feature can be either a handy time saver or an aggravating source of bugs. In particular (and a great irritant), when a conversion is required but none is possible, the interpreter will use the error value, invalid. Because invalid can be used in expressions (although to no great effect, as the result is usually invalid), its manifestation may go unnoticed until sometime later in the program.

Table 9-3 summarizes the type conversions that are possible and their results. These conversions are described in more detail in the following sections. In the table, "illegal" means that an automatic conversion is not possible. If the condition arises during execution, the result will usually be invalid. Note that the value invalid can never be converted to any other type. Also note that you can also perform some conversions explicitly, via the library calls Lang.parseInt(), Lang.parseFloat(), and String.toString().

Conversions to String

The interpreter can convert integer and floating-point values to an equivalent string representation. The exact format used for floating-point values is implementation-dependent; for example, the value 0.5 could be converted to "0.5" or "5e-1", depending on the implementation. Boolean

Table 9-3 Summary of Legal Automatic Data Type Conversions

A Value of Type …	…When Used as a … Boolean …Becomes …	Integer	Floating-Point	String
Boolean false	—	0	0.0	"false"
Boolean true	—	1	1.0	"true"
Integer 0	false	—	0.0	"0"
Integer != 0	true	—	Float value	String representation
Float 0.0	false	Illegal	—	String (e.g., "0.0" or "0.")
Float != 0.0	true	Illegal	—	String representation
Empty String	false	Illegal	Illegal	—
Nonempty String	true	Integer value (or illegal)	Float value (or illegal)	—
Invalid	Illegal	Illegal	Illegal	Illegal

values are converted to the equivalent lowercase string ("true" or "false").

Conversions to Integer

A string can be converted to an integer only if it is equivalent to a base-10 integral value. A floating-point value can never be automatically converted to an integer, even when the value contains no fractional portion. The Boolean values true and false are converted to the integer values 1 and 0, respectively.

Conversions to Floating-Point

An integer can be converted to its corresponding floating-point value, and the Boolean values true and false are converted to the floating-point values 1.0 and 0.0, respectively. A string can be converted to a floating-point value only if it can be interpreted as a floating-point number.

The interpreter is expected to recognize any valid floating-point format, regardless of the format that it uses when converting from floating-point to string. For example, if an interpreter converts the floating-point value 0.5 to the string "0.5", it must still allow the automatic conversion of "5e-1" to 0.5. If the string contains more significant digits than can be stored in a floating-point value, then the excess precision is lost when the value is converted. The interpreter decides whether the value will be truncated or rounded in such a case.

Conversions to Boolean

The empty string (""), integer 0, and floating-point 0.0 are all converted to false. All other values (except invalid) are converted to true.

Conversions to Invalid

The invalid type holds only the value invalid, which is either the result of an operation error or a literal value. Explicit conversions to the invalid type are not possible. In most cases, passing invalid as an operand will yield invalid as the result. The exceptions involve the conditional operator (?:), which treats invalid as false, and the typeof and isvalid operators, which recognize the invalid type.

Conversion Precedence Rules

When an operator or library function expects an operand of a specific type but an operand of a different type is supplied, the appropriate automatic conversion occurs, as described in the preceding sections. Some operators, however, are overloaded with multiple meanings; for example, the binary plus operator "+" can signal integer addition, floating-point addition, or string concatenation. When more than one conversion can be applied, precedence rules determine which conversion occurs and what type the result will have.

This topic is particularly opaque; the precedence is not necessarily intuitive, and you need to pay careful attention to the distinction between a value's current type and the types to which it can legally be converted. In all cases, if no conversion rule applies, the operand is converted to invalid.

In each of the following sets of rules, the first rule that applies is used and the remainder are ignored. The term *number* (or *numeric*) refers to an integer or floating-point value.

Rules for Unary Operators   For prefix and postfix increment and decrement (++ and --, respectively) and unary + and -:

1. If the operand is or can be converted to an integer, it is taken as an integer, and the result is an integer.
2. If the operand is or can be converted to a floating-point value, it is taken as a floating-point value, and the result is a floating-point value.

Expression	Result
+7	integer
+"7"	integer
-43.2	float
-"43.2"	float
-"4.32e2"	
v=true; ++v	integer (2)
v=false; --v	integer (-1)
+"Raz"	invalid
-"1e12345"	invalid (because the value is too large to be stored as a floating-point value)

Rules for Binary Operators Expecting Numeric Operands   For arithmetic binary operators (-, *, and /) and their assign-with-operation counterparts (-=, *=, and /=):

1. If at least one operand is a floating-point value and the other can be converted to floating-point, the operands are taken as floating-point values, and the result is a floating-point value.
2. If both operands are or can be converted to integers, they are taken as integers, and the result is an integer.
3. If both operands can be converted to floating-point values, they are taken as floating-point values, and the result is a floating-point value.

Expression	Result
2/1.6	Float
1.2 * "2.1"	Float
12 - "95"	Integer
"12" * "16"	Integer
"12" * "16."	Float
"2.3" * "3.2"	Float
6 / "A"	invalid

Rules for Binary Operators Expecting Numeric or String Operands

For the + and += operators (which can mean either addition or string concatenation) and the comparison operators (<, <=, >, >=, ==, and !=):

1. If at least one operand is a string, the other is taken as a string, and the result is a string.

2. If at least one operand is a floating-point value and the other can be converted to floating-point value, the operands are taken as floating-point values, and the result is a floating-point value.

3. If both operands are or can be converted to integers, they are taken as integers, and the result is an integer.

Expression	Result
`1 + "2"`	String ("12")
`"1.2" + 3`	String (for example, "1.23" or "1.2e13")
`1.2 + 3`	Float
`true + true`	Integer (2)
`true + " lies"`	String ("true lies")
`11 < 3.5`	Floating-point comparison (`false`)
`"11" < 3.5`	String comparison (`true`)

This particular set of rules often results in unpleasant surprises. Because the string conversion has higher precedence, if you present either the + or += operator with a string and a numeric argument, the result is always string concatenation:

```
x = 1 + 2;   // yields 3
x = "1" + 2; // yields "12"
x = 1 + "2"; // also yields "12"
```

In addition, because the + operator associates from left to right, mixing both strings and numbers in your expression may yield results other than what you expected:

```
x = 1 + 2 + " items";   // yields "3 items"
x = "items: " + 1 + 2;  // yields "items: 12"
```

To avoid this behavior, you can use parentheses to force the desired order of operations:

```
x = "items: " + (1 + 2); // yields "items: 3"
```

Alternatively, you can explicitly specify a conversion:

```
x = "items: " + String.toString(1 + 2); // yields "items: 3"
```

Another pitfall awaits JavaScript developers: In WMLScript, the string conversion rule applies to comparison operators. In JavaScript, a string comparison is performed only if both operands are strings initially. Hence, in WMLScript the expression "11"<3 is a string comparison (the 3 becomes "3") so the result is true, whereas in JavaScript it is a numeric comparison (the "11" becomes 11) and the result is false. Similarly, the expression "eleven" < 3, which is a valid string comparison in WMLScript, is an error in JavaScript because "eleven" cannot be converted into a number.

Identifiers

You use WMLScript *identifiers* to name variables, functions, and pragmas (instructions to the interpreter; see "Pragmas" later in this chapter). Identifiers are case-sensitive; they can be formed from any sequence of letters, numbers, and underscores (_), although they cannot start with a number. Figure 9-4 shows some examples of identifiers. You cannot use any of WMLScript's reserved words (listed in Table 9-4) as identifiers.

```
SpeedOfLight
fax_number
Address1
_Option
```

Figure 9-4 Examples of identifiers

Table 9-4 WMLScript Reserved Words

access	else	in	super
agent	enum	invalid	switch
break	equiv	isvalid	this
case	export	lib	throw
catch	extends	meta	true
class	extern	name	try
const	false	new	typeof
continue	finally	null	url
debugger	for	path	use
default	function	private	user
delete	header	public	var
div	http	return	void
do	if	sizeof	while
domain	import	struct	with

The interpreter actually supports three separate name spaces: one for function names, one for variables and function parameters, and one for pragmas. It is therefore possible—if confusing—to use the same identifier for a function name, variable, and pragma within the same compilation unit, as shown in Listing 9-4.

Listing 9-4   An identifier serving multiple roles.

```
use url xyzzy "http://foo.com/bar.wmls";

function xyzzy(xyzzy) {
   var result = xyzzy#somefunc(xyzzy);
   return result;
}
```

Operators

WMLScript supports a rich set of operators (Table 9-5). Note the required type of the operands and the type of the result, as shown in the table. When the type is "number" or the + operator is involved, the conversion precedence rules may come into play.

Assignment Operators

You assign a value to a variable by using the assignment operator (=):

```
var x = 1;
```

Table 9-5   Operator Precedence

Precedence	Associativity	Operator	Operation	Operand(s)	Result
1	R	++, --	Unary prefix or suffix increment and decrement	Number*	Number*
	R	+, -	Unary plus and minus	Number*	Number*
	R	~	Bitwise NOT	Integer	Integer
	R	!	Logical NOT	Boolean	Boolean
	R	typeof	Query data type	Any	Integer
	R	isvalid	Check for validity	Any	Boolean
2	L	*	Multiplication	Number*	Number*
	L	/	Division	Number*	Float

Precedence	Associativity	Operator	Operation	Operand(s)	Result
	L	`div`	Integer division	Integer	Integer
	L	`%`	Remainder (modulus)	Integer	Integer
3	L	`+`	Addition	Number*	Number*
	L	`-`	Subtraction	Number*	Number*
	L	`+`	String concatenation	String*	String*
4	L	`<<`	Bitwise left shift	Integer	Integer
	L	`>>`	Bitwise right shift with sign	Integer	Integer
	L	`>>>`	Bitwise right shift with zero fill	Integer	Integer
5	L	`<, <=, >, >=`	Less than, less than or equal to, greater than, greater than or equal to	Number or string*	Boolean
6	L	`==, !=`	Equality (identical values), inequality	Number or string*	Boolean
7	L	`&`	Bitwise AND	Integer	Integer
8	L	`^`	Bitwise XOR	Integer	Integer
9	L	`|`	Bitwise OR	Integer	Integer
10	L	`&&`	Logical AND	Boolean	Boolean
11	L	`||`	Logical OR	Boolean	Boolean
12	R	`?:`	Conditional expression	Boolean, any	Any
13	R	`=`	Assignment	Variable, any	any
	R	`*=, -=, +=`	Numerical operation with assignment	Variable, number*	Number
	R	`/=`	Numerical operation with assignment	Variable, number*	Float
	R	`%=, div=`	Numerical operation with assignment	Variable, integer	Integer
	R	`+=`	Concatenation assignment	String*	String
	R	`<<=, >>=, >>>=, &=, ^=, |=`	Bitwise operation and assignment	Variable, integer	Integer
14	L	`,`	Multiple evaluation	Any	Any

Note: "Number" refers to an integer or floating-point value; "variable" refers to a variable name (an l-value).

*Conversion precedence rules may apply. See "Automatic Type Conversions."

Assignment is by value only. That is, assignment of one variable to another does not bind the two variables together.

```
var x = 1;
var y = x;
y = -9;
Dialogs.alert(x);  // Displays "1"
```

When you operate on a variable and assign the result back to the same variable, such as in x = x + y, you can use the abbreviated form x += y. Most binary operators can be combined with assignment in this fashion—namely, +, -, *, /, |, %, <<, >>, >>>, &, ^, and div.

Although you might not think of it as such, the assignment operator is a true operator and returns a value—specifically, the value that was assigned. You can therefore initialize multiple variables to the same value, although you cannot declare and initialize them in the same statement.

```
var x, y, z;
x = y = z = false;
```

You can also use the assignment operator in other expressions, such as in the following example:

```
if ((a = b) == 6) c = 10;
```

The preceding statement is functionally equivalent to, if less readable than, the following two statements:

```
a = b;
if (a == 6) c = 10;
```

Arithmetic Operators

WMLScript supports a familiar set of unary and binary arithmetic operators. The binary operators are +, -, *, / (floating-point division), div (integer division), and % (modulus). Integer division truncates any fractional part of the result. On devices that support only integer math, an attempt to perform floating-point division (/) will always result in invalid.

```
r = 3 + 5;          // 8
r = 3 + 5.6;        // 8.6
r = 3 - 5;          // -2
r = 3.0 - 5;        // -2.0
r = 2 * 7;          // 14
r = 1.1 * 2.2;      // 2.42
r = 8 / 2;          // 4.0 (if floating-point supported)
r = 7 / 2;          // 3.5
r = 7 div 2;        // 3
r = 7.0 div 2;      // invalid (a float cannot be
                    // converted to an integer)
```

```
r = Lang.parseInt(7.0) div 2;   // 3
r = 17 % 5;                     // 2
```

The + and - operators can also be used with a single operand, as in the following example:

```
r = +3 / -2;
```

Relational and Logical Operators

Relational operators test the relative relationship between two quantities. WMLScript supports the standard set of relational operators: < (less than), <= (less than or equal to), > (greater than), >= (greater than or equal to), == (equal to), and != (not equal to).

When these operators are used with non-numerical operands, special rules apply. For Boolean arguments, true is larger than false. Strings are compared character by character based on the current character set. For example, in US-ASCII (and any other encoding that is a subset of Unicode), "a"<"b" is true because the character code for "a" is less than that for "b". Finally, any comparison that involves invalid will result in a result of invalid.

```
r = (3 < 5);              // true
r = (3 == 5.0);           // false
r = (true > false);       // true
r = ("a" < "b");          // true
r = ("aaa" > "aa");       // true
r = ("aaa" > "aaaa");     // false
r = (17 <= invalid);      // invalid
r = (false != invalid);   // invalid
```

The logical operators—&& (logical AND) , || (logical OR), and ! (logical NOT)—allow you to construct Boolean expressions. Logical expressions use "short circuit" evaluation: Evaluation stops as soon as the result can be determined. That is, if the left-side operand of an AND statement evaluates to false, the right-side operand will not be evaluated, and the result is false. Similarly, if the left-side operand of an OR statement evaluates to true, evaluation stops, and the result is true. You can rely on the left-side operand to "guard" the right-side operand, which enables you to write statements that might otherwise cause an error without instituting additional conditional tests. For example, the following statement guards against division by zero:

```
if ((x != 0) && (y/x > 1)) /* do something */
```

Short-circuit evaluation also applies when the left-side operand is invalid, in which case evaluation stops and the result is invalid.

```
r = true && true;      // true
r = true && false;     // false
r = false && false;    // false
r = true || true;      // true
r = true || false;     // true
r = false || false;    // false
r = !false;            // true
r = true && "";        // false
r = true && "xyz";     // true
r = true && 0;         // false
r = true && -17.62;    // true
r = true && invalid;   // invalid
```

Increment and Decrement Operators

The increment (++) and decrement (--) operators adjust the value of a variable by one. They are unusual in that they can be used either in prefix or postfix form:

```
x = 6;
x++;            // x = 7
--x;            // x = 6
```

The different forms are important only when they are used in an expression. In prefix form, the variable is adjusted first and the new value is then given to the expression. In postfix form, the expression is evaluated using the current value of the variable, and the variable is adjusted after this evaluation.

```
y = 1964;
r = y++;        // r = 1964, y = 1965;
y = 1964;
r = ++y;        // r = 1965, y = 1965;
```

Bitwise Operators

WMLScript provides seven operators that allow you to manipulate the bits of an operand directly:

&	Bitwise AND
|	Bitwise OR
^	Bitwise XOR, exclusive OR
<<	Left shift
>>	Right shift with sign
>>>	Right shift with zero fill
~	Bitwise NOT, one's complement

To use these operands, you need to understand binary numbers and two's complement representation, details we do not intend to delve into here. However, C programmers should take note: In WMLScript, these operators work on integers only. Operands of other types will be converted into integers, if possible, or will become `invalid`. Bitwise operators cannot be used to tinker with the characters in a string, for example.

```
var x, y, r;
x = 0xAA;   // = 10101010₂
y = 0x0F;   // = 00001111₂

r = x & y;      // = 0x0A
r = x | y;      // = 0xAF
r = x ^ y;      // = 0xA5
r = y << 2;     // 0x3C = 00111100₂
r = x >> 2;     // 0x2A = 00101010₂
r = ~y;         // = 0xF0 = -16
r = 16 >>> 2;   // 4
r = -16 >>> 1;  // -8
r = -1 >> 1;    // = 0xFFFFFFFF = -1
r = -1 >>> 1;   // = 0x7FFFFFFF = 2147483647
r = -1 >>> 31;  // = 1
```

String Operators

WMLScript's only string operator is concatenation, signaled by the `+` operator or, when combined with assignment, the `+=` operator. Overloading the same operator for both concatenation and addition was an unfortunate choice, as it opened the door for some unexpected behavior when addition and concatenation are used in the same expression. (The rules are straightforward, as we discussed earlier, but easily overlooked; the potential for confusion could have been averted had different symbols been used.) Other string operations are provided in WMLScript's standard **String** library, which we discuss in the section "*String*: Extended String Operations."

```
var Gettysburg = "Four score" + " seven";
Gettysburg += " years ago...";
```

Comma Operator

The comma operator enables you to combine multiple expressions into a single expression. Most often, you will use it to include several expressions in places where the syntax allows for only one. It is frequently used in a `for` statement, allowing you to create multiple initialization or update expressions.

```
var i, j, sum;
for (i=1, j=100, sum=0; i<j; i++, j-)
    sum += i*j;
```

The result of the comma operator is seldom used, but it returns the value of its right-side operand:

```
var x = 10, y = 20, z;
z = ++x, y-;       // x = 11, y = 19, z = 20
```

The comma used in function definitions and calls is a separator, not an operator, as it is when used with var to define multiple variables.

Conditional Operator

The conditional operator (?:) is sometimes called the ternary operator, because it is the only operator that takes three operands. It is also one of WMLScript's two operators that treat invalid differently. Essentially, the conditional operator is a concise form of the if statement (see "if-else Statements") that returns a value. If the first operand evaluates to true, the second operand is evaluated and returned as the result. If the first operand evaluates to false or invalid, the result is the evaluation of the third operand.

For example, the expression

```
var Reciprocal = (x != 0 ? 1/x : "undefined");
```

is functionally equivalent to the following if statement:

```
var Reciprocal;
if (x != 0)
    Reciprocal = 1/x;
else
    Reciprocal = "undefined";
```

The typeof Operator

The typeof operator tests the current internal type of its argument. It returns an integer code, as shown in Table 9-6. No type conversions are performed; instead, the result corresponds to the current type of the operand. (To test whether a conversion to a number is possible, you can use the standard library functions Lang.isFloat() and Lang.isInt().)

```
var x = 123;
var t = typeof x;   // t is now 0
x = 123.;
t = typeof x;       // t is now 1
x = "123";
t = typeof x;       // t is now 2
```

Table 9-6 typeof Return Values

Type	Code
Integer	0
Floating-point	1
String	2
Boolean	3
Invalid	4

The *isvalid* Operator

You can use the isvalid operator to check whether an expression evalu-ates to invalid. The expression isvalid x is shorthand for the expression (typeof x != 4).

```
var t1 = isvalid "123";  // true
var t2 = isvalid 1/0;    // false
```

Statements

A statement is one complete WMLScript "sentence." A single statement can span multiple lines, provided line breaks occur only between tokens, or multiple statements can occur on a single line.

Expression Statements

The simplest WMLScript statements are expressions that have side effects, such as assignment statements, increment and decrement expres-sions, and function calls:

```
x = 42;
x++;
alert("x=" + x);
```

Compound Statements

A *compound statement*, also called a *block statement*, is a series of state-ments enclosed in curly braces. You use one where the language expects a single statement but you need multiple statements to provide the de-sired result.

```
if (x == 0) {
    y++;
    x = 10;
}
```

var Statements

A var statement declares and initializes a variable. WMLScript does not support uninitialized variables; thus, if you do not provide an explicit initialization, the variable is automatically set to the empty string (""). Variable names must be unique within a function. The scope of the variable begins at the point of its declaration and terminates at the end of the function.

Declarations can occur within a block statement. Unlike other languages with which you might be familiar, such as C, C++, or Java, WMLScript does not allow the block to affect the scope of the variable. However, if the declaration includes an explicit initialization, the variable is reinitialized every time the block is executed.

Listing 9-5 demonstrates some of the finer points of var use. Because the declaration for b appears in the body of the loop and includes an initialization statement, this variable is reset to 1 every time the loop executes. Because s is initialized separately, however, it is set to the empty string only once, and it grows with each iteration of the loop.

Listing 9-5   Variable declarations.

```
extern function test() {
   var a = 3;    // initialized once
   // a is accessible

   for (;;) {
      var b = 1;    // initialized on every pass
      var s;        // implicit init happens once
      // a, b, s accessible

      if (0) {
         var c = 99;
      }
      // a, b, s, c accessible

      s += "glug ";

      a -= b; b++;
      if (a == 0)
         break;
   }

   // a, b, s, c still accessible.

   Dialogs.alert("Q: What sound does a beer make?" +
      "\nA: " + s);
```

```
        Dialogs.alert("a=" + a + " b=" + b + " c=" +
            c + " s=" + s);
}
```

Note that the variable c is declared within a block that does not get executed. Once that block has been passed, c is available for use. Because the block did not execute, however, this variable is initialized to an empty string, not 99.

if-else Statements

An if-else statement allows you to choose between executing two statements, depending on the value of a test expression, which must be enclosed in parentheses. (Either statement can be a block statement, if necessary.) The first statement executes if the test expression evaluates to true; if it is false or invalid, the statement following else is executed. The else part is optional and can be omitted if you do not need it.

```
if (Greeting == "")
    Greeting = "Hi,";
if (Name != "") {
    Name = String.elementAt(Name, 0, " ");
    Greeting += " " + Name + "!";
}
else
    Greeting += " stranger!";
```

You can nest if statements, with each else being associated with the closest previous if that lacks an else clause:

```
if (a == 1)
    if (b == 2)
        x = 7;
    else
        x = 8;
```

Alternatively, you can force an else to associate with a more "distant" if by using braces:

```
if (a == 1) {
    if (b == 2)
        x = 7;
}
else
    x = 8;
```

Another common programming construct is the "chaining" of if statements to take action on particular values, as shown on the next page.

```
if (input == 1)
   DoSomething();
else if (input == 2)
   DoTheTwist();
else if (input == 3)
   DoTheWatusi();
else
   DoDefault();
```

while Statements

The `while` statement is one of WMLScript's loop constructs; it allows you to define a block of code to be executed so long as a test expression is `true`.

```
while (test)
   statement;
```

The test condition is evaluated before the first execution of the loop. Thus, if it initially evaluates to `false` or `invalid`, the body of the loop never executes. Listing 9-6 gives an example of the use of `while` statements. The `break` and `continue` statements, which are discussed shortly, can be used to alter the normal sequence of execution.

Listing 9-6   `while` **loop example.**

```
extern function Main() {
   var r = 20;

   Lang.seed("seed");
   var n = Lang.random(r);
   var c = 1;
   while (n != 0) {
      c++;
      n = Lang.random(r);
   }

   var t = "try tries";
   Dialogs.alert("It took " + c + " " +
      String.elementAt(t, c - 1, " ") +
      " to get a zero.");
}
```

for Statements

The `for` statement is the other loop construct provided by WMLScript. You will typically use it when you want to iterate over a range of values. This loop is controlled by three expressions: *initialize, test,* and *increment.*

```
for (initialize; test; increment)
   statement;
```

When the interpreter encounters a `for` loop, it first evaluates the *initialize* expression, then the *test* expression. If *test* evaluates to `true`, then the interpreter executes the body of the loop (which can be a block statement), followed by the *increment* expression. The sequence then repeats with the *test* expression. The loop continues to execute as long as the test evaluates to `true`, although you can use the `break` and `continue` statements (discussed in the next section) to alter the execution sequence. The `for` loop can be considered to be a compact form of a `while` statement that takes the following form:

```
initialize;
while (test) {
    statement;
    increment;
}
```

An interesting feature of the `for` statement is that you can omit any or all of the three control expressions, as the situation dictates. If the *test* expression is omitted, the statement defaults to `true`. Omitting all three control expressions results in an indefinite loop, which will execute until a `break` statement within the loop body halts it.

The initialization expression can be a `var` statement that declares new variables. As always, these variables continue to live through the end of the function. Listing 9-7 shows an example of a `for` loop.

Listing 9-7   for loop example.

```
extern function Main() {
    var Input = "The true measure of a man is " +
                "the size of his hard drive.";
    var Vowels = "aeiou";

    for (var i=0, n=0; i < String.length(Input); i++) {
        var c = String.charAt(Input, i);
        if (String.find(Vowels, c) != -1)
            n++;
    }

    Dialogs.alert("The string contains " +
                String.toString(n) + " vowels.");
}
```

break and continue Statements

The `break` and `continue` statements remain valid only within the body of a loop, and both alter the normal execution sequence. A `break` statement instructs the interpreter to exit the loop immediately and pick up execution at the statement that follows the loop. The `continue` statement bypasses the remainder of the loop body and continues with the next iteration: A `while` loop is resumed on the condition expression, and a `for` loop is resumed on the update expression. Listing 9-8 demonstrates the use of both types of statements.

Listing 9-8   `break` and `continue` example.

```
/* (Inefficient) prime number generator */
extern function PrimeGen() {

    var Num = 10;
    var Found = 0, Primes = "";

    for (var Cand=1; Found < Num; Cand++) {
        for (var i = 2; i < Cand; i++) {
            var r = Cand % i;
            if (r == 0)
                break;
        }
        if (r == 0)
            continue;
        Found++;
        Primes += Cand + " ";
    }

    Dialogs.alert("First " + String.toString(Num) +
                " primes: " + Primes);

}
```

return Statements

A `return` statement exits a function; optionally, it may specify a return value, which is the function result. If no return value is specified or if the end of the function is encountered without the execution of a `return` statement, the function returns an empty string. Examples of the `return` statement can be found in the next section, where we discuss functions in detail.

Return values are not accessible from WML. If you need to return data from your WMLScript program to your WML deck, you can pass it in WML variables using the `WMLBrowser.setVar()` library call (see "setVar: Set a WML Variable").

Empty Statement

The empty statement is simply a semicolon. Executing an empty statement has no effect and performs no action; it is useful when the language syntax requires a statement but your program does not actually need one. This situation generally arises only with a `for` loop in which you have managed to do all of the work in the control expressions and which thus needs no body:

```
/* Clear the WML variables data0, data1, ..., data9 */
for (var i=0; i <= 9; WMLBrowser.setVar("data" + i++, ""))
   ;
```

Functions

A function is a named encapsulation of a set of operations. You call, or *invoke,* the function whenever you want to execute that particular sequence of operations. Values, called *arguments* or *parameters,* can be passed to the function when it is called; within the function, these values are treated in the same ways as variables that were initialized before the function began to execute.

A function may elect to return a result, based on which the caller can perform some action. (Actually, every function returns a result; if you do not return one explicitly, the interpreter will return an empty string.)

Listing 9-9 shows a simple function that returns the cube of a given number.[2] The function definition includes a *formal parameter,* x, which it references just as it would any other variable. The value of x is given by the *actual parameter* when the function is called. Here, our main program calls `Cube` for the values 1 through 9.

Listing 9-9   A simple function.

```
function Cube(x) {
   return x * x * x;
}

extern function Main() {
   for (var i=1; i<=9; i++)
      Dialogs.alert(ToStr(i) + " cubed = " + Cube(i));
}
```

Functions reside in *compilation units*—essentially, files. (Like all content, WMLScript source data can be generated dynamically at the server

---

[2]In practice, you usually would use the library function `Float.pow()` for this purpose, or, if you were dealing with only integers, you probably would write a more general-purpose routine to handle any exponent.

without ever being stored in the file system; thus, we use a more oblique term to describe it.) Each compilation unit can contain one or more functions, at least one of which must be declared to be externally visible using the `extern` keyword. Functions that are not externally accessible are available to only the other functions in the same file.

You declare a function with the keyword `function`, followed by its name (which must be unique within the compilation unit), a formal parameter list, and the function body. The formal parameter list assigns the names that will be used to access the values of the actual parameters within the function. Parameters are passed by value, and they act like local variables that are initialized before the function body is executed. WMLScript does not support conveniences with which you may be familiar from other languages, such as default arguments, optional arguments, and variable numbers of arguments.

Functions always return a value. By default, this value is the empty string (""); however, you can use a `return` statement to specify another value. The caller of the function can ignore the return value if it does not need it.

Function Invocation

The manner in which you invoke a function depends on where it resides. You can call a function in the same compilation unit by simply using its name followed by an argument list—for example, `Power(2,5)`. The ordering of functions within the file is not important, as any function can call any other function in the same file without any special declarations.

You can also call functions in other compilation units, although this effort requires a level of indirection. First, you must tell the WMLScript interpreter where the compilation unit is located, by using the `url` pragma (see "The `url` Pragma: External Function Resources"). This action assigns an identifier to the URL, which you can subsequently use together with a hash symbol (#) and the function name:

```
use url MathFuncs  "http://www.guetech.edu/mathlib.wmls";
...
var x = MathFuncs#Cube(6);
```

External function calls were not well supported by the Software Development Kits available at the time of this writing; that is, many of the browsers simply cannot call an external function. Although this situation will undoubtedly change, in the near term you should use external function calls with caution and test your application on actual devices.

Finally, WMLScript supports *libraries,* or named collections of functions that are built into the browser. Several libraries are standard with the language (see "WMLScript Standard Libraries"), and many of our examples have put them to work already. You call a library function by giving the library name, a period (.), and the function name.

Calling WMLScript from WML   In most of your applications, you will call your WMLScript program from a WML deck. In WML, WMLScript programs are identified in the same way as any other external resource—that is, by using the URL of the WMLScript compilation unit, a hash mark, and the name of the function:

```
href="http://guetech.edu/verify.wmls#check()"
```

As far as the WML browser is concerned, the function call is a URL like any other. Thus any special characters contained in the function call must be URL-escaped, which may be the case when you directly specify arguments to the WMLScript program. Consider the following example, in which we are passing a string containing an at sign (@):

```
href="http://www.guetech.edu/searchlib.wmls#search('me%40home')">
```

When you use WML variables to specify the parameters, the browser will handle the escaping for you automatically. An alternative approach to passing arguments is to have the WMLScript program take responsibility for retrieving the values. We cover exchanging data with WML in more detail when we discuss the **WMLBrowser** standard library and in the section "Exchanging Data with WML."

Pragmas

A *pragma* is not an executable statement but rather an instruction to the WMLScript interpreter that affects the execution of the program. Pragmas are introduced with the keyword use, and they must be specified before the definition of the first function in the compilation unit.

The ur1 Pragma: External Function Resources
We have already encountered the url pragma, which assigns a local name to an external compilation unit. Although the level of indirection needed to call external functions creates something of a nuisance, it also provides a small maintenance benefit. Because all of your external dependencies appear at the beginning of your program, they will be easy to update if their locations change.

When the interpreter encounters a `url` pragma, it associates the local name with the external resource; however, it does not attempt to retrieve the resource until the program actually executes a statement that requires it. If the browser cannot retrieve the resource or the function does not exist or is inaccessible, an error message will be reported. What happens after that is up to the browser; often, the user will be left at the last WML card viewed.

The location you specify can be either a fully qualified URL or one that is relative to the location of the calling program. Fragment identifiers cannot be used, because the `url` pragma identifies the compilation unit, not a specific function. Any special characters in the URL must be escaped manually.

The access Pragma: Access Control

The `access` pragma protects your WMLScript program from unauthorized use by restricting which clients may invoke the script. As in WML, the access control information accompanies the content, so protecting a program does not mean that no one can read it—merely that a compliant browser will not execute it. By default, the access is public, so all external functions can be called from any program residing on any server.

Privileges are granted based on the domain and path of the calling resource. Although you can specify one or both of these attributes, you can have only one `access` pragma in a compilation unit. The domain and path you specify are compared with the caller's URL, in the same manner as for the WML <access> element (see Chapter 7).

The access pragma has three possible forms:

```
use access domain domain-suffix path path-prefix
use access domain domain-suffix
use access path path-prefix
```

If you specify a domain and a path, they must be specified in that order. If you omit the domain, the default is the domain of the current compilation unit (that is, the domain hosting the file containing the access statement). The default for the path is "/" (the root, indicating that all scripts on the specified domain are authorized). Relative paths are supported; the browser will convert the relative path into an absolute path before making the comparison.

WMLScript differs from WML in one minor way: WML allows you to rely on the default value for both attributes:

```
<access/>
```

The equivalent restriction in WMLScript is as follows:

```
use access path "/"
```

The meta Attribute: Meta-information

WMLScript files can also contain meta-information, which enables you to control server-side processes or to access browser-specific features. Meta-data is specified somewhat differently in WMLScript than in WML and comes in three flavors:

- *Named data:* specified by name, intended for use by the origin server.
- *HTTP equivalent data:* specified by http equiv, intended to be interpreted as an HTTP request header.
- *User agent data:* specified by user agent, intended for use by the browser.

All meta-data consists of a type specification, a property name, and a property value; all of these values must be string literals. In addition, the property name cannot be an empty string. You can also include a *scheme*, the meaning of which depends on the particular data item; it allows you to provide more information about the manner in which the data should be interpreted.

WMLScript does not define any standards for meta-data or schemes, and browsers are not required to act on the meta-data or interpret it in any specific fashion.

Named Meta-information Named meta-data is intended for use by the origin server. The browser will ignore it, and network servers may remove it during transmission. For example, you might use named data to mark when a document should be removed from the server to facilitate an automated cleanup process:

```
use meta name "Expires" "2000-03-14 09:16" "EST";
```

The preceding example also uses a scheme parameter, which indicates the time zone.

HTTP Equivalent Meta-information Meta-data designated as "HTTP equivalent" is intended to be interpreted as a HTTP response header, as defined in RFC 2068.

```
use meta http equiv "From" "prez@whitehouse.gov";
```

During transmission, an intermediate server should replace this information with the corresponding protocol response header. Unfortunately, this substitution is not guaranteed by WMLScript, and the browser is not required to look for such data in the content. If you rely on the browser to see the data, you should transmit it as an actual HTTP header, not as meta-data.

User Agent Meta-data   Not surprisingly, user agent meta-data is intended for use by the browser.

```
use meta user agent "HypotheticalBrowserCompany.bookmarkable" "true";
```

Intermediate network servers cannot remove this type of meta-information from the content. Browsers can recognize and act on implementation-specific data. There is no real reason to use user agent meta-data except as defined by particular user agents. (Ideally, user agent authors would adopt a naming scheme similar to that suggested for WML vendor-specific <do> types.)

WMLScript Standard Libraries

WMLScript provides six standard libraries: **Lang**, **Float**, **String**, **URL**, **WMLBrowser**, and **Dialogs**. All compliant devices must provide all six, although on a browser that does not support floating-point math, the **Float** library is just a shell. As you might expect, library names are case-sensitive.

Most library functions expect arguments of specific types. If you specify an argument of a different type than is expected, the automatic conversion rules (see "Automatic Type Conversions") will apply. One notable exception exists: If you provide a floating-point number where a standard function expects an integer, the interpreter will call `Float.int()`automatically. Some functions accept values of any type; refer to the function description to see how these values are handled.

Lang: Core Functions

The **Lang** library contains functions that related to the core WMLScript language. These functions are similar to those in the ECMAScript core language and in the ECMAScript **Math** and **Number** libraries, with a few other miscellaneous functions thrown in.

Math and Number Functions

abs: Compute an Absolute Value

Syntax: `Lang.abs` (*number*)

Arguments: Any number.

Returns: The absolute value of the input number.

Exceptions: Returns `invalid` if the input cannot be converted to a number.

Example:
```
Lang.abs(-3);     // 3
Lang.abs("2.7");  // 2.7
Lang.abs(true);   // 1
Lang.abs("junk"); // invalid
```

float: Test Whether Floating-Point Support Is Available

Syntax: `Lang.float()`

Arguments: None.

Returns: A Boolean: `true` if floating-point value support is available; `false` otherwise.

Exceptions: None.

Example:
```
if (!Lang.float())
    Dialogs.alert("Floating-point support not present, "+
                    "results will be approximate.");
```

isFloat: Test Whether a Value Can Be Interpreted as a Number

Syntax: `Lang.isFloat(x)`

Arguments: Any value.

Returns: A Boolean: `true` if the value x can be converted into a floating-point value using `parseFloat()`; `false` otherwise. Unlike the `typeof` operator, `isFloat()` will consider possible conversions of x, if necessary.

Exceptions: Returns `invalid` if the implementation does not support floating-point values.

Example:
```
Lang.isFloat("4.2");            // true
Lang.isFloat(42);               // true
Lang.isFloat("  -16.7e2 dB");   // true
Lang.isFloat("");               // false
Lang.isFloat("junk");           // false
Lang.isFloat("10d");            // true
Lang.isFloat("10e ");           // false
Lang.isFloat(true);             // false
Lang.isFloat(invalid);          // invalid
```

isInt: Test Whether a Value Can Be Interpreted as an Integer

Syntax: `Lang.isInt(x)`

Arguments: Any value.

Returns: A Boolean: `true` if the value x can be converted into an integer
using `parseInt()`; `false` otherwise. Unlike the `typeof` operator,
`isInt()` will consider possible conversions of x, if necessary.

Exceptions: None.

Example:
```
Lang.isInt("  -1000"); // true
Lang.isInt(98.6);      // true
Lang.isInt("xyzzy");   // false
Lang.isInt("#9");      // false
Lang.isInt("10d");     // true
Lang.isInt(true);      // false
Lang.isInt(invalid);   // invalid
```

max: Return the Larger of Two Values

Syntax: `Lang.max(number1, number2)`

Arguments: Any two numbers.

Returns: The larger of the two numbers (as would be determined by
applying the > operator to the numbers).

Exceptions: Returns `invalid` if the input cannot be converted to a number.

Example:
```
Lang.max(6, -4);       // 6
Lang.max(4, 3.5);      // 4
Lang.max(3, 3.5);      // 3.5
Lang.max(3, 3.0);      // 3 or 3.0
Lang.max(0.5, true);   // 1
Lang.max("junk", 7);   // invalid
```

maxInt: Return the Maximum Integer Value That Can Be Represented

Syntax: `Lang.maxInt()`

Arguments: None.

Returns: 2147483647

Exceptions: None.

Example: `var big = Lang.maxInt();`

min: Return the Smaller of Two Values

Syntax: `Lang.min(number1, number2)`

Arguments: Any two numbers.

Returns: The smaller of the two numbers (as would be determined by applying the < operator to the numbers).

Exceptions: Returns `invalid` if the input cannot be converted to a number.

Example:
```
Lang.min(6, -4);       // -4
Lang.min(4, 3.5);      // 3.5
Lang.min(3, 3.5);      // 3
Lang.min(3, 3.0);      // 3 or 3.0
Lang.min(0.5, false);  // 0
Lang.min("junk", 7);   // invalid
```

minInt: Return the Minimum Integer Value That Can Be Represented

Syntax: `Lang.minInt()`

Arguments: None.

Returns: -2147483648

Exceptions: None.

Example: `var small = Lang.minInt();`

parseFloat: Convert a String to a Number

Syntax: `Lang.parseFloat(string)`

Arguments: Any string representing or beginning with a floating-point value.

Returns: The numeric value corresponding to the string or string prefix. Leading spaces are ignored, and parsing stops when the function encounters a character that cannot be treated as part of the floating-point representation.

Exceptions: Returns invalid if a parsing error occurs.
Returns invalid if the implementation does not support floating-point values.

Example:
```
Lang.parseFloat("4.2");        // 4.2
Lang.parseFloat(42);           // 42.0
Lang.parseFloat("  -16.7e2 dB"); // 1670
Lang.parseFloat(".1");         // 0.1
Lang.parseFloat("");           // invalid
Lang.parseFloat("x = 6");      // invalid
Lang.parseFloat("10e ");       // invalid
Lang.parseFloat("10 e");       // 10.0
```

parseInt: Convert a String to an Integer

Syntax: Lang.parseInt(*string*)

Arguments: Any string representing or beginning with an integer.

Returns: The integer value corresponding to the string or string prefix. Leading spaces are ignored, and parsing stops when the function encounters a character that is neither a decimal digit nor a leading sign (+ or –).

Exceptions: Returns invalid if a parsing error occurs.

Example:
```
Lang.parseInt("42");        // 42
Lang.parseInt("42 km/sec"); // 42
Lang.parseInt("     99");   // 99
Lang.parseInt("");          // invalid
Lang.parseInt("bogus");     // invalid
Lang.parseInt("-16");       // -16
Lang.parseInt("- 16");      // invalid
Lang.parseInt("--16");      // invalid
```

random: Return a Pseudo-random Number

Syntax: Lang.random(*number*)

Arguments: Upper limit for the random number to be generated.

Returns: A random number from the uniform distribution between zero and the specified upper limit, inclusive. Returns 0 if the upper limit is zero, or `invalid` if the upper limit is less than zero. If a floating-point value is specified, it is first converted to an integer with `Float.int()`.

Exceptions: Returns `invalid` if the input cannot be converted to a number.

Example:
```
Lang.random(5);        // i = 2 (maybe)
Lang.random("foo");    // invalid
Lang.random(-3);       // invalid
Lang.random(7.6);      // l = 5 (maybe)
```

seed: Initialize the Pseudo-Random Number Sequence

Syntax: `Lang.seed(number)`

Arguments: Seed for the random number generator. If a floating-point value is specified, it is converted to an integer via `Float.int()`. If the value is zero or positive, reseeding with the same value should generate the same sequence of pseudo-random numbers; if it is negative, a random, system-dependent initialization value is used. If a non-numeric value is specified, the seed is left unchanged.

Returns: An empty string.

Exceptions: Returns `invalid` if the input cannot be converted to a number.

Example:
```
Lang.seed(7);
var i = Lang.random(10);   // 6 (maybe)
Lang.seed(7);
i = Lang.random(10);       // 6 (same as before)
var s = Lang.seed("rtfm"); // invalid (seed unchanged)
```

Miscellaneous Functions

abort: Abnormal Exit from WMLScript Processing

Syntax: `Lang.abort(descriptionstring)`

Arguments: Any string. If the value `invalid` is specified, the string "invalid" is used instead.

Returns: Nothing. All execution of the program is terminated. Control returns to whatever invoked the interpreter (generally, the WML browser). You should use this function to effect an abnormal exit, which becomes necessary when your program has detected errors to the point where it cannot continue. Any pending navigation requests will be discarded.

Neither the interpreter nor the program that invoked it (for example, the browser) is required to do anything with the description string, and both may ignore it.

Exceptions: None.

Example: `Lang.abort("Red alert!");`
`Lang.abort("Error " + err " processing directive.");`
`Lang.abort(invalid);  // same as Lang.abort("invalid");`

In WMLScript 1.1 and 1.2, the requirement that `abort()` cancel pending navigation is not clearly spelled out. With current browsers, you should call `WMLBrowser.go(" ")` before calling `Lang.abort()`.

characterSet: Query the Character Set Supported by the Interpreter

Syntax: `Lang.characterSet()`

Arguments: None.

Returns: The integer corresponding to the IANA MIBenum value for the character set supported by the WMLScript interpreter.

Exceptions: None.

Example: `Lang.characterSet(); // 106 (perhaps)`

exit: Normal Exit from WMLScript Processing

Syntax: `Lang.exit(returnvalue)`

Arguments: Any value.

Returns: Nothing. All execution is terminated. Control returns to whatever invoked the interpreter (generally, the WML browser). This function works differently than `return`, in that any pending returns to WMLScript functions are disregarded. You should use this function to effect a normal exit from your program from within a nested function call.

Neither the interpreter nor the program that invoked it (for example, the browser) is required to do anything with the description string, and both may ignore it.

Exceptions: None.

Example: `Lang.exit("Answer to life, universe, everything = " + 42);`
`Lang.exit(7);`
`Lang.exit(invalid);`

> Unlike with `abort()`, if `exit()` is called with the value `invalid`, the WMLScript specification says this function should return `invalid` to the caller. This requirement seems unhelpful, as the caller is probably not cognizant of WMLScript's internal data types.

Float: Floating-Point Operations

The **Float** library contains common floating-point math functions. Implementations that do not support floating-point values must return `invalid` when a program calls any of these functions.

ceil: Round a Number Up

Syntax: `Float.ceil(number)`

Arguments: Any number.

Returns: Computes the ceiling function, returning the integer greater than or equal to the input.

Exceptions: Returns `invalid` if the input is not a number.

Example: `Float.ceil(3.1415); // 4`
`Float.ceil(-1.73);  // -1`

floor: Round a Number Down

Syntax: `Float.floor(number)`

Arguments: Any number.

Returns: Computes the floor function, returning the integer less than or equal to the input.

Exceptions: Returns `invalid` if the input is not a number.

Example: `Float.floor(3.1415); // 3`
`Float.floor(-1.73);  // -2`

int: Extract the Integer Portion of a Number

Syntax: `Float.int(number)`

Arguments: Any number.

Returns: The integer portion of the input.

Exceptions: Returns `invalid` if the input is not a number.

Example: `Float.int(3.1415); // 3`
`Float.int(-1.73);  // -1`

maxFloat: Return the Maximum Floating-Point Value That Can Be Represented

Syntax: `Lang.maxFloat()`

Arguments: None.

Returns: 3.40282347e+38

Exceptions: None.

Example: `var big = Lang.maxFloat();`

minFloat: Return the Smallest Positive Floating-Point Value That Can Be Represented

Syntax: `Lang.minFloat()`

Arguments: None.

Returns: 1.17549435e-38

Exceptions: None.

Example: `var tiny = Lang.minFloat();`

pow: Compute x^y

Syntax: `Float.pow(x, y)`

Arguments: Number and exponent. If the number is negative, the exponent must be an integer.

Returns: x raised to the power of y, x^y.

Exceptions: Returns `invalid` if x is zero and y is less than zero, or if x is less than zero and y is not an integer.

Example: `Float.pow(2, 3);     // 8.0`
`Float.pow(2.5, -3);  // 0.064`
`Float.pow(-2, 3.5);  // invalid`

round: Round a Number to the Nearest Integer

Syntax: `Float.round(number)`

Arguments: Any number.

Returns: x rounded to the nearest integer; 0.5 is rounded up.

Exceptions: None.

Example: `Float.round(6.5);  // 7`
`Float.round(-6.5); // -6`

sqrt: Compute the Square Root

Syntax: `Float.round(number)`

Arguments: Any number.

Returns: The square root of the input.

Exceptions: Returns `invalid` if the input is negative.

Example: `Float.sqrt(16);  // 4.0`
`Float.sqrt(5);   // 2.236068`

String: Extended String Operations

The **String** library provides string manipulation functions. Some functions take an index as an argument. All such indices are zero-based. Although indices are expected to be integers, if you supply a floating-point value and the interpreter supports floating-point math, it will helpfully call `Float.int()` for you automatically.

The string functions that operate on whitespace characters use a definition of "whitespace" that is slightly broader than that employed by the rest of WML and WMLScript. Along with the space, tab, carriage return, and linefeed characters, WMLScript recognizes the ASCII vertical tab and form feed as whitespace characters as well.

Several of the string functions operate on *delimited lists*—that is, strings consisting of a number of entries partitioned by a unique separator character. You can use such lists to address WMLScript's lack of an array data type to a certain extent. See the examples in "List Functions" for details.

Core String Functions

charAt: Get an Indexed Character from a String

Syntax: `String.charAt(string, index)`

Arguments: Any string and a zero-based index.

Returns: A one-character string, consisting of the character at the specified index; or an empty string if the index is larger than the length of the string. If the index is a floating-point value, it is first converted to an integer via `Float.int()`.

Exceptions: Returns `invalid` if `index` cannot be converted to a number.

Example:
```
String.charAt("Conundrum", 1);  // "o"
String.charAt("Conundrum", 50); // ""
String.charAt(1985, 0);         // "1"
```

compare: Lexicographically Compare Two Strings for Order

Syntax: `String.compare(string1, string2)`

Arguments: Any two strings.

Returns: An indication of which string precedes (is "less than") the other. The return value is -1 if `string1` precedes `string2` in the collating sequence, 1 if `string2` precedes `string1`, or 0 if the two strings are identical. Ordering is determined by using the current character set.

Exceptions: Returns `invalid` if either argument cannot be converted to a string.

Example:
```
String.compare("one", "one"); // 0
String.compare("abc", "abd"); // -1
String.compare("abc", "abb"); // 1
```

find: Search a String for a Substring

Syntax: `String.find(haystack, needle)`

Arguments: Any string (*haystack*) and a string for which to search (*needle*).

Returns: The zero-based index of the first character of the first occurrence of the string *needle* in the string *haystack*. If no match is found, –1 is returned. Characters must match exactly; for example, case is significant.

Exceptions: Returns `invalid` if the search string is empty.

Example:
```
String.find("radical advice", "ad"); // 1
String.find("radical advice", "aD"); // -1
String.find("radical advice", "");   // invalid
String.find("", "foo");              // -1
```

format: Format a Value to Match a Template

Syntax: `String.format(template, x)`

Arguments: A format template and any value.

Returns: The string resulting from applying the format template to the value.

Exceptions: Returns `invalid` if the format specification is illegal.

Example:
```
String.format("x = %4d", 42);
    //   "x =   42"
var b = String.format("%4d", -42);          // "  -42"
var c = String.format("%6.4d", 42);         // "  0042"
var d = String.format("%6.4d", -42);        // " -0042"
var e = String.format("Welcome back, %1!", "Kotter");
    // "Welcome back, Kotter!"
var f = String.format("%3f", 1.2345678);
    // "1.234568"
var g = String.format("%3f", 1.5555555);
    // "1.555556"
var h = String.format("%6.2%%", 1.2345678); // "  1.23%"
var i = String.format("%2f.0 %2f., 1.234); // " 1 ."
var j = String.format("%.0d", 0);           // ""
var k = String.format("%7d", "Echo");       // invalid
var l = String.format("%s", true);          // "true"
```

The `format()` function is, unfortunately, saddled with an arcane syntax reminiscent of the C language's `printf()` family. It takes the following form (square brackets indicate optional sequences):

```
[any_characters]%[width][.precision]type[any_characters]
```

The start of the *format specification,* which signals how the value should be formatted, is signaled with a percent sign (%). If you want to include a literal percent sign elsewhere in the template, you must escape it by doubling (%%). If the template includes multiple format specifications (that is, multiple single percent signs), the first specification is used and the remainder are removed from the string.

The specification consists of three codes: the *type,* which is required and indicates how the value is to be formatted, and the *width* and *precision,* which control the length of the result.

The Type Specification   The *type* is a one-character code, which specifies the desired data type of the result. Table 9-7 lists the possible values.

The Width Specification   The *width* is a positive integer specifying the minimum size of the output "field" that will hold the value. If the value as formatted includes fewer characters than the specified width, it is padded on the left with spaces. The width never causes the value to be truncated; if the formatted value requires more space than the given number of characters (or if no width is specified), the value is left untouched, subject to the given precision.

The width parameter gives you some ability to right-justify data. Devices that use only variable-pitch fonts will give approximate results, however. Note that for floating-point formatting, the width specifies the total number of characters to be printed—not just the characters found to the left of the decimal point.

Table 9-7   Possible Type Values

Type	Interpretation
d	The value will be formatted as an **integer**, in the form *[-]ddd.* (The "*ddd*" indicates one or more decimal digits; the exact length of the result will depend on the input value and the width and precision values.)
f	The value will be formatted as a **floating-point value**, in decimal notation *[-]ddd.ddd.* (The "*ddd*" indicates one or more decimal digits; the exact length of the result will depend on the input value and the width and precision values.)
s	The value will be formatted as a **string**. (The number of characters printed depends on the width and precision values.)

Table 9-8 Possible Precision Values

If Type Code Is...	...Precision Is Interpreted as:
d	For integers, specifies the minimum number of digits in the result. If the result contains fewer digits than this value, the number is padded on the left with zeros; however, the precision never causes the result to be truncated. The default precision is 1, indicating no padding. A precision of 0 also indicates no padding, with the only difference being the handling of the value zero. For example, `String.format("%.1d", 0)` returns `"0"`, whereas `String.format("%.0d", 0)` returns `""`.
f	For floating-point values, specifies the number of digits after the decimal point. The value is rounded to the specified number of places (five rounds up). If this value is not specified, the default precision is 6. If the precision is 0, no decimal point is printed. The value is right-padded with zeros to the specified number of digits, and at least one digit always appears to the left of the decimal; a zero is used if needed.
s	For string values, specifies the maximum number of characters. No padding is performed if the string is shorter than the specified precision. In addition, for some unfathomable reason, if the width is larger than the precision, the width is ignored. WAP 1.2.1 may remove the rule that states that a width larger than the precision is ignored.

The Precision Specification   The *precision*, a positive integer, further controls the number of characters to be included in the result. Its meaning varies depending on the formatting requested by the type code, as does the default behavior if no precision is specified.

For numeric values, this parameter does not specify "precision" in the mathematical sense but merely controls the number of decimal places to be displayed. In particular, a value will be right-padded with zeros, if needed, which would imply a mathematical precision greater than is warranted. Table 9-8 describes the precision values associated with the different type codes.

isEmpty: Test if a String Is Empty

Syntax: `String.isEmpty(string)`

Arguments: Any string.

Returns: A Boolean: `true` if the input is an empty string (length is zero); `false` otherwise.

Exceptions: None.

Example:
```
var b = String.isEmpty("Hey, Rocky!");  // false
var c = String.isEmpty("");             // true
var d = String.isEmpty(false);          // false
```

length: Return the Length of the String

Syntax: `String.length(string)`

Arguments: Any string.

Returns: The number of characters in the input.

Exceptions: None.

Example:
```
var i = String.length("abc");     // 3
var i = String.length(76);        // 2
var i = String.length("");        // 0
var i = String.length(false);     // 5
var i = String.length(invalid);   // invalid
```

replace: Replace One Substring with Another

Syntax: `String.replace(string, old, new)`

Arguments: Any string, a target, and a replacement.

Returns: A copy of the input string with all occurrences of `old` replaced with `new`.

Exceptions: Returns `invalid` if `old` is an empty string.

Example:
```
String.replace("do be do be do", "be", "wah");
    // "do wah do wah do"
String.replace("do be do be do", "do", "");
    // " be  be "
String.replace("mugwump", "", "u");  // invalid
```

squeeze: Remove Extra Whitespace Characters

Syntax: `String.squeeze(string)`

Arguments: Any string.

Returns: A copy of the string with all sequences of consecutive whitespace characters replaced by a single space (0x20).

Exceptions: None.

Example:
```
String.squeeze(" A   B  \r\n C");  // " A B C"
String.squeeze("ozone");           // "ozone"
String.squeeze("");                // ""
```

toString: Convert a Value to a String

Syntax: `String.toString(x)`

Arguments: Any value.

Returns: A string representation of the given value, exactly as performed by the WMLScript automatic conversions, with one addition: the `invalid` value becomes the string "invalid".

Exceptions: None.

Example:
```
String.toString(42);         // "42"
String.toString(true);       // "true"
String.toString("Edison");   // "Edison"
String.toString("");         // ""
String.toString(invalid);    // "invalid"
```

trim: Remove Leading and Trailing Whitespace Characters

Syntax: `String.trim(string)`

Arguments: Any string.

Returns: A copy of the string with all leading and trailing whitespace characters removed.

Exceptions: None.

Example:
```
String.trim(" A   B  \r\n C");    // "A   B  \r\n C"
var t = String.trim("ozone");     // "ozone"
var u = String.trim("");          // ""
```

List Functions

The **String** library also includes a number of functions that operate on lists: strings that contain a number of elements separated by an arbitrary separator character. You can access the elements individually, referencing them via a zero-based index. The list functions somewhat make up for WMLScript's lack of arrays.

Each of these functions accepts as an argument the character to be used as the separator. If the given separator string is longer than a single character, only the first character is used. If the argument is an empty string, all of the list functions will return `invalid`. Elements can be the empty string.

elementAt: Return the Element at a Given Index

Syntax: `String.elementAt(`*list*`, `*index*`, `*delim*`)`

Arguments: Any string, an index, and a separator character.

Returns: The given element from the list. If `index` is less than zero, zero is used; if `index` is greater than the number of elements in the list, the last element is returned. If the list is empty, an empty string is returned.

Exceptions: None.

Example:
```
var s = "How now, brown cow?";
String.elementAt(s, 0, " ");    // "How"
String.elementAt(s, 1, ",");    // "brown cow?"
String.elementAt(s, 10, ",");   // "brown cow?"
String.elementAt(s, 10, "?");   // ""
String.elementAt(s, -5, " ");   // "How"
String.elementAt(s, 1, "");     // invalid
```

elements: Return the Number of Elements in the List

Syntax: `String.elements(`*list*`, `*delim*`)`

Arguments: Any string and a separator character.

Returns: The number of elements in the string. The empty string is a valid element, so the result will always be at least 1.

Exceptions: None.

Example:
```
var s= "How now, brown cow?";
String.elements(s, " ");        // 4
String.elements(s, ",junk");    // 2
String.elements(s, "o");        // 5
String.elements(s, "?");        // 2
String.elements("", ":");       // 1
String.elements("a", ":");      // 1
String.elements(":", ":");      // 2
String.elements(" a  b ", ' '); // 4
```

insertAt: Insert an Element at a Given Index

Syntax: `String.insertAt(list, new, index, delim)`

Arguments: Any string, a new element, an index, and a separator character.

Returns: A copy of the list, with the new element inserted at the position given by the index. If index is less than zero, zero is used; if index is greater than the number of elements in the list, the new element is appended to the end. If the list is empty, the new string is returned.

Exceptions: None.

Example:
```
var s = "A B, C";
String.insertAt(s, "z", 0, " ");      // "z A B, C"
String.insertAt(s, "z", 1, " ");      // "A z B, C"
String.insertAt(s, "z", 10, " ");     // "A B, C z"
String.insertAt(s, "z", 1, ",");      // "A B,z, C"
String.insertAt(s, "z", 10, ",");     // "A B, C,z");
String.insertAt("", "new", 1, ",");   // "new"
```

removeAt: Remove the Element at a Given Index

Syntax: `String.removeAt(list, index, delim)`

Arguments: Any string, an index, and a separator character.

Returns: A copy of the list, with the given element and its adjacent separator (if any) removed. If index is less than zero, zero is used; if index is greater than the number of elements in the list, the last element is removed. If the list is empty, an empty string is returned.

Exceptions: None.

Example:
```
var s = "How now, brown cow?";
String.removeAt(s, 1, " ");     // "How brown cow?"
String.elementAt(s, 0, ",");    // "brown cow?"
String.elementAt(s, 25, " ");   // "How now, brown"
```

replaceAt: Replace the Element at a Given Index

Syntax: `String.replaceAt(list, new, index, delim)`

Arguments: Any string, a new element, an index, and a separator character.

Returns: A copy of the list, with the given element replaced with the new one. If index is less than zero, zero is used; if index is greater than the number of elements in the list, the last element is replaced. If the list is empty, an new element is returned.

Exceptions: None.

Example:
```
var s = "A B, C";
String.replaceAt(s, "z", 0, " ");      // "z B, C"
String.replaceAt(s, "x", 10, ",");     // "A B,x"
String.replaceAt("", "new", 1, ",");   // "new"
```

URL: Uniform Resource Locator Operations

The **URL** library contains a number of specialized string manipulation functions for working with Uniform Resource Locators. At present the library does not support all valid forms of URLs, as defined by RFC 2396, but it does support the common forms that you will need most often. Both absolute and relative URLs are supported. Note that, except in the case of `resolve()`, relative URLs are not automatically resolved into absolute URLs.

Query and Manipulation Functions

escapeString: Convert URL Special Characters to Escape Sequences

Syntax: `URL.escapeString(x)`

Arguments: Any string.

Returns: A copy of the string with any occurrences of special characters (as specified in RFC 2396) replaced with a hexadecimal escape sequence. No URL parsing or checking is performed; the entire string presented is escaped.

Exceptions: Returns `invalid` if the input string contains characters with a code higher than 0xFF.

Example:
```
URL.escapeString("http://host.com/path/a.wml");
    // "http%3A%2F%2Fhost.com%2Fpath%2Fa.wml"
URL.escapeString("script?X=\u007F#id");
    // "script%3FX%3D%7F%23id'"
```

The following characters will be escaped:

```
; / ? : " @ & = + $ , { } | \ ^ [ ] ` < > # %
```

In addition, the characters with the codes 0x00–0x20, 0x7F, and 0x8F–0xFF will be escaped.

getBase: Return the URL of the Current WMLScript File

Syntax: URL.getBase()

Arguments: None.

Returns: The absolute URL (without any fragment) of the resource containing the currently executing function.

Exceptions: None.

Example: var s = URL.getBase();
// "http://host.com/test.wmls" (perhaps)

getReferer Return the URL of the Caller

Syntax: URL.getReferer()

Arguments: None.

Returns: The smallest possible relative URL to the resource that called the resource containing the currently executing function, or the empty string if no referrer exists. Calls to functions within the same compilation unit do not change the referrer. (For historical reasons, "referer" is misspelled.)

Exceptions: None.

Example: URL.getReferer(); // "app.wml#card2" (perhaps)

> The requirement that the result be the "smallest possible" relative URL is somewhat vague and is likely to be interpreted differently between implementations. You should not assume that the result will be in any particular format.

isValid: Test Whether a URL Is Well Formed

Syntax: URL.isValid(url)

Arguments: Any string.

Returns: Returns true if url is a syntactically valid (with respect to the supported subset of RFC 2396 syntax) absolute or relative URL; false otherwise.

Exceptions: None.

Example: URL.isValid("http://host.com/script#func()"); // true
                URL.isValid("http://host.com/scr?%x")   // false
                URL.isValid("../common/test";   // true
                URL.isValid("http://host.com/bad>");   // false
                URL.isValid("exper?://host.com");   // true

> You may receive differing results if your URL includes some of the newer features of RFC2396 or uses one of the more obscure forms, such as in the last example above.

loadString: Retrieve Text Content Specified by a URL

Syntax: URL.loadString(*url*, *contenttype*)

Arguments: Any URL and an expected content type.

Returns: The text content retrieved from the specified URL.

Exceptions: Returns invalid if the specified content type is erroneous. Returns a scheme-specific integer error code if the content could not be retrieved.

Example: var s =
                URL.loadString("http://host.com/vcards/amy.vcf",
                               "text/x-vcard");
                var s = URL.loadString("http://host.com/test.wml",
                                       "text/vnd.wap.wml");

The loadString() function retrieves text content from a Web server. You must specify the MIME type of the content that you expect to get back; this value must be a text type, and it must match the type returned by the server exactly—no leading spaces or differences of capitalization are allowed. Any text subtype is permissible. You could, for example, retrieve a WML deck or a WMLScript program, although you probably have no reason to do so.

If an error occurs, you will receive a scheme-specific error code; for "http" requests, WMLScript generates an HTTP status code as defined in RFC 2616. If an incorrect content type is specified, loadString() should return invalid. Some ambiguity exists as to whether you should receive an error or invalid if you specify one text type and get back a different text type.

resolve: Resolve a Relative URL to a Base

Syntax: String.resolve(*baseurl*, *relativeurl*)

Arguments: Strings representing a base and relative URLs.

Returns: An absolute URL from the given base and relative URLs, complying with the rules specified in RFC 2396. If the path component of baseurl is not present, then a single slash character ("/") is assumed as the path. If the string given for relativeurl is already an absolute URL, it is returned without any modification.

Exceptions: Returns invalid if either of the URLs specified is malformed.

Example:
```
URL.resolve("http://host.com/", "deck.wml);
    // "http://host.com/deck.wml"
URL.resolve("http://host.com", "?x=1");
    // "http://host.com/?x=1"
URL.resolve("http://", "deck.wml");   // invalid
```

unescapeString: Convert URL Escape Sequences to Characters

Syntax: URL.unescapeString(*x*)

Arguments: Any string.

Returns: A copy of the string with any occurrences of URL escape sequences (as specified in RFC 2396) replaced with the characters they represent. No URL parsing or checking is performed.

Exceptions: Returns invalid if the input string contains characters with a code higher than 0xFF.

Example:
```
URL.unescapeString("http%3A%2F%2Fhost.com%2Fpath%2Fa.wml");
    // "http://host.com/path/a.wml"
URL.unescapeString("x=y+b");   // "x=y b"
URL.unescapeString("http://host.com/scr?%x");
    // "http://host.com/scr?%x"
```

Parsing Functions

The parsing functions allow you to extract segments from a URL. All of these functions support both absolute and relative URLs; relative URLs are not automatically resolved, however. In addition, all will return invalid if the URL does not appear syntactically correct, but the level of syntax checking applied will vary by browser.

> WMLScript does not support all of the newer URL features described by RFC 2396. If your URLs deviate from the common "scheme, host, port, path, parameters, query, fragment" form, your results may vary.

getFragment: Return the Fragment Segment

Syntax: URL.getFragment(*url*)

Arguments: A URL.

Returns: The fragment segment of the URL (the portion following the "#" character), or an empty string if no fragment is present.

Exceptions: Returns invalid if the URL is not syntactically correct.

Example: URL.getFragment(
       "http://host.com:80/apps/script;x;y?x=1#frag");
                               // "frag"
       URL.getFragment("../common/test");   // ""

getHost: Return the Host Segment

Syntax: URL.getHost(*url*)

Arguments: A URL.

Returns: The host portion of the URL, or an empty string if no host portion is present.

Exceptions: Returns invalid if the URL is not syntactically correct.

Example: URL.getHost("http://host.com:80/apps/script;x;y?x=1#frag");
                                   // "host.com"
       URL.getHost("../common/test)";   // ""
       URL.getHost("xyz://host.com");   // "host.com"
       URL.getHost("http://user@host.com#frag") // "host.com"

getParameters: Return the Last Parameters Segment

Syntax: URL.getParameters(*url*)

Arguments: A URL.

Returns: The parameters used in the last path segment of the URL, or an
empty string if no parameters are present. It is not possible to
retrieve parameters specified for any other path segment.

Exceptions: Returns `invalid` if the URL is not syntactically correct.

Example: `URL.getParameters(`
```
        "http://host.com:80/apps/script;x;y?x=1#frag");
                                                    // "x;y"
    URL.getParameters("../common/test");            // ""
    URL.getParameters("host.com/a;x/b;y=1/c;z")  // "z"
```

getPath: Return the Path Segment

Syntax: `URL.getPath(url)`

Arguments: A URL.

Returns: The path portion of the URL or an empty string if no path portion is present. Neither fragment identifiers nor parameters are
considered part of the path segment.

Exceptions: Returns `invalid` if the URL is not syntactically correct.

Example:
```
    URL.getPath("http://host.com:80/apps/script;x;y?x=1#frag");
                                        // "/apps/script"
    URL.getPath("..//common/test");   // "../common/test"
    URL.getPath("http://host.com/")   // "/"
    URL.getPath("http://host.com")    // ""
    URL.getPath("http://host.com/a;x/b;y=1/c;z");  // "/a/b/c"
```

getPort: Return the Port Segment

Syntax: `URL.getPort(url)`

Arguments: A URL.

Returns: The port segment of the URL, or an empty string if no port is
present.

Exceptions: Returns `invalid` if the URL is not syntactically correct.

Example:
```
    URL.getPort("http://host.com:80/apps/script;x;y?x=1#frag");
                                        // "80"
    URL.getPort("..//common/test");   // ""
```

getQuery: Return the Query Parameters Segment

Syntax: URL.getQuery(*url*)

Arguments: A URL.

Returns: The query parameters segment of the URL, or an empty string if no query parameters are present.

Exceptions: Returns invalid if the URL is not syntactically correct.

Example: URL.getQuery(
        "http://host.com:80/apps/script;x;y?x=1#frag");
                                     // "x=1"
       URL.getQuery("..//common/test");   // ""
       URL.getQuery("..//script?");   // ""

getScheme: Return the Scheme Segment

Syntax: URL.getScheme(*url*)

Arguments: A URL.

Returns: The scheme segment of the URL, or an empty string if no scheme is present.

Exceptions: Returns invalid if the URL is not syntactically correct.

Example: URL.getScheme(
        "http://host.com:80/apps/script;x;y?x=1#frag");
                                       // "http"
       URL.getScheme("..//common/test");   // ""
       URL.getScheme("xyz://host.com");   // "xyz"

WMLBrowser: Browser Control

The functions in the **WMLBrowser** library enable you to exercise control over the browser from your program. In particular, you have access to basic navigation operations and the ability to read and write WML variables.

If your device allows WMLScript programs to execute outside of a WML browser (and none does at present), calling any function in this library will return a result of invalid. Until such a device actually exists, you can safely ignore this possibility.

Navigation Functions

The go() and prev() functions allow a WMLScript program to initiate navigation in the browser. These WMLScript functions are similar to the

WML tasks <go> and <prev>, except that they do not take effect immediately. Instead, navigation is deferred until the program returns control to the browser. If your program executes more than one go() or prev() call before exiting, each call overwrites the previous request, and only the final one will take effect.

If you call go() with an empty string as an argument, no navigation will be performed when the program exits, and the browser's current card will remain unchanged. You can take advantage of this feature to cancel a previously issued go() or prev() call.

If you make use of referer information on the server, note that WMLScript programs never act as the referer. Instead, the referer will consist of the URL of the previous WML card.

go: Navigate to New Content

Syntax: WMLBrowser.go(*url*)

Arguments: Any URL.

Returns: An empty string.

Exceptions: None.

Example: WMLBrowser.go("http://host.com/deck.wml#c1");

Similar to the WML <go> task, go() directs the browser to navigate to the new content identified by the URL once the current program is complete. This instruction supersedes any previous navigation request (go() or prev()). If an empty string is specified, no navigation occurs and any previous request is canceled.

newContext: Create a New Browser Context

Syntax: WMLBrowser.newContext()

Arguments: None.

Returns: An empty string.

Exceptions: None.

Example: WMLBrowser.newContext();

This call instructs the browser to create a new browser context. It is similar to specifying newcontext="true" on a WML <go> task, except that it ignores navigation status. WML variables defined in the previous context are no longer available, although WMLScript variables remain unaffected. The browser's navigation history is reduced to a single entry—the card from which the WMLScript program was invoked. Any pending navigation from a previous go() call is unaffected.

prev: Return to the Previous Card

Syntax: WMLBrowser.prev()

Arguments: None.

Returns: An empty string.

Exceptions: None.

Example: WMLBrowser.prev();

Similar to the WML <prev> task, prev() directs the browser to navigate to the previous card once the current program is complete. This instruction supersedes any previous navigation request (go() or prev()).

Other Functions

getCurrentCard: Return the URL of the Current Card

Syntax: WMLBrowser.getCurrentCard()

Arguments: None.

Returns: The URL of the browser's current card, as the smallest possible URL relative to the current compilation unit or as an absolute URL if a relative URL is not possible.

Exceptions: None.

Example: WMLBrowser.getCurrentCard();

> The requirement that the result be the "smallest possible" relative URL is somewhat vague and is likely to be interpreted differently between implementations. You should not assume that the result will be in any particular format.

getVar: Retrieve a WML Variable

Syntax: WMLBrowser.getVar(*varname*)

Arguments: A legal WML variable name.

Returns: The value of the named variable in the current browser context, or an empty string if the variable does not have a value.

Exceptions: Returns invalid if the variable name given is illegal.

Example: WMLBrowser.getVar("dob");   // "Jun 9" (perhaps)
WMLBrowser.getVar("%bogus"); // invalid

refresh: Refresh the User Interface

Syntax: WMLBrowser.refresh()

Arguments: None.

Returns: An empty string if the refresh was successful, or an error message if it failed.

Exceptions: Returns invalid if immediate refresh is not supported.

Example: WMLBrowser.refresh();

The refresh() function tells the browser to update the user interface based on the current context, just as if a WML <refresh> task had been executed. If the implementation supports the immediate refresh capability, the WMLScript program will be suspended while the interface is updated. If the browser has not yet rendered the card (for example, if the program was called from an onenterforward binding in the card), the refresh operation will force it to be displayed. If the system does not support immediate refresh, this call will return invalid and the refresh will occur when the program ends.

The refresh() function differs from the WML refresh task in one way: If a timer was suspended when the script was executed, refresh() does not cause it to resume. It will, however, resume ticking when the script ends.

If the refresh() call fails for some reason, it will return a nonempty string. This string is expected to be a brief message explaining the error.

setVar: Set a WML Variable

Syntax: WMLBrowser.setVar(*varname*, *newvalue*)

Arguments: A legal WML variable name and value.

Returns: A Boolean: `true` if the variable was set successfully, `false` if an error occurred.

Exceptions: Returns `invalid` if the variable name or value given is illegal.

Example: `WMLBrowser.setVar("dob", "Mar 14"); // true`
`WMLBrowser.setVar("%bogus", "xyz"); // invalid`

Dialogs: Basic User Interface Functions

The **Dialogs** library lets your program interact with the user. The expressive range of the functions found in this library is rather limited, even by WML standards. Most of the user interface should be handled in WML.

alert: Display a Message

Syntax: `Dialogs.alert(msg)`

Arguments: Any string.

Returns: An empty string.

Exceptions: None.

Example: `Dialogs.alert("You are in a maze of twisty,`
`little passages, all different.");`

The `alert()` function displays a message and suspends program execution until the user presses a key.

confirm: Ask the User for Confirmation

Syntax: `Dialogs.confirm(msg, oklabel, cancellabel)`

Arguments: Any string and labels for OK and Cancel. If an empty string is specified for either label, the system default is used.

Returns: A Boolean: `true` if the user selected "OK"; `false` if the user selected "Cancel."

Exceptions: None.

Example: `b = Dialogs.confirm("Are you sure?", "Yes", "No");`
`b = Dialogs.confirm("Are you sure?", "", "");`

If the device supports dynamic labeling of controls, such as soft keys or pop-up menus, the given labels will be used. Otherwise, the OK and Cancel actions will be mapped to two implementation-defined controls. You may specify appropriate labels, as in the preceding example, but you should ensure that the prompt would make reasonable sense if the labels "OK" and "Cancel" were used instead. As in WML, try to keep your labels to six characters or fewer to minimize the likelihood that they will be truncated.

---

prompt: Ask for Input

Syntax: `Dialogs.prompt(`*`msg`*`, `*`default`*`)`

Arguments: Any string and a default answer.

Returns: The user's input.

Exceptions: None.

Example: `Dialogs.prompt("What is your name?", "Arthur Dent");`

The interpreter displays the given message and prompts the user for input. The string *default* contains the initial value of the input. Keep your message brief, as some browsers may truncate it.

Other WMLScript Libraries

In addition to the core WMLScript libraries, the WAP Forum has defined two optional application libraries: the **Crypto** library provides cryptographic operations, and the **WTAI** library provides an interface to telephony functions.

Crypto Library Overview

The WMLScript **Crypto** library provides a WAP client with cryptographic functions that are callable from a WMLScript program. In WAP June 2000, the library includes only a single function, providing for digital signatures. The **Crypto** library is optional, so it may not be present in all implementations.

signText: Allow the User to Sign a Text String

Syntax: Crypto.signText(*text*, *options*, *keytype*, *keyid*)

Arguments: A string containing text to be signed, a integer specifying signing options, an integer identifying the type of key identifier, and a key identifier.

Returns: A string containing the base-64 encoding of the signed string, "error:noCert" if no proper certificate or signature key is available, or "error:userCancel" if the user aborted the signing operation.

Exceptions: Returns invalid if any parameter is incorrect, or if an encoding error occurs.

Example: var Bill = "Bill: A Tale of Two Cities, $9.95";
var Res = Crypto.signText(Bill, 0, 1,
   "\x37\x00\xB6\x96\x37\x75\xE3\x93\x48\x74\xD3
\x98\x47\x53\x94\x34\x58\x97\xB5\xD6");

The signText() function supports applications, such as electronic commerce, that require persistent proof that a particular person has authorized a transaction. It displays a string of text to the user for confirmation; once acknowledged, the user's digital signature is attached to the data, which can then be sent across the network to a server. The server can use the signature as it sees fit, such as to validate the transaction, store it for audit and accounting purposes, and so on.

The *options* parameter is a set of flags, which can be ORed together. The following values are valid arguments:

0x0001   Include content. If set, the browser must include in the result the string to be signed.

0x0002   Include key hash. If set, the browser must include in the result the hash of the public key that corresponds to the signature key.

0x0004   Include certificate. If set, the browser must include in the result either the certificate or a URL referring to the certificate. If a certificate is not available, the function will fail and "error:noCert" will be returned.

The *keytype* parameter is an integer specifying the type of key identifier in the *keyid* parameter. The following values are valid arguments:

ø No key identifier is supplied. The browser may use any key and certificate that is available.

1 A SHA-1 (Secure Hash Algorithm) hash of the user public key is supplied in *keyid*. The browser must use the signature key that corresponds to the given public key hash. If this key is not available, the function will fail and return "error:noCert."

2 A SHA-1 hash of one or more trusted certificate authority (CA) public keys is supplied in *keyid*. The browser must use a signature key that is certified by one or more of the indicated CAs. If no such key is available, the function will fail and return "error:noCert."

If a SHA-1 hash is specified, then *keyid* is one or more 20-byte hash values that identify the key. Multiple values are concatenated, and the number of values provided is implied by the length of the *keyid* string.

WTAI Overview

The Wireless Telephony Application Interface (WTAI) provides access to telephony services for applications running in both the standard WAP Application Environment (WAE) user agent and the WTA user agent (see Chapter 13). Three types of WTAI libraries exist: *public*, *network common*, and *network-specific*. As its name implies, the public library contains functions that are made available to any third-party applications. In contrast, the network libraries are accessible only to applications running inside the WTA user agent. Obviously, the functions are supported on a telephone device only; attempting to use them on other devices will trigger some type of vendor-specific error mechanism.

WTAI functions can be accessed from WMLScript functions through the standard external function call syntax (see "Function Invocation"). Functions in the public library can also be called directly from WML via URLs using the "wtai" scheme:

```
wtai://library/function;parameterlist!resultlist
```

In this statement, the *parameterlist* field contains zero or more parameters to be passed to the function. The *resultlist* consists of the names of zero or more variable names to receive the results of the function call. Entries in both lists are delimited with semicolons (;). Each function defines the number and form of the parameters it accepts and the results it returns. If the caller does not need to check the result, the exclamation point and

Table 9-9   WTAI Error Codes

Code	Description
Ø	No error
-1	ID not found
-2	Incorrect number of parameters
-3	Service not available or function does not exist
-4	Service temporarily unavailable
-5	Called party is busy
-6	Network is busy
-7	No answer or call setup timed out
-8	Unknown error
-9	Out of memory
-10 to -63	Reserved for future standard library use
-64 to -127	Network-specific codes

resultlist can be omitted from the URL. Table 9-9 lists the relevant WTAI error codes.

Many of the functions require a phone number as an argument, which you can supply in either international or national format; international numbers begin with a plus sign ("+"). Phone numbers must consist of digits only: "Numbers" such as 800-CALL-ME are not acceptable and instead must be mapped to the corresponding numeric sequence. Likewise, spaces, hyphens, periods, parentheses, and other non-numeric characters are not allowed.

This section will describe the public libraries only briefly. Chapter 13 discusses the network common and network specific libraries in more detail.

Public WTAI Functions

The public library functions should eventually be available on all WAP telephone devices, although support was decidedly lacking at the time that this book was written. In addition, no "library discovery" mechanism had yet been created, so you may find it difficult to determine whether the user's device is a telephone. In the future, you should be able to determine the set of available WMLScript libraries through the UAProf mechanism, which is described in Chapter 11.

Make Call

Syntax: `wtai://wp/mc;`*number*`!result`
        `result = WTAPublic.makeCall(`*number*`);`

Arguments: Destination number to call.

Returns: Zero if successful or a WTAI error code otherwise.

Example: `"wtai://wp/mc;5551234"`
         `WTAPublic.makeCall("5551234");`

The Make Call function is used to initiate a call to the specified number. The number must be displayed to the user, and the user must explicitly acknowledge that the call should be initiated. The user ends the call by using the normal mechanism of the device.

Send DTMF Tones

Syntax: `wtai://wp/sd;dtmfseq!result`
        `result = WTAPublic.sendDTMF(dtmfseq);`

Arguments: A sequence of DTMF characters.

Returns: Zero if successful or a WTAI error code otherwise.

Example: `"wtai://wp/sd;555*1234"`
         `WTAPublic.sendDTMF("555*1234");`

You can use the Send DTMF Tones function to transmit DTMF tones through an active voice connection. The following are valid DTMF characters:

`0 1 2 3 4 5 6 7 8 9 * # , A B C D`

The implementation decides whether the user must acknowledge each DTMF sequence before it is sent or whether acknowledging the Make Call function implicitly acknowledges all further sequences in the same call.

Add Phonebook Entry

Syntax: `wtai://wp/ap;number;name!result`
        `result = WTAPublic.addPBENtry(number, name);`

Arguments: A phone number to store and the name with which it should be associated.

Returns: Zero if successful or a WTAI error code otherwise.

Example: `"wtai://wp/sd;555*1234"`
              `WTAPublic.sendDTMF("555*1234");`

The Add Phonebook Entry function adds a new entry to the device phonebook at the first available location. The name and number to be added must be displayed to the user, and the user must explicitly acknowledge the addition before it is made.

WMLScript Development

At a recent WAP Developers conference, a speaker asked the audience how many were currently using WMLScript in their applications. Only a few hands went up. The primary obstacles cited were inconsistent WMLScript implementations and inadequate development tools.

On the surface, it is hard to fathom why differences should persist among implementations. Much of WMLScript is similar to other, well-known languages and, unlike with WML, the major portion of WMLScript does not involve any visual elements. It would thus seem to be relatively easy to create a WMLScript-compliant interpreter. On closer examination, however, the standard proves to be less precise than it could be. Not surprisingly, differences between interpreters often arise from gray areas in the specification.

In testing the examples included in this chapter, we found this the case. Most interpreters we tested experienced few problems when the functions were presented with "expected" arguments. The picture was less rosy when type conversions and other boundary conditions were tested.

Fortunately, the situation should improve rapidly. WAP conformance tests are becoming available for testing interpreters, and specification ambiguities revealed during this testing will be addressed. Consistent WMLScript development should soon be possible.

The other major obstacle to development, the lack of adequate tools for writing and debugging WMLScript programs, will no doubt be addressed by enterprising tools developers. In the meantime, debugging is challenging but not impossible. This section includes some tips and hints for successful development. The program templates in Listings 9-10 and 9-11 demonstrate many of the techniques we describe in this section. You can copy the relevant portions into your own WML and WMLScript files.

Bear in mind that debugging code will add to the final size of your decks and scripts. In these examples, the debugging support adds approximately 100 bytes to the WML program and 200 bytes to the WMLScript program. (You can shave a few bytes by using shorter names for variables and cards.)

Listing 9-10   Template for debugging—WML.

```
<wml>
   <card id="c1">
      <p>
         Program Template
         <br/>
         <anchor>Invoke<go href="#runscript">
               <setvar name="sn" value="Template"/>
               <setvar name="fn" value="Main"/>
               <setvar name="rc" value="#done"/>
               <setvar name="ScriptMsg"
                  value="Program loading..."/>
            </go>
         </anchor>
      </p>
   </card>

   <card id="runscript" onenterforward=
         "$(sn).wmls#$(fn)('$(rc:escape)')">
      <onevent type="onenterbackward">
         <prev/>
      </onevent>
      <p>
         $(ScriptMsg)
      </p>
   </card>

   <card id="done">
      <p>
         <a href="#c1">Again</a>
      </p>
   </card>

   <card id="debug">
      <onevent type="onenterforward">
         <go href="#c1">
            <setvar name="Debug1" value="true"/>
            <setvar name="Debug2" value=""/>
         </go>
      </onevent>
      <onevent type="onenterbackward">
         <prev/>
      </onevent>
   </card>
</wml>
```

Listing 9-11   Template for debugging—WMLScript.

```
/*
 * ToStr is a wrapper for String.toString that
 * avoids doing anything if its argument is
 * already a string - some browsers currently
 * don't work properly otherwise.  (Also, "ToStr"
 * is more concise.)
 */

function ToStr(x) {
    return (typeof x == 2 ? x : String.toString(x));
}


/*
 * DebugMsg displays a debug prompt and allows you
 * to continue or abort execution.
 */

function DebugMsg(Msg) {
    if (!isvalid Msg)
        Msg = "(Invalid debug message)";

    if (!Dialogs.confirm(ToStr(Msg), "OK", "Stop"))
        Cleanup(true, "");
}


/*
 * Cleanup resets the debugging and execution
 * environment, and terminates the program.
 *
 * If bPrev is TRUE, the browser is directed to
 * the previous card; otherwise, it is
 * directed to the URL in Next, if any, or
 * control remains in the current card (or
 * any previously queued request executes).
 *
 */

function Cleanup(bPrev, Next) {
    WMLBrowser.setVar("ScriptMsg", "");
    WMLBrowser.refresh();

    for (var i=1; i <= 2; WMLBrowser.setVar("Debug"+ i++, ""))
        ;

    if (bPrev)
        WMLBrowser.prev();
    else if (Next != "")
        WMLBrowser.go(Next);
    Lang.exit("");
}
```

```
extern function Main(Done) {
   Done = URL.unescapeString(Done);

   var Debug1 = WMLBrowser.getVar("Debug1");
   var Debug2 = WMLBrowser.getVar("Debug2");

   WMLBrowser.refresh();

   /*
    * Your code goes here (demo code follows).
    */
   var Seq = "-\\|/";
   var sp = 0;
   for (var j = 1; j <=100 ; j++) {
      if (!(j%10)) {
         WMLBrowser.setVar("ScriptMsg", String.charAt(Seq, sp++));
         WMLBrowser.refresh();
         sp %= 4;
      }

      var x = Lang.random(10);

      if (Debug1) DebugMsg("j=" + ToStr(j) + " x=" + ToStr(x));
   }

   Dialogs.alert("Final x=" + x);

   Cleanup(false, Done);
}
```

Asking for Trouble

At present, you will find that the "ounce of prevention" axiom will serve you well. First and foremost, keep your scripts short, simple, and self-contained. The more enterprising you are, the less likely that the program will work across all browsers without modification. In fact, you may have no choice but to think small: A single WMLScript compilation unit will be subject to the same size restrictions as a WML deck. As we discussed in Chapter 7, you should strive to keep the binary size of a single transmission unit to under one kilobyte.

A second potential source of trouble with current browsers is implicit data type conversions. In testing the examples in this chapter, conversion problems accounted for the lion's share of incompatibilities, so try to perform conversions explicitly when you need them. The program in Listing 9-11 illustrates this point by explicitly calling String.toString() whenever a string is needed. (The program actually defines a wrapper function for `toString()`, `ToStr()`, that avoids making the conversion if the argument is already a string. At the time that this book was written, some browsers did not handle a string argument properly, making this extra check necessary.)

What Is Going On?

The current crop of SDKs lacks many features that would facilitate debugging. Niceties such as single-step execution, breakpoints, and the ability to examine and change variables while the program is running generally do not exist. The basic tool on which you must rely is the use of **Dialogs** library function calls to display and change information. Even that can be a challenge: In some development environments, it is difficult or impossible to halt a script while it is displaying a dialog. To escape from an infinite loop containing a dialog, you may have to kill the SDK. Nevertheless, the **Dialogs** functions are indispensable, as they are the only standard tools you have. Some implementations have started to include additional debugging libraries as well, which can be an extra help.

The function `DebugMsg()` in our template demonstrates one approach. The important lines follow:

```
if (!Dialogs.confirm(ToStr(Msg), "OK", "Stop"))
    Cleanup(true, "");
```

Note the use of `confirm()` instead of `alert()`: If you cancel the dialog by selecting the "Stop" action, the program directs itself to stop execution.

An important question, particularly when dealing with a deployed application, is how debugging messages should be enabled. Our template demonstrates one very simple approach. In the WML deck, card "c1" represents the main card of the application. Although here it is a menu containing just one option, in reality it could be any type of card. The card "debug" is used to enable the debug messages. This task is accomplished indirectly by setting one or more variables to `true`. Here, `Debug1` is enabled and `Debug2` is not:

```
<card id="debug">
    <onevent type="onenterforward">
        <go href="#c1">
            <setvar name="Debug1" value="true"/>
            <setvar name="Debug2" value=""/>
        </go>
    </onevent>
```

When debugging is desired, you simply invoke the application deck with the "#debug" card appended: after the variables are set, control is redirected to card "c1," the application's entry point. The WMLScript program can then check which sets of debug messages are enabled and display whatever information you wish:

```
var Debug1 = WMLBrowser.getVar("Debug1");
...
if (Debug1) DebugMsg("j=" + ToStr(j) + " x=" + ToStr(x));
```

You can extend this basic technique in any number of ways. For example, instead of using a Boolean value as the switch, you might set a counter, triggering debugging after a certain number of times through a loop. Alternatively, rather than using a static card as the debug entry point, your application might call a server-side script, which sets the debugging variables based on some dynamic information such as the `referer` header.

Usability Issues

When your program invokes a WMLScript, you may have to give some thought as to how it will affect the user's experience. Many browsers do not give any indication that a script is running, so if your program takes a while to execute, the user may conclude that the device is hung. To avoid confusion, you should let the user know when a delay is likely to occur.

A related issue is that scripts execute "within" the current card in the browser. That characteristic is frequently desirable, such as when you are validating input. However, when the program is more involved, you will probably want to navigate to a blank card first to give the script a blank "playground." This is especially true when you want to display messages from the script while it is executing.

The template program demonstrates a few different techniques that you can use singly or in combination to give feedback to the user. First, the WML deck includes a card, "runscript," that serves as the execution backdrop for the script. This card contains a single variable, `ScriptMsg`, which is initially set to "Program Loading." The program can update this variable to display information without pausing to wait for the user to confirm the message.

The name of the script file to load, the function to execute, and the card to which to return are all specified through WML variables. If you execute the template example as shown, the script call will resolve to the following statement:

```
onenterforward="Template.wmls#Main('%23done')"
```

If you use this technique more than once within your application, you should move the "runscript" card into its own deck, so that the browser can cache it separately.

The function `Main()`, in the WMLScript file, demonstrates the use of the `ScriptMsg` variable to display a progress indicator (a "spinner," in this case, though it is even easier to just update the variable with a message). The variable `Seq` contains the characters that will be displayed in sequence to make the spinner spin; the variable `sp` is the pointer to the character to display next. The `sp` variable is incremented after it is used and kept within the bounds of the string by using the remainder operator (%). Note the call to `refresh()` to ask the browser to display the message.

```
var Seq = "-\\|/";
var sp = 0;
for (var j = 1; j <=100 ; j++) {
   if (!(j%10)) {
      WMLBrowser.setVar("ScriptMsg",
         String.charAt(Seq, sp++));
      WMLBrowser.refresh();
      sp %= 4;
   }
}
```

Because each screen update takes some time, you need to balance the feedback you give to the user against its effect on total execution time. In the example, the spinner is updated only on every tenth iteration of the loop.

Other Gotchas

Before we close this section, we want to mention a few final things that can cause you confusion or headaches.

The Invalid Effect

If any expression involves `invalid` as an operand, its result almost always becomes `invalid`. Although this result is not too surprising when it occurs in mathematical statements, first-time WMLScript developers may be caught off guard when it affects a string expression. In this fragment, `Msg` takes on the value `invalid`, not `"x=invalid"`.

```
var x = 1/0;
var Msg = "x=" + x;
```

A similar problem occurs if you try to test a value for `invalid` using the `==` or `!=` operator. Although `if (x != invalid)` seems perfectly natural, it will always evaluate to `invalid`. The correct approach is to use the `isvalid` operator.

Finally, the functions in the **Dialogs** library, when passed `invalid` as a parameter, quietly do nothing at all. (Well, not quite: They return `invalid`, but who checks?) In this example, because `Msg` has the value `invalid`, the call to `alert` effectively vanishes:

```
var Msg = "x=" + 1/0;
Dialogs.alert(Msg);
```

The way to avoid being snared in this case is to call `String.toString()` for each of your operands in a string expression. This action will convert any operand that has managed to take on the value `invalid` to the string `"invalid"`—ensuring that it will, at least, show up. A second line of defense, as demonstrated in the function `DebugMsg()`, is to check whether the message to be displayed is `invalid` and adjust it accordingly. You will not be able to tell what the message was supposed to say, but it will at least immediately clue you in that a problem occurred.

Exchanging Data with WML

As we mentioned briefly in the section "Function Invocation," while invoking functions and passing arguments from within WMLScript is straightforward, calling WMLScript from WML involves a few wrinkles. To pass data as function arguments, you must remember that WML views the WMLScript call as a URL, causing the call to become subject to all of the usual URL restrictions.

Pay particular attention to any static data that you are passing to the WMLScript function: All special characters (see the list handled by `URL.escapeString()` in "escapeString: Convert URL Special Characters to Escape Sequences") must be manually converted to escape sequences. (If the values are being passed from WML variables, WML will handle the conversions.) Enclose each parameter in single or double quotes, then use the other type of quote to enclose the entire URL. Within your WMLScript program, you must remember to decode the argument values by calling `URL.unescapeString()`.

An alternative approach is possible if you are willing to closely couple the WML and WMLScript programs. Rather than relying on passing arguments, you can have the program retrieve the required data from the

WML variables itself. Aside from the coupling issue, neither option provides any real benefit relative to the other.

Regardless of how you pass the data, remember that WMLScript will receive it as string values. Although the implicit conversions will usually do the right thing, do not forget the troublesome + operator. It is safest to always call `Lang.parseInt()` on any argument that is expected to be numeric.

Binary WMLScript

The standard also defines a compact binary representation for WMLScript to enable efficient transmission. This section provides only a very high-level overview of the binary encoding; for further details, you should refer to the WMLScript standard.

A binary WMLScript unit consists of a header, a constant pool, a pragma pool, and a function pool (Figure 9-5). Square brackets ("[" and "]") enclose optional elements, and bracketed ellipses ("[...]") indicate that the preceding entity can be repeated. Many of the values are stored as multibyte numbers, as in Binary XML (discussed in Chapter 8).

The Bytecode Header

The header encodes the version number of the WMLScript bytecode and the size of the binary data. Note that the version number refers to the bytecode encoding, not to the level of the WMLScript standard being encoded.

```
bytecode      :=      header constants pragmas functions

header        :=      version codesize
constants     :=      number charset [constant [...]]
pragmas       :=      number [pragma [...]]
functions     :=      number externtable function [...]

constant      :=      ctype cvalue
pragma        :=      ptype pvalue
externtable   :=      number name [...]
name          :=      funcindex namelength namestring

function      :=      numargs numlocals codesize codearray
```

Figure 9-5 Binary WMLScript format

WMLScript 1.1, 1.2, and June 2000 (1.2.1) are all encoded with WMLScript bytecode version 1.1. The version number is encoded as a byte, with the upper four bits specifying the major version minus one and the lower four bits specifying the minor version. For example, version 1.1 is encoded as 0x01. The code size is a 32-bit multibyte number, giving the size of the bytecode excluding the header.

The Constant Pool

The constant pool consists of the count of constants in the pool (a 16-bit multibyte number), the character encoding (a 16-bit multibyte value), and the constant entries. The character encoding is an IANA MIBenum value, specifying which character set was used to encode the string constants. Each entry consists of an 8-bit type code and a type-specific representation.

The Pragma Pool

The pragma pool consists of the count of pragma entries (a 16-bit multibyte number) followed by the pragma entries. Each entry is an 8-bit type code and a type-specific encoding. No binary encoding is provided for named and HTTP-equiv meta-data, as neither type of information is intended for use by the browser.

The Function Pool

The function pool consists of the count of functions in the pool (an 8-bit number), a table defining the names of all externally visible functions, and the functions themselves. The table is a count of the external functions only, the index of the function in the pool, the length of the function name, and the UTF-8 encoded name. Functions that are not externally visible are referenced only by function index; their textual names are lost when the file is converted to binary format.

Each function is encoded as the number of arguments it expects (an 8-bit number), the number of local variables used (an 8-bit number), the size of the code (a 32-bit multibyte value), and the code array. The code array contains the actual WMLScript assembly-level instructions that make up the function. The instruction codes can be found in the WMLScript standard.

Conclusion

WMLScript provides a rich programming environment that supplements WML rendering. It can be used to great effect to provide a more dynamic and responsive user interface. Moreover, the WMLScript **Crypto** library enables secure e-commerce applications. As WAP clients mature, WMLScript will undoubtedly take on an ever more important role.

The WTAI functions represent a significant departure from traditional Web scripting and WAP scripting. These functions enable the convergence between data and telephony services—the essence of the WAP promise. A special Wireless Telephony Application (WTA) user agent running on the device supports these telephony operations. In Chapter 13, we discuss the operation of this user agent and explore in depth how telephony applications are written.

As we have seen in the last few chapters, user interface design for small WAP devices requires careful consideration of usability, and the programming task is complicated further by the broad variations among devices and browser implementations. In Chapter 10, we turn our attention to application usability for the mobile environment. As we will see, successful application development for this market also requires discipline and iteration.

Chapter 10

User Interface Design: Making Wireless Applications Easy to Use

The number of available WML pages is growing at an extraordinary pace. In January 2000, approximately 25,000 WML pages were available, and by the time of this book's printing in September 2000, this number had grown to 4.4 million. Thus, end users will have many choices regarding which sites they visit to find the information they want. The sites they choose, among other things, will be those that they find easy to use. To end users, of course, the user interface of the site *is* the product. That is, the vast majority of their experience with the product is with its user interface.

WML-based Web sites provide usage-sensitive services. Unlike hardware products that generate revenue based on the initial purchase, these services generate revenue based on the number of customers who use them and the number of times each customer accesses them. If customers do not use the services, then the services do not generate revenue. If customers have difficulty using a service, they will not use it as much as they would have otherwise—if they use it at all.

Unlike with hardware products, the barriers to *churn* (that is, people returning the product and no longer using it) are low for usage sensitive services. If customers try your WML-based service and find it too difficult to use, they can readily look for and possibly find a different, more user-friendly site. (They do not even have to find the receipt to return your service!)

Usable products and services can achieve an 80 percent increase in revenue because usability influences customer buying decisions.[1] These usability advantages can be achieved even as development costs are reduced. For example, early detection and resolution of usability issues can reduce the development cycle time by 33 to 50 percent.[2] In addition, 64 percent of software life-cycle costs are attributable to *unmet* or *unseen* user requirements and occur after the product is released; in contrast, only 16 percent of these costs are related to bugs or reliability problems.[3]

Web Site Design: Computer Terminals versus Mobile Terminals

User interface design for display on a computer terminal is very different from user interface design for display on a mobile terminal, for several reasons:

- The device is different.
- The network is different.
- The user is different.

The Device Is Different

Traditional Web sites are designed to be shown on desktop computers that have highly capable displays. These computer monitors typically can display anywhere from hundreds to millions of colors, and they have resolutions ranging from 640 pixels wide by 480 pixels high to 1600 pixels wide by 1200 pixels high—and someday even more (Figure 10-1). Currently, Web sites and applications also expect users to have highly capable input devices (such as a mouse or trackball), which enable the users to point to any group of pixels on the Web page and select them. In

---

[1]Wixon and Jones, 1991.

[2]Bosert, 1991.

[3]Karat, 1993.

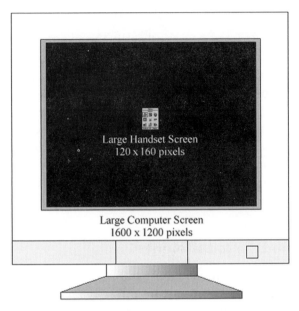

Large Handset Screen
120 x 160 pixels

Large Computer Screen
1600 x 1200 pixels

Figure 10-1　Relative screen resolutions for large computer screens and large handset screens

addition, Web content assumes the ability to easily input text (using, for example, a full-function QWERTY keyboard). Furthermore, content developers assume that computing resources are powerful, with capable central processing units and considerable memory (both RAM and ROM).

WAP, however, is designed for use on a wide variety of mobile terminals, ranging from pagers to handsets to Personal Digital Assistants (PDAs). Each of these mobile terminals has display capabilities that are much more limited than those of computer monitors. Likewise, the mobile displays themselves vary widely. For example, some handsets have text-only displays that offer 4 lines of text and 12 characters per line, whereas the most capable handsets provide graphical displays that are 120 pixels wide by 160 pixels high and display 11 lines of text. In addition, the vast majority of handset displays are gray-scale only. The input devices of many mobile terminals are also less capable, with pointing devices and text input methods being more laborious to use, particularly on telephone handsets. Furthermore, the central processing units (CPUs) and memory are severely limited in comparison to desktop systems.

The Network Is Different

Web sites are designed with the expectation of an Internet connection speed ranging from 28.8 kilobits per second to more than 1 megabit per second. Reflecting this expectation, they tend to include detailed graphics, multimedia, and downloadable applets that run on the client PC. However, mobile data speeds today provide an effective throughput ranging from less than 100 bits per second to 14.4 kilobits per second (although higher data speeds are around the corner). In addition, mobile data networks tend to have more latency, less connection stability, and less predictable availability. Round-trip latency of 5 to 10 seconds is not uncommon.

The User Is Different

Perhaps the most important difference, however, is the user. Mobile terminal users may not necessarily have any desktop computing experience, so standard computer user interface metaphors are not always appropriate. They also tend to be engaged in other activities while they are using their handset, so they cannot give full attention to the handset. Furthermore, mobile terminal users expect to be able to complete a task with their handset within a few minutes. They are unlikely to spend extended periods of time "surfing the Net" from a mobile device. Thus applications need to enable users to complete their tasks quickly and efficiently. Successful applications will cater to the needs of these users.

> The users are the most important difference between wireless network applications and wired network applications. Mobile terminal users have vastly different needs and skills and thus require an entirely different service design than users of typical Internet applications. Applications need to recognize these users' special needs to be successful.

The Interface *Should* Be Different!

Designing applications for display on a mobile terminal is very different from designing applications for display on a computer terminal. Hence, much of the experience in designing usable Web sites cannot be carried directly from the Internet world to the mobile world. All is not lost, however. Some user interface design techniques can be applied to the design of WAP-enabled Internet applications for mobile terminals. In addition, new design techniques for mobile terminals are emerging.

Designing a Usable WAP Site

Usability has many aspects. It refers to how easy the user interface is to learn for novice and casual users. It refers to how efficient, flexible, and powerful the user interface is to use for expert users. It refers to how low the error rate is, how satisfied users are with their experience in using the interface, and how much learning they retain over time.

Human factors is a discipline dedicated to improving the many components that define usability. Human factors professionals design products that people use and the environments in which they use them so as to better match the abilities, limitations, and needs of those people. These professionals achieve their goals by applying extensive knowledge about human capabilities, limitations, and behavior to product design. In addition, they supplement this knowledge by conducting scientific investigations to obtain product- and situation-specific knowledge to further aid design. This includes evaluating the product's usability through objective, systematic, and controlled evaluations.

Usability is a fundamental feature of any mobile Internet service, and it influences the operation of all other features of your service. To design easy-to-use interfaces, usability needs to be a primary goal throughout the application development process. Like any fundamental feature, usability is most effective when designed early into the process and very costly when begun late in the development cycle. That is, usability is not something that can be added toward the end of a development cycle, like shrink-wrapping.

Designing usability early into the process requires at least two things:

- An overall development process that is focused on the end user and employs structured usability techniques
- Knowledge and application of known user interface design principles and guidelines

The goal of this chapter is to help you design easy-to-use WML sites. The key to designing such sites lies in implementing a process focused on end users. Developing valuable and user-friendly services requires that you maintain this focus on the end user throughout the product development process. In the end, easy–to-use sites will aid in attracting and keeping customers.

The rest of this chapter introduces a design process outlining how and when to apply structured usability techniques. It also presents some of the best-known user interface design principles and guidelines. Because the design of WAP services is a new and still immature field, design guidelines are evolving and changing rapidly. Additional guidelines are sure to emerge, and you are encouraged to consult all sources of available information when designing your application.

Structured Usability Methods

The following characteristics of a user interface can signal problems with usability:[4]

- It was designed by software people, not human–computer interaction specialists.
- It was developed by strict top-down, functional decomposition.
- It was not developed to meet written, measurable usability specifications.
- It was not prototyped as it was being developed.
- It was not developed by means of an iterative refinement process.
- It was not empirically evaluated.

The same characteristics apply to almost all user interfaces, including WAP user interfaces. The process detailed in this section will help you avoid these common pitfalls by establishing usability as a primary goal throughout application development.

---

[4]From *Developing User Interfaces*, Hix and Hartson, 1993. Copyright © 1993. Reprinted by permission of John Wiley & Sons, Inc.

A user-involved design process is the most powerful step that can be taken toward ensuring a usable interface. It not only centers around the end users, but also actually involves them by placing the end users on the design team itself. This process should be adapted to fit within the product development cycle of your company and to accommodate the resources available.

Designing and developing Internet services is a fast-moving business. Service providers that constantly evaluate their applications, adapt to the trends, and change the most rapidly have a significant advantage over their competitors that cannot or do not match this pace. One school of thought is to design the site, get it out as fast as possible, welcome failure, and then iterate to produce a better site. Although this school of thought does apply to WAP applications, it is more appropriate for defining the content and purpose of your site. It is neither an efficient nor an effective technique for designing a usable site.

A far easier and faster technique is to adapt your service to make it more usable in the design or prototype stages, rather than to rewrite production code. Reflecting this concept, the process described in this chapter will help you develop a usable site quickly and cost-effectively by catching usability problems early, when they are easy to fix. Thus, once your application is deployed, you can be confident in its usability and can instead concentrate on adapting its content or purpose to follow evolving market trends. Realize, however, that each time you change the content or purpose of the site, you should follow the usability process outlined here to ensure that the site remains usable.

The Design Team

Regardless of the size of your company, a multidisciplinary team should be established to handle the design of the mobile Internet application. No one individual or department will have the necessary skills to design a usable interface. The ideal design team should include members with skills such as development, writing, human factors, usability assessment, visual design, task analysis, and business processes. It should also include representative users. These users will help maintain a user-centered design focus. It is this design team that should perform the structured methods detailed here.

Figure 10-2   The design process

The Design Process

An effective user interface design process will contain a number of important phases (Figure 10-2):

Phase 1: Define

Phase 2: Design

Phase 3: Prototype

Phase 4: Test

Phase 5: Iterate

Example: This section uses an example application to demonstrate the steps of the design process. The application we will design provides information on traffic congestion and accidents in and around the city. Our basic premise is that people need complete and detailed traffic information about roads on which they plan to travel soon. They want current information, they want it immediately, and they are interested only in traffic conditions that affect the route to their next destination.

Phase 1: Define

In this phase, the service is defined, and the requirements are gathered. Service definition involves gathering numerous design-affecting pieces of information and distilling this data into a concrete set of requirements. Those design-affecting pieces of information include the following items:

- User profile
- Task analysis
- Platform capabilities and constraints

User Profile

"Know your user" is one of the most important guidelines to follow when designing user interfaces. In the design process, the first step is to compile a user profile. Describing your users through a user profile early on will help guide many decisions in the upcoming design stages and hence make your application more valuable and easier to use for the target population.

A *user profile* is a description of the target population couched in terms of the characteristics that are most important to the user interface design. Creating the profile involves gathering data about user demographics, skills, knowledge, background, and other factors that characterize your potential customers. The user profile should describe each major skill required by the application and, if possible, the experience and approximate percentage of end users at high and low levels of experience. You can get this information through surveys, customer interviews, market research analyses, focus group sessions, contextual observations, and other research tools.

Once this data has been gathered, it can be presented in multiple ways for use by the entire design team. For example, each characteristic can be summarized in a table that identifies the relevant percentages. In addition, the user profile can be summarized through a "typical user description." In a typical user description, hypothetical users are characterized with respect to their experience in each major skill. You should create enough typical user descriptions to cover the range of skills and experiences of your users.

> **Example:** For our traffic alerts application, we have interviewed a wide variety of people who we think are prime candidates for our service. We have chosen to summarize our results using both a "typical user description" and a data table. Two sample user descriptions are provided below. Of course, for this application, more descriptions would likely be required to cover the entire user population.

Typical User Description 1: Mary.

Mary lives in a big city plagued with numerous and unpredictable traffic jams. The difference between getting caught in one of these traffic jams and avoiding it can mean the difference between getting somewhere on time and being very late. Mary is a teacher and mother of two very active children. She finds that her schedule tends to revolve around them. John, her son, is 14 and has soccer practice from 3:30 P.M. to 5:00 P.M. every Tuesday and Thursday. On Monday, Wednesday, and Friday, John goes home with a friend and stays there until 5:30 P.M. Susan, Mary's daughter, is 11 years old. She has gymnastics every afternoon from 3:00 P.M. to 4:30 P.M.

Mary's weekday schedule has become very predictable. In the mornings, she drives her children to school and goes to work. On Tuesdays and Thursdays, she leaves work at 2:30 P.M., picks up John and Susan from school, and drives Susan to gymnastics and John to soccer practice. Mary then goes back to work, because her husband will pick up both Susan and John and take them home. On Mondays, Wednesdays, and Fridays, she also leaves work at 2:30 P.M., picks up Susan from school, and takes her to gymnastics. She then waits for Susan at practice and takes her home when practice is over.

Mary could take any of several routes when driving her children to school and to their practices. She tends to prefer one route that has worked best for her in the long run, however, and takes that route unless she knows it is affected by an accident or traffic congestion.

One of the courses Mary teaches deals with computers and the Internet. She is very comfortable using Internet applications and spends some of her free time

finding educational sites on the Web. However, Mary is very wary of handheld computers, because she remembers how long it took to learn how to use her desktop computer. She prefers "daytimers" and other paper-based organization products because, even though she has never used PDAs or other handheld devices, she believes that they would be too difficult to use because of their small size. Mary does use one handheld product extensively—her cellular phone. She has programmed the names and numbers of all of her friends and claims that she could not maintain her busy schedule without it.

Typical User Description 2: Fred.

Fred is a service technician. He spends 90 percent of his day driving from one client to another, servicing his company's product. His days are completely unpredictable and revolve around the latest emergency. He often finds himself traveling all over the city on any particular day. Fred has never used a desktop computer and has never been on the Internet. He has heard all about it, but he sees no reason why it would benefit him. Nevertheless, Fred loves any type of electronic handheld product that can increase his productivity, because he is paid based on the number of service calls he makes. He was one of the first people to purchase a PDA and has upgraded with every new version released. He relies on his cellular phone extensively to keep in touch with his clients and his main office, but he has found little use for it beyond placing and receiving phone calls.

Table 10-1 partially summarizes our user profile data.

Table 10-1 Partial User Profile Data Summary

Measurement	Result
Experience with Internet	10% more than 5 years 25% 3–5 years 30% 1–3 years 35% no experience
Access to Internet from desktop computer	80% yes 20% no
Program numbers in cellular phonebook	10% more than 50 numbers 20% 20–50 numbers 20% 1–20 numbers 50% none
Time spent driving each day	5% more than 5 hours 25% 3–5 hours 50% 1–3 hours 20% less than 1 hour
Own a PDA now	20% yes 80% no
Enjoy learning new applications	65% yes 35% no

The characteristics of these users have significant design implications. If the users are not considered throughout the design process, the resulting product could easily fail to meet the needs of one or more groups of users.

Users of the mobile Internet tend to share several characteristics:

- They are unlikely to have training on your service—so keep your application intuitive.
- They are impatient—so enable value to come out as quickly as possible.
- Most buy phones for phone calls—so do not expect them to be adept at using mobile Internet services.
- They are busy doing other things—so do not expect them to spend time learning how to use your application.
- They will forget or avoid complex navigation—so keep your navigation scheme simple.

Task Analysis

A *task analysis* results in a description of how users perform tasks that are relevant to the application you are designing. It involves understanding which methods are used, why they are important, how the information flows, what the user does, and what can be automated. Information from a task analysis allows the designers to concentrate on ensuring the features of greatest importance to the users are the easiest to use. Insufficient or inaccurate task analysis can make it difficult for users to perform their most common, everyday tasks.

The most effective task analysis is carried out by watching users perform those tasks that are relevant to your application and documenting what they do. Alternatively, customer interviews, focus groups, surveys, and so on can be used. Some of the questions that should be answered through a task analysis include the following:[5]

- What tasks do users perform?
- What tasks are most critical?
- What steps are taken to perform tasks?
- What are users' goals for performing tasks?
- What information is needed to complete tasks?
- How frequently do users perform tasks?
- What tools are used to complete tasks?
- What output is generated from user tasks?

Example: The tasks in which Mary and Fred currently engage are very different. Mary watches the morning news and listens intently to the traffic report while eating breakfast. When she is in the car, she turns the radio on to a station that provides traffic reports every ten minutes and listens closely to see whether any of the roads she drives are mentioned. Both of these tasks are difficult, however, because sometimes the kids are making too much noise. Before she leaves work to pick up her kids after school, Mary logs on to the Internet to see whether any accidents have occurred on the routes she drives after work. If she determines that congestion affects one of her planned routes, she takes another route to her destination.

[5]From Theo Mandel, "Interface Design and Development," in *The Elements of User Interface Design*. Copyright © 1997. Reprinted by permission of John Wiley & Sons, Inc.

Mary performs the following tasks, among others:

- Turn on the TV, watch the news.
- Turn on the radio, listen to the news.
- Log onto the Internet, access the traffic Web site, look at the live camera shots of the relevant highways.
- Drive the kids from home to school (Monday to Friday), leave at 7:00 A.M.
- Drive herself from school to work (Monday to Friday), leave at 7:45 A.M.
- Drive herself from work to school (Monday to Friday), leave at 2:30 P.M.
- Drive Susan from school to gymnastics (Monday, Wednesday, Friday), leave at 2:45 P.M.
- Drive Susan from gymnastics to home (Monday, Wednesday, Friday), leave at 4:30 P.M.
- Drive Susan and John from school to gymnastics (Tuesday, Thursday), leave at 2:45 P.M.
- Drive John from Susan's gymnastics to soccer practice (Tuesday, Thursday), leave at 3:00 P.M.
- Drive herself from soccer to work (Tuesday, Thursday), leave at 3:30 P.M.
- Drive herself from work to home (Tuesday, Thursday), leave at 5:30 P.M.

Fred, on the other hand, listens to a radio station with "less talk, more rock." He relies on his dispatcher to keep abreast of the traffic conditions and warn everyone when significant congestion occurs. This system does not work well for him, however, because his dispatcher is very busy and sometimes fails to keep everyone informed. Fred also gets tired of hearing traffic conditions that do not apply to where he is. As a result, he often finds himself waiting in traffic, which reduces his productivity and really annoys him.

Fred performs the following tasks, among others:

- Drive himself from home to work, leaving at 7:30 A.M.
- Pick up his schedule of service calls that day.
- Drive from work to the first service call, leaving at 8:00 A.M.
- Listen to the dispatcher.
- Drive from the first service call to the second service call.
- Continue driving from service call to service call until he completes his schedule.
- Curse when he gets stuck in traffic, and radio the traffic condition in to the dispatcher.
- Occasionally, receive an emergency service call and adjust schedule.
- Occasionally, drive back to work for additional parts.
- Drive from work to home, leaving at 5:00 P.M.

One use for the results of a task analysis is to generate use case scenarios. *Use cases* are relatively independent, meaningful scenarios that describe how users carry out their work. They can, for example, describe how a potential customer would use your application to accomplish a particular objective. Key use cases that do a good job of representing the whole service are a valuable design tool. They are also extremely beneficial in design reviews, allowing you to ensure that your application or service enables the critical use cases to be executed easily.

Platform Capabilities and Constraints

Much of this chapter, and this book, is dedicated to understanding the capabilities and constraints of WAP-enabled devices. A thorough understanding of this issue is a requirement for designing WML-based services.

Phase 2: Design

As discussed in earlier sections, the mobile Internet is very different from the wired Internet. The device is different, the network is different, and the users are different. As a result, the applications need to be different as well.

Application Design Goals

Before discussing design principles, we must reemphasize that the mobile Internet is evolving rapidly. The principles presented in this book are based on common industry practices for mobile Internet applications. Like the early design principles for the wired Internet, the wireless design principles will undoubtedly change as the mobile Internet grows. Nevertheless, for applications and services that will be part of the first incarnation of the mobile Internet, the following design principles and guidelines will be critical for designing successful applications.

The wired Internet and its associated terminology create perceptions that do not apply to the mobile Internet. Designers of successful wireless applications will break away from those wireline perceptions:

- People use "browsers" to browse, or casually search the Internet for information.
- Finding value requires effort, takes time (numerous clicks), and is usually impersonal.
- Content is broadly scoped and often static.
- People expect unlimited access and free content.

The mobile Internet, therefore, needs a different model and different design goals. For applications to be successful on the mobile Internet, they need to achieve the following design goals:

- *Be targeted:* Provide only the most valuable information to a wireless user.

- *Be fast:* Make the most valuable information the easiest to obtain, thus enabling users to quickly find that information in just a few key clicks, rather than through browsing.

- *Be personal:* Create an intelligent application and present information that is adapted to each user's personal interests.

- *Be simple:* Ensure that information is easy to find and use. Your application cannot just deliver technology; it must be integrated and carefully designed to fit users' needs.

- *Be urgent:* Provide information that is critical to the end users and needs to be received while they are mobile.

- *Be timely:* Provide information that changes and needs to be received wirelessly because timing is important. Static information can be obtained elsewhere.

- *Adapt to the way people work:* Do not attempt to change people's worlds. Instead, try to be a part of their environment. People will adopt the mobile Internet when they can just try it out, find that it is important and useful, and easily merge it into their daily lives.

- *Use the Web to do your users' work for them:* Design applications that can perform tasks for your users (for example, alert users when an event of importance has occurred, such as a stock price reaching a particular level, so they do not have to keep checking manually). Applications that achieve this can become "killer apps."

Methods for Achieving the Design Goals
This section presents design principles that will help you achieve the application design goals presented in the previous section.

Guide Users to the Appropriate Content Users will come back to applications that are easy to navigate and enable them to quickly find the desired information with few or no errors. For this reason, a menu structure must be carefully organized to promote ease of understanding and efficient navigation.

Generally, menus should take the form of a hierarchical, branching tree structure. Menu items should be organized into clear, nonoverlapping categories, so that the items under each category could not be perceived as belonging to another category and so that every item fits well into a category. This point is easier said than done, but the benefits are well worth the effort. Nonoverlapping categories reduce user errors, reduce the number of options on sublevels, and simplify site maintenance.

The best way to accomplish this goal is by capturing how users organize or categorize the items. If the menu items are categorized according to users' perceived organizations, then users should be able to find those items more quickly and with fewer errors. Several studies have shown that when the categories are not well known and distinct, menu organizations generated from user data are superior to those generated by designer intuition. This idea holds true as long as the user-generated menus are based on research on multiple users who are typical of the end users. Techniques for collecting user data for menu categorization can be found in Paap and Cooke (1997) and Rugg and McGeorge (1997). An in-depth discussion of these techniques is beyond the scope of this book.

Within each menu level, menu items can be organized in several ways:

- Alphabetically
- Temporally (for example, days of the week, months of the year, save before exit)
- According to magnitude (for example, small, medium, large)
- Consistently (if the items appear in multiple places, keep the order the same)
- According to frequency of use (place the most frequently accessed items at the top)

Frequency of use is generally the preferred choice. Organizing items in this manner saves navigation time and increases the usability of those items. Generally, if a task requires the use of items located deep in the menu structure, users are significantly less likely to complete the task: They often give up before finding the item needed. Of course, this guideline can be ignored if items have a natural order (such as temporal or magnitude) or to maintain consistency with other menus of your application. Use alphabetical ordering for menu items only if the options make up a list of well-known, conventional names (for example, list of states).

Menu item names should be precise. They should be carefully chosen to reflect the structure of your menu categorization. Most errors in menu-driven systems occur because users do not understand the meaning of the options. Indeed, what seems to be an obvious menu item name to you might not be equally obvious to the end users. This fact highlights the importance of working with users to understand how to best organize and name menus.

Adding icons to menu items as a supplement to menu labels can be beneficial, if the icons are appropriately representative. When these graphical items show an example of a category member, they have been shown to reduce errors by 40 to 50 percent.[6] Of course, icons need to be carefully selected, because misleading icons can have a negative effect on navigation.

Personalize Your Application   Personalization is one of the most important design principles. Personalized applications increase stickiness (reduce churn), make applications easier and faster to use, optimize navigation by reducing key clicks, generate a sense of ownership in users, offer users a superior service experience that they cannot get elsewhere, reduce data entry, and increase usage and customer loyalty. In fact, personalization for WML applications often distinguishes a usable application from an unusable one. Ultimately, the wireless device is too constrained for "general" use.

Personalization is anything that customizes the application for the end user. Personalized services can learn from the user and adapt to him or her based on the user's explicit preferences and implicit behaviors demonstrated through real-life use of the service. If the user must perform complex or numerous activities to personalize the application, the use of a personal computer connected to the wired Internet may be necessary. For example, the user may need to use a PC to create a stock portfolio that can subsequently be accessed from the mobile phone.

---

[6]MacGregor, 1992.

Example: Our traffic alert application offers many opportunities for personalization. Mary could use her desktop Internet access account to specify the routes she travels most frequently and then use her wireless handset to get a summary of the traffic congestion or accidents on those routes. If she documented her routes on the desktop Web site and accesses the traffic summary report option more often than other service options in the traffic application, this option could become the first option listed when she accesses the traffic application from her wireless handset. Thus, in just a few seconds before she starts driving, Mary could find out whether an accident has occurred on that route and, if so, where that accident occurred. She could even request that the service monitor the routes for her and alert her if a traffic problem has occurred within the time frame during which she would normally be driving that route.

Fred's traffic alert service, on the other hand, would be very different. Because Fred does not travel defined routes, he would be more interested in receiving a basic map of the primary highways, with indicators showing the congested sections of those highways. Because he goes to the map part of the service more often than any other, the map option would become the first option listed when Fred accesses the traffic service from his wireless device. Thus he would also be able to obtain the information he needs (which is different from the information sent to Mary) in just a matter of seconds.

As another example, consider a personalized music e-commerce site. This site might recognize that you most commonly look for jazz selections and hence list jazz as the first choice whenever you enter the site. It might also offer purchase suggestions based on your past behavior and give you a one-button purchase option based on stored user preferences.

A word of caution is warranted, however, when dynamically adjusting menu order based on user behavior. Reordering menu options based on slight preferences or doing so often can be disconcerting to users who become used to the previous placement. As a result, reordering should occur only when strong preferences are demonstrated (for example, the user goes to the fourth item 80 percent of the time) and should occur infrequently.

Personalization can also be used to provide *proactive services* that inform users when a particular event of interest has occurred. Proactive services use the Web to do your users' work for them. Examples of these applications include notification when a stock price has increased or decreased by a certain percentage within a specified period of time or has reached a certain level, notification of the final score of a sporting event, and notification of community events such as school closings, inclement weather, and so on. A primary advantage of the mobile Internet over the wired Internet is that mobile Internet users can be "on" all day, whereas wired Internet users can be "on" only when they are using their PCs.

These wireless, proactive "push" services are very powerful, but they must be used judiciously. Too many notifications of unimportant events can prove annoying and compromise the value of your service. Users must always remain in control of the frequency and type of notifications.

Finally, you must recognize that users are very sensitive to privacy issues. Hence, it is important to use their personal information in a responsible fashion and to clearly articulate your information use policies.

Know Your User   Use the information collected in the definition phase (Phase 1) about your target audience to accomplish the following goals:

- *Target the information you present:* With a solid understanding of the tasks that your users perform and the information that they need to carry out those tasks, present only information that is essential to the completion of those tasks.

- *Adapt your application to the way your customers work:* Your application needs to adapt and fit within the users' lives. Do not expect them to change their lives to suit your application. Instead, use their terminology. Organize your navigation structure based on the way they think, not the way you think. For example, do not expect your users to understand how your company and its products are organized. List your products in categories that make sense to your users, not to the organizational structure of your company.

- *Present information that is relevant to a mobile user:* Mobile users are accessing your service while they are away from other, less expensive sources of that same service (for example, PCs and television). Users expect to see information that has value and changes, so the timing of its receipt is clearly important. Knowing your users allows you to determine which pieces of information fit this description.

> **Example:** Notice that as our traffic alerts service starts to take shape as described in the previous section, it targets the information distinctively to Mary and Fred, it adapts to the way they do their work, and it presents only what is relevant to them.

Reduce Keystrokes   A rule of thumb offered by Phone.com is the 50 per-cent rule, which states that "every key click reduces [the] potential user base of an application by 50 percent."[7] You should therefore expect a large number of your users to get lost after having to navigate through two or three screens. Although this rule may somewhat overstate the case, its message is clear: Reduce keystrokes.

The following methods can be used to reduce keystrokes:

• *Personalize your application:* Use personalization extensively to re-duce data entry, optimize the presentation order of your features, opti-mize navigation to the information of greatest interest to the individual user, provide proactive services, and predict customer desires (for exam-ple, offer purchase suggestions based on previous behavior).

• *Provide value at every level:* Give relevant information to users at every level as they navigate through your site.

• *Optimize navigation to the most important content:* Use the knowl-edge gained in the task analysis to ensure that information required for the most important and frequent tasks is the easiest to access by placing that option at the top of your navigation hierarchy.

• *Keep the content targeted:* Present only the information demanded by your users. Including infrequently accessed information increases the number of categories and the complexity of your application. Minimize the number of options that users must read and consider, but not select.

Example: Figure 10-3 shows one possi-ble scheme for our traffic alerts appli-cation that reports on common routes driven by Mary. Mary can select any route she normally drives to find out whether congestion has occurred on that route and, if so, where it is lo-cated. However, she needs to select every route to find out whether it is congested. Figure 10-4 shows an alter-native interface, which provides infor-mation at every level. Here, the first screen tells Mary that the drive to work is clear but there are two congested areas on the way to school. Now Mary does not need to select the **work** op-tion because she already knows there is no congestion along that route.

---

[7] Linder, 1999. Copyright © 1994–2000. Phone.com, Inc. All rights reserved. Reprinted with permission.

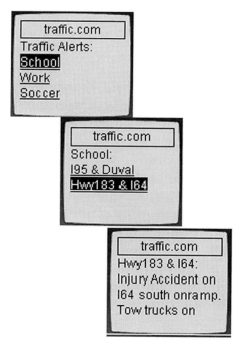

Figure 10-3 Possible implementation of the traffic alerts application

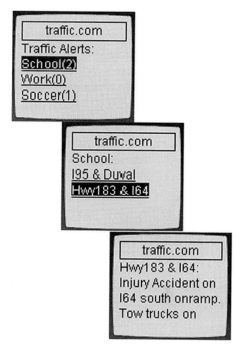

Figure 10-4 Example of providing value at every level

- *Allow users to select from lists:* When only a few choices are possible, use lists instead of requiring the user to enter text.

- *Take users directly to the information:* If something is done 90 percent of the time, take users to it immediately, rather than presenting another level of menus.

> Make a concerted effort to reduce keystrokes. Every key click may halve your potential user base.

Generate and Test Multiple Competing Designs   A common pitfall is to generate a single design and move on. A better approach is to generate several designs and then evaluate them with end users. Often, the most effective design combines or merges two or more competing designs. Once you have blended the best design ideas, test that design with end users as well.

Reduce Screen Clutter   Present only the information that is required on each screen. Make a concerted effort to remove anything from the screen that is not critical.

Follow Known Design Guidelines   Following well-established guidelines will help your application progress faster toward a simple, usable design. Many of these guidelines will be presented later in this chapter.

Transcoders

Transcoders have entered the market in an attempt to automatically convert HTML-based Web sites to WML-based Web sites. Although this goal is both very attractive and highly valuable, a word of caution is warranted. As mentioned earlier in this chapter, a number of significant differences exist between WML- and HTML-based Web sites, not the least of which is that users have very different goals when accessing them. These differences lead to very different requirements for site designs, which are very difficult to accommodate effectively with a transcoder.

Before launching a mobile service that is generated through transcoding of your HTML-based Web site, carefully compare the transcoded service with the application design goals mentioned earlier in this chapter. For example, the transcoded site should be targeted, fast, personal, simple, urgent, timely, and adaptive to the way people work, and it should use the Web to do your users' work. Also, many of the methods for achieving those design goals—for example, providing an efficient and understandable menu structure, personalizing the site, knowing the users, reducing keystrokes, reducing screen clutter, and following known design guidelines—should be used in the most effective manner. In most cases, a transcoded site cannot meet these goals as well as a customized WML site can. Being able to easily generate a WML-based application does not help very much if customers give up in frustration when trying to use it.

> Although it is often possible to automatically transcode an HTML site to a WML site, the resulting site will be less usable than a custom-designed WML site. Currently, customized WML sites are more capable than transcoded sites of meeting the design goals for building successful wireless applications.

Phase 3: Prototype

After you have completed part of the design, prototype some of its basic characteristics. Prototypes serve many important functions and are a critical part of the development process. In particular, they provide an effective tool for communicating design. They also enable designers to better visualize design and task flow, and they provide a low-cost vehicle for getting end-user input regarding the proposed design. Finally, they can be used as a living design specification.

Prototyping WML applications can be accomplished easily and efficiently with the many Software Development Kits (SDKs) available (see Appendix A for a list of some SDKs). In fact, it is much easier to prototype a WML application than to prototype a typical PC application. An SDK simulates the appearance of handsets on computer screens and shows WML content. This level of fidelity is often acceptable for early, and sometimes even for final, prototypes. As prototypes progress, the next step—displaying them on browser-capable handsets—is also relatively simple. The ease of generating WML prototypes makes this one of the most effective steps in creating a mobile Internet interface and one that can be performed with a large return on investment.

Prototypes can serve another significant purpose that is unique to WAP applications. That is, static WML decks that mimic the actual application can be written and displayed on several available simulators. Not only does this flexibility allow tweaking of the application flow, but it can also reveal problems with how particular WML code is rendered by different browsers (this situation will be discussed at greater length later in this chapter).

Expect early prototypes to change significantly as they go through evaluations and further iterations. Do not be surprised if it becomes necessary to throw away the first few prototypes as they evolve toward more usable designs. Thus, to streamline the process, prototype only the functionality that is necessary to demonstrate the features currently under evaluation.

Just as it is important in Phase 2 to develop alternative designs, it is also important in Phase 3 to prototype those alternative designs for evaluation. The development team should prototype designs early and iterate them often to quickly identify the most effective design alternatives; later prototypes can be built based on those designs. Remember—it is far easier to change and iterate prototype code that does not meet the customers' needs than it is to change production code that does not meet the customers' needs.

Example: When designing the traffic alert service that Mary would use, it is not necessary to implement the city map that Fred would use. In addition, the first few prototypes for Mary do not even have to be adaptive prototypes. Instead, they might cover only a few routes in the city, and they might even simulate the user interface only when accidents or congestion occur (instead of actually tracking the routes in real time). Because the first few prototypes may be aimed at defining the overall navigational structure and flow of the site, real-time data and comprehensive traffic updates are not necessary and will merely slow down development.

Phase 4: Test

Usability testing is a key step in the product development process. It is the only way to find out before release whether your customers can actually use your application. Testing should be done early and often, with the results of each usability test feeding into the next design iteration.

Usability testing involves giving your application to representative users and asking them to perform tasks (which were identified in the task analysis) by using the application. As the users work with the application, observe areas in which they succeed as well as the areas in which they struggle. Maintain and carry forward designs that are proved successful. Change and iterate designs that cause users to struggle.

Usability testing can also provide information about users' subjective impressions, perceptions, satisfaction, preferences, and questions about the interface. This information can be just as useful as the objective pass-fail data.

Usability Test Process

In this section, we provide only a brief summary of usability testing. In reality, usability testing is a very well-developed area, and a full discussion of it is beyond the scope of this book. The reader is referred to the many books covering this subject, including Dumas and Redish (1994), Nielsen and Mack (1994), and Rubin (1994).

Usability tests can take place in instrumented laboratories with hidden cameras, one-way mirrors, intercom systems, observation rooms, and sophisticated recording equipment. Note, however, that even the simplest arrangements of a room, video recorder, and notepad can produce significant benefits.

An early step in a usability test is to define the participants. Choose test participants who closely match your target audience (the user profile you created earlier will help in this regard). It is not necessary to schedule a large number of participants. Often, four to five participants can identify 80 percent of design problems,[8] particularly if the product has poor usability and the likelihood of problem detection is high. For highly usable products, more participants (for example, six to ten) may be necessary to find a high percentage of the design problems.

Next, define the tasks that the test subjects will perform. Your task analysis will prove valuable here. Select tasks that you expect will be very important to or used frequently by your customers and that your prototype is capable of performing. Consider all aspects of a user's experience with your application, and include all components of your application as part of the usability test. Write instructions that tell your participants to perform those tasks. (Do not tell them *how* to perform the tasks; observing what they think needs to be done to perform the task is the goal of the usability test.)

Example: One task for Mary might be to determine whether there is any traffic congestion on the route that she normally travels from work to school. For this task, the testing instructions may simply state the following:

You are ready to leave work to pick up your children from school. Find out whether there is any traffic congestion on your typical route from work to school. If there is traffic congestion on this route, identify where it is located.

Identify and provide an environment that is comparable to the target setting in as many ways as possible. A quiet location, free from distraction, is usually best, however, and it is recommended to deviate from the target setting in this respect. Whenever possible, ask all design members to observe the test (or video recordings of the test). This approach allows for a common reference point among design team members. In addition, it often allows team members to suggest more creative solutions to design

---

[8]Virzi, 1990, 1992.

problems identified in the study, as different team members apply their own insights to what they observed. Furthermore, the entire team becomes far more willing to iterate and improve a difficult-to-use design when they have personally observed users struggling when trying to use it.

Once the test subjects come in, make them feel comfortable. Participants are often very anxious when placed in a testing environment. Introduce yourself, describe the testing process, and clearly state that the focus of the test is on the product, not them. Tell them that if they struggle during any particular task, it is because the product did not make that task easy to perform. Likewise, if they readily succeed with any particular task, it is because the product made that task easy to perform. It sometimes helps to explain that the test participants are the customers and that—as the axiom says—they are always right. It is far easier to change the product to adapt to the users than it is to change the users to adapt to the product. After all, the former endeavor is the goal of usability testing.

Allow the users to perform the tasks on their own. Avoid giving them hints or help of any kind. After all, when your customers use your final product, you will not be there to help them. Give the test participants reasonable time to work through each task and any difficult situation. If it becomes necessary to help them because they would not be able to accomplish the task, ask them what they are thinking and how they would expect to be able to accomplish the task. Try to provide only general hints; avoid giving specific advice. Take note of the hints the users needed to accomplish the task, and adjust the design accordingly in the next iteration.

One goal of the usability test is to identify whether your service will be easy or difficult for your customers to use when they are on their own. Telling a participant how to accomplish a task, even though it is tempting, makes it impossible to achieve this goal. *Therefore, in the usability tests, you should give the participants only the information they would have if you were not present.*

Early in the design process, it can be useful to ask the participants to think aloud as they work through the tasks. This procedure can give you insights into their thought processes. If possible, record the session using a video recorder (if you do so, be sure to inform the users and obtain their consent to be recorded). Even the most observant experimenter can miss details, and the video recording can prove very valuable for reviewing items you missed.

After the participants have completed the usability test, a post-experiment interview and satisfaction questionnaire may be very useful in obtaining subjective impressions of the interface.

> Usability testing is a key step in the product development process. It is the only way to find out before release of your product whether your users can use your application. Such testing should be done early and often, with the results of each usability test being used as input to the next design iteration.

Phase 5: Iterate

Often, the usability evaluation reveals a number of opportunities for improving the design. When this evaluation is performed early in the design cycle, it is far easier and less costly to take advantage of these opportunities and alter the design.

An *iteration* refers to a refinement of the service's definition and design, resulting in an updated prototype and a subsequent usability test to identify new usability issues and evaluate the effect of the design changes. Iterative design enables testing to occur in different stages of the product development, facilitating earlier detection and simplifying resolution of usability issues. It also helps to identify usability issues that may have been "hidden" behind other usability issues. For example, if an early usability test shows that the target population has difficulty understanding the terminology used by the service, then changing that terminology may later help the design team see that users also struggle with another part of the interface (for example, inefficient categorization of menu items). The latter usability issue could not be identified in the earlier test, because users were confused by the terminology and thus could not evaluate the categorization of the menu items. As proof of the value of iteration, Packebush (1996) found that more usability issues were detected when conducting three iterative tests with three participants each, than when conducting a single test with nine participants.

Iterating the design process in this fashion is critical for ensuring usability. Iteration should continue until the design converges to a proven, usable service.

A common misperception is that an iterative design cycle requires more time. As mentioned earlier, each iteration does not have to be a lengthy cycle. With the use of rapid prototyping tools and the inclusion of a small number of test participants in each iteration, each design cycle can be completed very quickly (one or two days), enabling many iterations to be carried out in a short period. Furthermore, designs developed in this manner are more likely to result in a proven service having significantly fewer usability issues discovered late in the cycle. In the end, this approach *saves* time and money because it curtails costly redesigns and changes to the production service.

User Interface Design Guidelines

This section presents some of the general design guidelines that are applicable to a wide range of user interfaces, including WML-based user interfaces.

General Design Guidelines

Hundreds of guidelines exist in the literature. Lund (1997) has compiled a list of ten guidelines that he predicts can identify 85 percent of all application usability problems and 89 percent of all serious usability problems. His top ten guidelines are presented and explained here (with some modifications).

1. *Know thy user, and YOU are not thy user.* This guideline reiterates the importance of having a clear understanding of the user. It appears simple on the surface, but in practice it is difficult to implement. To help achieve this goal, it is best to allow the designers to watch interviews of the users and observe them at work. Designers should maintain an early and continual focus on the users.

The second part of this guideline is just as important. As the developer of a product, you are not the user. You have far too much knowledge about the system, its design, and the subject matter to be an average user. Try as you might, as a developer and designer, you are inevitably biased. Thus it is very important to keep a focus on end users, rather than on yourself and the members of your company.

2. *Things that look the same should act the same. Consistency, consistency, consistency.* Following this guideline is important for enabling users to carry knowledge about how your user interface works from one part of the system to another, thereby reducing how much users must learn to use your system easily and effectively. It also helps maintain a common look and feel across your interface.

3. *The information for the decision needs to be there when the decision is made.* Provide users with all of the relevant information you have to aid them in making the decisions required by your system.

4. *Prevent errors when possible. When it is not possible to prevent errors, error messages should actually mean something to the user and tell him or her how to fix the problem.* This guideline encourages designers to anticipate possible user errors and work to prevent them. In good interaction design, almost no action by a user should be unexpected. At every decision point that your users face while accomplishing a task, ask yourself what they might do here, and try to prevent problems. When an error cannot be prevented, give the user an error message that is informative, clearly states the problem in the user's terms, is positive and not threatening, and describes how to fix the error.

Designing for user errors is an involved effort that requires additional design and development work, but it often means the difference between a confusing user interface that customers abandon and a user interface that customers believe is simple and to which they will return repeatedly. To paraphrase a well-known saying, "To err is human; forgive by design."[9]

5. *Everyone makes mistakes, so every mistake should be fixable.* Allow users to recover from errors. Enable them to undo previous actions. Require confirmation of actions that would be particularly destructive if users took that action by accident (for example, "delete all messages"), and clearly state the results of that action in the user's terminology. If it is impossible to recover from the results of that action, clearly state this fact in the confirmation message as well.

6. *Don't overload the user's buffers. Minimize the need for a mighty memory.* Short-term memory lasts from approximately 30 seconds to a maximum of 2 minutes. The capacity of short-term memory has been described as "seven plus or minus two chunks," where a chunk is a basic

---

[9]From *Developing User Interfaces*, Hix and Hartson, 1993. Copyright © 1993. Reprinted by permission of John Wiley & Sons, Inc.

unit of information to be remembered. Limit the number of items that users must put into short-term memory, as well as the length of time that they must hold that information there. When possible, carry information forward from one screen to the next, so that users are not required to recall it. In addition, facilitate task closure in a short period of time.

7. *Keep it simple.* Make tasks easy to perform. Particularly in early versions of your service, do not expect users to be able to perform complex tasks.

8. *Every action should have a reaction.* Whenever a user takes an action, the system should provide some feedback. This feedback should clearly indicate the results of that action. This step includes giving the user easy-to-understand and descriptive confirmation of changes to system settings and options.

9. *The user should always know what is happening.* The system's reaction to user commands should not shock or surprise users. The user should always know what the system is doing. If the system requires a relatively long time to complete a task, it should provide status messages to the user.

10. *The more you do something, the easier it should be to do.* This guideline refers not only to the need for personalization, as mentioned earlier, but also to the fact that your interface should be easy to remember. Thus customers should not have to relearn the interface each time they use it.

As you attempt to follow these ten guidelines, you may encounter conflicts. That is because the guidelines are not rules to be followed strictly to the letter, but rather reasonable suggestions for user interface design. They require interpretation and sometimes even tailoring to a particular design scenario. Resolving conflicts requires making design trade-offs. Let your usability tests help you decide when to make those trade-offs and even, if necessary, to go against one of the guidelines. The usability test results should have the final say in design because they are a true measure of one of your service's end goals—namely, that it is easy to use.

Variability of WAP Devices

WAP is designed to support a wide variety of devices, which differ significantly from HTML-based devices. In particular, WAP devices have much smaller displays, less capable input devices, and relatively limited

CPUs and memory; they also operate over a network with more latency, less connection stability, and less predictable availability. WAP devices can currently be classified into three categories:

1. *Two-way pagers:* These devices typically have limited graphics capabilities, screens that are generally wider than they are tall, a means for user input (sometimes a small, thumb-operated QWERTY keypad), and limited CPUs and memory.
2. *Phones:* These devices typically have text-based displays with limited graphics capabilities (although some are text-only), function keys and a numeric keypad for user input, and limited CPUs and memory.
3. *Personal Digital Assistants:* PDAs typically support text and graphics (some support color), as well as an enhanced user input mechanism such as a keyboard, pointer or stylus, or handwriting recognition.

You may notice that the characteristics of these devices are described in relatively broad terms here. A wide variety of pagers, phones, and PDAs exist today (having different display sizes, numbers and types of function keys, sizes, weights, and so forth), and these devices are all likely to include WML browsers in the future. Devices will not be standardized around screen size, input devices, or memory. Hence, your applications will have to adapt to a wide variety of characteristics within each device category. For this reason, we highly recommend that you test your application across multiple devices and multiple browsers to ensure that it always operates in the manner intended.

Figures 10-5 through 10-10 show a few examples of phones and PDAs that have announced support for WML. These products demonstrate the considerable variability among WAP devices. As you build your WAP application, you must ensure that your application will work effectively and usably across all WAP-capable devices.

Variability of WAP Browsers

Far more significant than the differences in the actual WAP devices are the differences among WAP browsers. As discussed in Chapter 7, the WML specification gives browsers a great deal of flexibility in rendering, and markup that works well on one browser can prove very cumbersome on another. As a result, to write effective WML, you need to worry

Figure 10-5   Ericsson MC218

Figure 10-6
NeoPoint 1000

Figure 10-7
Nokia 7110

Figure 10-8
Motorola handset
Reprinted with permission from Motorola, Inc.

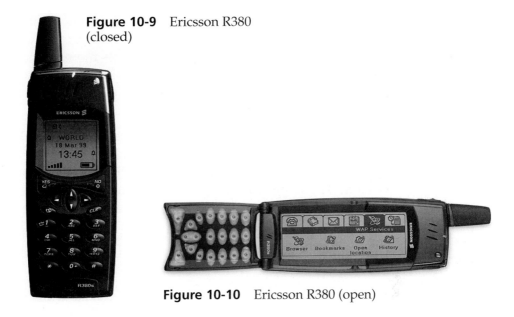

Figure 10-9 Ericsson R380 (closed)

Figure 10-10 Ericsson R380 (open)

less about presentation and more about the application's ability to work effectively across browsers. You also need to test your program extensively across multiple browsers to ensure that it works as planned.

WML Design Guidelines

This section provides some guidelines for designing WML-based services. Like the general guidelines described previously, the recommendations given here represent reasonable suggestions for user interface design. They require interpretation to a particular design scenario, and conflicts are possible. Usability testing will help you make intelligent design trade-offs based on overall usability. As always, the usability test results should have the final say in the design of your application.

   1. *Allow the users to complete their tasks quickly.* Mobile terminal users are unlikely to use their phones to "browse" the Internet. In addition, many users will be paying to access the mobile Internet, with the fee being based on how long or how much they use the service. As a result, users will expect to look up the information they need in a few minutes, and they will lose patience with applications that require numerous steps and a lot of time.

2. *Keep your application as simple as possible.* Remove all functionality that is not absolutely required to complete the primary goal of your application. Additional or complicated features merely increase your application's complexity. The first version of your application should demonstrate how easy it is to perform highly valuable tasks. Add additional features only when your users demand them.

3. *Whenever possible, avoid requiring users to enter text.* Entering text on mobile terminals is tedious and time-consuming. Find creative ways to avoid text input. Use personalization to fill in default options on forms when it makes sense to do so. Allow users to select from lists instead of entering the text when only a few choices are possible.

4. *Reduce keystrokes.* Every keystroke risks losing a customer. This guideline, and methods for accomplishing it, were presented earlier in this chapter.

5. *Design for smaller phones; there will be more of them, and they are among the most constrained.* Although many types of WAP-enabled devices will be available, the market will include more phones than other types of devices for the near future. Moreover, for now, most phones will be purchased because they are phones—not because they can access the mobile Internet—and users tend to prefer smaller phones. Furthermore, phones are among the most constrained devices, so if your application works on a small phone, it is more likely to work on other types of WAP-capable devices.

6. *Avoid unwrapped lines.* All browsers must support unwrapped lines in some fashion, though in reality this support is often difficult to use. Some browsers require the user to scroll horizontally, an option that is rarely noticed and therefore rarely performed by users. Some browsers utilize "times square" scrolling. *Times square* is a horizontal scrolling option used to display the full text of a line that will not fit on one screen. It cycles through the entire line by automatically paging one screen to the right until the full text is displayed. This mode is not supported by all phones, however. In addition, users have difficulty reading text cycled through in this manner, and they sometimes mistake the resultant flashing as a warning or as a message meant to grab their attention. It is far more preferable to fit the text within a single line.

7. *Do not expect the browser menu on devices with Phone.com browsers to be easy to use.* For example, on some phones with Phone.com browsers, it is difficult to find.

8. *Avoid complicated screens.* Complicated screens, such as tables with three or more columns, often do not render consistently across the wide variety of devices.

9. *If a list contains more than two or three items, ensure that it is obvious to the user that scrolling is required.* Because some devices can show only two or three items at a time and some browsers do not provide an indication (such as a downward arrow) that the list continues below the active screen, users will not always know that the list contains more items. As a result, some explicit indication (such as text stating that the list contains six items) is recommended.

10. *Allow users full control over items that they receive via push notification.* New users have a tendency to request push notification of too many items, and eventually those notifications become annoying. Users need an easy means of controlling their push notifications so that they can experiment with different settings and find one that is useful but not annoying.

11. *If a card is referenced by or contains a menu, consider adding a title that informs the users where they are within your application.* For example, if the user selects "Calendar" from a previous menu item, the first line of the next card could be "Calendar," followed by the actions available to the user within the calendar. This strategy serves to inform the users where they are within your application and reinforces which choice they made in the previous menu.

12. *For searching, be permissive with user-entered text.* On phones, it is easy for users to accidentally misspell words, and it can be difficult to find non-alphanumeric characters (especially non-ASCII characters). As a result, your application should allow for misspelled words and expect users to simulate difficult-to-enter characters (such as "ae" for "æ", or "o" for "ô").

13. *For searching, give users access to full results and provide a means for narrowing a large result list.* If a search result contains many items, allow users to scroll through the list or easily adjust the search criteria to further narrow the list.

14. *Provide help for all application screens and, in a stepwise fashion, explain the actions that are needed to accomplish the main goal of that screen.* This approach will aid users seeking help in using your application.

Design Guidelines for Selected WML Elements

This section presents design guidelines for selected WML elements and their attributes that influence the user interface. Because these design guidelines focus on the user interface, they depend heavily on the browsers that interpret the WML and render that user interface. At the time that this book was written, only WAP 1.1 browsers and simulators were available. As a result, these guidelines focus on the rendering of WML elements for WAP 1.1-compliant browsers.

The WML specification defines which WML elements are mandatory and which are optional to support. Because of the large variety of WAP devices available and the significant differences in their user interfaces, the WML specification intentionally does not define how those elements should be displayed. As a result, the rendering of WML elements is left up to each individual device to optimize for its own capabilities. The advantage of this flexibility is that your content can be rendered across a wide variety of devices. The disadvantage is that your content can look and feel entirely different from one device to the next, depending on how the browser in each device chooses to display your content. In fact, it is entirely possible—and even likely, unless you are diligent in testing across many browsers to prevent the problem—that your application will render beautifully and be very easy to use on one browser but render entirely differently and be very difficult to use on another browser. Developers who fell into the trap of testing their design with a single browser can tell many woeful stories of what occurred when they later tested the application on a different browser.

As an application developer, you have a few options for adapting to this situation:

1. You can design your application with a full understanding of browser differences, utilizing only those elements that render consistently and usably across all browsers.

2. You can base the majority of your application on common elements that render consistently and usably across all browsers, then customize pieces of the application that were particularly difficult to render across these browsers.

3. You can tailor your application for each device or browser, thereby maximizing the behaviors of each device or browser and potentially improving performance and usability.

A good strategy would be to aim for the first option, but rely on the second option as a backup if you simply cannot account for all of the browser differences within a single application design. The third option could then serve as a last resort or be used if it would significantly improve usability. If you wish to customize your entire application or even parts of it, you will need to utilize the techniques discussed in Chapter 11.

For options 1 and 2, the following guidelines will help you understand the differences among available WAP 1.1-compliant browsers and design applications that will display consistently and usably across those browsers. These guidelines, however, do not substitute for testing of your application with those browsers: Testing your application throughout the design process with as many browsers as you intend to support is the most important step and will yield the greatest benefit. Instead, these recommendations describe a means for getting closer to the goal of a consistent and usable design across browsers on your first design iteration. They allow you to devote subsequent iterations to fine-tuning for additional differences and to adjusting the design itself based on the results of early usability tests.

These guidelines are inspired by a document submitted to the WAP Forum entitled "Generic Content Authoring Guidelines for WML 1.1: Best Practices and Recommendations."[10] In the study described in this document, test cases were constructed and run across three simulators, five handsets, and one PDA:

- Ericsson WAPIDE SDK version 2.0B8 simulator
- Nokia WAP Toolkit version 1.3beta simulator
- Phone.com UP.Simulator 3.2 simulator
- Ericsson R380S handset
- Ericsson R320S handset
- Nokia 7110 handset
- Two handsets whose identities were withheld due to a nondisclosure agreement
- Ericsson MC218 version 1.13 PDA

---

[10]Senjen et al., 2000.

The following guidelines are also based on direct testing with three available simulators:

- Ericsson WAPIDE SDK version 2.0, model Ericsson R320s (referred to throughout the remainder of the chapter as the "Ericsson browser simulator")
- Nokia WAP Toolkit version 1.3beta, model Nokia 7110 (referred to throughout the remainder of the chapter as the "Nokia browser simulator")
- Phone.com UP.Simulator 4.0 Beta 2, model Alcatel One Touch Pocket (referred to throughout the remainder of the chapter as the "Phone.com browser simulator")

Note that none of these simulators behaves in exactly the same way as the actual device. As a rule, you should not interpret the behavior of browser simulators as a perfect reflection of the final implementation in actual devices. In addition, further differences will arise over time as vendors adjust and modify their simulators and device browsers. As a result, the specifics of the browser simulator behaviors described in this chapter should be viewed as example implementations of the WML 1.1 standard, which are provided to give you a better understanding of how much browser behavior can vary.

Note also that these guidelines are not exhaustive. Instead, they are meant to illustrate the types of differences among browser behaviors.

The guidelines are organized according to WML tag and split into three categories: navigation, user input, and appearance and presentation.

Navigation

Navigation elements can be used to move from one card to another. This section presents guidelines to consider when designing how users will navigate through your application.

<anchor> and <a> Elements

The <anchor> and <a> elements can be used as hyperlinks—that is, when users select them, the browser will navigate to a new screen. The <anchor> and <a> elements are both mandatory elements in the WML 1.2 specification. The specification encourages authors to use the <a> element instead of the <anchor> element when possible to allow for more efficient tokenization. The `title` and `accesskey` attributes are optional.

Browser Differences   The <anchor> and <a> elements work similarly across all browser simulators. Figures 10-11, 10-12, and 10-13 demonstrate their look and feel for the three browser simulators. (In the figures, each browser simulator is accessing the WML markup shown in Listing 10-1.) Because they operate relatively consistently across browsers, these elements are recommended for constructing menus for navigating an application's options.

Listing 10-1   Code used to generate the words displayed in Figures 10-11, 10-12, and 10-13.

```
<?xml version="1.0"?>
<!DOCTYPE wml PUBLIC "-//WAPFORUM//DTD WML 1.1//EN"
  "http://www.wapforum.org/DTD/wml_1.1.xml">
<wml>
<head>
  <meta http-equiv="Cache-Control" content="max-age=0"/>
</head>
<template>
  <do type="prev">
    <prev/>
  </do>
</template>
<card title="SBCWireless.com">
  <p>
  My Portal:
  <br/>
  <a href="#card1" title="OK">Email</a>
  <br/>
  <a href="calendar.wml" title="OK">Calendar</a>
  <br/>
  <a href="contacts.wml" title="OK">Contacts</a>
  <br/>
  <a href="news.wml" title="OK">News</a>
  <br/>
  </p>
</card>
<card id="card1" title="SBCWireless.com">
  <p>
```

```
Inbox:
<br/>
<a href="email1.wml" title="OK">FW: Meeting</a>
<br/>
<a href="email2.wml">Chicago Trip</a>
<br/>
<a href="email3.wml">Announcement</a>
<br/>
<a href="email4.wml">Meeting Request</a>
<br/>
</p>
</card>
</wml>
```

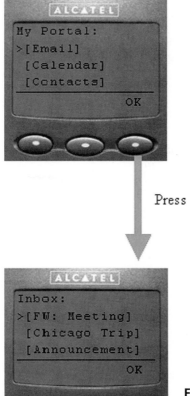

Press

Figure 10-11 Phone.com browser simulator demonstrating <anchor> and <a> elements

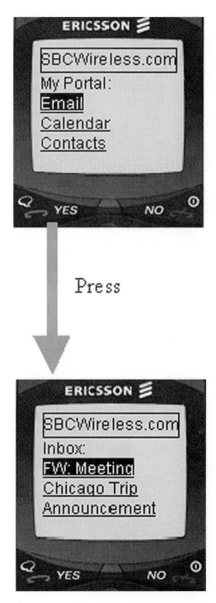

Figure 10-12 Ericsson browser simulator demonstrating <anchor> and <a> elements

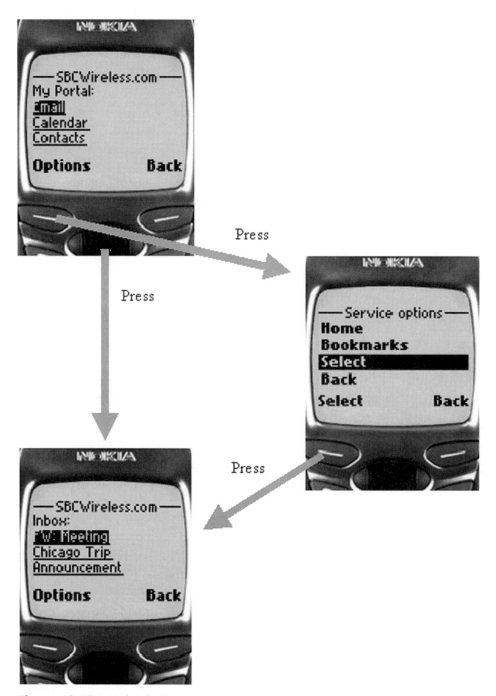

Figure 10-13   Nokia browser simulator demonstrating <anchor>
and <a> elements

User Interface Design Guidelines

1. *Use anchored elements to construct menus for navigating through an application's options.* Anchored elements are presented relatively consistently across the browser simulators and can be effectively used for menus.

2. *Separate anchored elements from other anchored elements with <br> or <p> tags.* The WML 1.2 standard says nothing about how links must be rendered, so browsers may differ in how they handle two consecutive anchored elements. The browser simulators used as examples here demonstrate acceptable variability in the link rendering. The Nokia and Phone.com browser simulators place an anchored element on a separate line from other elements, and the Ericsson browser simulator places two consecutive anchored elements on the same line, wrapping them to the next line as necessary. Separating anchored elements with <br> or <p> tags will enable consistent rendering across browsers.

3. *Avoid anchored elements that are longer than a single screen. If possible, keep them shorter than one line in length (12 characters, including indentations), particularly if they are used as part of a list of anchors (such as in a menu).* The cue for the active link can be lost during scrolling when links are longer than a single screen on the Phone.com browser simulator.

4. *If it is not feasible to keep anchored elements shorter than one line in length when part of a list of anchored elements (such as in a menu), consider specifying the text as nowrap* (see the discussion of the <p> element later in this chapter). This approach will maintain the appearance and structure of the list.

5. *Limit lists of anchored elements to nine items.* Too many items in a single list can be difficult to navigate.

6. *Do not use the same term for the title attribute for an <anchor> element and for the label attribute for a <do type="accept"> event on the same card unless both are intended to invoke the same function.* The Phone.com browser simulator displays the title of the <anchor> element in the same place as the label of the <do> type="accept" element. If these terms are the same but perform different actions, confusion can result.

7. *Use a meaningful term for the title attribute, but do not make it critical that the user see this term.* The title attribute is optional. For example, the Phone.com browser simulator displays it on the same screen as the anchored element, but the Nokia and Ericsson browser simulators do not. Specify a meaningful term for browsers that display this attribute, because these browsers otherwise may apply a default term.

<do> Element

The <do> element can be used to define additional events on a card (such as "go to another card") that can take place when selected. This element is mandatory in the WML 1.2 specification, but its representation is browser-dependent. The <do> element can be mapped to a graphically generated button, a static or dynamic (soft) key on the device, an item in a menu, or any other widget that the browser chooses. The type attribute is also mandatory and can consist of several events: accept, prev, help, reset, options, delete, unknown, experimental types, and vendor-specific types. The label attribute, however, is not mandatory; hence, the browser may or may not choose to display the label you defined for the <do> element.

For example, a <do type="options"> element can be given a label of "Menu" and, when selected, can bring up a list of additional options, such as Edit, Delete, Move, and Save. This Menu option can be represented on the card as a soft key, an item in another menu, a graphically generated button, or any other widget the browser desires. However, depending on the browser, the user might not see the word "Menu" on the user interface at all.

Note that the <prev> element and the prev type differ from each other. The <prev> element is a task that will always go back to the previous URL on the history stack, if one exists. The prev type can specify any task and can be defined to go to any URL specified by the content author, as long as the browser can interpret that address.

Browser Differences   One notable difference between the three browser simulators is in the mapping of the <do> element. The Phone.com browser simulator maps the <do type="accept"> event and the <do type="options"> event to a soft key (when available), so that these events are visible when the content of the card is displayed.

In contrast, the Nokia and Ericsson browser simulators place these events in a menu of options (which also includes options such as "Home" and "Bookmark") and lists them on a separate screen from the content of the card. These options can be accessed on the Nokia browser by pressing the soft key labeled "Options" or the roller key. They can be accessed on the Ericsson browser by pressing the YES key or by pressing and holding the YES key. (Which of these two actions will access the options depends on where the cursor is located in the card. If the cursor is located on an anchor element, the user must press and hold the YES key to access the <do> elements. On a text-only card, the <do> element is made accessible by a single press of the YES key.)

Figures 10-14, 10-15, and 10-16 demonstrate the look and feel for all three browser simulators when displaying <do> elements. In the figures, each browser simulator is accessing the WML markup shown in Listing 10-2.

Listing 10-2   Code used to generate the words displayed in Figures 10-14, 10-15, and 10-16.

```
<?xml version="1.0"?>
<!DOCTYPE wml PUBLIC "-//WAPFORUM//DTD WML 1.1//EN"
  "http://www.wapforum.org/DTD/wml_1.1.xml">
<wml>
<head>
  <meta http-equiv="Cache-Control" content="max-age=0"/>
</head>
<template>
  <do type="prev">
    <prev/>
  </do>
</template>
<card title="music.com">
  <do type="accept" label="Back">
    <go href="#card2"/>
  </do>
  <do type="options" label="Buy">
    <go href="buy.wml"/>
  </do>
  <p>
    The price of your CD "Brand New Day" by Sting is $$42.
  </p>
</card>
<card id="card2" title="music.com">
  <do type="accept" label="OK">
    <go href="#card3"/>
  </do>
  <p>
```

```
      Please enter your account PIN
      <input title="PIN" name="PIN"/>
  </p>
</card>
<card id="card3" title="music.com">
  <p>
    Thank you!
  </p>
</card>
</wml>
```

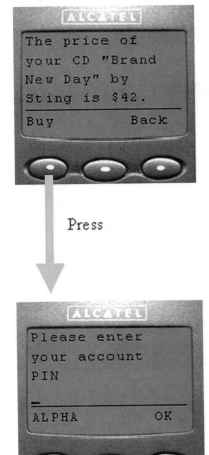

Figure 10-14   Phone.com browser simulator demonstrating a <do> element with accept and option events

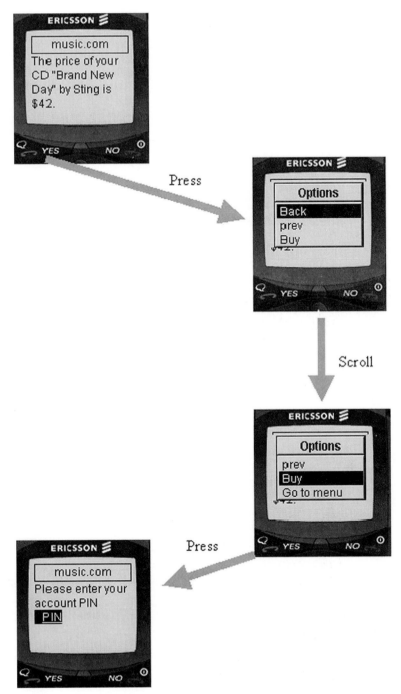

Figure 10-15 Ericsson browser simulator demonstrating a <do> element with accept and option events

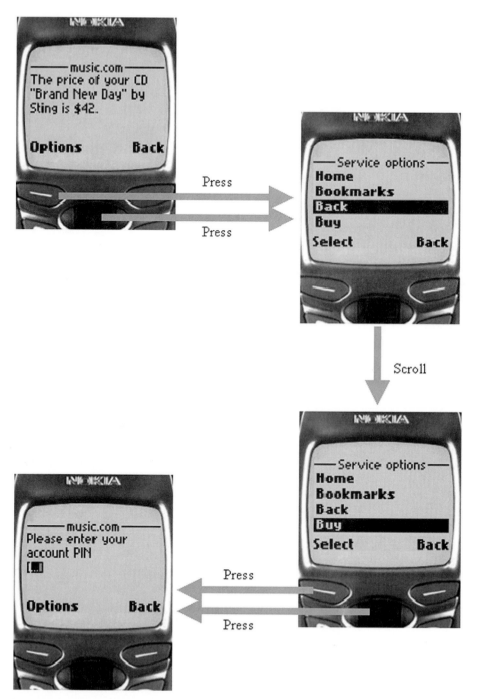

Figure 10-16   Nokia browser simulator demonstrating a <do> element with accept and option events

User Interface Design Guidelines

1. *A <do> event should not be the only means of accessing the main task.* The <do> events are accessible only through a multistep process on the Nokia and Ericsson browser simulators. Alternative navigation methods, such as hyperlinks (<anchor> and <a> elements), are more efficient on these browsers. In Figures 10-14, 10-15, and 10-16, adding anchored links at the bottom of the text would be the preferred navigational method for purchasing the CD on the Nokia and Ericsson browser simulators. Indeed, it is often advisable to duplicate the most important <do> elements with anchored links.

2. *When duplicating <do> elements with anchored links, use the same term as the label for the <do> element and the title for the <a> or <anchor> element, and maintain the same functionality.* Doing so will convey to users that these functions are duplicates of one another, rather than separate items that will perform different actions.

3. *When using <do> elements, use the <do type="accept"> event for the most frequently used task.* The Phone.com and Ericsson browser simulators make the <do type="accept"> event the most easily accessible.

4. *Always define the <do type="prev"> event. Map this event to the <prev> element for cards in which you want to enable backward navigation through the history stack, the <go> element for cards in which logical backward navigation should lead the user to a new card, or the <noop> element for cards in which you do not want to enable backward navigation.* If the <do type="prev"> event is undefined for any card, the browser is not required to provide a means to go back one card, although it can if it desires. For example, the Nokia browser simulator does not provide its standard means to go back (a soft key labeled "Back" next to the soft key labeled "Options") unless a <do type="prev"> event is defined. On the other hand, the Phone.com and Ericsson browser simulators include a key that will perform a <prev> task even when the <do type="prev"> event is not defined.

5. *Give <do> events, such as <do type="accept"> and <do type="options">, a meaningful label attribute.* Even though the label is optional in the WAP 1.2 specification, many browsers support it, and those that do support it rely on this attribute to signal users about what will occur when that event is selected.

6. *Use five or fewer characters for the* label *of a* <do type="accept"> *or* <do type="options"> *function to ensure maximum compatibility across devices.* Some devices cannot display more than five characters for these label attributes.

7. *Use standard* label *attributes for the* <do type="accept"> *and* <do type="options"> *functions, and use consistent labels throughout the interface.* This approach will promote a common look and feel throughout the interface and allow transfer of training from one part of the interface to another. For example, once users learn that "OK" will choose the item highlighted from the list, they should not have to learn that in some situations "Go," "Choose," or "Select" will achieve the same effect. Table 10-2 shows some recommended labels.

8. *Be careful about defining more than one active* <do type="options"> *event within a single card.* The WML 1.2 standard requires the browser to handle multiple "options" bindings if they exist. Those multiple bindings are not always rendered in an easy-to-use fashion, however, and

Table 10-2   Recommended Function Labels

Action	Function	Label
Proceed to the next item in a list	accept	Skip
Complete a task	accept	Done
Edit a specified value	accept	Edit
Execute a search	accept	Find
Answer a prompt positively	accept	Yes
Answer a prompt negatively	options	No
Create a new item, record, or entry	accept or options	New
Initiate a voice phone call	accept	Call
Initiate a fax	accept or options	Fax
Originate an e-mail message	accept or options	Email
Provide a menu of tasks the user can perform	options	Menu
Save a set of choices or preferences	options	Save

many browsers do not recommend their use. For example, the Ericsson browser simulator does not present additional `<do type="options">` events in an easy-to-use way.

9. *Be careful about making necessary functions accessible only by* `<do type="delete">` *or* `<do type="help">` *events.* Support for these bindings is required by the WML 1.2 standard, but the manner in which they are supported is not specified. Indeed, these bindings are often difficult to use. For example, the Phone.com browser simulator displays the `<do type="help">` event in a browser menu that is not always easy to access.

10. *Define the* `<do type="accept">` *event for every card, even if the default behavior for a particular browser is desired.* The WML standard does not specify any particular default behavior. Some browser simulators institute default behaviors when the `<do type="accept">` event is undefined; others do not. The Phone.com browser simulator will substitute the `<prev>` element as the default behavior, whereas the Nokia and Ericsson browser simulators will not provide a default `<do type="accept">` event.

11. *Do not use the same* `label` *for two or more different* `<do>` *events.* It may confuse users to see the same item in a menu twice, particularly if the items produce different actions.

12. *Ensure that when two labels are the same (within or across* `<do>` *elements,* `<select>` *elements, or anchored lists), they produce the same action.* This approach promotes consistent use of terminology across the user interface.

13. *Specify* `<do>` *events in the order in which you wish them to appear.* The Nokia browser simulator will display them in the order specified.

`<onevent>` *Element*

The `<onevent>` element binds an intrinsic event with a task. Thus, when the intrinsic event occurs, the associated task is performed. The `<onevent>` element is a mandatory element in the WML 1.2 specification. It has a single attribute, `type`. The `type` attribute can have one of four values: `onpick`, `onenterforward`, `onenterbackward`, and `ontimer`.

1. *Be careful of the pitfalls when binding an* onenterbackward *attribute to a* <go> *task.* Suppose that the user navigates forward from your card, then navigates back through a <prev> element. The onenterbackward on your card will route the user to the target of the <go> element to the card from which the user just came. Thus, it appears to the user as if the <prev> element does not work and it is impossible to back out of the card.

2. *Be careful of the pitfalls when using* onenterforward *to navigate to a card where another* onenterforward *is used for navigating to another card.* Loops may occur, which can lock up the browser.

User Input

User input elements can be used to capture information from the user. This section presents guidelines for elements that are used to collect input from your users.

<input> Element

The <input> element provides users with a means to input text. It is a mandatory element in the WML 1.2 specification.

Browser Differences   The <input> element is implemented differently across the three browser simulators. Figures 10-17, 10-18, and 10-19 demonstrate the look and feel of the <input> element across these simulators. In the figures, each browser simulator is accessing the WML markup shown in Listing 10-3.

Listing 10-3   Code used to generate the words displayed in Figures 10-17, 10-18, and 10-19.

```
<?xml version="1.0"?>
<!DOCTYPE wml PUBLIC "-//WAPFORUM//DTD WML 1.1//EN"
  "http://www.wapforum.org/DTD/wml_1.1.xml">
```

```wml
<wml>
<head>
  <meta http-equiv="Cache-Control" content="max-age=0"/>
</head>
<template>
  <do type="prev">
    <prev/>
  </do>
</template>
<card id="card2" title="music.com">
  <do type="accept" label="Done">
    <go href="#card3"/>
  </do>
  <p>
    Please enter your account PIN
    <input title="PIN" name="PIN"/>
    <a href="#card3">Done</a><br/>
  </p>
</card>
<card id="card3" title="music.com">
  <p>
    Thank you!
  </p>
</card>
</wml>
```

The Ericsson and Nokia browser simulators guide the user to an input screen that is designed to look and operate similarly to other input screens used by the handset (for example, for entering a name in the handset's phone book). In contrast, the Phone.com browser enables the user to input the text on the same screen as the prompt.

Note that the Phone.com browser simulator screen shots show an extra screen with "Done," which does not exist for the Ericsson or Nokia browser simulators. This extra screen is undesirable, but it is a by-product of trying to use the same code for all three browsers. This is one instance where tailoring part of the application to the specific browsers would be useful.

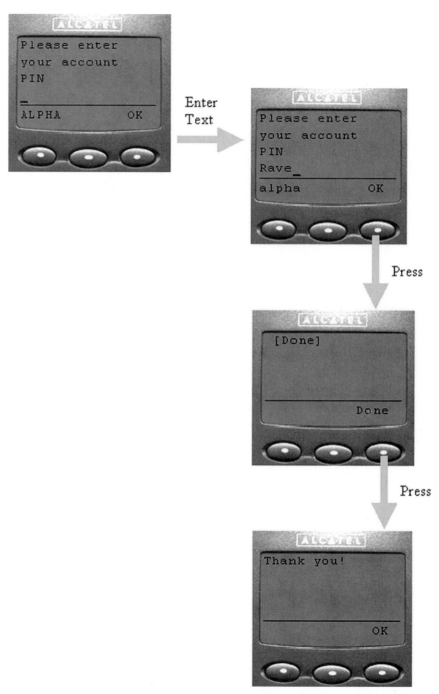

Figure 10-17   Phone.com browser simulator demonstrating an `<input>` element

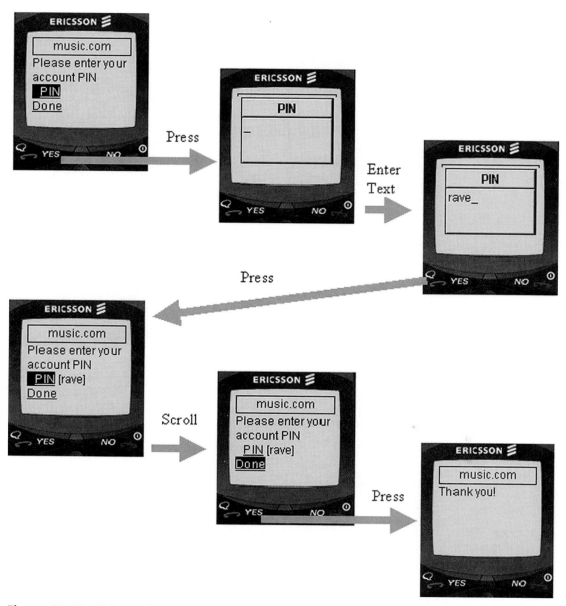

Figure 10-18 Ericsson browser simulator demonstrating an <input> element

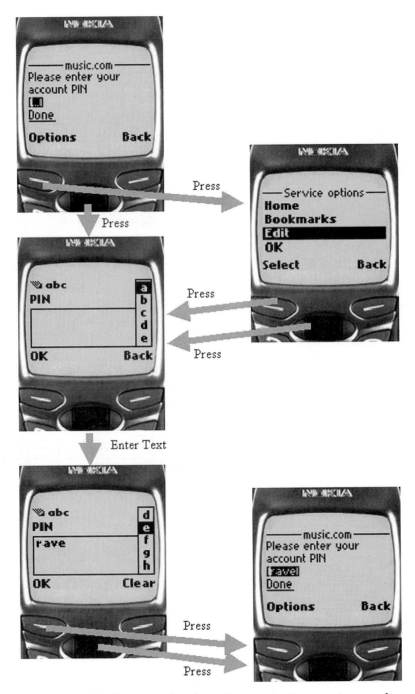

Figure 10-19a   Nokia browser simulator demonstrating an <input> element (part 1)

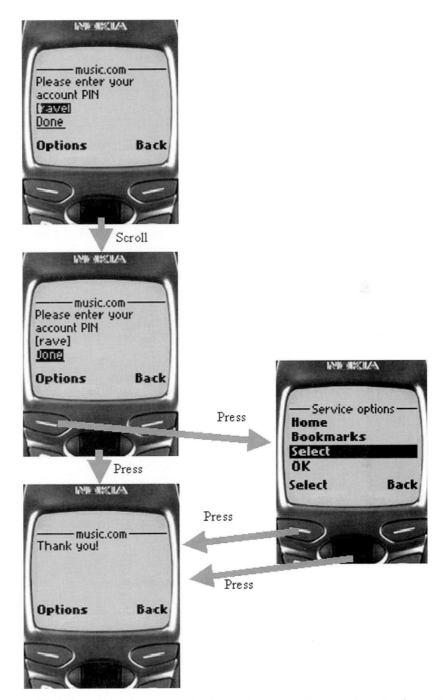

Figure 10-19b Nokia browser simulator demonstrating an <input> element (part 2)

User Interface Design Guidelines

1. *Use the `title` attribute to give the `<input>` element a meaningful label.* The `title` attribute is optional, so some browsers display it but others do not. Specifying the `title` attribute will aid usability in those browsers that do display it. The Ericsson browser simulator uses this attribute as a label to allow users to select it and navigate to the desired item. The Phone.com and Nokia browser simulators do not display this label in all cases.

2. *Specify a value for the `default` attribute when that value is likely to be accepted by most of your users.* Doing so will help minimize text entry.

3. *Use the `format` and `maxlength` attributes to prevent user errors.* Whenever a special format is required, use the `format` option to restrict the input. For example, if alphabetic characters are required, specify the alphabetic format; if numbers are required, specify the numeric format. Doing so will not only help prevent user errors but may also automatically switch the browser into the appropriate character entry mode. If the entry is limited to a maximum number of characters, specify that number as well. Entering characters can be tedious, and the `maxlength` attribute can sometimes be used to prevent users from entering a long character string, only to find later that they misunderstood the purpose of the entry field and that the appropriate entry was actually very short.

Mixed-case text should be used for the following types of information: descriptions, names, street addresses, e-mail message content, and other free-form text. Lowercase-only text entry should be used for e-mail addresses and keywords in keyword searches.

4. *Test to ensure your `format` attribute specifies text input in the manner you intended, and perform a full input validation on the server as if no `format` had been specified.* The WML 1.2 standard is somewhat vague about the exact behavior of the various formatting characters. As a result, you cannot rely on the `format` attribute to fully limit the user's input. For example, the Phone.com browser simulator defaults "X," "x," "M," and "m" format types to be numeric entries when they are preceded by an "N" format type, and it defaults to alphabetic entries when they are preceded by a "A" or "a" type. The Ericsson browser simulator defaults these format types to be alphabetic entries regardless of the preceding format type.

5. *Ensure that introductory text prior to the `<input>` element states the number of characters to be input, if applicable, and the format required* (for example, "5 digits"). Knowing ahead of time what input is required will aid users in providing the proper input the first time. Browsers have some flexibility in implementing the `format` and `maxlength` attributes. Some, such as the Phone.com browser simulator, reject invalid characters in real time or disable inappropriate keys. Others, such as the Ericsson browser simulator, wait until the user attempts to "commit" the entry and then inform the user of errors (such as exceeding the `maxlength` attribute).

6. *Within your application, be consistent in introducing text entry fields so that users clearly understand when they should enter text.* Doing so will also promote a common look and feel.

7. *Avoid using literal characters, such as parentheses or dashes, for imposing a known format on user-entered data without specifying the appropriate format* (for example, xxx-xx-xxxx). Again, browsers have flexibility in how they treat literal characters. On some browsers, such as the Phone.com browser simulator, these characters usually appear automatically. On other browsers, the user must manually enter these characters to make the entry valid.

8. *Do not use the `password` type, even for entering passwords, unless only numeric input is required.* The password type will mask the user's input, which is not needed on a phone (the user can turn the phone away for privacy) and complicates input. The Ericsson browser simulator also masks the characters as they are entered, so it is difficult for the user to tell which characters are being entered.

<select> Element

The `<select>` element provides a means for users to select an option from a list of options. It is a mandatory element in the WML 1.2 specification.

Browser Differences   The `<select>` element is also implemented differently across the browser simulators. Figures 10-20, 10-21, and 10-22 demonstrate the look and feel for the `<select>` element for all three browser simulators. In the figures, each browser simulator is accessing the WML markup shown in Listing 10-4.

Listing 10-4   Code used to generate the words displayed in Figures 10-20, 10-21, and 10-22.

```
<?xml version="1.0"?>
<!DOCTYPE wml PUBLIC "-//WAPFORUM//DTD WML 1.1//EN"
  "http://www.wapforum.org/DTD/wml_1.1.xml">
<wml>
<head>
  <meta http-equiv="Cache-Control" content="max-age=0"/>
</head>
<template>
  <do type="prev">
    <prev/>
  </do>
</template>
<card title="pizza.com">
  <p>
    Choose pizza
    <select title="Pizza" iname="x">
      <option title="OK">Pepperoni</option>
      <option title="OK">Meat Lovers</option>
      <option title="OK">Vegetarian</option>
      <option title="OK">Supreme</option>
    </select>
    Payment type
    <select title="Payment">
      <option title="OK">Check</option>
      <option title="OK">Credit Card</option>
      <option title="OK">Cash</option>
    </select>
  </p>
</card>
</wml>
```

The Ericsson and Nokia browser simulators guide the user to a select screen, which is used to choose one of the options, and then return the user to the previous screen. The Phone.com browser simulator allows the user to select one of the options on the same screen as the prompt, then takes the user to the next screen once a selection is made.

Figure 10-20   Phone.com browser simulator demonstrating a <select> element

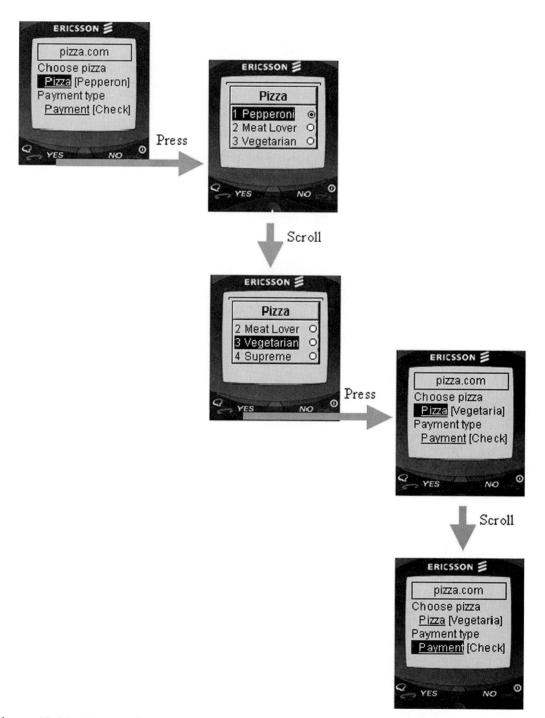

Figure 10-21   Ericsson browser simulator demonstrating a <select> element

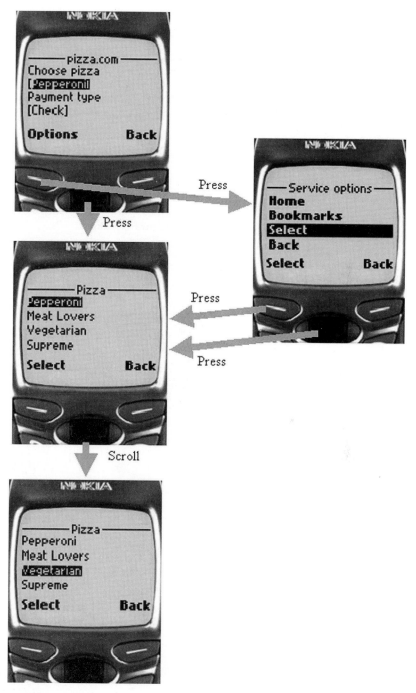

Figure 10-22a   Nokia browser simulator demonstrating a `<select>` element (part 1)

Figure 10-22b   Nokia browser simulator demonstrating a `<select>` element
(part 2)

User Interface Design Guidelines

1. *Avoid presenting more than nine items in a <select> list.* Browsers have great flexibility in how select lists are rendered. Some, such as the Phone.com browser simulator, provide numbers beside the items in a select list; users can then quickly select one of the available items by pressing the corresponding number on the keypad. Because the keypad includes only nine (nonzero) numbers, it can number only the first nine items. If more items are necessary, organize them into a hierarchical structure with proper categorization.

2. *Use the title attribute to give a meaningful label to the <select> list.* The Ericsson browser simulator will use the title as a label for the select list.

3. *Do not rely on the title attribute being displayed.* It is an optional attribute in the WML 1.2 specification, and the Phone.com and Nokia browser simulators may not display it.

4. *Define a default value for the <select> list. This value should be the most common choice, if one exists, unless a dangerous action would result* (for example, placing a large order). Doing so will minimize key presses.

5. *Place descriptive introductory text immediately prior to the <select> list.* This information puts the select list in context. On the Nokia and Ericsson browser simulators, where the contents of the select list appear on a different screen, the introductory text serves as a useful cue to the user that a selection from a list of values is possible.

6. *Specify a meaningful name for the <option> title attribute, but do not expect all browsers to display it.* Displaying the <option> title is optional in the WML 1.2 specification, and the Nokia and Ericsson browser simulators do not display it on the same screen as the items in the <select> list.

7. *If the user does not have to select an option from the select list, provide an option item such as "none."* Otherwise, the user may be forced to select one of the options to continue.

8. *Avoid using <select> lists with onpick events to implement navigational menus.* The Nokia and Ericsson browser simulators provide an introductory screen to the select list, so extra keystrokes are required to select an item within a list. For navigational purposes, these extra steps can be avoided through the use of <anchor> or <a> elements.

9. *Avoid using* onpick *events with* <select> *lists that allow multiple item selection.* The WML standard allows browsers to decide how to implement this event, so variations are possible. For example, the Phone.com browser simulator does not perform onpick events until the user has finished selecting all appropriate items. The Nokia browser simulator, on the other hand, executes the onpick event immediately after the corresponding item is selected.

Appearance and Presentation

You can use appearance and presentation elements to create a particular look for your user interface. This section presents guidelines for specifying the appearance of your application.

<img> Element

The <img> element can used to display graphics on the screen, if the device supports images. The <img> element is mandatory in the WML 1.2 specification, but support of images is not required. If the device does not support images, the alt attribute is displayed in its place.

1. *Use the* alt *attribute to give a meaningful name to the image.* This text will be displayed if the device does not support images.

2. *Use application-specific images selectively.* They can increase download times.

3. *Avoid using images that are larger than the device's display.* Images can be truncated otherwise.

4. *Use wireless bitmap (WBMP) images instead of Windows bitmaps, PNGs, GIFs, or other types of images.* All WAP browsers that support images also support WBMP images, but this relationship does not necessarily hold true for other image types.

5. *Do not use the* localsrc *attribute unless the content is targeted to a particular browser.* Different browsers have different locally defined images.

<p> Element

The <p> element can used to display text on the screen. Support for it is mandatory in the WML 1.2 specification.

1. *Do not count on browsers to support soft hyphens.* Text that overflows a line may not necessarily be broken on a soft hyphen. However, soft hyphens should be provided as guidance for browsers that do choose to support them.

2. *Do not use hyphens if the sole purpose is to break a word.* In fact, the WML specification currently does not allow a browser to automatically break a line on a hyphen.

3. *When using different alignments within a card, specify the alignment of all text elements.* The default alignment for an element will depend on the alignment of the previous element.

4. *Do not count on alignment being supported on all browsers.* The Nokia 7110 does not support text alignment, for example; all text is left-justified.

5. *If the nowrap mode is used, make sure that the text will be understandable if shortened to ten characters.* The line will be displayed in this way until the user scrolls to see the overflowing line. Note, however, that the Nokia 7110 does not support wrapping modes; text is always wrapped with this browser.

6. *Use left text alignment when the paragraph is in nowrap mode.* The WML 1.2 standard does not specify how browsers should react when center or right alignment is specified with nowrap mode; as a result, implementations vary in their treatment of this situation. Many browsers will simply ignore the alignment request. Others may try to honor the alignment request, with varying results. For example, the Ericsson browser simulator truncates the overflow from the beginning of the word for right text alignment, and truncates the overflow from both ends of the word for center text alignment. Thus left alignment ensures that the word will make the most sense.

7. *If possible, choose words that are shorter than 12 characters, including format indentations by the browser.* Words longer than this limit will be broken and displayed across two lines for displays with a 12-character limits, making reading of the text more difficult.

8. *Make sure that anchored text does not contain underscores.* Some browsers, such as the Ericsson browser simulator, underline anchored text, making the underscore impossible to see.

<b>, <big>, <em>, <i>, <small>, <strong>, and <u> Elements

Although the<b>, <big>, <em>, <i>, <small>, <strong>, and <u> elements can be used to display formatted text on the screen, they are optional in the

WML 1.2 specification and may not be supported on all browsers. For example, the Nokia 7110 does not support any of them. Nevertheless, the WML 1.2 specification recommends the use of the `<em>` and `<strong>` elements over the use of the others. In addition, you should avoid nesting these elements.

If you are tailoring your application for a specific browser that you know supports additional formatting elements, consider using the `<b>` element (bold) for emphasizing important information, the `<big>` element for status messages (such as "Seeking" or "Dialing"), and the `<small>` element for explanatory text prior to input fields or similar elements.

<table> Element

The `<table>` element is used to organize text in tables. Support for it is mandatory in the WML 1.2 specification.

1. *Avoid using the `<table>` element when possible.* The `<table>` element does not always display well on the small screens of handsets.

2. *Make sure that anchored text does not appear in tables.* The WML standard is flexible regarding how this situation should be treated and, as a result, browsers may handle this situation very differently. In some cases, such as with the Phone.com browser simulator, the browser will break up the table format when anchored text appears.

3. *Do not use the `<table>` element as a layout tool.* The WML 1.2 specification merely requires the browser to display the contents of the table— but it does not require the browser to display the contents of the table in the requested format. For example, the Nokia 7110 will display all table elements in a single column.

4. *Do not include more than 10 characters in a table row.* The WML 1.2 specification requires browsers to simply make their "best effort" to display the table. When a table including more than 10 characters per line is specified for display on a device that is limited to 12 characters per line, mixed results will occur. On some browsers and devices, the content of the table may be readable only after scrolling to the right (something users rarely do). On other browsers and devices, such as the Phone.com browser simulator, the table format will be broken.

<card> Element

1. *Use the `title` attribute to give the card a meaningful name.* The `title` attribute is optional for the `<card>` element. Nevertheless, some browsers and gateways support bookmarking cards; when they do, the card name can be presented to the user as the default name of the bookmark. Using the `title` attribute facilitates bookmarking your site and requires fewer keystrokes by users. In addition, the Ericsson and Nokia browser simulators present the `title` of the current card in a user interface title bar.

2. *Do not rely on the `title` attribute being displayed.* The Nokia and Ericsson browser simulators show this attribute in a user interface title bar, but the Phone.com browser simulator does not always display it in a similar manner.

3. *Ensure that the `title` makes sense when viewed alone.* The card `title` may become a bookmark name, and the bookmark name will be viewed without the remaining content of the card.

4. *Ensure that the `title` makes sense if shortened to 12 characters.* Some browsers truncate long titles. For example, the Ericsson browser simulator truncates a `title` that is too long for its display box.

5. *Use the `ordered=true` option when your card contains short forms containing only required fields that follow a natural order, and when you want to ensure that users follow that order. However, do not rely on all browsers to support this feature.* The `ordered` attribute is optional in the WML 1.2 specification, so browsers are free to ignore it. For example, the Nokia and Ericsson browser simulators basically treat this option no differently than `ordered=false`. On the other hand, some browsers will honor this request. For example, with this option set to `true`, the Phone.com browser simulator will guide the user through the form in the specified order, not allowing the user to fill in the fields out of order.

6. *Use the `ordered=false` option when your card contains short forms that can be completed in any order or that contain optional fields.* This option allows users to fill in the fields of the form in any order, leaving some fields blank if desired.

7. *If the `ordered` attribute is `false`, make sure that all text immediately preceding an `<input>` or `<select>` element is a prompt for that element.* On the Phone.com browser simulator, this text will be shown only after the `<input>` or `<select>` element is chosen.

`<fieldset>` Element
The `<fieldset>` element allows for groupings of related fields and text. Support for it is optional in the WML 1.2 specification, so you should not rely on it. For example, the Nokia 7110 does not support this element.

<optgroup> Element

The `<optgroup>` element allows for groupings of related `option` elements into a hierarchy. The `<optgroup>` element is optional in the WML 1.2 specification, so all browsers may not support it. When it is not supported, a normal select list is displayed. For example, the `<optgroup>` element is not supported in the Phone.com and Ericsson browser simulators.

Other Guidelines

Many device-specific guidelines exist for developing WAP applications. Phone.com, Nokia, Ericsson, and others have written guidelines recommending best design practices for their devices; these guidelines are available on the vendors' Web sites. You can, of course, make use of all these excellent sources, but realize that many of them were written for specific devices or specific browsers. Consequently, some of these recommendations may not translate well to other devices or other browsers.

Conclusion

User interface design is both a science and an art. The challenge lies in building high-quality interfaces that are readily understood and natural for users. In many cases, the interface will mean the difference between a successful, revenue-generating service and a failure.

Successful user interface design relies on two key elements: following a user interface design process and adhering to user interface design guidelines. The design process involves defining, designing, prototyping, testing, and iterating your application. It should always center around the potential end users. Make sure to test your designs with users early in the process. In addition, for WAP applications, it is important to develop and test your design iterations using a range of simulators and actual devices. To ensure a usable application, it is important to iterate the design and prototypes until your users demonstrate your application is easy to use.

The user interface guidelines will prove helpful when you are designing your application, enabling you to benefit from the experience and insight of the many designers who have come before you. Because it is tempting to rely entirely on design guidelines for the development of an application, some developers fall into this trap. Design guidelines are generic, however, and cannot foresee all of the intricacies of your application. Even strict adherence to them cannot ensure that you will produce a usable application. In the end, the design guidelines can accelerate your application development, but they are no substitute for following the full design process.

We have now discussed the basic components needed to build a WAP application using WML, WMLScript, and (binary) XML. These facilities essentially provide the user with a browsing experience from a limited-function wireless device. In the next part of the book, we will look at the technologies used to build more sophisticated WAP applications that go beyond the traditional browser model. These facilities support greater content personalization, push content to the client, and allow tighter integration of data and telephony services. Because WAP is being used to support mobile commerce applications, we will also consider the security characteristics of an end-to-end WAP solution.

Part IV
Advanced WAP

Chapter 11
Tailoring Content to the Client

Content on the World Wide Web is currently designed for display on desktop PCs that are running standard HTML browsers. Most of the time, these PCs and browsers have rather consistent capabilities and support a common set of features. In the past, content providers created separate versions of their content to optimize them for the Netscape Navigator and Microsoft Internet Explorer browsers. Today, however, the differences between the browsers no longer merit this level of effort for most content developers. Similarly, at the transport layer, the access speed to the Internet varies greatly, ranging from a dial-up 28.8 Kbps modem connection to a high-speed LAN or DSL connection. Nevertheless, very few providers have adapted their content to account for these network differences.

The game will change with the introduction of non-PC devices that attempt to access the same information or service. We have already seen that WAP-enabled mobile devices may differ significantly with respect to their display capabilities, browser implementations, and user input options; indeed, WAP encourages such heterogeneity. Network connectivity now has even greater variability once we account for the low-bandwidth, high-latency characteristics of wireless networks.

In Chapters 7 and 10, we discussed how to address this variability by carefully constructing WML that most browsers display properly, despite their implementation differences. We described two tactics:

- A "least common denominator" approach that uses only the subset of WML that renders reliably in all environments
- A "defensive" approach that constructs WML that renders acceptably in different browsers, even though each one handles the WML differently.

This WML is difficult to author, and it requires careful maintenance as browsers and device capabilities change or as new browsers and terminals are introduced.

Another approach to enhancing the user experience is to provide content that is customized or tailored based on the capabilities of the particular device, browser, and network. With this strategy, you have two possible tactics:

- Generate multiple versions of the content in advance, using a priori knowledge of the types of targeted devices or user settings
- Dynamically construct a customized presentation using templates or style sheets from content stored either in common formats such as XML or in device-neutral formats such as databases

In either case, the server application needs to receive information with the request describing the device, browser, and network environment so that it can select or generate content that is suitable for the client terminal.

In this chapter, we discuss how to build applications that customize the generated content to account for the individual capabilities and preferences of the user, browser, device, and network making the request. We begin by describing how you can use ad hoc mechanisms currently supported on the World Wide Web. As the Internet extends to support an ever-increasing range of terminals, including WAP devices, new standards have begun to emerge to simplify the task. We also describe these standards—namely, Composite Capability/Preference Profiles (CC/PP) and WAP User Agent Profiles (UAProf). Devices supporting these standards are expected to be on the market beginning in the second half of 2000.

Techniques Using HTTP 1.1

Today, most attempts to customize content for the client must rely on brute force techniques. That is, you can either use explicit URLs to identify the different versions of content or rely on the limited set of information provided with the HTTP request.

Explicit URLs

The simplest approach to the problem is to explicitly publish multiple versions of the site, associating each version of the content with a different URL. For example, the home page might be identified as http:// www.coolsite.com/NokiaPhone/index.wml, http://www.coolsite.com/ EricssonPhone/index.wml, http://www.coolsite.com/PC/index.html, and so on. The user is then responsible for making a request to the correct URL based on the type of browser (or device or network or combination thereof) being used.

Although this approach solves the interoperability issue, it is extremely cumbersome for users to remember and memorize different device-specific URLs for the same site. For example, if a user wishes to access your site from his desktop while at the office and from a WAP handset when mobile, he would navigate to different URLs, depending on which terminal he is using. This method quickly becomes unwieldy to administer and maintain.[1] Moreover, you cannot easily extend this system to address dynamic network characteristics or the user's personal display preferences.

HTTP Headers

Along with each request that is transmitted to your Web server, HTTP (RFC 2616) provides mechanisms for delivering rudimentary information regarding the type of browser and some of its capabilities. Your application can analyze these headers to determine how to select or customize content. This approach is certainly better than the explicit URL

---

[1]The problem can be alleviated somewhat through the use of device-specific bookmark lists or device-specific portal home pages. Both of these approaches eliminate the need for the user to remember and type the URL into the phone. However, neither approach simplifies the user's task when navigating to a site for the first time.

Table 11-1   Summary of Standard HTTP Headers That Identify the Client Browser
and Its Capabilities

Header	Description
User-Agent	Identifies the browser making the request. The format of the value is not standardized.
Accept	Identifies the MIME media types (and versions) accepted by the browser.
Accept-Charset	Identifies the character sets supported by the browser.
Accept-Encoding	Identifies how content delivered to the browser may be packaged.
Accept-Language	Lists the natural languages accepted by the browser and user.

approach described in the previous section, because it shifts the burden away from the user and to the browser developer and service provider. Unfortunately, this approach still has several drawbacks. The provided browser information can potentially be unreliable,[2] and there is no standard format for it. Consequently, these server-side content negotiation mechanisms are error-prone. Moreover, the information provided is usually inadequate for conveying the broad range of capabilities of mobile devices.

The relevant HTTP headers to be manipulated are **User-Agent**, **Accept**, **Accept-Language**, and **Accept-Charset** (Table 11-1).

User-Agent

The **User-Agent** header identifies the user agent by name and version number. There is no required format for user agent information, nor is there a standard listing of the values you might expect to find. Nevertheless, this header represents the most common way of customizing content for the browser today. The server application can parse this header and, based on a priori knowledge, map it to a set of browser capabilities. For example, your application might recognize that the "User-Agent: BizWiz 1.3beta2" header indicates that the browser does not support

---

[2]The browser is responsible for identifying itself, and it may give incorrect or incomplete information. The Web provides a well-known example of this behavior. After many servers began to deliver optimized content for the Netscape Navigator browser (which identified itself as "Mozilla"), Microsoft Internet Explorer began to masquerade as the Netscape browser by including a "Mozilla-compatible" identification in its HTTP headers.

images, because you happen to know that the BizWhiz browser did not support images properly until version 2.

Accept

Perhaps the most important consideration is identifying the version of WML supported by the browser, particularly if you want to use any of the new features added in WML 1.2 or 1.3. To make this determination, your server application needs to check the **Accept** header in the HTTP request. The browser uses this header to list which content types it can handle and, if applicable, which version. Consider the following example:

```
Accept: application/vnd.wap.wml;level="1.2"
Accept: application/vnd.wap.wml
```

The `level` parameter, if present, indicates the major and minor version of WML that the browser can handle. When it is not present, as in the second example, you must assume the use of WML 1.1.

When your server returns the WML deck, any version of WML less than or equal to the requested version should be acceptable to the browser. However, it is safest to match the requested content type exactly. Your server should specify the version both in the XML header within the document and in the HTTP **Content-Type** header that prefaces the returned data (response); the format of the **Content-Type** header is the same as that for the **Accept** header.

The **Accept** header may list multiple MIME media types, separated by commas. It may also use wildcards to designate a family of acceptable media types. Some examples of this header's use follow:

```
Accept: application/vnd.wap.wml;level="1.2", text/html;level="4"
Accept: text/*, application/vnd.wap.wml, image/*
```

Accept-Language

The **Accept-Language** header lists the natural languages that the user and browser accept. For example,

```
Accept-Language: da, en-gb;q=0.8, en-us;q=0.7, en;q=0.6
```

means that the user prefers Danish, but also accepts (in priority order, as indicated by the "q" values) British English, U.S. English, and other English forms.

The application should do its best to honor the user's language preferences, particularly because the browser includes this list only if the user explicitly registered those preferences.

Other Accept Headers

HTTP provides several other headers that WAP applications rarely need to use. Typically, these headers are handled by the HTTP server or by the WAP gateway.

- The **Accept-Charset** header identifies the character set supported by the browser.
  ```
  Accept-Charset: iso-8859-5, unicode-1-1
  ```
- The **Accept-Encoding** header identifies how the content delivered to the browser may be packaged.
  ```
  Accept-Encoding: compress, gzip
  Accept-Encoding:
  Accept-Encoding: *
  ```

A Standard Capability Negotiation Mechanism

Despite the limitations imposed by the existing HTTP environment, there is hope for developers seeking to customize content for a particular client device, browser, user, and network. The Internet community now recognizes the criticality of customizing content to particular client capabilities and preferences.

Why is this trend now occurring? The mobile Internet is not the only revolution taking place around the classic World Wide Web. WAP devices are being joined by Web tablets, Web TVs, automotive IVIS systems, telephones, and other appliances that are rendering content from the Web. The divergence in input modes, display size, and processing capabilities for these terminals has far exceeded what anyone might have imagined just a few years ago.

As a result, the richly formatted content that was designed primarily for the desktop PC no longer meets the needs of all Web-connected clients. We have already seen this situation arise with WAP devices, but the same is true even among devices that can render HTML. For instance, consider two browser environments, a Web TV and a desktop PC. The former offers limited screen resolution, limited processing power, and additional television-oriented capabilities; the latter offers high resolution, considerable processing power, and broader connectivity to peripheral devices. Given the capabilities of these devices, it would do the user injustice to be served with a Web page that is not optimized to his or her browser execution environment.

To enable these client-aware applications, work is under way to develop an interoperable standard mechanism for describing and transmitting the necessary information to application servers on the Internet. Two standards—Composite Capability/Preferences Profiles (CC/PP) and the WAP User Agent Profiles (UAProf)— seek to provide the following features:

- Extensibility, to support the rapid emergence of new features and capabilities in devices and applications
- Efficient transmission, to support low-bandwidth wireless networks
- Composition of information from multiple sources, including the device itself, the device manufacturer, browser developer, network operator, firewalls, or some other repository on the Internet
- Caching of the capability information either at a proxy or at the content server, to reduce both the required network bandwidth and the processing required to generate customized content

Composite Capability/Preferences Profiles

To address these requirements, a framework called *Composite Capability/ Preferences Profiles* (CC/PP) was first developed by the World Wide Web Consortium (W3C). CC/PP defines a general architecture for describing user-side capability information for the purposes of content adaptation. It is based on *Resource Description Framework* (RDF), an XML-based metadata format used for describing and exchanging semantic information on the Web.[3]

---

[3] The RDF format enables interoperability among applications that exchange machine-understandable information. With RDF, generic tools can author, manipulate, and search data on the Web, making the Web into a machine-processable information repository. RDF has applications in several areas, including digital signatures, privacy preferences and capability negotiation, Web site mapping, and library classification. A particular community defines the XML tags used to describe the information. RDF then defines how to add semantic structure to that information. For example, using RDF, one can characterize an XML element as representing a property or value, an ordered or unordered list, a set of alternative options, or a group. For more information on RDF, see **http:/www.w3.org/RDF**.

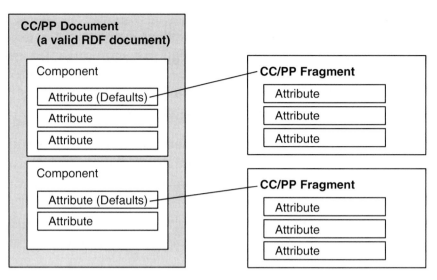

Figure 11-1   Structure of a CC/PP document

CC/PP Document Structure

A CC/PP document consists of attributes and components (Figure 11-1). An attribute describes a particular characteristic of the client environment. It is expressed as a name–value pair, where the name uniquely identifies the characteristic. A *component* is simply a group of related attributes. User or implementer groups may define application-specific RDF *schemas*[4] and *vocabularies* that describe particular components and their associated attributes. Consequently, one can consider a CC/PP profile document to be an *instance* of the schema.

Because RDF supports only string data types, all attributes in the profile must have string values. When the attribute value is actually a URI,

---

[4]The schema is like an application-specific dictionary that defines the meaning, characteristics, and relationships among properties within a vocabulary. It identifies any constraints or restrictions, including inheritance from other schemas or restrictions on allowable attribute values. A typical schema consists of classes, which are organized in a hierarchy. Extensibility is supported through subclass refinement. Each schema is identified by a globally unique URI.

An RDF document may employ multiple vocabularies using the XML name space mechanism. Each predicate in an RDF statement must be identified with exactly one schema, although a **Description** element may contain statements with predicates from many schemas. It is good practice to qualify property names with the corresponding schema name space prefix so as to avoid ambiguity. This name space merging allows schemas to be easily shared and reused by multiple applications.

the attribute is qualified with RDF tags to indicate to the parser that the value is not simply a literal string. Similarly, when the attribute is described as a composite value (such as a list), it is expressed as an RDF resource called a *container*.

Each CC/PP component includes a special attribute, named **Defaults.** The value of this attribute usually is a URI that points to a CC/PP fragment containing a list of default attributes for that component. (The list of default attributes may also be asserted in-line within the component itself, though that approach is considerably less popular.) Any other assertions provided with the component override the values declared through the **Defaults** attribute. This **Defaults** capability allows a CC/PP document to refer to a static, common set of capability information provided, for example, by the device manufacturer, browser provider, or network operator. The client therefore needs to explicitly describe only changes to these default profiles.

Listing 11-1 shows an example CC/PP document.

Listing 11-1 Sample CC/PP document, using the vocabulary defined by WAP UAProf.

```
<?xml version="1.0"?>
<rdf:RDF xmlns:rdf="http://www.w3.org/1999/02/22-rdf-syntax-ns#"
        xmlns:prf="http://www.wapforum.org/UAPROF/ccppschema-19991014991014#">

<rdf:Description ID="MyProfile">

<prf:component>
  <rdf:Description ID="TerminalHardware">
    <rdf:type resource=
"http://www.wapforum.org/UAPROF/ccppschema-19991014#HardwarePlatform" />
    <prf:Defaults rdf:resource="http://www.mysite.com/mydev/mymodel" />
      <!-- Override the ImageCapable property, and
           add VoiceInputCapable and Keyboard properties  -->
      <prf:Imagecapable>Yes</prf:Imagecapable>
      <prf:Keyboard>Disambiguating</prf:Keyboard>
      <prf:VoiceInputCapable>Yes</prf:VoiceInputCapable>
  </rdf:Description>
</prf:component>

<prf:component>
  <rdf:Description ID="TerminalSoftware">
    <rdf:type resource=
      "http://www.wapforum.org/UAPROF/ccppschema-19991014#SoftwarePlatform" />
    <!-- Define VideoInputEncoder property and add JVMVersion property -->
      <prf:JVMVersion>
        <rdf:Bag>
          <rdf:_11>SunJRE1.2</rdf:_11>
```

```
          <rdf:_l2>MSJVM1.0</rdf:_l2>
        </rdf:Bag>
      </prf:JVMVersion>
      <prf:VideoInputEncoder>
        <rdf:Bag>
          <rdf:_l1>Mpeg-1</rdf:_l1>
          <rdf:_l2>Mpeg-2</rdf:_l2>
          <rdf:_l3>Mpeg-4</rdf:_l3>
        </rdf:Bag>
      </prf:VideoInputEncoder>
    </rdf:Description>
  </prf:component>

</rdf:Description>
</rdf:RDF>


<!-- The default properties at http://www.mysite.com/mydev/mymodel
     might be as follows:  -->

<?xml version="1.0"?>
<rdf:RDF xmlns:rdf="http://www.w3.org/1999/02/22-rdf-syntax-ns#"
         xmlns:prf="http://www.wapforum.org/UAPROF/ccppschema-19991014#">
         <!--hardware vendor site: Default description of properties -->
  <rdf:Description about = "http://www.mysite.com/mydev/mymodel">
    <prf:Vendor>aaa</prf:Vendor>
    <prf:Model>1234</prf:Model>
    <prf:CPU>PPC650</prf:CPU>
    <prf:TextInputCapable>Yes</prf:TextInputCapable>
    <prf:ImageCapable>No</prf:ImageCapable>
    <prf:SoftKeysCapable>Yes</prf:SoftKeysCapable>
    <prf:SoundOutputCapable>Yes</prf:SoundOutputCapable>
    <prf:PointingResolution>Pixel</prf:PointingResolution>
    <prf:ColorCapable>No</prf:ColorCapable>
    <prf:ScreenSize>600x400</prf:ScreenSize>
    <prf:ScreenSizeChar>12x4</prf:ScreenSizeChar>
    <prf:MaxScreenChar>48x32</prf:MaxScreenChar>
    <prf:InputCharSet>
      <rdf:Bag>
        <rdf:li>US-ASCII</rdf:li>
      </rdf:Bag>
    </prf:InputCharSet>
    <prf:BitsPerPixel>8</prf:BitsPerPixel>
    <prf:OutputCharSet>
      <rdf:Bag>
        <rdf:li>US-ASCII</rdf:li>
        <rdf:li>Shift_JIS</rdf:li>
      </rdf:Bag>
    </prf:OutputCharSet>
  </rdf:Description>
</rdf:RDF>
```

CC/PP Exchange Protocol

The *CC/PP Exchange Protocol* describes how to embed CC/PP documents within HTTP 1.1 request headers. A set of new headers containing the capability information is added to the HTTP request and passed to the server, which in turn parses the profile and returns a set of customized content based on the profile.

These CC/PP Exchange Protocol headers use the HTTP 1.1 Extension Framework defined in RFC 2774. This framework allows the client to designate the *strength* of the capability information—that is, whether the user agent prefers to receive nontailored content or an error response when the origin server is unable to process the capability information. The framework also allows the client to designate whether the headers should be treated as using an *end-to-end* or *hop-by-hop* scheme; the former indicates that proxies must forward the headers "as is" to the content server, and the latter indicates that proxies must interpret the headers and decide which portion, if any, to forward.

As the HTTP request travels through the network from the client to the server, gateways, proxies, and firewalls may need to add information about known client capabilities, override the characteristics of the client (for example, to enforce security policies), or declare their own content conversion capabilities. The CC/PP Exchange Protocol allows multiple CC/PP documents to be associated with a request, although the user agent must necessarily designate the headers as hop-by-hop so that proxies may rewrite them to include the additional documents. Each of these documents may be embedded directly into the HTTP request or may be referenced indirectly by providing a URI to an external server. The application server is responsible for retrieving all of the referenced CC/PP documents and combining them—in a process called *profile composition*—to determine the resulting client profile.

The CC/PP Exchange Protocol defines the following HTTP headers:

- The **Profile** request header provides a list of CC/PP documents that are associated with the request. Each CC/PP document is identified either by an absolute URI (conforming to RFC 2396) or by a reference to one of the **Profile-Diff** headers included in the same request.

- The **Profile-Diff** request header is used to include a CC/PP document with the request. The header name itself is composed from the string "Profile-Diff-" followed by a sequence number. Within a **Profile** header, a **Profile-Diff** reference is constructed by combining the **Profile-Diff** header's sequence number with an MD5 digest hash (see RFC 1321) of the content associated with that **Profile-Diff** header. The hash enables caching and efficient processing of the reference.

- The **Profile-Warning** response header provides the client with information about the server's ability to retrieve, parse, and use the profile sent in the request header. Table 11-2 lists the warning codes and recommended warning text defined by the CC/PP Exchange Protocol.

Listing 11-2 shows examples of the CC/PP Exchange Protocol implementation. In the listing, the "ns=" attribute in each example defines a unique name space for the CC/PP Exchange Protocol headers. This ID can be any number (as long as it is not used by other headers in the HTTP request) and is used as a prefix for each of the associated headers.

Table 11-2   Profile-Warning Codes Defined by the CC/PP Exchange Protocol

Warn Code	Warn Text	Notes
100	OK	
101	Used stale profile	Indicates that an out-of-date version of a CC/PP document was used, either because an absolute URI could not be retrieved or because a server delivered an expired CC/PP document.
102	Not used profile	Indicates that the profile could not be obtained and therefore was not used.
200	Not applied	Indicates that the profile was not used because only one representation of the content was available at the server.
201	Content selection applied	Indicates that the server used the profile to select from among several alternative representations of the content.
202	Content generation applied	Indicates that the server used the profile to dynamically generate targeted content.
203	Transformation applied	A **Profile-Warning** header with this value is introduced by any proxy that transforms the content based on the profile.

Listing 11-2   Sample CC/PP Exchange Protocol headers.

```
M-GET /a-resource HTTP/1.1
Man: "http://www.w3.org/1999/06/24-CCPPexchange" ; ns=99
99-Profile: "http://www.coolterm.com/hw", "http://www.wizzyos.com/sw"


M-GET /a-resource HTTP/1.1
Man: "http://www.w3.org/1999/06/24-CCPPexchange" ; ns=98
98-Profile: "http://www.coolterm.com/hw", "1-uKhJE/AEeeMzFSejsYshHg=="
98-Profile-Diff-1: <?xml version="1.0"?>
  <rdf:RDF xmlns:rdf="http://www.w3.org/1999/02/22-rdf-syntax-ns#"
           xmlns:prf=
                  "http://www.wapforum.org/UAPROF/ccppschema-19991014991014#">
  <rdf:Description ID="MyProfile">
  <prf:component>
    <rdf:Description ID="coolhw">
      <rdf:type resource=
"http://www.wapforum.org/UAPROF/ccppschema-19991014#HardwarePlatform" />
      <prf:SoundOutputCapable>Yes</prf:SoundOutputCapable>
    </rdf:Description>
  </prf:component>
  </rdf:Description>
  </rdf:RDF>


M-GET /a-resource HTTP/1.1
Man: "http://www.w3.org/1999/06/24-CCPPexchange" ; ns=12
12-Profile-Warning: 102 http://www.coolterm.com/hw "Not used profile",
                    202 www.coolsite.com "Content generation applied"


M-GET /a-resource HTTP/1.1
Man: "http://www.w3.org/1999/06/24-CCPPexchange" ; ns=13
13-Profile-Warning: 101 http://www.coolterm.com/hw "Used stale profile",
                    102 http://www.wizzyos.com/sw "Not used profile",
                    200 www.coolsite.com "Not applied"
                                 "Wed, 31 Mar 2000 08:49:37 GMT"
```

WAP User Agent Profiles

User Agent Profiles (UAProf) were introduced with version 1.2 of the WAP specifications. UAProf extends the CC/PP architecture to support WAP devices that seek to access mobile Internet information and services over wireless links. It specifies three features:

- A mapping of the CC/PP Exchange Protocol to WSP
- A binary encoding of CC/PP documents
- A schema, and vocabulary, for describing WAP clients

Mapping of the CC/PP Exchange Protocol to WSP

During WSP session establishment, the client sends the CC/PP documents to the WAP gateway, where they are cached for the duration of the session. Whenever the user requests content from an origin server, the WAP gateway adds the cached CC/PP information by inserting the appropriate CC/PP headers (based on the CC/PP Exchange Protocol) into the HTTP request. Along with each WSP request, the client can provide additional capabilities or updates to previously cached capabilities. Note that the gateway appends this information to the request but does not update the cached capabilities.

The WAP gateway also translates the HTTP **Profile-Warning** header in the HTTP response into the corresponding WSP response header.

Binary Encoding of CC/PP Documents

The XML encoding of profiles makes them verbose. Consequently, the UAProf specification defines a WBXML encoding to ensure efficient transmission of these documents through wireless media. Each component name, attribute name, and common attribute value is associated with a numeric value. (Chapter 8 described WBXML in more detail.)

UAProf Schema

The WAP UAProf specification defines a vocabulary—that is, a set of components and attributes within those components—for describing WAP devices, browsers, networks, and users. An instance of the vocabulary, representing the CC/PP profile for a terminal, can consist of a subset of the vocabulary items. Moreover, anyone is free to define a new vocabulary that includes new components and associated attributes or that includes new attributes within existing components. Because RDF supports the concept of XML name spaces, a profile document may combine items from multiple vocabularies by referring to the name space that defines each component and attribute.

The following CC/PP components are specified in the UAProf schema:

- *HardwarePlatform:* A set of attributes that describe the hardware characteristics of the terminal. Attributes in this component include the device model number, type and size of the display, and so on.

- *SoftwarePlatform:* A set of attributes associated with the operating environment of the device, including the operating system software and available multimedia encoders.

- *BrowserUA:* A set of attributes describing the browser application. Attributes in this component include the supported markup and scripting languages, character encodings, and supported application plug-ins.

- *NetworkCharacteristics:* A set of attributes describing the network environment, including the type of bearer, bandwidth, and so on.

- *WapCharacteristics:* A set of attributes that particularly pertain to the WAP environment, including WAP Push and Wireless Telephony Application (WTA) capabilities.

Appendix D provides an exhaustive list of attributes in the WAP UAProf vocabulary.

Putting It All Together

As shown in Figure 11-2, the end-to-end communication path contains the following elements:

1. *The WAP user agent running on a client device that is capable of requesting and rendering WML content.* The profile is encoded using WBXML and transmitted to the WAP gateway during WSP session setup. The CC/PP profile is cached at the WAP gateway for the duration of the session and

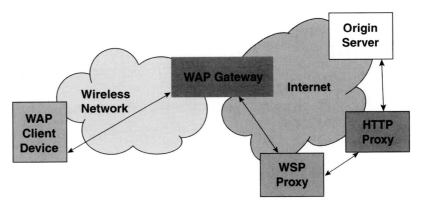

Figure 11-2 End-to-end architecture for WAP User Agent Profiles

inserted into each request sent by the client. When it performs a WSP request, the user agent can dynamically provide additional capabilities or updates to augment the cached capabilities.

2. *A wireless network infrastructure that supports WAP 1.2 or higher.* It facilitates transmission of the profile information over the air.

3. *A WAP gateway that translates WSP requests into corresponding HTTP 1.1 requests for transmission over the Internet.* Using the CC/PP Exchange Protocol, the gateway forwards any cached CC/PP documents provided during WSP session setup as well as any CC/PP documents included with the WSP request itself. The gateway may provide additional profile information by inserting an entry into the CC/PP Exchange Protocol **Profile** header. Upon receiving the HTTP response, the WAP gateway translates the HTTP **Profile-Warning** header into the corresponding WSP header.

4. *The Internet or an intranet that may include HTTP 1.1 proxy servers supporting caching, firewalls, and transcoding functions.* As the request passes through these proxies, each has the option of adding CC/PP documents to the request by appending a reference to the **Profile** header and, if necessary, inserting a **Profile-Diff** header. These network elements may also transform the content received from the server before forwarding it to the WAP client device for rendering; in doing so, they must insert an appropriate **Profile-Warning** value with a 203 code (see Table 11-2).

5. *A CC/PP-compliant Web application server that returns customized content to the client based on the profile received in the HTTP request.* To accomplish this task, the server first assembles the profile by composing the different CC/PP documents referenced in the **Profile** header. Depending on the application, the customized content is then either selected from a set of variants or generated dynamically. When returning the content, the server includes an appropriate **Profile-Warning** header indicating the extent to which it successfully honored the profiles when providing the enclosed content.

Profile Composition at the Web Application Server

Through the CC/PP Exchange Protocol, the Web application server receives a set of CC/PP documents that are listed (either by URI or by **Profile-Diff** reference) in the **Profile** header. These documents originate from the client user agent and from the various network intermediaries found along the path between the client and the Web application server. As we saw in Figure 11-1, each CC/PP document includes a set of components containing attributes, and each component may include a **Defaults** attribute that references a group of attributes.

The Web application server must merge all of these documents to determine the final device profile that it uses to customize the content. This merging process is called *profile composition.* Profile composition results in an equivalent single profile, which can be represented as a single CC/PP document. The merged document contains components and attributes with values, but it does not contain any **Defaults** attributes.

Profile composition is a three-step process:

1. Retrieve all of the CC/PP documents listed in the **Profile** header, either by accessing the referenced **Profile-Diff** header (and verifying its MD-5 hash) or by retrieving the provided URI.

2. For each CC/PP document, construct a new document as shown in Figure 11-3. The new document logically expands any attributes provided through the **Defaults** attribute; it also applies any attribute overrides provided in the component description.

   - For each component, copy the attributes provided by the **Defaults** attribute, if it exists.

   - Copy the additional attributes provided within the component, replacing any matching attributes that already exist for that component.

3. Merge these new CC/PP documents in the order that they are listed in the **Profile** header.[5] Within the vocabulary (see Appendix D), each attribute is associated with a *resolution rule* that indicates how to process the attribute if it appears in multiple CC/PP documents. The allowed resolution rules are as follows:

   - *Locked:* The final value is the value asserted in the first CC/PP document containing the attribute.

   - *Override:* The final value is the value asserted in the last CC/PP document containing the attribute.

---

[5]The CC/PP document merging procedure described here is defined in the WAP UAProf specification and therefore may not apply to profiles originating from non-WAP devices. At the time that this book was written, the World Wide Web Consortium was working to formalize the handling of generic CC/PP documents.

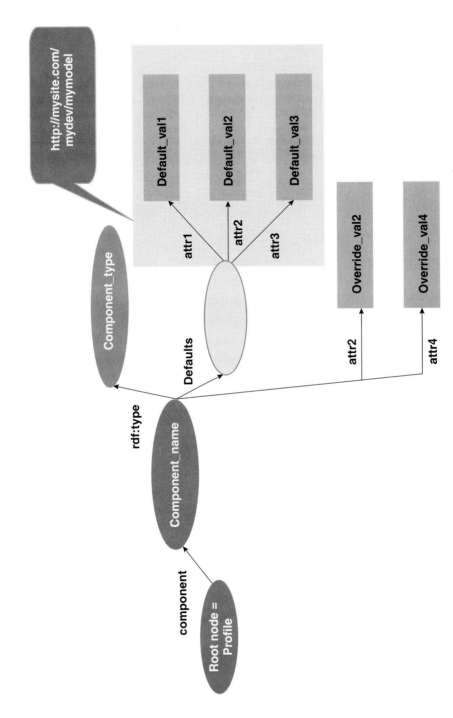

Figure 11-3a Example of resolving **Defaults** attributes: original CC/PP document graph

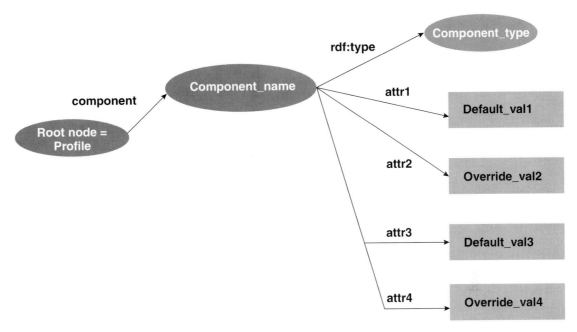

Figure 11-3b   Example of resolving **Defaults** attributes: resolved CC/PP document graph

- *Append:* The final value is a *container,* listing the values associated with the attribute in each of the CC/PP documents.

As a rule, Web application servers do not apply the profile composition process to generate a single merged profile document. The composition algorithm can be computationally intensive, particularly when many attributes or multiple CC/PP documents are involved. Moreover, each server may be interested in only a subset of the received profile information. Therefore, a CC/PP library on the application server will provide a query interface for retrieving specific profile attributes. To perform a query, the CC/PP library inspects the available CC/PP documents and returns the resolved value of the requested attribute.

Examples of Profile Composition

In this section, we provide two examples of how a server might implement the profile composition algorithm for WAP UAProf. The assumptions listed on the next page apply to both examples:

- A user wishes to access content that is located at
  http:/www.JazzySite.com/coolPage.wml from a wireless WAP
  terminal.
- The device supports a WAP browser and has the properties
  identified in Table 11-3.
- The device has a limited storage capacity, so it does not store its
  complete profile in memory. Instead, it asserts a profile containing a **Defaults** attribute with URI referencing information that
  can be retrieved from the device manufacturer's Web site.
- The device asserts some additional attributes describing an external keyboard that the user has plugged into the wireless terminal.
- Although the WAP gateway optionally could retrieve the **Defaults**
  profile and embed it into the CC/PP document that it forwards to
  the application server, we assume that it does not do so. Instead,
  the Web application server resolves the URI and retrieves the
  CC/PP document referenced in the **Defaults** attribute.

Table 11-3   Example Attributes from the UAProf Vocabulary

Component	Attribute	Explanation	Type	Value	Resolution Rule
HardwarePlatform	Model	Model number assigned to the terminal device by the vendor or manufacturer	Literal	"niftyDev4216"	Locked
HardwarePlatform	ColorCapable	Color support provided by the device display	Boolean	"No"	Override
WapCharacteristics	WmlVersion	List of WML language versions supported by the device	Literal (bag)	"1.1"	Append
HardwarePlatform	Keyboard	Type of keyboard supported by the device	Literal	"Disambiguating"	Locked

All the listings for the CC/PP RDF documents expressed in XML have been verified with the Simple RDF Parser and Compiler (SiRPAC),[6] version 1.14.

Composition Involving a Single Profile Document

In this example, the Web application server receives only the CC/PP document asserted by the client, as shown in Listing 11-3 and illustrated in Figure 11-4. The server first parses the profile.

Listing 11-3   Profile asserted by the client.

```
<?xml version="1.0"?>
<rdf:RDF xmlns:rdf=http://www.w3.org/1999/02/22-rdf-syntax-ns#
         xmlns:prf="http://www.wapforum.org/UAPROF/ccppschema19991014991014#">
<rdf:Description ID="MyProfile">
<prf:component>
    <rdf:Description ID="NiftyHrdwrCpblty">
        <rdf:type resource=
"http://www.wapforum.org/UAPROF/ccppschema-19991014/#HardwarePlatform" />
        <prf:Defaults rdf:resource="http://www.NiftyDev.com/4216" />
        <prf:Keyboard>disambiguating</prf:Keyboard>
    </rdf:Description>
</prf:component>
<prf:component>
    <rdf:Description ID="NiftysWapCpblty">
        <rdf:type resource=
"http://www.wapforum.org/UAPROF/ccppschema-19991014/#WapCharacteristics" />
        <prf:Defaults>
            <rdf:Description>
                <prf:WmlVersion>
                    <rdf:Bag>
                        <rdf:_11>1.1</rdf:_11>
                    </rdf:Bag>
                </prf:WmlVersion>
            </rdf:Description>
        </prf:Defaults>
    </rdf:Description>
</prf:component>
</rdf:Description>
</rdf:RDF>
```

When it encounters the URI associated with the Defaults attribute (**www.NiftyDev.com/4216**) for the component of type **Hardware Platform**, it generates an HTTP request to retrieve the CC/PP attributes

---

[6]The SiRPAC online interactive service is available at http://www.w3.org/RDF/ Implementations/SiRPAC/.

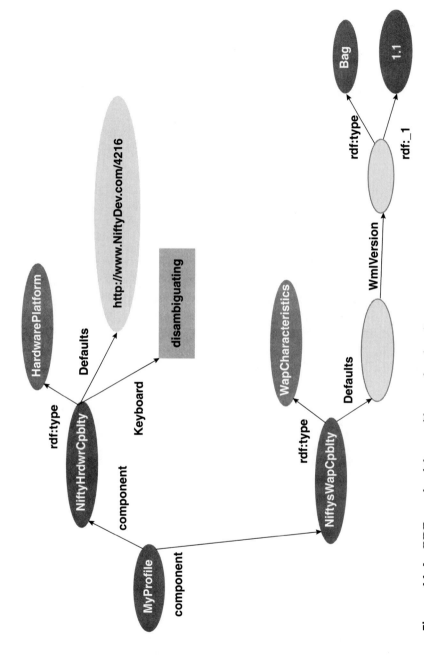

Figure 11-4 RDF graph of the profile sent by the client

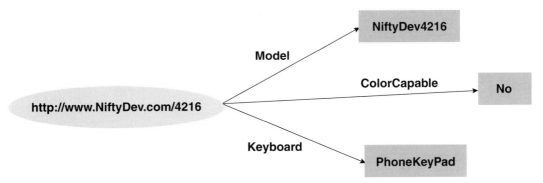

Figure 11-5 CC/PP document representing the **Defaults** attributes available at www.NiftyDev.com/4216

Listing 11-4   CC/PP document asserting Default attributes available at www.NiftyDev.com/4216.

```
<?xml version="1.0"?>
<rdf:RDF xmlns:rdf=http://www.w3.org/1999/02/22-rdf-syntax-ns#
         xmlns:prf=
"http://www.wapforum.org/UAPROF/ccppschema19991014991014#">
<rdf:Description about = "http://www.NiftyDev.com/4216">
   <prf:Model>NiftyDev4216</prf:Model>
   <prf:Keyboard>PhoneKeyPad</prf:Keyboard>
   <prf:ColorCapable>No</prf:ColorCapable>
</rdf:Description>
</rdf:RDF>
```

referenced by the URI. The retrieved attributes are shown in Listing 11-4 and illustrated in Figure 11-5. These attributes must be merged with the other attributes asserted in the **HardwarePlatform** component to arrive at a final set of attribute values for the component.

The final profile is shown in Listing 11-5 and illustrated in Figure 11-6. In this case, because of the profile composition, the **Keyboard** attribute takes the final value of "disambiguating."

Listing 11-5   Composed profile equivalent obtained by merging the CC/PP documents from Listings 11-3 and 11-4.

```
<?xml version="1.0"?>
<rdf:RDF xmlns:rdf=http://www.w3.org/1999/02/22-rdf-syntax-ns#
         xmlns:prf=
               "http://www.wapforum.org/UAPROF/ccppschema19991014991014#" >
```

```
<rdf:Description ID="MyProfile">
<prf:component>
   <rdf:Description ID="NiftyHdwrCpblty">
      <rdf:type resource=
      "http://www.wapforum.org/UAPROF/ccppschema-19991014/#HardwarePlatform" />
       <prf:Model>NiftyDev4216</prf:Model>
       <prf:Keyboard>disambiguating</prf:Keyboard>
       <prf:ColorCapable>No</prf:ColorCapable>
   </rdf:Description>
</prf:component>
<prf:component>
   <rdf:Description ID="NiftyWapCpblty">
      <rdf:type resource=
      "http://www.wapforum.org/UAPROF/ccppschema-19991014/#WapCharacteristics"/>
      <prf:WmlVersion>
         <rdf:Bag>
            <rdf:_11>1.1</rdf:_11>
         </rdf:Bag>
      </prf:WmlVersion>
   </rdf:Description>
</prf:component>
</rdf:Description>
</rdf:RDF>
```

Composition Involving Multiple Profile Documents

In this example, we illustrate profile composition from multiple profile documents. Here the HTTP request to the Web application server delivers a **Profile** header containing three CC/PP documents:

- The client asserts the same profile as in the previous section (see Listing 11-3 and Figure 11-4). This profile references the **Defaults** contained in Listing 11-4 and illustrated in Figure 11-5.

- The WAP gateway adds a CC/PP document (see Listing 11-6, and Figure 11-7 on page 485) to characterize the device's network connectivity. This document asserts a value for the **CurrentBearerService** attribute pertaining to the component of type **NetworkCharacteristics**.

- The request passes through a transcoding proxy that is capable of accepting color content and converting it into a black-and-white equivalent that can be rendered on the device. The proxy therefore adds a CC/PP document (see Listing 11-7, and Figure 11-8 on page 286) that asserts a value of "Yes" for the **ColorCapable** attribute. (We assume that the CC/PP Exchange Protocol headers are designated on a hop-by-hop basis.)

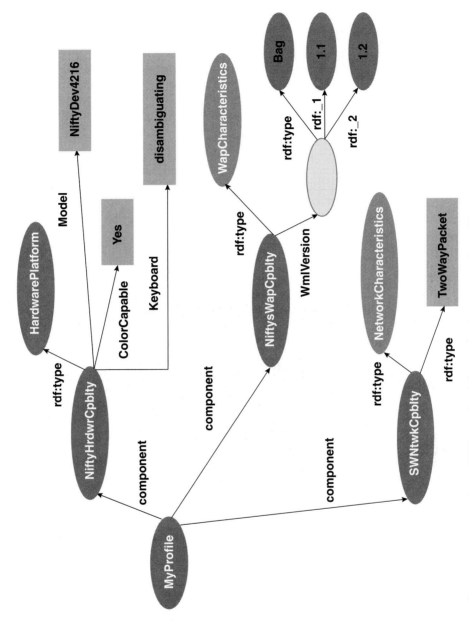

Figure 11-6 Resulting RDF graph of the equivalent merged profile

Listing 11-6   Profile introduced by the WAP gateway.

```
<?xml version="1.0"?>
<rdf:RDF xmlns:rdf=http://www.w3.org/1999/02/22-rdf-syntax-ns#
         xmlns:prf="http://www.wapforum.org/UAPROF/ccppschema19991014991014#" >
<rdf:Description ID="MyProfile">
<prf:component>
    <rdf:Description ID="SWNtwkCpblty">
        <rdf:type resource=
"http://www.wapforum.org/UAPROF/ccppschema-19991014/#NetworkCharacteristics" />
        <prf:CurrentBearerService>TwoWayPacket</prf:CurrentBearerService>
    </rdf:Description>
</prf:component>
<prf:component>
    <rdf:Description ID="GtwyWapCpblty">
        <rdf:type resource=
"http://www.wapforum.org/UAPROF/ccppschema-19991014/#WapCharacteristics" />
        <prf:WmlVersion>
          <rdf:Bag>
             <rdf:_11>1.2</rdf:_11>
          </rdf:Bag>
        </prf:WmlVersion>
    </rdf:Description>
</prf:component>
</rdf:Description>
</rdf:RDF>
```

Listing 11-7   Profile asserted by the transcoding proxy.

```
<?xml version="1.0"?>
<rdf:RDF xmlns:rdf=http://w3.org/1999/02/22-rdf-syntax-ns#
         xmlns:prf="http://www.wapforum.org/UAPROF/ccppschema19991014991014#" >
<rdf:Description ID="MyProfile">
<prf:component>
    <rdf:Description ID="Prxy1HrdwrCpblty">
        <rdf:type resource=
"http://www.wapforum.org/UAPROF/ccppschema-19991014/#HardwarePlatform" />
        <prf:ColorCapable>Yes</prf:ColorCapable>
    </rdf:Description>
</prf:component>
</rdf:Description>
</rdf:RDF>
```

The Web application server must apply composition rules to merge all three profiles before generating content. It begins by parsing each of the CC/PP documents and resolving the URI associated with the **Defaults** attributes, as described in the previous example. The resulting CC/PP documents are then merged based on the resolution rules defined for each attribute. The resulting merged profile is shown in Listing 11-8, and illustrated in Figure 11-9 on page 487.

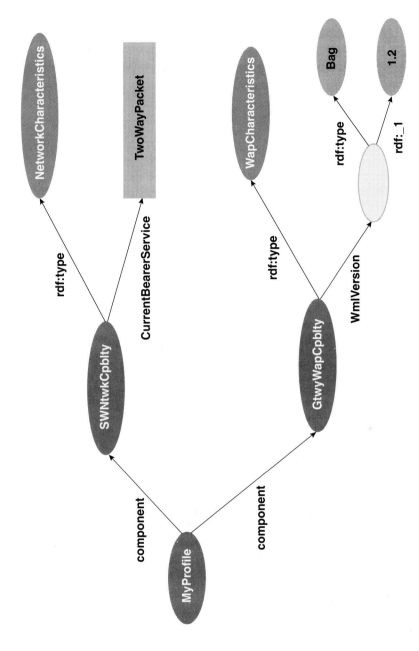

Figure 11-7   CC/PP profile asserted by the WAP gateway

485

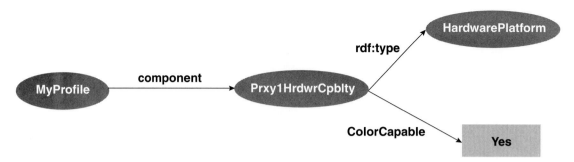

Figure 11-8   RDF graph of the profile conveyed by the transcoding proxy

Listing 11-8   **The final composed profile (equivalent) obtained by merging the CC/PP documents from Listings 11-3, 11-4, 11-6, and 11-7.**

```xml
<?xml version="1.0"?>
<rdf:RDF xmlns:rdf=http://www.w3.org/1999/02/22-rdf-syntax-ns#
        xmlns:prf="http://www.wapforum.org/UAPROF/ccppschema19991014991014#" >
<rdf:Description ID="MyProfile">
<prf:component>
    <rdf:Description ID="NiftyHdwrCpblty">
      <rdf:type resource=
"http://www.wapforum.org/UAPROF/ccppschema-19991014/#HardwarePlatform" />
      <prf:Model>NiftyDev4216</prf:Model>
      <prf:Keyboard>disambiguating</prf:Keyboard>
      <prf:ColorCapable>Yes</prf:ColorCapable>
    </rdf:Description>
</prf:component>
<prf:component>
    <rdf:Description ID="NiftyWapCpblty">
      <rdf:type resource=
"http://www.wapforum.org/UAPROF/ccppschema-19991014/#WapCharacteristics" />
      <prf:WmlVersion>
        <rdf:Bag>
            <rdf:_l1>1.1</rdf:_l1>
            <rdf:_l1>1.2</rdf:_l1>
        </rdf:Bag>
      </prf:WmlVersion>
    </rdf:Description>
</prf:component>
<prf:component>
    <rdf:Description ID="SWNtwkCpblty">
      <rdf:type resource=
"http://www.wapforum.org/UAPROF/ccppschema-19991014/#NetworkCharacteristics" />
<prf:CurrentBearerService>TwoWayPacket</prf:CurrentBearerService>
    </rdf:Description>
</prf:component>
</rdf:Description>
</rdf:RDF>
```

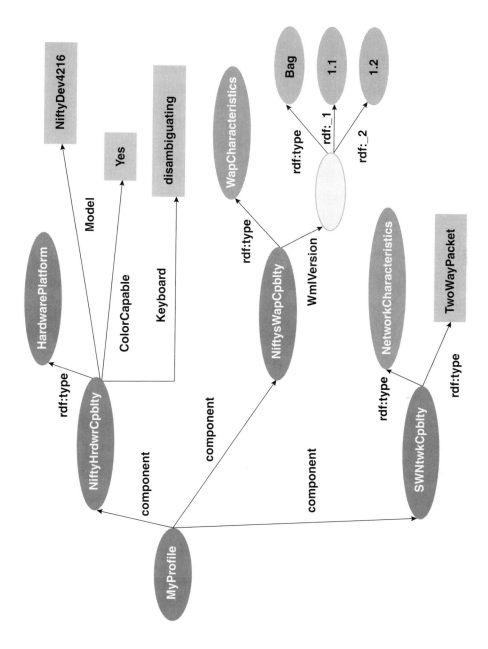

Figure 11-9 Final RDF graph created by merging the profiles sent by the client, the gateway, and the proxy, as well as the segment retrieved from the **Defaults** URI

487

Let us assume that our server has two versions of the content: a WML 1.1 version with no images and a WML 1.2 version that references color images.

By inspecting the merged profile, the server discovers that the client environment can handle both WML 1.1 and WML 1.2. Based on the profile, it also realizes that it can deliver its color WML 1.2 content. (If the profile had indicated support for only black-and-white display, then our server would have been forced to deliver its WML 1.1 content with no images.)

Upon receiving the content from the server, the transcoding proxy inspects the profile that it received from the gateway, only to discover that the device really supports just black-and-white images. It therefore converts the color images into a black-and-white form before passing them to the gateway. The proxy is responsible for performing the conversion because it asserted the additional color capabilities on behalf of the device.

Upon receiving the black-and-white content from the transcoding proxy, the WAP gateway inspects the profile that it received from the device, only to discover that the device supports just WML 1.1. It therefore translates the WML 1.2 content into WML 1.1. The gateway is responsible for this conversion because it asserted the additional WML 1.2 capabilities on behalf of the device.

Finally, the client device receives the WML 1.1 content referencing the black-and-white images.

Conclusion

In this chapter, we considered approaches for delivering content that is tailored to the characteristics of WAP clients, browsers, users, and networks. The ad hoc mechanisms based on current HTTP 1.1 headers are currently being used in the initial development of wireless network content. Nevertheless, developers are demanding the sophisticated information and features provided by CC/PP and UAProf, and phones supporting these features will be available soon. Moreover, the ETSI MExE standard has adopted WAP UAProf, and it will likely become incorporated into the 3GPP standards.

The World Wide Web Consortium has embarked on an effort to formalize CC/PP into a Web standard. The forthcoming W3C recommendation adds a trust model for handling the end-to-end communications through proxies and firewalls, a "core" vocabulary for all Web-connected clients, and richer composition rules. This effort is likely to drive the use of CC/PP for the next-generation Web.

Chapter 12
Push Messaging

One especially interesting feature of WAP is the ability to push information to the mobile handset instead of relying on the traditional pull, or "request–response," model. In the classic Web, a user pulls information online by initiating a request with a URL to a server, and the server returns information associated with that particular URL. With the push model, the information is sent to a client without the need for any previous user request. In this respect, the WAP environment clearly differs from the Web world and enables new types of services over the wireless network.

A good example of a push model is *paging*. In a paging system, the mobile client does not actively pull information. Instead, it simply waits to receive a "push"—or a *page*, as it is more commonly known in that environment. Someone who wishes to reach a particular person initiates a page, and the network is then responsible for carrying this message over the air to the subscriber's mobile client, the *pager*.

Another example of a push service is *Short Message Service* (SMS). SMS is widely used in mobile network environments, especially with GSM networks and terminals. On a mobile phone, this service provides similar functionality to that of a pager. SMS supports text messages, as well as some proprietary formats. In reality, it is a two-way message service, because messages can also be initiated from the mobile client. This approach differs from paging, which traditionally has been a one-way service— from the network to a pager. Recently, however, two-way paging has emerged very strongly in North America and is now gaining rapid user acceptance.

SMS and paging can be regarded as the de facto "push services" in use in mobile networks today, and they will certainly remain so for some time. They are popular because, despite the relatively small payload and restricted content types, both enable a variety of useful services for mobile users. Examples of these popular services include news headlines, stock price alerts, and voice mail notifications that are pushed to end users' pagers and mobile phones. Unfortunately, the wide range of push access methods, the need for proprietary protocols because of the close tie to the mobile and paging networks, and the limited availability of the push capabilities in some countries have limited the range of services utilizing SMS and paging.

WAP Push advances these (and future) messaging models by integrating them into the WAP application environment on the mobile device and by making them accessible through standard Internet protocols. As a consequence, these advancements open the door to global accessibility and a wider range of available services.

In this chapter, we discuss the WAP Push architecture and its application-enabling features. We begin by discussing the history and goals of WAP Push. Next, we describe the WAP Push architecture and the services provided by each of its elements. We then take a closer look at how an application creates a Push Message, addresses it to the mobile client, and sends it for delivery. After discussing the mechanics of push messaging through the Push Proxy Gateway and the Push Over-the-Air Protocol, we conclude the chapter by covering push initiator authentication and trusted content.

Overview of WAP Push

The history of WAP Push actually goes back to the origins of WAP. The first version of the WAP specifications included some notion of push, though it was specified only in terms of Wireless Session Protocol primitives for transmitting pushed data. That is, the specifications did not provide any end-to-end features to actually enable push-based services.

To complete the push enablement, the WAP Forum chartered a push drafting committee in July 1998. The committee's charter seemed simple enough:

Create a solution for network-initiated content delivery.

Although the task sounded simple, the drafting committee took more than a year to complete its task. In August 1999, a suite of seven specifications was finally voted upon by the WAP Forum membership and entered a period of public review. The standard was formally adopted in December 1999. Mobile devices and network infrastructure supporting these specifications are expected to be widely available by 2001.

WAP Push Goals

The WAP Push specification has three key goals with respect to service developers:

1. *Standard Internet protocols and content types are cornerstones of WAP Push.* From the start, the main focus was to make things simple and easy to use from the Internet world. After all, that is where the push services are built. Furthermore, it was important that WAP Push did not restrict or limit the set of content types that could be pushed over the mobile network.

2. *The complexity of underlying mobile networks is completely hidden from the services utilizing WAP Push.* Because push services will be built to run on standard Web servers and to use standard Internet protocols, service developers should not be burdened with having to understand the mobile networks in detail.

3. *A simple, transport-independent protocol is required between the Web service and the WAP Push service connected to the mobile network.* In the Internet today, there are two dominant application protocols: the Hypertext Transfer Protocol (HTTP) and the Simple Mail Transfer Protocol (SMTP). A service should be able to use either one without being locked into that choice.

These three points represent only a fraction of the full goals and requirements that were put in place before the WAP Forum began working on the WAP Push specification. Other requirements focused on ensuring mobile and Internet network efficiency, maintaining user control, and ensuring simplicity of implementation.

WAP Push Framework

WAP Push essentially consists of three elements. First, the *Push Initiator* creates the message that needs to be pushed. Second, to have the Push Initiator interact with the wireless world, a gateway—namely, the *Push*

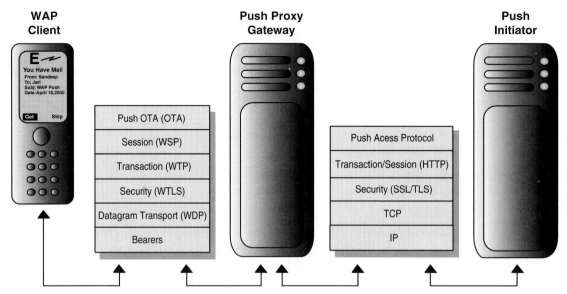

Figure 12-1   WAP Push framework

Proxy Gateway (PPG)—is required. Third, the WAP client receives the message. Figure 12-1 illustrates these elements and their interaction with associated protocols.

WAP Push Protocols

WAP Push defines two protocols: *Push Access Protocol* (PAP) and *Push Over-the-Air (OTA) Protocol.*

The Push Initiator and the Push Proxy Gateway communicate using PAP. The Push Initiator uses PAP to submit push messages, cancel previously submitted messages, and query the message status and WAP client capabilities. The Push Proxy Gateway uses PAP to respond to requests from Push Initiators. PAP is currently transferred over HTTP 1.1, although other transfer methods may be used. Currently, the WAP Forum is investigating a binding for PAP over SMTP.

The Push Proxy Gateway and the WAP client communicate using the Push OTA Protocol. This protocol is a thin layer built on top of Wireless Session Protocol (WSP), and it is responsible for transferring the content from the Push Proxy Gateway over the wireless network to the WAP client.

WAP Push-Specific Content Types

To simplify the use of WAP Push, two MIME media types are defined: Service Indication and Service Loading. These media types give application developers a head start on creating services based on WAP Push.

Service Indication is an XML document type that indicates that content is waiting for the WAP client and provides a reference to that content. This reference is typically a URI pointing to a service or resource that can be accessed by the WAP client.

Service Loading, another XML document type, is similar to Service Indication except that the client will automatically, without end-user involvement, download and execute the content indicated by the reference URI.

In addition to Service Indication and Service Loading, a third MIME type, called *Session Initiation Application,* may be employed. This special-purpose media type is used to inform the WAP client that WSP session creation is required.

We will discuss these media types in more detail later in this chapter.

Having introduced the basic elements of WAP Push, we are now ready to look at each of them in more detail. We begin in the Internet world, with the Push Access Protocol.

Push Access Protocol

As we have seen, the Push Initiator and Push Proxy Gateway communicate using PAP to initiate and control Push Message submissions. PAP is a simple, XML-based protocol that is independent of the underlying transport. Currently, the WAP Push specification defines how PAP can be implemented over HTTP 1.1; the WAP Forum is also working on an a binding to SMTP. In the future, more transport methods are likely to emerge. Indeed, because of the PAP design, it will be relatively easy to define bindings for PAP utilizing these new transports.

In this section, we first discuss the message format of PAP transmissions, then define the operations provided by PAP. After describing quality-of-service possibilities, we explain the PAP binding to HTTP 1.1.

Push Access Protocol Message Format

A Push Access Protocol Push Submission message takes the form of a MIME **multipart/related** document that may carry a maximum of three types of information, each encapsulated in a separate MIME multipart entity. (Note that most of the other PAP operations use simple documents of type **application/XML** without the MIME **multipart/related** structure.) These three types of information include the following:

1. *Push Proxy Gateway and Push Initiator control information:* This XML document contains the requested PAP operation and its attributes. (The available operations are discussed in the next section.) It is always the first entity of the PAP message.

2. *The actual Push Message that is targeted to the WAP client:* This message contains headers followed by the message body. The message body is associated with its own (arbitrary) MIME type(s), which itself may even be a MIME **multipart** type. Note that neither WAP nor WAP Push restricts the content types. When included in a PAP message, the Push Message is always the second entity.

3. *Capabilities and preferences information:* This information is carried in the RDF format defined for *WAP User Agent Profiles* (UAProf), which was discussed in Chapter 11. It contains information such as the preferred or supported media types of the client, device characteristics such as the screen size, and support for color (if any).

The capabilities and preferences information is used in two ways. First, when submitting a Push Message, the Push Initiator can describe the assumed device's capabilities and preferences. The Push Proxy Gateway can verify these assumptions before forwarding the message to the device. In this case, the capabilities and preferences information is the third entity in a PAP Push Message submission request.

Alternatively, it can be provided by a Push Proxy Gateway in response to a client capability query from the Push Initiator. In this case, it is the second entity of a PAP message. Because devices will have different characteristics, the Push Initiator can use this information to tailor the content to ensure optimized handling in the particular WAP client.

Push Access Protocol Operations

For facilitating WAP Push service, PAP provides five basic operations for the Push Initiator and Push Proxy Gateway. Only the *Push Submission* and *Result Notification* operations must be supported by Push Proxy Gateway implementations, however, so it is advisable to investigate beforehand which additional operations are supported by the Push Proxy Gateway that you plan to use.

PAP operations are based on a request–response model, meaning that each message triggers a response that is sent back to the originator.

Push Submission

The Push Submission operation describes the Push Message that is submitted to a Push Proxy Gateway for delivery. It carries a unique message identification (message ID) assigned by the Push Initiator and provides additional information about the message source and the preferred handling of the message:

- Delivery parameters, including whether the message should be sent before or after a defined time period and whether a delivery report is requested.
- The device address to which the actual Push Message, which is contained in the second entity of the PAP message, should be delivered. Addressing is discussed further in the section "WAP Push Addressing."
- Information identifying the originator of the message.
- Quality-of-service parameters defining the priority of the message and delivery method (confirmed or unconfirmed). These parameters can also define some mobile-network-related attributes, including the desired bearer type. The Push Proxy Gateway implementation decides whether to honor quality-of-service definitions. If the gateway is not able to fulfill the request, it rejects the Push Message.

Listing 12-1 shows an example of control information contained in the first MIME entity of a Push Submission.

Listing 12-1   The first entity in a PAP Push Submission Request message.

```
Content-Type: application/xml; charset=iso-8859-1

<?xml version="1.0"?>
<!DOCTYPE pap PUBLIC "-//WAPFORUM//DTD PAP 1.0//EN"
            "http://www.wapforum.org/DTD/pap_1.0.dtd">
<pap>
```

```
<push-message push-id="210861030999@alvinen.com"
              deliver-before-timestamp="2000-04-12T00:00:00Z"
              ppg-notify-requested-to=
              "http://www.alvinen.com/cgi-bin/my-notification-collector">
   <address address-value=
       "WAPPUSH=anita%40alvinen.com/TYPE=USER@pushservice.carrier.com"/>
   <quality-of-service
       priority="high"
       delivery-method="confirmed"/>
</push-message>
</pap>
```

Push Submission Response

As an initial response to Push Submission, the Push Proxy Gateway generates a push response message that includes the message ID, together with information about the Push Proxy Gateway and a timestamp indicating when this response was created. This response can also include a status code for the initial message submission and a Push Proxy Gateway implementation-specific progress information, if so requested by the Push Initiator.

Push Cancellation

This operation cancels messages based on their message IDs. The Push Initiator can optionally define the recipient address or addresses to request cancellation only for certain recipients of the identified message.

Push Cancellation Response

As a response to message cancellation, the Push Proxy Gateway sends back a message to the Push Initiator with the message ID and a status code representing the outcome of the cancellation request.

Push Status Query

The Push Initiator can query the status of previously submitted messages based on their message IDs. Optionally, it can narrow the scope of the status query to certain recipient addresses.

Push Status Query Response

The Push Status Query Response includes the message ID, possible recipient address to which this status applies, and the status code itself. Additionally, the message can include quality-of-service information describing the delivery methods used for this particular message, if requested in the original Push Submission.

Client Capability Query

The Push Initiator uses this query to obtain information about the WAP client before submitting a message. It assigns an ID to the query, and provides both the address of the client and an identifier for the application in the WAP client about which it is requesting information.

Client Capability Query Response

The Push Proxy Gateway uses these identifiers and selects a suitable set of capabilities to be returned to the Push Initiator. After receiving this information, the Push Initiator can tailor the Push Message to achieve a format appropriate for the particular WAP client.

Result Notification

All messages submitted by the Push Initiator to the Push Proxy Gateway will get a Push Submission Response when they are accepted for processing. In addition, the Push Initiator can ask in the Push Submission Request that the Push Proxy Gateway send a notification indicating the final status of the message (whether the message was delivered, canceled, or expired, or whether an error occurred).

Result Notification Response

The Result Notification Response acknowledges receipt of the Result Notification. It is sent from the Push Initiator to the Push Proxy Gateway.

Push Access Protocol over HTTP 1.1

HTTP 1.1 can be used to transfer PAP messages. PAP requests are sent as HTTP POST requests, and PAP responses are included in the HTTP reply. Because security is an important issue, especially in the Internet world, the Push Proxy Gateway should control which Push Initiators can access it using PAP. As PAP can be tunneled over HTTP, security methods such as SSL and X.509 client certificates can be used to support this authentication.

WAP Push Addressing

In this section, we discuss the format of the addresses used in WAP Push to identify the destination client and the destination application.

WAP Client Addressing

The address format in WAP Push is compatible with the e-mail address format defined in RFC 822. The WAP client address is composed from a client specifier and a Push Proxy Gateway specifier. The client specifier may be either a device address or a user-defined identifier.

Device addresses are static network addresses, such as *Public Land Mobile Network* (PLMN) telephone numbers. As an example, consider the following WAP client address, which combines a telephone number and a Push Proxy Gateway address:

```
WAPPUSH=+141588999777/TYPE=PLMN@pushservice.operator.com
```

User-defined identifiers are mapped to wireless network addresses by the Push Proxy Gateway. A good example of a user-defined address is an e-mail address. An identifier could actually be mapped to several wireless network addresses, if the Push Initiator and Push Proxy Gateway agree to support this scheme. As an example, consider the following WAP client address, which combines a user-defined identifier (anita@alvinen.com) and a Push Proxy Gateway address:

```
WAPPUSH=anita%40alvinen.com/TYPE=USER@pushservice.carrier.com
```

A Push Proxy Gateway must support at least one of the two types of client specifiers. The gateway is required to be able to parse both address formats, determine whether it supports the requested specifier, and, if necessary, notify the Push Initiator with an appropriate error code in the Push Status Query Response or the Result Notification message. Naturally, it is helpful if a Push Initiator knows beforehand which types of specifiers are supported by a Push Proxy Gateway.

Application Addressing

The Push Initiator can address a particular application in the WAP client by including an application ID in the X-Wap-Application-Id header in the Push Message.

When a Push Message arrives at the WAP client, the application ID is used to locate the appropriate application and dispatch the received content to it. Such a message can also arrive at the WAP client without an application ID, in which case it will be dispatched to the default WML user agent.

The application ID name space is currently managed by the WAP Interim Naming Authority (WINA), which was described in Chapter 6.

Push Message

As previously discussed, the Push Message is the second entity in a PAP Push Submission Request. Constructed by the Push Initiator, it carries the actual content intended for the WAP client.

Push Message Format

Push Messages use a generic format for Internet text messages, as defined in RFC 822, but they can also accommodate binary message bodies. Each message generally takes the same form as a valid HTTP 1.1 response message and consists of message headers and a message body.

Message Headers

Two types of headers exist: generic headers and WAP-specific headers. The generic headers are based on the common Internet message headers defined by HTTP 1.1.[1] The WAP-specific headers include the following:

- `X-Wap-Application-Id` identifies the target application in the WAP client. If this header is undefined, then the message is delivered to the default WML user agent.
- `X-Wap-Content-URI` uniquely identifies the Push Message when it is placed in the client's cache. The message may be invalidated and discarded from the cache in accordance with normal cache control policies.[2]
- `X-Wap-Initiator-URI` identifies the Push Initiator and can be used by the WAP client to verify trusted Push Initiators. Use of this header is discussed further in the section "Push Initiator Authentication and Trusted Content."

Message Body

The body of a Push Message can be any MIME-media type, such as a Service Indication (see "MIME Media Types for Push Messages").

---

[1]For more information about the generic headers in WAP Push, refer to the WAP Push Message Specification.

[2]For more information about invalidating cached content, refer to the WAP Cache Operation Specification; Chapter 7 provides an overview of WAP content caching policies.

Push Message Example

Listing 12-2 is an example of a Push Message. It uses the generic header `Content-Type` and the WAP header `X-Wap-Application-Id`, which indicates the application ID for the WML user agent. The message body is a Service Indication (as discussed in the next section).

Combining the PAP control entity and the Push Message, the complete transmission to the Push Proxy Gateway takes the form shown in Listing 12-3.

Listing 12-2   A Push Message (the second entity in a PAP Push Submission Request).

```
Content-Type: text/vnd.wap.si; charset=iso-8859-1
X-Wap-Application-Id: 02

<?xml version="1.0"?>
<!DOCTYPE si PUBLIC "-//WAPFORUM//DTD SI 1.0//EN"
            "http://www.wapforum.org/DTD/si.dtd">
<si>
   <indication href="http://www.alvinen.com/email/newmail.wml"
            created="2000-04-11T17:10:00Z"
            si-expires="2000-04-12T00:00:00Z"
            action="signal-medium">
      You have mail
   </indication>
</si>
```

Listing 12-3   A complete PAP Push Submission Request message.

```
POST  /cgi-bin/wap_push.cgi HTTP/1.1
Host: www.pushservice.carrier.com
Date: Tue, 11 April 2000 18:00:00 GMT
Content-Type: multipart/related; boundary=NEXT_PART; type="application/xml"

--NEXT_PART
Content-Type: application/xml; charset=iso-8859-1

<?xml version="1.0"?>
<!DOCTYPE pap PUBLIC "-//WAPFORUM//DTD PAP 1.0//EN"
                "http://www.wapforum.org/DTD/pap_1.0.dtd">
<pap>
<push-message push-id="210861030999@alvinen.com"
            deliver-before-timestamp="2000-04-12T00:00:00Z"
            ppg-notify-requested-to=
                "http://www.alvinen.com/cgi-bin/my-notification-collector">
   <address address-value=
       "WAPPUSH=anita%40alvinen.com/TYPE=USER@pushservice.carrier.com"/>
```

```
            <quality-of-service
                priority="high"
                delivery-method="confirmed"/>
</push-message>
</pap>

--NEXT_PART
Content-Type: text/vnd.wap.si; charset=iso-8859-1
X-Wap-Application-Id: 02

<?xml version="1.0"?>
<!DOCTYPE si PUBLIC "-//WAPFORUM//DTD SI 1.0//EN"
                    "http://www.wapforum.org/DTD/si.dtd">
<si>
    <indication href="http://www.alvinen.com/email/newmail.wml"
                created="2000-04-11T17:10:00Z"
                si-expires="2000-04-12T00:00:00Z"
                action="signal-medium">
        You have mail
    </indication>
</si>

--NEXT_PART--
```

MIME Media Types for Push Messages

Although a Push Message may have any MIME media type, WAP Push defines two types that provide particularly useful semantics. The Service Indication and Service Loading types represent XML documents that describe an event and instruct the client user agent how to handle that event.

Service Indication

A *Service Indication* (SI) signals the user that an event—most likely an asynchronous one—has occurred. It provides information about the event in the form of a small message describing the event and a URI reference to information about the event or related service. Examples of using Service Indication with WAP Push include voice mail, e-mail, or news service notifications. The following MIME media types have been registered:

- **application/vnd.wap.sic**: represents a Service Indication in Wireless Binary XML (WBXML) format.
- **text/vnd.wap.si**: represents a Service Indication in text format.

Service Indication Features

A Service Indication conveys a URI to the WAP client, along with a small message that is displayed to the user. The receiving client allows the user to start the related service by launching the provided URI or to postpone the Service Indication for later handling. In addition to the message and URI, the Service Indication provides the following features:

- *Control of user-intrusiveness level:* The Service Indication can be assigned a user-intrusiveness level, according to the importance of the event that the message represents. Three levels are specified: (1) `signal-low` indicates that the Service Indication should be automatically postponed for later handling without first querying the user; (2) `signal-medium` indicates that the Service Indication should be presented to the user in as nonintrusive a way as soon as possible; and (3) `signal-high` indicates that the Service Indication should be presented as soon as possible. Basically, `signal-high` means that the Service Indication will be presented at once, but the specification leaves some room here for implementation-specific interpretations because exceptions to the general rule for safety or usability may be warranted.

- *Replacement:* A Service Indication can be assigned an identifier that can be used later to detect Service Indications carrying the same kind of information. The identifier is used, together with date and time attributes also present in a Service Indication, to allow the new message to replace old ones having the same type. For example, a previously received, but unprocessed Service Indication containing an indication of two new voice mail items might be replaced with one saying that there are four new voice mail items.

- *Expiration:* Service Indications contain an attribute that indicates the expiration date and time. If this attribute is set, the Service Indication will be deleted or marked as expired automatically when the particular date and time are reached.

- *Delete:* When a Service Indication becomes invalid, it can be deleted by sending a new Service Indication containing the **delete** action and the original message ID. For example, if a user checks her voice mail from some phone other than her mobile WAP client, the voice mail system can issue a Service Indication to delete the now-invalid voice mail Service Indication from the WAP client.

- *Out-of-order handling:* Out-of-order Service Indications are handled based on their date and timestamp attributes. A Service Indication is silently discarded if it is older than a previously received Service Indication carrying an identical ID.

Service Indication Usage

A Service Indication, as its name implies, signals that an event has occurred. It is compact in form, but it can be further optimized by binary encoding using WAP Binary XML (WBXML), discussed in Chapter 8. Service Indication offers the easiest way for application and service developers to quickly build a service or application using WAP Push. However, note that handset vendors may adopt different interpretations of the Service Indication user-intrusiveness levels according to their user interface preferences. Therefore, you are advised to research the different implementations before deploying Service Indication in a service.

Listing 12-4 shows an example of a Service Indication that expires on April 12, 2000, at 23:30 UTC time. It informs the user with medium-level intrusiveness that a new e-mail has arrived, and it provides a URI pointing to the mail item.

Listing 12-4   A Service Indication message.

```
<?xml version="1.0"?>
<!DOCTYPE si PUBLIC "-//WAPFORUM//DTD SI 1.0//EN"
                    "http://www.wapforum.org/DTD/si.dtd">
<si>
   <indication href="http://www.alvinen.com/email/newmail.wml"
               created="2000-04-11T17:10:00Z"
               si-expires="2000-04-12T00:00:00Z"
               action="signal-medium">
      You have mail
   </indication>
</si>
```

Service Loading

Service Loading (SL) is a MIME media type signaling automatic content download on behalf of the user. A Service Loading document carries only a URI and an attribute describing the user-intrusiveness level. When the WAP client receives a Service Loading message, it activates the service indicated by the URI, downloads the content, and either executes or caches the content, based on the specified level of user-intrusiveness. Service Loading can be used, for example, to push e-mail messages to the mobile client's inbox in the background. The following Service Loading MIME media types have been registered:

- **application/vnd.wap.slc**: represents Service Loading in WBXML format.
- **text/vnd.wap.sl**: represents Service Loading in Text format.

Service Loading User-Intrusiveness Levels

Service Loading can have three levels of user-intrusiveness:

- execute-low indicates that the WAP client should download and execute the content as if the end user had initiated the request. In this case, message processing needs to be performed in a non-user-intrusive manner.
- execute-high indicates behavior similar to that specified by execute-low, except that the operation may be done in a user-intrusive manner.
- cache indicates behavior similar to that specified by execute-low, except that instead of being executed after download, the content is placed in the cache.

Service Loading Usage

Unlike Service Indication, Service Loading is not a mandatory feature in WAP Push, and therefore it is unlikely to be supported in most early WAP Push clients. Time will tell how widely Service Loading will be used. This feature does, however, offer several useful capabilities that will certainly become popular over time.

One thing is certain: Due to its nature, Service Loading will not be available for all service developers. For example, the user might restrict the acceptance of Service Loading media types to those originating from trusted service providers, or the Push Proxy Gateway owner might impose its own policies.

Furthermore, as with Service Indication, the various handset vendors are likely to interpret the user-intrusiveness levels differently.

Like Service Indication, Service Loading can be optimized for over-the-air delivery by binary encoding using WBXML.

Listing 12-5 shows an example of a Service Loading message that downloads a new e-mail item and places it in the client's cache for possible later processing.

Listing 12-5   A Service Loading message.

```
<?xml version="1.0"?>
<!DOCTYPE sl PUBLIC "-//WAPFORUM//DTD SL 1.0//EN"
          "http://www.wapforum.org/DTD/sl.dtd">
<sl href="http://www.alvinen.com/email/importantemail.wml"
    action="cache"/>
```

Push Proxy Gateway

For WAP Push, the Push Proxy Gateway serves as the "glue" between the wired and the wireless world. In short, the Push Proxy Gateway translates Push Initiator requests that are submitted using PAP into messages that are delivered using the Push OTA Protocol to the WAP client.

The Push Proxy Gateway's job involves translating attributes defined by the Push Initiator into actual instructions on how and when the message should be processed. Additionally, this gateway needs to provide storage for pending messages and for information used to respond to status queries arriving from the Push Initiator.

The Push Proxy Gateway specification describes the functional role of this intermediary at only a high level. It leaves considerable flexibility for commercial implementations to differentiate themselves, while still defining the minimum functionality required to guarantee interoperability with the various Push Initiator implementations. In particular, an implementer is free to build a Push Proxy Gateway into the WAP gateway that is directly connected to the mobile network.

In this section, we discuss how a Push Proxy Gateway processes a PAP message containing a Push Submission request from a Push Initiator. We begin by looking at what happens when a message submission arrives and then see what conversions might take place and how the message is delivered.

Push Submission

Upon receiving a PAP message submitted by the Push Initiator, the Push Proxy Gateway first validates the syntax of the PAP control information (see "Push Access Protocol Message Format"), the first entity in the PAP message, by comparing it with the Document Type Definition (DTD). The Push Proxy Gateway then generates the PAP Push Submission Response message. This response simply indicates the initial acceptance or rejection of the Push Submission. It serves as the first signal to the Push Initiator that the Push Submission is being processed further by the Push Proxy Gateway. If any error conditions already exist, then the Push Proxy Gateway will return an appropriate error code in the response message.

Once the Push Proxy Gateway has initially accepted the Push Submission, it begins checking the control information in the message. For example, these checks verify the delivery address and the other delivery attributes.

The Push Proxy Gateway may also optimize headers defined in the Push Message entity to reduce required over-the-air bandwidth. For example, it may encode the headers into binary format, and it may remove headers with default values that are known to the WAP client. The gateway can also manipulate the Push Message content to optimize the over-the-air transmission. For example, it may encode WML or a Service Indication contained in the message into binary format.

Message Delivery

Depending on the control information in the Push Message, the Push Proxy Gateway selects the appropriate method of delivery. It can choose from two methods:

- *Unconfirmed Push:* The WAP client does not return a confirmation when the message is received. At the Push Proxy Gateway, the message will have `Delivered` status immediately after it is submitted over the air.

- *Confirmed Push:* The WAP client returns a message delivery confirmation to the Push Proxy Gateway. The message will not have `Delivered` status until an acknowledgment is received from the WAP client within a push proxy gateway-specific timeout period.

The Push Proxy Gateway must honor any delivery method requested by the Push Initiator. If it cannot fulfill the request, it must reject the Push Message and, upon request, report an error to the Push Initiator.

Push Over-the-Air Protocol

The Push Proxy Gateway and WAP client communicate using the Push Over-the-Air (OTA) Protocol. This protocol is implemented on top of the Wireless Session Protocol (WSP) and is responsible for transferring the content from the Push Proxy Gateway over the wireless network to the WAP client. In this section, we discuss different modes of message transfer over the air and examine how the Push Proxy Gateway can request session creation when needed.

Push Connection Modes

Because the Push OTA Protocol relies on WSP services, it establishes Push Sessions to talk with the WAP client. These sessions can be connectionless or connection-oriented.

Connectionless Push uses the WSP **S-Unit-Push** service primitives. The service need not establish a true session to communicate with the client. Because no session is set up, however, this mode cannot be used to fulfill a Push Initiator's request for Confirmed Push—after all, the client has no way to communicate whether it received the message. Consequently, this mode is used only when the Push Initiator requests Unconfirmed Push. The Push Proxy Gateway also uses this mode when it does not have an open session with the client but needs to establish one.

As its name implies, *Connection-Oriented Push* requires an established session between the WAP client and the Push Proxy Gateway. It uses the WSP session-oriented Push primitives (**S-Push, S-ConfirmedPush**). The Push Proxy Gateway uses this mode, with the **S-ConfirmedPush** primitive, when a Push Initiator requests Confirmed Push.

Session Initiation Application Request

A special case arises when the WAP client does not have a session to the Push Proxy Gateway. When Connection-Oriented Push is required, the Push Proxy Gateway must establish a WSP session with the WAP client. However, the WAP architecture addresses only the traditional pull-type message transfer, in which a WAP client establishes a session with a server; it does not support session establishment from the server to the client.

WAP Push solves this problem by using a Connectionless Push request, initiated by the Push Proxy Gateway, over the air. The payload of the message is the *Session Initiation Application* (SIA) content type, indicating the location of the Push Proxy Gateway to which the client should establish a session and which bearer network it should use. On receiving this message, the WAP client invokes the Session Initiation Application and establishes a session to the server using the indicated bearer network.

Push Initiator Authentication and Trusted Content

It is important that a WAP client be able to authenticate the Push Initiator. WAP Push provides a simple method that ensures some degree of authentication. This mechanism relies on a transitive trust between the WAP client and the Push Proxy Gateway, which, in turn, should authenticate the Push Initiator using, for example, X.509 client certificates (see "Push Access Protocol over HTTP 1.1"). Chapter 14 discusses this transitive trust concept in more detail.

To establish the chain of trust, the client must first determine the identity of the Push Initiator. To do so, it performs two steps:

1. *It verifies that it trusts the Push Proxy Gateway.* The client maintains a list of contact points for trusted Push Proxy Gateways. It simply checks whether the gateway's address appears in this list.

2. *It verifies that the (trusted) Push Proxy Gateway has authenticated the Push Initiator.* The Push OTA Protocol carries an **Authenticated** flag that is set by the PPG to indicate that it authenticated the Push Initiator.

The client can now be sure that the Push Initiator was authenticated. The Push OTA Protocol carries an **Initiator URI** field identifying the Push Initiator, so the client has the required Push Initiator information.

Next, the client must determine whether it trusts the Push Initiator. It can do so in two ways:

• *Directly:* The client maintains a *trusted URI list*, which indicates those Push Initiators that it trusts. The WAP client simply needs to verify that the particular Push Initiator's URI is contained in the local trusted URI list.

- *Indirectly:* The Push OTA Protocol contains a **Trusted** flag, which is set by the Push Proxy Gateway if it trusts the Push Initiator. The client may therefore choose to defer the trust decision to the (trusted) Push Proxy Gateway.

Conclusion

Many of the WAP applications that will drive the mobile Internet market (as discussed in Chapter 3) rely on the ability to push personalized, time- and location-sensitive content to mobile users. The WAP Push infrastructure extends the WAP environment to provide an open interface for building and deploying these applications and services so that they will operate over a wide range of wireless infrastructures. Despite the flexibility offered by the standards, however, the notion of data push raises some user privacy and control issues that need to be addressed by implementers involved in creating end-to-end push services.

In the next chapter, we explore the integration of wireless telephony with wireless data. Wireless Telephony Applications bring together many of the features of WAP, including WML, WMLScript, and WAP Push. Indeed, WAP Push and WTA are the key features that differentiate the mobile Internet infrastructure from the traditional Internet. Together, these features transform a generic mobile phone and browser into an interactive personal communications companion.

Chapter 13

Wireless Telephony Applications

In Chapter 2, we defined the mobile Internet as the convergence of wireless communications and the wired Internet. Until now, however, our discussion of WAP has been confined to enabling data capabilities from mobile phones. We have not actually brought voice and data together into a single environment.

Why might we want to integrate voice and data in such a way? Today, the mobile network supports a rich set of features such as call forwarding, call waiting, and call conferencing. Unfortunately, these features are not always easy to manage. Browser-based applications provide a convenient and easy-to-use way to enable these features. Moreover, as new packet-based wireless networks emerge, users will eventually be able to engage in voice calls and data access simultaneously.[1] This possibility opens the door for applications that allow users to move effortlessly between these two communications media.

This chapter describes how WAP Wireless Telephony Applications (WTA) provide a bridge between wireless telephony and data. It details

---

[1]Today, most WAP deployments use circuit-switched data (CSD), essentially treating the mobile phone as a cellular modem and providing data access over a normal wireless call. Unfortunately, while a data call is in progress, the user cannot initiate a simultaneous voice call. In packet-based environments, the voice traffic can be encoded into IP packets, like any other type of data; hence, voice and data traffic can be sent at the same time.

these applications and discusses the run-time environment in which they are executed. In addition, it describes various design considerations that a WTA developer must take into account before building and deploying a WTA application. Finally, it provides a set of templates that can be used to construct these applications. It is important to note that the WTA specifications continue to evolve rapidly, thereby providing a more sophisticated mobile client environment and ultimately enabling a richer set of application capabilities.

Overview of the WTA Architecture

WTA applications are developed using Wireless Markup Language (WML) and WMLScript. Like other WAP applications, WTA applications can almost be guaranteed to work and behave consistently across current and future networks and across a wide range of mobile clients.[2]

Figure 13-1 illustrates the end-to-end system for delivering these WTA applications. WTA extends the WAP application Environment in several ways. As shown in the figure, a WTA server communicates with the WAP gateway to deliver and manage telephony services. On the client, WTA applications require the presence of the WTA application framework, which supports the real-time needs of telephony applications and optimizes the low bandwidth to distribute content to the mobile client. This framework includes three components:

1. A dedicated *WTA user agent* executes WTA applications within a real-time environment. The user agent supports the WTAI libraries, renders WML, and executes WMLScript.

2. A *repository* provides persistent client-side storage for WTA applications, so that they can be retrieved or pushed from the WTA server prior to use. WTA applications are stored as *channels* in the repository, as shown in Figure 13-2. These channels, in turn, are made up of entities, called *resources*. Resources include WML decks, WMLScript, and WBMP (Wireless Bitmap) images. To conserve memory in the mobile client, resources can be shared by multiple channels.

---

[2]For maximum interoperability, particularly until the infrastructure matures, a WTA service developer should consider working with a wireless operator during development, so that the resulting application can be optimally hosted in that operator's mobile network environment.

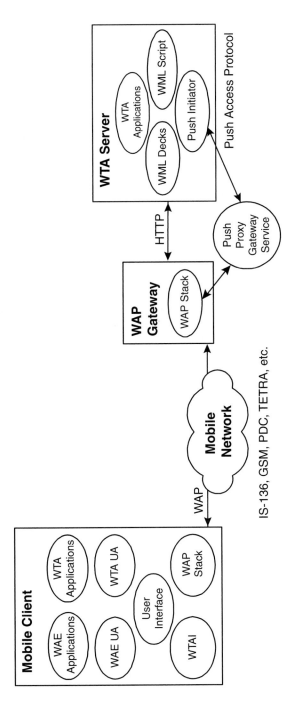

Figure 13-1 WTA logical architecture

513

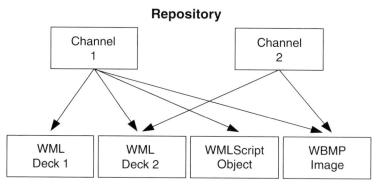

Figure 13-2   WTA repository

3. Wireless telephony events and interfaces are supported through the WTAI libraries. Events, such as incoming call and call connected events, are delivered to a WTA application for processing. WTA applications may also invoke WMLScript library interfaces to initiate and control telephony operations.

For more advanced applications, a Push Initiator and Push Proxy Gateway (discussed in Chapter 12) may also be required.

As shown in Figure 13-3, the WTA application environment uses the existing WAP protocols. WSP is used to request and deliver telephony applications. WTLS is used to ensure that these applications are delivered securely, and PAP is used to push applications and content to the device.

The WTA Client Framework

The WTA client includes a user agent, the repository, and a WTA application programming interface.

WTA User Agent

Two user agents in the mobile client—the Wireless Application Environment (WAE) user agent and the WTA user agent—synergistically share the application environment. Figure 13-4 depicts this environment.

The WAE user agent has limited access to the WTA capabilities and can access only the public WTAI library (described in Chapter 9). However, all public telephony operations require explicit user approval before

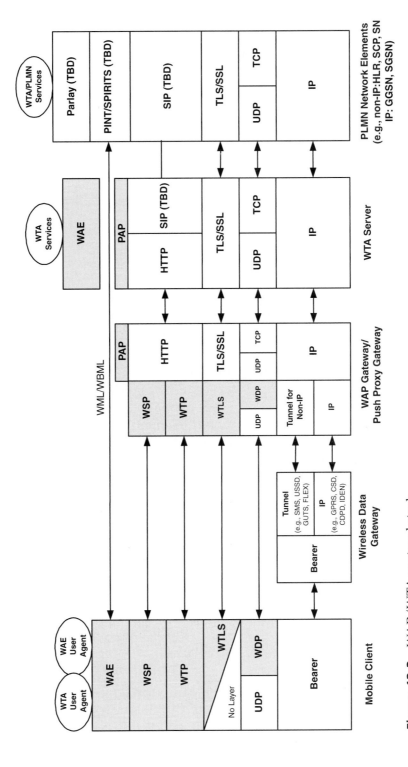

Figure 13-3 WAP/WTA protocol stack

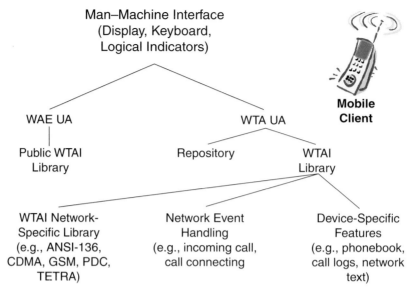

Figure 13-4   WTA user agent

being completed. Thus, in instances like makeCall(), the dialed number is displayed on the handset and the user can cancel the operation before it is executed.

In contrast, the WTA user agent in the mobile client is a domain-specific user agent for the mobile telephony environment. It is allowed unrestricted access to all of the WTAI libraries, including the network-common and the network-specific libraries. These libraries contain call control functions that provide direct access to the mobile network. Eventually, as networks evolve toward better integration of voice and data services, the WAP gateway is likely to support these mobile network services directly.

The WTA user agent also manages WTA applications, interacts with the WTA server through the WAP gateway, and has access to the human–machine interface. Like the Internet Web browser and the WAE user agent, the WTA user agent uses URLs to reference content from the WTA server. The WTA user agent, however, may actually retrieve the WTA applications from the repository, where they may be cached or prefetched for fast access.

WTA Session
When the user requests a WTA application that is not stored in the repository, the mobile client initiates a WSP session over WTLS to a trusted

WAP gateway. WTLS enables mutual authentication between the client and gateway and provides over-the-air encryption.

Once the session is established, the WTA user agent retrieves its services from the WTA server through the dedicated WTA port on the WAP gateway. The WAP gateway therefore can enforce the security policy of the telecommunications service provider by restricting the client's access to certain WTA servers. The WTA user agent can then access content and receive content only through this "secured" pipe; all content for the WTA user agent not received through this pipe will be discarded.

Currently, the WTA user agent may establish only one WSP session. In the future, it may be possible for several WTA sessions to be established simultaneously. For example, one session might update the local phonebook, while another session assists in setting up a conference call.

Event Handling

The WTA user agent processes all network events and directs them to an appropriate handler within an application.

When a network event is received, the user agent first attempts to perform *local binding*, dispatching the event locally to the currently executing program. An application may bind an event to a handler that is invoked by the user agent when the event occurs. In the following example, the application binds an event handler to the call connecting event:

```
<!-- Update the display when the call is being connected -->
<onevent type="wtaev-cc/cc">
   <refresh>
      <setvar name="WMLMsg" value="Call Connecting"/>
   </refresh>
</onevent>
```

If the currently active program does not have a defined event handler for that event, the user agent next attempts to perform a *global binding*. It searches the repository for a channel that has defined a matching event handler. For example, the following channel definition contains a binding for the incoming call event:

```
<?xml version="1.0"?>
<!DOCTYPE channel PUBLIC "-//WAPFORUM//DTD CHANNEL 1.2//EN"
                         "http://www.wapforum.org/DTD/channel.dtd">
<channel
   maxspace="2048"
   base="http://wta.operator.com"
   eventid="wtaev-cc/ic"
```

```
      channelid="Incoming Call Distributor"
      success="wtaSuccess.wml"
      failure="wtaFailure.wml"
    >
        <resource href="Hello.wml"/>
        <resource href="Hello.wmls"/>
</channel>
```

After locating a channel that is capable of handling the event, the user agent retrieves the WTA application from the repository, using the first listed resource in the channel definition as the application entry point. It checks the WML syntax, processes any defined onenterforward event, and then delivers the network event.

If no local or global bindings exist for the network event, then the event is passed to the phone to handle in its default fashion. In most cases, the user must explicitly handle the event. The user interface presentation is implementation-dependent.

The Repository

The *repository* is analogous to the level 2 cache in a microprocessor, which contains most of the frequently executed instructions for a program. The processor can quickly load these instructions if there is a "hit" without having to access slower memory or the even slower disk drive. The major difference between the level 2 cache and the WTA repository is that the repository holds persistent WTA content (channels and resources). It must therefore utilize nonvolatile storage.

The need for the repository is dictated by the limited bandwidth of the wireless network interface connecting the client to the WAP gateway. The repository eliminates the requirement to frequently download content in real time to the mobile client. Thus it expedites WTA application retrieval and enhances the user experience.

The *resource manager* of the WTA user agent allocates memory in the repository and is always aware of the amount of available space. Prior to downloading a channel and its resources, the WTA user agent should negotiate, on behalf of the application, with the resource manager to obtain a memory allocation sufficient to satisfy the application's needs. Memory for those resources that are not already resident in the repository will then be allocated, and those resources can subsequently be downloaded from the server to the mobile client.

The channel and associated resources can be loaded into the repository by the following methods:

- The application can be preinstalled into the repository during manufacturing or during the subscription process at a customer care center.
- The WTA user agent can pull the channel and its associated resources from the WTA server and install the application in the repository.
- The channel can be pushed directly from the WTA server into the repository.

A channel can be removed from the repository if it becomes stale or if the user requests space for an application that requires the memory being occupied by that channel. When the channel is unloaded, only its resources that are not being shared by another loaded channel are removed from the repository. If a resource is shared with other channels in the repository, it cannot be removed.

WTA Application Programming Interface

The WTA application programming interface consists of two components:

- *An event model,* allowing the application to learn about and take action on telephony actions.
- *A scripting interface,* allowing the application to initiate and control telephony operations.

In this section, we discuss these two features of WTA.

Telephony Events

When the user makes a call or an incoming call is received, the WTA "network layer" generates a sequence of events. These network events are delivered to the WTA user agent and then acted on by a WTA application. Today, only one user agent and only one active application context exist, so the two terms may be used synonymously. In the future, multiple WTA user agents may exist, with each one managing multiple contexts.

When a network event is delivered, additional information is stored in WML variables—for example, **$(0)**, **$(1)**, and so on. The first variable contains a unique transaction ID associated with the call, and the other parameter usually contains information about the remote party. Network events are placed into a queue and delivered sequentially to the application.

Consequently, the event parameters are guaranteed to retain their current values only within the corresponding event handler. If the user navigates to another card and then returns to the current card, the values of these variables may have changed because another telephony event was delivered during the intervening period. Consequently, the application should always copy these variables into card-specific variables.

Two call models are used to describe the telephony events from the voice network. The first model, the originating call model, describes the behavior of the network as it interacts with the user who is setting up a call. The second model, the terminating call model, describes the behavior of a call completing to the user and originating from either the wireline or wireless network.

Originating Call Model   The *originating call model* (Figure 13-5) defines the call states to handle calls originating from the mobile client user. In Figure 13-5, the ovals represent call states and the labels next to the transitions represent the network event delivered to the WTA user agent. The call transitions from state to state, remaining in each state until it receives some event from the user or the network.

For a typical originating call, the user begins by dialing a phone number either manually or by using the phonebook in the mobile client. The WTA application receives the Outgoing Call (**wtaev-cc/oc**) event, and the call transitions to the Digits Dialed state. It waits in this state until the mobile client detects ringing from the network. The WTA user agent then receives the Call Connecting (**wtaev-cc/cc**) event, and the call transitions to the Ringing state. When the call is answered, the WTAI user agent receives the Call Connected (**wtaev-cc/co**) event, and the call transitions to the Answer state. The call remains in this state until either the user or the called party disconnects, which triggers a Call Cleared (**wtaev-cc/cl**) event. After the call is cleared, the phone returns to the Idle state.

Terminating Call Model   The *terminating call* model (Figure 13-6) contains the call states for a call incoming to the user. An Incoming Call (**wtaev-cc/ic**) event causes the call to transition from the Idle state to the Ringing state. If the user chooses to receive the call, the Call Connected (**wtaev-cc/cc**) event is received by the WTA user agent, and the call transitions from the Ringing state to the Answer state. The call remains in this state until either the user or the calling party disconnects. At that time, the WTA user agent receives the Call Cleared (**wtaev-cc/cl**) event. On

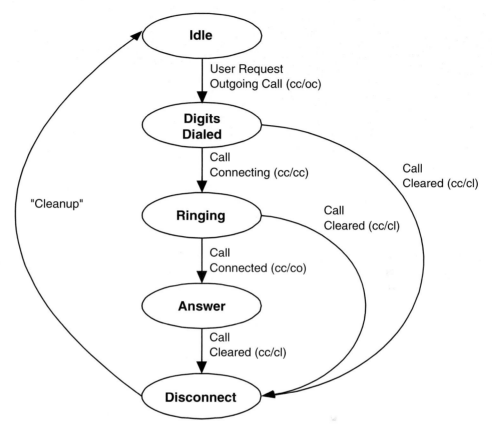

Figure 13-5 Originating call model

completion of any necessary cleanup, the call transitions back to the Idle state, where it awaits a new incoming or outgoing call.

Scripting Interfaces Available to WTA Applications

In Chapter 9, we described the WTAI public library, which provides telephony services that are accessible to all WAP applications, including WTA applications. WTA applications have exclusive access to additional WMLScript interfaces. Using these interfaces, an application can interact with the repository, as well as with other subsystems that are intrinsic to most digital mobile clients: the phonebook, call logs, and network text message handling.

These additional interfaces are divided into two groups: network-common libraries and network-specific libraries.

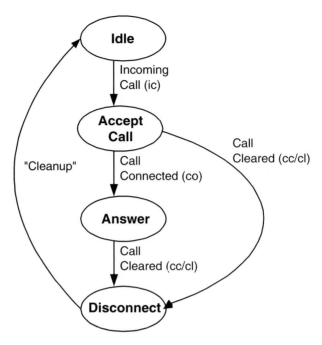

Figure 13-6   Terminating call model

Network-Common Libraries   The *network-common* WTA library contains functions that apply to most wireless networks.

Voice Control Events   The voice control events allow the application to manipulate telephone calls. This group includes the following functions:

- `WTAVoiceCall.setup()`: Initiates a phone call to the specified number.
- `WTAVoiceCall.accept()`: Accepts an incoming or waiting call and "lifts the handset."
- `WTAVoiceCall.release()`: Hangs up a call that is currently active.
- `WTAVoiceCall.sendDTMF()`: Sends a touch-tone sequence through an active voice call.
- `WTAVoiceCall.callStatus()`: Obtains information about a call, including the remote phone number, remote party's name, call duration, and current status.

- `WTAVoiceCall.list()`: Obtains a list of all currently active calls on the device.

Network Text Message Handling   When the network text message service is available in a mobile network and the subscriber has subscribed to the service, the mobile client can receive, send, and store text messages. Short Message Service (SMS) is an example of one such network text message service. The number of text messages, the number of characters allowed in a message, and the maximum number of characters for all messages are implementation-dependent.

   WTA applications can not only send, receive, and remove text messages, but also obtain information about these messages. The library contains the following functions:

- `WTANetText.send()`: Sends a network text message.
- `WTANetText.list()`: Obtains the list of the network text messages.
- `WTANetText.remove()`: Deletes a network text message stored on the device.
- `WTANetText.getFieldValue()`: Obtains the textual content, originator address, timestamp, or status of a network text message.
- `WTANetText.markAsRead()`: Marks a network text message as being read.

Phonebook   The phonebook functions allow the application to access and manipulate the database of contacts stored on the device. They represent the phonebook as an array. Each entry contains an opaque data structure holding a name, an associated phone number, an ID number, and additional implementation-dependent fields. Both the name and the phone number are strings. To obtain information from the phonebook, the application typically applies an index to the array and then uses the `getFieldValue()` function to obtain a field (the name or phone number).

   The service developer must be careful when writing phonebook applications, because different devices can have quite varied phonebook implementations. In particular, the number of phonebook entries and the length of each entry are implementation-dependent. The entry formatting may also vary, which complicates searching or comparing entries. For example, different clients store names in uppercase only, lowercase only, or a combination of uppercase and lowercase.

WTA applications can perform the following functions on the phonebook:

- `WTAPhoneBook.write()`: Writes a new phonebook entry.
- `WTAPhoneBook.search()`: Searches the phonebook for an entry whose name, number, or ID matches a given value.
- `WTAPhoneBook.remove()`: Removes a specified phonebook entry.
- `WTAPhoneBook.getFieldValue()`: Obtains a particular field from a phonebook entry.
- `WTAPhoneBook.change()`: Updates a particular field in a phonebook entry.

Call Logs   The mobile client automatically stores dialed numbers, received calls, and missed calls into its *call log*. Each call log comprises an array of entries, and WTA applications manipulate the call logs in much the same way as they manipulate the phonebook.

The phone numbers of received calls and missed calls are stored only if the mobile network is able to identify the caller. The number of entries for each log is implementation-dependent.

WTA applications can perform the following functions on the call log:

- `WTACallLog.dialed()`: Retrieves the log entry for a recently dialed number.
- `WTACallLog.missed()`: Retrieves the log entry for a recently missed call.
- `WTACallLog.received()`: Retrieves the log entry for a recently received call.
- `WTACallLog.getFieldValue()`: Obtains a particular field from a call log entry.

Miscellaneous Functions   The **WTAMisc** library contains various utility functions for WTA applications:

- `WTAMisc.setIndicator()`: Controls whether various indications are shown on the client's display. These messages might highlight incoming calls, call waiting, received text message, received voice mail, received fax, received e-mail, and so on.

- `WTAMisc.endContext()`: Terminates the current execution context within the WTA user agent.

- `WTAMisc.setProtection()`: Controls whether the current WTA user agent context can be interrupted by events other than direct user intervention.

- `WTAMisc.getProtection()`: Retrieves the context protection mode.

Network-Specific Libraries   *Network-specific* WTA libraries contain functions and events that apply only to particular wireless networks. For example, in GSM networks, the **WTAGSM** library provides the following functions: `reject()`, `hold()`, `transfer()`, `multiparty()` (which creates a multiparty call or adds a caller to an ongoing call), `retrieve()` (which disconnects a caller from the multiparty call), `location()` (which obtains the user's current location), and `sendUSSD()`. The network-specific libraries also define additional network events, when the network supports extra capabilities. For example, in IS-136 networks, the application can learn about incoming network alerts.

You should refer to the WTAI specifications for more details on the network-specific capabilities.

The WTA Server and Security

The WTA server is a Web application server that stores WTA applications in the form of WML decks and WMLScript. It is capable of responding to requests for content by the mobile client. These requests are delivered as HTTP requests from the WAP gateway. In addition, the WTA server may push channels to the client. The WTA server uses PAP over HTTP to send this content to the Push Proxy Gateway. All content from the WTA server is delivered over a secure channel between the WAP gateway and the mobile client.

WTA applications have a higher privilege level than standard WAP applications, because the former may access the protected WTAI network-common and network-specific libraries. The mobile client therefore needs to be able to distinguish those applications that have this level of trust from those that can use only the public WTAI libraries. Typically, the WAP gateway enforces policies that dictate which servers may deliver or offer WTA applications. To prevent the delivery of "badly

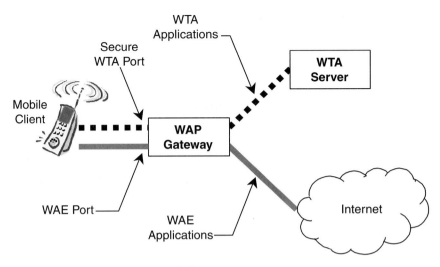

Figure 13-7   WTA security model

behaved" applications that might maliciously access telephony operations without user permission, the network operator typically retains
exclusive control over these WTA servers. Figure 13-7 depicts the WTA
security model.

To differentiate requests for WTA applications from requests for standard WAE applications, the WTA user agent establishes its own WSP session to the WAP gateway using a well-known WDP port (port 2805 for
connectionless WSP sessions and port 2923 for connection-oriented WSP
sessions). These sessions must use WTLS for authentication and encryption. The WTA user agent trusts any applications retrieved over these
ports, so the WAP gateway will allow requests over these ports to be sent
only to trusted WTA servers.

On the other hand, content delivered through the standard WSP port
is considered "untrusted." As a result, applications associated with such
servers have limited access to the WTAI libraries on the mobile client.
Access is provided to only the public WTAI library functions. These
functions require explicit user authorization before they will execute to
completion. Furthermore, applications that are delivered via the WSP
port are not allowed to process network events. Instead, the WTA user
agent rejects any applications or content that is not received through its
secure WSP sessions to the well-known WTA ports.

Design Considerations

A service developer begins the process of WTA application development by first putting together a service concept, then performing network mapping, service design, development, and testing.

The *service concept* details the behavior of the service and its interaction with the user. Screens and dialogs may be defined, as well as the expected latency for each part of the service. The service concept also defines which networks should be supported and which operators should be enlisted as partners, if any. Many of the structured usability techniques from Chapter 10 apply at this stage of design.

Next, the service is mapped to a particular mobile network and the network architecture is put together. This step is known as *network mapping*. Here, the developer decides which pieces should reside in the mobile client, the wireless data gateway if any (for example, in the case of SMS, this gateway would be the SMSC), the WAP gateway, and the WTA server. It is imperative to find out as much as possible about which versions of software will be loaded into the mobile clients and each of the network elements.

In *service design,* the service developer determines which pieces of the application are already resident in the mobile client. These components may be WTAI libraries, preinstalled resources, or other items. The service developer should decide whether those resources can be reused, which new pieces can be loaded and made resident in the mobile client, and, if a Push Proxy Gateway is available, what kind of content can be pushed over the network.

After the design has been defined in as much detail as possible, application development can begin. The WTA user agent will dispatch an event to a single application only. Hence, if multiple applications are to be used, an application routing manager must be created to run on the client and distribute events to the appropriate serving applications. For example, if an Incoming Call (**wtaev-cc/ic**) event arrives, the routing manager must determine which application should handle it. Likewise, the routing manager should ensure that subsequent events related to that call are sent to the same application. In this endeavor, the identity of the remote party can be used as the routing key.

The iterative process of development and testing can be performed using a SDK and the resources listed in Appendix A. On completion of development, the application can be staged on a test system for integration testing. If all goes well, the application may then be deployed on a production network.

Network Design Considerations

Although the service developer does not need to be an expert on the mobile network, when developing a WTA application, he or she must be aware of the constraints that the network places on that application.

Real-Time Loading Issues

Real-time design considerations often create conflicting design choices, and the designer must make trade-offs to satisfy these concerns. For example, if an application is not present in the repository when it is required, it must be downloaded quickly because WTA applications need to be launched rapidly to handle the incoming or outgoing call. If the network is not fast enough or if the application is unavailable, then the application becomes unusable.

At first glance, it would appear that the best solution would be to "push" all applications at subscription to the mobile client in advance. In reality, this solution solves the latency problem only when memory is abundant and can be readily allocated to applications. Because the devices have limited memory, such preloaded WTA applications can prove detrimental to other applications or content that may need to be loaded or cached on demand. If the repository is full, then garbage collection must be activated to free sufficient memory, which further adds to the latency problem.

Acceptable Perception of Latency

Usability studies have shown that a user will wait at most six seconds after making a request (for example, after dialing a phone number) to see or hear a response indicating that something is in progress or has been completed. If no response is provided, users will either totally abandon the request or abandon and then immediately reinitiate the same request.

Because network events are typically queued for delivery to the WTA application, several events could become "trapped" in the queue while waiting for another event to complete. By the time those queued events are finally processed, the user is likely to have already canceled the corresponding requests. The processing and discarding of these trapped events merely increase the perceived latency and reduce the perceived quality of service.

Bearer Selection

The success of a WTA application depends on which bearer network is used to retrieve the application, among other things. Each network offers a different combination of latency and bandwidth. Currently, the available bearer networks for retrieving WTA applications include SMS, CDPD, CSD, and GPRS.

If a small amount of content is being transmitted, then a low-bandwidth, connectionless, packet-oriented bearer like SMS may be sufficient. For example, to deliver a stock quote to a mobile client would require two SMS messages. As a result, it would be possible to deliver only a very small application or a small quantity of content (up to several hundred bytes) in real time using the SMS bearer. Such a bearer would therefore be most useful for conveying menu updates and alerts to inform the subscriber.

A small application or content of several thousand bytes can be deployed using CSD at 9.6 Kbps or 14.4 Kbps. Unfortunately, it may take 12 to 30 seconds to establish a CSD call. Moreover, during an active data session, voice calls cannot be made. Therefore, the CSD bearer does not gracefully support real-time downloading of a WTA application while a voice call is being established or is in progress.

Packet-based systems, such as CDPD and GPRS, offer the potential for voice and data to occur simultaneously. CDPD's bandwidth is similar to that of CSD; GPRS, however, offers a 115 Kbps channel that is shared with other subscribers in the cell. Using GPRS, a user can often easily deploy a medium-size application, in excess of 10 KB. Indeed, it might be possible to use cell broadcast over GPRS to deliver an application to several subscribers in a cell.

In the near future, EDGE (384 Kbps) and UMTS (up to 2 Mbps) are likely to provide better capabilities for distributing WTA applications or content to the mobile client in real time.

Memory Constraints

Because of the "small" amount of memory available in the mobile client today, it is crucial to design around this constraint and be frugal with memory. The designer must therefore determine which portions of the applications should be memory-resident in the mobile client and which parts should execute on the WTA server.

Relief is on the horizon, however. Mobile client vendors have suggested that their devices may offer as much as 64 MB of memory in a few years. Also, the general-purpose, low-power microprocessors used in the client devices are clearly getting faster.

Application Design Considerations

While taking full advantage of the WTAI libraries, the service developer must create the illusion of speed despite the limited over-the-air band-width, memory, and computing resources available to the mobile client. When developing the application, the developer must consider the following issues:

- *Partitioning:* An application typically consists of two files—a WML file and a WMLScript file. The WML file contains event handlers that access URIs and functions resident in the WML and the WMLScript file, respectively. The developer must decide which pieces of the application should be written in WML and which should be written in WMLScript. In addition, he or she must determine how closely to couple the two files; for example, the WMLScript function might retrieve data directly from the WML variables themselves, or it might receive data through arguments passed to it.

- *Repository:* The repository stores channels and resources. The developer must decide which pieces of the application will be loaded into the repository, as well as which resources will be shared among multiple channels. Channel definitions for global bindings must be stored in the repository.

- *Event handling:* The developer must decide which events to trap, whether to use global or local bindings with these events, and which of these events can terminate the WTA user agent context.

- *Network-specific WTAI features:* The developer must determine whether these features are required, keeping in mind that they will not work when delivered to mobile clients that are served by a different type of network.

- *Error handling:* WML does not contain any conditional statements, so the WMLScript program must perform any error handling. The developer must determine how application errors and resource failures will be handled. For example, the application might handle the errors, or the phone might handle them in its default way (typically by informing the user). If the application will handle the error, the developer must decide which error messages to display.

- *Delivery to the mobile client:* Once the application has been developed and tested, the service developer must decide how the application will be delivered to the mobile client. The client could "pull" the application, or it could be "pushed" over the air from the WTA server. The application could be "burned" into the mobile client, delivered when the user subscribes to the service, or delivered on demand.

Application Creation Toolbox

As we have seen, WTA applications provide network event handlers for monitoring the status of voice calls and invoke function calls to respond to user requests. These applications can be modeled with an action/event construct and a finite state machine.

Action/Event Construct

WTA applications can be modeled with an *action/event construct. Actions* are caused by the explicit behavior of the user, who instructs the program to perform some function (such as "set up a call"). In response to an action, an *event* (such as the outgoing call event) is returned to the application. Unsolicited events (such as the incoming call event) generated from within the mobile network can also invoke the application. Multiple events can be defined for each action, but only one event can be returned in response to an action.

One benefit of the action/event construct is that it simplifies partitioning of an application. The pieces that contain actions should be written in WMLScript, which offers "if-then-else" conditional constructs and can return error codes on failure. These actions are represented as functions. On the other hand, event handlers, which typically require some user interaction, should be in written in WML.

We can model these actions and events as application templates for the originating and terminating call models. You can then use these templates to build most of your WTA applications. To use the templates, you simply add WMLScript functions unique to the application, functions for error handling, and messages to be displayed to the user. In the tables, the suggested places for these additions in the templates are denoted by "+". When completed, the WTA application will contain a WML file and a WMLScript file.

Terminating Call Template

The template in Table 13-1 supports a terminating call application. An incoming call event starts the instantiation of a context. Listing 13-1 shows the completed application translated from this template. It contains a channel, a WML deck, and a WMLScript file.

Table 13-1   Terminating Call Template

WML	WMLScript
Incoming Call: `<onevent type="wtaev-cc/ic">` + Display messages unique to your application	
	Accept Call: + Functions unique to your application `WTAVoiceCall.accept(…)`

Call Connected:
`<onevent type="wtaev-cc/co">`
+ Display status message, if any
+ Display messages unique to your application
Wait for call termination from the user or the calling party:
`<onevent type="wtaev-cc/cl">`	

	Cleanup, done! + Functions unique to your applications `WTAMisc.endContext()`

Listing 13-1(a)   Originating call template channel definition.

```
<?xml version="1.0"?>
<!DOCTYPE channel PUBLIC "-//WAPFORUM//DTD CHANNEL 1.2//EN"
                         "http://www.wapforum.org/DTD/channel.dtd">
<channel
    maxspace="2048"
    base="http://wta.operator.com"
    eventid="wtaev-cc/ic"
    channelid="Hello Service"
    success="wtaSuccess.wml"
    failure="wtaFailure.wml"
    >
        <resource href="Hello.wml">
        <resource href="Hello.wmls">
</channel>
```

Listing 13-1(b) Originating call template WML file.

```
<?xml version="1.0"?>
<!DOCTYPE wta-wml PUBLIC "-//WAPFORUM//DTD WTA-WML 1.2//EN"
                        "http://www.wapforum.org/DTD/wta-wml1.2.dtd">
<wta-wml>
   <card>
      <!-- incoming call for the user -->
      <onevent type="onenterforward">
         <go href="Hello.wmls#DisplayHello($(transid), $(callerID))">
            <setvar name="transid" value="$(0)"/>
            <setvar name="callerID" value="$(1)"/>
         </go>
      </onevent>

      <!-- call connected, display message to the user -->
      <onevent type="wtaev-cc/co">
         <refresh>
            <!-- display status messages, if any -->
            <setvar name="msg" value="Call connected!"/>
            <!-- display additional messages unique to your application -->
         </refresh>
      </onevent>

      <!-- call has terminated, so cleanup -->
      <onevent type="wtaev-cc/cl">
         <go href="Hello.wmls#cleanup()"/>
      </onevent>
   </card>
</wta-wml>
```

Listing 13-1(c) Originating call template WMLScript file.

```
   /* Hello.wmls:
      This sample application displays "Hello World"
      and a status message */

/* This function displays the Hello World message." */
function DisplayHello(transId, callerId) {
   // false=drop call when current context is terminated
   WTAVoiceCall.accept(transid, false);
   WMLBrowser.setVar("msg", "Hello World!");
   WMLBrowser.refresh();
}

/* This function performs final cleanup. */
function cleanup() {
   // terminate the context
   WTAMisc.endContext();
}
```

One noteworthy item in this example is the handling of the WTA event variables, **$(0)** and **$(1)**. Because control is being passed to a WMLScript function, the WML card copies these variables into deck-specific variables. This approach ensures that the WMLScript context will not be affected if another network event arrives and rewrites the WTA event parameters.

Originating Call Template

In the case of an originating call, a user typically requests that a call be established by selecting an item from a menu. The `WTAVoiceCall.setup()` function is invoked, and the first event returned is the outgoing call event, **wtaev-cc/oc.** The complete template is shown in Table 13-2.

Table 13-2   Originating Call Template

WMLScript	WML
User initiates request from a menu: + Functions unique to your application `WTAVoiceCall.setup(…)`	
	Outgoing Call: `<onevent type="wtaev-cc/oc">` + Display status message, if any + Display messages unique to your application
	Call Connecting: `<onevent type="wtaev-cc/cc">` + Display status message, if any + Display messages unique to your application
	Call Connected: `<onevent type="wtaev-cc/co">` + Display status message, if any + Display messages unique to your application
	Wait for call termination from the user or the called party: `<onevent type="wtaev-cc/cl">` + Display messages unique to your application
Cleanup, done! `WTAMisc.endContext()`	

Finite State Machine

We introduced the *finite state machine* (FSM) implicitly when describing the action/event construct and in Figure 13-5 and 13-6. The WTA application can be modeled as a "machine" with a finite number of "states." The FSM model will make the application more manageable during programming, easier to debug, and, in the long run, more easily maintained. Although the discussion here focuses on WTA applications, it actually applies to all WAP applications.

For ease of discussion, we will assume that the "current state" is the state that the "machine" is presently in, and the "next state" is the state that the "machine" will be in after a *state transition*. Only one event can be delivered to the current state at any time. When an event is received, the machine processes an appropriate action and then transitions to the next state.

To illustrate the FSM more explicitly, we can extend the action/event construct described previously. Each state is implemented using a single WML card in the WML deck. The WMLScript `WMLBrowser.go()` function enables the transition from one state to another. You can envision the `WMLBrowser.go()` function as being much like the **goto** statement in many computer languages; the program counter is loaded with the provided address, and there is no return address.

The application template in Figure 13-8 illustrates how the FSM can model a terminating call application. In this example, the Call Cleared (**wtaev-cc/cl**) event is used to show that a single event can be handled differently according to the current state when the event is received. The template contains all of the code needed to develop a complete application. If desired, you can add code to the template in places indicated by the ellipses ("...").

Future WTA Enhancements

The WTA working group continues to work on correcting known deficiencies in the current release of the WTA specifications. In this section, we consider several potential enhancements for future releases of the specification.

WML (Terminating Call Model): wtaFSM.wml	WMLScript: wtaFSM.wmls

```
<?xml version="1.0"?>
<!DOCTYPE wta-wml PUBLIC "-//WAPFORUM//DTD WML 1.2//EN"
                         "http://www.wapforum.org/DTD/wta-wml1.2.dtd">

<wta-wml>
   <card>
      <!--Incoming call detected -->
      <onevent type="onenterforward">
         <go href="wtaFSM.wmls#processIncoming ('$(id)')">

            <!-- save event parameters to context variables;
                     id contains the context id  -->
            <setvar name="id" value="$(0)"/>
            <setvar name="callerId" value="$(1)"/>
         </go>
      </onevent>
   </card>
```

```
extern function processIncoming(id) {
    // ...
    // Transition from Idle to Ringing
    WMLBrowser.go("wtaFSM.wml#Ringing");
}
```

```
<!-- In Ringing state, wait for events -->
   <card id="Ringing">
      <!-- Call is accepted by the user, connected -->
      <onevent type="wtaev-cc/co">

         <!-- ... -->

         <go href="wtaFSM.wmls#processRinging ('$(id)')"/>
      </onevent>

      <!--Call Cleared treatment for Ringing -->
      <onevent type="wtaev-cc/cl">

         <!-- ... -->

         <go href="wtaFSM.wmls#cleanup ('$(id)')"/>
      </onevent>
   </card>
```

```
extern function processRinging(id) {
    // ...
    // Transition from Ringing to Answer
    WMLBrowser.go("wtaFSM.wml#Answer");
}
```

Figure 13-8   Finite state model's depiction of a terminating call application

WML (Terminating Call Model): wtaFSM.wml	WMLScript: wtaFSM.wmls

```
<!-- In the Answer state, wait for events -->
   <card id ="Answer">
      <onevent type="wtaev-cc/co">

         <!-- ... -->

         <go href="wtaFSM.wmls#processAnswer ('$(id)')"/>
      </onevent>

      <!--Call Cleared treatment for Answer -->
      <onevent type="wtaev-cc/cl">

         <!-- ... -->

         <go href="wtaFSM.wmls#cleanup ('$(id)')"/>
      </onevent>
   </card>
```

```
extern function processAnswer(id) {
   // ...
   // Stay in Answer state
}
```

```
extern function cleanup(id) {
   // Done with the call
   WTAMisc.endContext();
}
```

```
<!-- Use this card to display messages generated
     by WMLScript to the user, e.g. errors, status messages, etc. -->
   <card id="displayMessage">
      <p>
      $(msg)
      </p>
   </card>
</wta-wml>
```

WTA Server APIs

The WTA server today is simply an application server that delivers WTA applications to the mobile client. It may be extended to support integration with the call control features of mobile networks and, possibly, mobile IP networks. Several application programming interfaces (APIs) therefore would need to be defined.

External Device Events

In the near future, users will want to extend the capabilities of the mobile terminal by connecting it to external devices, such as a laptop PC or PDA. WTA applications could be written to handle mobile network events originating not only from the mobile terminal, but also from these external devices.

Multiple Context Support

Currently, the WTA user agent can have only one active context for handling network events. If this context is busy handling a call, a second call from the mobile network will not be handled—or at least will not be handled well. In most cases, the existing application context is terminated, or the second call is directed to the default user interface for processing. Mobile network features such as call waiting cannot work well without multiple context support. In the future, the WTA user agent may be endowed with the ability to instantiate a new context for each WTA call and distribute events for both incoming and outgoing calls to the associated context.

Improved Event Handling

WTA network events are real-time events. For example, if a mobile call is not answered within four rings, the network might automatically forward it to voice mail. Alternatively, the caller who is kept waiting while making a call may choose to simply hang up. Therefore, if WTA applications do not process these incoming call events quickly, the user loses the opportunity of ever answering the call. As a consequence, real-time asynchronous events must be able to interrupt normal WML and WMLScript processing so that they can be processed expediently.

Conclusion

WAP's integration of telephony and data brings enormous value to the mobile user. WTA applications can give the user interactive control over incoming and outgoing calls, as well as simplify complex telephone calling operations. The WTA environment builds on the standard WAP application tools—WML and WMLScript—to provide this capability.

We have now covered all of the building blocks for the WAP infrastructure and, in particular, the WAP application environment. In Chapter 14, we will explore how the necessary WAP infrastructure is deployed end-to-end to deliver services for mobile clients.

Chapter 14

Building and Deploying End-to-End WAP Services

The success of WAP, as with any new service delivery mechanism, is tightly linked to the availability of content and applications—in this case, the *WAP-enabled services*. As discussed in Chapter 4, these services are delivered through the cooperation of an end-to-end business *value chain* (Figure 14-1). The business value chain includes the user, device manufacturer, network operator/ISP, infrastructure provider, content aggregator/portal, application service provider, content owner, and content developer.

If the business value chain is to make a WAP service available, it must deploy several technology elements along the path linking the mobile device to the WAP service. Together, these technology elements constitute the *deployment chain* (see Figure 14-1). The individual technology elements were described in Chapter 6; following the data chain from the device back toward the service, the first element is the end user and the user's device. The device connects to a mobile network that provides the communications capability. This network, in turn, is tied to a WAP gateway that performs protocol bridging and content modification functions (tokenization, script compilation, and so on). The WAP gateway connects through a variety of WAP and Web proxies providing further content transformation and caching services. Finally, the service itself

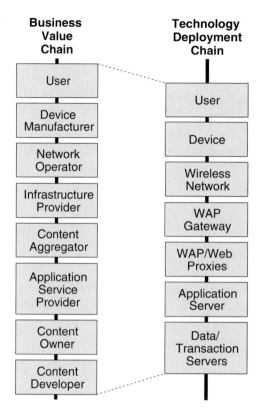

Figure 14-1   The WAP value
chain and deployment chain

resides on an application server, which may be coupled to a variety of
back-end data sources and transactional capabilities.

The various members of the business value chain install and operate
the different elements of the deployment chain. The choice of which technology is deployed by each value chain member, however, reflects that
entity's particular business model, as well as the overall security, performance, and integration needs of the service. Ultimately, the technology
configuration influences the type of service that can be offered to the
user. As one might expect in a dynamic market such as the mobile Internet, the mapping between deployment technology and business entities
continues to evolve.

WAP service development is further complicated by the need to align
the new offerings with existing services already being delivered to the
World Wide Web. Over time, as service providers seek to extend their
reach to more users and devices, their sites will need to support additional
client environments, such as alternative application environments that

emerge with different device types, or different user modalities, such as voice. In time, service delivery can become quite complex—and expensive—as the provider must build, deploy, and maintain these "multi-mode" capabilities.

This chapter focuses on the construction and deployment of WAP services. It begins by considering the factors that influence the mapping from technology contained in the deployment chain to the businesses that constitute the end-to-end value chain. It then discusses three key factors in more detail: end-to-end security and trust, connectivity to the Internet, and service integration.

Mapping the Deployment Chain to the Business Value Chain

Business entities within the value chain choose which physical infrastructure—and, therefore, which logical technology elements—they will deploy. The resulting mapping between the deployment chain and the value chain depends on a number of factors:

1. *Business models within the value chain:* Different entities in the value chain will quite naturally adopt different business models. These business models, in turn, define what services are provided by the network elements deployed by the respective business entities. (These business models were discussed in Chapter 4.)

2. *Security considerations:* Because the WAP gateway must translate between WTLS and SSL/TLS, it must have plain-text access to the application content being delivered to the client. This access violates the requirements of end-to-end security, which may significantly affect the structure of the technology deployment.

3. *Need to connect with existing network infrastructure:* Most services seek to reuse existing infrastructure that delivers content and services to desktop Web clients. Web proxies and Web servers have been widely adopted, and these servers represent a significant investment that organizations would prefer to reuse to the greatest extent possible.

4. *Service integration:* The required network infrastructure also depends on the type and format of content generated by the Web server. For example, if the server delivers WML directly, then no

network elements are required for content translation. On the other hand, if the Web server delivers only HTML (and it cannot be changed), then additional network infrastructure will be required to deliver this content to WAP clients.

5. *Performance considerations:* The introduction of additional network elements between the client and the origin server increases the end-to-end latency of the content request/response path. To manage this latency, logical technology elements may be integrated. The fine-tuning of end-to-end performance is usually the last factor in a deployment, as the business, security, and content issues typically dominate the earlier stages of the decision process.

These considerations lead to a broad range of possible end-to-end configurations of the network infrastructure. For example, the roles of application server, WAP gateway, and client may be spread across different domains (Figure 14-2). A network operator may choose to host nothing (essentially providing raw network connectivity or "pipe"), a WAP gateway (providing a WAP-to-Internet connectivity service for devices), or even the application (providing an integrated hosted service). Alternatively, any portion of this infrastructure may be moved to the application service provider (ASP) or a third-party outsourcing service.

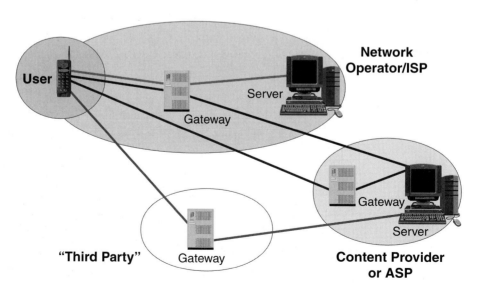

Figure 14-2   Roles between potential contributors to a WAP service delivery chain

In truth, no single mapping between infrastructure and value chain roles can satisfy the needs of all possible service providers. Instead, the decision about which configuration is appropriate must be made individually for each situation, and the choice will depend on the service requirements. For example, security concerns or the need to provide and control high-availability services might dictate that many of the infrastructure elements be provided at the service provider's site. On the other hand, if a low-maintenance operation is required, then many infrastructure elements can be outsourced to network operators and service bureaus. Not unexpectedly, the nature of the service to be provided—the source of the data and the devices that need to be served—probably exerts the single biggest influence on the required infrastructure elements.

Beyond the value chain business models, the three most critical infrastructure factors are the security, Internet connectivity, and service design. These topics are covered next.

Security Domains

We define a *domain* to represent the sphere of influence of a persona, be it an individual, institution, or organization. The domain contains a set of infrastructure elements that are under the direct control of that persona and that are therefore "trusted" by that persona. Thus the WAP value chain contains several domains, including the end user, the network operator, the ASP, and various third-party outsourcers. The ASP may itself encompass several domains. Some ASPs host the actual data being delivered by the application and therefore not only perform data collection, aggregation, or generation but also provide an application that uses that data. It is equally possible that the application hosted by the ASP must communicate with a separate domain that hosts the data and provides data aggregation services.

Interdomain Trust

Probably the most important functional difference between these configurations relates to their treatment of security-sensitive applications. With these applications, the user and ASP must establish a mutual trust relationship. Depending on the particular deployment of infrastructure across the value chain domains, however, they may not be able to establish this trust relationship directly with each other. Instead, the user and

ASP might need to establish additional trust relationships with intermediary members of the value chain so as to construct a "chain of trust" that links them together. Common sense indicates that this chain of trust becomes more difficult to achieve as more domains are involved in this process.

In the Internet world, a number of protocols have emerged that establish such trust relationships. The most commonly used is without doubt the SSL (Secure Sockets Layer) protocol, which achieves mutual authentication and encryption of data that is exchanged between two parties. With this protocol, any intermediate domain is transparent as far as the end-points of the SSL communication are concerned. For example, if an SSL link is established between the user and the ASP, then neither party needs to trust the routers that may be employed within the network between them: SSL's "end-to-end" property ensures that the authentication and encryption operate between the end points of the communication path without interruption.

WAP Gateway Implications for Trust Models

In a WAP deployment chain, however, the WAP gateway is *nontransparent*; to perform the required bridging task between the WAP protocol stack and the Internet protocol stack, it needs access to the application data, which necessarily interrupts any transport-level encryption (Figure 14-3). This plain-text access is required to allow the gateway to route the WAP request to the intended destination application server, to tokenize WML content, and to compile WMLScript. Because the WAP gateway must extract the content in plain text as it crosses from the WAP side to the Internet side, and vice versa, its owner (or a hacker who attacks the gateway) could also examine the content.[1]

Consequently, to establish an end-to-end trust relationship between a WAP application user and an ASP, the domain that hosts the WAP gateway must also participate in the chain of trust. In other words, security-

---

[1]This operation is usually much more difficult than it sounds. A properly constructed WAP gateway will keep the unencrypted content only in memory and then only for a small amount of time; it should never store the content in a disk file. A hacker, therefore, needs to obtain "super-user" access and, at the precise moment, capture a snapshot of the gateway software's physical (or virtual) memory.

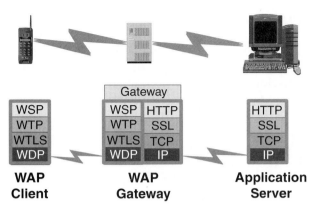

Figure 14-3 WAP deployment scenario with full-feature "bridging" gateway function

sensitive applications require not only a trust relationship between the user and application server, but also relationships between the user and the gateway's domain and between the application server and the gateway's domain. These relationships include trusting the gateway owner to select a secure gateway, to not be malicious, and to provide a secure hosting environment that blocks potential intruders from outside.

The new user–gateway and gateway–ASP trust relationships may be established in one of three ways:

1. Establish long-term cooperative agreements between the ASP, user, and gateway operator. These *service-level agreements* (SLAs) may specify security requirements and appropriate recourse for breach of that service guarantee.

2. Host the gateway within the ASP infrastructure. This approach essentially makes the user–ASP trust relationship identical to the user–gateway relationship and trivializes the gateway–ASP relationship.

3. Host the application within the network operator's infrastructure. Like the second option, this approach essentially makes the user–ASP trust relationship identical to the user–gateway relationship and trivializes the gateway–ASP relationship.

The net effect of these alternatives is to establish a complete chain of trust between the user and the application.

WAP Protocol Tunneling

The second configuration mentioned above requires that WAP packets be passed through the wireless network operator to a remote WAP gateway located within the ASP. In this configuration, the network operator should not interpret the WAP protocol stack or have access to any of the content contained within the WAP packets. Instead, the ASP should take responsibility for handling the entire protocol stack, including content tokenization and compilation. Support for this type of routing, or *tunneling*, is discussed in the next section.

Summary

Clearly, the security features of a WAP service deployment depend on the ownership of the individual delivery elements as well as the exact type of functional split between those elements. The matrix depicted in Figure 14-4 shows the security features of those configurations.

Linking WAP and the Internet

Many network operators and ASPs seek to link the WAP environment with the classic Internet. The Internet offers a rich set of content, as well as a well-developed routing, protocol, and security infrastructure. Consequently, linking WAP with the classic Internet makes the mobile Internet interesting to users and reduces the management and maintenance costs for service providers.

As we saw in Figure 6-6 on page 106, this link may be provided in three ways:

- At the application layer, a WAP gateway and WAP proxy can attempt to convert the Web content into meaningful WAP content and to convert the full protocol stacks. In this case, the WAP client can access any Web server and content.

- At the session layer, a gateway can convert a WSP request (over WTP/WDP) into an HTTP request (over TCP/IP). In this case, any standard Web server can receive and process the request, although it must generate content in a form that is meaningful to the WAP client.

- At the datagram layer (WDP), a tunneling gateway can bridge the full suite of WAP transport and session protocols from the

Bridging Gateway	Secure because WTLS security layer is terminated within same trusted domain as application server	Not secure because gateway function terminates WTLS link and has plain-text access on untrusted host	Not secure because gateway function terminates WTLS link and has plain-text access on untrusted host	Secure because WTLS security layer is terminated within same trusted domain as application server	Not secure because gateway function terminates WTLS link and has plain-text access on untrusted host
Tunneling Gateway	Secure because gateway tunnels beneath encryption layer; not necessary because gateway and server are in same domain	Secure because third-party gateway on untrusted host bridges beneath encryption layer	Secure because third-party gateway on untrusted host bridges beneath encryption layer	Secure because gateway tunnels beneath encryption layer; not necessary because gateway and server are in same domain	Secure because third-party gateway on untrusted host bridges beneath encryption layer
	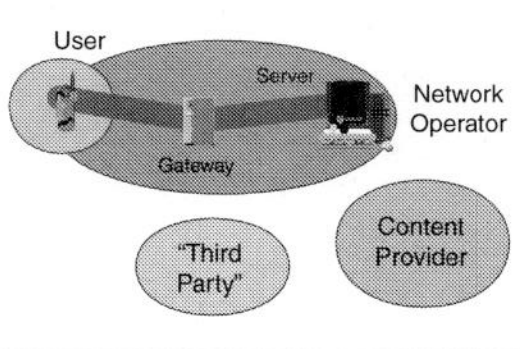	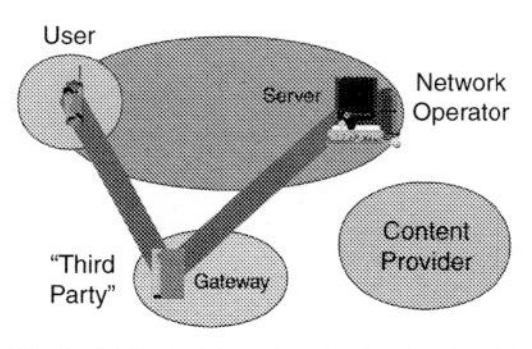	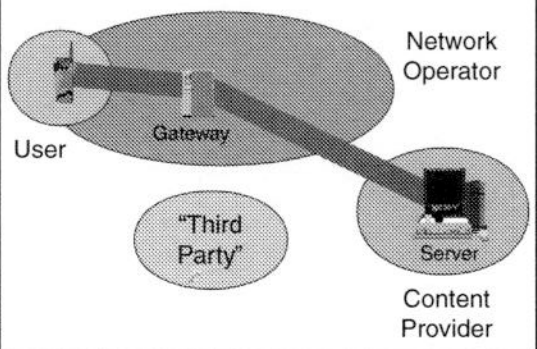	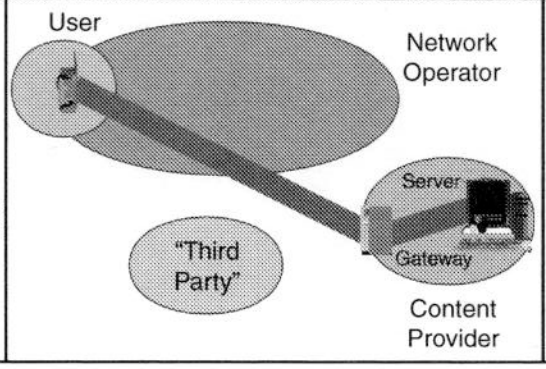	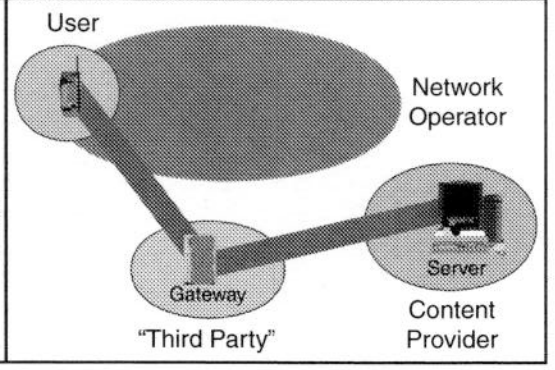

Figure 14-4 Infrastructure ownership, functional split, and their joint influence on the security properties of the resulting configuration

wireless bearer network directly into UDP/IP frames sent over the Internet. In this case, the higher-level WAP protocols are actually decoded at a server running inside the Internet.

In the end, these options are the only three reliable ways of linking WAP and the classic Internet. Attempts to convert or bridge between the two sets of standards at other layers are fraught with peril. In this section, we consider these three possibilities, outlining their relative advantages and disadvantages.

Linking the Application Layers

Conceptually, the simplest way of linking WAP with the classic Web is to provide a gateway and proxy that convert HTML to WML and to bridge the full WAP protocol stack with the standard Internet protocol stack. As illustrated in Figure 14-5(a), this approach essentially divides the deployment chain into two halves—the WAP side and the Web side. It requires the deployment of a single converter box but no modification of the existing Web infrastructure.

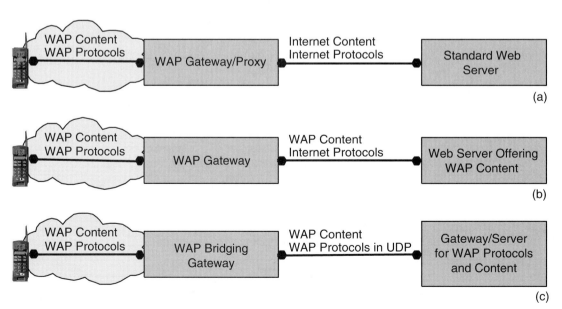

Figure 14-5   Bridging between the WAP environment and the Internet at (a) the application layer, (b) the session layer, and (c) the datagram layer

Despite its simplicity, this approach has its limitations. Because the full protocol stacks—including the security layers (SSL and WTLS)—are spliced together, it does not offer true end-to-end security unless the gateway and application server reside within the same domain.

Moreover, the generic translation of existing HTML content to WML is nearly impossible to accomplish effectively. Difficulties arise for several reasons:

- The deck-of-cards structure of WML documents differs from the page structure of HTML documents. The HTML document, therefore, must be split into cards—a process that usually requires semantic analysis to understand the appropriate content groupings. The presence of HTML frames and the use of HTML tables strictly for visual formatting purposes (a commonly employed tactic) further complicate the conversion.

- The WML language incorporates many features, such as variable state and a browser history mechanism, that are typically implemented using JavaScript embedded in an HTML page. It is quite difficult to parse these scripts, understand their semantics, and generate the corresponding WML tags or WMLScript code.

- The user interaction models for WML differ from those supported by HTML. WML uses abstract actions and events to define device-independent interfaces, whereas HTML relies on buttons, text boxes, and similar visual elements. The translator must recognize the role of these visual elements and translate them into appropriate logical interactions.

- HTML pages typically contain too much content for the WML environment. The content may be too large to fit into a mobile phone's memory, for example. Even if the content can be downloaded, volumes of information are of little value to the mobile user because of the small size of the screen. The conversion must also handle the rich graphical or multimedia content contained in the HTML page.

- Finally, and most important, it is difficult to design *effective* content for users with small-screen devices. Existing Web offerings are designed for the desktop user, who can access those applications with a large and powerful computer and fast Internet connection. When addressing the mobile Internet, content developers must perform extensive user testing to ensure that the deployed interface is easy to use, intuitive, and properly structured to deliver the desired information with minimal user effort. No level of automation can capture the subtleties of effective user interface design. (Chapter 10 discussed user interface design for WAP environments in detail.)

Because of these limitations, proxy-based solutions have been most successful in supporting the Compact HTML browsers used in NTT DoCoMo's i-mode service in Japan, as well as various HTML-compatible browsers for PDAs such as the Palm Pilot and Pocket PC. Devices using such browsers typically have small—but not tiny—displays; content conversion can often be accomplished through adaptation techniques. Nevertheless, usability still suffers.

Consequently, complete stack bridging is most appropriate for a quick entrée to WAP. In the long term, however, user interface generation needs to move closer to the Web server. In the end, automated HTML-to-WML conversion is best applied in an application-specific manner, with advance knowledge of the style and structure of the HTML being generated by the Web server. The evolution of a content site from supporting HTML-based content (and relying on automated content transformation) to directly supporting multiple types of clients (including WAP clients) is discussed later in this chapter.

Linking the Session Layers

The WAP and Internet protocol stacks can be bridged at the session layer, as shown in Figure 14-5(b). The session-level bridging is possible because both HTTP and WSP offer a request–response communication style, in which a client requests a document from a server and the server responds with the requested document. Moreover, the control information provided within WSP and HTTP requests and responses match almost perfectly.

In this scenario, the WAP gateway converts the WSP requests from the mobile terminal into HTTP requests that can be received by standard Web servers; the gateway also takes HTTP responses from the Web server and forwards them to the mobile terminal using WSP. Of course, this translation scheme requires the WAP gateway to decode the WDP, WTLS, and WTP protocols and to initiate Internet-side connections using TCP/IP and SSL. In carrying out the HTTP–WSP mapping, the WAP gateway performs binary encoding of the data content (WML or XML tokenization) and WMLScript compilation. It does not attempt to modify the content, however, so the Web server must provide content in an acceptable WAP format (that is, WML, XML, or WMLScript).

This configuration puts a greater burden on—and offers greater control to—the provider of applications or services. The provider can generate customized content, reflecting the capabilities and preferences of the target device, network, and user. Unfortunately, like application-level bridging, this configuration breaks the end-to-end security from the browser to the application, because the WAP gateway outside the ASP's trusted domain requires access to the application data.

Linking the Datagram Layers

As discussed in Chapter 6, the WDP protocol provides bindings to a variety of networks, including those that support the IP protocol. On these IP networks, WDP is identical to UDP. Hence, WDP packets encapsulating WTLS, WTP, and WSP can simply be transferred into UDP packets for transmission through the Internet.

As shown in Figures 14-5(c) and 14-6, a gateway can support this transfer operation without needing either to interpret the higher-level WAP layers or to touch the application-level content. This configuration essentially *tunnels* the WAP protocols through the Internet to a remote WAP gateway. In contrast to a traditional WAP gateway, therefore, the

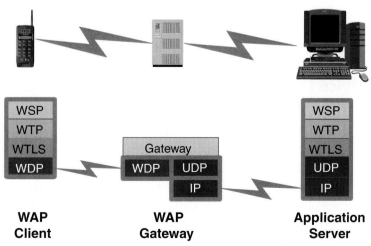

Figure 14-6 Protocol configuration with a tunneling WAP gateway

tunneling WAP gateway really amounts to a network router. Using appropriate encryption mechanisms (such as that provided by WTLS), the system can hide security-sensitive content from the network elements. Consequently, the tunneling gateway allows secure services to be provided from a domain that is outside the network operator.

Unfortunately, the tunneling approach has a major limitation. The WDP protocol contains only a single destination address—that of the first (tunneling) WAP gateway—so the datagram does not include any information that designates where it should get sent through the Internet. Normally, the WAP gateway would determine the destination by inspecting the URL contained in the WSP request; because a tunneling gateway relays packets at the datagram (WDP) layer, it cannot access the WSP layer and therefore cannot rely on that information. As a result, the tunneling gateway must route each client's WAP packets to a single preconfigured destination. Future versions of the WAP protocol stack may formalize a tunneling protocol that allows the client to exert better control over where its packets are routed through the Internet.

The tunneled protocol configuration places the greatest burden on the application or service provider. That provider must install software that can process the entire WAP protocol stack, generate WAP content, and compile and tokenize that content for delivery to WAP devices. As with session-level bridging, the application or service provider shoulders a greater burden but gains greater control over the user experience. Moreover, because the bridging gateway does not need to interpret the higher layers of the WAP stack, the configuration preserves end-to-end security between the browser and the application, regardless of which domain owns and operates the tunneling gateway.

WAP Service Design

In the previous section, we considered the difficulty of supporting generic conversion between HTML and WML. Ultimately, content developers will need to generate WAP content directly from their Web sites, relying on either session-level or datagram-level bridging (depending on end-to-end security needs) between the WAP environment and the Internet.

In this section, we discuss how a service provider might generate such WAP content. In the simplest case, a service provider could use the standard Web application server infrastructure to develop and host a WAP site. With this approach, the content development techniques are essentially identical to those used on the standard World Wide Web. However, developing high-quality mobile applications is usually more complicated than such a simple adaptation of Web technology might imply.

First, a high-quality mobile application offering works in conjunction with an existing Internet Web site, and that site may also offer services through other environments such as voice. The various "faces" of the application need to share information about users, their interests, and their behavior. These *multimode services* often rely on sophisticated programming techniques that allow the application logic to be separated from the particular markup language used to deliver the content. However, the application faces may also differ from each other. For example, application sign-up and profiling are better handled on the Web than via WAP.

Second, mobile devices such as WAP phones can support applications that go beyond conventional "Web wisdom." Unlike a Web site that often deals with anonymous users, WAP delivers user-specific information, such as the user ID, profile, and location, that can be used to personalize the delivered content. In addition, WAP enables the pushing of data from the Web site to the user, and it supports integration of data and telephony. To take advantage of these features, the application developer needs to introduce more capabilities than are provided by the Web site.

As an example, Figure 14-7 compares the top-level page of a Web travel site with the top-level input panel of a WAP-based flight reservation system. In this case, the WAP interface can reduce the number of required user inputs because the client's identity and location are known (the mobile network operator may provide both pieces of information as supplementary information elements with the request). The application might use the location information to guess the user's departure airport and pre-fill the input field. Thus this transition from a Web-based interface to a WAP interface requires a focus on the necessary content, customization for the network environment, and personalization for the particular user.

There are essentially three approaches to building server-side applications for the WAP environment:

1. Deploy a proxy that automatically converts an existing HTML interface to WML.
2. Build a separate WAP application server that accesses the data used by the existing Web application and generates WML interfaces.

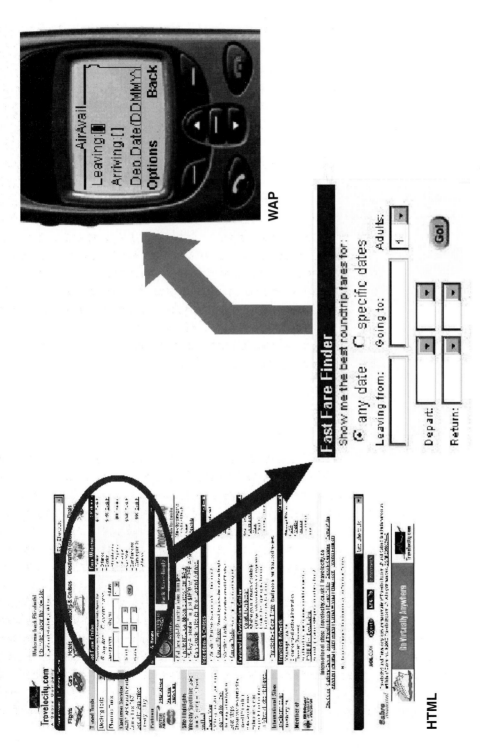

WAP

HTML

Figure 14-7 The transition from a Web-based interface to a WAP interface (Images are copyright © 2000, Travelocity.com; reprinted with permission).

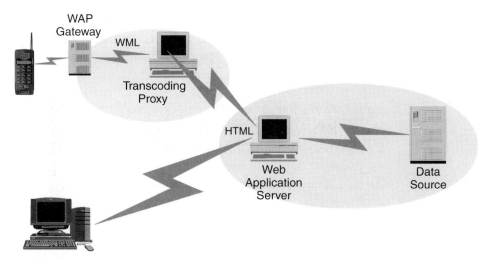

Figure 14-8 Daisy-chaining front ends to support WAP devices from existing HTML offerings and infrastructure

3. Build an integrated Web site that generates HTML, WML, and other markup languages according to the needs of the requesting device browser.

In the following sections, we consider each of these approaches in turn.

Adaptation of an Existing HTML Interface

A number of commercial platforms[2] are available that perform application-specific conversion from existing HTML into a form that suits the limited display capabilities of mobile devices and the slower speed of wireless networks. Figure 14-8 depicts one configuration involving such "intermediaries," "content filters," or *transcoding proxies*. An application server provides an HTML front end to the application data or transaction system. The WAP content is then built from the same HTML views; a proxy is daisy-chained in front of the existing HTML offering to generate the WML view. The WAP gateway bridges the gap between the communication protocols used on the mobile data network and the wired Internet.

---

[2]WebSphere Transcoding Publisher from IBM and Mosaic from Spyglass are two such examples.

Within the proxy, an application-specific module is installed and bound to particular URLs or HTML content templates. The module is aware of the content that the HTML page contains and the actions that the user may perform. The module performs two tasks:

1. It extracts the salient information required by the mobile user and formats it for effective display by a WML browser.

2. It redesigns the application interaction to minimize the user effort required to obtain the desired information or complete a transaction. The module must define how the user should interact with the site, and it must translate those user actions into requests that are recognized by the existing Web server.

This solution can be deployed quickly because the WAP-specific components remain completely shielded from the existing Web and application infrastructure. To the HTML-based application server, the transcoding proxy looks like any other HTML-capable client. Moreover, the transcoding proxy potentially can be outsourced to third-party service providers, portal operators, or carriers. An outsourced solution may be of particular interest to small application providers that wish to make only a small investment to ground-test the market acceptance of their WAP services. Larger organizations may require rigid service guarantees that may not be available from such third parties.

Although proxy-based solutions can be implemented quickly, the value of such a configuration is necessarily constrained by the features provided by the existing HTML service. Proxy-based solutions usually cannot use most of WAP's most interesting features, such as data push. Likewise, proxies typically cannot take advantage of additional information, such as user location, which may be unique to the wireless network environment.

It is possible to implement these application extensions within the application module installed in the transcoding proxy. Unfortunately, these extensions can become quite complex, and they cannot issue requests or transactions that are not already exposed by the HTML interface. As more function is added to the proxy, it eventually "degenerates" into a full application server that uses the original (HTML) server merely as an information source. This leads to further fragmentation of application logic across the ASP's infrastructure. As such proxy solutions grow more complex, the ASP is usually better served by building a full-fledged WAP application server.

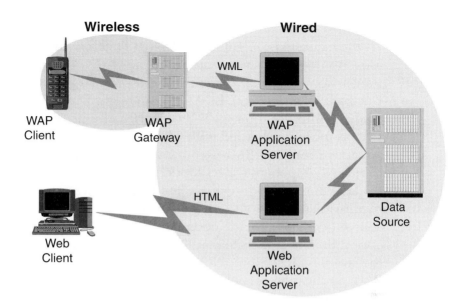

Figure 14-9 Separate Web application servers and WAP application servers

WAP Application Servers

As an alternative to a proxy-based scheme, the content provider may deploy a WAP service by establishing a physically and logically separate *WAP application server* within the back-end infrastructure. The WAP application server[3] is a conventional "Web" server; indeed, it may use the same techniques for generating static or dynamic content as its Web brethren. The difference is that the ultimate result of the content generation is WML rather than HTML. This solution enables tailor-made services for WAP but avoids changes to the existing Web infrastructure.

Figure 14-9 depicts a typical back-end infrastructure involving an application server that is capable of generating WAP-enabled content directly. Although this configuration includes a WAP gateway for bridging the wireless and wireline protocols, the architecture for the WAP services is similar to that for an Internet browser or any other client device.

---

[3]Several WAP application servers are available commercially, most of which simply extend existing Web application servers by providing additional services that ease the development of WAP applications. The available WAP application servers include offerings from Ericsson, IBM, Lotus, and Nokia.

The browser connects to an appropriate application server, which delivers the requested content in a form that the browser can display. The various application servers communicate with a common data source or transaction engine by using standard protocols such as ODBC (Object Database Connectivity), LDAP (Lightweight Directory Access Protocol), or IIOP (Internet Inter-ORB Protocol), or by using remote access APIs such as those constructed with CORBA (Common Object Request Broker Architecture), Java RMI (Remote Method Invocation), or DCOM (Distributed Component Object Model).[4]

Like the transcoding proxy, the WAP application server solution may require relatively large investments in the long term. If the existing data source does not provide adequate APIs to meet the needs of the WAP application, then the site may require significant reengineering to enable the seamless insertion of a WAP application server. Once installed, the WAP application server is an additional piece of infrastructure that the service provider or ASP must maintain; its presence implies investments in hardware as well as software. Finally, the WAP service and Web service must be managed in lockstep. That is, any new service that is offered for the Web audience requires additional investments in the WAP application server to upgrade the mobile service, and vice versa.

To eliminate these limitations, the WAP service offerings must be woven even more deeply into the IT infrastructure.

Multimode Application Servers

A third architecture, illustrated in Figure 14-10, provides an integrated scheme for delivering services to conventional desktop users, WAP devices, and future devices. Like the WAP application server architecture described in the previous section, this approach separates *content generation* and *markup generation*.[5] As shown in Figure 14-11, however, it goes a step further in deploying a single application server that can generate multiple markup language representations for the data. This approach essentially merges the Web application server and the WAP application

---

[4]Discussion of this back-end connectivity is beyond the scope of this book. Good overviews of these techniques are provided by Linthicum (2000) and Ashbury/Weiner (1999).

[5]Note the parallel between this separation and the *model-view-controller* (MVC) paradigm for object-oriented software development.

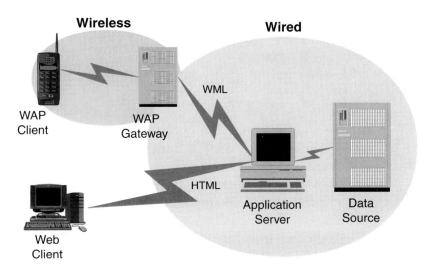

Figure 14-10 A multimode application server

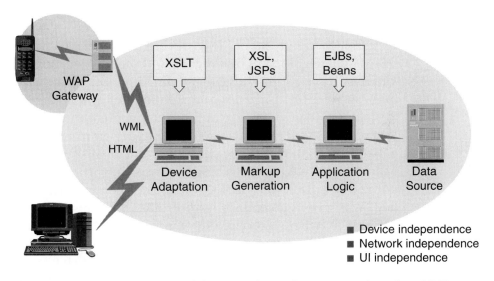

Figure 14-11 Provisioning of device-independent services based on XML and XSL or JSP front ends

server. This unified application server can be extended easily to support new markup languages, including VoiceXML, as they emerge.

Two approaches are commonly used today to create this architecture: eXtensible Markup Language (XML) and JavaServer Pages (JSPs).

Extensible Markup Language

As discussed earlier in this chapter, achieving generic, automated conversion from HTML to WML is difficult because transcoding proxies cannot easily translate the semantics from HTML and their associated scripts into WML. Moreover, these transcoding proxies cannot convert the HTML-based user interface interactions into a form that is suitable for the limited interface environment.

The problem is that HTML lacks a separation between *data* and *data representation*. HTML pages contain both the data content and instructions describing how that content should be presented to the user. The data content should not vary with changes in the user's browser environment, but the structure and display of that content need to change depending on, for example, the screen space available on any given end-user device.

Prior to the advent of WML, several attempts were made to overcome HTML's limitations in this regard and thereby support small-footprint devices. These approaches either defined subsets of the HTML standard or published HTML usage recommendations for content developers. Content developers then needed to author their content multiple times, once for each HTML variant. This problem had arisen in the past as well, most notably as content developers sought to take advantage of features that were unique to the various Web browsers (in particular, Netscape Navigator and Microsoft Internet Explorer). The need for such "multiple authoring" was seen as potentially leading either to a fragmentation of the World Wide Web (where a service offering might not be able to reach all clients) or to a significant complication of the task of content developers.

To address these concerns, the World Wide Web Consortium defined XML. XML is a syntax definition language that allows content sources to define data sets and formats and to encode their data in a universally accepted format. Syntactically, XML looks very similar to HTML, but the particular choice of tag names depends on the type of data being described in the document.

In addition to the XML standard, which defines the raw data stream, the World Wide Web Consortium has defined a standard for describing how to manipulate an XML document. The eXtensible Style-Sheet Language (XSL) standard provides a set of transformation rules for converting an input XML document into an output document, which may be in HTML, WML, or another format.

In this way, the data source can publish information in a particular XML form, and the application server can maintain a set of XSL style sheets for transforming the XML data into a markup language that is suitable for the client device. When the request reaches the application server, logic simply analyzes the request to determine the most appropriate XSL style sheet to apply to the data. Supporting a new browser markup language simply involves introducing a new XSL document to the application server.

JavaServer Pages

JSPs provide an alternative method for supporting the separation of data and data representation. In this environment, the data is encapsulated in a JavaBean, which provides APIs for accessing particular data elements. The data representation—the JSP—is actually a document written in HTML, WML, or any other markup language that can be rendered by the client. This document includes special tags that describe API calls on the JavaBean to access and format data.

The JSP document is compiled, using a JSP compiler, into a servlet that is installed on the application server. Markup contained in the JSP is transformed into Java commands to output that text directly to the output stream. JSP tags describing calls to JavaBean APIs are transformed into Java code that calls the corresponding JavaBean API and writes the result to the output stream.

When the request reaches the application server, logic analyzes it to determine the most appropriate JSP to apply. The corresponding servlet is then invoked. The servlet outputs the final document, which essentially merges the static markup contained in the original JSP with the dynamic data provided by the JavaBean. In this way, the data source can provide data in any format—including XML—and a JavaBean will supply an interface to that data.

A multimode application server holds a collection of JSPs for delivering content in markup languages that are suitable for a variety of client browsers. Supporting a new browser markup language simply involves writing and compiling a new JSP at the application server. Most important, this does not require modifications to the existing JavaBeans or data.

Comparing XML/XSL and JSPs

Both XSL and JSP documents describe how to turn XML-based data into content suitable for display. Hence, whereas the XML document contains data, XSLs and JSPs add representation. JSPs have an additional advantage in that the data source need not be in XML, as long as it can be encapsulated as a JavaBean.

The major difference between the two approaches lies in how the transformation between the raw data and its browser representation is defined. XSL is an extremely powerful tool for converting the data into virtually any representation. Unfortunately, it is generally quite difficult to build and manage the style sheets required; these tasks are best handled by programmers, rather than graphical designers or user interface specialists. In contrast, JSPs are written in the target markup language, so graphical designers can use existing tools to build and preview the page. Because JSPs primarily import data from the JavaBean, however, they offer less flexibility in dynamically structuring the layout of the data.

One other difference between the JSP and XSL approach lies in the sequence of processing. With XSL, the style sheet is applied to generate the representation of the data after the data has been compiled into an XML record; the process that generates the XML record therefore either must be device-dependent, in order to generate only those data fields actually needed for the device, or must generate the full record and let the style sheet *prune* data as needed for the device. While the first approach compromises the architecture of separating device-independent data generation from the device-dependent generation of the representation of that data, the latter approach may result in considerable wasted processing to extract unneeded data. JSPs, on the other hand, retrieve data from Java-Beans as a result of a reference in the actual output, so they only request those data items that are actually needed to generate the markup being returned. JavaBeans can defer a back-end data request or transaction until a reference to that data field is actually encountered in the output, thus limiting the processing to those data items that actually occur in the output.

Conclusion

A WAP service delivery infrastructure may be constructed in many ways. The particular configuration depends on which business models are employed by value chain members, the extent to which the content provider is willing to reengineer or adapt its existing content for the mobile Internet, and the security, performance, and manageability requirements of the service. At one extreme, the entire infrastructure could be owned and deployed by the content provider; at the other extreme, the carrier could deploy the entire infrastructure, including the applications. In reality, most configurations will involve some sort of hybrid structure, where the roles are shared among the carrier, portal, content provider, and ASP.

Web designers face a challenging task in building Web sites that can not only deliver content to a variety of existing devices, but also support new device types over time. The designer must choose between solutions that offer immediate deployment capability with higher long-term maintenance costs and solutions that require more significant reengineering in exchange for easier maintainability. The decision is not an easy one, as it can mean the difference between a mediocre mobile experience and a memorable one for customers.

Ideally, the markup languages used by Internet browsers and those used by WAP-based devices would converge, possibly through the use of XML. As we will discuss in Chapter 15, this "convergence" is an oft-discussed goal that represents one of the future directions for WAP.

Part V
Where Next?

Chapter 15
The Mobile Internet Future

It is difficult to believe that as recently as 1998, most people had never dreamed of accessing Internet content from small, handheld devices. Desktop PCs represented the dominant Web-connected clients. Service providers were rushing to add rich graphical and multimedia content to their sites in a race to capture the attention of Web users. In an ironic twist, the advent of the mobile Internet has sent these same service providers rushing to remove the rich content so as to make their sites accessible on the new Web-connected devices.

Despite its relatively short history, WAP has significantly affected both the definition and the enablement of the mobile Internet. Its emergence has captured people's imaginations, suggesting what might be accomplished with handheld devices that had previously been considered only in terms of their telephony capabilities. Indeed, this merging of data and voice into a portable device is a quite compelling opportunity.

In this book, we have discussed the mobile Internet as enabled by WAP. From WAP-enabled devices, a user can browse WAP-enabled content and services, received pushed information, and access data-enabled telephony applications. As technology and standards advance, the mobile Internet will surely evolve to include even more new capabilities. In this chapter, we explore some future directions for WAP and the mobile Internet.

Better Content, Easier Access

Today, a WAP browser is restricted to sites offering WML, WMLScript, and XML content. This content can represent a quite attractive set of mobile services. Of course, as with the classic Web, users will quickly come to expect a more significant experience, along with even greater ease of use. The mobile Internet therefore will need to support ever richer types of content, more personalized services, and greater usability.

Multimedia Content

Most WAP-enabled content is text-based. Although the WAP standard provides WBMP (a binary format for images), the small size of the mobile screen restricts how many images can be included in a single WML card. In most cases, these images merely serve to augment the textual content instead of becoming the main focus of user attention.

Mobile phones are well suited to displaying richer multimedia content, however. First, because they are phones, they inherently have audio input and output capabilities. Modern phones already contain the hardware required to take a digital signal and convert it into audible sound; indeed, these electronics form the heart of a phone's day-to-day operation. The device also has a microphone and speaker that are conveniently located for easy use. Second, because phones are connected to a network, they can receive streamed data, such as audio or video. With streamed data, the device needs only enough storage for a short buffer of the content, to account for short bursts in network latency or data corruption. Given the small screen, the volume of video data also need not be large.

We have already begun to see initial attempts to take advantage of these multimedia capabilities. Currently, one can buy phones that come with companion MP3 players. The user downloads an audio file over the (wired) Internet into the MP3 player. The MP3 player is then attached to the phone and uses the phone's circuitry to process the audio signal and deliver it to the user. This approach not only reduces the cost and weight of the MP3 player, but also leads to devices that are easier to use and more natural for the user.

Prototypes have been developed that support the attachment of video cameras to phones, allowing the simultaneous transmission of voice and video during a call. Phone manufacturers are experimenting with voice recognition and automated speech generation as well. Someday, one might imagine integrated WAP browsing and voice browsing, which would add to user convenience and ease of use.

To encourage the widespread use of multimedia, the WAP standards will need to define ways of compressing multimedia content for delivery over low-bandwidth, high-latency wireless networks. They will also need to support real-time streaming of content. Because of the inherent bandwidth and real-time delivery requirements of multimedia content, these extensions may unfortunately eliminate the "universality" that the WAP standard has heretofore offered. However, as mobile network bandwidth increases—particularly with the emergence of third-generation (3G) network technologies such as UMTS offering a shared data stream capacity as high as 2 Mbps—these content types will become mainstays of the mobile Internet.

Convergence with the Web

One of the major criticisms of WAP is that the content format is fundamentally different from the HTML and JavaScript used on the Web today. As we saw in Chapter 14, the new content types represent a real barrier to quickly adapting Web services to support the mobile Internet.

Much talk has been devoted to the notion of "converging" the WAP and Web worlds. Ideally, the content types could be merged so that authors could write content once and have it delivered to a broad set of Internet clients. As part of this effort, one would want to see an integration of HTML, WML, VoiceXML, and other emerging formats for the television and digital broadcasting industries.

To allow this convergence to occur, the WAP Forum made significant changes in the WML 1.1 specification to better align WML with the syntax of HTML and XML. These changes included clarification of capitalization rules and the use of HTML-compatible tables.

At the same time, the World Wide Web Consortium has begun to undertake this convergence through the development of the *Extensible Hypertext Markup Language* (XHTML). XHTML first redefines HTML so that it conforms to the XML syntax. It then goes a step further by trying to refactor HTML as a set of "modules," each containing a subset of HTML tags. The hope is that this refactoring will help bring all Web clients under a single umbrella, with each browser supporting a set of XHTML modules. The burden on content developers would be reduced because XHTML modules represent well-defined units of browser interoperability.

Convergence of WML and XHTML will not be easy, however. As we have seen, WML and HTML define different document structures and user interaction models. Moreover, WML provides features that overlap with capabilities traditionally implemented using JavaScript. To frame WML as a valid XHTML module, designers will need to resolve these semantic differences.

The integration of XHTML with voice will be even more difficult, because the interaction patterns of the two differ significantly. Multimodal user interfaces that combine text and voice output pose an even greater challenge. Clearly, the dream of a single, universal content format is still far from reality.

Automatic Provisioning

When the user receives a mobile phone today, he or she can generally begin using it within a few seconds. In most cases, the user simply inserts a SIM card (or enters an access code) and presses the "on" button. Contrast this experience with the initial use of a Web browser on a PC: The user may need to configure the modem, install software, configure a dialer program, configure the software to understand the network environment, and then pray that it all works correctly (and pray even harder for help if it does not work).

As we move toward the mobile Internet, we risk transferring the terrible configuration tasks from the PC world to the mobile world. Early WAP handsets already require the user to input phone numbers and other configuration information. Besides being aggravating for users, this task is made worse by the devices' small screens and tiny input keys.

The solution to this problem lies in the development of a standard method for remotely configuring the phone on the user's behalf. This configuration should be automatically updated to reflect changes in the WAP gateway address and other network parameters. Ultimately, each network service may need to provide its own configuration information, including a phone number, gateway address, security parameters, and pricing information.

End-to-End Security

If we revisit the key mobile Internet services described in Chapter 3, we discover that most of them require the exchange of private information, including personal preferences or financial information. To fully support these applications, the mobile Internet will require a robust security infrastructure that not only guarantees effective user authentication, but also assures true end-to-end security.

The WTLS layer includes support for both client-side and server-side certificates. Using WTLS, the WAP client and WAP gateway can mutually authenticate each other. Moreover, WAP defines the WMLScript **Crypto** Library (Chapter 9), which provides a basic mechanism for signing content that a client must send to a server. This library forms the foundation for implementing nonrepudiable transactions.

These mechanisms are quite limited, however. First, WAP does not provide any mechanisms for performing end-to-end authentication between the client and the application server. Instead, the client and server must rely on the "chain of trust" built from the client to the WAP gateway and from the WAP gateway to the application server. Moreover, the WAP certificate format is incompatible with the X.509 certificates used on the Web today. To address this concern, WAP must define how the mobile Internet will be integrated with the existing public key infrastructure (PKI) mechanisms used on the Internet. In addition, the standard must support application-level mutual authentication between the client and the application server.

Second, WAP does not deliver true end-to-end data security. Because WTLS and SSL/TLS are incompatible, content must be decrypted and reencrypted as it passes through the WAP gateway. This requirement has represented a considerable source of concern for service providers that are accustomed to the end-to-end security semantics provided by SSL. A number of solutions to this problem can be envisioned:

- As content providers move to host their own WAP gateways to enable end-to-end security using WTLS, allow WAP clients to seamlessly transfer among WAP gateways as they move from one site to another.

- Redefine the WTLS protocol to make it directly transferable into SSL/TLS without decryption by the WAP gateway. Alternatively, the WAP standard could simply choose to permit the use of SSL/TLS, although this approach would necessarily increase the network bandwidth and client computation requirements.

- Provide an application-level end-to-end security mechanism, possibly employing *selective encryption* to reduce the computational burden and enable the use of transcoding proxies.

Beyond Browsing

The WAP standard today relies on a browser model. The WAP user agent is expected to be a content renderer that accesses WML and WMLScript content. Although WAP defines WBXML to encode XML data, its primary role is as an efficient encoder of WML documents.

Over time, we can expect mobile Internet clients to mature. They will emerge not as user agent platforms, but rather as *application platforms* in which the WML user agent will represent only one of the executing applications. Users will not only access mobile Internet services directly but also run applications that access and retrieve data and information on their behalf.

Java

The Java programming language has defined the concept of client-side programming for the World Wide Web. Java provides a ubiquitous execution environment that supports the development, delivery, and execution of portable applications—a "Write Once, Run Anywhere" model. Downloadable *applets* run within the Web browser and add graphical content to Web pages, enable sophisticated data presentation, and support richer user interaction. These are all compelling capabilities that designers seek to extend to the mobile handset environment.

Traditionally, the Java execution environment has possessed a number of qualities that made it unsuitable for mobile computing:

- The Java user interface model is tied to a rich graphical interface, including a full set of widgets such as windows, buttons, and scrollbars.

- The execution environment, the *Java Virtual Machine* (JVM), is computationally expensive, particularly when coupled with performance optimization technology such as a just-in-time (JIT) compiler.

- Java application portability results from the use of a standard class library whose memory footprint is quite large (and growing with each Java platform release).

Various attempts have been made to address these issues, most notably through the definition of Java class library subsets such as PersonalJava and EmbeddedJava and through the definition of Java class library extensions such as JavaPhone. Unfortunately, these efforts have largely failed to satisfy the size and function requirements of the mobile environment while preserving application portability.

Recently, however, Java has begun to demonstrate its viability in the mobile environment. New virtual machine technologies, such as Visual-Age Micro Edition from IBM and the kVM (Java 2 Micro-Edition, or J2ME) from Sun Microsystems, are smaller and faster than their predecessors. The IBM tools, in particular, support efficient packaging of applications to minimize their downloading and execution footprint. New class libraries have also been customized to support alternative user interface models.

Java capabilities are already available on some phones, particularly in Japan. Although their use remains limited to providing basic client-side logic to augment downloaded Web pages, the robustness and capability of these Java platforms will certainly grow over time to provide a full-fledged execution environment for portable applications.

When the phones support downloadable applications, the server infrastructure will need to *manage* those applications. For example, the server must schedule which software should be downloaded to a particular device and ensure that the software can run properly within the device. These software distribution mechanisms will ensure continued ease of use as the complexity of the client device increases.

Asynchronous Messaging and Data Synchronization

Today, network connectivity is not ubiquitous: There are plenty of tunnels, buildings, and remote areas that lack cellular coverage. Even in a world with ubiquitous network connectivity, a device may not always be connected to the network. In an airplane, for example, the user is restricted from connecting to a cellular network. In addition, the user may want to disable the network communications temporarily to conserve precious battery power.

One limitation of the browser model is that it requires the client to be connected to the network. If the network is not available, the client is restricted to accessing content currently stored in the local browser cache. In this situation, the mobile Internet is of very little value indeed!

As mobile clients begin to support the execution of client-side applications, handheld devices will perform sophisticated operations, even when they cannot communicate with the wireless network. In this case, the application will be able to access data stored locally on the device, present it to the user, accept user-entered changes to the data, and store those changes in the local data store. When the device reconnects to the network, the device can transmit a description of the data updates to a server, which then will return the changes made to the data while the client was disconnected. This process, known as *data synchronization*, will allow a user to access and manipulate data while disconnected from the network while at the same time ensuring that updates made to the data eventually become available to all servers and users who are interested in that data.

Currently, most mobile phones support some basic data synchronization capability for synchronizing their local phone books with a desktop application such as Lotus Notes or Microsoft Outlook. Over time, users will demand disconnected access to other types of data, including e-mail, data from relational databases, and even content from the Web.

Other types of client applications might support *queued messaging* while the device is disconnected from the network. That is, the user might request a transaction, with the application storing the request in persistent storage on the device. When the device connects with the network, the queued requests are passed to the appropriate server applications for processing. After transmitting the requests, the client could then disconnect from the network. Meanwhile, responses to the user's requests could be queued at a server for later retrieval by the client.

Queued messaging can enable powerful mobile commerce applications. For example, a shopping application might assist the user in constructing a complex order and then queue the complete order for later transmission. After sending the order, the user can reconnect later to check its status. Such message queuing reduces the amount of time that a user is connected to the network and, because it relies on local application logic, improves the overall responsiveness of the shopping experience.

Access to Attached Devices

Traditionally, mobile phones have been simple appliances that permit personal communication (and now, through WAP technology, mobile Internet access). Today, however, these devices are increasingly being connected to other components through serial cables, special connectors, and, eventually, short-range wireless links. For instance, we have already seen an example in which the mobile phone can be docked with a portable MP3 player. One might imagine eventually connecting cellular devices to storage, computers, sensors, controllers, and even other phones. In these environments, the phone might serve as a network communications appliance and application execution environment on behalf of the attached peripherals.

Currently, a downloaded WAP application is not able to discover the presence of these attached devices. Even if it could identify them, WMLScript provides no way to actually communicate with these peripherals. Instead, today's WAP application environment enables applications only for the handset itself.

A more flexible WAP environment would permit WMLScript applications to learn about attached peripherals. It would provide a standard, interoperable mechanism for requesting services from or passing data to them. Applications would be shielded from the implementation details of the particular peripheral. Whenever a new device is connected, the WAP application environment would dynamically extend itself to support the new services offered by that peripheral. Finally, WAP User Agent Profiles (UAProf) would allow the device to describe its currently attached peripherals and thereby permit an application server to generate content and application logic that is customized to the client-side environment.

Beyond Cellular

The development of the WAP specification was motivated by the need to support today's cellular networks, which are typically characterized by low bandwidth and high latency. At the low end, SMS introduces latencies of at least one second with 160-byte packet lengths. At the high end, circuit-switched data offers between 9.6 Kbps and 28.8 Kbps throughput with latencies approaching one second.

New network technologies are changing the way that people think about mobile data communications, however. Indeed, the evolution of the mobile Internet is already beginning to spark work geared toward ensuring that the WAP specifications will better support these new network environments.

Third-Generation Networks

The initial deployments of third-generation (3G) network technologies will occur by late 2000. Such technologies promise to provide data bandwidth exceeding one megabit per second—nearly two orders of magnitude beyond the capacity of today's digital cellular technology. Unlike traditional cellular systems, 3G networks are packet-based and run standard IP. The network is always "connected," meaning that data requests can be issued instantaneously without the need to first establish a call or circuit.

This new generation of networking technology is likely to revolutionize the types of applications that are supported on the mobile Internet. Higher network bandwidth opens the door to richer content, including streaming audio and video. We have already seen the possible implications of multimedia messaging, which becomes practical in these networks. Because the network is packet-based, voice and data communications can occur simultaneously; voice packets can be packetized and sent through the network, so they do not consume the entire channel to and from the telephone. The resulting networks provide better support for pushing data to the device, because no signaling is required to request that the device establish a new session. Instead, the session can be established once and remain active as long as the device is turned on (and within the coverage range).

Bluetooth

Bluetooth is a new short-range, low-power radio technology specifically aimed at portable computing devices, especially mobile phones and PDAs. It enables communications at rates as high as 1 Mbps to a maximum of 100 m distance. The technology is expected to begin appearing in devices late in 2000.

In the future, mobile phones will support both Bluetooth and cellular communications, and, of course, they will support WAP. WAP's network and device independence make it the ideal technology to bridge the Bluetooth and cellular worlds. The Bluetooth specification already defines how the WAP protocols may run on top of a Bluetooth network link, thereby allowing a device to access WAP content over the short-range connection. The WAP gateway might be a fixed access point installed in a building, or a nearby laptop might supply this function.

Ultimately, Bluetooth may have an even more significant effect on the mobile Internet world: It enables entirely new topologies of communicating devices. For example, one might imagine a personal area network (PAN) containing a collection of devices—a laptop, pager, PDA, cellular phone, and data-collecting shoes—all communicating with one another through Bluetooth. Devices on the PAN might rely on the cellular phone to provide remote data access connectivity through the use of the WAP protocols. Your shoes might push a WML deck for display on the cellular phone, and the laptop might provide a large local cache and processing power to support the entire PAN.

The combination of Bluetooth, 3G, and WAP will certainly lead to a new mobile Internet that features ubiquitous connectivity, faster connections, and more possibilities for interdevice communications. Phones will complete their evolution from yesterday's voice communications devices to today's mobile Internet browsers to tomorrow's mobile Internet connectivity appliances. The applications themselves will run on any device and seamlessly access networked services.

Mobile Data Unleashed

Computing and technology are pervading our lives. A mere decade ago, the power of the Internet was almost unknown. Today, a life without the ability to connect to people and information across the globe is almost unimaginable.

In the next decade, the Internet and World Wide Web will permeate our lives even more deeply: Connecting to people and information seamlessly, anywhere, anytime, instantly, will be taken for granted. Our lives will be immensely enhanced by unprecedented breakthroughs in global wireless networks and untethered handheld devices, full of intelligence and processing power and armed with cool capabilities that we can hardly imagine today. We will witness, experience, and benefit firsthand from the fruits of these spectacular technologies and applications as they influence our lives at home, work, school, and play. The current limitations of the mobile Internet will surely prove to be not only temporary challenges that are soon addressed through innovation and creativity, but also catalysts for delivering the promise of pervasive computing in the post-PC era.

Given the rapid rate of adoption of the Internet and the proliferation of cellular phones and other Internet-connected devices in both homes and businesses, the opportunities for key converging technologies such as WAP are endless. WAP will continue to redefine mobility in the voice and data communications world.

Appendices

Appendix A
WAP Development Tools, Browsers, and Resources

This appendix lists some of the resources that are available for building WAP applications and content. It is not intended to be an exhaustive list of WAP and WML development tools. Instead, these sources represent merely a starting point. URLs and other information were correct at the time that this book was written; check the vendors' Web sites for the latest developments.

Development Environments

Ericsson WAP IDE

Information: `http://www.ericsson.com/developerszone/`
Platforms: Windows 95/98/NT4
The Ericsson WAP Integrated Development Environment (IDE) includes basic documentation, an Ericsson R320s phone emulator, an integrated development environment, WML and WMLScript bytecode compilers, and a WML syntax analyzer. The distribution also includes Xitami, an open-source Web server, which has been preconfigured for WAP content. The IDE can function with or without the use of a WAP gateway. A trial version of Ericsson's WAP gateway is also available.

IBM Wapsody

Information: `http://alphaworks.ibm.com/tech/wapsody`
Platforms: Java 1.1.x with Swing 1.1, or Java 1.2
IBM's Wapsody tool is a device-generic implementation of the WAP protocol stack and application environment. It includes a WAP browser with the unique ability to dynamically switch between different device configurations without resetting the application state.

Motorola Application Development Kit

Information: `http://www.mot.com/spin/mix/`
Platforms: Windows 95/98/NT4
The Motorola Application Development Kit (ADK) allows the creation of both WML and VoxML (voice-enabled) applications.

Nokia WAP Toolkit

Information: `http://www.forum.nokia.com/waplogin/`
Platforms: Java Run-time Environment 1.2.2 or later
The Nokia WAP Toolkit includes an integrated development environment with complete developer documentation and emulators for the Nokia 7110 phone and two theoretical phones (the 6110 and 6150). The emulators are self-contained; however, to use the 7110 emulator, you will need to connect through a WAP gateway. (Information on Nokia's WAP gateway is also available on the company's Web site.)

Phone.com UP.SDK

Information: `http://updev.phone.com`
Platforms: Windows 95/98/NT4, Solaris
The Phone.com UP.SDK includes complete developer documentation and a browser that simulates a generic WAP phone. Configurations that simulate real devices from manufacturers such as Mitsubishi, Motorola, Samsung, and Alcatel can be downloaded separately. The SDK can function with or without the use of a WAP gateway.

Other WAP Browsers

AU-System, AB

Information: `http://www.wapguide.com/wapguide/`
Platform: PalmOS 3.3
The AU-System provides a version of the Ericsson WAP browser for Palm platform devices.

4thpass KBrowser

Information: `http://www.4thpass.com/kbrowser/`
Platform: Java2 Micro Edition, Palm III, V, VII
4thpass provides WAP browsers for Palm and Java2 Micro Edition platforms, as well as other WAP services.

IBM Wired Anywhere

Information: `http://www.alphaworks.ibm.com/tech/wiredanywhere`
Platform: PalmOS 2.0 and above
IBM Wired Anywhere is a very limited WAP browser demonstration for the Palm platform.

WAPman (EdgeMatrix)

Information: `http://www.edgematrix.com`
Platform: PalmOS 3.1, Windows 95/98/NT4
EdgeMatrix provides WAP browsers for the Windows and Palm platforms.

Yospace SmartPhone

Information: `http://www.yospace.com`
Platform: JDK 1.1.8
The Yospace SmartPhone is a Java-based WAP browser, including a Web site editor.

Other Useful Resources

The WAP Forum

Information: `http://www.wapforum.org`
The WAP Forum's site includes, as you might imagine, extensive information on WAP, including all of the WAP specifications. Forum members also have access to a wide range of mailing lists covering all aspects of WAP.

WAP and WML Discussion Groups

Information: `http://www.egroups.com/group/wap,`
`http://www.egroups.com/group/wml`
Open forum for discussing WAP in general and WAP development issues.

WBMP Creator

Information: `http://www.teraflops.com/wbmp`
This Web tool converts BMP images into Wireless BMP (WBMP) images.

IBM XMLViewer

Information: `http://alphaworks.ibm.com/tech/xmlviewer`
This tool displays any XML document, such as a WML deck.

Kannel Project

Information: `http://www.kannel.org`
The Kannel project is developing an open-source WAP and SMS gateway.

WAP.net

Information: `http://www.wap.net`
WAP.net provides an online resource for WAP developers.

AnywhereYouGo.com

Information: `http://www.anywhereyougo.com`
This Web site provides news, discussion, and resources on wireless application development, including WAP.

WapLinks

Information: `http://www.waplinks.com`
The WapLinks site offers a comprehensive list of resources on all aspects of WAP.

Appendix B
WML Reference

This appendix summarizes the WML elements and attributes. The following notational conventions are used:

- **Boldface** indicates required attributes.
- <u>Underlining</u> marks default values, which are used when you do not explicitly specify an attribute.
- A vertical bar (|) separates two options, of which you may choose one.
- The "(novar)" notation indicates attributes that can not be specified using WML variables.
- A WML version number, such as "[1.2]," indicates a language feature added after WML 1.1.

a	Defines a link associated with a simple go task. *When the user activates the link, the specified URL is loaded.*
Can contain:	text, ` `, `<img>`
Valid in:	`<p>`, `<fieldset>`, `<td>`, `<pre>` [1.3]
href	*The URL to request when the link is activated.*
title	The browser may either display the title in some fashion or ignore it.
accesskey [1.2]	A single character to be assigned as the accesskey, if possible.

id	(novar)
class	(novar)
xml:lang	(novar)

access	Controls execution access to the deck.
Can contain:	Nothing
Valid in:	\<head>

domain	*The domain suffix of domains to be allowed access.*
path	*The path prefix of decks to be allowed access.*
id	(novar)
class	(novar)
xml:lang	(novar)

anchor	Defines a link associated with a task.
	When the user activates the link, the associated task is executed.
Can contain:	text, \ , \<img>, one of \<go>, \<prev>, or \<refresh>
Valid in:	\<p>, \<fieldset>, \<td>, \<pre> [1.3]

title	*The browser may either display the title in some fashion or ignore it.*
accesskey [1.2]	*A single character to be assigned as the accesskey, if possible.*
id	(novar)
class	(novar)
xml:lang	(novar)

b	Contains text that should be rendered in bold font, if possible.
Can contain:	Text (including variables) and other emphasis elements
Valid in:	\<p>, \<td>, \<fieldset>, \ , other emphasis elements

id	(novar)
class	(novar)
xml:lang	(novar)

big	Contains text that should be rendered in large font, if possible.
Can contain:	Text (including variables) and other emphasis elements
Valid in:	\<p>, \<td>, \<fieldset>, \ , other emphasis elements

id	(novar)
class	(novar)
xml:lang	(novar)

br	Forces subsequent content to begin on a new line.
Can contain:	Nothing
Valid in:	`<p>`, `<anchor>`, `<a>`, `<fieldset>`, `<td>`

id	(novar)
class	(novar)

card	Contains content and user interface elements.

Can contain:	`<onevent>`, `<timer>`, `<do>`, `<p>`, `<pre>` [1.2]
	Any onevent elements must precede a timer, which must precede any other content. Only one timer element can be specified. The onenterforward, onenterbackward, and ontimer attributes are shorthand for an onevent element of the same type containing a go element. A template cannot contain both an attribute and element binding for the same event.

Valid in:	`<wml>`

title	*The browser may either display the title in some fashion, make other use of it (e.g., default bookmark name), or ignore it.*
newcontext	"false" | "true" (novar) *Indicates that a new browser context should be created for rendering this card.*
ordered	"true" | "false" (novar) *Indicates whether the card's fields possess a natural order.*
onenterforward	*Specifies a URL to load when this card is entered via forward navigation, including via a bookmark or direct entry.*
onenterbackward	*Specifies a URL to load when this card is entered via backward navigation.*
ontimer	*Specifies a URL to load when a timer contained in this card expires.*
id	(novar) *Gives a name to this card that can be used as a target for navigation.*
class	(novar)
xml:lang	(novar)

do	Binds a user-initiated event to a task. When the event occurs, the associated task is executed.
Can contain:	One of the following: `<go>`, `<prev>`, `<noop>`, `<refresh>`
Valid in:	`<template>` `<card>`, `<p>`, `<fieldset>`, `<pre>` [1.3]

type	`"accept"` | `"prev"` | `"help"` | `"reset"` | `"options"` | `"delete"` | `"unknown"` | `experimental_type` | `vendor_type` | `other_type` (novar) *Specifies the type of binding being defined.*
label	*Specifies a label for the binding; used when dynamic labeling of the control is possible.*
name	*Assigns a name to binding. A card-level binding overrides a deck-level binding with the same name. Defaults to the value of the type attribute.*
optional	<u>`"false"`</u> | `"true"` (novar) *Specifies whether the browser can ignore this binding (choose not to make it available to the user).*
id	(novar)
class	(novar)
xml:lang	(novar)

em	Contains text that should be rendered with emphasis, if possible.
Can contain:	Text (including variables) and other emphasis elements
Valid in:	`<p>`, `<td>`, `<fieldset>`, ` `, other emphasis elements

id	(novar)
class	(novar)
xml:lang	(novar)

fieldset	Marks a group of related fields and text.
Can contain:	Text (including variables), `<fieldset>`, `<input>`, `<select>`, ` `, `<img>`, `<anchor>`, `<a>`, `<table>`, `<do>` *The browser may ignore fieldsets but must process all elements they contain.*
Valid in:	`<p>`, `<fieldset>`

title	*The browser may either display the title in some fashion or ignore it.*

`id`	(novar)
`class`	(novar)
`xml:lang`	(novar)

go	Defines a forward navigation task.
Can contain:	`<postfield>`, `<setvar>`
Valid in:	`<do>`, `<onevent>`, `<anchor>`

`href`	Specifies the URL to load when the task is activated.
`sendreferer`	<u>"false"</u> | <u>"true"</u> (novar)
	Specifies whether the URL of the referring deck should be transmitted with the request.
`method`	<u>"get"</u> | "post" (novar)
	Specifies the method for sending any associated postfield elements along with the request.
`accept-charset`	*A list of character set encodings, separated by spaces or commas.*
`enctype` [1.2]	<u>"application/x-www-form-urlencoded"</u> | "multilart/form-data" (novar)
	Specifies the content type used to transmit any associated postfields. Only valid when `method="get"`.
`cache-control` [1.3]	"no-cache" (novar)
	Tells the browser and any intermediate network agents to ignore any local cache and go back to the origin server for a fresh copy of the content.
`id`	(novar)
`class`	(novar)

head	Defines deck-specific information.
Can contain:	`<access>`, `<meta>`
Valid in:	`<wml>`

`id`	(novar)
`class`	(novar)

i	Contains text that should be rendered in italic font, if possible.
Can contain:	Text (including variables) and other emphasis elements
Valid in:	`<p>`, `<td>`, `<fieldset>`, ` `, other emphasis elements

id	(novar)
class	(novar)
xml:lang	(novar)

img	Includes an image in the card content.
Can contain:	Nothing
Valid in:	`<p>`, `<fieldset>`, `<td>`

alt	*Text to be displayed if the image cannot be shown for any reason.*
src	*The URL of the image to display.*
localsrc	*The identifier of the local representation to use, if available.*
vspace	<u>"0"</u> | pixels | percent% (novar) *Amount of padding space to appear above and below the image. The browser may ignore this attribute.*
hspace	<u>"0"</u> | pixels | percent% (novar) *Amount of padding space to appear to the left and right of the image. The browser may ignore this attribute.*
align	<u>"bottom"</u> | "top" | "middle" (novar) *Specifies the alignment of the image with the surrounding text. May be ignored.*
height	pixels | percent% (novar) *Specifies the amount of vertical space to reserve for the image. May be ignored.*
width	pixels | percent% (novar) *Amount of horizontal space to reserve for the image. May be ignored.*
id	(novar)
class	(novar)

input	Defines an entry field.
Can contain:	Nothing
Valid in:	`<p>`, `<fieldset>`

name	(novar) *Specifies the WML variable that will receive the user's input and that will also provide the default value of the input field.*
value	*Specifies a default value to be used when the control variable does not have an acceptable value.*
format	"*M" (novar) *Specifies a format mask to constrain the user's input.*

emtpyok	"false" | "true" (novar)
	Specifies whether an empty value is acceptable (see Chapter 7).
size	(novar)
	Display width of field. May be ignored.
maxlength	(novar)
	Maximum number of characters allowed.
type	"text" | "password" (novar)
	Specifies whether input should be echoed or masked.
tabindex	(novar)
	Specifies the tab position of this control.
title	*The browser may either display the title in some fashion or ignore it.*
accesskey [1.2]	*A single character to be assigned as the accesskey, if possible.*
id	(novar)
class	(novar)
xml:lang	(novar)

meta	Defines meta-information.
Can contain:	Nothing
Valid in:	\<head>

name |	(novar)
http-equiv	Names the meta-data and defines how it should be interpreted.
forua	"false" | "true"
	Specifies whether the data is intended for the browser (user agent).
content	The data.
scheme	*Additional information about how the data should be interpreted.*
id	(novar)
class	(novar)
xml:lang	(novar)

noop	Defines a null task (no operation).
Can contain:	Nothing
Valid in:	\<do>, \<onevent>

id	(novar)
class	(novar)

onevent	Binds an intrinsic event to a task.
	When the event occurs, the associated task is executed.
Can contain:	One of the following: `<go>`, `<prev>`, `<noop>`, `<refresh>`
Valid in:	The `onpick` type can be used only in an `<option>` element; the others can be used in only in a `<template>` or `<card>`

`type`	`"onenterforward"` | `"onenterbackward"` | `"ontimer"` | `"onpick"` (novar)
	Specifies the type of binding being defined.
`id`	(novar)
`class`	(novar)

optgroup	Marks a group of related elements in a selection list.
Can contain:	`<option>`, `<optgroup>`
	All optgroup elements must contain at least one option or optgroup element. The browser may ignore optgroups but must process any option elements they contain.
Valid in:	`<select>`, `<optgroup>`

`title`	*The browser may either display the title in some fashion or ignore it.*
`id`	(novar)
`class`	(novar)
`xml:lang`	(novar)

option	Defines one element in a selection list.
Can contain:	Text, `<onevent>` (onpick only)
	A single option element cannot contain both an onevent element and an onpick attribute.
Valid in:	`<select>`, `<optgroup>`

`value`	*A value associated with this option, to be assigned to the select list's control variable when this option is selected.*
`onpick`	*A URL to load when this option is selected.*
`title`	*The browser may either display the title in some fashion or ignore it.*
`id`	(novar)
`class`	(novar)
`xml:lang`	(novar)

p	Contains one paragraph of formatted content, including text, images, and event bindings.
Can contain:	Text (including variables), emphasis elements, ` `, `<img>`, `<anchor>`, `<a>`, `<table>`, `<input>`, `<select>`, `<fieldset>`, `<do>`
Valid in:	`<card>`

align	<u>"left"</u> | "center" | "right" (novar) *Indicates the desired alignment of the text relative to the screen.*
mode	"wrap" | "nowrap" (novar) *Indicates whether long lines are wrapped to the screen width. Defaults to the same mode as the preceding paragraph; the first card in the deck defaults to "wrap."*
id	(novar)
class	(novar)
xml:lang	(novar)

postfield	Specifies data to be passed to the application server.
Can contain:	Nothing
Valid in:	`<go>`

name	The key that identifies the data to the server.
value	The data to be passed.
id	(novar)
class	(novar)
xml:lang	(novar)

pre [1.2]	Contains preformatted text.
Can contain:	Text (including variables), emphasis elements (except for `<u>`, `<big>`, and `<small>`), ` `, `<a>`, `<input>`, `<select>`; in 1.3, also `<u>`, `<anchor>`, `<do>`
Valid in:	`<card>`

xml:space	<u>"preserve"</u> (novar)
id	(novar)
class	(novar)

prev	Defines a backward navigation task.
Can contain:	`<setvar>`
Valid in:	`<do>`, `<onevent>`, `<anchor>`

`id`	(novar)
`class`	(novar)

refresh	Defines a screen refresh task.
Can contain:	`<setvar>`
Valid in:	`<do>`, `<onevent>`, `<anchor>`
`id`	(novar)
`class`	(novar)

select	Defines a selection list.
Can contain:	`<option>`, `<optgroup>`
Valid in:	`<p>`, `<fieldset>`
`multiple`	`"false"` | `"true"` (novar) *Specifies whether the list should be single-select or multiselect.*
`name`	(novar) *Specifies the WML variable to receive the user's selection. Also used to determine the default selection(s).*
`value`	*Used to determine the default selection(s).*
`iname`	(novar) *Specifies the WML variable to receive the index of the user's selection. Also used to determine the default selection(s).*
`ivalue`	*Used to determine the default selection(s).*
`tabindex`	(novar) *Specifies the tab position of this control.*
`title`	*The browser may either display the title in some fashion or ignore it.*
`id`	(novar)
`class`	(novar)
`xml:lang`	(novar)

setvar	Assigns a value to a variable or clears a previously assigned value.
Can contain:	Nothing
Valid in:	`<go>`, `<prev>`, `<refresh>`
name	The variable name being assigned or cleared.
value	*The new value to be assigned, or an empty string to clear the variable.*

id	(novar)
class	(novar)

small	Contains text that should be rendered in small font, if possible.
Can contain:	Text (including variables) and other emphasis elements
Valid in:	<p>, <td>, <fieldset>, , other emphasis elements

id	(novar)
class	(novar)
xml:lang	(novar)

strong	Contains text that should be rendered with strong emphasis, if possible.
Can contain:	Text (including variables) and other emphasis elements
Valid in:	<p>, <td>, <fieldset>, , other emphasis elements

id	(novar)
class	(novar)
xml:lang	(novar)

table	Contains content to be aligned into columns. *The browser displays tabular data to the best of its ability, which may be minimal.*
Can contain:	<tr>
Valid in:	<p>, <fieldset>

columns	(novar) *The number of rows in the table.*
title	*The browser may either display the title in some fashion or ignore it.*
align	*A sequence, one character per column, of "C", "L", or "R", indicating the desired alignment of the corresponding column. Unrecognized characters are treated as specifying the default alignment. WML 1.2 added "D" to explicitly specify the default alignment.*
id	(novar)
class	(novar)

td	Defines one cell in a table.
Can contain:	Text (including variables), emphasis elements, ` `, `<img>`, `<anchor>`, `<a>`
Valid in:	`<tr>`

id	(novar)
class	(novar)
xml:lang	(novar)

template	Defines event bindings that apply to all cards in the deck. *The onenterforward, onenterbackward, and ontimer attributes are shorthand for an onevent element of the same type containing a go element. A template cannot contain both an attribute and element binding for the same event.*
Can contain:	`<onevent>`, `<do>`
Valid in:	`<wml>`

onenterforward	*Specifies a URL to load when a card is entered via forward navigation, including via a bookmark or direct entry.*
onenterbackward	*Specifies a URL to load when a card is entered via backward navigation.*
ontimer	*Specifies a URL to load when a timer contained in a card expires.*
id	(novar)
class	(novar)

timer	Specifies an activity to occur after a certain amount of time.
Can contain:	Nothing *A timer can trigger an event even when the user is actively interacting with the card.*
Valid in:	`<select>`, `<optgroup>`

name	A WML variable to control the timer value.
value	The default value of the timer.
id	(novar)
class	(novar)
xml:lang	(novar)

tr	Defines one row in a table.
Can contain:	`<td>`
Valid in:	`<table>`
`id`	(novar)
`class`	(novar)

u	Contains text that should be rendered in underlined font, if possible.
Can contain:	Text (including variables) and other emphasis elements
Valid in:	`<p>`, `<td>`, `<fieldset>`, ` `, other emphasis elements
`id`	(novar)
`class`	(novar)
`xml:lang`	(novar)

wml	Defines a WML deck.
Can contain:	`<head>`, `<template>`, `<card>` *The head and template are optional; the deck must contain at least one card. The head must precede the template, which must precede the first card.*
`id`	(novar)
`class`	(novar)
`xml:lang`	(novar)

Appendix C
WMLScript Standard Libraries Reference

This appendix summarizes the standard WMLScript libraries. It shows the expected types for each argument and the possible return types. When an argument of a different type is presented, the default conversion rules are applied, if possible. The following terms are used:

Any type   A value of any type (integer, floating-point, string, Boolean, or invalid)

Any number   An integer or floating-point value

Crypto Library (Optional)

Crypto.signText(*text*, *options*, *keytype*, *keyid*)
Allow the user to sign a text string.

Arguments: text: string, the text to be signed.
options: integer, signing options. One or more of the following, ORed together:
0x00: no options
0x01: include content
0x02: include key hash
0x04: include certificate

keytype: integer, type of key identifier in *keyid*. One of the
following:

> 0: no key identifier supplied (*keyid* is an empty string)
> 1: *keyid* is the SHA-1 hash of the user public key
> 2: *keyid* is the SHA-1 hash of one or more trusted certificate
>   authorities

keyid: string, key identifier, as identified by *keytype*.

Returns: String.

If successful, the base-64 encoding of the signed string.
"error:noCert" if no proper certificate or signature key is
available.
"error:userCancel" if the user aborted the signing operation.
`invalid` if parameters are incorrect or an encoding error occurs.

Dialogs Library

`Dialogs.alert(`*`msg`*`)`   Display a message.
Execution pauses until the user confirms the message.

Arguments: *msg:* string, message to be displayed.

Returns: String (empty).
invalid if the argument could not be converted to a string.

`Dialogs.confirm(`*`msg, accept, cancel`*`)`   Ask for confirmation.
Displays a message and two possible responses for the user to select.

Arguments: *msg:* string, message to be displayed.
accept: string, text for "accept" reply (if empty, system default is
used).
cancel: string, text for "cancel" reply (if empty, system default is
used).

Returns: Boolean (true if "accept" was selected; false if "cancel" was
selected).
`invalid` if any argument could not be converted to a string.

`Dialogs.prompt(`*`msg, default`*`)`   Prompt for user input.

Arguments: *msg:* string, message to be displayed.
default: string, default response (may be empty for no default).

Returns: String, the user's input.
`invalid` if either argument could not be converted to a string.

Float Library

Not all implementations support floating-point values; *see* Lang.float().

Float.ceil(*n*)   Apply the ceiling function.
Returns the smallest integer not less than the argument.

Arguments:	Any number.
Returns:	Integer. invalid if the argument cannot be converted to a number or if floating-point numbers are not supported.

Float.floor(*n*)   Apply the floor function.
Returns the largest integer not greater than the argument.

Arguments:	Any number.
Returns:	Integer. invalid if the argument cannot be converted to a number or if floating-point numbers are not supported.

Float.int(*n*)   Convert a value to an integer.
Return the argument with any fractional portion truncated.

Arguments:	Any number.
Returns:	Integer. invalid if the argument cannot be converted to a number or if floating-point numbers are not supported.

Float.maxFloat()   Return the largest supported floating-point value.

Arguments:	None.
Returns:	Floating-point 3.40282347E+38. invalid if floating-point numbers are not supported.

Float.minFloat()
Return the smallest floating-point value greater than zero.

Arguments:	None.
Returns:	Floating-point 1.17549435E-38. invalid if floating-point numbers are not supported.

Float.pow(*n1*, *n2*)   Compute *n1* to the power of *n2*.
The result is an approximation, which will vary depending on the implementation.

Arguments: Any two numbers.
If n1 is negative, then n2 must be an integer.
If n1 is zero, then n2 must be greater than or equal to zero.

Returns: Floating-point value.
`invalid` if either argument cannot be converted to a number, if
the arguments are not valid, or if floating-point numbers are not
supported.

Float.round(*n*)   Round a number.
Returns the closest integer to the argument (.5 rounds up).

Arguments: Any number.

Returns: Integer.
`invalid` if the argument cannot be converted to a number or if
floating-point numbers are not supported.

Float.sqrt(*n*)   Compute a square root.
The result is an approximation, which will vary depending on the implementation.

Arguments: Any number.

Returns: Floating-point value.
`invalid` if the argument cannot be converted to a number, if the
argument is less than zero, or if floating-point numbers are not
supported.

Lang Library

Lang.abort(*x*)
Perform an abnormal exit from the WMLScript interpreter.
The value of the argument is returned to the application that invoked WMLScript.
Any pending navigation request is ignored.

Arguments: Any type.
The value `invalid` is converted to the string `"invalid"`.

Returns: Nothing.

`Lang.abs(x)`   Compute the absolute value of a number.

Arguments: Any number.

Returns: Number (same type as the argument).
invalid if the argument cannot be converted to a number

`Lang.character Set()`
Return the character set supported by the WMLScript interpreter.

Arguments: None.

Returns: Integer, the IANA MIBenum value assigned to the character set.

`Lang.exit(x)`   Perform a normal exit from the WMLScript interpreter.
The value of the argument is returned to the application that invoked WMLScript.

Arguments: Any type.
The value invalid is returned directly.

Returns: Nothing.

`Lang.float()`
Test whether the current platform supports floating-point numbers.

Arguments: Any type.

Returns: Boolean, true if floating-point numbers are supported.

`Lang.isFloat(x)`
Test whether a value can be converted to a floating-point number.

Arguments: Any type.

Returns: Boolean, true if value is already a floating-point value or
if it can be converted to a string that can be parsed with
`Lang.parseFloat()`.
invalid if floating-point numbers are not supported

`Lang.isInt(x)`   Test whether a value can be converted to an integer number.

Arguments: Any type.

Returns: Boolean, true if value is already an integer or if it can be converted to a string that can be parsed with *`Lang.parseInt()`*.

Lang.max(*n1*, *n2*)   Return the greater of two numbers.
If the arguments are of different types, conversion precedence rules for integers and floating-point values are applied.

Arguments:	Any two numbers.
Returns:	Number (type determined by types of arguments).
	`invalid` if either argument cannot be converted to a valid number.

Lang.maxInt()   Return the largest supported integer value.

Arguments:	None.
Returns:	Integer 2147483647.

Lang.min(*n1*, *n2*)   Return the lesser of two numbers.
If the arguments are of different types, conversion precedence rules for integers and floating-point values are applied.

Arguments:	Any two numbers.
Returns:	Number (type determined by types of arguments).
	`invalid` if either argument cannot be converted to a valid number.

Lang.minInt()   Return the smallest possible integer value.

Arguments:	None.
Returns:	Integer –2147483648.

Lang.parseFloat(*s*)   Return the floating-point value of the argument.
Parsing ends at the first character that cannot be parsed as part of a floating-point number.

Arguments:	String.
Returns:	Floating-point number.
	`invalid` if a parsing error occurs or if floating-point numbers are not supported.

Lang.parseInt(*s*)   Return the integer value of the argument.
Parsing ends at the first character that cannot be parsed as part of an integer.

Arguments:	String.
Returns:	Integer.
	`invalid` if a parsing error occurs.

Lang.random(*n*)   Return a pseudo-random number.

Arguments:	Any number.
	If a floating-point number is given, it is converted to an integer with `Float.int()`.
Returns:	Integer, a number from the uniform distribution in the range [0,*n*].
	`invalid` if the argument cannot be converted to a number or is less than zero.

Lang.seed(*n*)   Initialize the pseudo-random number generator.
On many systems, a seed greater than or equal to zero will result in a repeatable sequence of pseudo-random numbers.

Arguments:	Any number.
	If a floating-point number is given, it is converted to an integer with `Float.int()`.
Returns:	Empty string.
	`invalid` if the argument cannot be converted to a number.

String Library

String.charAt(*s*, *i*)   Returns a specific character from a string.

Arguments:	*s*: any string.
	i: any number, zero-based index.
	If the index is a floating-point number, it is converted to an integer with `Float.int()`.
Returns:	String, containing the requested character or an empty string if the index is out of range.
	`invalid` if either argument cannot be converted to the required type.

String.compare(*s1*, *s2*)   Lexically compare two strings.

Arguments: Any two strings.

Returns: Integer, -1 if *s1* precedes *s2*, 0 if *s1* equals *s2*, or 1 if s1 follows s2).
`invalid` if either argument cannot be converted to a string.

String.elementAt(*s*, *i*, *d*)   Return an element from a string.

Arguments: *s*: any string.
i: any number, a zero-based index.
d: string specifying a delimiter character.
*If the index is a floating-point number, it is converted to an integer
with* `Float.int()`*. If the delimiter is more than one character, the first
character is used. If the index is less than zero, the first element is
returned. If the index is greater than the number of elements in the
string, the last element is returned.*

Returns: String, the substring comprising the indexed element.
`invalid` if any argument cannot be converted to the required
type or if *d* is an empty string.

String.elements(*s*, *d*)   Count the elements in a string.

Arguments: *s*: any string.
d: string specifying a delimiter character.
If the delimiter is more than one character, the first character is used.

Returns: Integer, the number of occurrences of the separator character in
the string plus one.
`invalid` if either argument cannot be converted to a string or if *d*
is an empty string.

String.find(*s1*, *s2*)   Search for a substring.

Arguments: *s1*: string to be searched.
s2: string to be located.

Returns: Integer, the zero-based index of the first occurrence of *s2* within
s1 or −1 if the index is not found.
`invalid` if either argument cannot be converted to a string or if
s2 is an empty string.

String.format(s, x)   Format a value as a string.

Arguments: *s*: a format string.
x: a value of any type.
The format string takes the form:
%[width][.precision]type
The type code may be d *(integer),* f *(floating point,) or* s *(string).*

Returns: String, the result of converting *x* to a string using the formatting specified in *s*.
invalid if *s* contains an illegal format specification.

String.insertAt(s1, s2, i, d)   Insert an element into a string.

Arguments: *s1*: target string.
s2: string containing the new element.
i: any number, a zero-based index.
d: string specifying a delimiter character.
If the delimiter is more than one character, the first character is used. If the index is a floating-point number, it is converted to an integer with Float.int()*. If the index is less than zero, the new element becomes the first element. If the index is greater than the number of elements in the string, the new element becomes the last element.*

Returns: String, a copy of *s1* with *s2* inserted at given index.
invalid if any argument cannot be converted to the required type or if *d* is an empty string.

String.isEmpty(s)   Test for an empty string.

Arguments: Any string.

Returns: Boolean, true if the length of *s* is zero.
invalid if the argument cannot be converted to a string.

String.length(s)   Count the characters in a string.

Arguments: Any string.

Returns: Number of characters in the string.
invalid if the argument cannot be converted to a string.

`String.removeAt(s, i, d)`   Remove an element from a string.

Arguments:	*s*: a target string.
	i: any number, a zero-based index.
	d: string specifying a delimiter character.
	If the delimiter is more than one character, the first character is used. If the index is a floating-point number, it is converted to an integer with `Float.int()`. *If the index is less than zero, the first element is removed. If the index is greater than the number of elements in the string, the last element is removed.*
Returns:	String, a copy of s with the indexed element removed. `invalid` if any argument cannot be converted to the required type or if *d* is an empty string.

`String.replace(s1, s2, s3)`   Replace a substring.

Arguments:	*s1*: target string.
	s2: string to locate in *s1*.
	s3: string to replace *s2*.
Returns:	String, a copy of *s1* with every occurrence of *s2* replaced with *s3*. `invalid` if any argument cannot be converted to a string or if *s2* is an empty string.

`String.replaceAt(s1, s2, i, d)`   Replace an element in a string.

Arguments:	*s1*: target string.
	s2: a string containing the new element.
	i: any number, a zero-based index.
	d: string specifying a delimiter character.
	If the delimiter is more than one character, the first character is used. If the index is a floating-point number, it is converted to an integer with `Float.int()`. *If the index is less than zero, the first element is replaced. If the index is greater than the number of elements in the string, the last element is replaced.*
Returns:	String, a copy of *s1* with the indexed element replaced by *s2*. `invalid` if any argument cannot be converted to the required type or if *d* is an empty string.

`String.squeeze(s)` Compress whitespace in a string.

Arguments: Any string.

Returns: String, a copy of *s* with all sequences of whitespace characters replaced by a single space.
invalid if the argument cannot be converted to a string.

`String.subString(s, i, 1)` Returns a portion of a string.

Arguments: *s*: any string.
i: any number, a zero-based index.
l: any number, the length of the substring to return.
If the index or length is a floating-point number, it is converted to an integer with `Float.int()`. If index is less than zero, zero is used.

Returns: String containing the requested substring.
invalid if any argument cannot be converted to the required type.

`String.toString(x)` Convert a value to a string.

Arguments: Any type.

Returns: String, the string representation of the argument .
invalid is converted to the string `"invalid"`.

`String.trim(s)` Remove leading and trailing whitespace from a string.

Arguments: Any string.

Returns: String, a copy of *s* with all leading and trailing sequences of whitespace characters removed.
invalid if the argument cannot be converted to a string.

URL Library

`URL.escapeString(s)` Encode special characters.

Arguments: Any string.

Returns: String, copy of *s* with special characters replaced by escape sequences).
invalid if the input cannot be converted to a string or contains characters not in the US-ASCII character set.

URL.getBase()   Return the absolute URL of the current compilation unit. *The fragment (i.e., the function name) is not returned.*

Arguments: None.

Returns: String.

URL.getFragment(*s*)   Extract the fragment component of a URL. *Both absolute and relative URLs are supported.*

Arguments: String, a URL.

Returns: String, empty if no fragment exists.
invalid if *s* cannot be converted to a string or is not a syntactically valid URL.

URL.getHost(*s*)   Extract the host component of a URL. *Both absolute and relative URLs are supported.*

Arguments: String, a URL.

Returns: String, empty if no fragment exists.
invalid if *s* cannot be converted to a string or is not a syntactically valid URL.

URL.getParameters(*s*)   Extract the parameter component of a URL. *Both absolute and relative URLs are supported. Only parameters from the last segment are returned.*

Arguments: String, a URL.

Returns: String, empty if no fragment exists.
invalid if *s* cannot be converted to a string or is not a syntactically valid URL.

URL.getPath(*s*)   Extract the path component of a URL. *Both absolute and relative URLs are supported.*

Arguments: String, a URL.

Returns: String, empty if no fragment exists.
invalid if *s* cannot be converted to a string or is not a syntactically valid URL.

URL.getPort(*s*)　Extract the port component of a URL.
Both absolute and relative URLs are supported.

Arguments:　String, a URL.

Returns:　String, empty if no fragment exists.
invalid if *s* cannot be converted to a string or is not a syntactically valid URL.

URL.getQuery(*s*)　Extract the query component of a URL.
Both absolute and relative URLs are supported.

Arguments:　String, a URL.

Returns:　String, empty if no fragment exists.
invalid if *s* cannot be converted to a string or is not a syntactically valid URL.

URL.getReferer()
Return the URL of the resource that called the current compilation unit.
The referrer is returned as the smallest possible relative URL or as an absolute URL if the referrer is not relative. If no referrer is available, an empty string is returned.

Arguments:　None.

Returns:　String.

URL.getScheme(*s*)　Extract the scheme component of a URL.
Both absolute and relative URLs are supported.

Arguments:　String, a URL.

Returns:　String, empty if no fragment exists.
invalid if *s* cannot be converted to a string or is not a syntactically valid URL.

URL.isValid(*s*)　Test whether a string is a syntactically valid URL.
Both absolute and relative URLs are supported.

Arguments:　Any string.

Returns:　Boolean, true if s can be interpreted as a valid URL.
invalid if the argument cannot be converted to a string.

URL.loadString(*u*, *t*)   Retrieve text content.

Arguments:	*u*: string, the URL to retrieve.
	t: string, the content type expected.
Returns:	String, the content represented by the URL.
	Integer, an error code if the content cannot be retrieved.
	invalid if the given content type is invalid or does not match the actual content type.

URL.resolve(*b*, *r*)   Resolve a URL relative to a given base.

Arguments:	*b*: string, a base URL.
	r: string, a relative URL.
Returns:	String, the URL resulting from resolving *r* against the base *b*), invalid if either argument cannot be converted to a string or is not a syntactically valid URL.

URL.unescapeString(*s*)   Decode special characters.

Arguments:	Any string.
Returns:	String, copy of argument with escape sequences replaced with the corresponding character.
	invalid if the input string contains characters not in the US-ASCII character set.

WMLBrowser Library

WMLBrowser.getCurrentCard()   Get the URL of the current card.

Arguments:	None.
Returns:	String, the URL of the current card (relative to the current compilation unit, if possible, or absolute).
	invalid if there is no current card or if the script was not invoked from a browser.

WMLBrowser.getVar(*s*)   Retrieve the value of a WML variable.

Arguments: String, a WML variable name.

Returns: String, the current value of the named WML variable (which may be the empty string).
invalid if the specified variable name is invalid.

WMLBrowser.go(*s*)   Navigate to a new URL.
Overrides any previous go() or prev() call. Navigation occurs when control returns to the browser.

Arguments: String, a URL.
A null string cancels any previous go() or prev() call.

Returns: Empty string.
invalid if the argument cannot be converted to a string or if the script was not invoked from a browser.

WMLBrowser.newContext()   Establish a new browser context.
The new context has no defined variables and only the current card in the navigation history. A pending go() request is not affected.

Arguments: None.

Returns: Empty string.
invalid if the script was not invoked from a browser.

WMLBrowser.prev()   Navigate to the previous card.
Overrides any previous go() call. Navigation occurs when control returns to the browser.

Arguments: None.

Returns: Empty string.
invalid if the script was not invoked from a browser.

WMLBrowser.refresh()   Refresh the display.

Arguments: None.

Returns: Empty string.
invalid if the display could not be refreshed immediately.
If immediate refresh is not possible, the display will be refreshed when the WMLScript program ends.

WMLBrowser.setVar(*s1*, *s2*)   Assign a new value to a WML variable.

Arguments: *s1*: string, a WML variable name.
s2: string, a new value for the variable.
An empty string may be used to undefine the specified variable.

Returns: Boolean, `true` if the variable was set successfully or `false` if it could not be set.
`invalid` if the specified variable name or value is invalid or if the script was not invoked from a browser.

WTAPublic Library

WTAPublic.addPBEntry(*number*, *name*)   Add a phonebook entry.
Adds a new entry to the first available location in the device phonebook. The user must explicitly acknowledge the addition.

Arguments: *number*: string, phone number to be added.
name: string, name to be used for the entry.

Returns: Integer.
0 if successful, or WTAI error code otherwise.

WTAPublic.makeCall(*number*)   Place a voice call.
The number must be displayed to the user, who must explicitly acknowledge that the call can be placed. The user ends the call by using the device's normal mechanism.

Arguments: *number*: string, phone number to call.

Returns: Integer.
0 if successful, or WTAI error code otherwise.

WTAPublic.sendDTMF(*seq*)   Send DTMF tones.
Sends a sequence of DTMF tones through an active voice connection.

Arguments: *seq*: string, sequence to send, composed of any of the following characters:
0 1 2 3 4 5 6 7 8 9 * # , A B C D

Returns: Integer.
0 if successful, or WTAI error code otherwise.

Appendix D
User Agent Profiles Vocabulary

The table in this appendix summarizes the components and attributes defined by the WAP 1.1 UAProf specification.

Attribute	Description	Reso-lution Rule	Type	Sample Values
Component: HardwarePlatform				
BitsPerPixel	The number of bits of color or gray-scale information per pixel	Override	Number	"2", "8"
ColorCapable	Indicates whether the device display supports color	Override	Boolean	"Yes", "No"
CPU	Name and model number of device CPU	Locked	Literal	"Pentium III", "PowerPC 750"
ImageCapable	Indicates whether the device supports the display of images	Locked	Boolean	"Yes", "No"
InputCharSet	List of character sets supported by the device for text entry	Locked	Literal (bag)	"US-ASCII", "ISO-8859-1", "Shift_JIS"

continued

Attribute	Description	Reso-lution Rule	Type	Sample Values
Component: HardwarePlatform *continued*				
Keyboard	Type of keyboard sup-ported by the device	Locked	Literal	"Disambig-uating", "Qwerty", "PhoneKeypad"
MaxScreenChar	Size of the virtual page onto which a docu-ment is rendered, in units of characters	Locked	Dimen-sion	"16x80", "48x32"
Model	Model number as-signed to the terminal device by the vendor or manufacturer	Locked	Literal	"Mustang GT", "Q30"
OutputCharSet	List of character sets supported by the de-vice for output to the display	Append	Literal (bag)	"US-ASCII", "ISO-8859-1", "Shift_JIS"
PointingResolution	Type of resolution of the pointing accessory supported by the device	Locked	Literal	"Character", "Line", "Pixel"
ScreenSize	The size of the device's screen in units of pixels	Locked	Dimen-sion	"160x160", "640x480"
ScreenSizeChar	Size of the device's screen in units of characters	Locked	Dimen-sion	"12x4", "16x8"
SoftKeysCapable	Indicates whether the device supports pro-grammable soft keys	Locked	Boolean	"Yes", "No"
SoundOutputCapable	Indicates whether the device supports sound output	Locked	Boolean	"Yes", "No"
TextInputCapable	Indicates whether the device supports alpha-numeric text entry	Locked	Boolean	"Yes", "No"
Vendor	Name of the manufac-turer of the terminal device	Locked	Literal	"Ford", "Lexus"
VoiceInputCapable	Indicates whether the device supports any form of voice input, including speech recog-nition	Locked	Boolean	"Yes", "No"

Attribute	Description	Reso-lution Rule	Type	Sample Values
Component: SoftwarePlatform				
AcceptDownloadableSoftware	Indicates the user's preference on whether to accept download-able software	Locked	Boolean	"Yes", "No"
AudioInputEncoder	List of audio input en-coders supported by the device	Append	Literal (bag)	"G.711", "G.931"
DownloadableSoftwareSupport	List of executable con-tent types that the de-vice supports and that it is willing to accept from the network	Locked	Literal (bag)	"application/x-msdos-exe"
JVMVersion	List of the Java Virtual Machines installed on the device	Append	Literal (bag)	"SunJRE1.2", "MSJVM1.0"
MexeClassmark	ETSI MExE classmark	Locked	Number	"1", "2"
MexeSpec	Class mark special-ization	Locked	Literal	"7.02"
OSName	Name of the device's operating system	Locked	Literal	"Mac OS", "Windows NT"
OSVendor	Vendor of the device's operating system	Locked	Literal	"Apple", "Microsoft"
OSVersion	Version of the device's operating system	Locked	Literal	"6.0", "4.5"
RecipientAppAgent	User agent associated with the current request	Locked	Literal	"SpeedyMail"
SoftwareNumber	Version of the device-specific software (firm-ware) to which the device's low-level software conforms	Locked	Literal	"2"
VideoInputEncoder	List of video input en-coders supported by the device	Append	Literal (bag)	"MPEG-1", "MPEG-2", "H.261"
Component: NetworkCharacteristics				
CurrentBearerService	The bearer on which the current session was opened	Locked	Literal	"OneWaySMS", "GUTS", "TwoWayPacket"

continued

Attribute	Description	Reso-lution Rule	Type	Sample Values
Component: NetworkCharacteristics *continued*				
SecuritySupport	Type of security or encryption mechanism supported	Locked	Literal	"PPTP"
SupportedBearers	List of bearers supported by the device	Locked	Literal (bag)	"GPRS", "GUTS", "TwowaySMS", CSD", "USSD"
Component: BrowserUA				
BrowserName	Name of the browser user agent associated with the current request	Locked	Literal	"Mozilla", "MSIE"
BrowserVersion	Version of the browser	Locked	Literal	"1.0"
CcppAccept	List of content types supported by the device	Append	Literal (bag)	"text/html", "text/plain", "text/html", "image/gif"
CcppAccept-Charset	List of character sets supported by the device	Append	Literal (bag)	"US-ASCII", "ISO-8859-1", "Shift_JIS"
CcppAccept-Encoding	List of transfer encodings supported by the device	Append	Literal (bag)	"base64", "quoted-printable"
CcppAccept-Language	List of preferred document languages	Append	Literal (sequence)	"zh-CN", "en", "fr"
DownloadableBrowserApps	List of executable content types that the browser supports and that it is willing to accept from the network	Append	Literal (bag)	"application/ava-applet" "application/javascript"
FramesCapable	Indicates whether the browser is capable of displaying HTML frames	Override	Boolean	"Yes", "No"
HtmlVersion	Version of Hypertext Markup Language (HTML) supported by the browser	Locked	Literal	"2.0", "3.2", "4.0"
JavaScriptVersion	Version of JavaScript supported by the browser	Locked	Literal	"1.4"

Attribute	Description	Reso-lution Rule	Type	Sample Values
Component: BrowserUA *continued*				
PreferenceForFrames	Indicates the user's preference for receiving HTML content that contains frames	Locked	Boolean	"Yes", "No"
TablesCapable	Indicates whether the browser is capable of displaying HTML tables	Locked	Boolean	"Yes", "No"
XhtmlVersion	Version of XHTML supported by the browser	Locked	Literal	"1.0"
XhtmlModules	List of XHTML modules supported by the browser	Append	Literal	"XHTML1-struct", "XHTML1-blkstruct", "XHTML1-frames"
Component: WapCharacteristics				
WapDeviceClass	Classification of the device based on capabilities as identified in the WAP 1.1 specifications	Locked	Literal	"A"
WapPushMsgPriority	User's preference on the priority of incoming push messages	Locked	Literal	"critical", "low", "none", "all"
WapPushMsgSize	Maximum size of a push message that the device can handle	Locked	Number	"1024", "1400"
WapVersion	Version of WAP supported	Locked	Literal	"1.1", "1.2", "2.0"
WmlDeckSize	Maximum size of a WML deck that can be downloaded to the device	Locked	Number	"4096"
WmlScriptLibraries	List of mandatory and optional libraries supported in the device's WMLScript virtual machine	Locked	Literal (bag)	"Lang", "Float", "String", "URL", "WMLBrowser", "Dialogs"

continued

Attribute	Description	Reso-lution Rule	Type	Sample Values
Component: WapCharacteristics *continued*				
WmlScriptVersion	List of WMLScript version numbers supported by the device	Append	Literal (bag)	"1.1", "1.2"
WmlVersion	List of WML language version numbers supported by the device	Append	Literal (bag)	"1.1", "1.0"
WtaiLibraries	List of WTAI network-common and network-specific libraries supported by the device that are URI-accessible	Locked	Literal (bag)	"WTAVoiceCall", "WTANetText", "WTAPhoneBook", "WTACallLog", "WTAMisc", "WTAGSM", "WTAIS136", "WTAPDC"
WtaVersion	Version of WTA user agent	Locked	Literal	"1.1"

Appendix E
Mobile Internet and WAP Acronyms

To the newcomer, it may appear that the "A" in WAP stands for "acronyms." This appendix provides a list of the various acronyms that you might encounter when reading WAP specifications or writing applications for the mobile Internet.

3G	Third Generation (network)
3GPP	Third Generation Partnership Project
AEG	WAP Asian Expert Group
AIM	America Online (AOL) Instant Messenger
AMIC	Automotive Multimedia Interface Consortium
AMPS	Advanced Mobile Phone System
ANSI	American National Standards Institute
API	Application Programming Interface
Arch	WAP Architecture Group
ASP	Active Server Page
B2B	Business-to-Business
B2C	Business-to-Consumer
BEG	WAP Billing Expert Group
CC/PP	Composite Capabilities/Preferences Profiles
CDMA	Code Division Multiple Access
CDPD	Cellular Digital Packet Data
CEG	WAP Carrier Expert Group

CEGET	WAP Carrier Expert Group Executive Team
CGI	Common Gateway Interface
CRM	Customer Relationship Management
CSD	Circuit-Switched Data
DECT	Digital Enhanced Cordless Telecommunications
DHCP	Dynamic Host Configuration Protocol
DNS	Domain Name System
DPRS	DECT Packet Radio Service
DTD	Document Type Definition
DTMF	Dual Tone Multi-Frequency
ECC	WAP Education and Communication Committee
ECMA	European Computer Manufacturers Association
ECOMEG	WAP E-Commerce Expert Group
EDAI	External Device Application Interface (obsolete; now EFI)
EDGE	Enhanced Data for Global Evolution (*also* Enhanced Data for GSM Evolution, Enhanced Data GSM Environment)
EFI	External Functionality Interface
eJava	Embedded Java
ERP	Enterprise Resource Planning
ETSI	European Telecommunication Standardisation Institute
FSM	Finite State Machine
GMCF	Global Mobile Commerce Forum
GPRS	General Packet Radio Service
GPS	Global Positioning System
GSM	Global System for Mobile Communications
GUTS	General UDP Transport Service
HDML	Handheld Device Markup Language
HDTP	Handheld Device Transfer Protocol
HSCSD	High-Speed Circuit-Switched Data
HTML	Hypertext Markup Language
HTTP	Hypertext Transfer Protocol
IANA	Internet Assigned Numbers Authority
iDEN	Integrated Digital Enhanced Network (Motorola)
IM	Instant Messaging
IMAP	Internet Mail Access Protocol
IN	Intelligent Network
IP	Internet Protocol
IS-54	Original interim standard covering TDMA cellular system; superseded by IS-136
IS-95	Original interim standard covering CDMA cellular system
IS-136	Original interim standard covering TDMA cellular system; superseded by ANSI-136
ISO	International Organization for Standardization

ISP	Internet Service Provider
IVIS	In-Vehicle Information System
IVR	Interactive Voice Response
J2ME	Java 2 Micro-Edition
JSP	JavaServer Page
MCEG	WAP Marketing and Communication Expert Group
MExE	ETSI Mobile Station Application Execution Environment
MMEG	WAP Multimedia Expert Group
MMI	Man–Machine Interface
MMS	WAP Multimedia Messaging Specification
NBS	Narrowband Sockets (Nokia)
OTA	Over-the-Air
OTP	Over-the-Air Provisioning
PAP	WAP Push Access Protocol
PC	Personal Computer
PCS	Personal Communication Services
PDA	Personal Digital Assistant
PDC	Personal Digital Cellular
PHS	Personal Handy Phone System
PIM	Personal Information Manager / Personal Information Management
pJava	Personal Java
PLMN	Public Land Mobile Network
POP	Post Office Protocol
PPG	WAP Push Proxy Gateway
PPP	Point-to-Point Protocol
RAS	Remote Access Server
SAT, SATK	SIM Application Toolkit
SCEG	WAP Smart Card Expert Group
SDS	Short Data Service
SI	WAP Push Service Indication
SIA	WAP Push Session Initiation Application
SIM	Subscriber Identity Module
SL	WAP Push Service Loading
SLA	Service-Level Agreement
SMS	Short Message Service
SMSC	Short Message Service Center
SMSEG	WAP Short Message Service (SMS) Expert Group
SMTP	Simple Mail Transfer Protocol
SRC	WAP Specification Requirements Committee
SSL	Secure Sockets Layer
TCP	Transmission Control Protocol
TDMA	Time Division Multiple Access

TEG	WAP Telematics Expert Group
TETRA	Terrestrial Trunked Radio
TLS	Transport Layer Security
TPS	Trusted Provisioning Server
T/TCP	Transactional Transmission Control Protocol (Transactional TCP)
UA	User Agent
UAProf	WAP User Agent Profiles
UDP	User Datagram Protocol
UMC	Unified Messaging Consortium
UMTS	Universal Mobile Telecommunication System
URI	Uniform Resource Identifier
URL	Uniform Resource Locator
URN	Uniform Resource Name
USSD	Unstructured Supplementary Services Data
W3C	World Wide Web Consortium
WAE	Wireless Applications Environment
WAG	WAP Wireless Applications Group
WAP	Wireless Application Protocol
WBMP	Wireless Bitmap
WBXML	Wireless Binary eXtensible Markup Language (XML)
WDEG, WDG	WAP Wireless Developers Expert Group
WDP	Wireless Datagram Protocol
WIG	WAP Interoperability Group
WIM	WAP Identity Module
WINA	WAP Interim Naming Authority
WML	Wireless Markup Language
WPG	WAP Protocols Group
WSG	WAP Security Group
WSP	Wireless Session Protocol
WTA	Wireless Telephony Applications
WTAI	Wireless Telephony Applications Interface
WTASI	Wireless Telephony Applications Service Indication
WTLS	Wireless Transport Layer Security
WTP	Wireless Transaction Protocol
WWW	World Wide Web
XML	eXtensible Markup Language
XHTML	eXtensible Hyptertext Markup Language

Bibliography

S. Adler, et al. "Extensible Stylesheet Language (XSL), Version 1.0." W3C working draft, March 2000. Available from http://www.w3.org/TR/xsl/.

M. Allman. "TCP Byte Counting Refinements." *Computer Communications Review* 29(3), July 1999.

M. Allman and V. Paxson. "On Estimating End-to-End Network Path Properties." *Proceedings of ACM SIGCOMM'99*, 263–274, September 1999.

M. Allman, V. Paxson, and W. R. Stevens. "TCP Congestion Control." Internet RFC 2581, April 1999. Available from ftp://ftp.isi.edu/in-notes/rfc2581.txt.

H. Alvestrand. "Tags for the Identification of Languages." Internet RFC 1766, March 1995. Available from ftp://ftp.isi.edu/in-notes/rfc1766.txt.

G. Alwang. "Unified Messaging." *PC Magazine*, 114, August 1999.

"America Online Goes Wireless." Press Release, 28 February 2000. Available from http://www.aol.com.

America Online, Inc. "Frequently Asked Questions about AOL Instant Messaging." March 2000. Available from http://www.aol.com/aim/about.html.

"America Online, Inc. Acquires Tegic Communications." Press Release, 1 December 1999. Available from http://www.tegic.com/indexnews.html.

Andrew Seybold's Outlook Web site, http://www.outlook.com.

"Applications, the Next Frontier: Telco on Mission to Destroy Dominance of Lotus." *ISP Business News* 5(19), May 1999.

"Architecture for Wireless Application Protocol Published on the World Wide Web: One Broad and Global Solution for Existing and Future Value Added Services in Wireless Networks." 15 September 1997. Available from http://www.wapforum.org/new/sep15971.htm.

L. Arent. "A Palm in the Tool Belt." *Wired Magazine*, August 1999. Available from http://www.wired.com.

S. Ashbury and S. R. Weiner. *Developing Java Enterprise Applications.* New York: Wiley, 1999.

"AT&T PocketNet Service Replaces New York City Radio Dispatch System." Press Release, February 1998. Available from http://www.attws.com/nohost/data/dispatch/.

"Auto Makers Announce Pacts with 'Net Firms." Associated Press, January 2000. Available from http://www.boston.com.

S. Baker, I. M. Kunii, and S. V. Brull. "Smart Phones: They're the Next Phase in the Tech Revolution, and Soon They May Change Your Life." *Business Week,* International Edition, 18 October 1999.

"Bandai to Let Portable Game Machines Users Browse the Web." Newsbytes, 24 June 1999. Available from http://www.newsbytes.com.

"Bell Atlantic Mobile, Motorola and Phone.com Collaborate to Create Over-the-Air Provisioning." *Cambridge Telecom Report,* July 1999.

Bell Labs Trends and Developments, 1(1), April 1997. Available from http://www.lucent.com/minds/trends.

T. Berners-Lee, R. Fielding, and L. Masinter. "Uniform Resource Identifiers (URI): Generic Syntax." Internet RFC 2396, August 1998. Available from ftp://ftp.isi.edu/in-notes/rfc2396.txt.

H. Bethoney. "Putting a 'V' Into E-Commerce." *PC Week,* 9 November 1998. Available from http://www.cma.zdnet.com.

———. "Voice Browser Packages Will Offer Hands-Off Access to Web Sites." *PC Week,* 9 November 1998. Available from http://www.cma.zdnet.com.

B. Bewin. "Search-Engine Vendor: Wireless Web Pages Grew Tenfold Last Month." *Computerworld,* 3 May 2000. Available from http://www.computerworld.com/home/print.nsf/CWFlash/000503DB72.

R. Blumenstein and N. Wingfield. "Could America Online Become the Ma Bell of New Millennium?" *Wall Street Journal,* March 2000.

J. L. Bosert. *Quality Functional Development: A Practitioner's Approach* (New York: ACQC Quality Press), 1991.

R. Braden. "Extending TCP for Transactions—Concepts" Internet RFC 1379, November 1992. Availabe from ftp://ftp.isi.edu/in-notes/rfc1379.txt.

———. "T/TCP—TCP Extensions for Transactions Functional Specification." Internet RFC 1644, July 1994. Available from ftp://ftp.isi.edu/in-notes/rfc1644.txt.

T. Bray, D. Hollander, and A. Layman. "Namespaces in XML." W3C Recommendation REC-xml-names-19990114, January 1999. Available from http://www.w3.org/TR/REC-xml-names.

T. Bray, J. Paoli, and C. M. Sperberg-McQueen. "Extensible Markup Language (XML) 1.0." W3C Recommendation REC-xml-19980210, February 1998. Available from http://www.w3.org/TR/REC-xml.

D. Brickley and R. V. Guha. "Resource Description Framework (RDF) Schema Specification 1.0." W3C Candidate Recommendation, 27 March 2000. Available from http://www.w3.org/TR/rdf-schema.

R. Broida. "E-Mail in Your Pocket." *Home Office Computing,* 17(2):40, February 1999.

J. Bryan. "Enhanced Throughput Cellular Makes You Forget That Your Data Is Riding on an Analog Connection." *Byte,* September 1994.

S. Buckingham (Mobile Lifestreams, Inc.). Presentations to Morgan Stanley Dean Witter "WAP RAP" Teleconference, April 2000.

S. Burbeck. "Applications Programming in Smalltalk-80(TM): How to Use Model-View-Controller (MVC)," 1992. Available from http://st-www.cs.uiuc.edu/sers/smarch/st-docs/mvc.html.

Cahners In-stat Group. "A Wireless Revolution: Medium and Large Market Wireless Opportunities." 1999. Available from http://www.cahners.com.

——. "Converged Services May Stanch Customer Churn." 1999. Available from http://www.cahners.com.

J. Clark. "XSL Transformations (XSLT) Version 1.0." W3C Recommendation REC-xslt-19991116, November 1999. Available from http://www.w3.org/TR/xslt.

T. Clark. "Bank of America Plans to Introduce Wireless Banking." *CNET News,* July 1999. Available from http://www.cnet.com.

P. Clarke. "Siemens Uses Trenches on a Die's Surface to Boost Bit Density Over Conventional ROM—Mini Memory Card Targets Mobile-Telecom Apps." *Electronic Engineering Times,* November 1997.

D. E. Comer and D. L. Stevens. *Internetworking with TCP/IP, Volume I* (Upper Saddle River, NJ: Prentice Hall), 1994.

——. *Internetworking with TCP/IP, Volume III: Client-Server Programming and Applications* (Upper Saddle River, NJ: Prentice Hall), 1996.

"The Convergence of Mobile Data and Computing." *Yankee Group,* 2(34), August 1998.

"Comverse Network Systems Joins Wireless Application Protocol Forum." Press Release, 7 July 1998. Available from http://www.comversens.com.

D. Costa. "Phoning in for E-Mail; Cisco and Motorola to Create Open IP Architecture." *Computer Shopper,* June 1999.

D. Crocker. "Standard for the Format of ARPA Internet Text Messages." Internet RFC 822, August 1982. Available from ftp://ftp.isi.edu/in-notes/rfc822.txt.

"CyPost Develops Instant Messaging Service for Japanese Mac Market." *Business Wire,* March 2000.

C. Dahm. "Customer Care on the Go." *Global Telephony,* February 1999. Available from http://www.globaltelephony.com.

Davinci Technologies Web site, http://www.davinci.ca.

F. Dawson and T. Howes. "vCard MIME Directory Profile." Internet RFC 2426, September 1998. Available from ftp://ftp.isi.edu/in-notes/rfc2426.txt.

F. Dawson and D. Stenerson. "Internet Calendaring and Scheduling Core Object Specification (iCalendar)." Internet RFC 2445, November 1998. Available from ftp://ftp.isi.edu/in-notes/rfc2445.txt.

C. Degnan. "One-Stop Access to Messages." *PC Week,* 16(24):6, June 1999.

A. den Broeder. "Nokia, Microsoft to Cash in on Internet's Next Big Thing; Wireless Surfing." *Bloomberg Online,* December 1999. Available from http://www.bloomberg.com.

"Dial a Carwash ... or Whatever." Available from http://www.sonera.fi.

T. Dierks and C. Allen. "The TLS Protocol Version 1.0." Internet RFC 2246, January 1999. Available from ftp://ftp.isi.edu/in-notes/rfc2246.txt.

"A Different Perspective on Web Access through Mobile Phones." *Wireless Data News,* 7(14), July 1999.

B. Dorshkind. "WAP Untethers the Web." *UNIX Review's Performance Computing,* 17(6):59, June 1999.

Dowjones.com Archives Web site, http://www.dowjones.com.

J. S. Dumas and J. C. Redish. *A Practical Guide to Usability Testing* (Norwood, NJ: Ablex), 1994.

"Entrust Technologies First to Deliver Digital Certificates to Enable Trusted Wireless Transactions." Press Release, 16 December 1999. Available from http://www.entrust.com/news/1999_12_16_99.

"Ericsson Announces Mobile Portal for Personalized Mobile Internet." Press Release, 25 February 1999. Available from http://www.ericsson.com.

Ericsson Mobile Internet Web site, http://mobileinternet.ericsson.com

"Ericsson, Motorola, Nokia, and Unwired Planet Unite to Create an Open Common Protocol for Interactive Wireless Applications," 26 June 1997. Available from http://www.wapforum.org/new/jun26971.htm.

"Ericsson, Motorola, Nokia and Unwired Planet Establish Wireless Application Protocol Forum Ltd.: Other Industry Partners and Operators Can Apply for WAP Forum Membership and Contribute to the Specification Work." 7 January 1998. Available from http://www.wapforum.org/new/jan07.htm.

"Europe—Sendit Teams with De La Rue on Mobile E-mail." *Newsbytes,* 4 March 1998. Available from http://www.newsbytes.com.

European Computer Manufacturers Association (ECMA). *ECMAScript Language Specification,* Second Edition. Standard ECMA-262, June 1998. Available from http://www.ecma.ch/stand/ECMA-262.htm.

European Telecommunications Standards Institute (ETSI). "MExE—Mobile Station Application Execution Environment." Available from http://www.etsi.org/smg/smg4/mexe.htm.

"Evolution of Cellular/PCS Carrier Data Strategies: Building Momentum Towards IP Mobility." *Yankee Group,* 3(11), April 1999.

M. A. Farmer. "Services Firms Tackle Europe for Wireless Trials." *CNET News,* February 2000. Available from http://www.cnet.com.

R. Fielding, et al. "Hypertext Transfer Protocol—HTTP/1.1." Internet RFC 2616, June 1999. Available from ftp://ftp.isi.edu/in-notes/rfc2616.txt. See also RFC 2068 (January 1997); available from ftp://ftp.isi.edu/in-notes/rfc2068.txt.

"First Tracking Service with Mobile Phone." *Cargoweb News,* 14 December 1999. Available from http://www.cargoweb.nl.

R. D. Frank. "The Mobile Executive: OnStar at the Masters," April 1999. Available from http://www.outlook.com.

J. Franks, et al. "HTTP Authentication: Basic and Digest Access Authentication." Internet RFC 2617, June 1999. Available from ftp://ftp.isi.edu/in-notes/rfc2617.txt.

G. Fraone. "Calling All Cars (Telematics Products Offered as a Standard Option)." *Electronic Business,* 24(12):28, December 1998.

M. Frauenfielder. "The Future Is at Hand." *Industry Standard,* July 1999.

N. Freed and N. Borenstein. "Multipurpose Internet Mail Extensions (MIME) Part One: Format of Internet Message Bodies." Internet RFC 2045, November 1996. Available from ftp://ftp.isi.edu/in-notes/rfc2045.txt.

A. Frier, P. Karlton, and P. Kocher. "The SSL 3.0 Protocol." Internet Draft (expired), November 1996. Available from http://home.netscape.com/eng/ssl3/draft302.txt.

J. Gallant. "Voices from the Vortex: Vortex 99, Day One." *Network World*, 26 May 1999.

R. Garber. "Looking for the Wireless 'Thunder Lizards.'" *Red Herring*, May 2000.

"Gauging Trends in Messaging and Other Tales." *Yankee Group*, 2(36), August 1998.

S. Goldman. "The Future for WAP Applications: A Global Overview." Presented at IBC WAP Australia Conference, 28 August 2000.

T. Grimstad, H. Stegavik, and E. Saastad. "User Interface Design Guidelines for WAP Applications (Version 1.2)." Technical Report, Telenor Mobil, 2000.

J. Halpin. "U.S. Consumer Interest in Smart Cards Picks Up, with All Eyes Toward E-commerce." *Computer Shopper*, 285, August 1999.

M. Hamblen. "Ericsson to Target U.S. Businesses." *Computerworld*, November 1998.

——. "Smart Phones Are Coming." CNN, June 1999. Available from http://www.cnn.com.

D. Haskin. "Web Service Announced for Docs with Handhelds." *AllNetDevices*, 29 July 1999. Available from http://www.allnetdevices.com.

D. Hayhoe. "Sorting-Based Menu Categories." *International Journal of Man–Machine Studies* 33:677–705, 1990.

S. Henry. "AOL Says It Will Buy MapQuest Travel Site." *Washington Post*, E01, 23 December 1999.

"Hirose Develops Small Sockets for SIM Cards." *Electronic Buyer's News*, November 1997.

D. Hix and H. R. Hartson. *Developing User Interfaces: Ensuring Usability Through Product and Process* (New York: John Wiley and Sons), 1993.

J. Hoe. "Improving the Startup Behavior of a Congestion Control System for TCP." *Proceedings of SIGCOMM'96*, 270–280, August 1996.

R. Iannella. "An Idiot's Guide to the Resource Description Framework." *The New Review of Information Networking*, 4:1–10, 1998. Available from http://www.archive.dstc.edu.au/RDU/reports/RDF-Idiot.

IBM VisualAge Micro Edition Web site, http://www.ibm.com/software/ad/embedded.

iButton Web site, http://www.ibutton.com.

"The Impact of the Internet on Mobile Computing and Wireless Data." *Yankee Group*, December 1997.

"Industry Support for Wireless Application Protocol Gains Momentum: New Language for Microbrowsers Under Development." 7 July 1997. Available from http://www.wapforum.org/new/jul07.htm.

Infrared Data Association (IrDA). "IrDA Object Exchange Protocol (IrOBEX)." Version 1.2. 18 March 1999. Available from http://www.irda.org/standards/pubs/IrOBEX12.pdf.

"Instant Messaging Heads for Cell Phones." December 1999. Available from http://www.IDG.net.

International Standards Organization (ISO). "Code for the Representation of Names of Languages." ISO 639:1988, 1988.

——. "Code for the Representation of Names of Languages—Part 2: Alpha-3 Code." ISO 639-2:1988, 1988.

——. "Codes for the Representation of Names of Countries and Their Subdivisions—Part 1: Country Codes." ISO 3166-1:1997, 1997.

——. "Codes for the Representation of Names of Countries and Their Subdivisions—Part 2: Country Subdivision Code." ISO 3166-2:1998, 1998.

——. "Codes for the Representation of Names of Countries and Their Subdivisions—Part 3: Code for Formerly Used Names of Countries." ISO 3166-3:1999, 1999.

——. "Information Processing—8-Bit-Byte Coded Graphic Character Sets—Part 7: Latin/Greek Alphabet." ISO/IEC FCD 8859-7, 1999.

——. "Information Processing—Text and Office Systems—Standard Generalized Markup Language (SGML)." ISO 8879:1986, 1996.

——. "Information Technology—Character Code Structure and Extension Techniques." ISO/IEC 2022:1994, 1999.

——. "Information Technology—Universal Multiple-Octet Coded Character Set (UCS)—Part 1: Architecture and Basic Multilingual Plane." ISO/IEC 10646-1:1993, 1999. For further details on the ISO/IEC 10646 suite of standards, refer to http://www.iso.ch.

Internet Assigned Numbers Authority Web site, http://www.iana.org.

Internet Mail Consortium. "vCard—The Electronic Business Card." Version 2.1. September 1996. Available from http://www.imc.org/pdi/vcard-21.doc.

——. "vCalendar—The Electronic Calendaring and Scheduling Format." Version 1.0. September 1996. Available from http://www.imc.org/pdi/vcal-10.doc.

"ISP Profile: Reborn as Application Platform Provider." *ISP Business News,* 5(21), May 1999.

"ISP Profile: Worldweb.net: Helping Publications Spin Their Webs." *ISP Business News,* 5(20), May 1999.

V. Jacobson. "Congestion Avoidance and Control." *Proceedings of SIGCOMM '88,* 314–329, August 1988.

"Japanese Venture Offers In-Car Multimedia." *Computergram International,* 29 April 1998. Available from http://www.computerwire.com.

C. M. Karat. "Usability Engineering in Dollars and Cents." *IEEE Software,* 10:88–89, 1993.

B. Kasrel. "Microsoft/Nextel Deal Missing a Key Partner." *Forrester Brief,* May 1999.

B. Kasrel, et. al. "A Second Wind for Wireless." *Forrester Research,* January 1999.

A. S. Kay. "Where Can You Roam with Your Phone? GSM: Trying to Conquer Roam from Coast to Coast (Information Services)." *Communications Week,* August 1997.

P. King and T. Hyland. "Handheld Device Markup Language Specification." W3C Note NOTE-Submission-HDML-spec, May 1997. Available from http://www.w3.org/pub/WWW/TR/NOTE-Submission-HDML-spec.html.

Also see the "HDML 3.0 Language Reference," available from http://developer.phone.com/dev/ts/htmldoc/31h/hdmlref/output (by registration only).

D. Kristol and L. Mortulli. "HTTP State Management Mechanism." Internet RFC 2109, February 1997. Available from ftp://ftp.isi.edu/in-notes/rfc2109.txt.

M. LaMonica. "Bullish on the Net: Online Financial Services Are Obliterating the Industry's Economic Model, But IT Is Helping Companies Add Value." *InfoWorld*, 21(17):34, April 1999.

O. Lassila, "Web Metadata: A Matter of Semantics." *IEEE Internet Computing*, 2(4), July/August 1998.

O. Lassila and R. R. Swick. "Resource Description Framework (RDF) Model and Syntax Specification." W3C Recommendation REC-rdf-syntax-19990222, February 1999. Available from http://www.w3.org/TR/REC-rdf-syntax.

L. Latour. "WAP Buzz Likely Will Fuel Service Providers' Shares." *Wall Street Journal*, 3 September 1999.

J. R. Lewis. "Sample Sizes for Usability Studies: Additional Considerations." *Human Factors*, 36(2):368–378, 1994.

L. Liebmann. "Jump on the Instant Messaging Bandwagon." *ComputerWorld*, March 2000. Available from http://www.computerworld.com.

B. Linder. "WAP Services That Drive Usage: Where Mobile Commerce Fits in." Presented at the Unwired Universe Conference, San Jose, CA, July 1999.

D. S. Linthicum. *Enterprise Application Integration.* (Reading, MA: Addison-Wesley), 2000.

"Looking for the Next Generation of the Wireless User." *Yankee Group*, 2(41), November 1998.

E. Luening. "Microsoft to Take Instant Messaging Wireless." CNET News.com, September 1999. Available from http://www.cnet.com.

A. M. Lund. "Expert Ratings of Usability Maxims." *Ergonomics in Design*, 5(3):15–20, 1997.

J. N. MacGregor. "A Comparison of the Effects of Icons and Descriptors in Videotext Menu Retrieval." *International Journal of Man–Machine Studies*, 37:767–777, 1992.

T. Mandel. *The Elements of User Interface Design* (New York: John Wiley and Sons), 1997.

M. Marchiori, "The RDF Advantages Page." Available from http://www.w3.org/RDF/advantages.html.

M. A. Marics and G. Engelbeck. "Designing Voice Menu Applications for Telephones." *Handbook of Human–Computer Interaction*. M. Helander, T. K. Landauer, and P. Prabhu, eds. (Amsterdam: Elsevier Science), 1085–1102, 1997.

B. Martin. "Personalization: How Portals Drive Loyalty and Returning Usage." Presented at the Unwired Universe Conference, San Jose, CA, July 1999.

B. Martin and B. Jano. "WAP Binary XML Content Format." W3C Note NOTE-wbxml-19990624, June 1999. Available from http://www.w3.org/TR/wbxml.

A. Marx. "Game Companies Search for Profits Online." *Internet World*, 5(20):41, 24 May 1999.

L. Masinter. "Returning Values from Forms: multipart/form-data." Internet RFC 2388, August 1998. Available from ftp://ftp.isi.edu/in-notes/rfc2388.txt.

D. J. Mayhew. *The Usability Engineering Lifecycle* (San Francisco: Morgan Kaufmann Publishers), 1999.

S. McCarron and D. Raggett. "HTML Working Group Roadmap." W3C Note 20000210, February 2000. Available from http://www.w3.org/TR/xhtml-roadmap.

A. F. McMillan. "Banking Without a Wire." October 1999. Available from http://www.cnnfn.com.

E. A. Meyer. *Cascading Style Sheets: The Definitive Guide*. O'Reilly & Associates, 2000.

Microsoft Corporation. JScript Version 5 Documentation. Available from http://msdn.microsoft.com/scripting.

——. *The Windows Interface Guidelines for Software Design*. (Redmond, WA: Microsoft Press), 1995.

S. Miles. "Young Handheld Market Set to Triple, Report Says." CNET News.com, December 1999.

B. A. Miller and C. Bisdikian. *Bluetooth Revealed: An Insider's Guide to an Open Specification for Global Wireless Communications*. (Upper Saddle River, NJ: Prentice Hall), 2000.

E. Miller. "An Introduction to the Resource Description Framework." *D-Lib Magazine*, May 1998. Available from http://www.dlib.org/dlib/may98/miller/05miller.html.

G. A. Miller. "The Magical Number Seven, Plus or Minus Two: Some Limits on Our Capability for Processing Information." *Psychological Science*, 63:81–97, 1956.

D. L. Mills. "Improved Algorithms for Synchronizing Computer Network Clocks." *IEEE/ACM Transactions on Networking*, 3(3):245–254, June 1995.

——. "Internet Time Synchronization: The Network Time Protocol." *IEEE Transactions on Communications*, 39(10):1482–1493, October 1991.

"Mobile Technologies and the Consumer 2000." *Yankee Group*, October 1997.

"Mobile User Survey Series: The Convergence of Mobile Data and Computing." *Yankee Group*, 2(34), August 1998.

G. Moore. *Crossing the Chasm* (New York: Harper Collins), 1991.

"Motorola and AOL Announce Plans to Develop Wireless Application for AOL Instant Messenger." *Business Wire*, October 1999. Available from http://www.corporate-ir.net/ireye/.

"Motorola Unveils VoxML 'Voice Browser' Technology." *Communications Today*, October 1998.

"Motorola's Telematics Power BMW Mayday Phone." *Mobile Phone News*, 15(45), 9 November 1998.

Netscape Communications Corporation. "Client-Side JavaScript Guide." Version 1.3. June 1999. Available from http://developer.netscape.com/docs/manuals/javascript.html.

"Next-Gen Features Will Keep Cellular Services Attractive." *Newsbytes*, June 1999. Available from http://www.newsbytes.com.

H. Nielsen, P. Leach, and S. Lawrence. "An HTTP Extension Framework." Internet RFC 2774, February 2000. Available from ftp://ftp.isi.edu/in-notes/rfc2774.txt.

J. Nielsen. "Enhancing the Explanatory Power of Usabilty Heuristics." *Proceedings of the ACM CHI '94 Conference*, 152–158, 1994.

J. Nielsen and R. L. Mack, eds. *Usability Inspection Methods* (New York: John Wiley & Sons), 1994.

Nokia, Inc. "Wireless Application Protocol: The Corporate Perspective." White Paper, March 1999. Available from http://www.nokia.com.

"Nokia Defines New Wireless Service Category with Development of Smart Messaging: Direct Access from GSM Phone to Internet Services." Press Release, 25 April 1997. Available from http://www.nokia.com.

"Nokia and Intel Provide Narrowband Sockets Technology (NBS)." Press Release, 19 March 1997. Available from http://www.nokia.com.

"Nokia's Smart Messaging Technology Will Be Key Element in New Wireless Application Protocol: Common Protocol Expected to Boost Wireless Data Market and Stimulate Rapid Development of Value-Added Services." Press Release, 26 June 1997. Available from http://www.nokia.com.

"Nokia Unveils the World's First Media Phone for Internet Access." Press Release, 23 February 1999. Available from http://www.nokia.com.

"NTT DoCoMo to Launch Internet Access from Cellphones." *Newsbytes,* January 1999. Available from http://www.newsbytes.com.

H. Ohto and J. Hjelm. "Composite Capability/Preference Profiles (CC/PP) Exchange Protocol Based on HTTP Extension Framework." W3C NOTE NOTE-CCPP-exchange-19990617, 17 June 1999. Available from http://www.w3.org/Mobile/Group/IG/1999/06/NOTE-CCPPexchange-19990617.

S. O'Keefe, S. Masud, and D. Allen. "The 10 Hottest Technologies." *Telecommunications,* 33(5):20, May 1999. Available from http://www.telecomsmag.com.

"1 Billion SMS Text Messages Sent This Month." *Newsbytes,* April 1999. Available from http://www.newsbytes.com.

"Online Brokerages Go Wireless." May 1999. Available from http://palmtops.about.com/blwirelesstrades.htm.

"Online Trading in Hong Kong: Flu Now, Fever Later." *Newsbytes,* May 1999. Available from http://www.newsbytes.com.

M. Ozburn. "Nextel: Packet Data Potential in the U.S." Presented at the Unwired Universe Conference, San Jose, CA, July 1999.

K. R. Paap and N. J. Cooke. "Design of Menus." *Handbook of Human–Computer Interaction.* M. Helander, T. K. Landauer, and P. Prabhu, eds. (Amsterdam: Elsevier Science), 533–572, 1997.

S. J. Packebush. *A Comparison of Iterative and Traditional Usability Test Methods.* Unpublished Dissertation. (College Station, Texas: Texas A&M University), 1996.

L. G. Paul. "Weathering a Market Storm: Online Brokerages Shore Up Their Systems to Cope with the E-trading Flood." *Network World,* 12 April 1999. Available from http://www.nwfusion.com/research/2000/0207.

Phillips Electronics. "Overview of Telecommunications Standards." Available from http://www-us.semiconductors.com/comms/support/telecomstandards.html.

Phone.com. "Developing User Friendly Applications: Application Usability Guidelines from the Phone.com Application Development Team." White Paper, Redwood City, CA, 1999.

——. "Enabling the Wireless Internet." White Paper, Redwood City, CA, February 1999.

——. *UP.SDK Developers Guide.* Technical Report DKDV-R32-001, Redwood City, CA , 1999.

——. *WML Language Reference, Version 1.1.* Technical Report DKWL-R32-001, Redwood City, CA, 1999.

B. Pietrucha. "Report: Wireless Portals Users to Grow to 25 Million by 2006," February 2000. Available from http://www.Internet.com.

Pinpoint.com Web site, http://www.pinpoint.com.

J. Postel. "Internet Protocol: DARPA Internet Program Protocol Specification." Internet RFC 791, September 1981. Available from ftp://ftp.isi.edu/in-notes/rfc791.txt.

——. "Simple Mail Transfer Protocol." Internet RFC 821, August 1982. Available from ftp://ftp.isi.edu/in-notes/rfc821.txt.

——. "Transmission Control Protocol: DARPA Internet Program Protocol Specification." Internet RFC 793, September 1981. Available from ftp://ftp.isi.edu/in-notes/rfc793.txt.

——. "User Datagram Protocol." Internet RFC 768, August 1980. Available from ftp://ftp.isi.edu/in-notes/rfc768.txt.

J. Postel and J. Reynolds. "Telnet Protocol Specification." Internet RFC 854, May 1983. Available from ftp://ftp.isi.edu/in-notes/rfc854.txt..

D. Raggett. "HTML 3.2 Reference Specification." W3C Recommendation REC-html32, January 1997. Available from http://www.w3.org/TR/REC-html32.

D. Raggett, A. Le Hors, and I. Jacobs. "HTML 4.0 Specification." W3C Recommendation REC-html40-19980424, April 1998. Available from http://www.w3.org/TR/1998/REC-html40-19980424.

——. "HTML 4.01 Specification." W3C Recommendation REC-html40-19980424, December 1999. Available from http://www.w3.org/TR/1999/REC-html401-19991224.

F. Reynolds, et al. "Composite Capability/Preferences Profiles: A User Side Framework for Content Negotiation." W3C Note NOTE-CCPP-19990727, 27 July 1999. Available from http://www.w3.org/TR/1998/NOTE-CCPP-19990727.

B. Riggs. "Consolidated Messages—Vendors Give Unified Messaging a Boost." *InformationWeek*, 31, 19 April 1999. Available from http://www.informationweek.com/maindocs/index_730.htm.

B. Riggs and M. E. Thyfault. "Unified Messaging—Products and Services Promise Simpler All-in-One Message Systems." *InformationWeek*, 19, 14 June 1999. Available from http://www.informationweek.com/maindocs/index_738.htm.

R. Rivest. "The MD5 Message-Digest Algorithm." Internet RFC 1321, April 1992. Available from ftp://ftp.isi.edu/in-notes/rfc1321.txt.

R. Roske-Hofstrand and K. R. Paap. "Cognitive Networks as a Guide to Menu Organization: An Application in the Automated Cockpit." *Ergonomics,* 29(11):1301–1312, 1986.

J. Rubin. *Handbook of Usability Testing* (New York: John Wiley & Sons), 1994.

J. Rudd and S. Isensee. "Twenty-Two Tips for a Happier, Healthier Prototype." *ACM Interactions,* 35–40, January 1994.

G. Rugg and P. McGeorge. "The Sorting Techniques: A Tutorial Paper on Card Sorts, Picture Sorts, and Item Sorts." *Expert Systems,*14(2):80–93, 1997.

J. Ryan. "Sprint PCS Unveils the CDMA Story." Presented at the Unwired Universe Conference, San Jose, CA, July 1999.

P. Rysavy. "Wide-Area Wireless Computing." *Networking Computing.* Available from http://www.networkcomputing.com/netdesign/wireless1.html.

M. S. Sanders and E. J. McCormick. *Human Factors in Engineering and Design,* Seventh Edition (New York: McGraw-Hill), 1993.

G. Schaefer. "Nintendo to Take Pokémon Game Online, Link to Wireless Game Boy Machines." *Bloomberg Technology News,* December 1999.

R. Senjen, et al. "Generic Content Authoring Guidelines for WML 1.1: Best Practices and Recommendations." Technical Report, Version 4, Telstra Research Laboratories, 2000.

A. Seybold. "Wireless Internet Feeding Frenzy." Pinecrest Press, August 1999.

B. Shneiderman. *Designing the User Interface: Strategies for Effective Human–Computer Interaction,* Third Edition (Wokingham, UK: Addison-Wesley), 1997.

S. Singhal. "Measuring Functional Separability in WAP to Ensure Architectural Consistency." Input paper submitted to WAP Architecture Group, Kyoto, Japan, December 1998. Available from http://www.wapforum.org.

——. "The Mobile Future: Is WAP Enough?" Presented at IBC Mobile 2000 Internet Conference, London, UK, 12 April 2000.

S. K. Singhal and B. Q. Nguyen. "The Java Factor." *Communications of the ACM,* 41(6): 34–37, June 1998.

P. Smethers. "The User Interface: Why It Makes or Breaks Your Services." Presented at the Unwired Universe Conference, San Jose, CA, July 1999.

W. Stallings. *Data and Computer Communications,* Fifth Edition (Upper Saddle River, NJ: Prentice-Hall), 1996.

W. R. Stevens. *TCP/IP Illustrated, Volume 1: The Protocols* (Reading, MA: Addison-Wesley), 1994.

Sun Microsystems. "Enterprise JavaBeans Specification, Version 1.1, Final Release." Available from http://www.java.sun.com/products/ejb/.

——. "The Java Language: A White Paper." Available from http://sunsite.org.uk/packages/java-http/1.0alpha3/doc/overview/java/.

——. "JavaServer Pages Specification 1.1." Available from http://www.java.sun.com/products/ejb/.

——. "Java Servlet API Specification 2.2." Available from http://www.java.sun.com/products/servlet/.

SyncML.org Web site, http://www.syncml.org.

S. Taylor. Panel presentation. Presented at the Unwired Universe Conference, San Jose, CA., July 1999.

Techmall Web site, http://www.techmall.com/techdocs/archives.html.

"Telematics: The Future Is in the Car." July 1999. Available from http://www.mot.com/telematics/byline.html.

M. J. Thompson. "E-commerce to Ring Up \$36 Billion." *Network World,* 20 July 1999. Available from http://www.nwfusion.com/news/1999/0207comm.html.

3GPP Web site, http://www.3gpp.org/home.htm.

D. Toft. "Web Banking via Cell Phone, Palm Catching on." *InfoWorld,* 21(31), August 1999. Available from http://www.infoworld.com.

"Trade Show Poker: What the Subtle Game of Publicity at Wireless '99 Says about the Industry's Direction." *PCS Week,* 10(6), February 1999.

M. Tso, D. J. Gillespie, and D. Romrell. "Always On, Always Connected Mobile Computing." *Proceedings of the 1996 IEEE International Conference on Universal Personal Communications,* September 1996.

D. Ungar and R. B. Smith. "Self: The Power of Simplicity." *Proceedings of OOPSLA'87,* 227–241, October 1987. Available from http://www.sun.com/research/self.

Unicode Consortium. *The Unicode Standard, Version 3.0,* 2000. *Also see* http://www.unicode.org.

"Unified Messaging." *Electronic Mail & Messaging Systems,* 23(13), July 1999.

Unified Messaging Consortium (UMC) Web site, http://www.unified-msg.com/.

"U.S. Public Stirred, Not Shaken, by Future Mobile Phone Possibilities." *Business Wire,* February 2000.

R. A. Virzi. "Refining the Test Phase of Usability Evaluation: How Many Subjects Is Enough?" *Human Factors,* 34(4):457–468, 1992.

——. "Streamlining the Design Process: Running Fewer Subjects." *Proceedings of the Human Factors Society 34th Annual Meeting,* 291–294, 1990.

VoiceXML Forum. "Voice eXtensible Markup Language (VoiceXML), Version 1.0 Specification," March 1999. Available from http://www.voicexml.org/specs/VoiceXML-100.pdf.

"WAP—Wireless Application Protocol." IBC UK Conference E-brief. Available from http://www.the-arc-group.com

E. Wareham. "Online Retailing to Reach US\$36 Billion This Year (a Boston Consulting Group Study on Electronic Commerce Commissioned by Shop.org)." *Computing Canada,* 25(29):5, July 1999.

"Webb Interactive Services Launches Jabber, Inc.—XML Based Instant Messaging." *PR Newswire,* 1 March 2000. Available from http://www.webb.net.

T. E. Weber. "E-World: Telecoms Beware: Instant Messaging Is New Web Threat." *Wall Street Journal Europe,* March 2000.

"Webraska—Alcatel." *Wireless Today,* 3(26), July 1999.

"Welcome Real-time Launches E-couponing Portal Technology Targeting Click and Mortar Merchants." Press release, 19 April 2000. Available from http://www.welcome-rt.com.

"Wireless: The Weather Channel Web Site Cuts the Cord with Wireless Weather." *EDGE, On & About AT&T,* March 1999.

Wireless Application Protocol Forum. *Official Wireless Application Protocol: The Complete Standard with Searchable CD-ROM.* (New York: John Wiley & Sons), 1999.

———. "WAP: Wireless Internet Today." White Paper, October 1999. Available from http://www.wapforum.org/what/whitepapers.htm.

———. *Wireless Application Protocol Architecture Specification.* Available from http://www.wapforum.org/what/technical.htm.

———. *Wireless Application Protocol: Binary XML Content Format Specification, Version 1.1.* Available from http://www.wapforum.org/what/technical.htm.

———. *Wireless Application Protocol: Cache Model Specification.* Available from http://www.wapforum.org/what/technical.htm.

———. *Wireless Application Protocol: Push Access Protocol Specification.* Available from http://www.wapforum.org/what/technical.htm.

———. *Wireless Application Protocol: Push Architectural Overview.* Available from http://www.wapforum.org/what/technical.htm.

———. *Wireless Application Protocol: Push Message Specification.* Available from http://www.wapforum.org/what/technical.htm.

———. *Wireless Application Protocol: Push OTA Protocol Specification.* Available from http://www.wapforum.org/what/technical.htm.

———. *Wireless Application Protocol: Push Proxy Gateway Service Specification.* Available from http://www.wapforum.org/what/technical.htm.

———. *Wireless Application Protocol: User Agent Profile Specification.* Available from http://www.wapforum.org/what/technical.htm.

———. *Wireless Application Protocol: WAP Cache Operation Specification.* Available from http://www.wapforum.org/what/technical.htm.

———. *Wireless Application Protocol: WAP Service Indication Specification.* Available from http://www.wapforum.org/what/technical.htm.

———. *Wireless Application Protocol: WAP Service Loading Specification.* Available from http://www.wapforum.org/what/technical.htm.

———. *Wireless Application Protocol: Wireless Application Environment Overview.* Available from http://www.wapforum.org/what/technical.htm.

———. *Wireless Application Protocol: Wireless Application Environment Specification.* Available from http://www.wapforum.org/what/technical.htm.

———. *Wireless Application Protocol: Wireless Control Message Protocol Specification.* Available from http://www.wapforum.org/what/technical.htm.

———. *Wireless Application Protocol: Wireless Datagram Protocol Specification.* Available from http://www.wapforum.org/what/technical.htm.

———. *Wireless Application Protocol: Wireless Markup Language Specification.* Available from http://www.wapforum.org/what/technical.htm.

———. *Wireless Application Protocol: Wireless Session Protocol Specification.* Available from http://www.wapforum.org/what/technical.htm.

———. *Wireless Application Protocol: Wireless Telephony Application Interface Specification.* Available from http://www.wapforum.org/what/technical.htm.

——. *Wireless Application Protocol: Wireless Telephony Application Interface Specification—GSM Specific Addendum.* Available from http://www.wapforum.org/what/technical.htm.

——. *Wireless Application Protocol: Wireless Telephony Application Interface Specification—IS-136 Specific Addendum.* Available from http://www.wapforum.org/what/technical.htm.

——. *Wireless Application Protocol: Wireless Telephony Application Interface Specification—PDC Specific Addendum.* Available from http://www.wapforum.org/what/technical.htm.

——. *Wireless Application Protocol: Wireless Telephony Application Specification.* Available from http://www.wapforum.org/what/technical.htm.

——. *Wireless Application Protocol: Wireless Transaction Protocol Specification.* Available from http://www.wapforum.org/what/technical.htm.

——. *Wireless Application Protocol: Wireless Transport Layer Security Protocol Specification.* Available from http://www.wapforum.org/what/technical.htm.

——. *Wireless Application Protocol: WMLScript Language Specification.* Available from http://www.wapforum.org/what/technical.htm.

——. *Wireless Application Protocol: WMLScript Standard Libraries Specification.* Available from http://www.wapforum.org/what/technical.htm.

"Wireless Application Protocol Specification Version 1.0 Now Published on the World Wide Web: WAP Forum Delivers Version 1.0 Specification to Enable Internet/Intranet Access Combined with Advanced Telephony Services on Wireless Devices." Press Release, 7 May 1998. Available from http://www.wapforum.org/new/may0798WAPSpec.htm.

"Wireless E-Mail: AT&T Is First to Deliver Real-Time E-mail via Wireless Phone." Edge Publishing, 1998. Available from http://www.iac-insite.com.

"Wireless E-Mail Set for Growth—Survey." *Newsbytes,* 4 April 1997. Available from http://www.newsbytes.com.

"Wireless Industry Gears Up for Wider Internet Browsing." *Mobile Communications Report,* June 1999.

"Wireless Instant Messaging," January 2000. Available from http://www.tegic.com.

"Wireless Intelligent Terminals: Smarter Than Your Average Phone." *Yankee Group,* 2(42), November 1998.

Wireless Internet & Mobile Computing Newsletter Web site, http://www.wirelessinternet.com.

"Wireless Multimedia—Revolution or Gimmick?" *Inside Multimedia,* May 1999.

D. Wixon and S. Jones. "Usability for Fun and Profit: A Case Study of the Design of DEC RALLY Version 2." *Human–Computer Interface Design: Success Stories, Emerging Methods, and Real-World Context.* M. Rudisill, et al., eds. (New York: Springer Verlag), 1991.

D. Wolfe, "The Promise of Unified Messaging." *Network,* May 1999. Available from http://www.networkmagazine.com.

"The World of Wireless Value-Added Services—Global Overview and an Update on the US." *Yankee Group,* 2(38), September 1998.

World Wide Web Consortium. "XHTML 1.0: The Extensible HyperText Markup Language." W3C Recommendation REC-xhtml1-20000126, January 2000. Available from http://www.w3.org/TR/xhtml1.

D. Wright. "Auto PC: Windows CE Hits the Road." *Electronic Engineering Times*, 1069:74, July 1999.

———. "Those Prying Eyes." *Telecom*, March 1999.

"Xypoint Demos Location-Enhanced Cellular Technology." *Newsbytes*, September 1998. Available from http://www.newsbytes.com.

"Your Car: The Ultimate Portable Wireless Data Device." *Wireless Data News*, 7(13), June 1999.

A. Zieger. "New Wireless Phones Merge PC, PDA and Voice Functions." *InternetWeek*, 718:S6, 8 June 1998.

S. Zurier. "Extending the Internet (Online Trading Should Encourage Growth of Market for Handheld Devices)." *InternetWeek*, June 1999.

Index

abort function
    Lang library, 345–346
abs function
    Lang library, 341
Absolute URLs, 161
    on WML card, 151
Abstract protocol services, 107
Accelerator, 232
Accept action, acting as prev, *211*
Accept binding
    assigned to soft key, *208*
    on stealth menu, *209*
accept-charset attribute, 192
Accept-Charset header, 464
Accept-charset parameter, 263
Accept do type, example of, *201–202*
Accept-Encoding header, 464
Accept header, 463
Accept-Language header, 463
accept type, 118, 201
access, 53, 588
Access control, 124
    and access pragma, 338–339
Access element, 169, 264, 266
accesskey attribute, 232–233, 241, 423
Access keys, 232
Access networks, 10
access pragma, 338–339
Access security, 264
ACK, 70
Acronyms list, 623–626
Action/event construct, 531, 535
Actions, 531
Active elements, 207

Activity proposal, 101
Add Phonebook Entry function, 373–374
Addresses, WAP Push, 497–498
Addressing. *See also* WAP Push Addressing
Advanced Mobile Phone System, 108
Advertiser-supported applications, 60
Advertising, 17, 123
a element, 233, 422–423, 587–588
    browser differences, 423
    Ericsson browser simulator demonstrating, *425*
    Nokia browser simulator demonstrating, *426*
    Phone.com browser simulator demonstrating, *423*
Airline reservations, 33
Airmobile from Motorola, 92
Alcatel, 95
alert function, Dialogs library, 368
align attribute, 182–183, 225, 228
Alignment
    image, 225
    text, 181, 451
Allied Business Intelligence, 36
Allman, Mark, 71
Alphabetical ordering, for menu items, 400–401
alt attribute, 223–224
Amazon.com, 21
America Online
    instant messaging through, 25
    Mobile Messenger Service, 26
AMIC. *See* Automotive Multimedia Interface Consortium
AMPS. *See* Advanced Mobile Phone System
Analog cellular networks, 72
Analog lines, and communication errors, 74

Note: Italicized page locators indicate figures

Analog modem technologies, 90–91
anchor, 150, 174, 229, 230, 588
    fragment, 174
Anchored links, duplicating do elements with, 433
Anchored text
    and tables, 452
    and underscores, 451
anchor element, 230–231, 422–423, 427
    access key for, 232
    browser differences, 423
    Ericsson browser simulator demonstrating, *425*
    Nokia browser simulator demonstrating, *426*
    Phone.com browser simulator demonstrating, *423*
    user interface design guidelines, 427–428
    use of, *231*
Answer state, 520
AnywhereYouGo.com, 586
AOL. *See* America Online
APIs. *See* Application programming interfaces
Appearance and presentation elements, design guidelines for WML elements, 450–454
Applets, 58, 85, 86, 574
Application addressing, 498
Application development, usability throughout, 390
Application environment, 108
Application layer
    linking WAP and Internet at, 548, *550*, 550–552
Application-level scripting, 142
Application platforms, 574
Application programming interfaces, 84–85
    and JavaBeans, 563
    WTA, 537
Applications
    and customized content, 459
    personalized, 401
    user switches between, 271
Application security, 264–266
    access element, 264
    domain attribute, 265
    path attribute, 265–266
Application service provider, 58, 60–61, 544
Application-specific modules, tasks performed by, 558
"Applications" phase, 15
Application tokens, 285
    in WBXML document, 122
Application writer, and scalability, 78
Appointments, 5, 6, 23
Approved specification, 102

Architecture Group, WAP Forum, 101
ARDIS, 92
Arguments, 335
Arithmetic operators, 324–325
Arrays, 84
ASCII, 115
Asia, digital networks in, 72
ASP. *See* Application service provider
Assignment operators, 228, 322, 324
Associate members, in WAP Forum, 100
Asynchronous messaging, 575–576
Asynchronous notification features, voice telephony integrated with, 11
Attached devices, access to, in future, 576–577
AT&T, 25
    Paradyne, 91
    Personal Network, 58
    Wireless Services, 95
Attribute codes, 287–288
    assignment of, 297
Attributes
    in CC/PP document, 466, 475
    summary, 165
    WML, 162–163
Attribute tokens, 285
Auctions and auctioneering, 33
Audio and video streaming, 61
Australia, 72
AU Systems, 56, 585
Authenticated flag, 508
Authentication, 517
    end-to-end, 573
    Push Initiator, 508–509
    and trust relationships, 546
    with Wireless Transport Layer Security, 111
    WTLS for, 526
Automated HTML-to-WML conversion, 552
Automatic conversion, 340
    defined, 316
Automatic data type conversions, summary of legal, *317*
Automatic provisioning, 572
Automatic speech generation, 570
Automotive IVIS systems, 464
Automotive Multimedia Interface Consortium, 38, 141
AWS. *See* AT&T Wireless Services

Back-end connectivity, 560n4
Backslash, 238
Backward navigation, 215
    prev element, 194
    in WML, 152
Bandai, 39

Bandwidth, 53
  and bearer selection, 529
  increase in, 571
  and richer content, 578
  and run-time costs, 72–74
Banking, electronic, 31
BankOne, 26
Basic Authentication mechanism, HTTP, 264, 266, 267
Battery power/technology, 11, 55, 76, 575
Bearer independence, 137
  and WAP standard, 137
Bearer protocols, 108, 110
BEA's WebLogic Application Server, 126
b element, 451
BER. *See* Bit error rate
Betting, 38, 39
big element, 451
Billing services, 5, 31–32, 42–44, 57
Binary arithmetic operators, 324
Binary encoding, 113, 120, 124, 125, 129, 132, 278
  CC/PP, 471–472
  HTTP-WSP mapping, 552
  WBXML, 503, 504
  XML, 121
Binary operators
  and assignment, 324
  plus (+), 318
  rules for, in WMLScript, 319–321
Binary WML, 180, 280, 300–306
  attribute start tokens, *300–302*
  attribute value tokens, *303*
  encoding example, 304–306
  extension tokens, *303*
  tag tokens, *300*
Binary WML encoding example
  encoding of WML deck, *304–306*
  sample WML deck to be encoded, *304*
Binary WMLScript. *See also* WMLScript
  bytecode header, 382–383
  constant pool, 383
  format, *382*
  function pool, 383
  pragma pool, 383
Binary XML, 382
Bindings, 188
  adding, 216
  duplicate, 213, 215
  overriding, 205–206, 207
Bit error rate, 74
Bitwise operators, 326–327
BizBuddy (FaceTime), 26
Blank lines, 187
Block comments, 312

Block statement, 329, 330
Bluetooth, 578–579
  radio environment, 141
  radio technology, short-range, 33
  Special Interest Group, 141
BMW, 36
Boldface text, 119, 179
Bookmarks
  mobile, 28
  and user switching between applications, 271
Boolean literals, 314
Boolean type, 315
Boolean value, conversions to, 316, 317, 318
Booz Allen Hamilton, 15
Boston Consulting Group, 29
Braces, with if-else statements, 331
Brand loyalty, 53
Brand name recognition, 30, 53, 61
Breaking, in wrap mode, 183
break statement, 332, 333–334
br element, 184–185, 589
Bridging, 124. *See also* Convergence
  application-layer, *550*, 552–553
  datagram-layer, *550*, 553–554
  to Internet, 104
  session-layer, *550*, 552–553, 554
  between WAP environment and the Internet, *549*
Bridging gateway, *549*
BroadBeam, ExpressQ from, 91
Browser context, 172
Browser-enabled mobile devices, 12
Browser-equipped Personal Digital Assistant, 6
Browser-equipped phone, 5
Browsers
  and cache value, 154
  and content design, 459
  and deck access control, 264
  HTTP and performance of, 80
  and interoperability, 571
  and soft keys, 208
  tailoring WML to, 200
  testing, 420, 421
  WML, 147, 155–158
Browser vendors, 55–56
Browsing, mobile, 4
br tags, and separation of anchored elements, 427
Buffering, packet, 69
Bugs, 386. *See also* Debugging; Errors
  and automatic type conversions, 316
Bundled services, 55, 58
"Burning" application, into mobile client, 531
Burstiness, and packet sequencing, 70
Business Class Transportation, 47
Business drivers, 15–17

Businesses
  Internet services for, 3
  mobile access for, 15
Business models
  and mobile Internet, xiii
  within value chain, 543
Business opportunities, 51–87
  application service provider, 60–61
  content aggregator (portal), 59–60
  content developer, 62–63
  content provider, 62
  end-user market, 54–55
  infrastructure vendor, 58–59
  terminal manufacturer and browser vendor,
    55–56
  wireless Internet access provider, 56–58
Business-to-business (B2B) commerce, 29,
  47, 59
Business-to-consumer (B2C) commerce, 29
Business value chain
  mapping deployment chain to, 543–545
  members of, 16–17, 541, *542*
Buying decisions, usability influences on, 386
b variable, declaration for, 330
Bytecode header, binary WMLScript, 382–383
Byte codes, 279–280
Byte-counting techniques, 72

C, 330
C++, 316, 330
CA. *See* Certificate Authority
Cache
  card contents stored in, 151
  defined, 154
  in Service Loading, 504, 505
Cache-Control
  attribute, 193
  must-revalidate response header, 154
  response header, 262
Cache-control="nocache," emulating, *193*
Cached headers, 113
Caching, 107, 262, 474
  content, 124, 126
  and HTTP security, 266
  model document, 118
  services, 541
Cahners In-Stat Group, 15
Call Cleared event, 520, 535
Call conferencing, 511
Call Connected event, 520
Call Connecting event, 520
  event handler bound to, 517
Call control functions, 516
Caller ID information, saving to contact list, 45

Call forwarding, 23, 511
Call logs, 521
  functions of, 524
Call screening lists, 46
Call template channel definition, originating, *532*
Call waiting, 511
Cap Gemini America, 9
card, 589
Card element, 170, 198, 452–453
Card-level binding, 189, 210
Cards, 117
  and do element, 428
  identifying, 174–175
  navigation between, *153*
  and timer, 257
  in WML deck, 149
  WML document, 167
Carrier Expert Group, WAP Forum, 101
Cascading menus, 250
Cascading Style Sheets, 82
Case-insensitivity, with character set encoding
  names, 180
Case sensitivity
  with WML, 163, 239
  WMLScript, 311, 340
Catalogs
  multimedia, 41
  WTA and downloading of, 121
CBalance function, 130
cc:Mail, 92
CC/PP. *See* Composite Capability/Preference
  Profiles
CC/PP components, specification of in UAProf
  schema, 472–473
CC/PP documents, 474
  asserting Default attributes, *481*
  binary encoding of, 471, 472
  final composed profile obtained by merging,
    484, 486
  mapping of, 472
  merging, *481–482*
  Profile header containing three, 482
  sample, using vocabulary defined by WAP
    UAProf, *467–468*
  structure, *466*, 466–467
CC/PP Exchange Protocol, 469–470, 472, 474
  mapping of, to WSP, 471, 472
  profile-warning codes defined by, *470*
  sample headers, *471*
CC/PP profile, asserted by WAP gateway, *485*
CC/PP specification, 140
CCR. *See* Class Conformance Requirements
CDMA. *See* Code Division Multiple Access
CDPD. *See* Cellular Digital Packet Data

Cegetel SFR, 28
ceil function, Float library, 347
Cells
  geographic, 108
  WML tables, 225, 227
Cellular communications, wireless networks
    for, 72
Cellular Digital Packet Data, 92, 108, 529
Cellular infrastructure, xi
Cellular networks
  beyond, 577–578
  and "handling off" process, 75
Cellular phones, xi, 4, 5, 578, 579
  in Europe, 9
  and user profiles, 394
  WMLScript-enabled, 310
Center alignment, 451
Central processing units (CPUs), 387
Certificate authority (CA), 371
CGI programs or servlets, 58, 159, 276
Chaining, of if statements, 331–332
Channels, 530
  loading into/removing from repository,
    518–519
  in originating call template, *532*
  WTA applications stored as, in repository, 512
Character emphasis elements, *179*
Character entities, WML, *176*
Character reference, 177
CharacterSet function, Lang library, 346
Character sets, and internationalization, 180
charAt function, String library, 350
Charset, 283–284
Chat/chat roms, 25, 59
Chauffeur services, 46
Checking account balance
  and data source, 130
  end-to-end WAP, *127*
  request flow, 128–130
  response flow, 130–132
  WAP client device, 128–129, 132
  WAP gateway, 129, 132
  Web application server, 129, 130–131
  WML and Nokia 6150 phone simulator request
    for, *128*
  WML and Nokia 6150 phone simulator
    response to request for, *133*
  XML representation of, 131
  XSL for conversion of XML into WML, 131–132
Chevy Chase consulting firm, 60
"Child finder" capabilities, 42
Christiansen/Cummings Associates, 39
Churn, barriers to, 385
Circuits, network reliance on, 109

Circuit-switched data, 511n1, 529
Circuit-switched networks, 68
class attribute, 163
Class Conformance Requirements, 123
Client. *See also* Tailoring content to client
  profile asserted by, *479*
Client-aware applications, enabling, 465
Client Capability Query, 497
Client Capability Query Response, 497
Client-side certificates, 573
CNN, 28
Code Breaker, 145, 307
Code Division Multiple Access, 72, 73, 108–109
Code pages, 115, 116
  WBXML, 285–286
Collapsed sections, 250
ColorCapable attribute, 482
Color
  coding with WML, 159
  content, 482
  images, 160
Columns, in WML tables, 226
columns attribute, 227–228
Comma operator, 327–328
Comments, WML, 175
Common Object Request Broker Architecture
  (CORBA), 560
Communications errors, 74–75
Communications management services, 14
compare function, String library, 350
Competition, and mobile Internet, xiii
Competitive advantage, wireless equipment
  and, 15
Compilation units, 335, 338
  calling functions in, 336
Components, in CC/PP document, 466, 475
Composite Capability/Preference Profiles, 460,
  465–468, 488
  specification, 123–124
Composition algorithm, 477
Compound statements, in WMLScript, 329
Computer network protocols, xii
Computer terminal, user interface design
  for display on, 386
Computing power, reduction in cost of, 55
Concatenation, 112
  and string operators, 327
Conditional operator, 328
Conference calls, 45
Confirmed Push, 506, 507
confirm function, Dialogs library, 368
Conflict resolution, 414
Connectionless Push, 507
Connection-Oriented Push, 507

Consistency, in user interface design, 412–413
Constant pool, 383
    in binary WMLScript unit, 382, 383
Constrained devices
    limitations with, 146
    and WML browser, 157
Construction site applications, 47
Constructors, 84
Consumer portals, 60
Consumers, 18
    Internet services for, 3
Contact list, caller ID information saved to, 45
Container, 467, 477
Content. *See also* Tailoring content to client
    customization of, 124, 126
    filtering, 124, 126, 557
    generation, 275–276, 560
    guiding users to appropriate, 399–401
    hosting, 61
    insertion, 126
    multimedia, in future, 570–571
    navigation optimized to, 404
    production routes, 156
    style elements, 178
    tailoring, 124
    WBXML, 280–281
    WBXML document, 285–292
    in WML cards, 149
Content aggregator (portal), 59–60
content attribute, 273
Content authors, and new releases, 277
Content caching, 124, 126
Content conversion, with WAP proxy, 126
Content developers, 62–63
    and mobile Internet standard, 94
    and user-agent profiles, 123
Content nonrepudiation, and Crypto Library, 573
Content providers, 58, 62
Content push, server-initiated, 124
Content-Type header, 463
Context stacks, 271
Continuation flag, 281
continue statement, 332
    in WMLScript, 333–334
Contracts, 33
Controls, WML, 235–256
Convergence, 565. *See also* Data; Interdevice
        communications; Internet; mobile Internet;
        World Wide Web
    drivers enabling, *13*
    enabling, 11–12
    between Internet and wireless communications,
        18

    market, 9–11
    between wireless and online information
        industries, 9
Conversion
    precedence rules, 318
    specification, 221
Cooke, N.J., 400
Cookies, 113
    HTTP, 267
CORBA. *See* Common Object Request Broker
        Architecture
Core attributes, id and class, 163
Coupons, electronic, 34
Courier services, 46
CPU cycles, limited, 147
Credit card transactions, and securing variables, 268
Cryptographic functions, callability of, from
        WMLScript program, 369
Cryptographic iButton, 85
Crypto Library, 573, 601–602
    signText function, 369–370
CSD. *See* Circuit-switched data
CSS. *See* Cascading Style Sheets
CurrentBearerService attribute, 482
Current value, of variable, 190
Cursor keys, 157
Customer loyalty, and content provider, 62
Customer personalization, 53. *See also*
        Personalization
Customers. *See also* Personalization; Users
    caring for, 42–44
    interviewing, 396
    retention of, 61
Customization, 57
    and usage drivers, 14
Customization of content. *See* Tailoring content
        to the client
Cyber-cash, 35
CyPost, 25

Dai-chi Kosho, 39
Data, 562
    bridge between wireless telephony and, 511
    exchanging with WML, 381–382
    opaque, 291
    pruning, 564
Data-collecting shoes, 578
Data-enabled phones, 5, 14
Data encryption, 111
Datagram abstraction, by WDP, 111
Datagram layer, 97
    linking WAP and Internet at, 548, *550*,
        553–554

Data-optimized networks, 92–93
  ARDIS, 92
  Cellular Digital Packet Data, 92
  RAM mobile data, 92
  Ricochet, 92–93
Data push, 558
Data representation
  HTML and lack of separation between data
    and, 562
  JSPs support for separation of data and, 563
Data security, 264
  end-to-end, 573
Data services, 17
Data source, 126
Data storage, demand for, 76
Data synchronization, 123, 141, 575–576, 576
Data type conversions, 377
Data validation, with WMLScript, 308, 310
Day planner, 6
Day trading, online, 32
DB2, IBM, 126
DCOM. *See* Distributed Component Object
    Model
Dead areas, 147
Dead-end card, 211
Debit cards, 35
Debugging, 378. *See also* Errors; Testing
  template for WML, 375
  template for WMLScript, 376–377
  WMLScript programs, 374
DebugMsg() function, 381
Deck access control, 264
Deck-level bindings, 205, 206
  and rendering, 210
Deck of cards
  document structure, 117
  WML document consisting of, *117*
Decks, 117, 149
  and abbreviating onevent elements, 198–199
  discarding from caches, 154
  identifying, 174–175
  WML, 166
Deck size, and WBXML, 280
Declarations
  document type, 273–274
  variable, 315, 330–331
  XML, 168
Decrement (--) operators, 326
Decryption, 573. *See also* Encryption
Default attribute values, 165
Default mask, 237
Default option, 253
Default option index, 253, 254

Defaults attribute, 467, 475, 478, 479, 482, 484
  CC/PP document representing, *481*
  example of resolving, original CC/PP
    document graph, *476, 477*
Default value determination, 253–255
Delay, 68
Delete action, Service Indication, 502
Deleted message scenario, *212*
delete type, 118, 204
Deleting, message, 212–213
Delimited lists, 349
Delivered status, Push Message delivery, 506
Denial-of-service attacks, 111
Deployment chain, 541, 542
  mapping business value chain to, 543–545
  WAP, 124–127
Description element, in RDF statement, 466n4
Design. *See also* User interface design; WML
    design guidelines for selected elements;
    WTA design considerations
  iterative, 411–412
Designers, and focus on user, 412
Design guidelines, following, 406
Design ideas, blending, 405
Design process, user interface, 392–411, 454
  and application design goals, 398–399
  define phase, 392–398
  design phase, 398–406
  generate/test multiple designs, 405
  iteration phase, 411
  keystroke reduction, 404–405
  and menu structure, 339–401
  and personalization, 401–403
  prototype phase, 407–408
  task analysis, 396–398
  test phase, 408–411
  and transcoders, 406
  and user knowledge, 403
  user profile, 393–395
Designs, prototyping alternative, 407
Design team, 391
  makeup of, 391
Desktop personal computers, 464, 569
  and content design, 459
  traditional Web sites shown on, 386
Desktop terminals, 3
Desktop users, versus mobile Internet users, 10–11
Developers, 412
  and browser testing, 420–421
Device addresses, 498
Device capability information, 141
Device extensibility, 142
Device independence, 142

Device-independent man–machine interface, 118–119
Device-independent services
  provisioning of, based on XML and XSL or JSP front ends, *561*
DHCP, 78
Dialog functions, 378
Dialogs Library, 368–369, 602
  alert function, 368
  confirm function, 368
  and invalid value, 381
  prompt function, 369
Digital broadcasting industries, 571
Digital cameras, 14
Digital certificate technology, 30
Digital control channel, 73
Digital marketplaces, 53
Digital mobile phones, wireless Internet services on, ix
Digital networks, 72, 75
Digital signal processors, 76
Digital signatures, 369, 370
  and RDF, 465n3
Digits Dialed state, 520
Directory information, 29
Directory services, 18, 59
Discretionary hyphen, 184
Display capabilities. *See also* Screens
  mobile terminals versus computer monitors, 387
Display versus rendering, in WML, 157–158
Distributed Component Object Model, 560
DNS, 78
Document body, in WBXML document, 122
Document caching model, 118
Document parsing, speed of, 278
Document prologue, 168–169
  encoding declaration in, 180
Document structure, WBXML, 281–284
Document tokens, in WBXML document, 122
Document type declarations, 168, 273–274
Document Type Definition, 83, 169, 273–274, 280, 282, 506
  encoding example without, 293–297
  external, 297
  and tokens, 285
  and WBXML encoding process, 292
do element, 199–200, 428, 590
  browser differences, 428–429
  Ericsson browser simulator demonstrating, with accept and option events, *431*
  Nokia browser simulator demonstrating, with accept and option events, *432*
  Phone.com browser simulator demonstrating, with accept and option events, *429*

rendering of, *208*
  and type attribute, 200–201
  usage guidelines, 216–217
  user interface design guidelines, 433–435
  using, 207–210
Dog races, 39
DOI. *See* Default option index
Dollar signs, 177–178, 219
Domain
  attribute, 265
  defined, 545
Doppler radar maps, 29
Doppler shift effects, 75
DoTestLab.wml, 205
do type="accept" event, 433, 434, 435
do type="options" event, 433, 434
do types, predefined, *201*
Drivers
  business, 15–17
  convergence enabled by, 12, *13*
  technology, 12–14
  usage, 14–15
DSPs. *See* Digital signal processors
DTD. *See* Document type definition
DTMF tones, transmitting through active voice connection, 373
Dumas, J. S., 408
DUPACK recovery mechanism, 70, 71
Duplicate bindings, 213–215
Duwango, 41
Dynamic class loading, 85
Dynamic content generation, 126, 156, 159, 275, 276
Dynamic decks, and absolute URLs, 161
Dynamic pages, 275, 276

Early Adopters, 11
  and "tools" phase, 15
Early Majority users, and "platforms" phase, 15
e-business, 47, 61
e-care, 42–44
  case for, *43*
ECMAScript, 83, 84
  core language, 340
  Math and Number libraries, 341
  WMLScript contrasted with, 308
ECMAScript interpreter, 84
ECMAScript standard, WMLScript based on, 120
e-commerce, 17, 18, 30, 59, 61
  business-to-business, 47
  smart-card technology for, 14
  and WMLScript Crypto library, 384
e-coupons, 34
EDGE. *See* Enhanced Data for Global Evolution

Electric, 96
Electronic banking, 31
Electronic bill paying, 5
Electronic commerce. *See* e-commerce
Electronic mail. *See* e-mail
Electronic postcards, 40
elementAt function, String library, 356
Elements, 165
    within card, 170
    WML, 162
elements function, in String library, 356
e-mail, 5, 7, 14, 59, 61, 576
    downloading, 6
    mobile, 21–22
    and telematics, 35
    voice-controlled, 46
EmbeddedJava, 574
em element, 451, 590
Emphasis elements, 178
    full formatting of, *179*
    partial formatting of, *179*
emptyok attribute, 238–239
Empty statement, in WMLScript, 334–335
Encoding, efficient, 115–116
Encoding process
    encoding example, with no DTD, 293–297
    using external DTD, 297–299
    WBXML, 292–299
Encryption, 111, 264, 546, 554. *See also* Decryption;
    Security
    over-the-air, 517
    WTLS for, 526
enctype attribute, 192–193
End-to-end communication path, elements
    within, 473–474
End-to-end communications, 488
End-to-end push services, 509
End-to-end reliability, 112
End-to-end scheme, 469
End-to-end security, 572–573
End-to-end system supporting WAP client
    devices
    logical view of, *125*
End-to-end WAP checking account balance
    request, *127*
End-to-end WAP request, 127–132
    data source, 130
    request flow, 128
    WAP client device, 128-129, 132
    WAP gateway, 129, 132
    Web application server, 129, 130–132
End-to-end WAP services
    building and deploying, 541–565
    linking WAP and Internet, 548–554

mapping deployment chain to business value
    chain, 543–545
    security domains, 545–548
    WAP service design, 554–564
END token, 288, 292
End users, 54–55
    and deployment chain, 541
    as part of design team, 391
Enhanced Cellular, 91
Enhanced Control Cellular, 91
Enhanced Data for Global Evolution, 73, 109, 529
Enhanced Throughput Cellular, 91
Enhanced WML, 307–384. *See also* Wireless
    Markup Language
    binary WMLScript, 382–383
    Wireless Telephony Application Interface,
        371–374
    WMLScript, 308–340
    WMLScript development, 374–382
    WMLScript standard libraries, 340–371
Enterprise customers, 54
Enterprise intranets, 19
Enterprise resource planning, 61
Entertainment services, 38–39
ENTITY, 289
    tokens, 292
Ericsson, 95, 96, 126
Ericsson browser, 245
    simple document displayed by, *166*
Ericsson browser simulator, 422, 427, 449
    anchor and a elements demonstrated with,
        425
    demonstrating do element, with accept and
        option events, *431*
    demonstrating input element, *439*
    demonstrating select element, *446*
    and title attribute, 453
Ericsson MC218, *416*
    version 1.13 PDA, 421
Ericsson R380, open and closed, *417*
Ericsson R320S handset, 421
Ericsson R380S handset, 421
Ericsson SDK, sample rendering of single-choice
    select with, *252*
Ericsson WAPIDE SDK version 2.0, model Erics-
    son R320s. *See* Ericsson browser simulator
Ericsson WAPIDE SDK version 2.0B8 simulator,
    421
Ericsson WAP Integrated Development
    Environment, 583
ERP. *See* Enterprise resource planning
Error detection, and invalid value, 312
Error handling, by WMLScript program, 530
Error rates, and reliability, 74–76

Error recovery
  protocols, 75
  for TCP, 70
Errors
  and browser limitations, 274–275
  in menu-driven systems, 401
  preventing, 413, 442
Escape encoding, 220
Escape sequences, 220, 381
  special character, *314*
  and string literals, 314
escapeString function, URL library, 358
ETC. *See* Enhanced Throughput Cellular
ETSI. *See* European Telecommunications
      Standardisation Institute
Europe
  cellular phone use in, 9
  digital networks in, 72
  electronic purchasing in, 33
  fleet management in, 47
  high-bandwidth applications support in, 73–74
  location-dependent services in, 12
  online users in, 3
  wireless bundling in, 58
European Telecommunications Standardisation
      Institute, 141
  and evolution of WAP standard, 99
Event bindings, 149, 150, 167, 188, 189, 196
  and abbreviating onevent elements, 199
  in paragraph element, 181
  rendering, 210
Event equivalence, *198–199*
Event handling, 530
  improved, 538
  and WTA event handling, 517–518
Event model, within WTA application
      programming interface, 519
Events, 188, 531
  linked to tasks, 149, 195–207
execute-high, 504
execute-low, 504
exit function, Lang library, 346–347
Experimental types, 204
Expert Groups, WAP Forum, 101
Expiration, Service Indication, 502
Expires response header, 262
Expression statements, in WMLScript, 329
ExpressQ, 91
Extended methods, 115
eXtensible Markup Language, ix, xiv, 82, 83, 87,
      116, 126, 140, 148, 278, 306, 562-563. *See also*
      Wireless Binary eXtensible Markup
      Language
  comparing XSL, JavaServer Pages and, 564

content, 570
and convergence with the Web, 571
data, 574
declaration, 168
influence of, on WML, 147, 148
and WAP standard, 139
eXtensible Style-Sheet Language, 563
  comparing XML, JavaServer pages
        and, 564
  processor, 131
eXtensible Style Sheets, 82
Extension tokens, 285, 289–290, 290
External devices, future of, 538
External Document Type Definition, 297
External function calls, 336
External resource, 149

FaceTime, 26
FDM. *See* Frequency Division Multiplexing
Ferris Research, 26
Fields, grouping related, 260–261
Field service dispatch services, 61
fieldset element, 172, 257, 260, 453, 590
Financial services Web sites, and WML support,
      146
find function, String library, 350–351
Finite state machine, 535
Finland, WAP services in, 42
Firefighting, 46
Firewalls, 469, 474, 488
First-generation cellular networks, 13n2
Fleet management and dispatch service, 14,
      47–48
Flexible deployability principle
  layering and abstraction, 134
  and separability principle, 135
Flexible implementability principle, 136
Flex protocol, 109
float function, Lang library, 341
Floating-point addition, 318
Floating-point literals, 313
  examples of, *313*
Floating-point types, 315
Floating-point values, 313, *352*
  conversions to, 317
  converting to string, 316
  and numeric operands, 319
Float Library, 603–604
  ceil function, 347
  floating-point operations, 347–349
  floor function, 347
  int function, 340, 348
  maxFloat function, 313, 348
  minFloat function, 313, 348

pow function, 348–349
round function, 349
sqrt function, 349
floor function, Float library, 347
Flower deliveries, 33
Focus groups, 396
Fonts, 119
Formal parameter, 335
format attribute, 236–238, 443
for error prevention, 442
Format codes, 236
inputting, *237*
use of, 247
format function, String library, 351
format mask, 238, 240
FORMAT parameter, 130
Format specification, 352
format string, 240
Formatting, WBXML document, 281
Formatting characters, WML, 239
Forrester Research, 29, 61
for statements
loop example, *333*
in WMLScript, 332–333
Fortune telling, 39
forua attribute, 273
Forward navigation, 213
go element, 189–191
in WML, 151, 152, 153
Fragment, URL, 174
Frames, 108
Frequency Division Multiplexing, 108, 109
FSM. *See* Finite state machine
Fujitsu, and IVIS systems, 37
Full members, in WAP Forum, 100
Fully qualified reference, 161
Function, 335–337
invocation, 336–337
simple, *335*
WMLScript called from WML, 337
WMLScript identifiers for naming, 321
function keyword, 336
Function labels, recommended, *434*
Function pool, 383
in binary WMLScript unit, 382, 383

Gambling, 38, 39
Game Boy (Nintendo®), 38, 39
Games, online, 38, 41
Gartner Group, 15, 31
Gateway-ASP trust relationships, 547
Gateways, 104, 469
General Packet Radio Service, 73, 109, 529

"Generic Content Authoring Guidelines for WML 1.1: Best Practices and Recommendations," 421
Generic headers, in Push Message, 499
Generic set tokens, 285
Geographic cells, 108
getBase function, URL library, 359
getCurrentCard function, WMLBrowser library, 366
getFieldValue function, 523
getFragment function, 362
getHost function, URL library, 362
GET method, 151
Get method, versus post method, 261–262
getParameters function, URL library, 362–363
getPath function, URL library, 363
getPort function, URL library, 363
getReferer function, URL library, 359
getScheme function, URL library, 364
getVar function, WMLBrowser library, 367
GIF. *See* Portable Network Graphics
Global binding, 517, 518, 530
Global literal tokens, 287
Global Mobile Commerce Forum, 30, 331
Global Positioning System, 36, 48
Global System for Mobile Communication, 69, 72, 73, 109
Global tokens, 285, 288–292, 297
character entities, 289
control codes, 292
extension tokens, 289–290
literals, 288–289
opaque data, 291
processing instructions, 290–291
strings and string references, 289
WBXML 1.2 and 1.3, *286*
in WBXML document, 122
Global use principle, 136–137
Global wireless networks, 579
GMCF. *See* Global Mobile Commerce Forum
go element, 189–191, 230, 591
go function, WMLBrowser library, 365
go task, 188, 192, 198
binding onenterbackward attribute to, 435
goto statement, 535
GPRS. *See* General Packet Radio Service
GPS. *See* Global Positioning System
Graphics
capabilities, 14
img element and display of, 450
WML browsers supporting, 222
Grocery shopping, 42
Group boxes, 250
Groupware, 61

GSM. *See* Global System for Mobile Communication
GSM networks, functions provided by WTAGSM library in, 525
GSM Short Message Service, 92

Hackers and hacking, 266, 546
Handheld computers
    embedded browsers in, 147
    and user profiles, 394
Handheld Device Markup Language, 91, 117
    influence of, on WML, 147, 148
    within WAP standard, 96
Handheld devices, xii
    and data synchronization, 576
    Internet access via, 569
    mobile phones, 9
    untethered, 579
Handheld Device Transport Protocol, 96, 97
"Handing off" process, 75
Handset, client, communication between applications/services at each layer on, *105*
Handset behavior, and WAP standard, *102*
Handset displays. *See also* Screens
    and WAP, 387
Handset manufacturers, 17
    and mobile Internet standard, 93, 94
    and WAP standard, 95
Handsets, Motorola, *416*
Handwriting recognition, 157
Hardware Platform component, 479, 481
Hardware providers, and mobile Internet standard, 93, 94
HDML. *See* Handheld Device Markup Language
HDTP. *See* Handheld Device Transport Protocol
head element, 169, 591
Header, in binary WMLScript unit, 382–383
Header caching, 114
Header values, 115, 116
Heads, WML document, 167
Health care, 42
Hearts, 39
height attribute, 225
help do type, example of, *202–203*
help type, 118, 202
Hexadecimal values, 312
High-speed networks, 74
History
    cache related to, 154
    navigation, 151
History stack, 118, 173, 274–275
    entries on, 151
    entries placed on WML, 153
HistoryStack.wml, 153

Hong Kong
    electronic trading in, 30
    horse race betting in, 39
Hop-to-hop scheme, 469
Horizontal applications, 14
Horizontal markets, consumer portals for, 60
Horizontal portals, 53
Horoscopes, 39
Horse racing, 39
Hotspots, 229, 230
href attribute, 166, 190, 191, 230, 233
hspace attribute, 224
HTML. *See* Hypertext Markup Language
HTML-based devices, and variability of WAP devices, 414–415
HTML-based Web sites, and transcoders, 406
HTML browsers, and content design, 459
HTML content, difficulties in translating, to WML, 551
HTML development, WML content development contrasted with, 276
HTML interface, adapting existing, 557–558
HTML version 4.0, 147
HTTP. *See* Hypertext Transfer Protocol
HTTP Content-Type header, 181
HTTP cookies, 267
HTTP equivalent data, 339
HTTP equivalent meta-information, 339–340
http-equiv attribute, 272
Http-equiv meta-data, 181
HTTP headers, 461–464
    Accept-Charset header, 464
    Accept-Encoding header, 464
    Accept header, 463
    Accept-Language header, 463
    summary of standard, *462*
    User-Agent header, 462–463
HTTP 1.1 standard, 113, 493, 497
    Extension Framework, 469
    techniques, 461–464
HTTP protocol, and caching, 154
HTTP server, HTTP headers handled by, 464
Human factors, 389
Hypertext Markup Language, xiv, 81, 87, 116, 126, 571
    and convergence of WML, 140
    influence of, on WML, 147, 148
    integration of XML, WML and, 571
    and overloading of term anchor, 229
    and WAP standard, 139
    WML distinguished from, 152
Hypertext Transfer Protocol, ix, 80–81, 87, 124, 160, 491
    IETF work on revision of, 140

security, 266–267
and WAP standard, 139
Hyphens, 450–451

IANA. *See* Internet Assigned Numbers Authority
IBM
    DB2, 127, 130
    and Java, 85
    Secureway Wireless Gateway, 125–126, 127
    390 series
    VisualAge Micro-Edition, 86
    Wapsody, 166, 167, 185, 243, *252*, 584
    Websphere Application Server, 127
    Websphere Performance Pack, 126
    WebSphere Transcoding Publisher, 557n2
    Wired Anywhere, 585
    XMLViewer, 586
iButton, 85
ICMP. *See* Internet Control Message Protocol
Icons, for menu items, 401
id attribute, 163, 174
iDEN phone, Motorola, 166
Identifiers
    examples of, WMLScript, *321*
    with multiple roles, *322*
    user-defined, 498
    for wireless devices, 77
    WMLScript, 321–322
Idle state, 520, 521
i element, 451, 591
IETF. *See* Internet Engineering Task Force
if-else statement, in WMLScript, 331–332
if-then-else conditional construct, 531
IIOP. *See* Internet Inter-ORB Protocol
Illegal type conversions, 316
IM. *See* Instant messaging
Images
    sample rendering of, Nokia SDK, *222*
    and WBMP, 570
    WML, 221–225
IMC. *See* Internet Mail Consortium
img element, 450, 592
    use of, *223*
i-mode, 63
Implicit bindings, 215
Inactive elements, 207
iname attribute, 248, 249, 254, 255
Incoming Call event, 520
Incoming call treatment, 45
Increment expression, 332, 333
Increment (++) operators, 326
Indentation, 187
Index sequence, 253
"Infomediaries," 17, 53

Information, sending, 261–262
Information Superhighway, 3
Infrared Data Association, 97
Infrastructure ownership, security, functional
    split and, *549*
Infrastructure vendors, 17, 58–59
Initialization, of variables, 315
initialize expression, 332, 333
Initiator URI, 508
In-line string tokens, 290
Input devices, of mobile terminals, 387
input element, 235, 242, 249, 436, 592
    access key for, 232
    alternative use of, *246–247*
    browser differences, 436–437
    Ericsson browser simulator demonstrating, *439*
    naive use of, *243*
    Nokia browser simulator demonstrating, *440,
        441*
    Phone.com browser simulator demonstrating,
        438
    use of, 241
    user interface design guidelines, 442
Input fields
    initialization, 241–242
    rendering and operation of, 242–246
    various implementations of, *243–245*
Input forms, 118
INs. *See* Intelligent networks
insertAt function, String library, 357
Instance of schema, 466
Instant messaging, 25–27
Integer, *352*
Integer addition, 318
Integer literals, 312–313
Integer type, 315
Integer value, conversions to, 317
Integrated access scenarios, 61
Intel, Narrowband Sockets from, 92
Intelligent middleware, 74
Intelligent networks, 45
Intelligent-Terminal Transfer Protocol, 96
Intelligent Transport Systems Data Bus Forum, 38
Interactive voice response, 43
Interdevice communications, potential seamless-
    ness with, 579
Interdomain trust, 545–546
Interference, 147
International Data Corporation (IDC), 15, 31, 63
Internationalization
    and WAP standard, 137–138
    WML text, 180–181
Internet, xi, 3, 9, 74. *See also* mobile Internet;
    World Wide Web

Internet *continued*
 bridging to, 104
 connectivity to: five-year forecast, *10*
 content design and access speed to, 459
 content provider roles on, 62
 expansion of reach of, xi
 future of, 579
 and Java technology, 84, 85
 linking WAP to, 548–554
 and multimedia services, 39, 40
 range of terminals supported by, 459
 service design and development, 391
 Web-capable mobile phones connectivity and,
  15
 wireless communications convergence with, 18
Internet architectures, WAP standard and
  consistency with, 138
Internet Assigned Numbers Authority, 101, 164,
  293
 character encodings registered with, 283
 MIBenum value, 383
Internet Control Message Protocol, and WAP
  standard, 139
Internet Engineering Task Force
 WAP Forum relationship with, 133, 139, 140
 and World Wide Web Consortium, 140
Internet Inter-ORB Protocol, 560
Internet Mail Consortium, 122
Internet Protocol, ix, 19, 124, 553
Internet protocol stack layers, WAP protocol stack
  layers compared to, *106*
Interoperability. *See also* Wireless Telephony
  Applications
 and standard mechanisms, 465
 and WAP standard, 136
Interpreters, testing, 374
int function, Float library, 348
Intradeck/interdeck navigation model, 117–118
Intrinsic event handlers, and timers, 257
Intrinsic events, 188, 250
 trapping, 195–196
Intrinsic event types, *196*
invalid effect, 380–381
invalid literals, 314
Invalid packets, 111
invalid type, 315, 318
invalid value, 316, 380
 error detection, 312
In-Vehicle Information Systems, 35–38, 141
Investing, online, 32–33
Invocation, function, 335, 336–337, 381
IP. *See* Internet Protocol
IrDA. *See* Infrared Data Association

IrOBEX. *See* Object Exchange protocol
ISDN, 75
isEmpty function, String library, 353–354
isFloat function, Lang library, 328, 341–342
isInt function, Lang library, 328, 342
IS-136 networks, 525
ISO/IEC-10646 Universal Character Set, 177, 180
ISPs, 60
isValid function, URL library, 359–360
is valid operator, 329
Italic, 119
Iteration, 411–412, 454
 and WTA application development, 527
ITTP. *See* Intelligent-Terminal Transfer Protocol
ivalue attribute, 248
IVIS. *See* In-Vehicle Information Systems
IVR. *See* Interactive voice response

Japan
 autonomous navigation systems in, 35
 e-banking in, 31
 electronic purchasing in, 33
 high-bandwidth applications support in, 73
 Java capabilities on phones in, 575
 network games in, 39
 wireless network infrastructures in, 109
Java programming language, 84–86, 87, 316, 330
 and future of mobile Internet, 574–575
JavaBeans, 563, 564
Java Card 2.0 specification, 85
JavaPhone, 575
Java Remote Method Invocation, 560
JavaScript, 58, 83, 116, 119, 120, 126, 316, 551,
  571, 572
 string comparison in, 321
JavaScript 1.1, WMLScript based on, 308
JavaServer Pages, 58, 562, 563
 XML/XSL compared to, 564
Java Virtual Machine, and iButton, 85
Jewelry
 Java-powered, 85
JIT. *See* Just-in-time
Jog shuttles, 157
JPEG. *See* Portable Network Graphics
JScript, 83, 120
Jupiter Communications, 26, 29
Just-in-time compilers, 86
JVM. *See* Java Virtual Machine

Kannel Project, 586
Keyboard, lack of full, 147
keyboard attribute, 481
Key hash, 370

keyid, 370, 371
Keystroke reduction, 404–405, 418
keytype parameter, Crypto library, 370
Kiosk to content, 27–29
kVM, java 2 Micro-Edition, or J2ME, from Sun
    Microsystems, 575

label attribute, 205, 428
Labels
    for bindings, 216
    for do events, 435
Lang Library, 312, 340–347, 604–607
    abort function, 345–346
    abs: compute an absolute value, 341
    abs function, 341
    characterSet function, 346
    core functions in, 340–347
    exit function, 346–347
    float function, 341
    isFloat function, 328, 341–342
    isInt function, 328, 342
    math and number functions in, 341–345
    max function, 313, 342
    maxInt function, 343
    min function, 343
    minInt function, 313, 343
    miscellaneous functions, 345–347
    parseFloat function, 316, 343–344
    parseInt function, 316, 344, 382
    random function, 344–345
    seed function, 345
Language independence, and WAP standard,
    136
Language preferences, and Accept-Language
    header, 463
Languages, worldwide. *See also* Internationalization
    WAP standard and support for, 137–138
Laptops, 6, 578
    mobile terminal connection to, 538
Last-in, first-out, list of cards, 118
Late Majority market, 16
Latency, 68–69, 68–72, 388, 415, 570
    acceptable perception of, 528
    and bearer selection, 529
    effect of, on applications, 69–70
    effect of, on transport protocols, 70
    and end-to-end performance, 544
    TCP behavior with high-latency environments,
      70–71
Layering
    advantages with, 104, 107
    disadvantages with, 107
    and WAP standard, 96–98

Layers, within WAP architecture, *103*
Layers of WAP standard, and Principle of
    Separability, 135
Layout, WML text, 181–188
Left-to-right languages, WML table orientation,
    226
Left-to-right paragraph alignment, 183
Legal automatic data type conversions, summary
    of, *317*
length function, String library, 354
Letter pickers, 157
Level 2 cache, WTA repository contrasted with, 518
Library(ies), 337. *See also* WMLScript Standard
    Libraries; WMLScript Standard Libraries
    reference
    debugging, 378
    defined, 311
    network-common, 521, 522–525
    network-specific, 521, 525
    in WMLScript environment, 120
Library classification, and RDF, 465n3
Life-enhancing applications, 35–41
    entertainment services, 38–39
    multimedia services, 39–41
    telematics, 35–38
LIFO. *See* Last-in, first-out
Line breaks, 119, 184–185
    formatting of, *185*
    WML documents, 181
Line comments, 312
Line wrapping, in WML tables, 225
Linking, example, *174*
Link pointer, 150
Links, 230
    to cards, 150
    whitespace in, 234
    WML, 229–234
Link task, 230
Lists, and scrolling, 419
List values, selecting during processing, 255
LITERAL, 287, 288, 289
LITERAL_A, 287
LITERAL_AC, 287
LITERAL_C, 287
Literal characters, avoiding use of, 443
Literal dollar signs, 177–178, 219
Literals, WMLScript, 312–314
    Boolean, 314
    floating-point, 313
    integer, 312–313
    invalid, 314
    string, 313–314
LITERAL tokens, 292

loadString function, URL library, 360
Local binding, 517, 518
Location-based billing, *12*
Location-based information, *12*
Location-dependent applications/
    services, 77
    forecast for, *12*
Location independence, 77
Location-independent workforce, 15
Logical AND operator, 325
Logical navigation, physical navigation versus,
    210–213
Logical NOT operator, 325
Logical operators, 325
Logical OR operator, 325
LogonHealth, 42
Loop constructs, WMLScript
    for statement, 332–333
    while statement, 332
Loops, 436
Lotteries, 39
Lotus Notes, 92, 576
Lund, A.M., 412

Mack, R.L., 408
makeCall(), 516
Management information blocks, 78
Mantissa, 313
Map services, and WML support, 146
Market convergence, 9–11
Market share leaders, 64
Markup elements, 161
Markup generation, 560
Marquee scrolling, 183
Mask character, 237
Masks, 236, 237, 238
    and format codes, 247
Mass-market consumers, 54, 55
Materna Anny Way gateway, 126
max function, Lang library, 313, 342
maxFloat function, Float library, 348
maxInt function, Lang library, 313, 343
maxlength attribute, 240, 443
    for error prevention, 442
Mayday, 36
McGeorge, P., 400
Medical applications, 42
Memory, 387
    constraints, 529
    in repository, 518
    short-term, 413, 414
    tight, 147
Menu, 199
    options as entry in, *214*

options as request to display, *214*
    selection list contrasted with, 256
Menu categorization, user data collected for, 400
Meridien Research, 31
Message ID, and Push Submission operation, 495
Messages, deleting, 212–213
Messaging, 14, 18, 123
    multimedia, 141
    push, 123–124
meta attribute, 339
Meta-data, 272, 273
    user agent, 340
meta element, 169, 272, 273, 593
    content and scheme attributes, 273
    forua attribute, 273
    name and http-equiv attributes, 272–273
Meta-information
    HTTP equivalent, 339–340
    meta attribute, 339
    named, 339
Meta-language, 148
"Meta" markup languages, 82
method attribute, 192
Metricom, 92
MIBenum value, 293
    IANA, 283, 284
MIBs. *See* Management information blocks
Micro-browsers, ix, 55
Microcom, Enhanced Cellular developed by, 91
Micro-Java standards, 86
Microsoft
    JScript, 83
    Internet Explorer, 562
    Internet Explorer browsers, 459
    Winsock API, 92
Microsoft Network, instant messaging through, 25
Microsoft Outlook, 576
Middleware, 71
MIME media types
    for Push Messages, 499, 501–505
    Service Indication, 501–503
    Service Loading, 503–505
    for WAP content, 160
MIME multipart/related document, Push Access
        Protocol Push Submission in form of,
        493–494
minFloat function, Float library, 348
min function, Lang library, 343
minInt function, Lang library, 343
Mitsubishi, 95
Mobile banking, 31
Mobile business users, 6–7, 15
Mobile clients
    application delivery to, 531

WAP standard and delivery of information for, 124
WAP standard and unifying of, 137
Mobile client vendors, and memory constraints, 529
Mobile commerce applications, 31–35
  bill payment, 31–32
  contracts, 33
  e-coupons, 34
  electronic banking, 31
  electronic purchases of goods/services, 33
  online trading, 32–33
  and queued messaging, 576
Mobile data
  business drivers, 15–17
  enabling convergence, 11–12
  and end-user benefits, 17–18
  market convergence, 9–11
  rise of, 9–18
  technology drivers, 12–14
  unleashing, 579
  usage drivers, 14–15
Mobile data speeds, 388
Mobile devices, and convergence, 10
Mobile e-commerce, motivations for, 30
Mobile e-mail, 21, 22
Mobile game playing, 38
Mobile handsets, browser-enabled, 17
mobile Internet, xi–xii, 10, 142, 395, 464
  acronyms, 623–626
  advantages with, 403
  application design goals, 398
  applications for, 48–49
  characteristics of, *68*
  and content developers, 63
  enhancements for, 14
  handsets, increase in sales of, 56
  and mapping between deployment technology and business entities, 541
  need for standard, 93–95
  and seamless integration of services, 57
  successful applications on, 399
  and usability, xiii, 389
  and usage drivers, 14
  user benefits from, 4–7
  user characteristics and, 395
  and user testing, 551–552
  users versus Internet users, 10–11
  value chain, *16*
  value of, 7
mobile Internet challenges/pitfalls, 67–87
  bandwidth and run-time costs, 72–74
  current Web technologies for wireless applications, 79–80

differences between wireless/wireline worlds, 67–68
  error rates and reliability, 74–76
  HTML and XML, 81–83
  HTTP, 80–81
  and Java, 84–86
  latency, 68–72
  service requirements, 78–79
  Web scripting languages, 83–84
  wireless device constraints, 76–78
mobile Internet future, 569–579
  access to attached devices, 576–577
  asynchronous messaging and data synchronization, 575–576
  automatic provisioning, 572
  beyond browsing, 574–577
  beyond cellular, 577–579
  and Bluetooth, 578–579
  convergence with the Web, 571–572
  end-to-end security, 572–573
  and Java, 574–575
  mobile data unleashed, 579
  multimedia content, 570–571
  third-generation networks, 577–578
mobile Internet services, 9, 19–49
  electronic commerce, 29–35
  e-mail/text messaging, 21–22
  entertainment services, 38–39
  information and transactional services, 27–35
  instant messaging, 25–27
  kiosk to content, 27–29
  life-enhancing applications, 35–42
  multimedia services, 39–41
  personal information management, 22–23
  productivity applications, 19
  summary of key applications for, *20*
  telematics, 35–38
  telephony account/subscription management, 42–46
  unified messaging and universal mailbox, 23–25
  vertical services for enterprise, 46–48
Mobile network, and deployment chain, 541
Mobile phones, 490
  and Bluetooth, 578
  and multimedia content, 570
  Short Message Service on, 489
Mobile portals, 60
Mobile Station Application Execution Environment
  and Third-Generation Protocol Project, 141
  WAP relationship with, 139, 141
Mobile terminals, 13
  design applications for display on, 388–389
  user interface design for display on, 386

Mobile users
  knowing, 403
  rise in, 15
Mobile visual mailbox, 45
Mobitex, 69
mode attribute, 182, 183–184
Model-view-controller, 560n5
Modems, 3
Modularity, 90, 113, 114–115
Moore, Geoffrey, 11n1
Moore's law, 76
Mosaic, 557n2
Motorola, 26, 95, 109
  Application Development Kit, 584
  Enhanced Control Cellular developed by, 91
  handset, *416*
Mouse, 386
Movie and theater tickets, 33
MP3 player, 570, 576
Multibyte integers, 280–281
Multimedia catalogs, 41
Multimedia entertainment, streaming, and
      broadcast, 40–41
Multimedia Expert Group, WAP Forum, 101
Multimedia messaging, 141, 578
Multimedia services, 39–41
Multimodal user interfaces, 572
Multimode application server, 560, *561*, 562
  and JavaServer Pages, 563
Multimode capabilities, 543
Multimode services, 555
multiple attribute, 248
Multiple authoring, 562
Multiple-choice select, 254, 255
  sample rendering of, IBM Wapsody, *252*
Multiple-choice selection list, *252–253*
Multiple context support, 538
Multiple latency bursts, 71
Multiway conference setup, 45
Must-Revalidate HTTP response, 194
MVC. *See* Model-view-controller

name attribute, 205, 207, 218, 236, 248, 254, 255,
      258, 259, 263, 272, 273
Named data, 339
Named meta-data, 339
Names
  for bindings, 206
  for cards, 174
  menu item, 401
Narrowband Sockets, 60, 67, 92. *See also* Wireless
      Transport Protocol
Naughton, Patrick, 84
Navigation, 150

  and anchored elements, 427
  between cards, *153*
  and explicit URLs, 461
  optimizing, to most important content, 404
  reassigning variable during, *190–191*
  and type attribute, 197
Navigation elements design, anchor and a
      elements, 422–423
Navigation functions, WMLBrowser library,
      364–366
Navigation history, 151
Navigation time, and menu structure, 400
NBS. *See* Narrowband Sockets
NeoPoint 1000, *416*
Nested tags, 179
Netscape Communications Corporation, and
      JavaScript, 83
Netscape Navigator, 562
  browsers, 459
NetTech Systems, ExpressQ from, 91
Network bandwidth, and run-time costs, 72–74
NetworkCharacteristics type, 482
Network-common libraries, 521, 522
  call logs, 524
  miscellaneous functions, 524
  network text message handling, 523
  phone book functions, 523–524
  voice control events, 522–523
  WTAI, 371, 372
Network-common services, within WTAI
      services, 121
Network connectivity
  decreasing costs for, 53
  restrictions and limitations with, 575
  variability in, 459
Network infrastructure
  communication between applications/services
        at each layer on, *105*
  end-to-end configurations of, 544
  WAP standard and behavior of, *102*
Network latency, 68, 570
  defined, 68
Network mapping, 527
Network services, and "roaming" problem, 78–79
Network-specific libraries, 521
  WTA, 525
  WTAI, 371, 372
Network-specific services, within WTAI services,
      121
Network text message handling, 521
  functions of, 523
Network text message service, 523
newcontext attribute, 155, 172–174, 190
  effect of specifying, *173*

newContext function, WMLBrowser library, 365–366
News, 28, 123, 490
"News on the move," 40
Nielsen, J., 408
Nihon Mobile Broadcasting Corporation, 37
Nocache helper application, *193*
Nokia, 26, 56, 95, 126
  browser and input field implementation, 245
  Narrowband Sockets from, 92
Nokia browser, simple document displayed by, *166*
Nokia browser simulator, 421, 422, 427, 449, 450
  anchor and a elements demonstrated with, *426*
  demonstrating do element, with accept and option events, *432*
  demonstrating input element, *440, 441*
  demonstrating select element, *447, 448*
  and title attribute, 453
Nokia phones, 56
Nokia 6150 Phone Simulator, 127
  WML and request for checking account balance, *128*
  WML and response to request for checking account balance, *133*
Nokia 7110 handset, *416*, 421, 452, 453
Nokia Smart Messaging Platform, 92
Nokia Smart Messaging Technology, 96
Nokia WAP Toolkit, 584
Nokia WAP Toolkit version 1.3beta, model Nokia 7110. *See* Nokia browser simulator
Nonbreaking
  with nowrap mode, 183
  space, 184, 187
Nontransparency, 546
noop element, 194–195, 593
noop task, 188, 207
Nortel, 96
Notebook tabs, 250
nowrap mode, 451
NTP, 118
NTT DoCoMo, 42
  i-mode service, 31, 552
Number (or numeric), 318
Numeric operands, rules for binary operators expecting, 319, 320
Numeric tokens, in WBXML document, 122

Object Database Connectivity, 560
Object Exchange protocol, 97
Object-oriented language, 83
Obstructions, 147
Octal values, 312
ODBC. *See* Object Database Connectivity

Offline information access, 123
onenterbackward attribute, 172
  binding to go task, 435
onenterbackward binding, 194, 197, 219
onenterbackward event, 198
onenterbackward event binding, and timers, 257
onenterforward attribute, 172
onenterforward binding, 190, 197, 219
  for initializing variables, *219–220*
onenterforward event, 198, 518
onenterforward event binding, and timers, 257
One-stop shopping, 55
onevent element, 195–196, 198–199, 435–436, 594
One-way paging, 109
Online auctions, market opportunities for, *34*
Online bill payment, 31
Online calendar application, 5
Online catalogs, 29
Online games, 41
Online intermediaries, 17
Online retailing, 30
Online shopping, multimedia catalogs for, 41
Online subscription management, 58
Online trading, 32–33
  growth in, *32*
Online virtual communities, 14
onpick attribute, 250
onpick binding, 198
onpick handler, 255–256
  example of, *256*
OnStar, 35, 36
ontimer attribute, 172
ontimer event, 198
  to initialize variables, *220*
Opaque data, 291, 292
Opaque token, 291
Open Group, The, 136
Operations control, 47
optgroup element, 247, 250–251, 454, 594
Optimizability, and WAP standard, 136
optional attribute, 206
option element, 198, 249, 250, 255, 594
Option index, 253
Options
  as entry in menu, *214*
  as request to display menu, *214*
Options binding, 215
Options do type, example of, *203–204*
Options menus, 209, 210
options parameter, Crypto library, 370
options type, 118, 202
option value, 253
option value sequence, 253
Oracle's 8i databases, 126

ordered attribute, 171–172, 242
ordered=false option, 453
ordered=true option, 453
Originating call model, 520, *521*
Originating call template, 534, *534*
Origin server, 126, 127
OTA. *See* Over-the-Air Protocol
Outgoing Call event, 520
Out-of-order delivery, in cellular systems, 70
Out-of-order Service Indications, 503
Overflow, 313
Overflow.wml, 313
Overriding, bindings, *205–206*
Over-the-air programming, 14
Over-the-Air Protocol, Push, 507–508
Over-the-air-provisioning, 44
Ovum, 23

Paap, K.R., 400
Packebush, S.J., 411
Packet-based networks, 68
    wireless, 511
Packet-based systems, and bearer selection, 529
Packets
    bearer network transmission of, 109
    and network latency, 69
    resequencing, 70
    TCP behavior and loss of, 71
    and WAP, 548
Padding, 223, 224
    column, 226, 227
Pagers, 6, 387, 415, 489, 490
    embedded browsers in, 147
    wireless Internet services on, ix
Paging/paging systems, 21, 489, 490
Palm Computing, 92
Palm.net service, 92
Palm Pilot, 47, 56, 552
PAMR. *See* Public Access Mobile Radio
PAN. *See* Personal area network
PAP. *See* Push Access Protocol
PAP message, 494
    processing of, by Push Proxy Gateway, 505
PAP Push Submission Request message
    first entity in, *495–496*
Paragraph element. *See* p element
Parameter list, 336
parameterlist field, 371
Parameters, 335
    passing, 336
Parentheses, and variables syntax, 217
parseFloat function, Lang library, 316, 343–344
parseInt function, Lang library, 316, 344, 382
Parser, and RDF tags, 467

Parsing
    address formats, 498
    URL library, 361–364
    URLs, 310
    and WBXML, 280
Partitioning, 530
"Password" control, 240
Passwords, and HTTP security, 266
path attribute, 265–266
Payment collection, 57
PDAs. *See* Personal Digital Assistants
PDC. *See* Personal Digital Cellular system
Peapod.com grocery ordering service, 42
p element, 181–182, 450–451, 595
Pelorus Group, 23
Pens, wireless, 157
Percent sign, format specification signaled with,
        352
Personal area network, 578, 579
Personal computer, 87
Personal Digital Assistants, xi, 4, 6, 19, 40, 55,
        387, 415
    and Bluetooth, 578
    mobile terminal connection to, 538
    price reduction for, 63
    and user profiles, 394
    wireless Internet services on, ix
Personal Digital Cellular system, 73, 109
Personal Handy Phone System, 73, 109
Personal information management, 14, 22–23
Personalization, 55, 401–403, 414, 418
    and keystroke reduction, 404
Personalized information, with mobile portals, 60
PersonalJava, 574
Person-to-person instant messaging, 123
Pharmacy services, 42
Philips, 96
Phonebook, 521
    functions of, 523–524
Phonecasting, 28
Phone.com, 56, 59, 91, 95, 117
    browser and input field implementation, 245
    50 percent rule, 404
    SDK, 166
    subscriber identifiers with browsers, 267
    UP.Link server, 126
Phone.com browser, 418
    simple document displayed by, *167*
Phone.com browser simulator, 422, 427, 449, 450
    anchor and a elements demonstrated with,
        423
    demonstrating do element, with accept and
        option events, *429*
    demonstrating input element, *438*

demonstrating select element, *445*
and title attribute, 453
Phone.com UP.SDK, 584
Phone.com UP.Simulator 3.2, 421
Phone.com UP.Simulator 4.0 Beta 2, model
    Alcatel One Touch, pocket. *See* Phone.com
    browser simulator
Phones, 415. *See also* Mobile phones; Wireless
    Telephony Applications
    designing for smaller, 418
    downloadable applications on, 575
    dropping prices for, 63
    embedded browsers in, 147
    feature setup and management, 46
    and user-entered text, 419
Photonet service (NTT DoCoMo), 39
PHS. *See* Personal Handy Phone System
Physical navigation versus logical navigation ,
    210–213
Physical style tags, 178
Piggybacking, 112
PIM. *See* Personal information management
PIs. *See* Processing instructions
Pixels, 386, 387
    image's size in, 225
PKI. *See* Public key infrastructure
Plain-text files, for WML documents, 159
"Platforms" phase, and Early Majority users, 15
PLMN. *See* Public Land Mobile Network
PMR. *See* Private Mobile Radio
PNG. *See* Portable Network Graphics
Pocket PC, 552
Pointer sticks, 157
Pointing devices, 387
Pokémon®, 38, 39
Polling loops, 76
Pop-up menus, 369
Portable Network Graphics, 222
Portal, 58, 59
Portal providers/vendors, 17, 60
Positive acceptance, 152
Postcards, electronic, 40
postfield element, 151, 192, 199, 262–263, 595
Postfix increment and decrement, 318, 326
POST method, 151
Post method, get method versus, 261–262
PostScript, 81
pow function, Float library, 348–349
PowWow (TribalVoice), 25
PPG. *See* WAP Push Proxy Gateway
Pragma pool, 383
    in binary WMLScript unit, 382, 383
Pragmas, 337–340
    access pragma, 338–339

url pragma, 337–338
WMLScript identifiers for naming, 321
Preamble, in WBXML document, 122
Precedence rules, 316, 318
Precision, 353
Precision specification, 352
Precision values, possible, *353*
Predictive text entry capability, 14
pre element, 185–186, 595
Prefixes, WML, 177, 178
Prefix increment and decrement, 318, 326
Preformatted text, 185–186
Prev
    accept action acting as, *211*
    defining binding for, 216
    element, 194, 230, 428, 595–596
    example of do type, *201–202*
    mystery, 215–216
    task, 153, 188
    type, 118, 201, 428
Privacy/private information
    and data push, 509
    and end-to-end security, 572–573
    and personalization, 403
    and RDF, 465n3
Private Mobile Radio, 73
Proactive services, 402
Processing instructions, 290–291
    encoding examples, *291*
Product development process, and usability
    testing, 411
Professionals, and mobile Internet, 4, 6–7
Profile composition, 469
    examples of, 477–488
    from multiple profile documents, 482–488
    from single profile document, 479–482
    steps in, 475
    at Web application server, 474–488
Profile-Diff header, 474, 475
    request header, 469–470
Profile header, 474, 475, 482
    request header, 469
Profiles, merging, 484, 486
Profile-Warning header, 472, 474
    response header, 470
Prologue, WML document, 167, 168
prompt function, Dialogs library, 369
Proposed specifications, 101, 102
Protocol converters, 104
Protocol features, 115
Protocol layering, within WAP architecture, *103*
Protocol parameters, 115
Protocols, collections of, 110
Protocol stack, evolution of WAP, *98*

Prototype-based inheritance, 83, 84
Prototype-based object model, 83
Prototyping, 454
  WML applications, 407
Proxies, 59, 104, 469
  WAP, 126
  Web, 126
Proxy-based solutions, 558
Pruning data, 564
Public Access Mobile Radio, 73
Public deck, 266
Public identifiers
  encoding of XML document using, *298–299*
  WBXML, 281–283
  WBXML 1.3
  well-known, *283*
Public key infrastructure, mobile Internet
    integration with, 573
Public Land Mobile Network, 498
Public libraries, WTAI, 371, 372
Public safety agencies, 46
Public services, within WTAI services, 120–121
Pulled applications, 531
Pull model, 489
Push Access Protocol, 492, 493–497, 514
  message format, 493–494
  over HTTP 1.1, 497
  protocol operations, 494–497
  Push Submission message, 493
Push buttons, 157, 199
Push Cancellation, 496
  operation, 496
  Response, 496
Push capabilities, 142
Pushed information, 569
Push Initiator, 491, 492, 493, 497, 498, 499, 514
  authentication of, 508–509
  control information, 494
  and Push Proxy Gateway, 505
  and Push Submission processing, 506
Push Message, 490, 499–501
  example, *500*, 500–501
  message format, 499
  MIME media types for, 501–505
Push Message format
  message body, 499
  message headers, 499
Push messaging, xiii, 123–124, 489–509
  MIME media types for Push Messages, 501–505
  overview of WAP Push, 490–493
  Push Access Protocol, 493–497
  Push Message, 499–501
  Push Over-the-Air Protocol, 507–508
  Push Proxy Gateway, 505–506

WAP Push addressing, 497–498
Push notification, 419
  to mobile devices, 33
Push Over-the-Air Protocol, 490, 492, 507–508
  Push connection modes, 507
  Session Initiation Application request, 508–509
  Trusted flag within, 508
Push services, popularity of, 490
Push specifications, 135
Push Status Query, 496
Push Status Query Response, 496, 498
Push Submission
  operation, 494, 495–496
  Response, 496, 497

Qualcomm, 108
Quality-of-service parameters, and Push Submis-
    sion operation, 495
Query interfaces, for retrieving profile attributes,
    477
Query parameters segment, of URL library, 364
Query string, 261, 262
Queued messaging, 576
Quote characters, in escape sequences, 314
Quote escaping, 163
QWERTY keypad, 387

Radicati Group, 24n2
Radio, short-range, 576
Radio-frequency spectrum, 72
RAM Mobile data network, 92
random function, Lang library, 344–345
RDF. *See* Resource Description Framework
Real estate applications, 41
Real-time design considerations, 528
Reassembly software, 70
Redish, J.C., 408
Redrawing cards, 153
Redundancy, elimination of, 134
Reencryption, 546, 573
Reference to pictures, in WML deck, 149
ReFlex protocol, 109
refresh element, 195, 230, 596
refresh function, WMLBrowser library, 367
refresh task, 153, 188
  and timers, 258–259
Relational operators, 325
Relative URLs, 161
Reliability, 107, 386
  and error rates, 74–76
removeAt function, String library, 357
Rendering
  cards, 149
  and ordered attribute, 171

and variability of WAP browsers, 415
replaceAT function, String library, 357–358
replace function, String library, 354
Replacement, Service Indication, 502
Replay attacks, 111
Repository, 512, 521, 530
    WTA, *514*
Request headers, 151
Request-response communication style,
    552
Request-response model, 114, 115, 489
    PAP operations based on, 495
RequestServlet, 129, 130
Requirements document, 101
reset type, 118, 204
Resolution rules, 475, 477
    append, 477
    locked, 475
    override, 475
Resolve function, URL library, 361
Resource Description Framework, 465
    final graph created by merging profiles, *487*
    graph of merged profile, *483*
    graph of profile conveyed by transcoding
        proxy, *486*
    graph of profile sent by client, *480*
    schemas, 466
    tags, 467
Resources, 512, 530
Response headers, 154
Response time, 69
Restaurant reservations, 7
resultlist, 371, 372
Result Notification, 497
    message, 498
    operations, 494
Result Notification Response, 497
ResultSet, 130
Retailing, online, 30
Return statement, in WMLScript, 334
return statement, 336
Reuters, 28
Reverse navigation, in WML, 152
RICOCHET, 92
Right alignment, 451
Right-to-left languages, WML table orientation, 226
Right-to-left paragraph alignment, 183
Ringing state, 520
Ring tone composer (harmonium), 56
Roadside assistance, *12*
Roaming, and network services, 78–79
Rocker switches, 157
round function, Float library, 349
Round-Trip Time, 71

Rows
    table cells organized into, 228
    in WML tables, 225
RTT. *See* Round-Trip Time
Rubin, J., 408
Rugg, G., 400
Run-time costs, bandwidth and, 72–74

Sales force automation, 48, 61
Sametime (Lotus), 26
SBC, 25
Scalability, 78
Scheme attribute, 273
S-Confirmed Push, 507
Screens
    clutter reduction, 406
    complicated, 419
    on different browsers, 167
    and ordered attribute, 171, 172
    and paragraph formatting, 182
    relative resolutions for large computer
        and handheld, *387*
    small, 147
    splash, 259
    touch, 157, 171
    and WML, 156–157
Script, 149. *See also* WMLScript
Scripting, ix, 83–84, 87
Scripting interfaces, 519
    for WTA applications, 521–525
ScriptMsg variable, 380
Scrolling
    and lists, 419
    and mode attribute, 183
    times square, 418
    in WML tables, 225
SCRs. *See* Static conformance requirements
SDKs. *See* Software Development Kits
Search engines, 59
Second-generation (2G) networks, 13n2
Secure Hash Algorithm, 371
Secure Sockets Layer, ix, 111, 551, 573. *See also*
        Transport Layer Security
Secure transactions, 30
Secureway Wireless Gateway, 91
Security, 107, 142, 173, 219, 517, 547, 573
    application, 264–266
    attacks, 111
    and datagram-layer linking, 554
    and deployment chain, 541
    end-to-end, 543
    HTTP, 266–267
    and session-layer linking, 553
    smart-card technology for, 14

Security *continued*
  and telematics, 35
  variable, 267–272
  for WAP service deployment, 548
  WTA server and, 525–526
Security domains, 545–548
  interdomain trust, 545–546
  WAP gateway implications for trust models, 546–547
  WAP protocol tunneling, 548
Security layer, 97, 111
seed function, Lang library, 345
Select element, 235, 247, 443
  browser differences, 443–444
  and default value determination, 253–255
  Ericsson browser simulator demonstrating, *446*
  Nokia browser simulator demonstrating, *447, 448*
  Phone.com browser simulator demonstrating, *445*
  user interface design guidelines, 449–450
  use of, 251–253
Selection lists, 247
  initialization of, 254–255
  menus contrasted with, 256
  multiple-choice, *252–253*
  single-choice, *251–252*
Selective encryption, 573
select, 596
select list
  and option element, 249
  user interface design guidelines for, 449–450
Semicolons, 249, 253, 311, 371
Send DTMF Tones function, 373
senderferer attribute, 165, 191–192
Separability principle, 104, 135
Sequence identifiers, for packets, 69
seq variable, 380
Serial cables, 576
Server certificates, 111
Server setup, for WML browsers, 159–160
Server-side applications, for WAP environment, 555, 557
Server-side application server programming, 159
Server-side certificates, 573
Service abstraction, 109, 110
Service aggregation, 57
Service bureaus, 53, 58, 60, 61
Service concept, 527
Service definition, 392–393
Service design, 527
Service developer
  application design considerations for, 530
  and phonebook applications, 523

and WTA application development, 527
Service indication, 493, 499, 500, 501
  features of, 502–503
  message, *503*
  usage, 503
Service integration, 543–544
Service interfaces, 104
Service-level agreements (SLAs), 547
Service Loading, 493, 503–505
  message, *505*
  usage, 504–505
  user-intrusiveness levels, 504
Service provider
  content provider synonymous with, 62
  and design, 391
  WAP content generated by, 554–555
Service requirements, 78–79
Services hosting, 57
Servlets, 58
Session Initiation Application, 493, 508
  request, 507–508
Session layer, linking WAP and Internet at, 548, *550*, 552–53
Session protocols, 142
Sessions, 113
  establishment and teardown, 80
  within WAP standard, 113–114
setvar element, 219, 596
setVar function, WMLBrowser library, 367–368
Set variables, 217
SGML. *See* Standard Generalized Markup Language
Short circuit evaluation, 325
Short Message Service, 12, 21, 69, 73, 109, 489, 490, 523, 529, 577
Short-range radio, 576
Short-term memory, 413, 414
SI. *See* Service Indication
SIA. *See* Session Initiation Application
Siemens, 96
signal-high, 502
signal-low, 502
signal-medium, 502
signText function, Crypto library, 369–370
SIM card, 572
Simple Mail Transfer Protocol, 491
Simple RDF Parser and Compiler, 479
Single-choice select, 254, 255
  sample rendering of, Ericsson SDK, *252*
Single-choice selection list, *251–252*
SiRPAC. *See* Simple RDF Parser and Compiler
Site-based content filtering, 126
size attribute, 239
SL. *See* Service Loading

small element, 451, 597
Small-screen devices, designing effective content
    for users with, 551
Smart Card Expert Group, WAP Forum, 101
Smart-card technology, 14, 34–35
Smart phones, 55
SMS. *See* Short Message Service
SMTP. *See* Simple Mail Transfer Protocol
Soft hyphens, 184, 450–451
Soft keys, 118, 208, 369
    accept binding assigned to, *208*
Software Development Kits, 156, 159
    and infinite loops, 378
    prototyping WML applications with, 407
    and WTA application development, 527
Software life-cycle costs, and unmet/unseen user
    requirements, 386
Software providers, and mobile Internet
    standard, 93, 94
Sonera, 42
Spaces, in elements, 163
Special characters, 163
    WML, 176–177
Specification Committee, WAP Forum, 100
Specification Working Group, WAP Forum, 101
Speech generation, automatic, 570
Speech recognition
    character-based, 157
    technology, 46
Splash screen, 259
Spread-spectrum technology, 109
S-Push, 507
sp variable, 380
Spyglass, Mosaic from, 557n2
sqrt function, Float library, 349
squeeze function, String library, 354–355
src attribute, 224, 287
SSL. *See* Secure Sockets Layer
SSL/TLS, 124
Stack bridging, 552
Stand-alone tokens, 290
Standard Generalized Markup Language, 81, 82
StarTAC-D phone, 35
State machine, 111
State management model, 119
Statements, WMLScript, 329–335
    break statement, 333–334
    compound, 329
    continue statement, 333–334
    empty statement, 334–335
    expression statements, 329
    for statements, 332–333
    if-else statements, 331–332
    return statements, 334

var statements, 330–331
    while statements, 332
State transition. *See* Finite state machine
Static conformance requirements, 136
Static content generation, 275
Static decks, 175
    and absolute URLs, 161
Static pages, 275, 276
Status messages, 414
Stealth menu, accept binding on, *209*
Stock prices alerts, 123, 490
Strategis Group, 12, 35, 36, 55, 56, 60
Strategy Analytics, 17
Streaming
    audio and video, 40, 578
    data, 570
    real-time content, 571
Strength of capability information, 469
String, *352*
    concatenation, 318, 320
    converted to integer, 317
    converted to floating-point values, 317
String Library, 327, 607–611
    charAt function, 350
    compare function, 350
    core string functions, 350–351
    elementAt function, 356
    elements function, 356
    find function, 350–351
    format function, 351
    insertAt function, 357
    isEmpty function, 353–354
    length function, 354
    list functions, 355–358
    removeAt function, 357
    replaceAt function, 357–358
    replace function, 354
    squeeze function, 354–355
    toString function, 316, 355, 377, 381
    trim function, 355
String literals, 313–314
String operands, rules for binary operators
    expecting, 320–321
String operators, 327
String representation, conversions to,
    316–317
String table
    in WBXML document, 122
    in WBXML file, 284
String values, and RDF, 466
strong element, 451, 597
STR_I token, 289
STR_T token, 289
Style tags, 179

Subscriber identifiers, 267
Subscription-based services, 17
Sun Microsystems, and development of Java
  programming language, 85
S-Unit-Push, WSP service primitives, 507
"Super-user" access, 546n1
Supply chain management, 61
Surveillance, 40
Surveys, 396
s variable, declaration for, 330
Swissair, 33
SWITCH_PAGE token, 292
Symmetric layers, 104
Syntax, 159
 for accessing value of variable, 217
 WML conventions, 164–166

tab control, 241
tabindex attribute, 241, 249
table element, 452, 597
 use of, *226*
Tables, 119
 and anchored text, 452
 sample rendering of, Nokia SDK, *227*
 WML, 225–229
Tag codes, 286–287
 structure of, *287*
Tags
 elements identified by, 162
 HTML support of, 81
 layout and images, 119
 RDF, 467
Tag tokens, 285
Tailoring content to client, 459–488
 Composite Capability/Preference Profiles,
  465–471
 profile composition at Web application server,
  474–488
 putting it all together, 473–474
 standard capability negotiation mechanism,
  464–473
 techniques using HTP 1.1, 461–464
 User Agent Profiles, 471–473
Tamagochi, 39
Task analysis, 393, 396–398
Tasks, 188, 189–195
 accept-charset attribute, 192
 backward navigation—prev element, 194
 binding user-initiated event to, *200*
 cache-control attribute, 193
 defined, 188
 enctype attribute, 192–193
 events linked to, 149, 195–207
 failure, 275

forward navigation—go element, 189–191
 href attribute, 191
 method attribute, 192
 noop element, 194–195
 refresh element, 195
 sendreferer attribute, 191–192
TCP, 124
TCP behavior
 with high-latency environments, 70–71
 improving, 71–72
TCP/IP, xiv
 effect of latency on, 70
 protocol connectivity, 78
td element, 228, 229, 598
TDM, 109
TDMA. *See* Time Division Multiple Access
Technology Adoption Life Cycle framework, 11
Technology drivers, 12–14
Tegic, 26
Telematics, 35–38
 world forecast, *37*
Telematics Expert Group, WAP Forum, 101
Telephones. *See* Phones
Telephony, 124
 account and subscription management,
  42–46
 enhanced applications, 44–46
 link between data and, 142
Telephony events, with WTA application
  programming interface, 519–520
Television industry, 571
Telnet, 112
Template, default prev binding using, *197*
Template bindings, hiding, 189
template element, 188, 197, 198, 206–207
Templates
 terminating call, *532*
 WML document, 167
Terminal manufacturers, 55
Terminals, 55
Terminal vendors, 56
Terminating call application, finite state model's
  depiction of, *536–537*
Terminating call model, 520–521, *522*
Terminating call template, 532
Ternary operator, 328
test expression, 332, 333
Testing
 interoperability, 136
 interpreters, 374
 usability, 408–411, 417, 454
 user, 551–552
 WML, 159
 WML application, 156

and WMLScript conversion problems, 377
and WTA application development, 527–528
TETRA. *See* Trans-European Trunked Radio
Tetris, 39
Text
  alignment, 181
  input devices, 387
  messaging, 21
  p element and display of, 450–451
  searching and user-entered, 419
  WML, 176–180
Text format, Service Loading in, 504
Text message handling network, 523
Thin-client mobile devices, 13
Third-generation network, 13n2, 141, 571, 577–57,
    579
Third-Generation Partnership Project
  and Mobile Station Application Execution
      Environment, 141
  WAP relationship with, 139, 141
3G. *See* Third-generation network
3GPP. *See* Third Generation Partnership Project
Time Division Multiple Access, 108
Timeout, 70
timer element, 190, 257–258, 598
Timer response algorithms, 76
Timers, 278
  browser-supported, 118
  and refresh, 220, 258–259
  simple demonstration, *259–260*
  and variables, 217
Times Square scrolling, 183, 418
title attribute, 170–171, 228, 232, 241, 249, 250, 251,
    261, 423, 442, 452–453
Tokens. *See also* Binary WML
  assignment of, 297
  global, 285, 288–292
  integer data, 290
  with string data, 290
  WBXML, 284
Toolbars, 199
"Tools" phase, and Early Adopters, 15
Tools vendors, and mobile Internet standard,
    93, 94
Toshiba, and IVIS systems, 37
toString function, String library, 316, 355, 377, 381
Touch screens, 157, 171
Toyota, and IVIS systems, 37
Trackball, 386
Traffic alert application
  personalization for, 402
  possible scheme for, 404, *405*
  and prototyping, 408
  and user profile, 393–395

Traffic and navigation, *12*
Traffic information, 5, 14, 28
Transactional model, WTP-enabled, 112
Transactional TCP, 112
Transaction-based applications, 60
Transcoders, 406
Transcoding functions, 474
Transcoding proxies, 482, 557, 558, 562, 573
  and content conversion, 488
  profile asserted by, *484*
  RDF graph of profile conveyed by, *486*
Trans-European Trunked Radio, 73–74
Transitive trust, 508
Transport Level Security
  protocol, 111
  and WAP standard, 139
Transport protocols, effect of latency on, 70
Trapping events, 195–196, 199–200, 528
Travel Web sites, and WML support, 146
tr element, 228, 599
trim function, String library, 355
Trust. *See also* Security
  chain of, between user and application, 547
  interdomain, 545–546
  models, 488, 546–547
  and WTA server, 526
Trusted content, and Push Initiator authentication,
    508–509
Trusted flag, 508
Trusted URI list, 508
Truth values, 314
T/TCP, and WAP standard, 139
Tunneling, 548
  gateway, *549*
  of WAP protocols to WAP gateway, 553–554
Tunneling protocol configuration, with
    datagram-layer linking, 554
Two-way paging, 109, 415
type attribute, 197–198, 200–205, 240
  and do element, 428
Type code, 352, 353
  in format specification, 352
Type conversions, in WMLScript, 316–318
typeof operator, 328–329
typeof return values, *329*
type password, 443
Types, variables not bound to, *315*
Type values, possible, *352*

UAProf. *See* WAP User Agent Profiles
UAProf mechanism, 372
UAProf schema, 472–473
UAProf vocabulary, example attributes from, *478*
UDP. *See* User Datagram Protocol

UDP/IP protocol connectivity, 78
u element, 451, 599
UMC. *See* Unified Messaging Consortium
UMTS. *See* Universal Mobile Telecommunication
     System
Unary arithmetic operators, 324
  rules for, in WMLScript, 318
Unconfirmed Push, 506, 507
Underflow, 313
Underlining, 119, 179
Underscores, and anchored text, 451
unescapeString function, 361
Unicode, 177
  character encoding, 137
Unicode 2.0, subsets of, 180
Unified messaging forecast, *24*
Unified Messaging Consortium, 23
Uniform Resource Locators, ix, 191. *See also*
     URL Library
  absolute, 161
  and calling WMLScript from WML, 337
  content identified by, 160
  for end-to-end WAP request, 128, 129
  explicit, 461
  protecting, 266
  relative, 161
  and sendreferer attribute, 192
  WML content identified by, 160
  WMLScript and parsing of, 310
Uniform Resource Name, 151n2
United Kingdom, mobile banking in, 31
United States
  online users in, 3
  rise in mobile users in, 15
  wireless portal use in, 60
Universal mailbox, 23, 24
Universal Mobile Telecommunication System,
     73, 109, 529, 571
unknown type, 204
Unsecured connection, and hacking, 266
Unwired Planet, 91, 95, 96, 117. *See also*
     Phone.com
Unwrapped lines, avoiding, 418
Updating context, refresh element, 195
URL escaping, 220–221
URL Library, 358–364, 611–614
  escapeString function, 358–359
  getBase function, 359
  getFragment function, 362
  getHost function, 362
  getParameters function, 362–363
  getPath function, 363
  getPort function, 363
  getReferer function, 359

  getScheme function, 364
  isValid function, 359–360
  loadString function, 360
  parsing functions, 361–364
  query and manipulation functions, 358–361
  resolve function, 361
  return query parameters segment of, 364
  unescapeString function, 361
url pragma, 336, 337–338
URLs. *See* Uniform Resource Locators
URL.unescapeString, 381
URN. *See* Uniform Resource Name
Usability
  aspects of, 389, 390
  problems with, 390
  structured methods, 390–391
Usability testing, 408–411, 417, 454
Usage drivers, 14–15
Usage-sensitive services, 385
US-ASCII, 180, 192, 293, 325
Use cases, 398
use keyword, pragmas introduced with, 337
User agent, 155
  data, 339
  header, 462–463
  meta-data, 340
User Agent Profiles, 123
  WAP, 471–473
User Datagram Protocol, 71, 124
  and service abstraction, 110
  and WAP standard, 139
User-defined identifiers, 498
User errors, 75–76
User-gateway trust relationships, 547
User-initiated event, 188
  binding task to, *200*
  trapping, 199–200
User input elements, 436
User interface (UI)
  appearance and presentation guidelines for,
     450–454
  elements, 149
  guidelines, 454
  importance of, 385
User interface design, 385–455
  design process, 392–412
  design team, 391
  guidelines, 412–419
  guidelines for selected WML elements,
     420–423, 427–429, 433–437, 442–444,
     449–454
  as science and art, 454
  for small WAP devices, 384
  structured usability methods, 390–412

for usable WAP sites, 389–390
Web site design: computer terminals versus
    mobile terminals, 386–389
User interface design guidelines, general, 412–414
User-intrusiveness, 502, 503, 504
User language independence, and Principle of
    Global Use, 137
User location, and proxies, 558
User profile, 393–395, 409. *See also* Personalization
    partial summary, *395*
Users
    changes in, 87
    mobile terminal, 388
    task analysis of, 396–398
    and testing, 551–552
UTF-8, 180
UTF-16, 180

Validating default option index, 253–254
value attribute, 218, 236, 248, 249, 258, 259, 263
Value chain, 54, 55
    business models within, 543
    for delivering services to end users, 52
    end-to-end business, 541
    and interdomain trust, 546
    members within, 541, *542*, 564
Values
    and attribute codes, 287
    for attributes, 165
    example of, at every level, *405*
    returning of, by functions, 336
Variable conversion modes, *221*
Variables, 151, 217–221, 278
    and browser content, 275
    declarations, 330–331
    escaping, 220–221
    initial initialization of, 219–221
    reassigning during navigation, *190–191*
    securing, 267–272
    using, 218–219
    WMLScript identifiers for naming, 321
Variable security techniques, parts 1 and 2,
    269–271
var statement, 315, 316
    in WMLScript, 330–331
vCalendar, 122, 126
vCard, 122, 126
Vehicles, telematics in, 35
Vendor-specific bindings, 206
Vendor types, 204
Version number, WBXML, 281
Vertical applications, 14
Vertical markets, wireless data applications for, 60
Vertical portals, 53

Video cameras, attachment of to phones, 570
Videoconferences, 14, 40
Video mail, 40
Video recording, for usability tests, 410–411
Virtual communities, online, 14
Virtual machine technologies, 575
Visual-Age Micro Edition, 575
Visual Basic, 83
Visual mailbox, mobile, 45
Vocabularies
    RDF, 466
    WAP UAProf specification defining of, 472
Voice, 543
    data integrated with, 511
    integration of XHTML and, 572
    packets, 578
    recognition, 46, 570
Voice browsers/browsing, 46, 571
    and telematics, 37
Voice control events, functions of, 522
Voice mail, 6, 23, 45, 538
    notifications, 490
Voice telephony, asynchronous notification
    features integrated with, 11
VoiceXML, 562
vspace attribute, 224

WAE. *See* Wireless Applications Environment
"Walled garden" approach, 57
WAP. *See* Wireless Application Protocol
WAP, Web, and Internet Consistency principle,
    138–139
WAP application servers, 559–560
    separate Web application servers and, *559*
    Web application server merged with, 560,
        562
WAP architecture, 90
    layering advantages with, 104
    overview of, 102–107
    services and applications, *103*
WAP architecture design principles, 132–139
    flexible deployability, 134
    flexible implementability, 136
    global use, 136–137
    separability, 135
WAP browsers
    text-based, 176
    variability of, 415, 417
WAP certificate format, 573
WAP client, 125, 127
    addressing, 498
    Push Message targeted to, 494
    schema, and vocabulary, for describing, 471,
        472–473

WAP client   *continued*
   transitive trust between Push Proxy Gateway
     and, 508
   WSP used to establish session between WAP
     gateway and, *114*
WAP client device, 128–129
   and response flow, 132
WAP client support, 124–132
   end-to-end WAP request, 127–132
   WAP deployment chain, 124–127
WAP Developer Group, 101, 586
WAP devices
   categories of, 415
   variability of, 414–415
WAP-enabled services, 541
WAP Forum, 41, 90, 95, 97, 120, 135, 147, 369,
     421, 585
   architecture group, 133
   and backward navigation in WML, 152
   binary encoding defined by, 279
   and convergence with the Web, 571
   current status of, 100–102
   going public, 98–99
   membership in, 100
   other groups related to, 141
   push drafting committee charter, 490–491
   and relationships to other standards, 139
   subgroups within, 100–101
   and UAProf specification, 140
   updates through, 277
   and variety of devices supporting WML,
     155
   and WAP Push Protocols, 492
   and WAP standard integration, 138
   and WML versioning, 148
WAP fulfillment chain, summary of, *52*
WAP gateway, 58, 59, 125, 127, 129, 132, 279,
     527, 544
   and Bluetooth, 578
   CC/PP profile asserted by, *485*
   and "chain of trust," 573
   and deployment chain, 541
   and Document Type Definition, 274
   HTTP headers handled by, 464
   and image scaling, 225
   implications for trust models, 546–547
   profile introduced by, *484*
   protocol with tunneling, *553*
   and request processing, 129
   and response flow, 132
   and security, 525, 526
   WSP used to establish session between WAP
     client and, *114*
   and WTA server, 512

WAP interface, transition from Web-based
     interface to, *556*
WAP Interim Naming Authority, 101, 498
WAPLinks, 586
WAPman (The Wireless Edge), 585
WAP media types, *160*
WAP.net, 586
WAP 1.1 UAProf specification, components/
     attributes defined by, 617–622
WAP phones, 555
WAP protocol stack, evolution of, *98*
WAP protocol stack layers, Internet protocol stack
     layers compared to, *106*
WAP protocol tunneling, 548
WAP proxy, 126, 127
WAP Push, 116n6, 126, 473, 504, 509
   framework, 491–492, *492*
   goals of, 491
   overview of, 490–493
   protocols, 492
   Push-specific content types, 493
WAP Push Addressing, 497–498
   application addressing, 498
   WAP client addressing, 498
WAP Push Proxy Gateway, 135, 490, 492, 493, 494,
     497, 505–506, 514, 525, 527
   complete PAP Push Submission Request
     message to, *500–501*
   message delivery, 506
   and Push Over-the-Air Protocol, 507
   Push Submission, 495, 505–506
   transitive trust between WAP client and, 508
   and WAP client addressing, 498
WAP service delivery chain, roles between
     potential contributors to, *544*
WAP service design, 554–564
   adapting existing HTML interface, 557–558
   comparing xml/XSL and JavaServer pages, 564
   eXtensible Markup Language, 562–563
   JavaServer Pages, 563
   multimode application servers, 560, 562
   WAP application servers, 559–560
WAP sites design, 389–390
Wapsody browser, 166, *167*, 185, 243, 252, 584
WAP-specific headers, in Push Message, 499
WAP standard, 141–142
   application environment, 116–124
   bearer adaptation, 107, 108–110
   and bearer independence, 137
   components of, 107–124
   consistency with Web and Internet
     architectures, 138–139
   efficient encoding, 115–116
   evolution of, 99–100

modularity, 114–115
relationship of, to other standards, 139–141
releases, 277
service protocols, 107, 111–113
sessions, 113–114
worldwide languages supported by, 137–138
WAP State Management specification, 267
WAP user agent, 574
WAP User Agent Profiles, xiii, 123, 459, 465,
   471–473, 488, 577
   binary encoding of CC/PP documents,
      471, 472
   capabilities and preferences information in, 494
   end-to-end architecture for, *473*
   mapping of CC/PP Exchange Protocol to WSP,
      471, 472
   and profile composition algorithm, 477–479
   UAProf schema, 471, 472–473
WAP/WTA protocol stack, *515*
Warburg Dillon Read, 17
WBMP. *See* Wireless Bitmap
WBMP Creator, 586
WBXML. *See* Wireless Binary eXtensible Markup
   Language
WBXML document content, 285–292
   attribute codes, 287–288
   character entities, 289
   code pages, 285–286
   control codes, 292
   extension tokens, 289–290
   global tokens, 288–292
   literals, 288–289
   opaque data, 291
   processing instructions, 290–291
   strings and string references, 289
   tag codes, 286–287
   tokens, 285
WBXML document structure, 281–284
   charset, 283–284
   header, 281
   public identifier, 281–283
   string table, 284
   version number, 281
WBXML 1.2 document structure, *282*
WDP. *See* Wireless Datagram Protocol
WDP bindings, and WAP standard, 137
Weakly typed language, WMLScript as, 315
Weather forecasts, 5, 28–29
Web application server, 126, 129, 130–132
   checking account balance query via, 127, 128
   and profile composition, 474–488
   and request processing, 129–130
   and response flow, 130
   WAP application server merged with, 560, 562

Web-based interface, transition from WAP
   interface to, *556*
Web browsers/browsing, xiv
   on cellular phone, 5
   and history, 151–152
   WML browsing contrasted with, 158
Web-capable mobile phones, Internet connection
   via, 15
Web clients, Web proxy for, 126
Web content publishing, 63
Web designers, challenges facing, 565
Web hosting, 61
Web identity, 53
Web marketplace, historical trends affecting, 53
Web pages, and HTTP, 80
Web proxies, 126, 127, 543
Webraska, 28
Web scripting languages, 83–84
Web servers, 58, 543
Web site design, computer terminals versus
   mobile terminals, 386–389
Web site mapping, and RDF, 465n3
Web sites
   differences between WML- and HTML-based,
      386–389, 406
   requirements for receiving information from,
      51
WebSphere Studio (IBM), 59
WebSphere Transcoding Publisher, 557n2
Web tablets, 464
Web Traffic Express, 126
Web TVs, 464
while loop, 334
while statement
   loop example, *332*
   in WMLScript, 332
Whitespace, 164, 187–188
   and images, 222
   in links, 234, *234*
   and String library, 349
   and WBXML encoding process, 292
   in WMLScript, 311
   and xml:space attribute, 186
White wireless bitmap format, 222
width attribute, 225
Width specification, 352
WINA. *See* WAP Interim Naming Authority
Wingspan Investment Services, 26
Wireless Application Protocol, ix, xii, 7, 12–13, 18,
   19, 87
   abbreviations, 623–626
   architecture design principles, 132–141
   browsers, 585
   components of WAP standard, 107–124

Wireless Application Protocol *continued*
   development tools, 583–584
   emergence of, 89
   future of, 579
   heterogeneity encouraged by, 459
   initiation of, 95–98
   and Internet linkage, 548–554
   mobile e-mail enabled by, 22
   mobile Internet enabled by, 569
   network infrastructure services supporting
      WAP clients, 124–132
   origins of, 90–102
   overview of, 89–142
   overview of architecture for, 102–107
   personal information management enabled
      by, 22
   resources, 585–586
   and use on variety of mobile terminals, 387
   value chain, 16–17
   and Web convergence, 571–572
Wireless applications, current Web technologies
     for, 79–80
Wireless Applications Environment, 116–124, 371,
     514
   common application content formats, 122–123
   "deck of cards" document structure, 117
   device-independent man-machine interface,
      118–119
   document caching model, 118
   intradeck and interdeck navigation model,
      117–118
   layout and images, 119
   push messaging, 123–124
   state management model, 119
   user-agent profiles, 123
   Wireless Binary XML, 121–122
   Wireless Markup Language, 116–117
   Wireless Markup Language Script, 119–120
   Wireless Telephony Applications, 120–121, 512
Wireless application users
   issues encountered by, *68*
Wireless application writing, 87
Wireless Binary eXtensible Markup Language, xiii,
     121–122, 124, 125, 276, 278, 279–306, 574
   binary WML, 300–306
   content, 285–292
   content structure, 280–281
   document structure, 281–284
   encoding process, 292–299, 472
   overview of, 279–280
   Service Indication in, 501
   Service Loading in, 504
   standard, 117
Wireless Bitmap, 122, 124, 512, 570

Wireless communications. *See also* Wireless
     Application Protocol; Wireless
     Telephony Applications
   convergence between Internet and, 18
   popularity of, xi
Wireless data connections, speed issues, 147
Wireless data connectivity. *See also* Wireless
     Application Protocol
   unifying, 89
Wireless Datagram Protocol, 109, 124
   port, 526
   service abstraction, 110
Wireless data market, 1997, *94*
Wireless design applications, as departure from
     wireline perceptions, 398
Wireless device constraints, 76–78
Wireless devices, ix
   diversity of facilities on, 77
Wireless e-mail, 21
Wireless financial services, 31
Wireless industry
   convergence between online information
      industry and, 9
   growth of, 9
Wireless information appliance, 87
Wireless Internet access provider, 56–58
Wireless Internet standard, x
Wireless ISP, 58
Wireless links, error distribution over, 75
Wireless Markup Language, xiii, 116–117, 126,
     145–278, 509, 539, 551, 570, 574. *See also*
     Enhanced WML
   application security, 264–272
   basic content, 176–188
   basics of, 166–176
   binary, 300–306
   content converted into, 124
   content generation, 275–276
   controls, 235–256
   and convergence of HTML, 140
   and convergence of XHTML, 572
   document type declarations, 273–274
   errors and browser limitations, 274–275
   events, tasks, bindings, 188–217
   exchanging data with, 381–382
   influences on, 147–148
   integration of HTML, XML, and 571
   markup basics, 161–166
   miscellaneous markup, 257–261
   and Nokia 6150 phone simulator request for
      checking account balance, *128*
   and Nokia 6150 phone simulator response to
      request for checking account balance,
      133

other content to include, 221–234
other data: meta element, 272–273
overview of, 145–149
sending information, 261–263
summary of elements and attributes, 587–599
template for debugging, 375
URLs identifying content, 160–161
and variables, 217–221
versions of, 148, 488
WML authoring, 159–160
WML document model, 149–158
WMLScript called from, 381
WML version negotiation, 276–277
WTA applications developed using, 512
Wireless Markup Language Script. *See*
    WMLScript
Wireless middleware solutions, 91–92
    Airmobile, 92
    ExpressQ, 91
    Handheld Device Markup Language, 91–92
    Handheld Device Transport Protocol, 91–92
    Narrowband Sockets, 92
    Secureway Wireless Gateway (IBM), 91
Wireless network addresses, 498
Wireless network infrastructures, common,
    108–109
Wireless network latencies, side effects, 69
Wireless networks, constraints on, ix
Wireless operator, 56
Wireless pens, 157
Wireless phones, 9, 14
Wireless Session Protocol, 98, 111, 112–113,
    124, 492
    and mapping of CC/PP Exchange protocol, 472
    primitives, 490
    Push Over-the-Air Protocol on top of, 507
Wireless subscriber benefits, ix
Wireless TCP, 140
Wireless Telephony Applications, xiii, 116n6, 121,
    126, 473, 509, 511–539
    application creation toolbox, 531–535
    design considerations, 527–531
    future WTA enhancements, 535–538
    logical architecture, *513*
    overview of WTA architecture, 512–514
    repository, *514*
    security model, *526*
    user agent, 384
    WTA client framework, 514–525
    WTA server nd security, 525–526
Wireless Telephony Applications Interface,
    120–121, 160, 307, 371–374
    Add Phonebook Entry function, 374–375
    error codes, *372*

Make Call function, 373
    overview of, 371
    public library, 521
    Send DTMF Tones function, 373
Wireless Telephony Applications specifications,
    135
Wireless Transaction Protocol, 111, 112, 124
Wireless Transport Layer Security, 98, 111–112,
    124, 514, 551
Wireless Transport Protocol, 98
Wireless World Wide Web, x
Wireline networks, and bearer independence, 137
WML. *See* Wireless Markup Language
WML application developer, 156
WML applications, 149
    prototyping, 407
WML authoring, 159–160
WMLBrowser.go() function, 535
WMLBrowser Library, 614–616
    getCurrentCard function, 366
    getVar function, 367
    go function, 365
    navigation functions, 364–366
    newContext function, 365
    other functions in, 366–368
    prev function, 366
    refresh function, 367
    setVar function, 367–368
WML browsers/browsing, 155–158
    and content display, 157–158
    controlling, 157
    scrolling behavior, 183
    support for HTTP Basic Authentication
        mechanism by, 266
    variety of devices run on, 155
    Web browsing contrasted with, 158
WML cards, deck of, *150*
WML content, for end-to-end WAP request, 128
WML controls, 235–256
    accesskey attribute, 241
    and default value determination, 253–255
    emptyok attribute, 238–239
    format attribute, 236–238
    format code usage, 247
    input element, 235, 241
    and input field initialization, 241–242
    maxlength attribute, 240
    multiple attribute, 248
    name attribute, 236, 248
    onpick attribute, 250
    onpick handlers, 255–256
    optgroup element, 250–251
    option element, 249
    rendering/operation of input fields, 242–247

WML controls   *continued*
  and select controls, 251–253
  select element, 247
  select list values during processing, 255
  size attribute, 239
  tabindex attribute, 241, 249
  title attribute, 241, 249, 250, 251
  type attribute, 240
  value, iname, and ivalue attributes, 248–249
  value attribute, 236, 249
WML deck, 162, 166, 276, 512
  and finite state machine, 535
  in originating call template, *532*
WML design guidelines, 417–420
  appearance and presentation, 450–454
  browser differences, 423–426, 428, 436, 443–444
  navigation, 422–423
  for selected elements, 420–454
  user interface design guidelines, 427–428,
      433–436, 449–450
WML document model, 149–158
  and cache value, 154–155
  and navigation, 150
  and navigation history, 151–152
WML documents
  anatomy of, *168*
  images, 221–225
  links, 229–234
  tables, 225–229
WML file, 530
  and action/event construct, 531
  in originating call template, *533*
wml, 599
WML link, 230
WML markup basics, 161–166
  attributes, 162–163
  elements, 162
  id and class, 163
  syntax conventions, 164–166
  whitespace, 164
  xml:lang attribute, 163–164
WML named character entities, *176*
WMLScript, xiii, 119–120, 122, 124, 125, 126, 154,
      189, 276, 278, 307, 509, 570, 574, 577
  and action/event construct, 531
  application-level security with, 264
  calling from WML, 381–382
  compilation, 553
  content converted into, 124
  Crypto Library, 307, 384
  date checking with, *309–310*
  development, 374–382
  ECMAScript contrasted with, 310–311
  and href attribute, 191
  language basics, 311–340
  reserved words, *321*
  simple example, 308–310
  simple validation routing in, *309*
  standard libraries, 311
  string conversion rule in, *321*
  template for debugging, 376–377
  and timers, 257
  typical uses with, 310
  WML contrasted with, 338–339
  WTA applications developed using, 512
  WTA environment built on, 539
WMLScript file, 530
  and action/event construct, 531
  in originating call template, 532, *533*
WMLScript interfaces, WTA applications and
      access to, 521
WMLScript language basics, 311–340
  automatic type conversions, 316
  Boolean literals, 314
  comments, 312
  conversion precedence rules, 318
  conversions to Boolean, 318
  conversions to floating-point, 317–318
  conversions to invalid value, 318
  conversions to String, 316–317
  floating-point literals, 313
  functions, 335–337
  identifiers, 321–322
  integer literals, 312–313
  invalid literal, 314
  invalid value, 312
  literals, 312–314
  operators, 322–329
  pragmas, 337–340
  rules for binary operators expecting numeric
      operands, 319
  rules for binary operators expecting numeric
      or string operands, 320–321
  rules for unary operators, 318–319
  statements, 329–335
  string literals, 313–314
  variables, 315–316
WMLScript libraries, 123
WMLScript library interfaces, and WTA
      applications, 514
WMLScript operators, 322–329
  arithmetic, 324–325
  assignment, 322, 324
  bitwise, 326–327
  comma, 327–328
  conditional, 328

increment and decrement, 326
isvalid, 329
operator precedence, *322–323*
relational and logical, 325–326
string, 327
typeof, 328
WMLScript Standard Libraries, *311*, 337, 340–371
Crypto library, 369–370
Dialogs library, 368–369
Float library: floating point operations, 347–349
Lang library core functions, 340–347
String library: extended string operations,
    349–358
URL library: operations, 358–364
WMLBrowser library: browser control, 364–368
WTAI library, 369
WMLScript Standard Libraries reference, 601–616
Crypto Library, 601–602
Dialogs Library, 602
Float Library, 603–604
Lang Library, 604–607
String Library, 607–611
URL Library, 611–614
WMLBrowser Library, 614–616
WTAPublic Library, 616
WML skeleton, 167–175
card element, 170
document prologue, 168–169
head element, 169
id attribute, 174
newcontext attribute, 172–174
onenterforward, onenterbackward, and
    ontimer attributes, 172
ordered attribute, 171–172
title attribute, 170–171
wml (Deck) element, 169
WML specification, for WML elements, 420
WML text, 176–180
character sets/internationalization, 180–181
emphasis-adding weight to words, 178–180
literal data—CDATA sections, 178
literal dollar signs, 177–178
special characters, 176–177
WML text layout, 181–188
align attribute, 182–183
br element, 184–185
mode attribute, 183–184
paragraphs, 181–182
pre element, 185–186
whitespace, 187–188
xml: space attribute, 186
WML Web sites, and transcoders, 406
Working drafts, 101

World Wide Web, xi, xii, 3, 19, 25, 113, 459, 464,
    541. *See also* Internet; mobile Internet
and content design, 459
and convergence, 11
data security in, 264
and e-care, 42
future of, 579
HTTP and success of, 80
influence of, on WML, 147
and Java, 84, 85, 574
and market convergence, 10
and mobile world, 27, 28
and telematics, 36
WAP convergence with, 571–572
wireless connection to, 4
World Wide Web architectures, WAP standard
    and consistency with, 138
World Wide Web Consortium, 79, 82, 83, 123, 571
CC/PP development/formalization efforts
    by, 465, 488
and evolution of WAP standard, 99
WAP Forum relationship with, 133, 139, 140
WBXML submitted to, 280
XML defined by, 562
and XSL, 563
WSP. *See* Wireless Session Protocol
WSP/C, 115
WTA. *See* Wireless Telephony Applications
WTA application interface
components within, 519
telephony events, 519–520
WTA applications
bearer networks for retrieving, 529
scripting interfaces available to, 521–525
WTACallLog library, 524
WTA client framework, 514–525
repository, 518–519
WTA application programming interface,
    519–525
WTA user agent, 514, 516
WTA design considerations, 527–528
application design considerations, 530–531
network design considerations, 528–529
WTA event variables, copying of, into deck-
    specific variables, 534
WTA gateway, 135
WTAGSM library, functions in, 525
WTAI. *See* Wireless Telephony Applications
    Interface
WTAI libraries, 514, 516
wtai scheme, 371
WTAMisc library, utility functions for WTA
    applications in, 524–525

WTANetText library, 523
WTA network design considerations, 528–529
  bearer selection, 529
  memory constraints, 529
  perception of latency, 528
  real-time issues, 528
WTAPhoneBook library, 523–524
WTAPublic Library, 373–374, 616
WTA repository, level 2 cache contrasted with,
    518
WTA server, 527
  APIs, 537
  application pushed over air from, 531
  and security, 525–526
WTA user agent, 512, 516
  and event handling, 517
  and multiple context support, 538
  and repository, 519
  and WTA session, 517
WTAVoiceCall library, 522–523
WTA working group, 535
W-TCP. *See* Wireless TCP
W3C. *See* World Wide Web Consortium
WTLS. *See* Wireless Transport Layer Security
WTLS layer, and authentication, 573
WTLS protocol, 264
WTP. *See* Wireless Transaction Protocol
WTP/C, 98

WTP/D, 98
WTP/T, 98
WWW. *See* World Wide Web

X.509 certificates, 111, 139, 508, 573
XHTML, 83
XML. *See* eXtensible Markup Language
XML document
  encoding example, *293*
  encoding of, using public ID, *298–299*
  WBXML encoding of sample, *294–296*
xml:lang attribute, 163–164
XML name spaces, RDF support for, 472
xml space attribute, 18
XSL. *See* eXtensible Style-Sheet Language
XSL style sheet, 128, 130
X-Wap-Application-Id, 499, 500
X-Wap-Content-URI, 499
X-Wap-Initiator-URI, 499

Yabumi Instant Messaging, 25
Yahoo!, instant messaging through, 25
Yankee Group, 47
  Mobile User Survey, 9
Yellow Freight Systems, 27n4
Yospace SmartPhone, 585

Zero-based index, 284, 289, 349

ACM Press Books Related Titles of Interest

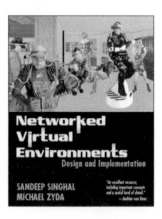

Networked Virtual Environments
Design and Implementation
Sandeep Singhal and Michael Zyda

Networked virtual environments (Net-VE's) offer a three-dimensional, virtual "space" in which users around the world can interact in real time. Net-VE applications have already been adopted by the military and by the aerospace and entertainment industries. They are also used to enhance engineering design, scientific research, and electronic commerce. Written by two of the field's leaders, this book provides a comprehensive examination of Net-VE's, explains the underlying technologies, and furnishes a roadmap for designing and building interactive 3D virtual environments.

0-201-32557-8 • Hardback • 352 pages • © 1999

Mobility
Processes, Computers, and Agents
Dejan Milojicic, Frederick Douglis, and Richard Wheeler

This book brings together in one single resource leading-edge research and practice in three areas of mobility: process migration, mobile computing, and mobile agents. Presented chronologically, the chapters in this book—each written by a leading expert in that particular area—track the development of critical technologies that have influenced mobility. Introductions by the editors and original afterwords by many of the authors provide information on implementation and practical application, technological context, and updates on the most recent advances.

0-201-37928-7 • Paperback • 704 pages • © 1999

Software for Use
A Practical Guide to the Models and Methods of Usage-Centered Design
Larry L. Constantine and Lucy A.D. Lockwood

In this book, two well-known authors present the models and methods of a revolutionary approach to software that will help programmers deliver more usable software. Much more than just another set of rules for good user-interface design, the book guides readers through a systematic software development process—usage-centered design, which weaves together two major threads in software development methods: use cases (also used with UML) and essential modeling. With numerous examples and case studies of both conventional and specialized software applications, the authors illustrate what has been shown to work in practice and what has proved to be of the greatest practical value.

0-201-92478-1 • Hardback • 608 pages • © 1999

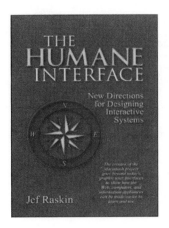

The Humane Interface

New Directions for Designing Interactive Systems

Jef Raskin

This unique guide to interactive system design reflects the experience and vision of Jef Raskin, the creator of the Apple Macintosh project. With his farsightedness and practicality, Raskin demonstrates that making computers significantly easier to use requires new approaches. He offers a wealth of innovative and specific interface ideas for software designers, developers, and product managers.

0-201-37937-6 • Paperback • 256 pages • © 2000

Requirements Engineering and Rapid Development

An Object-Oriented Approach

Ian Graham

The message of this book is simple—software development should be done quickly and effectively. Systems that take years to develop can often end up out of synch with their users' evolving requirements and business objectives by the time they are delivered. This book shows how to solve the problem by using a systematic approach to requirements gathering and business modeling. Packed full of practical advice and tried-and-tested techniques for object modeling, it illustrates how these techniques may be applied not only to models of computer systems, but to models of the world in which they have to operate.

0-201-36047-0 • Hardback • 288 pages • © 1999

Information Warfare and Security

Dorothy E. Denning

This book tells what individuals, corporations, and governments need to know about information-related attacks and defenses. Every day, we hear reports of hackers who have penetrated computer networks, vandalized Web pages, and accessed sensitive information. We hear how they have tampered with medical records, disrupted 911 emergency systems, and siphoned money from bank accounts. Could information terrorists, using nothing more than a personal computer, cause planes to crash, widespread power blackouts, or financial chaos? Such real and imaginary scenarios, and defenses against them, are the stuff of information warfare—operations that target or exploit information media to win some objective over an adversary.

0-201-43303-6 • Paperback • 544 pages • © 1999